FEDERAL RELIEF ADMINISTRATION AND THE ARTS

*The Origins and Administrative History*
*of the Arts Projects*
*of the Works Progress Administration*

WILLIAM F. McDONALD

# *Federal*
# *Relief Administration*
# *and the Arts*

OHIO STATE UNIVERSITY PRESS

*To my wife Mildred*

# Acknowledgments

The Rockefeller Foundation, through its division for the humanities under the direction of Dr. David H. Stevens, made possible by generous grants of money the inauguration, prosecution, and completion of this study. The American Council of Learned Societies, then domiciled in Washington, D. C. and under the direction of Dr. Waldo G. Leland, undertook the responsibility of administering the project and showed itself at all times and in every way efficient and helpful. The National Archives, through the kindness of Dr. Solon J. Buck, then Archivist of the United States, graciously provided office space that gave ready access to the records. The members of the staff of the National Archives, and particularly Dr. Herman Kahn, within whose jurisdiction the pertinent records then resided, afforded every facility and co-operation. To these institutions, their directors and their staffs, the undersigned, in the name of his predecessors and associates as well as his own, expresses his gratitude and esteem.

WILLIAM F. McDONALD

*Columbus, Ohio*
*January, 1969*

# Introduction

Between 1933 and 1943, and more intensively between 1935 and 1939, the government of the United States, through its relief agencies and more particularly through the Works Progress Administration (later called the Work Projects Administration), supported and subsidized an arts program that in material size and cultural character was unprecedented in the history of this or any other nation. The heart of the program was Federal Project Number One (known more familiarly as "Federal One"), which existed as part of the Works Progress Administration between 1935 and 1939 and included within its compass art, writing, music, theater, and historical records.

This program arose from the coincidence, fortuitous or providential, of two ideas: (1) that in time of need the artist, no less than the manual worker, is entitled to employment as an artist at the public expense; and (2) that the arts, no less than business, agriculture, and labor, are and should be the immediate concern of the ideal commonwealth.

This coincidence and its consequences so impressed men of learning and influence that it was suggested in responsible quarters that a history of this experiment be written. Accordingly, in the spring of 1942 the Rockefeller Foundation undertook to subsidize, and the American Council of Learned Societies to administer, a preparation of a history of the arts programs of the federal government during the late depression.

The first director of the project was Donald H. Daugherty of the American Council of Learned Societies. During his brief regime he accomplished important tasks in locating and gaining access to the pertinent public records, in seeking the acquaintance and advice of persons connected with the program, and in establishing general procedures for the undertaking ahead. In August, 1942, Dr. Daughtery entered the armed services of the United States, and was succeeded by Harold W. Landin, a member of the department of history of the Ohio State University and already participating in the project on a temporary basis since mid-June. Under his administration the project took permanent form. A staff was secured, the members of which, with few exceptions, remained until their assignments were completed; the pertinent public records were searched, organized, and indexed so as to make their contents readily accessible and usable; persons of importance connected with Federal One were sought out and interviewed, and their testimonies recorded; and a general outline of the projected history was elaborated.

Finally, because the times were out of joint, Dr. Landin accepted a commission in the Army of the United States, and the undersigned, by profession a student of ancient history and also a member of the history department of the Ohio State University, was asked to complete an inquiry far removed in time and place from his own field of specialization. Under his administration, which lasted from September, 1943, to September, 1945, the work was written and the project brought to an end.

The finished manuscript was the work of many hands and minds. The undersigned was responsible for the original research, as well as the final composition, of the first half (Chapters I through XVI), which studies the origins of public concern for art and artists in time of need and the general background and administration of the government arts programs. In the difficult task of financial analysis, however, he had the invaluable assistance of Julius Davidson, formerly finance officer of Federal One. Without his oral advice and written reports the chapters and parts of chapters on the financial structure and operation of Federal One could not have been satisfactorily completed.

For the second part of this work (Chapters XVI through XXXI), in which each of the five arts projects is studied separately and in turn, members of the staff were assigned to do the preliminary research upon the basis of which the undersigned composed the final draft. These members of the staff and the parts for which they were responsible were: Louis Filler, Federal Arts Project; Benjamin A. Bodkin, Federal Writers Project; Mrs. Margaret Kerr and Mrs. Betty Carr, Federal Music Project; Mrs. Helen Stearns, Federal Theater Project; and Mrs. Mabel B. Eisenhart, Historical Records Survey. In addition, research and secretarial work of a miscellaneous nature were undertaken by Mrs. Alison Landin Bell and Mrs. Mildred Lee McDonald, as well as by the project's two loyal and competent secretaries, Mrs. Elizabeth A. Posniak and Mrs. Jean Enders. To each one of these, separately and jointly, the project owes its completion, and the undersigned takes this occasion publicly to express his respect for their competence and his appreciation of their labor and loyalty.

This study is based upon two sources of inquiry: the official records and personal interviews. In each case there were limitations. In the matter of archives, only those of the central (Washington) office were examined. In a project that covered not only the continental United States but also Alaska and Puerto Rico, the suggestion that state and local records should be searched would have been fantastic. This account, therefore, reflects the point of view and examines the administrative structure and problems of the Washington office. No attempt has been made, except incidentally, to list, much less to analyze, state and local peculiarities. A further limitation resided in the fact that the project did not have access to the records of Harry L. Hopkins, the first administrator of the WPA and the most important single individual in the inauguration of the arts program, nor to the records of the President and of Mrs. Franklin D. Roosevelt.

In the matter of personal interviews the limitation was largely spatial. In the main, those who resided in or between Washington and Boston in the period of project operation (1942-45) were accessible and were approached. This left a large part of the country uncovered— a significant fact when it is remembered that, even before the project was started, the exigencies of war were scattering the Washington office personnel to the four winds. However, what was lost in extent of coverage was compensated for by its intensity. With surprisingly few exceptions those who were approached gave generously of their time and frankly and honestly of their judgments and opinions, each according to his own experience. To them, one and all, and in the name of the project, the undersigned expresses his gratitude.

The final form of this composition is the work and responsibility of the undersigned alone. Although circumstances have postponed its publication for over twenty years, the matter remains substantially the same, except for compression and editing, as it was when it was first presented for publication in 1946. Whatever errors of fact and judgment remain are to be attributed to mistakes of the mind and not of the heart. The undersigned was not at any time in any way employed by, or officially connected with, the Works Projects Administration, much less Federal Project Number One.

Last but not least, it remains to thank the Ohio State University

Press for its generosity and courage in undertaking the publication of this work. The director of the Press, Weldon A. Kefauver, and the editor, Robert S. Demorest, have shown the undersigned every courtesy and afforded him every facility and assistance toward the completion of his task.

W. F. McD.

# Table of Contents

CONTENTS

# 1

# The Philosophy of Social Service

## SOCIAL SERVICE AND PUBLIC POWER

The Works Progress Administration represented within a limited domain and for a limited time the assumption of public power within the federal government by the professional social worker. The public agencies of the state, no less than other combinations of men ordained to achieve a common end, are subject to change when the end changes. That delicate balance of control between the lay politician and the professional expert, which in periods of social stability maintains the integrity of public administration, tends to be disturbed in times of social change and, if the change be fundamental, to be destroyed. Stresses and strains are created within the administrative structure between tradition and innovation, and a period of administrative instability ensues. The result is, for a time, either government by politicians without expert advice or government by experts without political wisdom. In the end, unless complete collapse occur, the politician accepts the legitimacy of the new discipline, and the expert concedes the utility of political action.

The history of the Works Progress Administration provides an excellent example of a conflict of purpose within the administrative structure of the state; and the arts program of the WPA presents a more dramatic, if less significant, picture of the same struggle within the confines of a single agency.

## CATEGORICAL RELIEF

The purpose of the WPA, simply stated, was to provide work relief to employable persons in need. Unemployable persons in need were ex-

1

cluded from the area of its concern. This was a decision of policy made by President Franklin Roosevelt at the inception of the program, and based upon the opinion that adequate facilities for their care existed elsewhere.

Relief of the unemployable, when provided by the public authority either within an institution or as outdoor (or home) relief, is known as "categorical" relief. By 1935 most states granted it in one or more of its forms. In the same year, the Social Security Act acknowledged federal responsibility and through the familiar grant-in-aid system supplemented state funds and established standards for assistance to three categories: the aged, the blind, and dependent children. The effect of categorical relief upon the general picture should not be exaggerated, for in many instances the amount granted was small and the grant itself limited by conditions of residence and other requirements that seriously restricted coverage. It is a fact, nonetheless, that the assumption of this responsibility by the states and the federal government considerably relieved the burden on other services, both public and private.

The social worker, though he contributed substantially both by his philosophy and by his membership in groups that exerted political pressure to the recognition of public responsibility toward the unemployable persons in need, was neither compelled nor prepared to enter the administrative domain of the state in order to achieve his purpose. The humanitarian philosophy, of which social service was the practical expression, had so permeated the minds of the people that the politician accepted in theory, however he might circumvent in practice, the principle of categorical relief.

DIRECT RELIEF

The employable person in need, who was the immediate ward of the WPA, presented a more difficult problem. Direct relief (the dole)— aid in the form of money, goods, or services—was, before 1929, the traditional method by which relief was administered to the able-bodied in the United States. The postulates of private enterprise precluded the hypothesis that unemployment among those capable of work could be other than a temporary and local phenomenon, and in such circumstances improvisation became a rule of action. The need for invention resulted in many bizarre and unpleasant devices, of which the most obnoxious were the breadline, the soup-kitchen, and "bundle days."

2

Direct relief appealed to the public agency because it was cheaper and because it had dramatic possibilities. In an emergency well-meaning individuals, inspired by humane motives and a civic loyalty, formed temporary relief organizations, which, by providing public spectacles, achieved a theatrical effect that emphasized the tragic aspects of the crisis. In this they were abetted by the politician, who saw the machine possibilities of the sportula, and by the press, which usually supported and sometimes sponsored mass measures for purposes of sensationalism and self-advertisement.

Against this the social worker protested, not because the hypothesis of direct relief was false, but because the methods of the public agency were unscientific. Indeed, it was natural that the trained social worker should denounce the haphazard methods of the public dole, especially when he saw, time and again, in periods of depression, the collapse of standards he had labored to establish in more normal times. Yet, as a matter of fact, at least until recent times, the usual relief provided employable persons by the private agency was direct relief, given, to be sure, in response to scientifically ascertained need but not in return for work or other services.

THE IDEA OF WORK RELIEF

In the process of time, however, the professional social worker found himself administering, or otherwise involved in, a program of work in connection with relief. Two developments contributed to this change. In the first place, public bodies found that the private society was useful as a certifying agency and sometimes as an administrator of the program. The private agency, on its part, was not loathe to demonstrate to the public authorities the efficacy of its methods, and welcomed, if not the public auspices, at any rate the public funds that provided the laboratory.

In the second place, there was a slow, but nonetheless perceptible, change in philosophy. Work came to be recognized as an element in the *materia medica* of the scientific social worker. During the depression of 1893-97 a student of social work wrote, with reference to the value of work in connection with relief:

> The demoralizing physical and moral results of long continued idleness have been prevented. . . . The same amount of direct relief would have left

3

the recipients weaker in body and poorer in their only real capital, the power to work, than they are now, and also with habits of idleness, which, in many cases, it would have been difficult for them to overcome when the opportunity for real work returned.[1]

The relation between work and relief, implied in this quotation, is the essence of the idea of work relief, upon which the fundamental philosophy of the WPA rested.

## WORK RELIEF AND THE WORK TEST

Work relief, though it developed historically from the work test and public works, differs from each. The work test was, as its name implies, a test through work of the worthiness of the applicant to receive relief and, as such, precedent to relief and not itself relief. It rested upon two premises: the first, which involves the economic order, was that, except in short-lived and, for the most part, local crises, work is available to all who are willing and able; the second, which is sociological, was that the individual applicant, if he is able-bodied, lacks work because of defects of character.

The history of the work test parallels that of the laissez-faire economy. England's Old Poor Law of 1601 was essentially medieval in character. It assumed corporate responsibility for destitution, the state merely replacing the church, and retained outdoor or home relief, the prevalent medieval practice.

It was not until almost a century later, when the implications of the new economy became more obvious, that the English institution known as the workhouse was founded. The workhouse was a protest against the indiscriminate outdoor relief countenanced by the Old Poor Law. Its purpose was to subject the able-bodied applicant to an indoor work test, and thus, by a winnowing device, to separate the worthy from the unworthy poor.

It was natural that the English colonies in America, when confronted with the problem of poor relief, should adopt the system of the mother country. The almshouse was the American equivalent of the English workhouse and in general followed the pattern of the "mixed workhouse." However, the conditions of economic constriction, which made the work test ineffective in England, were not present—or not to the same degree—in the New World. On the contrary, from the beginning through the nineteenth century the frontier character of the American economy made unemployment of the able-bodied relatively rare and socially unimportant. Consequently, the American almshouse, although it became almost exclusively a home for those who, because of age or other reasons, were physically incapable of self-support, continued to use the work test as a rough and ready, if unscientific, method whereby the work habits of individuals were molded to the pattern of a frontier society.

In the end, in the United States as in England, the presence of mass unemployment or the ever imminent danger of it has forced the abandonment of the work test. It is now generally recognized that, at least since the twenties, periods of depression have occurred and can occur in which the larger part of the unemployed, though capable and willing, are unable to find work. Consequently, it has become unthinkable that a device, which, if it ever had a use, served to discipline the tramp, should be adopted nationally as a chastisement for millions.

However, if economic change has finally made the work test historically obsolete, the opposition of the social worker did much to render it unpopular, even in the period of its acceptance. The social worker of the nineteenth century attacked the work test for the same reason that he attacked direct relief. Both were unscientific, and, for that reason, aggravated the malady that they presumed to cure. If the failure of the individual to seek or to find work is due to defects of character, as the social worker conceded, then the cure lies not in the dole or in trial by ordeal but in social medication. In the end, should the individual stubbornly resist diagnosis, a quasi work test could be maintained by abandoning him to the competitive labor market.

WORK AS PAYMENT FOR RELIEF

The social worker's rejection of work as a test for relief did not, however, carry with it a rejection of work in connection with relief. The Elberfeld system required that each recipient of relief, after having been judged worthy through investigation, be obliged to do work suited to his capacity in return for the help given.* Work thus became a pay-

*The Elberfeld system, which was introduced in Elberfeld, Germany, about 1800 and later adopted by other German municipalities, initiated visitation of the destitute as a substitute for, and protest against, indiscriminate relief. Later, Thomas Chalmers (1780-1847) attacked the English poor laws and their administration because the work test, as then used, failed to discriminate between the worthy and the unworthy, and consequently tended to create a pauper class. As suggested by

5

ment to the public body for value received. The concept of work relief, relief through work, emerged. But though the purpose of the work required changed, the nature of the work performance remained much the same. It was natural enough that the work test, since it was a test of character, should assume something of the nature of trial by ordeal. But the logic of requiring rock-breaking and wood-splitting in work relief is not so obvious. In part the reason was lack of imagination and failure to apprehend the implications of the change in purpose; fundamentally, however, the cause was economic and nowhere better expressed than by a writer in 1895:

> The work given must be adequate in amount to prevent families from suffering either hunger or cold; but at the same time it must be really hard work in order to prevent dabbling, and it must be decidedly underpaid in order not to attract those who already have work at half-time, or who have otherwise disagreeable work. The whole must be so unattractive as to guarantee that, when other work can be had, the laborer will seek it.[2]

Work, then, although no longer a test precedent to relief, became a test inherent in relief of the recipient's willingness to accept private employment.

Under such conditions there was little incentive to seek variety in the nature of the work provided. In the first place, most of the unemployed were unskilled, and simple manual labor exhausted their abilities. In the second place, the capacity of private and public agencies to provide work relief, other than the simplest and most menial, was limited. Finally, any enlargement of the scope of work was regarded as competitive with private enterprise. Accordingly, until the depression of the thirties, work relief meant unskilled manual labor, and, so far as there was work relief for women, it was restricted almost entirely to the sewing room.

Work relief, then, as it developed before 1929, differed from the work test in method but not in purpose. The classical work test was indoor or institutional relief, whereas work relief was outdoor or home relief. The concept that the individual was on trial was present in both types; but in the former he was on trial for relief, whereas in the latter he was on trial for private employment. The social worker rejected the work test as unscientific but attempted by scientific methods to accomplish the same purpose—the adjustment of the individual to the demands of a laissez-faire economy.

the Elberfeld system, Chalmers proposed investigation of the individual as the way to discover the causes of destitution.

THE ADAPTATION OF PUBLIC WORKS TO WORK RELIEF

At the same time and from another direction, public works also contributed to the genesis of work relief. In our time, public works are considered those that are by common consent within the province of public enterprise, such as street repair in a municipality, roads in a county, and battleships in a nation. Although the public body may, and sometimes does, directly employ the needed labor, the usual method, especially in the United States, is through contract with a private firm.

In early depressions in our country, and indeed in other countries and in more remote times, one of the recognized ways of meeting a period of unemployment was the expansion of public works. This expansion may be contrived in two ways: by advancing the starting date of works already projected, and by inventing new works to be undertaken in the emergency.

In public works the center of attention is the work and not the worker. Consequently, men are hired on the basis of competence, not need. Second, since the work is done by a public contractor, or, if by force account, under conditions approximating those of public contract, full-time work is offered and prevailing wages paid. A true public-works program is essentially an employment program and only by coincidence a relief program.


THE REDEFINITION OF NEED

In the first half of the nineteenth century the concept of need, as it existed in the community and in the mind of the social worker, was fundamentally economic. If the need of the recipient of relief was emphasized, as it was in the work test and work relief, need was interpreted as lack of the physical necessities of life; if the need of the community was emphasized, as it was in public works, the accent was upon the desirability of economically sound public improvements. Prior to 1860, social work was concerned almost exclusively with the physical relief of the poor, and, for the most part, the permanently poor, who, though honest workers, were unable because of low wages to reach that level of existence that would make them independent of outside aid. Orphanages, where they existed, were custodial rather than educational, and hospitals purely medical agencies rather than centers and occasions for social rehabilitation.

7

About the middle of the century, however, two significant changes in method occurred: casework and the charity organization.

Social casework, although it began as a protest against the unscientific and indiscriminate methods of English poor-law administration, soon transcended its original purpose. Those who devoted themselves to personal investigation of the indigent quickly saw that poverty was due to sociological as well as economic causes. The transition was thus made from the problem of economic self-support to that of social self-maintenance. The purpose was to adjust the individual's habits to the acceptable mores of the time and to achieve in the social universe the balance that was maintained in the economic universe by the natural law of supply and demand. The problem was summarized in a word—social maladjustment.

The concern of the caseworker with the individual's adjustment to his environment necessarily led to a concern first with the family and then with the community. This shift in emphasis is well illustrated by the tendency of many charitable organizations to change their name to "family welfare society." A study of relations between husband and wife and between parent and child led to a preoccupation with the problems of marriage, divorce, and juvenile delinquency. Naturally, these considerations have carried the student from the family to the community and have resulted in our own day in the rise of the "community center." The group, as well as—and to a certain degree rather than—the individual or the family, has become the center of attention. The community playground, the community dance, community music, and community drama have become the solvents in which the conflicts within the individual and within the family group would be resolved in a higher synthesis, the result of which would be social equilibrium.*

### THE SOCIAL SETTLEMENT

The expansion of the area of the social worker's concern until it embraced the community emphasized the need for, and caused the ap-

---

*It might be mentioned here that more recently there has been a tendency to use the psychological rather than the sociological approach to social maladjustment. The hypothesis is psychiatric, the assumption being that not only the conflict lies within the individual but also its cure. This represents a movement away from the group and the family back to the individual, and it was not without its influence upon the development of certain programs (e.g., musical therapy) among the arts projects.

8

pearance of, the social "general practitioner," as opposed to the social caseworker, who was concerned with specifics. In 1889 Jane Addams founded Chicago's famous Hull House, and the movement grew until in 1930 there were 160 such houses with 1,500 trained staff members and 7,500 volunteer assistants. In the social-settlement movement the settlement worker served, so to speak, as a staff officer, to co-ordinate the activities of the caseworker and to relate them to each other and to the whole within a limited social continuum. His consequent concern with groups and varieties of group expression led him naturally to emphasize those outward forms in which, in complex as well as in simple societies, friendly people express the bonds that bind them together. Music, the dance, the pageant, art, handicraft, and the theater were stressed, not as media in which the maestro and the diva expressed their superiority, but as spontaneous and natural manifestations of the élan of the group.

This emphasis upon the democratic rather than the aristocratic qualities of culture, which had its origin in the social-settlement movement, has tremendously influenced the American school system. Co-operation rather than isolation in the learning process and active participation rather than passive enjoyment are the principles that now rule, or promise to rule, the philosophy of the playground and the classroom; and the spirit of the settlement house has in large measure become, and been accepted as, the spirit of the community.

This casework, which began as a device for distinguishing between the worthy and the unworthy poor, now encompassed within its embrace a concern with the conditions that hinder or encourage the full self-development of the individual. In theory, and in some degree in practice, the social agency, although it still concentrated its efforts upon the economically underprivileged, repudiated the common belief that the ills it seeks to cure are confined to the lowest economic stratum.

CHARITY ORGANIZATION

The remarkable growth of social casework in the latter half of the nineteenth century was accompanied by another and related development that was equally momentous. Just as social casework represents the adaptation of the scientific method to a sociological purpose, so the charity organization society represents the adoption of the scientific principles of management by social agencies. The movement, begun in

9

London in 1869, reached the United States during the depression of 1873-79, and in that period and the succeeding depression of 1893-97 the number of such societies in this country was multiplied many times. The charity organization movement, representing the broader concept of social work fostered by the social settlement, endeavored to raise relief to a community level and at the same time to broaden the definition of charity to include examination of the sociological circumstances closely connected with economic want; or, in the words of the historian of the movement, "to discharge more effectively the social obligations of neighborliness incident to citizenship even in the complex and unneighborly city."[3]

For the achievement of its dual purpose the charity organization society established itself as a central staff agency to co-ordinate the activities of the several line agencies (the various relief societies) and to plan the administration of relief in terms of its own more advanced definition of social aid. It was not designed to supplant existing agencies nor did it itself ordinarily administer relief, except in those communities where no other agency existed. By the time of the short-lived crisis of 1907-8 charity organization societies were so well organized and had so educated public opinion that in many places they controlled the administration of relief. Although remaining agencies supported by private contributions, they assumed public responsibilities, and their advice was sought by mayors and even by governors. In many instances the planning and co-ordination of relief on a community-wide basis was entrusted to them by the public authorities. The community-fund movement, which began in World War I, represented the final development of the private charity organization society as a staff agency for community welfare, and showed how far the mind of the social worker had advanced beyond the concept of poor relief.

The introduction of efficient administrative techniques into social-agency organization was, however, a means rather than an end. The primary purpose of the charity organization society was the education of the private relief agency, the public authorities, and the community in general in the new philosophy of social service. The older societies, habituated to methods dictated by sentiment or prejudice, were gradually instructed in the techniques of casework and the new sociological approach to poverty. In time most of them became line agencies for the effectuation of staff policy.

The conversion of the public authorities was a more difficult task. In times of crisis the city fathers bestirred themselves, but for the most part in ways that were an abomination to the social worker. Some form of indiscriminate outdoor relief usually resulted—at worst, the soup kitchen, the bread line, or the "bundle-day"; at best, some form of "made" work that was economically wasteful, socially undesirable, ill-paid, and badly administered. With each trough in the business curve the local authorities by their unscientific methods threatened to destroy the structure that the charity organization movement had built in the intervening normal period by long and laborious effort. Since it was impossible to reduce a public body to a line agency of a private staff-organization, the leaders of the charity organization met the problem by anathema. In the end the public authorities desisted from an endeavor that they had neither the means nor the trained personnel to pursue, and by 1929 poor relief and social service, at any rate so far as the able-bodied were concerned, was practically the monopoly of the private practitioner. This repudiation of the public authority as an agency of social service, though at the time based upon sound reasons and inspired by the best intentions, backfired in the depression of the thirties. A mutual distrust pervaded relations between the politician and the social worker, and the public, which long had been taught by the most advanced social workers of the time that social service was not within the public domain, saw with amazement and foreboding the construction by public authorities of a congeries of social service agencies, the architects of which were for the most part men trained in private social service.

## THE PROFESSIONALIZATION OF THE SOCIAL WORKER

In the meantime the way toward rapprochement was made smoother by a development within the social service field: professionalization. The transition from amateur to professional status was here, as in other fields, the result of three processes: the creation of a discipline, the establishment of a formal curriculum, and the formation of a guild. The impetus came almost entirely from the charity organization group, whose leaders had, above all others, appreciation of sound administrative practice and the speculative mind. The most important single cause making toward a discipline was the introduction and development of social casework. Diagnosis of the individual's difficulties, the planning of the curative process, and the actual administration of the remedy demanded a kind of person and a kind of training for which

11

the desire to do good and the leisure to do it were not enough. These requirements of competent casework led to the development of techniques, and the latter in turn to specialized training.

Beginning with the establishment of a summer school in 1898 by the New York School of Philanthropy (later the New York School of Social Work), the movement grew until in 1919 fifteen of these schools formed the Association of Training Schools for Professional Social Work (the later American Association of Schools of Social Work). In 1933 the membership in this body was twenty-five. Today, with departments and, indeed, schools of social service in most of the larger universities, social work has achieved academic status.

Last of all, the formation of a guild provided the social worker with a professional *esprit de corps*. The first truly professional organization of social workers was the American Association of Social Workers, formed in 1921. The purposes of this association, like all of its kind, were, first, self-defense (the procurement of fair wages and conditions of employment for its members); second, self-improvement (the establishment of high standards by control of the curriculum and the encouragement of research); and third, self-expression (the conversion of the public to the social worker's creed and the exertion of pressure upon lawmaking bodies for favored legislation). In 1929 the social worker entered the depression with the sense of solidarity that only a membership card engenders.

In 1930 the United States Bureau of the Census officially recognized social work as a distinct profession, and classified 31,241 persons as so employed. One further important, but natural, fact: in 1930 the ratio of men to women among those employed in social work was 1:4; the ratio in the association's membership was even higher, 1:6; that among students, 1:9.2, was highest of all.[4] At the beginning of the depression social work was predominantly a woman's profession, a fact that had influences germane to this inquiry.

The emergence of the professional social worker as the executive instrument in the administration of social service and as the conceptual leader in the elaboration of a social philosophy was the outstanding development in the history of social service in the first quarter of this century. It was no accident that in March, 1933, the professional social worker, like the professional economist and political scientist, descended upon Washington. The age of the amateur servant of the poor was over.

1.   Josephine Shaw Lowell, "Five Months' Work for the Unemployed in New York City," *Charities Review*, III (1894), 334.

2.   Philip W. Ayres, "Is Emergency Relief by Work Wise?", *Proceedings of the National Conference of Charities and Correction*, 1895, p. 100, as quoted in L. H. Feder, *Unemployment Relief in Periods of Depression* (New York: Russell Sage Foundation, 1936), p. 179.

3.   Frank D. Watson, *The Charity Organization Movement in the United States* (New York: Macmillan Company, 1922), p. 214.

4.   Mary Clarke Burnett, "Training for Social Work," *Encyclopedia of the Social Sciences*, XIV, 186 A.

# 2

## The Beginnings of White-Collar Relief

PUBLIC ACCEPTANCE OF THE PRINCIPLE OF WORK RELIEF

The public acceptance of the idea of work relief was the outstanding feature of the first four years of the depression (1929-33). The private welfare agency pioneered in its application, but in time, if slowly, first the local subdivision and then, in turn, the state and the federal governments recognized its validity. In the beginning, however, its application was narrowed by two limitations. In the first place, it was agreed that work relief should concern itself with projects outside the normal activities of government. Otherwise, trespass would be committed against the domain of public works. In the second place, both habit and pressure counseled projects that would not compete with private enterprise. Between the two lay the limited area of work relief. Thus bounded, work relief was "made" work, not because it was necessarily useless, but because it was work that, if there were no depression, would not be undertaken either by a public or a private body.

Within these limitations the early work-relief programs of the states and local subdivisions further suffered from two major defects: lack of diversification and the budget-deficiency principle. Most work provided was of the lowest manual type, and the determination of wages and working hours by the calculation of budget deficiency led to a staggering of employment that impaired efficiency of project operation.

THE RECOGNITION OF FEDERAL RESPONSIBILITY FOR RELIEF

On October 21, 1930, one year after the crash of the stock market, President Hoover appointed Colonel Arthur Woods chairman of a com-

14

mittee to deal with unemployment. This committee was popularly known as the Woods Committee; its official title was the President's Emergency Committee for Employment. With no powers and only limited funds, it served merely as a staff agency to advise the states and localities, as well as private industry, with regard to relief and, in so far as possible, to co-ordinate their activities. The Woods Committee ceased to exist in August, 1931, and was succeeded in the same month by the President's Organization on Unemployment Relief, popularly known as the Gifford Committee. Walter S. Gifford, president of the American Telephone and Telegraph Company, was named its chairman. In the fall of 1931, in order to meet present need, the Gifford Committee organized and supported a nationwide drive for relief funds through the local community chests. From these drives and others in the spring of 1932, approximately $100,000,000 dollars was realized. Of this sum, however, only $35,000,000 was allocated to home relief, the remainder going to organizations of a non-relief or quasi-relief character. Thus the charity-organization movement, which was expressing its advanced philosophy and achieving a vertebrate administrative structure in the community-fund movement, suddenly found itself integrated nationally and recognized officially by the federal government. By simply shifting its attention from public works to relief, the Gifford Committee had, unconsciously but unmistakably, lifted the charity organization movement from the local to the national level and made the professional social worker a counselor in federal policy.

As soon as it was recognized that immediate relief on a national scale was paramount, the ultimate acceptance of financial responsibility on the part of the federal government was practically inevitable; and on the eve of his departure from public life, President Hoover gave statutory form to this development by approving the Emergency Relief and Construction Act (July 21, 1932). Title I of this act, the only part that concerns this inquiry, authorized the Reconstruction Finance Corporation to advance to the states, as loans, $300,000,000 to furnish relief and work relief to destitute persons.*

The difference between the RFC, acting in this capacity, and the two earlier committees lay in the fact that the RFC had funds at its disposal, and, in accordance with the precedents already established by the grant-in-aid system, was entitled to make rules regarding the use and administration of these funds. Under Title I of the act the funds could

*Since repayment of loans made under Title I of this act was subsequently waived, so far as the states were concerned, the RFC became in this respect the first federal grant-in-aid agency for relief.

be used for either direct or work relief; but in either case it was necessary that the recipient be not only unemployed but also destitute. Within this statutory context the RFC made several rules, three of which are significant in relation to this inquiry:

1. All projects must be on public and not on private property.

2. Projects must be worthwhile.

3. No project worker may replace an already employed worker.

The reasons for these three rules, which were subsequently adopted by the FERA and the WPA, are obvious. The first prevented the use of public funds for private benefit; the second tried to raise the quality of projects, although no attempt was made to define "worthwhile"; the third discouraged projects that undertook to do work within the regular province of a public body.

The RFC, however, was, and considered itself, primarily a banking, and not a relief, agency. Consequently, its chief concern was with the financial condition of the states that applied for help, how much they themselves could contribute and how much they needed from the agency. Beyond this appraisal of credit and that supervision necessary to ensure observance of the rules, the RFC attempted no supervision of the administration of relief.

### WHITE-COLLAR RELIEF AND THE PRIVATE AGENCY

If, before 1933, relatively little attention was given to work relief, or, at least, to the differentiation of work projects, still less solicitude was shown to the unemployed and destitute white-collar worker. The reasons for this were several. In the first place, the white-collar workers felt the initial impact of the depression less severely than the manual laborers. In the second place, even when they reached the end of their resources, they were reluctant to apply for relief either to public agencies or private charitable organizations. They preferred to have recourse to their unions, professional societies, churches, and fraternal organizations. Indeed, it was through such private associations and friends that the needy in this class first came to the attention of relief agencies.

When relief from these sources was unavailable, the white-collar worker preferred the private to the public agency because the latter, being more advanced in its social thinking, was more likely to treat his application with understanding and in confidence and, unencumbered by statutory limitations, was less restricted in its use of funds. Indeed, so reluctant were the white-collar workers to reveal their need that even those who finally brought themselves to approach the private agency usually tried to disguise their plight by applying for work in the agency or simply asking for advice.

Although some of these agencies provided no special work adapted to the skills of this group, a significant number made special efforts to take care of them. In some cases the agency itself took the initiative in visiting the family whose need was called to its attention; one agency used press releases to persuade white-collar people to apply for help; others solicited the help of churches to call their services to the attention of this class. The Savannah Welfare Society softened the humiliation by giving cash instead of grocery orders and by paying the rent money directly to the client instead of the landlord. Another device was the establishment of loan funds from which the applicant could borrow without loss of prestige and in some cases without interest.

The placement of the white-collar worker on proper work projects was still more difficult because everywhere the majority of, and in many places the only, work projects were those of a manual type. In New York City the Emergency Work Bureau, which was the operating agency for the work-relief program of the Prosser Committee (October, 1930–August, 1931) made a distinction in its placement service between skilled and white-collar applicants on the one hand and those in lower classifications on the other. The former were generally assigned to semi-public or non-profit private institutions, such as churches, settlement houses, relief agencies, colleges, museums, and hospitals, where professional and clerical work suitable to their training was available.

But in the early days, by far the most popular method was the employment of white-collar workers on the staff of the agency itself. In New York City the EWB recruited its staff almost entirely from the ranks of the unemployed. The reasons for this were, first, that there were not enough trained social workers to carry the increased load, and second, that employment in social agencies provided an economical and agreeable way to care for the white-collar unemployed. Of the $8,522,240 spent by the Prosser Committee, $381,957 was used for administrative and operating expenses. This was 4.5 per cent of the total. Of this latter sum, $15,000 was paid to non-relief administrative personnel, and approximately $200,000 went for wages of persons selected from the unemployed. Consequently, non-relief administrative expense amounted to an infinitesimal percentage (.02) of total expenditures.

### THE PHILADELPHIA AND NEW YORK CITY PROGRAMS

The earliest significant white-collar program under private auspices was devised in Philadelphia. There the Committee on Unemployment Relief, a private group established in November, 1930, and known as the Lloyd Committee, tried to make work relief as large a part of its program as possible and for this purpose formed a Subcommittee on Work. By private subscription the committee eventually secured about $4,000,000, of which 36 per cent was paid as wages for work relief. Lack of funds caused the termination of the committee's work in April, 1931. Of the white-collar work relief thus provided, Joanna Colcord writes:

> Without doubt more original work for white-collar men was found in Philadelphia than in any city visited. For instance, the local chapter of the Institute of Architects, which had undertaken a survey of colonial landmarks in the city, raised separate funds and disbursed them under the bureau's direction, using unemployed architects and draftsmen, and paying them $20 a week.[1]

Among other white-collar projects undertaken in Philadelphia the most significant in relation to this inquiry was using musical and theatrical artists in recreation projects. Entertainers, musicians, and recreation workers to the number of 118 were employed in settlements, recreation centers, hospitals, and children's institutions. "This was reported as being an especially valuable morale-building influence, both for the entertainers and for those whom they served."[2]

In New York City work relief for the white-collared class began later than in Philadelphia, but it eventually reached even more substantial proportions. In October, 1930, the Emergency Employment Committee (the Prosser Committee) was organized, and in the course of the winter raised approximately eight and a half million dollars for aid to the needy. The Emergency Work Bureau was established and operated by the four principal charities in New York City for the purpose of providing work relief. In the spring of 1931 the Women's Fund Committee (the Belmont Committee) raised some $600,000 for work relief to women. These committees continued to operate until August, 1931.

18

Some of these projects were of the white-collar variety, but most were of a manual kind, such as the sewing rooms for women supported by the Belmont Committee. The need of the manual worker for assistance was so immediate, especially in the absence of any public program supported by state or municipal funds, that there was little opportunity to attend to the special problems of the white-collar class.

However, the natural sympathy of the private agency toward white-collar relief was more manifest the next year in the work of the Gibson Committee, which was organized in August, 1931, to succeed the Prosser Committee.* By this time the City of New York had entered the relief picture. In August, 1931, a special act of the state legislature authorized the city to increase revenue bonds from $2,000,000 to $12,000,000 for 1931, and to use $10,000,000 for material and labor to relieve unemployment. The Board of Estimate made $5,000,000 available to each borough president, and between May 1 and July 1, 1931, 15,000 men were put to work at manual labor on three-day shifts per week.

Thus in the fall of 1931 there were two relief programs in operation in New York City, the city's and the Gibson Committee's. Their coexistence encouraged a division of responsibility, by the terms of which manual labor was supplied by the public funds, and work for women and for men not suited to outdoor manual labor was provided by the EWRB. The Welfare Council of New York City reported:

> Projects on which the Bureau is already using large numbers of the white-collar class are the compilation of a city directory, a census of vacant apartments, and the clerical and investigating work of its own office, the city's Emergency Work Bureau and the city's Home Relief Bureau. In smaller numbers many men and women of professional, clerical or business training and experience have been assigned to city departments and institutions and private non-profit-making organizations.[3]

Committees were established by professional societies to assist their members—among them were the Actors' Dinner Club, organized by Heywood Broun, and the Architects' Emergency Committee. In the spring of 1932 two committees working in co-operation with the EWRB became active in the interest of unemployed musicians, the more important being the Musicians' Emergency Aid under the leadership of Walter Damrosch. The work of this committee is thus described:

*The Emergency Work and Relief Bureau, the successor of the EWB, administered the fund of $20,695,000 raised by the Gibson Committee.

19

With part of the $250,000 it raised, and with help "in kind" that ran into big money, a series of extraordinary symphony concerts was presented at the Metropolitan Opera House. The orchestra of 200 unemployed musicians was directed by conductors and assisted by solo artists and choruses of the highest rank, who contributed their services. The program included a number of beautiful works that even New York rarely has an opportunity to hear at any price. Charges for admission were a small fraction of usual prices for orchestral concerts. This was the beginning of a movement for providing good music by unemployed musicians at low cost or free which had a notable development in the later years of the depression.[4]

In the second year of its existence, 1932-33, the Gibson Committee was able to give almost exclusive attention to the employment of white-collar applicants. The passage of the Wicks Act made this possible. The New York legislature at an extraordinary session passed this act in September, 1931. It established the Temporary Emergency Relief Administration of New York State, authorized home and work relief throughout the state, and decreed that the state refund of 40 per cent of municipal expenditures for home and work relief. Under its provisions New York City organized its Emergency Work and Relief Administration, consisting of the Emergency Work Commission for the administration of work relief and the Emergency Home Relief for the administration of home relief. Thus public relief, subsidized by the Wicks Act, was providing relief for the manual worker. The Gibson Committee accordingly was able to concentrate its attention upon the white-collar worker.

In November, 1932, the Gibson Committee started a campaign that raised some $15,000,000. Of this sum approximately half was spent for work-relief wages. Ratios of employment were adopted that were extremely favorable to the white-collar unemployed: one woman to two men; one non-clerical to three clerical or professional; one unattached woman to two with dependents; one unattached man to nine with families.[5] Professional and white-collar men and women made over half the applications this year and filled over two-thirds of the quota. The quotas of this class in previous years were 1:2 in 1932, 1:4 in 1931, and 1:5 in 1930.

In addition to the work relief carried on by New York City, assisted by grants in conformity with the Wicks Act, and that sustained by the Gibson Committee, New York State, through projects sponsored by departments of the state government, initiated work relief of its own. The invention of this device of statewide projects, segments of which were established in various parts of the state, was a most significant development. By it, the initiation of work projects, and to some degree their supervision and operation, was directly undertaken by the state, whereas formerly they had been within the exclusive domain of the locality. In other words, the statewide project was a means whereby the state relief administration, repudiating its position as a mere grant-in-aid agency, expressed in terms of project operation its own philosophy of work relief. It is significant that at this time Harry L. Hopkins was chairman of New York State's TERA and that under his leadership the state relief administration, as a staff agency, was using its influence to educate the local communities in the philosophy of social service. The statewide project attempted within the state what the nationwide project later essayed within the nation—the indoctrination of the less-advanced communities in the finer implications of work relief.

The emphasis upon white-collar employment on these statewide projects, although it did not predominate, was considerably stronger than it had been on local projects. By November, 1933, of the ten thousand from New York City on statewide projects, about three-fourths were unskilled and worked in state parks under the Department of Conservation.[6] The rest were chiefly clerical and professional workers, most of whom were taken from the Gibson Committee's EWRB and whose eligibility for relief from public funds was thus attested by a private agency. They were employed chiefly on projects under the state departments of education and of health, which provided classes for unemployed adults, dental service for adults, and additional facilities in the dental clinics for school children.

The Gibson Committee ceased to exist on September 30, 1933, and when, in March, 1933, it began its spring liquidation, the white-collar workers who had received assistance from it found difficulty in finding new assignments. Under the rules of the TERA it was necessary that projects other than statewide be undertaken under public auspices, and such auspices for white-collar projects, formerly financed by the Gibson Committee and administered by the EWRB, were not readily secured. At the same time non-profit private institutions were pressing the TERA to continue the assistance they had received under the Gibson Committee's grants. As a result of this pressure, TERA turned its attention to the white-collar problem on the local level.

The state relief administration, accordingly, created a "White-Collar Bureau" for New York City. Its purpose was to initiate and approve local white-collar projects (apart from those already in existence) as statewide projects under the State Department of Education.[7]

In order to supply subsidized staffs for private agencies, the TERA

21

agreed to carry on white-collar projects in New York City when the EWRB would close. An advisory committee was appointed to pass on proposed projects and to devise ways in which "public auspices" might be secured for them, as required by state law. By this formality public funds were used to subsidize non-profit private agencies by supplying them with personnel, and the public official secured as sponsor usually did little but lend his name to legalize the proposal.

## THE RFC AND THE LOS ANGELES PROGRAM

The first attention directed toward the white-collar unemployed on a national scale was inspired by the President's Emergency Committee for Employment, appointed on October 21, 1930, by President Hoover, under the chairmanship of Colonel Arthur Woods. This committee had no funds for relief and administered no relief. Its sole function was to co-ordinate state and local relief agencies. In this capacity it called attention to the need of providing relief to white-collar workers. The historian of the committee's work writes:

> In order to focus attention on the problem of relief to the white-collar unemployed without publicity and to secure a more definite local responsibility, the Committee suggested to the Family Welfare Association of America, the YMCA, the YWCA, the National Catholic Welfare Conference, and the Bureau of Jewish Social Research, that "they urge such alertness and activity upon their membership."[8]

It was not, however, until the passage of the Emergency Relief and Construction Act (July 21, 1932) that the use of federal funds for work relief was possible. Of the RFC money thus made available a very small part was spent for work relief, and, of that, an even smaller part for white-collar projects. Among them, however, was a significant experiment in Los Angeles County, California. The project was initiated under private auspices. Its primary purpose was the prevention of juvenile delinquency, and with this end in view an organization was set up in January, 1933, under the sponsorship of the County Employees' Relief Program. In the first month, spot maps were drawn to reveal the geographical location of delinquency areas. During the following months a small group, under the Los Angeles County Recreation and Probation Departments, experimented in the field so successfully that in June it was decided to expand the work on a county-wide basis for the coming summer. A conference of prominent citizens met and evolved the plan of using RFC funds for the project. Virgil Dahl, who as director of recreation was largely responsible for the development and prosecution of the plan, writes:

> The theory was that well-educated men and women could well be transferred from manual labor, such as working in gravel pits, doing road work, sewing, etc., to which they had been assigned to earn RFC relief, to a task for which they were better qualified, and which is, in a measure, more important to the community,—that of delinquency prevention. In short, it was reasoned that it was senseless to waste the talent of trained men and women in menial tasks when they could be enlisted in socially important work for the same RFC wage. . . . Thus was inaugurated the Juvenile Delinquency and Recreation Project No. 821 on July 6, 1933.[9]

The summer activities were largely outdoor and recreational, but at the close of the summer the benefits derived from the experiment were so manifest that it was decided in September to plan a winter program that would be not only recreational but also vocational and educational. The transition was not easy. It involved a change in the scheduled hours of playground work to conform with after-school and Saturday and Sunday playground operation. It also included the development of a program of adult recreational activities with emphasis upon the use of recreational facilities during the evenings, as well as a greater use of indoor facilities. This demanded diversification of program, which was achieved by classes for handicraft, amateur dramatics, and music. Some of these classes were for adults, and thus worked toward the creation of an adult education program. In Covina, California, for instance, activities in folk dancing, dramatics, and music, for adults as well as for children, were developed.

When the RFC program came to an end, it was apparent that the delinquency-prevention activities were such a success that their termination was unthinkable. Accordingly, on November 27, 1933, three days after the RFC program ceased to function, the project was reinstated under the CWA program. Its further growth under these new auspices, including the elaboration of an active and enthusiastic music program, fulfilled the hopes of its staunch supporters.

The Los Angeles County project is an interesting example of the development of a cultural program from a recreational program. The emphasis was not upon professional standards of performance but rather upon group participation and the moral and physical benefits derived from cultural activities that, if not of high artistic merit, were nonetheless spontaneous and sincere.

The foregoing brief account of the early development of white-collar projects indicates a special solicitude on the part of the social worker for the welfare of the professional and technical classes. Private agencies, operating under the direction of co-ordinating committees, like the Prosser and Gibson committees in New York City, devoted more and more of their resources to the white-collar unemployed, as public relief agencies relieved them of their responsibilities to the manual worker. Charity organization societies or institutions based upon the charity organization philosophy, like the YMCA, the YWCA, and other denominational groups, provided structure within which the principles of white-collar relief were developed and expressed. Through these organizations the thinking of public bodies, local, state, and federal, was affected, both by the transfer of personnel from the former to the latter as the need for professional social service grew progressively greater, and by the public acceptance of the white-collar projects that the private agencies initiated as demonstration projects.

1. Joanna C. Colcord, William C. Koplovitz, and Russell H. Kurtz, *Emergency Work Relief* (New York: Russell Sage Foundation, 1932), p. 17.

2. *Ibid.*, p. 173.

3. "Unemployment Relief Methods," Monthly Summary No. 3 (February, 1932), Vol. VI, No. 10, pp. 3-4.

4. Lillian Brandt, "Relief of the Unemployed in New York City, 1929-1937" (typewritten, Welfare Council of New York City), p. 82. All quotations are used with the permission of the Community Council of Greater New York.

5. *Ibid.*, p. 118.

6. *Ibid.*, p. 126.

7. *Ibid.*, p. 154.

8. E. P. Hayes, *Activities of the President's Emergency Committee for Unemployment, 1930-31* (Concord, N. H.: Rumford Press, 1936), pp. 114-15.

9. Virgil Dahl, "A Brief History of the Delinquency Prevention and Recreation Project in Los Angeles County, January, 1932 to June, 1934," (typewritten).

# 3

## Federal Recognition and Staff Policy

### THE ESTABLISHMENT OF THE FEDERAL EMERGENCY RELIEF ADMINISTRATION

On May 12, 1933, two months after the Roosevelt administration took office, the Federal Emergency Relief Act of 1933, providing $500,000,000 for outright grants to the states for relief, was approved by the President.

The Federal Emergency Relief Administration thus created was a grant-in-aid agency. Its initial appropriation was $200,000,000 more than that available to the Reconstruction Finance Corporation for loans. It differed from the RFC also in that its advances were outright grants and not loans. But fundamentally, the FERA was based upon the same premises as the RFC. Federal Responsibility for relief, in so far as the cost was concerned, was conceded; but the administration of relief was left where it had always been, in the localities. The reasons for this were obvious and sound. State and local relief agencies, both public and private, were already in existence and in operation; it would have been precarious and wasteful to supplant them immediately. Again, the opposition to federal participation was less forceful against grants than it would have been against federalization. Finally, the federal grant-in-aid system, which had its beginnings in the Morrill Act of 1862, was time-tested and, especially since the beginning of the present century, had been used for a variety of purposes—for agriculture, public roads, vocational education, forestry, and maternity and infant hygiene. The extension of the system to the financing of relief was not a break with precedent. Indeed, some states, such as New York, already had adopted what was in effect a grant-in-aid system for relief with re-

25

spect to the local subdivisions. The FERA merely brought the practice to the federal level.

Continuity with the RFC was maintained in two ways. In the first place, the RFC, though empowered to loan to local subdivisions, preferred to loan directly to the states. Of the $300,000,000 granted, total advances to counties amounted to only $16,000,000, and in these cases the RFC required the state to certify the county's need. The FERA, in furtherance of this policy, made its grants to states only.

Furthermore, the RFC, though it considered itself merely a banking corporation and not a relief agency, was aware that even a banking agency must extend some supervision and control over money lent. Accordingly, it created a staff of five field representatives, four of whom later became identified with the FERA. The work of these field representatives was mostly educational: they explained to the states under what conditions loans could be secured. The philosophy of relief, its nature and adequacy, and the personnel of relief administration in the states were considered to be outside their concern. Within narrower limits, however, the RFC made rules, noted above, three of which were important in establishing FERA policy. Work relief, the RFC ordained, must be on *useful* projects, though no attempt was made to define "useful." Work relief must not be undertaken in fields that are part of the normal function of government; i.e., a man on work relief must not displace a regular public employee. Finally, work relief must be on public, not private, property. These three cautions, inherited from the RFC, may be considered the basic principles upon which the FERA began its operations.

Finally, there were present the three conditions that in the course of time have attached themselves to the grant-in-aid: the right of the grant agency to withhold funds if the standards required by the law are not observed; the right of the grant agency to set at least minimum standards with respect to administration of the funds and fiscal operations; and the requirement that the state supply some part of the funds. These controls, especially the first two, were the instruments used by the FERA to make staff policy effective.

The FERA's concept of control, however, soon became much wider and deeper than that of the RFC. The reason lay not in any initial difference in structure or statutory purpose but in the basic philosophy of the personnel. The RFC thought primarily in banking terms—in terms of good loan risks. Its leadership and, by and large, its lesser personnel were recruited from the financial world; and, like the emergency committees created by President Hoover, it represented a laissez-faire philosophy with respect to relief. The FERA, on the other hand, represented, especially in the person of its administrator, Harry L. Hopkins, the more advanced philosophy of the social worker.

## HARRY L. HOPKINS

Every administrator, if he rises above the mediocre, impresses his personality upon the agency he heads. The degree to which this happens, however, depends upon two conditions: the age of the agency and the character of the administrator. Time tends to make rigid the philosophy of a public agency and to solidify the forms through which it expresses its purpose. In such an environment a new administrator, unless his temperament be iconoclastic, is more likely to be administered by the agency than to administer it. On the other hand, an incapable administrator, if given charge of a new agency, is rendered doubly incompetent when there is no inherited structure to sustain him. In the former case mediocrity results, and in the latter, chaos.

In the FERA, and subsequently the WPA, the agency found the man as surely as the man found the agency. Credit for the selection belongs to President Roosevelt, who as governor of New York was already acquainted with Harry Hopkins' work on the New York State TERA. But the reasons that prompted the appointment transcended personal ties, if such existed at that early date, and were based upon sound administrative considerations. When a public body attempts an entirely new task for which it lacks among its existing personnel men trained in the new discipline and acquainted with its aims, it is a counsel of wisdom to appoint as administrator one who is not only schooled in the techniques and enthusiastic about the purpose but who also commands the respect of the professional body whose leadership he assumes. Such a professional champion, if he possesses administrative aptitude, can construct a strong procedural foundation that, by articulating purpose in structure, acquires those attributes of permanency that enable it to outlast the apostolic period and become, if such is its fate, part of the accepted machinery of governments.

From the autumn of 1912, when, directly from Grinnell College, he came to Christodora House of New York's lower East Side, until April, 1933, when he was drafted by the President to head the new FERA, Hopkins had engaged in professional social work. Beginning as counselor at the Christodora boys' camp in New Jersey, he remained with Christodora House to do club work with boys. In the following April he was engaged by the Association for Improving the Condition of the Poor, at forty-five dollars a month, to do field studies in sociology. In this capacity he frequented the slums, mostly at night; and in tenements, in open lots, and by the water front he listened to the age-old chronicle of the poor. His impressions were expressed in a report that won him the commendation of his superiors. In 1915 he left the AICP to become executive head of Mayor Mitchel's new Board of Child Welfare, which, significantly, was the city's first appreciable recognition of public responsibility for relief, and provided pensions for indigent widows with children. Rejected by the Army because of defective vision when the United States entered World War I, he accepted a position as head of the Gulf Division of the Red Cross and eventually became director of the entire Southern Division. In 1922 he returned to the AICP as assistant director at a salary of $8,000. At this time the Association was making a study of the East Side to discover precisely the nature and extent of welfare work in that area, and to determine what co-ordination and combination among the several agencies could suitably be attempted. This research, of which Hopkins was given direction, involved the application of charity organization principles to a given area and condition, and schooled him in techniques of investigation and analysis that later enabled him to establish on a national scale a mammoth, and withal a remarkably efficient, research organization within the WPA. In 1924 he reached the summit of his private career when he was appointed director of the New York Tuberculosis Association, a newly created unit of New York's Charity Organization Society, at a salary of $10,000. Here again Harry Hopkins showed that felicity of imagination and courage of action that distinguished his career, and under his leadership the new organization expanded into general health work, heart diseases, dentistry, social hygiene, and research in preventive medicine to such a degree that it quickly became a model of its kind in the country.

After seven years as director of the New York Tuberculosis Association, he accepted Governor Roosevelt's invitation to become working director of the newly established New York Temporary Emergency Relief Administration at a salary of $11,500. When Jesse Isidor Straus resigned the chairmanship of the TERA in 1932, he was succeeded by Hopkins. It was indicative of the esteem in which he was generally held that his appointment to the TERA had been recommended to Roose-

28

velt by prominent citizens of the state, like Jesse Straus, as well as by his colleagues in charity organization work. With nineteen years of internship in the theory and practice of social service and a two-year novitiate in public administration, he entered the federal government in April, 1933, with a professional status that none could question and few could equal. The fact that he came to Washington at a salary $3,000 less than what he had been receiving in New York, though it does not represent a heroic sacrifice, indicates a sense of professional duty that is not universal.*

In the discipline of social service, however, as in other disciplines, knowledge and experience are not enough. To these two must be added integrity of purpose and devotion to a cause, without which knowledge becomes mere cleverness and experience little more than administrative legerdemain. Both these qualities Hopkins possessed in an eminent degree. His allegiance to the philosophy of the New Deal, which he rightly conceived to be the application of the principles of social service to the problems of the depression, was equaled only by his loyalty to the person of Roosevelt. Indeed, there were not two loyalties but one; for to Harry Hopkins, as to millions of others, Franklin D. Roosevelt *was* the new dispensation. In Hopkins, on the other hand, the President found a man after his own heart, one who shared his intellectual vitality, moral courage, and inventive genius, and who was absolutely faithful not because he was blindly obedient but because he had supreme trust in the integrity of his chief.

Raymond Clapper, whose ability to distinguish between the genuine and the sham made him a great journalist, wrote in December, 1937, an appreciation of Harry Hopkins. The analysis is keen as well as just, and is the more significant because it comes from the pen of a man who was as quick to criticize the shortcomings of the New Deal as he was to defend its virtues. In part the article reads:

> Most of those young, daring, and active New Dealers who mobilized in Washington in the spring of 1933 have succumbed to weary, disillusioned middle age. Some of them left, unable to endure the heat of conspicuous public life. Others went away to make money. Then you will find a number of them who have just grown tired. They are still around, but their eager enthusiasm is gone. They have discovered that making America over is a discouragingly slow and tedious task, quite thankless and full of grief. So they

*Many popular accounts of Hopkins' career appeared in periodicals during the period of his political prominence. One of the best is "Harry Hopkins," *Fortune*, Vol. XII, No. 1 (July, 1935), pp. 59-63, upon which the above analysis is largely based.

have become muscle-bound in office routine and have taken the drab protective coloration of the professional government employees whose chief end in life is to stay on the payroll and keep out of trouble.

But none of this is true of Harry Hopkins. He is going to see it through. He not only remains the senior veteran of the original New Dealers but is as zestful, as eager, and as hopeful as he was on that May day in 1933 when he arrived in Washington to take charge of relief administration for the new President. He has had bitter and disappointing experiences. In four and a half years as head of federal relief, Hopkins has been the object of more criticism and controversy than all other New Dealers combined. You might think that by now his sharp-jutting chin would have been worn away by what it has had to take. Yet it is sticking out as strong as ever, ready for more. He has learned that some things just can't be done. But he is convinced still that many things can be done. So he isn't quitting. On the contrary, he has his second wind.[1]

Harry Hopkins' qualities, to be sure, were not without their limitations. To a degree these were personal and, to a degree, inherent in the situation. Political dexterity is not a quality that one seeks in an apostle, or that, having found, one praises; and Hopkins entered the national arena with all the enthusiasm and conviction with which St. Paul ascended the Areopagus. The leader of a new movement, if he is worthy of leadership, necessarily breaks images. Besides, Hopkins shared with the professional expert in other fields that attitude which is sometimes contemptuous toward, and almost always impatient with, the devices of the lay politician. This tendency, although it is salutary if kept within limits, and certainly not without grounds, approaches the naïve when it outlaws politics in the government of a two-party state. Government *by* experts fosters absolutism as surely as government *without* experts implies anarchy. Democracy requires government by politicians with the advice of experts.

Hopkins' impatience with the counsels of political prudence led him upon occasion to attempt the politically impossible, and on other occasions, as in the early WPA arts program, the administratively impossible. In time, to be sure, he became more tolerant toward the exigencies of political action—the WPA provided a school for politics—but he never achieved the refinements of the true politician, and for that reason was never politically acceptable, even to his own party. He learned to make compromises, to be sure, as does almost every man who enters and remains in public life; but he never became a man of compromise, and, consequently, the politician who accepted his favors was as suspicious of the giving as the giver was of the asking. In this ultimate sense, Hopkins was politically maladroit, and his fondness for good living, which would have commended another man, only served to arouse antagonism and criticism.

The aptitude for improvisation and innovation, which, as a master in the field of social service, he possessed both by nature and by training, also at times approached the extreme. The relief agencies of the New Deal, and especially the WPA, were in a sense acts of creation, and eminently needed in their first administrator a tolerance for novelty. Improvisation, however, as Aristotle would have said, is a mean between inaction and impetuosity, and Hopkins sometimes inclined to the latter extreme. Quick decisions were so necessary, especially at the beginning, that there was an inclination to accept speed as of the essence of judgment. Consequently, on more than one occasion he issued instructions that a day or so later he reversed on second thought, often after his subordinates had already put, or begun to put, his directions into effect. The confusion, and sometimes the positive embarrassment, was not always inconsequential. Indeed, the wiser of his aides soon learned to recognize these "snap" decisions for what they were, and to wait at least twenty-four hours before acting upon them.

There was also the tendency to speak absolutely when qualification was necessary, as when under the WPA he told the directors of the four arts projects categorically that they would run their programs without any interference from the state administrators. On such occasions, it sometimes became the thankless task of an assistant administrator to soften the disappointment of the expert and to mitigate the resentment of the politician, and, between the two, to achieve a *modus vivendi* that would permit the continuance of the program.

An appreciation of the qualities of Harry Hopkins, and the defects in those qualities, is essential to this inquiry, for he impressed his character upon the relief agencies of the New Deal as clearly as the President stamped his upon the New Deal itself. There is a mutual influence between administrators and administrations that, if it proceeds far enough, approaches identification. In this sense, Harry Hopkins became a synonym for work relief.

## THE FERA AND WORK RELIEF

The three main programs of the FERA were direct relief, work relief, and special programs. Of these, only the second concerns this inquiry.

Harry Hopkins' basic philosophy with respect to work relief was expressed in homely but vigorous language at a WPA staff conference in June, 1935. On that occasion he said:

> What is more important, that this fellow who has been kicked around now for years and given a lot of relief, some of it pretty miserable and uncertain, be given a job, or that some great bridge be built and he not get a job? . . .
>
> Never forget that the objective of this whole program as laid down by the President, and he has laid it down over and over again, is the objective of taking 3,500,000 people off relief and putting them to work, and the secondary objective is to put them to work on the best possible projects we can, but don't ever forget that first objective, and don't let me hear any of you apologizing for it because it is nothing to be ashamed of.[2]

These words represented Hopkins' point of view in 1933 as truly as when they were spoken in 1935. Then, as later, he meant by work relief emphasis upon the worker and not upon the work. The FERA administrator was always utterly clear about this fundamental distinction between work relief and public works. Indeed, it was his ability to make this distinction clear to the President that enabled him eventually to triumph over Harold Ickes, who, through his PWA, sought in public works the resolution of the crisis.

The FERA provided an excellent instrument for the instruction of the layman in the principles of social service, for, although a grant-in-aid agency, it differed from all previous such agencies in its powers of supervision and control. In the first place, even in the making of grants a discretionary power was lodged with the FERA. Of the $500,000,000, one-half was to be granted on the basis of one dollar for each three dollars of public moneys, from all sources, spent in the state for unemployment relief during the preceding three months. Quarterly grants under this section were automatic. The other $250,000,000 however, could be granted at the discretion of the administrator to those states whose financial situation was such that they could not meet the matching provisions. The amount available to any one state was limited by the provision that it should not exceed 15 per cent of the total available for allocation.

In the second place, Congress, aware of the lack of adequate information upon which to base a relief program, enacted in section 3(c) of the Federal Emergency Relief Act of 1933 that "in executing any of the provisions of this Act, the Administrator, and any person duly authorized or designated by him, may conduct any investigation pertinent or material to the furtherance of the purposes of this Act and, at the request of the President, shall make such further investigations and studies as the President may deem necessary in dealing with the problems of unemployment relief." This section is important, for it was not only the statutory basis for the research program of the FERA but it also enabled the administrator to investigate the administration of relief in any of the states.

Finally, the most important from the point of view of federal control, section 5 of the act provided that information, in a form to be determined by the administrator, should accompany each state application. This information included (1) a statement of the financial situation within the state with respect to relief; (2) the provision made for administrative supervision; (3) the provision made for suitable standards of relief; and (4) a statement of the purposes for which the funds requested were to be used. Section 6 complemented this provision by requiring that ". . . the Governor of each State receiving grants under this Act shall file monthly with the Administrator, and in the form required by him, a report of the disbursements made under such grants."

The FERA reinforced these statutory provisions for control by administrative devices of its own. The first of these was the institution of field representatives, at first with roving commissions but later regionalized in nine strategically placed offices. These men were the "eyes and ears" of the administrator and, unlike the field officers of the RFC, played a major part in shaping state relief policy after the pattern of the Washington office. Closely allied to the field staff in purpose, but more limited in function, was the FERA division of investigation established in July, 1934, to investigate complaints and report criminal irregularities. Through this division and his field staff the administrator not only extended his personality throughout the land but also impressed it upon the several state relief administrations.

But of all controls the most effective was that exercised over state personnel. With regard to the Washington office, the administrator's power to select and to dismiss personnel was complete, for the Act, in section 3(c), gave him "authority to appoint and fix the compensation of all employees of the Administration, without regard to the Civil Service laws or the Classification Act of 1923 as amended. . . ." The state and local personnel, however, since they were not federal employees, were not directly under the jurisdiction of the FERA. The federal administrator, therefore, exerted his influence indirectly by the promulgation of rules and by pressure through statutory and administrative sanctions.

33

It has already been observed that the staff of the FERA represented the philosophy of the social worker. It was natural that the central office should wish to see realized in the states and localities a point of view consistent with its own. Indeed, the first problem of the agency was to build up adequate state and local relief administrations. It required very early each local relief administration to have at least one trained and experienced investigator on its staff.[3] Thus the social caseworker gained entrée to public employment. In the second place, although the FERA forbade the turning over of federal emergency relief funds to a private welfare agency, the prohibition was softened by the suggestion that in many cases the staffs of private relief agencies could be made public employees, serving either with or without pay.[4] Since, before the FERA, many localities had depended upon private welfare agencies for certification of the indigent and in some cases for administration of work programs, it was natural that the same localities should now look to these agents for similar services. Thus a considerable number of social workers were employed in a public capacity by state and local relief agencies. Moreover, in a subsequent pronouncement, the FERA allowed public agencies to make use of the personnel of private agencies provided that "for the time being it becomes an integral part of the public agency" and "visible evidence of the integration into the public agency is provided."[5] This attempt to build the local agencies according to the philosophy of the central office was not conspicuously successful, at least in the early FERA. The local staffs retained predominantly the plain man's point of view with respect to relief. At the same time, the presence of professional personnel on staffs below the federal level had a leavening effect and served, so to speak, to extend downward the personality of the Washington office. Indeed, so far as trained social workers were concerned, the need was greater than the supply, and in consequence the FERA undertook to subsidize the education of caseworkers by granting funds to thirty-nine state relief administrations to enable them to send qualified persons to accredited schools of social work for a half-year each.

Occasionally, when political patronage threatened the integrity of the program or amateur methods its efficiency, the federal administrator invoked the ultimate sanction of withholding, or threatening to withhold, grants. Such drastic action was adopted only *in extremis*, and to force the appointment or removal of a high administrative official, for the sword was doubled-edged. The withholding of funds, to be sure, embarrassed the state relief administrations, but its economic impact was not upon them but upon the destitute. Moreover, Congress as the dispenser of patronage looked askance upon all attempts of federal grant-in-aid agencies to impose their own personal standards upon the states. Indeed, at the Senate hearings on the FERA Bill for 1935, Hopkins was closely questioned on this score, and any attempt to use such a sanction generally would probably have resulted in a statutory prohibition.

## THE FERA PROGRAM OF DIVERSIFICATION

Edward A. Williams, the historian of the FERA, expresses the purpose of these several controls:

> The character and number of the regulations issued by the FERA indicate that the federal agency believed it necessary to take a strong hand in shaping state and local relief policies and administration. The federal relief officials were not satisfied with attempting to establish safeguards for the honest expenditure of federal moneys by the states; a further objective was to channel state and local spending in such a manner as to carry out definite social policies.[6]

The immediate social policies that the FERA endeavored to achieve were: (1) the substitution of work relief for direct relief; and (2) the diversification of the work-relief program and the improvement of its standards so that jobs would be provided in accordance with the skills of the unemployed. The second policy was a refinement of the first, and implicitly an emphasis upon white-collar projects. Speaking over the radio in October, 1933, Hopkins said:

> We have started several new things in the way of work relief. The policy we are following is to try to find things to do that use the special capacities of the persons on relief. There would be no sense in giving an unemployed needy teacher a brush hook and telling him or her to go out and cut weeds along a road, when there are thousands of adult unemployed people who need some more schooling.[7]

In a later statement Jacob Baker summarized the same fundamental philosophy:

> The history of FERA . . . could be summed up as a continuous effort to devise the best methods for providing jobs, so that as many people as possible might be given employment in the skills and trainings which they have

35

been accustomed to practice. For we realized early that it is more harmful to a man's morale to put him to work at a job he was not fitted for, to put a doctor of philosophy or a mechanic to digging ditches, than to give him a dole, and let him remain idle.[8]

Diversification developed as the experience and knowledge of the Washington staff grew:

When FERA first appeared on the scene, practically nothing at all was known about the people on relief; in June, 1933, we did not even know how many were on relief; we certainly did not know how many of them were employable; we did not know anything about the occupational characteristics of those that were employable; how many carpenters, electricians, artists, writers, chemists, typists, surveyors there were. . . .

The study of urban populations revealed the fact . . . that at least a million of the people referred to were industrial factory workers, and therefore that a purely construction program would not easily be adapted to their needs. You can see, therefore, that an immense amount of research had to precede the development of a reasonably complete work program which would give every man and woman in need a job that he or she could undertake and work on usefully. Moreover, as our information grew concerning the occupational characteristics of our relief population we had, at the same time, to develop projects suited to the different categories of workers as they were separated out and classified.

The ingenuity of American engineers, sociologists, public agencies of all sorts, and the staff of our work division was taxed to the utmost to provide a sufficient variety of projects. As a beginning we have drawn up some 285 working procedures for an equal number of types of projects, to employ most of the known trades, skills and professions. In view of these facts it will become apparent that the President's announcement in January, that we were through with direct relief, and that we would give everyone of the three million five hundred thousand employables on relief a job, did not by any means come as a new turn of policy, but was the result of long preparation and planning.[9]

Other immediate reasons besides the needs of industrial factory workers suggested diversfication. In addition to the professional classes there were large numbers of retail-store employees equally unfitted for a manual program. As a matter of fact, even the manual program proceeded under limitations, for the skilled construction workers were being absorbed by the Federal Emergency Administration of Public Works (PWA), and the FERA lacked men to undertake skilled supervision of large construction projects.

Diversification of projects implied diversification of wages, and the first corollary of the new principle was the payment of wages according to the skills of the unemployed* At first the FERA merely required that

*Wages, as here used, means hourly wages. The FERA adopted the budget-deficiency principle with respect to weekly and monthly wages.

"the rate of wages should be a fair rate of pay for the work performed. Total compensation should meet the budgetary requirements of the relief recipient."[10] Shortly thereafter, however, the wage regulation was tightened by the requirement that "on and after August 1, 1933, grants made under the Federal Emergency Relief Act of 1933 can be used in paying work relief wages *only* at or above 30 cents an hour. The local prevailing rate of pay for the type of work performed should be paid if it is in excess of 30 cents an hour."[11] Thus the FERA adopted the principle of prevailing hourly rates. The communities, however, were free to interpret "prevailing" as they pleased, and there is no evidence that any substantial rise in the wage level resulted. In fact, the thirty-cent minimum tended to become a maximum, especially in the South, and in the end Hopkins withdrew the provision.[12] The principle of wage diversification, although accomplishing little in the early FERA program, became a major tenet of later federal relief programs.

THE ORGANIZATION OF WORK RELIEF AND SPECIAL PROJECTS

If Harry Hopkins was the inspiration of the white-collar program, Jacob Baker was responsible for its elaboration and operation. Brought to the FERA in the summer of 1933 to become Director of Work Relief and Special Projects, he possessed the engineer's mind for mechanical detail and, because of a diverse professional and business experience, a sounder sense of administrative form than his chief's. Not a professional social worker himself, he was able to envisage the program in terms of wider relationships than those apparent to the more specialized personnel, and the very versatility of his mind when joined with his scientific approach reduced theory to practice and gave structural and administrative form to the speculative principles of the social philosopher. A short appreciation of his career appeared in *Fortune* in 1935, and shows how different was his background from that of Hopkins:

> Jacob Baker . . . is a bald, thickset, amiable engineer of forty whose casual manner conceals a vigorously theoretical and inventive turn of mind. It is one thing to say work relief and another thing to suggest and develop the work. Mr. Baker has to date been the chief instigator of the FERA's work projects, having supervision of its engineering programs and unemployed cooperatives, and his importance is bound to increase during the new work-relief program. He has had the most varied career of any of the FERA officials. He was raised on his father's Colorado ranch and did five years' work in education and agricultural engineering at Colorado Teachers College, Colorado Agricultural College, and the University of California. He has taught

science and agriculture in rural high schools in Idaho and California, has been a ranchman, day laborer, and construction "stiff," a superintendent of ranchers and mines in Mexico, a personnel expert with Bethlehem Shipbuilding Corp. and the San Joaquin Light & Power Corp. of California, and a consulting industrial engineer in Los Angeles (J. Lee Nicholson & Co.) and Chicago (House, Baker & Associates). As a partner in the latter firm he assisted in many of Samuel Insull's mid-boom mergers. In 1926 he helped set up and directed a popular educational publishing house (now the Vanguard Press of New York) under the American Fund for Public Service. He was recommended to Mr. Hopkins by Langdon Post of New York, who himself was assistant to Mr. Hopkins in the early days of the FERA.[13]

It is obvious that if Baker eventually arrived at the same conceptual destination as Hopkins, he traveled by a less direct and a quite different road. In fact, his interest in work relief and white-collar projects was not derived from the philosophy of social service but from the experiences of a socially minded engineer who saw in the co-operative movement the fabric of a new order.*

Even his approach to the problem of the white-collar unemployed was colored by his predilection for co-operative enterprise. In a letter written in 1934 he said in part:

> One of the things that the present system of industrial, social, and economic organization would make desirable would be possible increased security for professional occupations. Within the framework of things as they are at the present time these folks are all in the position of carrying on services that have to be sold individually. Some exploration of the possibility of setting up corporate research and service agencies that, through cooperative membership or otherwise, would be of greater security to professional people, would be interesting.[14]

### FEDERAL PROJECTS

In its program of diversification the FERA directly encouraged three types of projects: federal projects, women's projects, and white-collar projects. None of these programs had progressed far before the inception of the CWA, but their early beginning presaged more substantial development later.

The first effort was to encourage federal projects—i.e., projects un-

---

*In addition to his other duties, Mr. Baker was in charge of FERA's development of co-operatives among the unemployed, and, in a sense, co-operatives always remained his first concern. When, in the summer of 1936, he resigned as assistant administrator of the WPA, he was sent to Europe by that agency to study the co-operative movement there.

dertaken and supervised by departments of the federal government—with grants from the FERA, not directly to the federal department, but through the mediation of the states. No federal funds were allocated specifically or earmarked for these projects. As early as July 8, 1933, Hopkins wrote to the FERA field representatives:

> We are now exploring with the several Departments of Government possible work relief projects which will be under Federal auspices. These projects will be many and varied—anywhere from the control of Japanese beetles to major improvements on air fields belonging to the Army and Navy. We look forward to possible co-operative enterprises with all departments.[15]

In the *Monthly Report* for July, 1933, this source of diversification was further explored, and one of the projects suggested was "various studies provided for the occupation of white-collar workers."[16] It was ruled that such projects must in general be apart from normal governmental enterprises and not such as would have been carried out in due course regardless of an emergency.[17] This last clause was designed to allow the departments to undertake projects that they had had in mind and would have undertaken if the emergency had not intervened.

In the September *Report* the earliest of these projects to receive approval were listed.

> Work relief projects on a large scale will shortly be undertaken in the fields of malarial control, insect and rodent control, rural sanitation, coastal and geodetic surveys, and in taking of a building census to determine local trends in the industry, the need or lack of need for new structures, etc.[18]

This move was important because it represents the first small step in the direction of the federalization of work relief. The reasons for it, as they appeared to the FERA staff, are indicated in a memorandum written about this time.

> Until relief was federalized it was not possible to carry on programs of national significance under the auspices of the Federal departments. Federalizing the program will make it possible to employ large numbers of workers usefully in ways which would hardly be undertaken locally or by the states.[19]

It must be remembered that Hopkins, before becoming administrator of the FERA, was connected with the New York State TERA, which had undertaken state projects under the auspices of departments of the state government. These state projects leaned toward the encouragement of white-collar work and naturally inspired the administrator to attempt the like on a national scale.

It was not long before Hopkins, having started certain federal programs, now set out to encourage the states to adopt statewide programs that would tend in the same direction. The whole emphasis was toward raising work relief from the local level. On September 22, 1933, for instance, he wrote to the state offices of the FERA:

> We are definitely interested in furthering good work-relief projects in cooperation with other governmental units, not only Federal, but also State and local. We wonder if it would be a good thing if you in your turn would try to stimulate work of this kind in your own State. If you send a letter to the divisions of your State Government like the one which we have sent to the Federal Departments, and follow it up as we intend to by personal inquiry, the result might be well worth the effort.[20]

Few states, however, showed initiative in working out and operating such statewide projects. Indeed, it required considerable persuasion from the FERA to induce state administrators to approve federal projects. Jacob Baker felt it necessary gently to remind them:

> In deciding whether to carry out these projects [federal projects], when it is a choice between them and purely local projects, it should be remembered that Federal Relief Funds are being used to pay a considerable portion of the entire relief bills of all of the States.[21]

In order further to stimulate inventiveness on the part of the state relief administrations, Baker wrote to them:

> There is a wide variety of projects that fall in the territory between *normal governmental activities* on the one hand and *public works* on the other which can properly be carried out with work-relief labor. In this field may be many things you would like to do that have social and economic value, such as record revision, research, surveys, field work and so on, for which it is very unlikely that funds will ever be provided [in the normal budget of a public body].[22]

The encouragement of white-collar projects, which was the primary aim of these federal projects, is further revealed in a letter from Baker to Grace Abbott of the Children's Bureau, Department of Labor:

> We are anxious to provide work opportunities for as many of the clerical and professional people who have been forced to seek relief as we can.

The need of many of these people is so great that we can pay them enough wages on work relief to enable them to work for you continuously.[23]

The intimation contained in the last sentence quoted, that the principle of budget deficiency would be interpreted liberally in the case of the white-collar unemployed, is important, for it foreshadows an attitude that attains more significant development later.

But the hard fact was that the FERA, since it operated through grants-in-aid to the states, was unable to compel participation in federal projects. Actually, these projects were federal only in the sense that the FERA made arrangements with the proper federal authorities for their prosecution. The initiation of a work project within a state on behalf of a federal agency lay within the discretion of the state relief administrations: "Regardless of where projects of this kind originate, the responsibility for their final approval rests upom the State Relief Administrations which shall consider them in the light of the same rules that apply to any other work relief projects."[24]

The FERA acted merely to secure and maintain liaison between the state relief administrations and the proper federal departments. Moreover, no funds other than the state's regular grant were earmarked for the prosecution of federal projects: "No Federal Relief Funds will be allocated or granted by us specifically for any of these projects. Consequently, where it is practicable to carry them out, the workers will be furnished by the local relief administration and paid from the funds available to it."[25]

Under such conditions prosecution of federal projects within the states was not vigorous. The states and localities were unable or unwilling to undertake the cost of supervision and material, and the federal agencies were reluctant to finance such costs out of their regular appropriations.

To correct this situation the PWA allocated $2,000,000 for material and supervisory expense of federal work relief projects in October, 1933. The purpose of the allocation is described in a letter from Baker to R. G. Tugwell, then Assistant Secretary of Agriculture.

This fund is small but vital. Ordinarily the ratio of it [material and supervisory expense] to the relief which is to be earned as wages is less than 10%. These expenses may not be paid from relief funds. While the Federal Departments are more than willing to assume complete responsibility for the technical direction of projects, they can, in no case, pay these costs because of their reduced budgets.

These expenses differ for different projects. In general they must cover salaried supervision in states where no competent person can be obtained as a volunteer. All traveling expenses of the supervisory personnel, whether voluntary or otherwise, will be charged against this fund as well as the actual costs of materials, instruments, and incidentals, such as stationary and postage.[26]

This fund, however, was relatively small compared with the ambitions of the program, and was recognized as such. The above memorandum goes on to indicate that funds for some projects might be secured from other than governmental sources, and announces a plan to submit the malarial control project to the Rockefeller Foundation "with a request that a grant be made . . . to cover the expense of material and necessary accessory services."[27]

These early federal projects, though their accomplishments hardly progressed beyond the embryonic stage, served to reveal the difficulties that any white-collar program was apt to encounter. In the first place, the state and local relief administrations, partly because the immediate pressure upon them was exerted by the manual worker through unions and other forms of concerted action, were reluctant to undertake projects that were at once more costly and less popular. In the second place, the budget-deficiency principle, making it necessary to stagger employment, might work reasonably well in unskilled manual projects; but it produced an awkward and at times an impossible situation in the case of projects for which professional qualifications on the part of all the workers and constant supervision of a non-routine nature were essential. Finally, the financing of material and supervisory expenses was difficult, for FERA grants could not be used for that purpose, and the states and localities were unwilling for the most part to use their funds to the same end.

## WOMEN'S WORK

The second method, used for purposes of diversification, was the establishment of a work program for women. The women's work section was set up by the FERA on September 21, 1933, and the first official notice of it was sent to the states on October 13. The letter read:

Very little has been done to develop a program of work relief for women.

In order to centralize the responsibility for the development of useful projects for women, I have added to our staff Mrs. Ellen S. Woodward who is Director of Women's Work.

We feel that a properly qualified woman should be added to your staff to work with Mrs. Woodward. You may be able to deputize someone already on your staff. If not, the woman you appoint should be familiar with the existing governmental, social and civic agencies; with the employment services; and with the relief-work program now in operation. Possibly a well qualified person might be loaned from some other agency—at any rate, she should give her full time to this work.

Since the approval of this office is required before an appointment to this position can be effective, we would like to have you send us at the earliest possible moment the name and qualifications of the woman whom you would like to appoint. We are eager to start this work immediately.[28]

It is significant that the Washington office, in accordance with its policy of establishing personnel standards in the states, required not only the appointment in each state office of a director of women's work but also Washington approval of the appointee. It was hoped and, by and large, to be expected that these new members of the state staffs would be women with liberal social tendencies and, because social service was predominantly a woman's profession, familiar with, and favorably inclined toward, the philosophy of the social worker. The appointment of Mrs. Woodward is also noteworthy, because in the summer of 1936 she became assistant administrator of the WPA in charge of the Women's and Professional Division and thus administratively responsible for the cultural program of that agency.

The emphasis upon women's work naturally encouraged an emphasis upon white-collar projects. Women were not fitted for outdoor labor. There were, to be sure, manual projects upon which women could be put to work, such as sewing, gardening, and canning; and throughout the work programs of the FERA and the WPA the large majority were placed upon such projects. In fact, for September, 1933, 72.2 per cent of all women on work relief were employed on manual, or service projects, as they were called. But whereas the ratio of all workers employed on white-collar projects was less than 10 per cent, that of women so employed was 23.5 per cent.

Thus the emphasis upon women's work further encouraged the trend toward diversification, and actually was designed for that purpose. In November, 1933, a list of work projects for women, those in operation and those in preparation, showed the extent of this development. It is significant that cultural projects are among those especially designed for women.

1. *Work projects*

    a. *In operation*

    Among the most important work projects now in operation for unemployed women are: programs in recreation, dramatics and handcrafts; municipal horticultural nurseries, child feeding; sewing rooms; gardens; canning, and emergency nursery schools, and housing for transients. . . .

b. *Under preparation*

Among the projects under preparation are community centers where unemployed women trained in dressmaking, millinery, beauty culture, arts, crafts, and other vocational fields may teach the less skilled. Special projects are being planned for unemployed librarians, artists, musicians, actors, home economists, home demonstration agents, vocational specialists, older women and others.[29]

On November 20, 1933, a conference on emergency needs for women was held at the White House. Those attending were prominent in women's organizations and social work throughout the country. Harry Hopkins, Mrs. Roosevelt and Mrs. Woodward all addressed the conference, and their talks were followed by general discussion. Although the purpose of the meeting was to devise a women's program for the CWA, the minutes give in retrospect an excellent picture of work already done by and before the early FERA. Hopkins, in stating the problem, expressed his belief that there were between three and four hundred thousand women in the United States needing special services that under the law could be given either by the FERA or by the CWA. The disposition of these women, he further observed, was not on a population basis. They were concentrated in the urban areas. How undeveloped was the women's program is indicated by Hopkins' statement that "outside of New York City and half a dozen other places, we have had no experience in putting women to work."[30] According to him, there were fifty thousand women on work relief on November 20, 1933: "And we have found, in the main, an almost complete lack of imagination about work relief projects for women throughout this country. You can count on the fingers of one hand the cities that have shown great imagination in this."[31]

In her address Mrs. Woodward anticipated two major problems in the women's program: avoidance of competitive fields, and the difficulty of using women on mass projects such as were suitable for men.[32] The first difficulty concerned mainly work of a factory nature, such as mattress-making, which provoked objections from manufacturers. The second difficulty, however, struck at the very nature of clerical and professional projects. It was obvious that there would have to be many such projects, each relatively small, and that the costs of administration and supervision would be relatively higher than on large manual projects. This problem of project cost remained a stumbling block in the white-collar program.

Mrs. Woodward read a partial report concerning women on work relief in seventeen states for the month of September, 1933. Listed among the cultural projects in operation were service in museums and art galleries, musical programs, projects for artists, and handicraft. No mention was made of a theater project, but it said that "among the people for whom we are planning special projects are the stage group."[33] Mrs. Woodward paid special tribute to the active music program in New York City and to the research projects of the Alabama Department of Archives and History.[34]

The intransigeance of state and local relief authorities in the matter of white-collar and women's work was recognized, and the solution suggested by Mrs. Roosevelt is interesting in the light of subsequent developments. In her address she said:

> In talking to Mr. Hopkins the other day we came to two conclusions: one was that it would be necessary to tell people in different places that either a certain number of jobs must be found for a certain number of women or that a certain amount of money allotted must be used for giving the women work.[35]

The suggestion that the state relief administrators (the "people in different places") should be ordered to employ a certain number of women or to earmark a certain amount of money for their employment was not followed through at that time. A year later, however, an attempt was made to earmark a certain portion of FERA funds for white-collar projects. This was soon abandoned.

It was recognized that the FERA's rule against the granting of money to private agencies, even though non-profit, curtailed many opportunities for work relief for women. Mrs. Belmont's committee in New York City had found much employment for women in private non-profit agencies. Much more could now be done, it was observed, if the prohibition were lifted.[36] For obvious reasons, however, no step in this direction was taken.

Departments of the state governments in general were found to be more liberal than local authorities in promoting women's and professional projects. Of these, recreational and educational projects offered the best opportunities for such work relief. During the early years of the depression much discussion of the new leisure that technological advance had created brought an emphasis upon leisure-time activities of a recreational and educational type; and the influence of this thinking was felt at the conference. Mrs. Alexander Jardine, president of the National Federation of Music Clubs, offered the co-operation of her association "to any educational program that includes music . . . and in a program that will carry on in the professional fields of music, and in any way that we may assist in taking care of the leisure hours that are produced now."[37]

The copying of old records was particularly appealing, partly because records were so plentiful in state and local depositories, and partly because professional qualifications on the part of the workers were not necessary, except for supervision. Mrs. Bowman, president of the National Federation of Business and Professional Women's Clubs, remarked, "We have in Virginia literally thousands of records intimately connected with the founding of America and which are covered with dust and unobtainable with no copies of them in existence. That work can be done by women."[38]

Dr. Stanley, chief of the Bureau of Home Economics, Department of Agriculture, suggested establishing a number of research projects that would use women, trained home economists, clerical workers, and chemists.[39]

The importance of this conference, coming, as it did, at the very beginning of the work-relief program, needs emphasis. The women who attended it were nationally prominent in government or in social and cultural organizations. Their progressive point of view, if it was not in every case acquired through the discipline of social service, was colored by its philosophy; and the natural inclination of their sex toward beneficence, coupled with a proper sympathy and loyalty toward their less fortunate sisters, reinforced their acquired convictions. Above all, they had as their champion Eleanor Roosevelt. If her influence was less than that of her husband, it was because she lacked an official position; yet the very fact that she stood outside the government gave her a freedom of expression and action that emancipated her from the bondage of political expediency.

Women's projects and federal projects provided in common an emphasis upon the white-collar unemployed, and the close relationship in purpose between the two was recognized in a letter from the women's section of the FERA, suggesting that, where possible, women replace men on federal projects. The letter reads in part:

> In furnishing personnel for Federal projects you are to pay particular attention that women are employed wherever possible. The Federal departments, under whose auspices these projects are being carried out, are being similarly instructed. . . .
> In many instances men are now being employed to do work that could

be done by women. Wherever other jobs, which are not suitable for women, can be found for these men, we urge that the men be transferred and that women be used to take their places.[40]

## PROFESSIONAL PROJECTS

Although the programs for federal projects and women's projects both tended toward the encouragement of employment of professional workers, it was not until the end of October, 1933, that professional projects as such, and unrelated to any other program, were definitely urged upon the states. Late in October, 1933, Jacob Baker wrote a letter in answer to a particular inquiry, and in it he expressed a new principle with regard to the budget-deficiency policy. The pertinent part of the communication reads:

> Where suitable work relief on a basis of continuous service can be found for people in the clerical and professional group who have been forced to seek relief, our attitude is as follows:
> You may pay work-relief wages that run up to twelve or fifteen dollars a week to persons suitable for teaching, managing or interviewing in Reemployment offices, or doing technical, engineering or supervisory work as foremen or specialists or any other crews. The Work Relief wage allowance, of course, is based upon budgetary deficiency. In establishing this, prior living standards must be included as an important factor. Ordinarily, the people capable of the work mentioned will have had a prior living standard justifying a weekly budgetary allowance running between ten and fifteen dollars a week. . . . [41]

Five days later, the policy expressed in this letter was made official by a general communication to all state administrations that read:

> We are anxious to provide suitable work relief for the ever increasing numbers of people with clerical and professional training who are being forced on to the relief rolls.
> Continuity of supervision is particularly necessary on work relief projects if good work is to be done, owing to the fact that the workers themselves are staggered or rotated. Continuous service is understood not to exceed 40 hours per week.
> In order that persons in the clerical and professional group may be employed continuously as supervisors and in other ways, where continuous service is required, this office has advised in every case in which an inquiry has been made that the State Relief Administrations are justified in taking account of the prior standard of living in determining budget deficiencies. There are on relief many people who are capable of teaching, nursing, interviewing, and of doing technical, engineering, supervisory and managerial work, and of acting as specialists in various ways. Among them are many whose needs

47

will justify paying them a work relief wage running from ten to fifteen dollars a week.

The purpose of this letter is simply to acquaint all of the States with the advice given to some. The Federal work relief projects will afford an excellent placement for many of the clerical and professional people on the relief rolls.[42]

The consideration of *standards* of living in addition to *cost* of living —and especially the consideration of standards of living between classes in the same community—was novel and, as a device for encouraging white-collar projects, was a happy inspiration. In work relief for the professional classes the primary problem, as Baker observed, was supervision. Federal funds could be used only to pay work-relief wages to applicants certified as in need. The states, to be sure, were free to use their own funds to hire professional people not so certified to supervise projects, but they were reluctant to do so. Yet adequate supervision, especially in professional projects, was particularly important because of the staggering of work-relief employment. Baker found a partial resolution of this difficulty in permitting continuous (as opposed to staggered) employment of professional personnel from the relief rolls and paid from federal funds, with the justification that the higher living standards of this class vindicated the granting to them of higher weekly wages. Thus the preferential attitude of the FERA toward this class manifested itself not only in encouraging their employment but also in recommending for them higher relief wages. In this connection it is significant that the wage structure of the WPA was based not only on differences in cost of living but also on differences in standard of living.

The zeal with which the FERA encouraged white-collar projects was equaled only by the inability or reluctance of the localities to co-operate. In November, 1933, the answers to a questionnaire on white-collar relief, sent to over 450 communities, were analyzed. The pertinent question was, "Are people assigned to projects for which they are especially qualified because of trades or professions?"

> Most of the communities replied simply "No" or that work was common labor, and a large number specified road work as the only work-relief project. Only one city commented on the fact that in planning their projects an effort was made to provide for different trades.[43]

In so far as attempts were made to employ these classes, they affected only the trades and rarely touched the professional classes. One community in New York replied that "when special projects calling for technical or professional skill are not available, workers are frequently employed at ordinary unskilled labor."[44] Another New York community said frankly:

> Unless the projects are of the made variety (almost of a play variety), men in general are not assigned according to their qualifications. As a result "white-collar" men have to do laborer's work if a really constructive improvement for the city is to be made.[45]

Constructive comments were rare. One from a community in the same state reads:

> Individual competition in achievement within reasonable limits is encouraged. Pride in work done has produced wonderful results and has done much to remove the stigma of "work relief."[46]

Almost all communities agreed that the placement of skilled and professional workers was the most difficult feature in a work-relief program. Thus, despite efforts of the FERA to encourage projects for white-collar workers through federal projects, women's work, and other ways, little was accomplished in the early part of the program. The determination of the staff, however, to convince the localities of the rightness of its advice remained undiminished, and in November, 1933, the inauguration of the Civil Works program provided a new and wider opportunity.

The early efforts of the FERA toward diversification of work projects were significant, even if they did not result in much positive accomplishment. In the first place, precedents were established that could be used to advantage and favorably developed in subsequent work-relief programs—the CWA, the later FERA, and the WPA. In the second place, the six months' experience of the early FERA provided the Washington staff with a valuable exercise in staff management and control. A federal grant-in-aid agency, whether it be for relief or any other purpose, by its very nature lacks line authority in the states and localities. Consequently, unless its administration is strong, its operations become routine and, under certain circumstances, even automatic. What direction it gives, if any, rarely transcends that of a research organization whose findings are at the disposal of its clients. The "authority of ideas," however, which students of administration rightly consider to be of the essence of staff work, rests both upon the prerogatives of advice and consultation and upon the existence of controls, which lack the formality of command but are nonetheless effective. The Washington staff of the FERA was conscious of this fact, in part because they were moved by the compelling urge of a new philosophy. But they were also aware that the very novelty and inchoate nature of work relief throughout the nation demanded a kind of supervision that would impart form to chaos and create that relative uniformity without which national integration would be impossible. The early FERA's attempts to extend staff control into the states and localities, by the use of statutory and administrative sanctions and by the less direct devices of counsel and caution, were founded on these considerations; and their meaning becomes clearer in the policy and operations of the Civil Works Administration, which early in November, 1933, was established by executive order of the President.

1. Raymond Clapper, "Who is Hopkins?", *Forum*, December, 1937, p. 283.

2. *Proceedings*, Staff Conference, WPA, June 16, 1935, pp. 23-25.

3. Rules and Regulations, No. 3, FERA, July 11, 1933.

4. Rules and Regulations, No. 1, FERA, June 23, 1933.

5. Rules and Regulations, No. 3, FERA, July 11, 1933.

6. Edward Ainsworth Williams, *Federal Aid for Relief* (New York: Columbia University Press, 1939), p. 150.

7. "Emergency Relief in the United States," Speech of Harry L. Hopkins, arranged by the Washington *Star* and broadcast over a nationwide network of NBC, Wednesday night, October 11, 1933.

8. Release for Afternoon Papers, FERA, July 3, 1935.

9. *Ibid.*

10. *Ibid.*

11. Rules and Regulations, No. 4, FERA, July 21, 1933.

12. Letter, Hopkins to All State Administrators, FERA, November 19, 1934.

13. "Harry Hopkins," *Fortune*, July, 1935, p. 126 (Copyrighted by Time, Inc.)

14. Letters, Baker to Margaret C. Klem, FERA Files.

15. Memorandum, Hopkins to Field Representatives, FERA, July 8, 1933.

16. "Interdepartmental Co-operation," *Monthly Report* of the FERA, July 1 through July 31, 1933, p. 7.

17. *Ibid.*

18. "Special Programs," *Monthly Report* of the FERA, September 1 to September 30, 1933, p. 27.

19. Memorandum (anonymous and undated), FERA.

20. Letter A-5, FERA, September 22, 1933.

21. Letter A-5-1, FERA, September 22, 1933.

22. Letter A-5-3, FERA, September 22, 1933.

23. Letter, Baker to Grace Abbott, FERA, September 22, 1933.

24. Letter A-5-1, FERA, September 22, 1933.

25. *Ibid.*

26. Letter, Baker to Rexford Tugwell, FERA, October 16, 1933.

27. *Ibid.*

28. Letter A-21, FERA, October 10, 1933.

29. Letter W-1, FERA, November 14, 1933.

30. *Proceedings of the Conference on Emergency Needs of Women*, The White House, November 20, 1933, p. 7.

31. *Ibid.*, pp. 7-8.

32. *Ibid.*, p. 11.

33. *Ibid.*, pp. 12-13.

34. *Ibid.*, p. 14.

35. *Ibid.*, p. 15.

36. *Ibid.*, pp. 24-25.

37. *Ibid.*, p. 29.

38. *Ibid.*, p. 32.

39. *Ibid.*, pp. 35-36.

40. Letter W-2, FERA, November 29, 1933.

41. Letter, Baker to E. C. Brook, FERA, October 25, 1933.

42. Letter A-28, FERA, October 30, 1933.

43. "Unemployment Relief Experience," Monthly Summary No. 12, Vol. VIII, No. 7 (November, 1933), p. 85.

44. *Ibid.*

45. *Ibid.*

46. *Ibid.*

# 4

# An Experiment in Federalization

### THE CREATION OF THE CIVIL WORKS ADMINISTRATION

The Civil Works Administration was created on November 9, 1933, by executive order of the President under authority of the National Industrial Recovery Act, approved June 16, 1933. By the same order, Harry Hopkins, administrator of the FERA, was made administrator of the CWA. The original $400,000,000 used to finance CWA operations was made available to that agency through executive order out of the appropriation of $3,300,000,000 authorized by Section 220 of the National Industrial Recovery Act.

Unlike the FERA program, the CWA program was federal. The grant-in-aid system, so far as fork relief was concerned, was temporarily abandoned, and the CWA undertook not only to finance but also to administer the program. On November 10, 1933, the state emergency relief administrators were appointed state civil works administrators; and they and their staffs, as well as the local staffs, immediately took the oath of office as federal employees.

The second difference between the early FERA and the CWA lay in the fact that the CWA program was an employment program, not merely a relief program. The goal was the employment of four million, of whom approximately two million were to be taken over from relief rolls and the other two million from non-relief applicants. Accordingly, investigation of need for aid ceased with the CWA program.

The original $400,000,000 was from PWA balances under the NIRA, and consequently use of it was restricted by statute to a construction program. Moreover, for the same reason, the CWA established wages and working conditions according to the PWA formula.*

|  | Southern Zone | Central Zone | Northern Zone |
|---|---|---|---|
| Skilled .................. | $1.10 | $1.10 | $1.20 |
| Unskilled ............... | .40 | .45 | .50 |

These rates, which were almost everywhere higher than the hourly rates paid under the FERA, approximated union rates, and in some areas, especially in the South, were higher than locally prevailing rates.

The budgetary-deficiency principle was abandoned (there was no place for it in an employment program), and maximum hours were set as eight a day, thirty a week, and 130 a month. Thus the principle of full pay for a full week's work was asserted. To be sure, only a small proportion of the CWA workers (4.2 per cent) earned the skilled rate. The majority were in the unskilled category, and the average weekly earnings for the program as a whole were approximately fifteen dollars a week. This, however, represented a significant advance above the FERA standard, and was the adoption of the principle of prevailing weekly wages.

Two main reasons counseled the inauguration of the CWA. In the first place, the CWA represented a major innovation in economic policy. The earlier attempts to defeat the depression had concentrated almost exclusively upon a large construction program, on the hypothesis that stimulation of heavy industry would provide the impetus to set the wheels in motion again. The inability of the PWA to move as quickly as had been hoped, and the failure of the business improvement of the summer of 1933 to carry into the fall, caused serious doubt of the efficacy of the remedy. In contrast, the CWA attempted to prime the pump by placing money in the hands of the lower-income groups, with the hope that flooding the market with consumer's money would raise the level of production.

In the second place, the CWA represented a sudden and gigantic experiment in the federalization of relief, and in this sense was a harbinger of the later WPA. The experience of the early FERA, especially with

*Under the PWA the forty-eight states were classified into three zones, and minimum hourly rates for skilled and unskilled labor or projects in each zone were set as follows:

respect to the work-relief program, had convinced the administration of the agency that the standards with respect to work, wages, hours of labor, and quality of projects would not be realized so long as the states administered the program. The remedy was, in their opinion, for the federal agency to be not merely a staff agency but an operating agency, actively and directly administering, controlling, and supervising the work program throughout the country, and enjoying a line command that started in the Washington office, moved to the states, and through them to the local subdivisions. Indeed, not only the administrative employees but also the project workers were on the federal payroll, and Harry Hopkins, at the height of his glory, commanded more men than the commanding general of the United States Army in World War I.

The CWA was placed in operation with incredible speed. The program reached its peak of employment—4,263,644—in the week ending January 18, 1934, a little over a month after its inception. From that time forward, employment steadily decreased, although the decline did not become precipitous until the week ending April 12, 1934, when over 90 per cent of those employed in the previous week were dismissed. In effect, therefore, the CWA program lasted for slightly over four months, although it officially began on November 9, 1933, and officially closed, except for the Washington administrative staff, on July 14, 1934.

The essence of the CWA was improvisation, and its watchword was speed. For that reason it represented to the social worker what sudden war and instant mobilization represent to the military strategist, the supreme test of professional competence. In later years the staff of the WPA looked back upon the CWA period as the golden age of work relief. The sentiment was not without justification, for the CWA, even more than the later WPA, represented the ultimate refinement of the principle of work relief, in which, though the emphasis remained upon the worker and not the work, the standards of wages and working conditions attained the respectability of a public works program.

The effect of the announcement of the CWA program throughout the country was electric, for the unemployed as well as the social worker immediately sensed the revolutionary character of the change in policy. The reaction in New York City was typical, and is thus described by Lillian Brandt:

> President Roosevelt announced a "fundamental change" in the federal relief program. In place of aid to the states for home relief and work relief a federally financed and federally operated work-program would be substi-

tuted. . . . The new program would "remove from relief all employable persons." The 2,000,000 transferred from relief-rolls on November 16 would "immediately be placed on regular pay at the hourly rate prevailing for similar work in the community" and would have thirty hours of work a week. They would no longer be subject to investigation. They would be "off relief." The second 2,000,000 would be "recruited" through the Federal Reemployment Service. They would not be required to qualify as eligible for relief. . . .

Social workers in New York City tempered their enthusiasm with practical reservations, *sotto voce*. If CWA could, as Mr. Hopkins said it would, "take all able-bodied persons now receiving relief and put them at work on regular jobs at regular wages," and then take as many more not yet on relief and do the same thing for them, it would be fine. But—"There just isn't money enough"; "I wonder if anybody has thought it *through*." Would three months give PWA and NRA time to get into their full stride, or would the federal government find itself in the middle of February with 4,000,000 CWA employees on its hands, no more money to pay them, and still no place for them in private industry? Was the expectation of such a degree of recovery by the middle of February any more reasonable, any more excusable, than the ridiculed predictions of the Hoover administration?

To the unemployed in New York City announcements of the plan sounded like the opening of the Gates of Heaven.[1]

## THE CWA WHITE-COLLAR PROGRAM

The CWA, although it employed for the most part unskilled workers as did all work-relief programs, provided the Washington staff (practically the same as the old FERA staff, except that it was larger) with a magnificent opportunity to put into practice directly the philosophy with which it had previously attempted to imbue the state relief administrations—in particular, its white-collar program. Staff concern in this regard was first manifested in the wage provisions. The PWA wage structure, which the FERA adopted, did not provide for semiskilled or clerical and professional rates. To supply this lack, the CWA ruled that semiskilled workers be paid the local prevailing hourly rate, and that clerical and professional workers be paid a prevailing *weekly* wage that in no case was to be less than eighteen, fifteen and twelve dollars a week, respectively, in the Northern, Central, and Southern zones.

At first, the prosecution of a white-collar program under the CWA raised difficulties. The PWA money was by statute available only for construction purposes, and, although a certain number of white-collar personnel was necessary and by various devices might be engaged in such a program, a large-scale white-collar program was impossible. Harry Hopkins, however, was equal to the challenge, and by a very simple but ingenious expedient he was able to inaugurate, side by side with the CWA, the Civil Works Service program. It must be remembered that the FERA, though it ceased to concern itself with work relief, continued to operate as a grant-in-aid agency, mainly for direct relief, during the CWA period. Hopkins was able, therefore, to make FERA grants-in-aid to the states for purely white-collar projects. These funds were transferred to the states with the understanding that the respective governors would endorse the checks and return them to the Federal Treasury for a Civil Works working account. In this way some $31,000,000 was available for Civil Works Service projects. In fact, this was equivalent to earmarking funds for white-collar projects.*

The CWS projects (before February 15, 1934) were under the direction of the state emergency relief administrations and under the rules of the FERA. Except that work was restricted to relief clients, the conditions under which they operated were no different from those governing CWA projects. CWA wages were paid, and CWA working conditions were observed. Indeed, though the fiction of relief certification was maintained for CWS, investigation of relief status practically ceased under the CWS program. Lillian Brandt states the nature of the arrangement:

> When Mr. Hopkins discovered that "public works" did not include teaching, nursing, research, sewing, canning, typewriting, sculpture, plays, concerts and so on, except as they might be incidental to a construction project, he had to find some other way to provide for women and professional and white-collar men. So he created Civil Works Service (CWS), financed by appropriations from FERA, and therefore "relief." Its projects were subject to approval by CWA. Otherwise it was not, at first, organically connected with CWA, but it was assimilated to it in character as much as possible. Its "relief" aspect was minimized.[2]

The general rules under which CWA and CWS projects were operated did not differ significantly from those prevailing in the earlier FERA. All work was to be of social and economic value and to be performed on public property. All projects were to be operated by force account rather than by contract. Projects that could be financed through the PWA were not acceptable. Projects were not approved if they involved performance of work normally done by states or localities. With regard to this last rule, however, the interpretation of the CWA was liberal,

*On February 15, 1934, when the original allocation of $400,000,000 was running low, the CWA received $345,000,000 from the appropriation of $605,000,000 under the Act of February 15, 1934. Since this money came from FERA funds, the fiscal distinction between CWA and CWS was no longer necessary.

since many localities were so financially pressed that they could no longer maintain some of their normal activities without federal assistance.

One of the most important innovations of the CWA program was the device of state or local sponsorship. The Civil Works program was, as has been indicated, essentially a federal program not only in the source of its funds but also in personnel and operation. It was not expected, however, that the states and localities should completely withdraw from concern with a work program. Indeed, since the CWA was always considered a short-term program, the intention of the Washington office was so to indoctrinate the states and localities in the principles of a proper work program that when the CWA was over, the states, under a renewed FERA, would be ready and willing to carry on a better work program. Accordingly, apart from those that were by definition federal, all projects under Civil Works were sponsored by states or, as in the majority of cases, by local subdivisions. Sponsorship meant that the project was initiated and planned by the locality and submitted to the CWA for approval. It meant furthermore that, to some degree at least, the locality provided material and supervision at its own expense. Thus the locality was encouraged to participate in the program, and, in fact, state and local contributions amounted to 9.5 per cent of total CWA expenditures.

The Civil Works Service program was the first definitely designed to employ white-collar labor. As such, it indicated most clearly the philosophy of the Washington office. A CWS project was by definition a non-construction project. It was required to be submitted by a recognized public body to the Civil Works Administration within the district where the project was located. Persons assigned to CWS projects had to be eligible for relief, but the strict requirements for certification for home or work relief demanded by the FERA were not deemed necessary. Wages were to be the standard rate for the type of work performed, but not less than fifteen dollars nor more than thirty-five dollars on a weekly basis, and not less than thirty cents nor more than seventy-five cents on an hourly basis. The budgetary-deficiency principle was abandoned.

Because of the fiscal distinction between PWA and FERA funds, and the different statutory limitations with regard to each, the integration of CWS and CWA was not immediate. In fact, the white-collar client, when the distinction was pointed out to him, vigorously resented the fact that he, unlike the CWA employee, was still subject to the humiliation of the means test. The reaction in New York City is thus described:

There was plenty of impatience along unemployed white-collar workers in New York when the promised jobs were not immediately ready for them; and plenty of resentment among the clerical, professional and technical workers transferred from work-relief when they learned they were not "getting off relief" after all, as had been promised. The TERA Employees Association protested against their transfer to CWS instead of to CWA. After a sympathetic hearing by the State CWA, who admitted that the difference in status was inconsistent but said nothing could be done about it until Congress met, they sent a delegation to Washington to submit their grievances to federal officials.[3]

Although these statutory difficulties were shortly eased, the abruptness with which the CWS program was inaugurated, and the equally precipitate nature of its closing, after four months' operation, allowed the state and local administrations little time for preparation and reflection. The ingenuity with which projects were initiated was not matched by equal care in the inspection of the project proposals or proper solicitude for the continuity of adequate supervision. Quantity rather than quality was the rule if not the aim, and the spirit of the pioneer rather than that of the expert prevailed. Lillian Brandt's criticism is the more effective because it is that of an expert in the field of social service. She writes:

> All this work was just getting started by the end of the CWA period. There had been many handicaps due to insufficient or poor equipment. Hasty assignments had meant a large proportion of misfits, necessitating an immense amount of shifting about. Musicians and actors could show their ability in an audition. Artists, teachers and writers had to be taken usually on their own statement of what they had done, or aspired to do. Much pioneering was done in devising ways to utilize persons to the best advantage. Artists assigned to Mural Painting, for example, were experimentally grouped in units of eight to fifteen when it was found that many were "not first-class artists." For the instructors and group-leaders of all sorts training had to be provided. If the service projects had been discontinued at the end of CWA, a large part of the money would have been wasted, except as it served as an expensive form of relief.[4]

The lack of proper supervision, or the lack of continuity in such supervision as there was, was particularly apparent in research projects of a scientific or clerical nature. The same authority continues:

> Most of it, whatever the official sponsorship, was under the supervision of university professors, or persons in charge of research in public departments and private agencies. On the one hand they were by presumption eminently competent to direct such work. On the other hand they were already occupied with other duties. Many of the studies could not have been financed in the most prosperous times from public appropriations or private

contributions. Many of them were conducted by most extravagant methods, according to normal standards. But there was money begging to be spent, and to be spent on human labor rather than on machines.[5]

Of the total expenditures in New York City upon cws projects, 38 per cent was used to help emergency relief agencies to do their work; 14 per cent went to various offices of the state and city governments for their routine functions; the remainder, 40 per cent, was spent in the general field of education, including instruction, research, and cultural activities.[6]

## THE BEGINNINGS OF CULTURAL PROJECTS

The emphasis upon cultural projects as part of a comprehensive white-collar program really began in the cwa period. Before that time such work projects as were devised to employ musicians, artists, actors, writers, and research workers were confined to a few metropolitan centers, and were conspicuous, if at all, by their rarity. In a few states, to be sure, departments of recreation and of education had undertaken the encouragement of cultural activities by employing relief clients in supervisory positions; but here, too, as in local projects, the effort was rarely more than a gesture.

With the inauguration of cws, however, considerable impetus was given to elaborating the cultural projects. In New York City, where, as was to be expected, there was a concentration of this type of personnel, expansion was rapid. Aid to musicians, begun through the Musician's Emergency Aid in the spring of 1932, and carried forward under the New York City EWRB and the New York state TERA, was greatly increased under cws. Orchestras, bands, and chamber ensembles were formed to give free concerts in libraries, museums, hospitals, schools, and over the radio. Artists were employed to produce murals and posters and to assist teachers in the public schools. Actors gave plays in schools, institutions, and ccc camps. Five portable theaters on trucks were constructed to give plays in the public parks during the summer, and trained teachers of the theater gave instructions to 175 groups of 2,500 persons in amateur theatricals.[7] The experience of New York City was repeated, but to a lesser degree, in other metropolitan centers; and even in less-populated states and localities, orchestras, bands, theatricals, and other cultural programs, largely of an amateur kind but under professional guidance, were started.

The cultural projects of the cws, except in rare instances, were not of a highly professional character. Indeed, for the most part they remained definitely at an amateur level. Their importance, therefore, lay not in the quality of their performance but in the nature of their contribution. In them the accent was upon community services, and to that degree the program was patterned after the advanced philosophy of the social workers and, in effect, was an enlargement of the playground and the neighborhood house. The group and not the individual was the center of attention; recreation and education, rather than artistry, the purpose. For this reason performances were free, and the public and charitable aspect of the service was underscored by visits to hospitals, orphanages, and other public or non-profit private institutions of similar nature. Sponsorship by educational and recreational agencies, both state and local, encouraged a non-professional type of program, and provided the public auspices under which the benefits were distributed. This use of the arts as an agency of community service, much more than public subsidy of a professional program, represented the ideal of the social worker; and although it was in part obscured by the professional emphasis of Federal One, it emerged again after 1939 as the firm foundation of community support.

By the strange irony of coincidence, the community-service character of the cws program inspired the professional emphasis of the later wpa program. It was not simply that an attempt was made to raise the quality of performance (although that was present), but rather that the cws program suddenly revealed to the professional artist the immediate possibility of public subsidy. As a consequence, it was at this time that organized pressure—by unions, guilds, and other varieties of professional combination, some of them long established, others newly formed for this purpose—was first brought upon the Washington office to initiate a professional program in the arts. Letters, telegrams, resolutions, suggestions, plans, and petitions began to pour into the office of Hopkins and Baker, and even into the White House. Some of the writers of these letters were artists imbued with the philosophy of community service; others were either unaware of the social implications of their calling or candidly hostile toward democratization of the arts. In both cases, however, the stress upon professional competence created a dichotomy between community service and artistic integrity, which in turn provoked a conflict of purpose within the cultural program of the later wpa.

## FEDERAL PROJECTS OF THE CWA

Besides encouraging white-collar projects through the cws, the Washington staff of the cwa, building upon a precedent established in the early fera, used federal projects to further the same end. The cwa was especially adapted to advance this type of project because, now that work relief was federalized, the Washington office had authority to initiate and prosecute work projects. In particular, the cwa could make direct grants for supervisory and travel costs to the federal departments and thus surmount one of the most serious obstacles of the early fera program. Again, once a federal project was approved, the federal administrator was in a position to direct the state administrators, who now were directly under his command authority, to assign a certain number and a certain type of workers to the project. The apathy of state and local administrations was thus, to a degree, circumvented. The way in which these projects were initiated is thus explained:

It was thought that the State organizations using the powers and assistance of city, county and State governments would be able in the time allotted [one month] to assign not more than 3,500,000 people. Some procedure other than relying upon State and local Civil Works administrations needed to be evolved in order to put the remaining 500,000 men to work. . . . Accordingly it was decided to administer this part of the employment program from the Washington office of the Civil Works Administration. . . .

The attempt was made to secure this cooperation from the Federal department which it might be reasonably supposed would normally have undertaken the Work had the appropriation been made directly by Congress in the ordinary course of events. . . .

In putting this program into effect, no money was actually given to the Federal departments except a small amount to cover supervisory personnel and travel expenses. The projects were put in operation by sending an order to each State Civil Works Administration to furnish to an accredited representative of the Federal department the number of men agreed upon at the rates of pay prescribed and to honor suitable vouchers for other than labor expenses in the authorized amount.

The designation Federal Civil Works project indicates primarily a distinction of administration, because the work actually is done locally with local people. Some work that is undertaken is of such a nature that to be useful at all it should be coordinated throughout the several States in which it is being carried on. . . .

Approximately 90 projects of this kind are under way at thousands of work locations throughout the various States.[8]

These federal projects were classified under seven main headings. Heading (VI) was entitled "Projects for the Improvement or the Preservation of Public Records and Documents." Under it were a project for indexing portraits, undertaken under the auspices of the Library of Congress; a project for the translating and transcribing of Spanish records relating to Spanish land claims in New Mexico, sponsored by the Land Office of the Department of the Interior; and a project to edit manuscripts, supervised by the Biological Survey of the Department of Agriculture. Such projects employed writers and research students, and presaged the development of the later WPA Writers' Project and the Historical Records Survey.

But the most significant of these federal projects was the Public Works of Art Project, initiated on December 8, 1933, with a grant from the Civil Works Administration to the Treasury Department. The Procurement Division of the latter supervised the work. The PWAP was organized as an employment program for artists at craftsmen's wages under the direction of Edward Bruce and Forbes Watson.*

The estimate of the number of artists to be employed was 3,300 and the estimated cost $1,039,754. The project was carried on under the auspices and technical direction of the Treasury Department, and its purpose was the employment of artists for the decoration, beautification, and general embellishment of public buildings. During the course of the project, because of turnover, total employment reached 3,749 persons. Works ranging from sculpture, murals, oils, and mosaics to craft articles, Navajo blankets, portraits, and stage sets, totalling in all 15,663 pieces, were completed. The total cost of the project was $1,312,000, of which 90.3 per cent went in wages to the artists themselves. With the liquidation of the CWA in the spring of 1934 the unfinished projects of the PWAP were continued as part of the new Emergency Work Relief Program of the FERA. The products of PWAP were the property of the federal government, and arrangements were made to allocate them to public and non-profit private institutions. This phase of the program was finally completed in July, 1935.†

---

*A fuller discussion of the organization and accomplishments of the PWAP and other cultural programs of the CWA and the CWS is attempted later in those chapters that treat the art projects individually.

†One of the immediate and permanent effects of the PWAP was the establishment by Mr. Morgenthau, Secretary of the Treasury, of a Painting and Sculpture Section in the Procurement Division of the Treasury. This section was created on October 16, 1934, and given charge of the decoration of federal buildings erected by that division. Previously, the responsibility of such decoration had been that of the architect who received the commission.

As the first federal relief program in the arts, the PWAP provided the precedent for the later Treasury Relief Art Project and the Federal Art Project, and stimulated the efforts that subsequently resulted in the creation of projects in the other arts.*

WOMEN'S PROJECTS OF THE CWA

As in the early FERA, another instrument for the encouragement of white-collar employment was the Women's Division. Mrs. Woodward, the director of women's work in the CWA, defined the position of women in the CWA program in a letter dated December 5, 1934. After indicating that women were employable on both Civil Works projects and Civil Works Service projects, and announcing the rates of pay and working conditions, she continued: "Wherever it is possible, use should be made of local professional groups in the selection of persons from their groups on a basis of fitness and need for Civil Works Service projects."[9]

This concern with proper classification of professional applicants reveals the difficulties of both the early FERA and CWA in this regard, while the use of professional groups for certification of need manifests the liberal attitude of the Washington office when white-collar workers were concerned.

Mrs. Woodward, as a good staff officer, was concerned with the furtherance of her special charge, and as a woman responsible for the welfare of her sex in the matter of work relief, she was particularly annoyed by the easy manner in which state and local administrations assigned women to CWS projects while saving the CWA jobs, which were preferred, for men. She expressed her resentment in a strong letter addressed to the directors of women's work in the several states:

> State reports show that most of the women put to work so far are employed on Civil Works Service projects and not on Civil Works projects. This letter is to ask you to concentrate *now* in getting women in on the present going Civil Works projects and, in cooperation with your Civil Works

*The importance that the CWA attached to federal projects is indicated by the fact that a director of federal projects, Julius F. Stone, was appointed. He served under Jacob Baker, who now was assistant administrator in the national office. Within the CWA, Stone was largely responsible for the success of the PWAP. In March, 1934, he was asked by Hopkins to undertake the reorganization of the Florida CWA and ERA and was succeeded as director of federal projects by Sidney Williams.

Administration, to develop others rapidly. This is necessary because more funds are available for wages on such projects.

Our first effort should be toward getting women placed on going projects. Our information indicates that every project in every state has a counterpart in some other state on which women are working.

If you will study carefully the Civil Works projects now in operation in your State, you will find that women can be put to work on some part of practically any one of them. It is essential that you give this matter your immediate attention. Just as rapidly as you find vacant jobs that women can do, and that the foremen and supervisors are willing to give women a chance at, get women put on them. Transfer as many as possible from Civil Works Service jobs to Civil Works jobs.

By January 1st many women, all over the country, should be on Civil Works projects. Report to me on or before December 31st what progress you have made in this matter.[10]

It was during the CWA period, and under the auspices of women's work, that the device of "Working Procedures" was developed. A work project of a novel character, begun and successfuly prosecuted in one state, would come to the attention of the Washington office. If the new project commended itself to the staff, a procedure designed to fit the needs of other states was formulated and, upon approval, circulated abroad in the hope that other states would initiate a similar project. Perhaps the earliest use of such a method occurred with reference to an Alabama project.

Again we have heard from Alabama and I am sending you herewith a copy of an instruction that has gone out from the State Director of Women's Work concerning the project which is being handled by the Alabama Department of Archives and History in cooperation with the Civil Works Administration.

After describing the project, which concerned the proper marking of historical spots of importance along Alabama highways and upon which a corps of skilled women was at work in the Montgomery office, Mrs. Woodward concluded: "You may be able to develop, and have approved by your State Administration, a similar project for your State."[11]

The history of these working procedures belongs to the later FERA period, when a corpus of such procedures was created, including many procedures for projects in the arts. These, in turn, became a large part of the source material upon which the manuals of the later WPA arts projects were based.

THE END OF THE CWA

The CWA ended as abruptly as it had begun. It was, in essence, a temporary expedient to bridge a difficult winter, and was never meant to last. As a brief attempt to operate a work-relief program under conditions that hitherto had applied only to public works, it was financially unorthodox; and the President ordered its liquidation in March, 1934. There were those, to be sure—and among them some members of the Washington staff—who hoped and argued for its continuance and, possibly, for its permanence. But the implications of a public employment program that undertook to give work to all, irrespective of their immediate need and at wages and hours approximating those of private employment, were revolutionary, and the national administration in the spring of 1934 was moving to the right.

But if the experiment died in the womb, the memory of its promise endured, and in a very real sense the ambition of the Washington staff in its subsequent essays at work relief was to recapture, if not the substance, at least the spirit of the Civil Works Administration.

1.   Brandt, *op. cit.*, pp. 174-75.
2.   *Ibid.*, p. 180.
3.   *Ibid.*, pp. 181-82.
4.   *Ibid.*, pp. 209-10.
5.   *Ibid.*, p. 208.
6.   *Ibid.*, p. 206.
7.   *Ibid.*, p. 209.
8.   "Federal Civil Works Projects," *Monthly Report of the Federal Emergency Relief Administration*, December 1 to December 31, 1933, pp. 22-23.
9.   Letter W-6, FERA, December 6, 1933.
10.   Letter W-10, FERA, December 21, 1933.
11.   Letter W-15, FERA, January 9, 1934.

# 5

## The Genesis of an Arts Program

### THE ESTABLISHMENT OF THE EMERGENCY WORK
### RELIEF PROGRAM OF THE FERA

The end of the CWA, on March 31, 1934, returned federal concern with relief to the FERA, which had not ceased as a grant-in-aid agency. In theory the situation on April 1, 1934, was no different from what it had been before the inauguration of the CWA program. Work relief was returned to the states, which now, as before, received grants from the FERA. In fact, however, as a result of the CWA experience, the Washington staff was now much better prepared both psychologically and administratively to undertake the continued encouragement of work relief in the states. The immediate task was to secure the transfer of CWA workers to the payrolls of the state relief administrations. The number of workers on the CWA for the week ending March 29, 1934, was 1,964,040, which was some 2,300,000 less than the number employed in the CWA's period of maximum employment. The transfer was gradual and partial, but was practically completed by the beginning of May, 1934.

The FERA, when in April, 1934, it again undertook to bear the full burden of relief, reconstituted itself with a threefold division of responsibility. The three programs were: (1) relief for distressed families in rural areas; (2) relief for stranded populations (the transient program); and (3) relief for the needy unemployed living in cities and towns (the work-relief program). This last program, the only one with which this inquiry is concerned, was the successor of the works program of the CWA, and was under the immediate supervision of Jacob Baker, who had managed the earlier program.

It was decided that the work-relief program should be prosecuted in cities of over 5,000 population and in counties and other political subdivisions that were predominantly urban or industrial. The employment principle of the CWA was abandoned, and all applicants were required to be selected on the basis of need, ascertained by investigation. In addition, no separate grants were made for non-labor costs, which consequently fell upon the states and localities. The grant-in-aid system of the earlier FERA was followed, and all projects were subject to the approval of the several state relief administrations. Finally, although the principle of prevailing hourly rates, maintained under the CWA, was kept, weekly earnings were calculated on the budget-deficiency principle of the early FERA. As a result, the average weekly earnings of the workers under the Emergency Works Program dropped to twenty-eight dollars a month, as compared with sixty dollars a month when the CWA program was at its height.

One of the principle methods used previously to encourage white-collar employment was denied to the Emergency Works Program of the FERA. This was the initiation of federal projects. In the hearings of the House Committee on Appropriations on January 30, 1934, Harry Hopkins was carefully questioned with regard to funds allocated to other government departments for the prosecution of work projects. The committee felt that to allow these departments access to funds not specifically appropriated for them by Congress was bad practice; it also believed that, in some instances at least, such funds were being used to prosecute work for which Congress in the regular appropriation bills had specifically denied funds.[1] Accordingly, in the Act of February 15, 1934,[2] Congress forbade the initiation of any new federal projects, although it allowed those already in operation to be completed.*

With more and better information at hand than was available at the beginning of the FERA program in April, 1933, Baker, now assistant administrator of the FERA in charge of the Emergency Works Program, attempted to plan the general distribution of workers among the several classes of projects. In his preliminary plan the white-collar categories, together with the desired percentage of total employment, were:

---

*Although federal projects were forbidden by statute on February 15, 1934, the office concerned with them continued until the end of April, 1934. Sidney Williams remained in charge and signed himself "Acting Director of National Projects." Arthur Hanna was his assistant. Their responsibility was to answer inquiries and requests, many of them concerned with the continuation of the CWA cultural projects. In May and June, 1934, after the closing of this office, the task of replying to such letters was that of Percy A. Fellows, administratiive assistant to Harry Hopkins.

1. Research and Planning ..................... 10%
2. Public Culture and Education ............... 10%
3. Public Welfare and Health ................... 10%

Thus 30 per cent of all the workers under this scheme would be of the white-collar class, as against a little over 10 per cent under the cwa.[3]

In the plan as finally issued on March 20, however, distribution was:

1. Planning ............................... 3%
2. Public Welfare, Health, and Recreation ....... 7%
3. Public Education, Arts, and Research ......... 10%

Thus the total was reduced from 30 to 20 per cent, and the percentage of construction and service projects was correspondingly increased.*[4]

The difficulties of developing a cultural program under state and local auspices, which had plagued the earlier attempts of the FERA in this direction, immediately reasserted themselves upon the close of the CWA program. As before, the problem of competent supervision was paramount, for supervisory cost was no longer paid from federal funds, and it was difficult to secure adequate personnel from the relief rolls. The staggering of employment, moreover, now reintroduced under the budget-deficiency rule, further complicated the problem of management.

Under the circumstances it was not surprising that some local administrations considered the continuance of cultural projects impossible under the existing rules of the FERA. In a *Weekly Progress Report* a member of the Washington staff reported a typical experience in Philadelphia:

In Philadelphia I ran into an interesting problem with regard to the C.W.A. symphony orchestra, of which they are very proud, but which they have felt must be discontinued at the end of this month [April, 1934]. I discussed with Mr. Connor, the employment director, possible ways of keeping most of these musicians on the relief roll and continuing these performances. This situation seems to be typical—most of our Administrators seem to feel

*There was a consistent tendency on the part of the Washington staff to overestimate in all these programs the percentage of white-collar employment. At no time did employment of this class advance significantly beyond 10 per cent. In part, the wish was father to the thought, and in part, there was always the expectation that the public works program would employ a large part of the unskilled workers.

that former white-collar projects must be abandoned due to the rules governing the new Work Program. We shall have to do some very careful and thorough field work if this impression is to be corrected.[5]

As a matter of fact, the major difficulty was money, without which
none of the others could be properly resolved. The FERA simply was not
providing the amount of funds that had been allocated under the CWA,
and under this pressure the tendency of the states was to sacrifice the
white-collar projects as the more expensive. State and local officials
were under the immediate necessity of employing as many men as possible with a given amount of money, and any attempt on their part to
favor the white-collar class above the manual class, especially as such
preference would necessarily have resulted in a contraction of total employment, would have provoked the resentment of the community. It
must always be remembered that the front lines were in the field, and
that the Washington headquarters staff, secure in its remoteness from
combat, was not always appreciative of local reaction to its staff recommendations, and was not, like the officer in the field, at the mercy of
local pressures.*

There was, therefore, a precipitous drop in white-collar relief employment in the first three months of the new Emergency Works Program. The Washington staff was painfully aware of this, and tried to
soften its impact by the development of administrative projects. These
projects were a device whereby white-collar relief applicants were
used to staff state and local relief administrations. The idea was a development of the earlier practice whereby public and private welfare
agencies recruited white-collar workers in need to increase their staff.
Under the rules of the FERA, administrative, supervisory, and technical
employees, if required full time, were not restricted with regard to
hours of employment or amount of weekly wage; and since these wages
were paid at prevailing rates, such positions were attractive. More
significantly, administrative projects provided an opportunity for state
and local relief administrations to charge administrative expense to
project funds, and, for that reason, met with their approval. In fact,
the fiscal convenience of this approach to the white-collar problem was
so appealing that, in the end, the Washington office was forced to discourage the practice.†

*The PWAP was carried to completion during this period only because special
permission was given to waive relief requirements and special additional FERA funds
allocated specifically to it.

†In August, 1934, when special efforts were being made to encourage a white-

The use of administrative projects, however, was limited by their very nature, and the Washington staff remained genuinely concerned about the future of white-collar projects. Contact between Washington and the professional organizations, which had been precipitated by the CWA program, was maintained partly because the professional organizations redoubled their pressure when they realized the inadequacy of the new program and partly because the Washington staff, sincerely desirous of reinstituting a professional program, sought their advice and assistance. In April, 1934, Arthur Hanna, Sidney Williams' assistant, spent two days in New York City discussing proposals in the music and dramatic fields made by prominent citizens of the community to the President, Harry Hopkins, and others. Their proposals were turned over to the relief administrator of New York with the hope that, after examination, he would be persuaded to inaugurate at least a few projects of this type.[7]

Hanna realized that, at the moment, the fate of white-collar work relief was in the hands of state and local relief administrations. New York was almost unique in its progressive attitude. In New York City many of the cultural projects begun under the CWA were continued, if not to the same extent, at least with a genuine regard for the problem. The dramatic project, for instance, carried on; and with the coming of warmer weather, plays were produced in the parks in portable theaters. *Uncle Tom's Cabin* was the first of these, and 12,000 people fought to see it one evening in Crotona Park.[8]

At the same time word was bruited about that the Washington staff was working on a new plan that, by liberalizing the rules of the FERA, would secure preferential treatment for professional clients. This interpretation of the Washington staff's philosophy was encouraged by word that came from Harry Hopkins in Europe in the summer of 1934.

> On the fourth of July the Federal Administrator sailed for two months in Europe. From Paris came word that he was saying: "Americans will not stand for the dole, and we are going to put them to work on great public projects and pay them decent wages." Reports from Washington a few days earlier had intimated "broad plans" for "a new program" for the winter, which would provide wages, not relief, for real work, not perfunctory motions, and would put white-collar workers "in a separate bracket."[9]

The fact is that the FERA, which had been financially constricted ever since the closing of the CWA program, was waiting for money.

collar program, warnings were issued against using funds earmarked for professional and non-manual workers for staffing state and local relief administrations. Field representatives were especially cautioned to be on guard against this practice.[6]

Finally, on June 19, 1934, the 1935 Emergency Appropriation Act, which included moneys out of which allocations could be made to the FERA, was approved. The next day Baker wrote:

> Now that we know where we are for a while as to funds, we can lay out a program for white-collar workers. This should be by the device of earmarking appropriations made to the several states.
> The only pressing one is actors for CCC camps, playgrounds and parks.[10]

## THE FERA'S FIRST PROFESSIONAL PROGRAM AND
## THE FAILURE OF STAFF AUTHORITY

The appropriation of June did not take the Washington staff by surprise. The preceding three months had been spent in diligent preparation. Within ten days Baker was able to announce the details of the new program, and, with them, the establishment, within the Works Division, of a section for professional and non-manual projects under the supervision of Arthur Goldschmidt.*

Chief attention during the period of preparation was given to the elaboration of suitable "Working Procedures," a device used informally during the CWA period but now adopted as a more formal instrument of staff policy. The fundamental nature of these procedures and their place in the thinking of the Washington staff are well expressed in the following letter:

> All that this office does in connection with the direction and guidance of work relief is to formulate Working Procedures or ideas as they are presented. We do not take on the responsibility for specific direction of such projects. You will note on the Working Procedures sent you that a sponsor is indicated. That sponsor, in each case, takes all the responsibility for the direction and supervision.
> The Working Procedures for Writers were formulated on the basis of advice and suggestions and experience of the State Relief Administrations. Having formulated them, they are simply placed in the hands of State Administrations for such use as they find they can make of them. . . . Mr. Goldschmidt has no staff and his function is simply to act as a clearing office between the State Administrations in the exchange of information. . . .[11]

As this letter indicates, working procedures were normally inspired by reports sent in from the states. On the basis of such reports, the

---

*Goldschmidt's title was acting director of professional projects, and he remained in that position until, in June, 1935, the office was reorganized and placed in charge of Bruce McClure, formerly secretary to Hopkins

Washington office undertook to formulate a procedure that other states might use, either as it stood or with changes to suit local circumstances. Sometimes, however, working procedures originated in the central office, often as a result of suggestions from outside bodies or individuals interested in a particular type of program, or as the inspiration of the staff itself. Indication of outside pressure and the part played by the Washington office is shown in the following advice:

> Surveyors in need and needy artists, writers and musicians are the subjects of numerous inquiries being made regarding the aid which may be rendered. If the regional engineers will ascertain from time to time what projects have been developed in their States to help these people and keep us informed of any such projects which they consider unusually effective, it will be very helpful to the Professional Projects Division in answering these inquiries.[12]

Indeed, as regards cultural projects, the Washington office relied more upon the initiative and suggestions of professional organizations than upon the paradigm of projects already organized in the states; for, except in a few localities, little imagination was used by the states in inventing projects of this kind.

In the circulation of working procedures, however, the Washington office soon discovered that a bottleneck existed in the state offices. The FERA was performing its proper function as a staff agency by acting as a source of information for the state administrations. Once the procedure was in the state office, however, it was within the discretion of the state relief administration to send it, or not to send it, to the local offices. In many cases the procedures rested in the state offices.

> It came up at a staff conference this morning that it is very difficult to get knowledge of and information about our working procedures filtered down through the State to the local offices. I wish you would call attention to the working procedures in some prominent way in *The Project*. And also do whatever you can to see that *The Project* reaches the local administrations.[13]

This indifference of the state administration, which, though not universal, was general, was a permanent brake upon the forward motion of the Washington staff. *The Project* (mentioned in the above memorandum), a magazine prepared by the Works Division of the FERA and published for a few months, was, in part, an effort of the central office to avoid the deviousness of official channels and to establish a direct line of unofficial communication between the central office and the local administrations. In theory the plan was excellent, but in fact the local authorities were less progressive in their attitude than the state administrations.

These working procedures, though they were elaborated with respect to a large variety of projects, were designed primarily to encourage the states and localities to undertake projects they would not otherwise have initiated. For this reason the procedures emphasized white-collar projects, including those of a cultural type. A considerable number were worked up for music, dramatics, art, writing, and historical projects; these in time—reviewed according to need and improved as a result of experiment and criticism—became the material from which was derived the substance of the several manuals that governed the five projects in Federal One. In terms of technical detail the working procedures, though experimental in the beginning, were the foundation of the operational instructions of Federal One.*

The Washington staff, although setting much store upon the inspirational effect of these procedures, was careful not to pretend that they approached technical perfection. On this score, a Washington representative at an FERA regional conference made a revealing and amusing admission:

> Mr. LANING [of the FERA Washington staff]: Do you have any trouble getting the right kind of projects?
>
> Mrs. SANMANN [of the staff of the Nevada Relief Administration]: The suggestions [the Working Procedures] are very helpful. We have to revamp them of course, but the general suggestions are helpful. Some don't fit in our particular part of the country because the detail is worked out for us.
>
> Mr. LANING: They are very loose and some are sort of a joke, but the idea is usually very valuable and that is the intention. There are two important things. One is the title and the description [of the project] and the other is the personnel. We suggest the type of people you might look for in setting up such a project. We are not qualified to work out the details. You have the situation much more in hand.[14]

As a matter of fact, the Washington staff was too experienced in the ways of state and local administrations to believe that such a simple device would restore professional projects to their status under the CWA. Other methods were at hand, which, if more drastic, were worth a trial; and on July 2, 1934, the decisive letter, which revealed in full the staff

---

*The analysis of the content of these procedures, so far as the five arts projects are concerned, and typical examples of each kind appear in the chapters discussing each project individually.

plan of attack, was addressed to all state administrations. This letter began by announcing the establishment within the Work Division of a "Section for Professional and Nonmanual Projects," with Arthur Goldschmidt in charge, and then proceeded to set forth the rules and procedures for the employment of white-collar workers. This latter portion deserves quotation at length:

> The Work Division of the Federal Emergency Relief Administration has been designated to promote projects for employment for professional and nonmanual workers, compatible with their previous training and experience. It is intended that the Work Division of the State Relief Administrations be charged with this program. . . .
>
> *Funds*—These projects shall be prosecuted hereafter with the aid of funds earmarked for the purpose in grants to the States. The funds now being spent by the States for these projects will be included in the earmarked allocations. Local and State participation in the allotment of monies will be required as for all other work division activities. Applications for funds to prosecute professional projects shall be included in the regular monthly application made to this office and these funds shall be accounted separately.
>
> *Eligibility for Relief*—Selection of workers is made on the basis of need, determined by the Relief Administrations. The method of need determinations shall be by means of a questionnaire filed with the relief administration, and verified by a professional or technical organization or by a case-worker. This verification may be made monthly or bi-monthly. A copy of the questionnaire suggested by this office is attached. States wishing to alter this form must receive approval for changes from this office.
>
> *Wages*—Salaries of workers on professional projects shall be determined by unanimous agreement of the existing county prevailing wage rate committees. Weekly salary rates, based on the usual work week, shall be set up for all classes of workers on professional projects. These rates shall be translated into daily rates which in no case shall be less than $2.50 for the work done in any one day. In all cases the wage rate committee should confer with the appropriate organizations of professional groups in the determination of these rates.
>
> The rates should be submitted to the State Relief Administration and copies forwarded to the Federal Emergency Relief Administration as a matter of record. Changes in the wage rates may be made by the Relief Administrations only after a complete hearing and on the recommendation of the local county adjustment committee.
>
> Wages must be paid in cash or by check.
>
> *Hours of Employment*—Hours per day of employment of workers on professional projects shall be those traditionally expected of workers in the field in which they will be employed but in no case shall workers be employed more than seven hours in any one day or more than five days in any one week. Number of days of employment shall be based on the budget deficiency of the workers, but no person employed on professional projects shall be paid less than one daily wage for work performed during any one day.

74

The total work allowed a worker in any month may be consolidated in one part of that month where this arrangement provides greater usefulness of the worker, provided that the above limitations shall not be waived.[15]

The controls established in this letter over state and local operation so far exceeded those attempted by any previous federal grant-in-aid agency that the adventure can only be described as desperate. In the first place, the earmarking of funds for professional projects confronted the states with the alternative of spending the money for the designated purpose or not spending it at all. In the second place, preferential treatment was ordered for professional clients: (1) by the practical abolition of the means test; (2) by a determination of a higher hourly and weekly wage rate; and (3) by special arrangement of the hours of employment. A special accounting of the earmarked funds, subject to the inspection of the Washington office, was expected to provide the leverage by which that office would lift the states to the level of its own philosophy. This drastic experiment in staff control, where no command authority over the states existed anywhere in the agency, was short-lived; it was abandoned in October, 1934, when prudence and protest combined to counsel its end. It had no statutory basis, and if it sought precedent at all, it sought it in vain. Had efforts been made to continue or expand these controls, interrogation in Congressional hearings would most certainly have uncovered the venture and resulted in statutory prohibition.

On August 2, 1934, a second letter, intended to reassert and strengthen the instructions of the first, followed.[16] Besides emphasizing and clarifying instructions contained in the previous letter, this communication made three additional points. The state and local administrators, it seems, were as wise in their generation as the Washington staff were in theirs, and they attempted to evade the full purpose of the earmarking by using the funds to finance existing professional projects instead of creating new projects. This practice was forbidden. Second, control through monthly reports was enjoined, in accordance with instructions previously dispatched on July 10.[17] Third, the use of these funds to staff state and local relief administrations was prohibited. The last caution was necessary; a paragraph in one of the *Weekly Progress Reports* reveals the extent of the practice:

Recent reports indicate a general attempt to increase administrative personnel with no increase in administrative expenses. States should be reminded that no project of an administrative type may be initiated until it has been approved by this [the national] office.[18]

Information with regard to the operation of this program comes from several of the states. Alabama reported:

> In August, 1934, a movement was started by the Federal Emergency Relief Administration to make more adequate relief available to white-collar persons, or professional and non-manual persons. A quota of 3,000 was assigned to Alabama with sufficient funds to give each person or each case an average of $45.00 per month. White-collar certifications were allowed to range from $30.00 to $60.00 per month.
>
> Home investigations of applicants were not required, but sufficient information had to be available to enable the County Director of Relief to certify to the needs of the families. Affidavits signed by the applicants stating the financial circumstances of the families were acceptable in lieu of home investigations and detailed case records. . . .
>
> Approximately 1,750 relief persons were working on administrative projects at certifications equal in amount to white-collar certifications. Inasmuch as it was deemed advisable to recognize this cost as a cost of administration rather than white-collar relief, the number of white-collar cases, as such, has not exceeded 1,250.[19]

The last paragraph is badly phrased. It means that the Alabama relief administration subtracted from its quota of 3,000 the 1,750 already employed on administrative projects, leaving a remainder of only 1,250 to be assigned to professional projects. This was precisely the practice that the Washington office had forbidden.

In California a liberal relief administration co-operated with the plans of the Washington office and even refined upon its instructions. The urban counties of that state, with the exception of Alameda and Los Angeles, reported that professional and technical workers applied for relief during this period in offices separate from those receiving other applicants. Most of the counties used a special application form for professions. In four counties professional organizations, such as the Musician's Union, assisted in verifying eligibility for relief.[20]

In Nebraska, although the quota was set at 2,000, the number of persons classified as professional never exceeded 1,200. This was because the standard by which selection was made was set so high that relatively few could qualify as professional. Furthermore, the local relief administrations were reluctant to recognize higher monthly budgets for this group than those permitted other relief clients.[21]

In some states little, if anything, was accomplished. The Iowa report reads: "Very little work of this nature [in art] was done as most persons who were capable of producing works of art were not eligible as relief clients."[22]

The Tennessee report comments: "Few persons trained in music and art appeared on relief rolls in this State; therefore, these projects were not developed."[23]

Nevada naïvely reported: "Professional and non-manual workers received the same consideration, as far as possible, as workers on manual projects, referring to preference."[24]

What relation the quotas assigned by the Washington office for August bore to the number on work relief is not clear. The Alabama quota of 3,000 was approximately 7 per cent of the work-relief load for the previous June (43,451), whereas the Nebraska quota of 2,000 was 15 per cent of that state's total June work-relief roll (13,010). The national average was probably close to 10 per cent, in which case the national quota set for professional and technical workers was about 150,000.

In general, however, this short-lived program to secure preferential treatment for professional workers, though it failed of permanence, bore considerable fruit in many states. This was particularly true of projects in the arts, many of which were begun in the several states between July and October, 1934. Here the pressure from Washington was strengthened by equal pressure applied upon the state and local administrations by professional organizations and unions, which had become conscious of their strength during the CWA period. The Washington office, in its contact with these organizations, was adept at diverting their demands from itself to the several state administrations, where the effect was more immediate.

The projects in the arts that were started as a result of this program were numerous, and some of them outstanding. In California the mural-painting project at the Presidio started on August 6; the Colorado Springs Music Project began on July 5; in the same month the Art Project for Connecticut was set up to absorb the artists then working on the PWAP program, and musical activities reached their peak; the Art Project of the Illinois Emergency Relief Commission began on July 18, and in the same month, a project for actors in Cook County; in New Orleans the music project was started in August; in Maine the music project began on August 1; the Nebraska Lancaster County art project was started on September 19; in Concord, New Hampshire, a symphony orchestra was organized in October; in Portland, Oregon, band concerts were given from July 10 to September 30; in Puerto Rico the Division of Fine Arts, designed to establish art activities especially in connection with relief, was organized; in South Carolina the Richland County ERA orchestra was established on September 21; the Statewide

Art Project of Vermont was organized in October. In Hartford, Connecticut, the success of the concert orchestra was reflected in the fact that the city appropriated $3,700 as its contribution to the construction of a music shell in Bushnell Park, an ERA work project.*

Some of these projects were continued beyond October, 1934, but in many cases when the pressure from Washington was lifted, the projects were either discontinued or seriously curtailed. In Connecticut, for instance, because of the curtailment of funds, one orchestra and the four string ensembles were discontinued; but in Bridgeport, when the same cause threatened the closing of the ERA Symphony, popular support saved it. In Maine the music project was suspended from April 25 to June 6, 1935. In Nebraska the state administration, which was well disposed toward white-collar employment, continued the projects, but did not feel that the original quota could be maintained without handicapping the general relief program. In Portland, Oregon, concerts were discontinued at the close of September, 1934, and the art project on December 27, 1934.

The sponsorship of these projects was varied. The sponsor was of necessity a public agency. In the Illinois Art Project, the Vermont Art Project, the Nevada Art Project, the Minnesota Music Project, the Pennsylvania Music Project (which was outstanding), Connecticut's Survey of Historic and Scenic Places (which resulted in the Connecticut ERA Guide, and was sponsored by the State Planning Board), a state agency sponsored the project on a statewide basis, though activities were usually confined to a few localities within the state. Sometimes an agency of a city or county government acted as sponsor. The city and county of San Francisco sponsored its Entertainment Project (music and dramatics); the city of Colorado Springs sponsored its symphony orchestra; in Connecticut the several music projects were sponsored by the several cities or by their mayors, acting through local music committees. Occasionally, the local ERA (as in the Los Angeles Drama Project) sponsored the activity, especially when no other public body was ready or willing to act.†

It was during this program that the first attempt was made to make

*This shell is an exact duplicate of the one on the Charles River Esplanade in Boston, where the Boston Symphony Orchestra holds its outdoor summer concerts.

†The above account of this program's activities in the several states is based upon information provided in reports of the FERA Emergency Work Program from all the states, which were prepared at the close of the program and submitted at the request of the Washington office. They are available at the library of the Federal Works Agency, Washington, D.C.

the arts projects self-supporting. In view of the importance of the procedures pertaining to admission funds in the later WPA arts program, this early try is interesting. The initial letter on the subject, addressed to all state administrators reads:

> The following paragraph has been recently added to all working procedures having to do with public arts and entertainments:
>
>> *Charges.* Small charges—typically ten to forty cents—may be made for attendance of performances in cases where a prospective audience can pay. Funds should be handled by a representative of the Relief Administration and used to pay costs of operation. Surplus funds may be reserved for expansion or distributed to the participants in the project, dependent upon the decision of the Relief Administration. If the organization develops sufficient public support so that it can operate on its own, this should be encouraged.
>
> We particularly call this to your attention because we find there has been in many cases a feeling that no charges should be made on the part of these entertainment projects. It should be the intention of every Relief Administration to make these organizations self-supporting, putting them on a co-operative basis wherever possible or developing them to the point where sponsorship of a university, museum, or a public institution, or of the city itself will serve to carry it forward.[25]

Jacob Baker's interest in the co-operative idea is revealed in this suggestion. A similar procedure was suggested with regard to works of art, and, in addition, the possibility of selling the product was raised. This section of the procedure read:

> The art work so exhibited may be offered for sale at figures defined by the artist or may be placed at auction with the artist's permission. Agreements should be entered into in advance with the artist for the allocation of the income from sales. Where amounts are involved that will provide for the support of the artists for a reasonable period, such funds should accrue to the artist and he should be removed from the relief rolls.*[26]

This procedure reached final form in the following communication:

> It should be the intention of every relief Administration to make public art and entertainment projects self-supporting; putting them on a basis, wherever possible, whereby they may eventually become independent, and where they may function as an integral part of the life of the community.
> For that reason, it is often advisable to allow the project to charge small

---

*In general, however, statutory limitations with respect to the disposal of public property prevented the states from using this device.

admission fees for such persons as are able to pay these fees. The funds raised by admission charges may be used by the relief administrations to defray the cost of the project, and pay expenses for developing the project and for expanding its scope.

If the organization develops sufficient public support it may be able to operate on its own; this point of view should be encouraged as much as possible. However, relief supported shows and entertainments must not be allowed to compete with existing non-relief facilities.

Projects on which these charges may be applicable will include: symphony concerts and other musical entertainments, public dance orchestras, plays and exhibits of works of art. . . .[27]

Receipts from these admission charges—the device was attempted in only a few places—were inconsequential. The idea that arts projects could be made self-supporting was a mirage, as the later experience of the WPA arts program (where the scheme was tried on a much grander scale) was to demonstrate.

### THE ABANDONMENT OF FERA'S SPECIAL PROGRAM
### FOR PROFESSIONAL WORKERS

The special procedures devised in July and August to encourage and compel special consideration for professional projects were abandoned in October. The reasons for this change of policy were given by Baker in a letter to Margaret Klem:

On the whole it does not seem here a good idea to have funds earmarked for specific purposes within the States. I should say that this applies to all funds, although at the present time I believe it is not intended to make any change in Educational funds. We do not have information here of the changing relief load of a given class of persons and with earmarked funds it turns out quite frequently that a larger proportion of the State's total funds is kept for a specific class than is proper. Too, we like to keep as much responsibility on the States as possible. It is only in that way that real accounting can be demanded of it.[28]

With the end of earmarking, the exemption from the means test, which professional workers had been enjoying, was lifted. A letter, dated November 1, 1934, and addressed to all state administrators, read: "Professional and non-manual workers, whether from the relief rolls or assigned directly to projects, shall be eligible for relief. In the matter of reporting, they shall therefore be considered as relief cases."[29]

Finally, in December, 1934, the states were given to understand, unofficially, that the Washington office not only had relaxed its efforts on behalf of professional workers but would be pleased if the states did the same.

This *volte face* by the Washington staff was, of course, not voluntary. In his letter to Margaret Klem, Baker gave the reasons for the abandonment of earmarking, but he neglected to emphasize the source and extent of the pressure. The fact is that not only state administrators but also the Washington field staff, which ordinarily represented and defended the view of the Washington office, protested vigorously against the program. Howard Hunter, who was particularly outspoken, severely criticized professional projects in a letter to the Washington office. The details of the protest are not available, but it provoked a conference of Hopkins and Baker with Hunter upon the latter's return to the Washington office.[30] There is also evidence of correspondence with Margaret Klem, though again the nature of the complaint escapes search.[31]

If the state administrators were able to convert the field representatives to their point of view, the situation must have been critical. Indeed, the bad taste induced by the venture remained in the mouths of some for a considerable period afterward, and so late as April, 1935, speaking at an FERA regional conference, Miss Newsom asked significantly:

> Have any other states found that their communities are antagonistic to nonmanual projects because they originally came in as earmarked funds which were taken away? We have found they are no so anxious to work with nonmanual projects.[32]

First and foremost, the state administrators objected to earmarking, and insisted upon their prerogative to use their own discretion with regard to allocation. They argued, and not without grounds, that their office, and not the Washington office, was in a position to know and to meet the needs of a particular state. Second, preferential treatment for professional workers provoked the resentment of other classes on relief and, to a certain degree, the general public. In particular, the determination of relief wages on the basis of social status rather than economic need was difficult to justify, especially when need was so widespread; and the exemption of professional workers from the means test, while those in the lower categories were subjected to strict scrutiny, served to heighten the general consciousness of favoritism. This accumulation of grievances weighed upon the state and local administrators, who were not only anxious to maintain good public relations in their communities but were administratively responsible for their maintenance. Their political judgment that the program was ill-advised was no less pertinent than the professional judgment of the Washington staff that the program was desirable. In the end, but only for a time, the political judgment prevailed.

The failure of the program provoked a temporary attitude of caution on the part of the Washington staff that was unusual. Naturally, the change in policy was not favorably received by the professional classes. The protests in New York City have already been noticed. There were other protests elsewhere: the South Central Regional Conference of Business and Professional Women (comprising Arkansas, Missouri, Oklahoma, Louisiana, Texas, and Kansas) protested that "many persons in dire need suffer serious loss of personal dignity and morale by being forced to prove destitution before they can secure work."[33]

The Washington staff, on its part, though it recognized the advisability of a tactical retreat, was already reforming its lines in terms of a larger strategy. In the meantime, it was careful to maintain diplomatic relations with professional societies and to cultivate their friendship and support; it also continued to use and develop working procedures in an effort further to diversify the program. Meetings and conferences were held with individuals and groups representing the professional classes and preparations were made toward further encouragement of the program. The meeting of the National Recreation Conference in Washington, D.C., in October, 1934, provided an opportunity to appraise the situation.[34]

But, as the new year approached, the problem of the professional classes and all other problems of lesser moment were obscured by the emergence of the new works program, which was taking shape in the mind of the President and his advisors, and was destined to be the occasion of a professional program in the arts which, in administrative novelty and technical pretensions, would far transcend the earlier accomplishments of the CWA and the FERA.

1. U.S. Congress. House Committee on Appropriations. 73d Cong. 2d sess. (1934), *Hearings of a Subcommittee . . . on Federal Emergency Relief and Civil Works Program* (H.R.7527), 23-24, 44-47, 52-53.

2. Public, no. 93; 73d Cong., H.R. 7527.

3. Memorandum, Jacob Baker, March 10, 1934, FERA Files.

4. Letter WD-3, FERA, March 20, 1934.

5. *Weekly Progress Report*, FERA, April 14 to April 21, 1934.

6. *Ibid.*, August 20 to August 25, 1934.

7. *Ibid.*, April 9 to April 14, 1934.

8. Brandt, *op. cit.*, p. 289.

9. *Ibid.*, pp. 315-16.

10. Memorandum, Baker to Hopkins, June 20, 1934, FERA Files.

11. Letter, Baker to Clement Wood, New York City, November 23, 1934, FERA Files.

12. *Weekly Progress Report*, FERA, September 3 to September 15, 1934.

13. Memorandum, Baker to Henry Alsberg, December 31, 1934.

14. *Proceedings*, Mountain States Regional Conference, FERA Work Division, April 26, 1935 (Friday Morning Session), pp. 21-22.

15. Letter WD-9, FERA, July 2, 1934.

16. Letter WD-16, FERA, August 2, 1934.

17. Letter #2751, Work Division, FERA, July 10, 1934.

18. *Weekly Progress Report*, FERA, August 27 to September 1, 1934.

19. *Two Years of Federal Relief in Alabama*, Alabama Relief Administration, 1935.

20. *Review of Activities of the State Relief Administration of California, 1933-1935* (California State Printing Office, Sacramento, 1936), pp. 100-101.

21. *Report of the Work Division of the Nebraska Emergency Relief Administration, April 1, 1934 to July 1, 1935*, pp. 18, 20.

22. *Review of Iowa Emergency Relief Administration Work Division Activities, April 1, 1934—June 30, 1935*, p. 125.

23. *Review of Federal Emergency Relief Activities in Tennessee, April 1, 1934—June 30, 1935*, p. 134.

24. *Review of Work Relief Activities in Nevada, April 1, 1934—July 1, 1935*, p. 5.

25. Letter, Baker to all State Relief Administrators, September 13, 1934, FERA Files.

26. Letter A-64, FERA, September 28, 1934.

27. Letter WD-20, FERA, September 28, 1934.

28. Letter, Baker to Margaret C. Klem, San Francisco, November 10, 1934, FERA Files.

29. Letter WD-24, FERA, November 1, 1934.

30. Memorandum, Mary Cox to Goldschmidt, November 26, 1934, FERA Files.

31. Memorandum, Mary Cox to Goldschmidt, December 6, 1934, FERA Files.

32. *Proceedings*, Mountain States Regional Conference, FERA Work Division, April 26, 1935 (Friday Morning Session), p. 24.

33. Letter, Grace C. Niles to Hopkins, November 28, 1934, FERA Files.

34. "Progress Report," Professional Projects Section, FERA, October 13, 1934.

# 6

## The Eve of the Works Progress Administration

THE STATUS OF THE PROFESSIONAL CLASSES
ON RELIEF IN MARCH, 1935

In 1938 the Division of Social Research of the WPA under the direction of Corrington Gill, assistant administrator, and Howard B. Myers, director of the division, published the results of an extensive and meticulous investigation of the relief situation in the United States in March, 1935.[1] The findings of this investigation, though they were probably not available to those who planned the WPA arts program in the spring and summer of 1935—or, at least, not available in this form—provide the student of the depression with an excellent and exhaustive analysis of the relief situation at that time.

Of the 4,986,000 workers on relief in the United States in March, 1935, approximately 11 per cent, or 558,429, belonged to the white-collar class. These latter were largely concentrated in urban areas. More than two-thirds were on the relief rolls of ten states (New York, California, Illinois, Pennsylvania, Ohio, Massachusetts, New Jersey, Michigan, Minnesota, Texas), and one-fourth were on the relief rolls of five cities (New York, Chicago, Los Angeles, Boston, Philadelphia). Eighty-five per cent of the white-collar workers resided in urban centers. In New York City one in every five of those on relief was a white-collar worker; in Boston, one in four; and more than one in four, but less than one in three, in Los Angeles and San Francisco. The fundamental fact that these statistics make clear is that a white-collar program must be an urban program and, more significantly, must concentrate itself in a relatively few states, and in a relatively few metropolitan centers within those states.

Of the more than half-million white-collar workers on relief, 82,100, or approximately 15 per cent, belonged to the professional and technical groups. Of these, approximately 41 per cent were women. The percentage of professional and technical workers on relief to total workers on relief was 1:6. Although the professional and technical group is not broken down in terms of place of residence, it is obvious without statistics that if 85 per cent of the white-collar workers resided in urban centers, more than 85 per cent of the professional and technical workers were domiciled there. A professional program, even more than a white-collar program, must concentrate its efforts in the large centers of population. A further fact revealed by these figures is that in a professional program the number of women involved will almost equal the number of men.

Of those employed in the arts, actors numbered 3,709; artists, sculptors, and teachers of art, 2,900; and musicians and teachers of music, 14,922. This last class comprised almost one-fifth of the professional and technical workers on relief. Three of every four of the musicians, including teachers of music, were men.*

In another table, published in December, 1935, the percentage distribution of white-collar projects, workers on work relief, and earnings for the week ending April 18, 1935, were indicated.[2] An examination of these statistics shows that 10.8 per cent of all relief employees were of the white-collar class, whereas 24.8 per cent of all work projects were in the white-collar category. This discrepancy between the percentage of projects on the one hand and of workers on the other graphically illustrates a fact already known from experience: that white-collar projects of necessity were smaller in personnel per project than other types of projects, with the consequence that more supervisors were needed and project cost correspondingly increased. A similar discrepancy, though less in extent, between the percentage of workers and the percentage of earnings in the white-collar classification is also revealed in the table. This indicates that apart from supervisory cost, which was not at that time paid from federal funds, white-collar workers as a class were paid higher relief wages than other types of workers. A further fact emerging from these statistics is that white-collar projects, although they em-

---

*It is impossible to arrive at any statistics with regard to writers, employed or unemployed. The number of authors, occupationally speaking (i.e., those who make their living at writing and engage in no other gainful occupation), is infinitesimal. Beyond this group, practically every one who is literate "writes" or thinks that he can, as the WPA Writers' Project was to discover.

ployed only one-twelfth of all men, employed one-third of all women on work relief.*

Finally, this table indicates that so far as the arts projects were concerned (such as were later grouped under Federal One, and including music, dramatics, and art, but excluding writing and historical projects), employment was only .7 per cent of total work-relief employment.

A third table appeared in a WPA publication on December 31, 1935.[3] These statistics, prepared by Floyd Dell, show the distribution of work-relief employment for men and women, with hours and wages and by types of project, for the week ending February 21, 1935. Category (F) included public education, arts, and research, and the table indicates that within this category 9,435 workers were employed on work-relief projects in the field of the arts (Public Works of Art, Music, and Dramatic Activities). These figures, however, must be used with caution, for, because of the system of rotation under the budget-deficiency principle, employment in any one week averaged about two-thirds of monthly employment. Thus for the month of February, employment in these fields probably approximated 14,000.†

Unfortunately, FERA statistics on work-relief employment within the separate categories are not accurate, and substantial differences occur in different tables that are difficult to reconcile. The Washington office, since it did not itself keep such figures, depended upon reports from the states, which, if made at all, were haphazard and incomplete. In general, however, the available statistics indicate a tendency, other things being equal, for white-collar employment to average 10 per cent, and for employment in the arts to average 1 per cent, of total work-relief employment. In the subsequent WPA program, although attempts were made especially in the beginning to raise these percentages, both

*It must be kept in mind that white-collar projects as such did not employ *all* the white-collar workers on work relief. Projects concerned with public property, housing, and production and distribution of goods also utilized professional and non-manual persons such as engineers, architects, technicians, entomologists, laboratory assistants, foresters, etc. There are no statistics, however, regarding the number of white-collar workers employed on other than white-collar projects.

†In another report, *Government Aid during the Depression to Professional, Technical and Other Service Workers*, Works Progress Administration, May 18, 1936, also written by Floyd Dell, it is stated that theatrical workers employed in the FERA program, 1934-35, numbered about 7,000. This is approximately three times the employment (2,362) for the week ending February 21, 1935, and, if correct, represents the aggregate number employed in the whole program and not the number employed in any one weekly or monthly period, and not a weekly or monthly average.

the white-collar program and the arts program sought these averages as, so to speak, their natural level. The FERA staff, therefore, when it started to plan the WPA program, had reasonably good information concerning what percentage of employment in the white-collar and arts programs they could normally expect.

## THE PROBLEMS OF CLASSIFICATION
## AND ASSIGNMENT

The philosophy of work relief, as apprehended by the social worker of the time and shared by the Washington staff, required not only that the person on relief be given work instead of the dole but also that the work given him be in accordance with his skill and previous employment. Obviously, the perfect application of this principle involved a task of classification and assignment that, if attempted, would have postponed action beyond all reasonable limits, if it would have resulted in action at all. On the other hand, a decent attempt was imperative; without classification and assignment a program of work relief, if it was to advance beyond the unskilled category, was impossible.

The natural connection between classification and assignment has deceived some into thinking that they are the same. Classification is a problem of research; assignment, a problem of operations. In a well-managed program classification always and rightly precedes assignment, but does not necessarily imply it. Yet there is a common inclination to think that when the process of classification is complete, the task of assignment is done.

On the other hand, assignment that is not the result of classification is haphazard, and haphazard assignment is characteristic of every program hastily conceived or under pressure to start quickly. The consequence is that in such a program, classification, if it occurs at all, *follows* assignment, with the result that reorganization of personnel is constant until proper assignment is achieved. The ideal—that assignment should wait upon classification, or, in other words, that operations should wait upon research—is rarely if ever attained. But a reasonable balance between the two is not beyond reach; indeed, a respect for this relationship is a mark of the wise administrator.

In the early work-relief program, classification was impossible in any significant sense, for the knowledge upon which classification depended was not at hand. From the very beginning, therefore, the FERA, although it realized the immediacy of need and the consequent necessity of hasty assignment, was fully aware of the importance of research in a long-term program. Mr. Laning, of the Washington staff, addressing the FERA regional conference in April, 1935, said, "There are two points to emphasize: that is the necessity of planning and of placement. These are the fundamentals of this whole program. It almost stands or falls on those two points. I don't think they can be emphasized too strongly."[4]

A research organization was set up within the agency and among other things was made responsible for the reports and statistics upon which the analysis of white-collar employment, attempted in the previous section of this chapter, has been based. The results of this research were constantly made available to the operating divisions even in the early period.

The difficulty was that research was the prerogative of the Washington office, but operations were carried on by the local relief administrations; and this chasm between research in Washington and operations in the field (which is characteristic of many federal agencies) was never bridged in the FERA period. While Washington classified, the local offices assigned. To be sure, the FERA staff made valiant efforts to make the results of its research known abroad and used its field representatives and written communications as agencies of contact. But, as in the case of Working Procedures, these extensions of the personality of the central staff rarely reached beyond the state administrations into the localities. The fact that the FERA was merely a grant-in-aid agency widened the schism, and, without doubt, the decision in 1935 to federalize work relief was based in part upon the conviction, founded upon experience, that research without control was as futile as control without data was unintelligent.

In the period before the inauguration of the WPA, assignment was the concern of the local administrations; and the more diversified the work-relief program became, the more necessary was the proper assignment at the local level. In the early work-relief program, before the institution of the FERA, as long as relief was a local affair, little was done to elaborate a proper system of classification and assignment, except in a few communities such as New York City and Los Angeles, where significant work-relief programs developed. It was not necessary, for there was little work available that was not of the unskilled and manual type. Even in the early FERA program, before the inception of CWA, classification and assignment were not critical problems.

88

But when cws was instituted as part of the cwa program, the need became immediately apparent. The swiftness with which this program was placed in execution caused difficulties such as Miss Brandt describes:

> Of course every effort was made to match qualifications of applicants to requirements of projects, but everyone knew that while "speed" was the controlling consideration the best intentions could not prevent disappointing results. Those in charge consoled the men and women whom they sent to uncongenial work, the sponsors of projects to whom they sent unsuitable workers, and themselves with promises of transfers later—as soon as they could get to it.[5]

Further on, discussing the same subject, the same observer writes:

> Hasty assignments had meant a large proportion of misfits, necessitating an immense amount of shifting about. Musicians and actors could show their abilities in an audition. Artists, teachers and writers had to be taken usually on their own statement of what they had done or aspired to do. A man who thought he would like to be on the Publicity Project, for example, might say that he "used to work on" *The World*, and it might be discovered later that he had at one time been a copy-boy.[6]

If a situation like this prevailed in New York City, which had a background of four years' experience in work relief and was, so to speak, the center of social experiment, it is clear that in almost all other parts of the country local assignment was an adventure in gambling. The work, of course, was in the nature of pioneering; and in New York City, at least, an honest effort was made to improve the process, and an embryonic training program was initiated.

> Much pioneering was done in devising ways to utilize persons to the best advantage. Artists assigned to Mural Painting, for example, were experimentally grouped in units of eight to fifteen for cooperative work when it was found that many were "not first-class artists." For the instructors and group-leaders of all sorts training had to be provided.[7]

The lessons of the cwa program, if they did not serve to raise the standards of assignment in the localities, impressed upon the Washington office and, to a lesser degree, the state offices, the need of proper occupational classification as a guide to assignment. In October, 1934, the Work Division of the Washington office informed the state administrations of the result of their labors:

> The Division of Research and Statistics and the Works Division here are formulating a procedure for Occupational Classification, Index and Assign-

ment of workers on Works Division jobs. We expect to have it ready and out within the next week or two.

I have heard that a good many states and counties are developing such a procedure this fall. The one we are working up here is drawn from the best practice we have found in use, and I think will be very useful to all of you. For this reason if you can delay any such activities for a little while I think it will be to the advantage of all of us. In this way we can set up a similar procedure all over the country.[8]

This procedure appeared as section 2 of the *Manual of Work Division Procedure of the Federal Emergency Relief Administration,* dated November 15, 1934.

The purpose of the classification is stated thus:

A systematic and detailed classification of available workers will enable the relief agencies to define the types of work projects which should be developed to use the workers to the best advantage. It may also reveal groups of workers for which occupational retraining and/or physical rehabilitation may be necessary before they can be made productively useful. It is, therefore, highly important that this analysis and classification of workers be done carefully and with due regard to natural aptitudes, special training, work experience and physical fitness, and that assignment to specific projects be based upon the individual qualifications of the workers, as well as the personnel requirements of the project.[9]

The local work divisions were asked to designate a person to have general superintendence of the classification service and to act as liason officer between the work division and the social service division of the local relief administration. A special form, FERA Form 144, was provided for use in classification.

This form required information concerning the health, education, ability in English, special vocational training, and date of last employment.

In the Occupational Classification Index the code numbers for professional and technical workers ranged from X001 to X999. Among the occupations listed were:

X015  Actors
X018  Architects
X021  Artists, Sculptors, and Teachers of Art
X022  Artists, Sculptors, and Teachers of Art, Commercial
X030  Authors
X048  College Professors
X060  Designers

X070 Draftsmen [followed by 19 sub-classifications]
X092 Economists
X094 Editors
X116 Historians
X124 Journalists
X126 Lawyers, Judges, and Justices
X128 Librarians
X134 Musicians and Teachers of Music
X146 Photographers
X154 Radio Announcers
X156 Religious Workers
X158 Reporters (Newspaper)
X166 Special Writers
X180 Teachers (School) [followed by 7 sub-classifications]
X196 Translators
X198 Tutors
X202 Professional Persons (not elsewhere classified)

This code was adopted by the Works Progress Administration and appeared as WPA Circular No. 2, *Occupational Classification and Code,* dated July, 1935.

This classification, however useful it may have been for the accumulation of statistics—it smacks of the Bureau of the Census—demonstrates the futility of any attempt at occupational placement not immediately related to specific operational requirements. What the local administrations needed to know was not that actors existed, but how to identify an actor when they met one.*

The local administrations were aware of the importance of proper assignment, but almost without exception they lacked the time and qualified personnel to undertake the task; and in some instances, because the large majority of their clientele was unskilled, they were unwilling

---

*This criticism is directed at the FERA's Occupational Classification Index not because it was formulated (for such a classification has its uses) but because it was expected to assist the local administrations in making *assignments.* The most that this classification does, if it is taken in conjunction with statistics showing the distribution of categories of workers throughout the country, is to tell the local administrations what occupational groups they may expect to find in their particular locality. It does not, and indeed cannot, identify individuals within these groups. The truth is that no one removed from the locale of operations can assign, and a central office can insure proper assignment in the field, not by job classifications or, indeed, by elaborate job descriptions, but by placing in charge of its local operations men whose judgment in personnel selection is trustworthy.

to diversify their program to the extent that proper assignment became important. Clearly, the higher the rung on the occupational ladder, the more difficult the process of assignment. This was particularly true for the professional category and, above all, in the arts, where there were not only many gradations in terms of competence but also room for honest, and sometimes violent, differences of opinion among experts. Variations among the states were great. In one state musicians were classified as unskilled labor, probably because, seeing no opportunity of obtaining work relief at their professional occupation, they had registered as day laborers.[10] In fact, the use of occupational disguise among professional applicants was widespread in the FERA period. In New Jersey, Mr. Laning reported that "they had some people working on a theatrical project, but when you looked at their classification they were listed as typists, carpenters, etc., because they wanted a job."[11]

Sometimes, local classifications were amusing:

In Connecticut they had two preachers and two ministers. I asked them what the difference was and they said the preachers had the call and the ministers the training.[12]

Under these circumstances the use of classification boards, as suggested by the Washington office, was helpful. This method developed in the CWA period, particularly in New York City. Many of these local committees worked with, but were not a part of or paid by, the local relief administrations. Representing professional societies, as was often the case, they were glad to act as volunteers to facilitate the placement of their less fortunate brethren. In New York City, committees of prominent musicians and representatives of Actors' Equity Association gave their time gratis in order to try out musicians and actors seeking work relief. In less metropolitan areas it sometimes required ingenuity to uncover artistic personnel. Bruce McClure told of such a situation in Maine:

They had a project in Portland where they tried to get up some orchestras and bands, and in going through the classifications on relief rolls, could find no musicians; so they got the Secretary of the Musicians' Union to come down and help them out. He went out in trenches and dug up plenty.[13]

The use of audition boards, as in music and in the theater, or of examining committes, as in art, was developed further under the WPA arts program and, in many instances, achieved most satisfactory results. On the other hand, the wpa Writers' Project and, to a degree, the Historical Records Survey had no such facile means of classification, and their problem in this regard, as will be seen, was more difficult.

There was at times a temptation on the part of local relief administrations to constitute themselves as audition boards, and McClure warned against this practice:

> The way this problem [the problem of assignment] was met under cwa has been by the appointment of local voluntary committees, composed of people competent to judge and criticize artistic ability. But there are degrees within art and music. You have to have somebody who can tell you or your local man who out of that group is capable of doing a mural job in a municipal building, etc. Then there is employment for a group not so skilled; for instance, poster artists who can do every valuable service for schools and health departments; also a group who can do excellent lettering, etc. I don't think any of you could pass on the artistic ability of people registered as artists or musicians, but if you select from your community people who have interested themselves in those fields, you will solve what looks like a very difficult problem.[14]

Again, some state administrations, like the Washington office, tried to establish precise formulas for job classification. In one state a ruling was made that to be eligible for certain professional projects an applicant should be either a high school graduate or in certain cases have completed at least two years in college. In answering a question on this procedure, Mr. Laning replied:

> That is probably good for some things. A musician might never have been to school a day in his life. I don't think your educational requirements should be too strict. There should be some educational requirement, but it should be more of practical experience. That is where the emphasis should be. But if you are organizing a music or recreational project it certainly is a great mistake to insist that this man has some college background.[15]

The experience in this respect that the Washington office acquired as a result of two years of work relief should have taught it: (1) that classification, however valuable it may be as a guide to assignment and as a means to achieve relative uniformity throughout the country, was not the act of assignment or a substitute for it; and (2) that assignment was a local operation, the effectiveness of which was dependent upon the quality of local personnel who combined a respect for research with knowledge of the local situation.

## THE PROBLEM OF WORK-RELIEF WAGES

In the period between 1929 and 1933 wages paid to white-collar workers for work relief directed by private or public agencies did not differ materially from wages paid the less-skilled groups. There were some exceptions, as at Bridgeport, Connecticut, where foremen, time-keepers, and other supervisory employees were paid $2.20 a week more than ordinary workers. On the other hand, the Department of Public Welfare of Detroit paid all clients forty cents an hour, regardless of the type of work assigned. In another city an agency was able to assign two doctors in financial distress to a receiving hospital but, since there was not a variable wage rate, paid them manual wages.

Harry Hopkins, speaking in November, 1933, said:

> Women in New York paid by the Gibson Committee got twelve dollars a week, as I recall it. This seemed like an awful lot of money in comparison with the amount of money families were getting on relief. Yet we used to talk to thse women . . . and when you dug into it and found out how these women lived, the things they did to make the twelve dollars go, you realized that that twelve dollars, in New York City at any rate, wasn't any too much.[16]

In New York City, immediately before the beginning of the cwa program, women were paid $3.00 a day.[17] In the early FERA program, however, although prevailing hourly rates were encouraged by the national office, no minimum hourly rate was established; and wages, calculated on the budget-deficiency principle, were extremely low and rarely based upon the type of work performed.

With the inauguration of the cwa program in November, 1933, the principle of budget deficiency was abandoned. Under the first allocation to cwa wages were fixed at pwa rates. Under the cws program, however, which gave greatest employment to the white-collar class, and after February 15, 1934, when the pwa statutory limitations no longer held, wages were fixed at a thirty-cents-an-hour minimum, or the prevailing wage rate for that class of work in the community. Wages under the cwa for professional and clerical workers were high, as a special study for the weeks ending January 11 and February 22, 1934, indicate.

| Amount of Weekly Earnings | Percentage of Total Employees |
|---|---|
| Under $5 | 3.1 |
| $5 to $9.99 | 5.7 |
| $10 to $14.99 | 13.5 |
| $15 to $19.99 | 33.7 |
| $20 to $24.99 | 22.3 |
| $25 to $29.99 | 9.5 |
| $30 to $34.99 | 5.6 |
| $35 and over | 6.6 |
| Total | 100.0 |

Source: *Monthly Report of the Federal Emergency Relief Administration,* March 1 to March 31, 1934, p. 8.

Of this class, 77.7 per cent received fifteen dollars or over a week, and almost half were paid twenty dollars or over a week. Those who received under ten dollars week were mostly part-time employees. Moreover, the wages for professional workers were higher than this table indicates, since it includes the wages of clerical workers.

Under the Emergency Work Program of the FERA, established on April 1, 1934, to succeed the CWA program, the minimum of thirty cents an hour and the principle of prevailing rates were maintained; but the budget-deficiency principle was reintroduced, and working hours were not to exceed twenty-four a week.

When, in July, 1934, the Works Division of the FERA inaugurated its short-lived program to secure preferential treatment for professional clients, the means test and the budget-deficiency principle were relaxed, and the professional classes enjoyed a preferred status. In many communities, however, the reaction to this policy was unfavorable. An instance is cited by Miss Newsom.

You remember that $2.50 a day minimum for a while. One of our counties had a person who was leading choruses. He led 1½ hours on Monday and 1½ hours on Tuesday and he worked his budget out. We completely failed to show the community that it was worth while for him to earn $2.50 for 1½ hours when it took a man on the road much longer to work his out. Our communities aren't used to paying high wages for professional services.[18]

A represenative of the Wyoming ERA expressed the condition of the problem in his state:

Most of the counties are a little reluctant to carry on professional programs such as dramatics, tap dancing, piano instruction, physical instruction. In order to overcome that reluctance we prepare a budget of the cost of the projects for the month, and we set that aside and earmark it. The great criticism from the counties is, why pay additional money for those projects, when we have people in the counties not receiving their full budget.[19]

On the other hand, a few, especially among those with a background of social service, believed that a wage of sixty dollars a month (the average professional wage under the CWA) was too low. Mr. March represented this point of view:

I am glad the professional projects have provided for him [the professional worker]. The difficulty is that he has been accustomed—a fiddle player possibly or certainly an attorney or an engineer—has been accustomed to a good income. I don't mean the $60 a month standard; $200 or $300 more a month. The pity of the thing is the effect upon that individual of having to take even one of these professional jobs where he will get $60 a month or less. I think the loss to society due to the effect on that man's mind and his outlook and manner of thinking is far greater than in the case of the ditch digger who is forced to work for 30c an hour when the wage rate committee has tried to establish a higher one.*[20]

From the point of view of the relief worker the CWA period represented the ideal with respect to wages, which were calculated at the local prevailing rate and for a continuous work week; the difficulty was that the Treasury Department and the Bureau of the Budget were unable to share the workers' enthusiasm, and the President himself was genuinely alarmed at a rate of spending that transgressed the limits of orthodoxy. On the other hand, the budget-deficiency principle of the FERA, by staggering employment especially among the more highly paid workers, threatened the integrity of project operation. The idea of the security wage, which at once was lower than prevailing rates and at the same time allowed for continuity of employment, represented the WPA's attempt to arrive at a happy mean.

### THE PROBLEM OF NON-LABOR COSTS

One difficulty that manifested itself early in the work-relief program of the FERA was non-labor costs (supervision and material). In the early

---

*It was during this discussion that Mr. Laning contributed the phrase "brain erosion" to the vocabulary of the depression. "This man may not mind digging a ditch," he remarked, "but there is a real brain erosion."[21]

FERA the general impression in the states was that non-labor costs should be born by the sponsors and that federal funds should be kept for labor costs only, and in the beginning this was the policy of the Washington office.*

This attitude carried through the CWA period, but with the beginning of the Emergency Work Program of the FERA in April, 1934, the tendency was to relax the prohibition. In May, 1934, Jacob Baker wrote:

> The difficulty about writers' projects is that the larger part of the expense seems to be that of publication, paper material, printing and binding. . . . We are not justified in spending more than ten or fifteen per cent of the total cost of a project upon other than labor cost.[22]

With the inauguration of the special program for professional and non-manual projects in July, 1934, the letter of August 2 (WD-16) permitted that "materials and supervision for professional and nonmanual projects may be furnished out of funds granted for these projects up to 10 per cent of the total cost of the project, at the discretion of the state administrator." In the *Manual of Work Division Procedure* (November 15, 1934) procedure for professional projects is thus stated: "Together with supervision for Professional and Non manual projects, materials may be furnished for these projects at the discretion of the State Administrator."[23]

To the end of the FERA, however, non-labor costs remained a major problem. Miss Newsom said:

> Have the other states had trouble with materials? We have had small material funds. We have asked counties to give the rest, but just try to balance balls and bats against cement and rock. . . . In these specialized projects material is a big problem.[24]

Moreover, throughout the later FERA program the states, although they were told to use their discretion in paying non-labor costs, were never sure what latitude the Washington office was prepared to allow them. As Miss Newsom said, speaking in April, 1935: "We have never been able to determine what Washington considers O.K. It is surprising what the counties think we should furnish."[25]

At the same time there were those, though they were in the minority, who maintained that the sponsor's acceptance of non-labor costs was a token of community interest and responsibility. At the same conference Miss Smith emphasized this point of view:

*There was no statutory limitation on the use of FERA funds for non-labor costs.

> I think that [community participation] is your advantage, for if there is no local contribution it does not give the right interest. It is an asset instead of a liability. It creates a degree of local responsibility. We think local participation is a big asset.[26]

This problem of non-labor costs, though it existed to some degree in all types of projects, was most serious in professional projects. For this reason the Works Progress Administration, when it established Federal One, named itself as sponsor and undertook to pay non-labor costs from federal funds. This seemed like a ready and easy solution of the earlier difficulties, but though the problem of community financial contribution was removed, that of community moral support and participation remained. A financial investment creates a sense of responsibility and a continuity of interest which, at least in our kind of society, are rarely so surely guaranteed by other means.

The question of sponsorship and, with it, the assumption of non-labor costs by the community raised the basic problem of public relations, which was of such importance in the professional program. At the conference in April, 1935, Miss Newsom spoke at length on this subject

> I guess I am the only representative of boondoggling. I think first we must realize what we are trying to do in the program. Ours is a state that is not recreationally minded. . . . We have had the job educating the people, because the newspapers have not always given a clear picture. . . . We have had "boondoggling." We know now, more than ever, that we must have the country behind us. That means we have to work with the community, sell the people of the community as to the value of the tap-dancing. . . . We have so many people that have no understanding of it, and it has been our policy not to start a program any place until the community desires it.

Mr. Laning commented on this: "As soon as the people feel they are having a part in it they are pretty much with you. And when they aren't you can't organize tap-dancing classes."*[27]

The situation Miss Newsom so clearly describes was fundamental, and it is a matter of regret that the wpa arts program, in its effort to achieve professional standing, was sometimes inclined to neglect the cultivation of community support.

*"Tap dancing" in this context is not to be taken literally. It is used facetiously to describe the type of project called "boondoggling."

THE WOMEN'S DIVISION AND THE SECTION OF
PROFESSIONAL AND NON-MANUAL PROJECTS

The part played by the Women's Division in the encouragement of professional projects has already been discussed. When, however, in July, 1934, the FERA established its section of professional and non-manual projects under Arthur Goldschmidt, jurisdiction over professional projects was, in a sense, taken from Mrs. Woodward. Since between 20 and 25 per cent of all women on work relief were employed on such projects, the prospect was not agreeable to the women's section. Indeed, it became a matter of doubt, and sometimes of dispute, whether a woman in professional work should be the concern of Mr. Goldschmidt or Mrs. Woodward. This confusion, which derived from the use of a *principium divisionis* the terms of which were not mutually exclusive (women versus professional), was aggravated by the fact that, although the distinction, such as it was, prevailed in the Washington office, no separate section for professional and non-manual projects was established in the state and local offices. As a consequence, state and local administrations usually placed jurisdiction over professional projects in the hands of the state and local directors of women's work, for the obvious reason that more women than men, in proportion to the total employment of each class, were so engaged. Thus state and local directors of women's work, already technically responsible to Mrs. Woodward, became technically responsible also to Goldschmidt. The sound administrative principle that no one should have more than one immediate superior, even in staff relationships, was violated, and an atmosphere of rivalry was created.

In the Washington office both sections were under the authority of Jacob Baker; and early in 1935, when relations became strained, Baker in a memorandum to Mrs. Woodward made it clear that jurisdiction over professional projects was not within her domain.[28] Mrs. Woodward, however, was not a person to be easily deterred, and, recognizing the prestige that attached to a professional program, she was quick to encourage the state and local staffs of her division to initiate and promote professional projects. Baker felt that such promotional activities, if the time for them had come, belonged to the professional section, and so, in another memorandum to Mrs. Woodward, written three weeks after the first, he again counseled caution.[29]

At the FERA regional conference in April, Mr. Laning frankly conceded the conflict, though he softened his admission at the end:

> We do compete pretty hard with the women's section. This whole program ties in with the women's work section because we put a great many women to work as soon as they get a professional rating. We sort of claim them. We are probably not always justified. We get splendid cooperation.[30]

## THE PROBLEM OF PROFESSIONAL VERSUS
## SERVICE PROJECTS

In the arts program of the FERA, so far as it proceeded, the social philosophy of the neighborhood house was predominant. The leaders in Washington and in the states and localities co-operating in the development of the program were largely from the field of social service, and inherited Edward Denison's faith in community healing. The arts were, in their thinking, specifics for the cure of social and psychological maladjustment, and by them, no less than by the construction and production of physical goods, the community was "serviced." Consequently, as already has been observed, the accent was on the effect of the arts upon the community, and not on the the professional caliber of the artist, except in relation to this purpose. Baker, who arrived at this point of view because of his interest in the co-operative movement, not only as an economic release from the entrepreneur but also as an adventure in community living, expressed his and the program's philosophy at the close of the FERA period:

> From actual construction work we proceeded quite logically to service projects which contributed similarly to the health and happiness of the public, and more particularly, of the unemployed. Just because they were unemployed, these millions of people needed special medical and health care; they also needed some added recreational and educational opportunities. The mere fact that a man is out of a job constitutes no good reason why he should sit around on a park bench and contemplate suicide. Indeed, he needs the distraction that decent educational and recreational program offers much more than the man with a job. . . .
> Here is where the unemployed white-collar people had a chance at work; they have become the teachers, leaders and entertainers of the others. They teach in the adult schools, are the ones who play in orchestras in free concerts, give performances of plays; paint pictures and murals for our public buildings. For the first time in our history, our government has become a patron of the arts, officially and quite unashamed.[31]

In the transition from the FERA to the WPA arts program, there occurred a transfer of power, so far as jurisdiction over the arts was concerned, from those who emphasized the "service" aspect of the arts to those who stressed the professional integrity of the artist. The soundness of the former approach lay in the fact that it could be built upon existing foundations within the community such as playgrounds, recreational and educational facilities, community centers, churches and civic organizations and through these acquire not only local authenticity but also that popular support that impresses the politician, both at home and in Washington. On the other hand, the accent upon professionalism commended itself by its insistence upon artistic standards in a program of community education and by its solicitude for the salvation of artistic ideals at a time of disillusionment. Both approaches also had their limitations. In the social-service attitude there sometimes prevailed a cult of the amateur and an evangelical attitude that rightly offended the conscience of the expert; and on the part of the professional artist a pose was occasionally struck that was at best patronizing and at worse contemptuous toward the provinces. It is not suggested that these two approaches were mutually exclusive, or that there were not those on both sides who sought their reconciliation. But as a matter of emphasis, each approach defined the philosophy of the period of its ascendency and dictated the strategy of the Washington office and the tactics of the state and local administrations.

1.   Philip M. Hauser and Bruce L. Jenkinson, *Workers on Relief in the United States in March 1934* (Washington: United States Government Printing Office, 1938), 2 vols.

2.   "Relief for White-Collar Workers," *Monthly Report of the Federal Emergency Relief Administration*, December 1 through December 31, 1935, p. 64.

3.   *The Emergency Work Relief Program of the Federal Emergency Relief Administration*, April 1, 1934, to July 1, 1935, Appendix II, p. 121.

4.   *Proceedings*, Mountain States Regional Conference, FERA Work Division, April 29, 1935 (Friday Morning Session), p. 28.

5.   Brandt, *op. cit.*, p. 186.

6.   *Ibid.*, p. 209.

7.   *Ibid.*, pp. 209-10.

8.   Letter WD-21, FERA, October 8, 1934.

9.   *Manual of Work Division Procedure*, FERA, November 15, 1935, sec. 2, p. 1.

10.   *Proceedings*, Conference of State Administrators, FERA (Mayflower Hotel, Washington, D.C.), Meeting of Group No. 3, June 17-19, 1935, p. 2.

11.   *Proceedings*, Mountain States Regional Conference, FERA Work Division, April 26, 1935 (Friday Morning Session), p. 17.

12.   *Ibid.*, p. 17.

13. *Proceedings*, Conference of State Administrators (Mayflower Hotel, Washington, D.C.), Meeting of Group No. 6, June 18-19, 1935, p. 18.

14. *Proceedings*, Conference of State Administrators (Mayflower Hotel, Washington, D.C.), Meeting of Group No. 3, June 19, 1935, p. 24.

15. *Proceedings*, Mountain States Regional Meeting, FERA Work Division, April 29, 1935 (Friday Morning Session), p. 18.

16. *Proceedings of the Conference on Emergency Needs for Women*, The White House, November 20, 1933, pp. 6-7.

17. *Ibid.*, p. 17.

18. *Proceedings*, Mountain States Regional Conference, FERA Work Division, April 26, 1935 (Friday Morning Session), p. 24.

19. *Ibid.*, p. 22.

20. *Ibid.*, p. 26.

21. *Ibid.*

22. Letter, Baker to Hugh Harlan, May 12, 1934, FERA Files.

23. *Manual of Work Division Procedure*, FERA, November 15, 1934, p. 12.

24. *Proceedings*, Mountain States Regional Conference, FERA Work Division, April 26, 1935 (Friday Morning Session), p. 25.

25. *Ibid.*

26. *Ibid.*

27. *Ibid.*, p. 23.

28. Memorandum, Baker to Woodward, March 4, 1935, FERA Files.

29. Memorandum, Baker to Woodward, March 27, 1935, FERA Files.

30. *Proceedings*, Mountain States Regional Conference, FERA Work Division, April 26, 1935 (Friday Morning Session), p. 25.

31. Release for Afternoon Papers, Jacob Baker, July 3, 1935, FERA Files.

# 7

# Staff versus Line and Conflict in National Policy

THE ORGANIZATION OF THE WPA

The Works Progress Administration represented the continuation, under other conditions, of the Emergency Work Program of the FERA.

In his message to Congress, January 3, 1935, the President said:

> Work must be found for able-bodied but destitute workers. The Federal Government must and shall quit this business of relief. I am not willing that the vitality of our people be further sapped by the giving of cash, of market baskets, a few hours weekly of work cutting grass, raking leaves, or picking up papers in the public parks. We must preserve not only the bodies of the unemployed from destitution, but also their self-respect, their self-reliance, and courage and determination.

In the same speech the general nature of the new plan was foreshadowed.

> It is my thought that, with the exception of certain of the normal public-building operations of the Government, all emergency public works shall be united in a single new and greatly enlarged plan.
>
> With the establishment of this new system we can supersede the Federal Emergency Relief Administration with a coordinated authority, which will be charged with the orderly liquidation of our present relief activities and the substitution of a national chart for the giving of work.

Suggestions for the new program had been in the making since September, 1934. They came from a variety of sources within the government, but the main inspiration, as the sequel was to show, derived from the Work Division of the FERA. The PWA, to be sure, occupied a promi-

103

nent position during this period, for since its inception in 1933, it had been planning and gradually putting into execution large construction projects. But if the interest of the PWA was direct and concise, that of the Work Division was wider and more diversified. The FERA had been concerned with the unemployed in almost every aspect of their problems, and within the organization the Work Division had accumulated the experience of two years in devising projects that would suit their capacities. The experience of the PWA, on the other hand, if inconclusive, was nonetheless disappointing. The belief that a construction program, designed to stimulate heavy industry, would indirectly create enough employment to initiate business recovery was not so strongly held in 1935 as it had been two years before.

Nevertheless, the new program as it was finally presented to Congress was envisaged as almost entirely a construction program, in which the PWA and the several governmental departments and agencies would co-operate in the initiation and superintendence of work projects. The Works Progress Administration, established by Executive Order No. 7034, issued on May 6, 1935, was designed, as its name indicates, to act as a co-ordinating agency that would examine the various projects proposed by the several federal instrumentalities, co-ordinate their execution, and inspect their progress. The order read in part:

> I hereby establish . . .
>
> (c) A Works Progress Administration, which shall be responsible to the President for the honest, efficient, speedy, and coordinated execution of the work relief program as a whole, and for the execution of that program in such manner as to move from the relief rolls to work on such projects or in private employment the maximum number of persons in the shortest time possible.[1]

The same Executive Order gave the Works Progress Administration certain powers and duties to achieve its purpose. The last of these read:

> 3. Recommend and carry on small useful projects designed to assure a maximum employment in all localities.

As originally constituted, then, the WPA was essentially and almost exclusively a staff agency created to advise the President with respect to the *progress* of the program and to co-ordinate the program so that its purposes would be realized.

The process by which this staff agency—by virtue of an obscure clause that gave it operating power—became shortly the chief operat-

ing agency for the execution of the new program has been told elsewhere, and it is not necessary to repeat it here.[2] But this evolution was
in a sense inevitable if the program was to be executed "in such manner as to move from the relief rolls to work . . . the maximum number
of persons in the shortest time possible." The projects proposed by the
other government departments, and especially by the PWA, were mainly
large construction projects that required time to get started and lacked
the simplicity that would provide mass employment. The "small, useful
projects," on the other hand, which were the concern of the WPA, were
precisely the type that joined speed with coverage. Thus in September,
1935, as a result of the Hyde Park conference, the WPA became the chief
operating agency in the program.

The reasons for this development deserve emphasis. In the first
place, Roosevelt was determined that the work program should employ the 3,500,000 persons then on relief as quickly and as completely
as possible. The size of the appropriation, $4,800,000,000, was such that
this could be done only if the average man-year cost did not exceed
$1,142, including both labor and non-labor cost. Only projects with a
small cost for material and using a minimum of skilled labor fitted this
purpose.*

Moreover, the WPA possessed in its Washington and state work divisions, which were inherited from the FERA period, the necessary experienced personnel to carry out this kind of program. Even as early as
June, 1935, when the issue between him and Harold Ickes was still un-
decided, Harry Hopkins envisaged the predominance of the WPA. At
that time he told a conference of newly appointed state WPA administrators that his agency was preparing to employ 2,400,000 persons, or 69
per cent of the total employment goal.

The WPA program was, in effect, a compromise between the FERA
work program and the CWA. The employment feature of the CWA program was abandoned, and in its stead the relief principle of the FERA
was adopted. Employment on WPA was restricted, except for a small

---

*The cost of providing one man one year's employment under PWA was approxi-
mately $4,000. To employ 3,500,000 men at that rate would have meant an annual
cost of $14,000,000,000, an astronomical sum in the mind of orthodox finance in
1935. In 1938 the average cost of employing one man for one year on a WPA project was $984, and of this only $762 was federal cost, the remainder being the local
sponsor's contribution. This contrast well illustrates the difference in cost between
a true public-works program and a true work-relief program. Among the plans submitted early in 1935 was one that would have approached the cost of a comprehensive public-works program, but it was rejected by the Treasury Department
and the Bureau of the Budget as financially impossible.

percentage allowed for supervisory and administrative purposes, to those certified for relief by local relief agencies. On the other hand, the budget-deficiency calculation of the FERA was rejected in favor of a monthly security wage, the principle of which was advocated by the President in his message to Congress, January 4, 1935. It was intended that the average rate of pay should be fifty dollars a worker a month, or $600 a year. In return, the worker should enjoy continuous employment, with hours of work fixed at between 120 and 140 a month.

The basic purpose of the WPA, therefore, was to remove 3,500,000 employables from the relief rolls and to engage them in continuous employment at a monthly security wage.

In the second place, the WPA was instituted as a federal program, and in that respect resembled the CWA. The grant-in-aid system of the FERA was abandoned, and in its place the WPA became an operating agency with authority and responsibility for operations down to the lowest operating unit, the district office. Every individual employed by the WPA, whether administrative, supervisory, or project employee, was an employee of the federal government.*

## THE CONCEPTS OF LINE AND STAFF

The federalization of work relief and the entrustment of the execution of the program to the WPA created a direct line of authority from the federal administrator (Harry Hopkins) to the state administrators and, through them, to the district supervisors.† Thus the effectuation of federal policy in the states and localities was secured by command, and not, as in the FERA program, by advice and suggestion. At the same time, each line officer, from the federal through the state to the district office, was assisted by a staff, whose function was to advise its immediate superior concerning the technical or professional aspects of the program. A line of technical advice proceeded from the central staff to the state staffs and thence to the district staffs. The several staffs, however, did not possess authority to command. They counseled their chief

*This decision, like that relating to maximum employment in the smallest possible time, was made by the President. There were those in the FERA—Jacob Baker among them—who tended to favor the continuance of the grant-in-aid system. But the President was firm. Although the difficulties inherent in a grant-in-aid agency were undoubtedly persuasive, the decision was fundamentally political and based upon considerations of policy as well as patronage.

†The regional offices were not in the line of direct authority but were an extension of the Washington staff.

and, except at the lowest level, the subordinate line officers. Thus the staff of the central office advised the state staffs, and they in turn the district offices. At the lowest level, however, a staff officer also performed line functions. For instance, a district supervisor of women's work not only advised her chief with respect to women's work in the district but also directly operated the women's projects within the district.

## FLOW OF AUTHORITY AND SPAN OF CONTROL

In the vocabulary of modern administrative thought two expressions, *flow of authority* and *span of control,* have been devised to express this problem. The flow of authority is vertical, and the longer the line, the greater the need of co-ordination by the staff; for command, like water, dissipates itself as it descends from level to level. The span of control, on the other hand is horizontal, and the greater its spread, the greater the need of integration by the staff; for the number of reins that an administrator, like a charioteer, can hold in his hands is limited. In the WPA the flow of authority involved three levels, federal, state, and district; the span of control encompassed, in the case of the federal administrator, fifty-three main operating areas or "state" WPA's and, in the case of the state administrators, as many districts as were set up within a given state.*

The nice balance between flow of authority and span of control, which identifies the well-managed agency, is achieved and sustained by staff co-ordination and integration. By procedures the staff attempts to secure that reasonable uniformity of purpose and action without which an agency lacks unity; and by reports and field visits it secures adherence to its rules and an appreciation of local problems, without which an agency lacks elasticity.

## HEADQUARTERS-FIELD RELATIONS AND
## UNITY OF POLICY

The problem of staff and line relations and, as part of it, the problem of relations between the central office and the field are rightly subjects

---

*The regional offices of the WPA, unlike those of most federal agencies with field responsibilities, were theoretically not in the direct line of authority, but in practice tended, especially as the agency grew in wisdom, to exercise line command. Accordingly, the span of control of the federal administrator was not as wide as at first appears, but limited by the intervention of the regional office. As for the state administrator's span of control, in four states the state itself constituted a single district; Texas had the largest number of districts (twenty), followed by Ohio and Pennsylvania with sixteen each.

of concern and speculation to students of administration, and attempts have been made to resolve them by the use of charts and words. But a chart, however useful it may be to the administrative manager, merely states, and does not solve, the problems; either the chart is simple, in which case it deceives, or it is complex, in which case it bewilders the inquirer. Nor is the problem one of verbiage, to be met by distinguishing between the "authority of command" and the "authority of ideas," or by suggesting, as has recently been done, that in every administration there are really two "authorities," that of the line and that of the staff. Recognition is not reconciliation, although, to be sure, it is important that the nature of the difficulty be apprehended before an attempt be made to solve it.

Simply stated, the problem is one of policy, not of structure. If, within a given agency or between agencies within a government, there is substantial unity of purpose, staff and line co-operate, and the frictions between individuals, sections, divisions, and bureaus, which are present in every organization, merely betoken a rivalry that is often friendly and always salutary. If, however, there is lack of agreement with regard to fundamental policy, either between agencies or within a single agency, conflict ensues that threatens the very structure of the government or the agency concerned.

In March, 1933, when the Roosevelt administration assumed office, a situation presented itself in which the policy of the executive, as represented by the President and his chosen staff, was different from: (1) the policy of the Congress; (2) the policy of the judiciary; (3) the policy of the career civil servant; and (4) the policy of the state governments.*
This conflict manifested itself between and within every agency of the federal government. In the first place, the very establishment of a congeries of new agencies by the President, through which *novi homines* with new ideas could be brought into the government not only at the top but also throughout the structure, revealed his lack of faith not in the professional capacity but in the political temper of the career civil servant. The Washington office of the WPA, for instance, was staffed by men and women who were for the most part novices in government service. Second, the existence of these new agencies, expressing the policy of the executive, side by side with the older departments in which traditional policy prevailed created a conflict between agency and

*The attempt to "pack" the Supreme Court dramatized the struggle between the executive and the judiciary, and the several attempts to "purge" recalcitrant congressmen illustrated a similar conflict between the executive and the legislative.

agency, which in the case of the WPA manifested itself most clearly in that agency's relations with the Bureau of the Budget. Finally, throughout the Roosevelt administration there was the attempt, in many cases successful, to extend federal control within the states, not because federal control as such was better than state or local control but because, in view of the lack of sympathetic state administrations, federal policy as expressed in the executive could not be otherwise achieved.* For this reason, work relief was federalized under the WPA; the experience of the FERA had convinced both Harry Hopkins and the President that federal policy with respect to work relief could not be achieved in the states through personnel that represented the state point of view.

## CONTROL OF PERSONNEL AND SENATORIAL CONFIRMATION

Hopkins was sensitive to this consideration, especially in the selection of personnel. In April, 1936, in answer to a question from Mr. Taber, "Is the politics of the applicant [for an administrative post] investigated before he is appointed?", Hopkins replied:

> No. What we would do, what I would do, for instance, is to be sure that the person is friendly to this program. I would not have anybody working on my staff who did not believe in it. . . . My job is to find competent people who believe in this and I think any business organization would do the same thing. In other words, I think it would be absurd to have me direct this program if I did not believe in it.[3]

Almost a year before, addressing his Washington staff, Hopkins had spoken more freely:

> Now I want people doing this job that are in sympathy with doing this job. We have had some experience in the CWA. I have had plenty since I have been around here. I have had plenty of experience with a lot of people that are close personal friends of mine, but who never had the heart in the job, who really never believed in it. Now any more than General Motors would have a person working for them in an important position who wasn't devoted to General Motors, or any other corporation, why in the world should the federal government have people administering its job—I am speaking now of a sympathy for a particular job such as this Works Progress

---

*It is not here argued that this was the *only* reason for the extension of federal control during this period. Nor is it meant that state governments, judges, congressmen, and career civil servants were *all* unsympathetic with the policy of the executive.

Administration—who really don't believe in it, no matter how competent they are. I don't care how good they are, if they don't believe in this job I don't want them working for me.[4]

Unfortunately for his purpose, the Senate was as conscious of difference in policy as was Hopkins, and inserted in the Emergency Relief Appropriation Act of 1935 the following provision:

Any administrator or other officer, or the members of any central board, or other agency, named to have general supervision at the seat of Government over the program and work contemplated under the appropriation made in section 1 of this joint resolution and receiving a salary of $5000 or more per annum from such appropriation (except persons now serving as such under other law [*]), shall be appointed by the President, by and with the advice and consent of the Senate.[5]

The requirement of senatorial confirmation is an acknowledged limitation of the President's power of appointment. In effect, because of the observance of senatorial courtesy, it often happens that it is the Senate, and not the President, that appoints; and consequently, when difference of policy exists, the appointee represents senatorial policy or the policy of the senator's state rather than presidential policy. It is obvious that, even if the Senate accepts in large part the nominees of the President, the very fact that senatorial confirmation is required limits in advance the list from which the appointees are chosen. In the case of the wpa, Harry Hopkins personally undertook to recommend the appointment of state administrators; and although documentation for the statement is lacking, it can be confidently asserted a priori that not only did he refrain from recommending certain persons whom otherwise he would have appointed but in some instances he was under constraint to accept the choice of the more assertive members of the upper chamber.

The effect of this was radical and continuous. It is not that a political appointee as such was bad, in the sense that he was either incompetent or dishonest; it was that in this particular instance a senatorial choice, however competent and honest, was less likely to sympathize with the philosophy of the federal administrator than one chosen by the admin-

---

*This phrase was interpreted to except from the requirement of senatorial confirmation ERA state administrators who were continued as WPA state administrators. This occurred in fourteen states. This provision was repeated in all succeeding ERA acts except that of 1938. Hopkins was not in Washington at the time this provision was debated and inserted, and his assistants, although they realized its implications, were at a loss to act in his absence.

istrator under no such limitation. As a consequence of this provision, the state administrators of the WPA, as a whole, represented the layman's point of view with respect to work relief, as opposed to the more advanced point of view of the social worker as seen in the Washington office. As a result, the conflict in respect to fundamental policy that existed during the FERA period between Washington and the states was carried over into the WPA period. The only difference was that now the federal administrator possessed command authority over the state administrators, whereas under the FERA his authority was "the authority of ideas."

The possession of command authority, however, does not imply its unqualified use. Administratively speaking, Hopkins had power to dismiss at any time for any cause a state WPA administrator. Politically speaking, he had no such power. Extreme caution was necessary for two reasons. In the first place, the WPA did not exist by virtue of a substantive law but merely by virtue of appropriation acts periodically voted. Congress, and especially the House, could at any time either refuse further money or, as indeed it did, progressively reduce appropriations. The state administrators, who, for the most part, held their appointments because of senatorial connections, were in a position to make their point of view powerful in Congress. Harry Hopkins could resent, at times fight, this power, but never defy it. In the second place, the philosophy of the state governments expressed itself naturally through pressure upon their senators and representatives, who, in turn, brought this philosophy to bear upon national issues.

This conflict between the federal government and the states not only was dramatically expressed in the WPA, but substantially affected the flow of authority from the federal administrators to the state administrators.* The states, with a few notable exceptions, were opposed to the philosophy of work relief as expressed by Harry Hopkins and his staff. They preferred the dole (direct relief) as being both cheaper, as it was, and administratively simpler, as it was. Second, the states, precisely because fundamental policy was involved, resented the federalization of work relief; and though ready enough to accept a federal subsidy, they were unwilling to suffer federal control either of policy or of operations.

*The attitude of the district offices toward work relief varied. Rural districts, in the main, were unsympathetic, urban districts favorable. But since instructions from the federal office to the district offices were necessarily channeled through the state offices, the state offices could, and sometimes did, serve as an effective bottleneck.

111

Congressmen, again with relatively few exceptions, represented the state point of view in these respects.

PUBLIC PRESSURES AND THE WHITE-COLLAR PROGRAM

As a result of this fundamental difference of policy, pressures for and against work relief exerted themselves in different areas. Agitation for relief work of an adequate nature was directed in general to the national office of the wpa with the consequence that the Washington office was made particularly sensitive to the needs of the unemployed. This confirmed the Washington office in its philosophic position with respect to work relief. On the other hand, protests from quarters opposed to work relief usually were directed from the several states to congressmen who, in turn, were equally strengthened in their opposition to the philosophy of the social worker. At no time can it be said that Congress, as a whole, truly and genuinely supported the principle of work relief. Congress merely permitted its use, because in 1935 it was afraid to do otherwise and, having started the wpa, was, after 1935, afraid to stop it.*

This conflict in policy between the national and the state administrations exhibited itself most clearly in the white-collar program, and within that program, in the arts program. The states and, reflecting state opinion, the state wpa administrations were prepared to accept the principle of work relief, but only under certain conditions. In the first place, they emphasized manual labor, partly because they thought of need predominantly in terms of the unskilled laborer and partly because manual labor approached the nature of a work test, which represented their philosophy of relief. In the second place, they preferred construction projects, partly because they employed the manual worker and partly because they resulted in products, the usefulness of which was obvious to the lay mind. On the other hand, the white-collar program, which employed women as well as men and which busied itself with educational and recreational activities, was distinctly less popular with

*The fundamental distaste of Congress for the wpa and the reluctance with which they voted for its continuance are clearly apparent in the hearings on the several appropriation bills and in the debates in both houses. The appropriation hearings, to be sure, unlike the hearings of the Woodrum Committee and Dies Committee, were conducted on both sides with dignity and a sense of public responsibility; but the bias of the committee, nonetheless, is clearly revealed.

the state WPA administrations. In some cases the hostility was open and almost violent; in many other cases, however, the attitude can best be described as indifferent. The need among these classes was not so apparent, and the product of their activities was in many cases non-material and therefore, in the lay mind, a luxury.

What was true of the white-collar projects in general was true of the arts program in particular. Music, drama, literary activity, painting, and sculpture were in the layman's mind avocations that existed either for the delectation of those who could pay for them or for the self-satisfaction of those who engaged in them. If the idea that they properly entered into popular education and culture, or were of importance in the life of the common man, ever suggested itself to men of affairs, it failed to lead to action. Private individuals, to be sure, out of largess of spirit, might make contributions and bequests that made the arts accessible to the many; but the thought that there existed a *public* responsibility on the part of the state to encourage art and the enjoyment of the aesthetic experience occurred only to those whose general philosophy, political and cultural, was regarded in the better circles as, if not radical, at least unsound.

The opposition, which expressed itself in political channels through the states and the Congress, assumed popular form in the pages of the press. It is not necessary to document the statement that the press, as a whole, opposed the WPA concept of work relief. This was true of the daily press; it was doubly true of the trade press (apart from the union press), which forms and reflects the opinion of pressure groups. The masters of the fourth estate, applying the sound military principle that an enemy's line is most easily broken at its weakest point, concentrated their fire upon the white-collar—and particularly the arts—program. Viewed in the light of the purpose of the press, the plan of campaign was sound. The early attempts at an arts program had weaknesses. They were often hastily conceived, inadequately supervised, and wastefully managed. Moreover, the press found in the arts program an open field for ridicule and misrepresentation. Appealing to the uncritical attitude of the many or to the prejudices of the better informed, the press exposed to contemptuous merriment the least worthy projects and perverted the meaning or purpose of worthy projects. By these methods it was able to create in many communities an attitude of contempt for cultural projects. In some instances, as early as 1934, this led to local demands for investigation, and in one (New York City) to an actual investigation.

113

## THE ALDERMANNIC COMMITTEE AND PUBLIC RELATIONS

In April and May, 1935, the first organized and concerted attack upon white-collar projects was made in New York City by the Aldermannic Committee Investigating Relief. On October 16, 1934, the Board of Aldermen voted to make an inquiry into local relief operations. The first public hearing was held early in November, 1934, but most of the hearings occurred in April and May of the following year. Of these hearings Lillian Brandt writes:

> The newspapers, even those with a reputation for dignity and fair play, presented the testimony at its face value. There was "an almost complete surrender of editorial and news judgment" to the accusations of the Committee's Counsel, a "general inclination, as revealed in the handling of the reports, to 'get' the men and women who were administering relief" or to get the Mayor through them. Little or no effort was made to find out whether accusations were true, and sometimes flaming headlines were contradicted by the reporter's story below. Statements issued by officials in rebuttal were either thrown in the wastebasket or cut to make room for fresh charges. Accepting Mr. Stryker's presentation, the papers saw nothing but comedy in such work projects as "boondoggling," cartographic studies, semantics, classes in eurhythmic dancing, experiments with a "learning machine" and the poultry survey (humorously referred to as a "chicken census"),—even after their value was explained by the respective authorities who were their sponsors. The public in its ignorance held its sides in laughter.[6]

This investigation, coming at the very beginning of the WPA program, threatened the public relations of the new agency, and was vigorously resented by the Washington office. Harry Hopkins, whatever his shortcomings, lacked neither courage nor candor, and it was in this connection that he remarked that some people were "just too damn dumb" to understand white-collar projects. Corrington Gill, assistant administrator of the WPA, in a more restrained expression of policy appearing in the *New York Times*, defined the principle of white-collar work relief against the investigation's attack.

> By ridiculing a few projects whose immediate practical value was not obvious to them, opponents of work relief have been casting doubt upon a large amount of valuable work conducted under the so-called white-collar projects. These misunderstandings tend to jeopardize a program which means the difference between self-respect and collapse of morale for tens of thousands of people who are performing useful public tasks in a period of great personal stress. . . .

114

There should be no division of opinion on the necessity of providing work projects for these people. We can no more afford to lose their trained abilities than we can afford to line them up against the wall and shoot them or allow them to starve. Yet such loss is inevitable if they are forced to live indefinitely upon grocery orders.[7]

Throughout its existence the WPA was embarrassed by the problem of public relations. There is in Washington an unwritten law that it is against the canons of good taste and sound policy for an agency of the government to take its case directly to the people. Since Congress, national and state politicians, and the press are under no such limitation, a federal agency, especially if it is unpopular with those who control the instruments of propaganda, is at a definite disadvantage. The WPA was deeply conscious of this situation and in the beginning, with that disregard for precedent which characterizes the uninitiated, attempted by press releases, radio talks, and even through motion pictures, to counteract the effect of unfavorable propaganda upon its public relations. As time went on, Congress, by forceful intimation and, when that failed, by statutory and budgetary restrictions, gradually stripped the WPA of its power to defend itself, so that in the end it stood, so to speak, naked before its enemies. There is no doubt that the WPA, especially since it conceived its task to be that of public enlightenment as well as project operation, was seriously weakened in its public relations by its inability to secure an adequate hearing in the public forum.

1. Executive Order No. 7034, May 6, 1935.

2. Arthur W. Macmahon, John D. Millett, and Gladys Ogden, *The Administration of Federal Work Relief* (Chicago: Public Administration Service, 1941), Part III.

3. U.S. Congress. House. Committee on Appropriations. 74th Cong., 2d Sess. (1936), *Hearings of a Subcommittee . . . on First Deficiency Appropriation Bill* for 1936, p. 230.

4. *Proceedings*, Staff Conference, WPA, June 16, 1935 (Mayflower Hotel, Washington, D.C.), pp. 21-22.

5. *Emergency Relief Appropriation Act of 1935* (Public Resolution No. 11, 74th Cong., H.J. Res. 117), Sec. 3.

6. Brandt, *op. cit.*, pp. 326-27.

7. Corrington Gill, in *New York Times*, April 14, 1935. © 1935 by The New York Times Company. Reprinted by permission.

# 8

# The Establishment of the Federal Arts Program

## THE INCUBATION OF THE IDEA

As early as December, 1934, the Work Division of the national office was thinking in terms of national projects for the arts. Because of the precedent established by the PWAP, organized under the sponsorship of the Treasury Department in the CWA period, thought was first directed toward an art program, and conversations were begun with Edward Bruce, who had directed the Treasury program and whose experience would naturally be valuable to Jacob Baker and his staff. But it was quickly recognized that a work-relief program could not be established for artists (in the specific sense) without similar programs for other categories in the arts—music, theater, and so on. Moreover, Bruce, who was an artist as well as an art lover, thought in terms of professional standards rather than in terms of community service. The results of these conversations were transmitted from Baker to Hopkins in a memorandum dated December 21, 1934, which read in part:

> Bruce has correctly defined the difficulty of a national art project. If one is conducted the artists have to be moved around freely without regard to State and County Relief Administrations. In fact, the project becomes the thing, although a wide variety of artists will get jobs. But we cannot be sure that they will all be equally needy.
>
> All of that, however, I think would be all right and could be worked out if you want to do that for artists. If you do it for artists you will certainly have to do it for musicians, actors, and we ought to for engineers and architects and other white-collar people on different sorts of national surveys. On an enlarged work program this could easily be done and would constitute highly valuable projects.[1]

116

Exploration of the field to find a suitable director of the contemplated project had already begun, and in the same memorandum Baker argued against engaging a particular artist on the grounds that he was too conservative for the younger members of the profession. He said of Bruce that he was "one of the few men who happened to have the regard and respect of both the young and the old."[2] Indeed, Bruce's name naturally and immediately presented itself to the Washington staff. His predominant role in the success of the PWAP was generally recognized; in addition, his long years of federal service and his interest in the world of art had won him friends in high position in both official and cultural circles. Bruce, however, was too aware of the difficulties inherent in the contemplated federal art project to be a candidate for the directorship, but he continued throughout to give the Washington office the benefit of his experience and knowledge.*

## THE FIRST PLAN

The first plan suggested by Baker (March, 1935) showed the influence of Bruce's experience and advice. It envisaged a national technical committee in Washington supported by local technical committees throughout the nation, which together would establish broad policies

---

*Bruce concentrated his efforts upon the development of the Section of Painting and Sculpture, created on October 16, 1934, within the Procurement Division of the Treasury Department. This section, by public competition, selected artists to decorate new federal buildings, with funds from a monetary reserve set aside from the building fund. This program, although it looked toward the employment of unemployed artists, was in no sense a relief program. The need of the individual artist was not pertinent; artistic competence was the sole criterion.

At the same time, Bruce worked toward the establishment of the Treasury Relief Art Project. This program began on July 25, 1935, when the WPA allocated $530,784 to the Treasury Department for the purpose. But although the money came from the WPA, the project was administered by the Section of Painting and Sculpture, under Bruce and his staff. Since the rules of the WPA held, the artists (except for a 25 per cent non-relief exemption) were required to secure certification of need. By keeping the project small (total employment was 328, with 259 relief and 69 non-relief artists on the payroll), Bruce was able to restrict employment to artists on relief who possessed superior ability. Thus, in the TRAP, he was able to maintain the primacy of competence over that of need. The TRAP, unlike the Federal Art Project, never pretended to employ *all* needy artists. At the same time, the fact that the TRAP removed from the area of unemployment the better artists limited the number of competent personnel initially available to the Federal Art Project.

Bruce always recognized that the Federal Art Project complemented his own achievements in the Section of Painting and Sculpture, but his personal interpretation of artistic integrity was such as to preclude his participation in a program in which competence was not the *sole* criterion.

117

and elaborate working procedures. In addition, the national committee, by inspection trips into the field, would ensure the observance of its instructions. In his memorandum Baker wrote:

> In each locality of sufficient size to have painters, sculptors and architects at work we will have set up a small technical committee consisting typically of one painter, one sculptor, and one architect, including in addition perhaps a museum director and somebody from an art school, if necessary. The function of this committee will be to dig up the work that ought to be done and to advise as to its actual assignment to specific workers.
>
> Administrative organization of these projects will be the same as for all others, feeding down from here through whatever field organization we find is practicable for the whole Work Program.
>
> Corresponding to the local technical committees we need a technical advisory committee here consisting of one painter, one sculptor, and one architect. The technical committee will lay out broad policies and as any of the members have ideas about specific kinds of projects to be developed, Working Procedures will be written up and got out. This committee will also advise on necessary and desirable technical staff.
>
> The most useful function of the committee will be to personally make periodic trips through the country visiting projects, reviewing organization, and advising with the local technical committees and workers on projects. The personnel of the committee is such that the younger artists and architects of the country will receive stimulation and ideas from these men.[3]

It is interesting that, as the second paragraph of the above quotation indicates, Baker envisaged in the arts program the traditional distinction between line and staff. The several technical committees, including that of the national office, were to exercise purely staff duties. The scheme was an adaptation of the device of regional and local committees used by Bruce in the PWAP and the Section of Painting and Sculpture, respectively.

In another memorandum, dated the same day, Baker indicates that considerable thought had already been given to the selection of the Washington personnel, and that national projects in music and the theater were also in the making:

> We have worked out a scheme to put Jo Davidson at work. . . . He is to be a member of the Technical Committee along with Ned Bruce and a leading architect, probably Harvey Wiley Corbett. He can put in a lot of time the next month or so.
>
> We are outlining in the rough the same kind of organization for music with Kindler heading up the technical group, and in the theatre, pulling in Equity and Code Authority people—maybe Eddie Dowling.[4]

The inclusion of Bruce's name, and the professional emphasis implied in the other names, indicates the gradual shift in stress from social service to artistic quality.

118

During this period Arthur Goldschmidt, who was in charge of the section of professional and non-manual projects, was elaborating a manual for a national arts program. In February, 1935, he submitted a survey, which is described as furnishing a good example of a national project, but the survey itself is not at hand and no clue to its precise nature is revealed.[5] In mid-April Goldschmidt told the staff[6] that he was working on a tentative draft of the new manual for professional projects.*

In developing this plan, the Work Division of the FERA became conscious of the need of a survey of white-collar projects in operation under the FERA, and in March, 1935, Baker wrote to Howard Myers of the Research Division:

> One of the very important sections of our work-relief program which under the new development will be much more important than it has been is that covering professional, clerical, cultural and nonmanual workers. Specific questions should be asked as to how these projects were developed; who in the organization is responsible for them—both as to State and local organizations; what type of training the people have who have this responsibility; how these projects are fitted (a) to the existing skills of the workers, (b) to community needs; how community interest is built up in them; and in general an evaluation should be made of those now operating.[7]

As a result of this memorandum, a letter and forms were sent to the several field representatives of the FERA with the request that they obtain from the states information regarding the status of music, drama, and artists' projects.

> If this is to be of any use to us in working up liaison for the new program we will have to get it right away. . . .[8]

Unfortunately, the replies were neither prompt nor satisfactory. The information that the Work Division needed continued to come from interested individuals and professional organizations rather than from the state ERA's.

THE SEVEN LEAN MONTHS

In the period from December, 1934, to April, 1935, Goldschmidt's section, if it was working hard, was also working in the dark. However

---

*The preliminary draft of *Supplement No. 1 to Bulletin No. 29*, dated September 30, 1935, which laid the procedural foundation for Federal One, was largely the work of Goldschmidt.

clear the importance of professional projects may have appeared to Baker and his staff, the new works program, as it was presented to Congress in January, 1935, was viewed as almost exclusively a construction program. Admiral Christian J. Peoples was chosen as spokesman of the administration before the appropriation committee, apparently as a foil to avoid and obscure the rivalry between Harry Hopkins and Harold Ickes. He was director of the Procurement Division of the Treasury Department and, presumably, had made a searching investigation into relief activities. His knowledge of the President's final plan, if such knowledge existed at that time in any mind, including the President's, was disappointing, and his stress upon self-liquidating projects and express highways betokened a public works program. Indeed, this stress was so strong that it was Congressman Bacon, and not the administration's spokesman, who raised the only question concerning white-collar relief at the House hearings in January, 1935:

> Mr. BACON. I notice that most of these projects enumerated in the joint resolution would require unskilled labor. Has any thought been given to the great unemployment in what has been called before this committee the "white-collar" class, such as bookkeepers, auditors, clerks, and so, who are unfitted to do the heavy, unskilled work on a grade crossing, for example? . . . It seems to me that some thought should be given to that type of distressed person.
>
> Admiral PEOPLES. You are exactly right, Mr. Bacon. These classes of projects, of course, will cover unskilled as well as skilled labor. A certain percentage of the "white-collar" class will also be covered.[9]

The joint resolution, however, sailed through the House in three days but met stormy weather in the Senate. The first Senate hearings were held at the close of January, but the debate was so bitter and the balance so even that supplemental hearings were held on February 11 and 12. At the first Senate hearings Hopkins, who was asked to testify, mentioned the white-collar program but twice. Once, in answer to a question, he remarked, "There is a good deal of it [FERA money] on what we call 'white-collar' work of various kinds. We have, under our work relief program, people working on every conceivable kind of public-work project in America today."[10]

Later in the same hearings he was somewhat more specific, but failed to mention an arts program:

> Obviously, in view of the occupations and the skill of people on relief rolls, you cannot handle all of these people on straight construction projects. You have to have a few, a small percentage, of good white-collar projects

that could be started at once. . . . They might be research projects; they might be health projects, using, for instance, the nurses on relief rolls. I do not know how many thousands of nurses we have got on relief rolls. Those workers could be put on public health projects.[11]

At the supplemental hearings in February, Corrington Gill was selected by the administration to make the purposes of the bill clearer to the subcommittee, and was somewhat more specific with reference to a white-collar program and an arts program. The dialogue follows:

Mr. GILL. We have a large number of white-collar projects at the present time to take care of the architects, draftsmen, and so forth, that are out of work. . . . But we have for example 7,500 actors.

Senator BYRNES. Nurses?

Mr. GILL. Nurses, and that type of profession, teachers, lawyers, actors, musicians, and so forth, would give you the 10 per cent.

Senator STEIWER. You do not justify your breakdown then by insistence that there would be a large number of building projects and that they would employ 10 per cent of professional labor?

Mr. GILL. Oh, no.

Senator STEIWER. Now, that introduces an interesting detail. You have stated that there are about ten per cent out of the 3,500,000 that are white-collar people.

Mr. GILL. Yes.

Senator STEIWER. Of those, how many would be entitled to receive professional wages, which are higher, according to your classification, than skilled wages?

Mr. GILL. I would say probably most of them would be in the professional classification. They are the teachers and the research people and so on that would be on white-collar projects. Their standard of living is higher. Even on a relief basis, at the present time, they have a higher wage, because they have to have more to live on.*[12]

Debate on the bill continued in the Senate for another two months, and it was not until April 8, 1935, that the measure was passed and approved by the President.

But if the Work Division labored in darkness from December to April, 1935, the period from April to August was also one of doubt and confusion. The passage of the bill did not remove the veil that hid the

---

*Gill's estimate of 10 per cent for the white-collar program was based on FERA's experience and research. The principle of wages based upon standards of living is also revealed in this testimony.

President's plan. In March, Hopkins accompanied Roosevelt on a southern fishing trip, and was told that he would have an important part in the new work program. It was not made clear, however, what precisely that part would be, and although on his return Hopkins set the FERA staff to the task of drawing up a tentative program, work on it was desultory and inconclusive. Hope gave way to disappointment, however, when on April 17 the President gave to the press the impression that Ickes would be responsible for the greater part of the program's execution and Hopkins would be responsible for the determination of need and eligibility.

The first light broke on May 6, 1935, when by Executive Order No. 7034 the President created a tripartite design of central control and service: (1) the Division of Applications and Information; (2) the Advisory Committee on Allotments; and (3) the Works Progress Administration. The FERA administrator (Harry Hopkins) was designated—though not by name—as administrator of the Works Progress Administration. In this plan the WPA appeared as almost exclusively a staff agency, and an operating agency only in the sense that it was entrusted with the prosecution of "small useful projects designed to assure a maximum of employment in all localities." This residual responsibility of the WPA did not, at the time, appear important. The decisive part—the task of approving projects—was given to the Advisory Committee on Allotments, which held its first meeting on May 7, 1935. Although Secretary Ickes was chairman of the ACA, and Harry Hopkins a member of it, the President was present at every meeting but one; and each project approval, in fact and in form, was his decision.

The table was, in effect, the jousting-ground where Harry Hopkins and Harold Ickes fought for control, while the President played audience. The administrator of the PWA was beaten from the beginning, as Hopkins guessed and the President probably knew. But Roosevelt, following his favorite tactic of allowing his subordinates to resolve an issue *ambulando*, postponed decision until the verdict became inescapable.

By June 3, $1,800,000,000 had been allotted to employ 650,000 men, at a man-year cost of almost $2,800. It was obvious that the remaining $2,200,000 must employ 2,850,000 men, at a man-year cost of approximately $800, if the employment goal of 3,500,000 was to be reached. The President insisted upon this goal; the rest was a simple exercise in arithmetic. It was mathematically impossible within the limits of the appropriation to employ 3,500,000 men on a public works program.

Thereafter, events moved surely, if not rapidly. The first WPA projects were approved by the ACA on July 1, 1935. The last meeting of the committee was held on August 22. On September 12, at the Hyde Park conference with his leading aides in the program, the President earmarked unallocated money still available under the appropriation and gave the WPA the rest. Thereafter, the ascendency of the WPA was never challenged.

It is not surprising that in the meantime the general feeling of insecurity within the FERA pervaded the Work Division. On May 6, 1935, Baker wrote to a friend:

> Our professional affairs have turned out very badly at the moment in that the new work program has not jelled as far as we are concerned. I had hoped to have a regular job for ——— in connection with the National Theatre Project. I still see such a project ahead, and figure on him having a job, but it may not turn up until fall.[13]

A week later, the professional program was still in a state of suspense.

> Responsibility for the conduct of the new work relief program for professional persons has not yet been delegated. No regulations governing musical activities under the new program have yet been promulgated.[14]

Impatience at the delay grew, and on May 22, 1935, Baker held a staff conference at which he expressed himself frankly.

> The tendency among the government departments is to divide the $4,000,000,000 up among them, and the Works Progress Administration has not yet been allotted any funds for putting people to work although the statement was made repeatedly that it was Mr. Hopkins who would put the people to work. Until this is done, it is not possible to carry forward any program such as Safety, Women's Work, the labor policy, etc. At the present time we are acting as a censor and watchdog on the projects that are submitted; reviewing them and analyzing them from the point of view of utilizing relief labor.
> We have presented to the President in various ways the need for an allocation of funds for the Works Progress Administration but as yet it has not been done."
> When questions were asked, Mr. Baker said that it was impossible to send out or to definitely approve rules and regulations for the Works Progress Administration, when a definite set-up of this did not exist. If and when the set-up is established, projects will be handled in a decentralized manner, similar to the one under C.W.A. . . .[15]

In the Washington office of the Work Division, however, preparations continued for the white-collar program. On May 3, 1935, a letter was sent to the state relief administrators, setting up a section of public-service projects and requesting the appointment of one person in each state office to head the section. Thus a section, parallel to the section of professional and non-manual projects in the Washington office, was established in the state administrations.*

In connection with this administrative change, a second attempt was made to secure adequate information from the states on the subject of professional and non-manual projects. The letter announcing the formation of the new section in the state offices also requested the preparation of a report:

> In connection with the new Work Program it will be necessary to have available in this office a report concerning all professional and clerical projects now under way. A survey will also be required of those projects undertaken since the close of the Civil Works Administration up to the present time to the extent that they are readily available. Forms for this purpose will be furnished at a later date. These include projects under the classifications, A. Planning; E. Public Welfare; F. Publication Education, Arts and Research. Records of current projects should also be maintained.[16]

The replies to this request were more satisfactory than those received in answer to the March request addressed to the field representatives, but still not adequate.*

A "national" theater project is first mentioned in a letter of Jacob Baker's dated May 6,[17] but it is clear from another letter dated the same day that "national" is not used as a synonym for "federal" but merely to indicate technical direction from the Washington office:

> Preparations for that phase [music] of the new work program which will provide work projects for professional and clerical persons have not yet been completed. It is expected, however, that this program will be designed, as all other work activities, to promote projects sponsored by public agencies. It is hoped that in this program such nonprofit organizations as the National Music League may be called on to assist in the prosecution of these projects.[18]

At the end of May, anticipating victory, Hopkins felt enough as-

---

*The person appointed to head this section in each state was, with few exceptions, already on the state staff, and, in many cases, the state director of women's work.

*The replies to the May request provided, in part, the material for the article, "Relief for White-Collar Workers," which appeared in the December issue of the FERA's *Monthly Report,* and for Floyd Dell's report, dated May 18, 1936, *Government Aid During the Depression to Professional, Technical and Other Service Workers.*

surance of his part in the new work program to announce the formation of the WPA's structure in the field. There was to be a State Works Progress Administration in each state. Hopkins immediately undertook the appointment of the state administrators and called a meeting of them with the Washington staff at Washington for June 17–19, 1935.

In preparation for this, and in token of his concern for the white-collar class, Hopkins on May 27 agreed to lend to the Work Division Bruce McClure, who had been executive secretary of the relief administration (FERA) under Hopkins. His assignment was to direct the white-collar program under the general supervision of Jacob Baker. On June 1, 1935, therefore, McClure was designated director, and Arthur Goldschmidt associate director, of the new Section for Professional and Service Projects of the FERA.[19] This new section, which was carried over into the WPA, displaced the former section for professional and non-manual projects under Goldschmidt, and was paralleled in the states by the recently-created sections of public service projects. The section was small, and there was no indication at this time that it would shortly become a division or assume the magnitude that it eventually did.

The idea of staff responsibility still prevailed, and the duty of the section was conceived as that of advice and encouragement. The section, moreover, although it comprised all professional and service projects, was ready now to concentrate its energies upon an arts program. McClure, speaking in mid-June, 1935, said:

> The reason for existence [of the Section for Professional and Service Projects] as a separate unit is in most cases professional, drama, music, art. These have to be sold to a sponsor, and it is our idea to sell the idea of the use in their accustomed group. You want to establish the project, you want the sponsors, you must use your salesmanship and sell them the idea. This is creating and establishing projects for the professional and technical group.[20]

Indeed, as late as the Washington conference of state WPA administrators there was no sign that the Washington office had in mind a federal program for the arts. McClure, though he insisted on the importance of a vigorous cultural program, was equally insistent upon its local sponsorship by public bodies.

> Our first figure is $300,000,000 which is earmarked for professional and white-collar projects. . . . Why is there a separate section for the prosecution of professional, clerical and service projects? The answer to that is: Remember always this whole program is predicated on employing people on

the work to which they have been accustomed and taking advantage of their skills. The reason for being separate is that it involves really a selling job. On construction jobs you are going to have to exercise a great deal of sales resistance. This is more a promotional job. It is difficult to imagine a group coming to you unless it was some interested group, perhaps a professional association with a project for a music program, an art program or a research program. . . . Your job will be to find governmental agencies within your State willing to sponsor these proposed projects.[21]

The difficulties foreseen at this conference were those inherent in the system of local sponsorship. Insistence was placed upon the rule that the sponsor must be a public body, and it was emphasized that not even local WPA administrations should—although they could—sponsor such projects.* There is nowhere any intimation that the WPA itself would sponsor a federal arts program. Goldschmidt, speaking at the same conference, remarked, "By insisting that you can't do anything of that sort [engage in an arts program], except for a public agency, you are going to have a lot of "heat" turned off. . . ."[22]

The same stress upon local public sponsorship and the same revelation of emphasis upon an arts program appear in the following dialogue, which took place at the conference:

Mr. HINKLE: Who will sponsor professional and service projects?

Mr. MC CLURE: There will be a great variety of public agencies who could authorize the sponsoring of professional projects.

Mr. HINKLE: Give us a rough list of just what kind of projects comes under professional and service projects?

Mr. GOLDSCHMIDT: . . . In the cultural projects, there are projects for artists; music projects; projects for writers. . . .[23]

Thus by mid-June, although the substance of the contemplated WPA arts program was clearly enough revealed and the store set upon it by the Washington office apparent, its form as a WPA federally sponsored program had not yet taken shape in the minds of its makers.

THE GRAND DESIGN

Between June 19, 1935, when the first conference of state WPA administrators ended, and August 2, 1935, when the first official an-

---

*At first the privilege of sponsoring local projects was granted to local WPA administrations, but was withdrawn after a few months.

nouncement of the new program was made, the decisive step was taken that resulted in the creation of wpa-Sponsored Federal Project Number One. The wpa files, now in the National Archives, and the memories of men with whom it has been possible to consult fail to enlighten the inquirer either as to the *immediate* reason that counseled this sudden but momentous change in policy or as to the precise date when the final decision was made.

There is, however, one clue. Early in July, John R. McCarl, Comptroller General of the United States, presumably wrote a letter at the request of the wpa in which he interpreted the distinction between federal and non-federal projects in relation to the white-collar program. This letter is not at hand, but a memorandum from John J. Abt, assistant general counsel of the wpa, addressed to Bruce McClure contains the substance of the Comptroller General's communication. Abt's memorandum follows in full:

McCarl has indicated that "white-collar" projects will be divided into two distinct categories: Federal and non-Federal projects.

The distinction which McCarl has in mind is not entirely clear. In general, however, he will probably insist that a project which supplements some normal activity of the State, municipality or other public body must be classed as a non-federal project. On the other hand, projects which involve something which does not fall within the normal scope of municipal or State activity may be classified as a federal project. Thus, a project which involves the placement of additional librarians in a municipal library will probably be classified as a non-federal project. On the other hand, a research project to be conducted in a public library, an orchestra or a repertory theatre could be conducted as a federal project.

The distinction between a federal project and a non-federal project is of importance from only two points of view:

1. A federal project will be sponsored by Works Progress Administration and undertaken and prosecuted entirely by it. A non-federal project, on the other hand, must be sponsored by the municipality or other local agency concerned. These projects will, in form, be grants of labor and material from Works Progress Administration to the project sponsor. In fact, however, Works Progress Administration can obtain the same control of a non-federal project as of a federal project by making its grant of labor and material to the local agency conditioned upon compliance by the local agency with all of the conditions which Works Progress Administration would require in a federal project.

2. All projects which McCarl classifies as non-federal projects fall within classification (g) of the Act and must be financed out of the appropriation provided for in that category. In other words, a non-federal "white-collar" project must be financed out of the funds allocated under category (g) and cannot be financed out of the funds allocated out of category (e) for assistance to educational, professional and clerical persons. Since the funds available under category (g) are limited, it would seem to be advisable to prose-

cute as many "white-collar" projects as possible as federal projects in order to exhaust the three hundred million dollars allocated under clause (e) and save the moneys allocated under clause (g) for projects which cannot be undertaken as federal projects.[24]

The meaning of Abt's statement is not entirely clear. But the general purport of the interpretation is revealed. It will be recalled that the amount appropriated by the ERA Act of 1935 was earmarked in accordance with seven categories. Of these categories, (e) earmarked $300,000,000 "for assistance for educational, professional and clerical persons," and (g) $900,000,000 for "loans or grants, or both, for projects of States, Territories, Possessions, including subdivisions and agencies thereof, municipalities, and the District of Columbia, and self-liquidating bodies of public bodies thereof. . . ." The Comptroller General apparently ruled that the money under (e) must be spent for federal projects, since there was in that clause no provision for grants or loans to states and their subdivisions. Consequently, the whole $300,000,000 must be spent for federal projects for the white-collar classes; i.e., for "assistance for educational, professional and clerical persons." At the same time the Comptroller General pointed out that white-collar projects could be operated as non-federal projects under limitation (g) whenever such a project "supplements some normal activity of the State, municipality or other public body." The result was that the WPA suddenly found itself with an *embarras de richesses* so far as white-collar funds were concerned. The danger was that too many white-collar projects might be operated under limitation (g), resulting in failure to spend the $300,000,000 earmarked under limitation (e). Consequently, Abt suggested that it would be advisable "to prosecute as many white-collar projects as possible as federal projects in order to exhaust the three hundred million dollars allocated under clause (e), and save the money allocated under clause (g) for projects which cannot be undertaken as federal projects."

If, as seems not unlikely, the sudden and immediate decision to organize the arts program as a series of federal projects was the result of this interpretation, the incident affords an interesting, but not unique, example of the accidental influence of statutory language—even where no intent is present—upon an administrative agency. There was irony, too, in the fact that a program as fiscally unorthodox and as administratively unprecedented as was Federal One should have been immediately prompted by an innocent legal interpretation from the General Accounting Office. Unless there was a precipitous change of heart in the month following June 19, there was at this time no intent on the part of the Washington staff to operate the arts program as a WPA-sponsored project.*

The Washington office, however, was ready to ride the crest of fortune, and in the latter part of July, 1935, a hurried effort was made to devise as many WPA-sponsored white-collar projects as immediately suggested themselves. At first thirteen were contemplated, but in the end only six achieved fulfilment. Of these, WPA-Sponsored Federal Project Number One, which included subprojects in art, music, theater, writers, and, later, the historical records survey, was the first. During the latter part of July the federal directors for these four projects were engaged: Holger Cahill for art, Nicolai Sokoloff for music, Hallie Flanagan for theater, and Henry Alsberg for writers.

On August 2, 1935, Baker was ready to make the first official announcement of the existence of Federal One:

> It is the intention of this Administration to sponsor nation-wide projects intending to employ persons now on relief who are qualified in fields of Art, Music, Drama, and Writing. The following persons have been appointed by Mr. Hopkins to direct each of these nation-wide projects: Art, Holger Cahill; Music, Nikolai Sokoloff; Drama, Hallie Flanagan; and Writers, Henry G. Alsberg.
>
> Each of these directors will have a staff in Washington and the field to insure the unified planning and execution of the programs.
>
> While it is intended that these four Federal projects will eventually supersede all State and local projects in these fields of activity, it is important that all desirable activities now in operation be continued until the Federal projects are initiated. You are, therefore, requested to include this type of project in the general transfer of the ERA Work Projects to the State Works Progress Administration, submitting them for approval through the regular channels. During this interim period, you may also submit for approval, through the regular channels, such additional State and local projects in these fields as are warranted by the availability of relief workers. Submit any questions as to procedure or policy to Bruce McClure, Director of Professional and Service Projects, Works Progress Administration, Washington.[25]

*The federalization of work relief under the WPA must not be confused with the *federalization of sponsorship* under the arts program. In the former case, though operation was federal, the initiative remained with the states; in the latter case, *both* operation *and* initiative became federal.

The statutory language of the 1935 ERA Act, which suggested the fiscal distinction between monies for federal and monies for non-federal projects, was not repeated in subsequent ERA acts. In the 1936 Act, for instance, the clause that introduced the categories read, " . . . This appropriation shall be available for the following classes of public projects, Federal and non-Federal. . . . " Consequently, after the 1935 appropriation was spent, there was no compulsion to restrict money earmarked for educational, professional, and clerical persons to federal WPA-sponsored projects.

Further delay, however, ensued. It was not until August 29, 1935, that the first presidential allocations were made to Federal One, and not until September 12, that the arts program received the final and authoritative approval of the President. As a matter of fact, a month of grace was needed, for the sudden change of policy from locally sponsored projects to a WPA-sponsorered federal project required the hasty elaboration of an entirely new set of rules and procedures, for which no precedent in federal work-relief experience existed. The interval was also used by the federal directors in organizing their Washington offices, engaging a national and field staff, and planning the substance of their programs. The progress of their thinking is first indicated in Bulletin No. 29, dated September 4, 1935, which established the basic procedures for professional and service projects. In this bulletin the relation between federal projects and the Professional and Service Division was defined:

*Federal Professional and Service Projects Sponsored by the W.P.A.* The Works Progress Administration at Washington will, from time to time, sponsor Federal and Professional and Service Projects for nation-wide application in certain activities in which an integrated program is desired, or for which Federal control is necessary. Such projects will be designed to provide employment for all eligible persons equipped by experience, training, and ability for the type of work involved. Such Federal projects shall supersede all State and local projects in these fields. The Preparation of Project Applications, WPA Form 306, will not be necessary for local project units of Works Progress Administration sponsored Federal projects, inasmuch as these projects will be submitted directly for approval and authorization by the Works Progress Administration at Washington.

Each of these nation-wide projects will be managed by a Federal Project Director, appointed by the Works Progress Administrator, who will serve on the staff of the Director of Professional and Service Projects at Washington. At present, nation-wide Federal projects are being initiated in the fields of art, drama, music and writing. (See Mr. Baker's letter of August 2, 1935 to all State Administrators, WP-7, originally released under serial No. WD-37).

The State Works Progress Administration, and its district offices, shall act as the agents of the Works Progress Administration at Washington, in carrying forward these Works Progress Administration sponsored Federal projects. The State Assistant Director in charge of the Professional and Service Projects Section, under the direction of the Director of Projects and Planning and the State Administrator, shall be held responsible for the proper operation of these projects within the State. The Federal Project Directors, or their representatives, shall advise the State Administrators to appoint State Supervisors and District Assistant Supervisors for the programs of their respective activities whenever, in the judgment of the Federal Project Directors or their representatives, the State or local situation makes technical supervision necessary. Federal Project Directors *may nominate persons* to be appointed to these positions and *all appointees are to be approved by them.* The State Supervisors and District Assistant Supervisors will, following approval by the Federal Project Directors, or their representatives, become members of the staffs of the State Assistant Directors in charge of the Professional and Service Projects Section, and be administratively responsible to the Assistant Directors.

All Emergency Relief Administration professional and service projects now operating, as well as approved local or State Works Progress Administration projects, shall, after review by the Federal Project Director, or his representatives, be transferred to the corresponding Federal projects, or be cancelled.

All new professional and service project units in these fields shall be approved by the Federal Project Director of the applicable Federal project, or his designated field or local representative.

The Federal Project Directors of the Works Progress Administration sponsored Federal projects will issue forms, schedules, working procedures and instructions on conditions of employment regarding these projects.[26]

On September 12, when Federal One was approved by the President, Hopkins immediately wired the state administrators to this effect and informed them that this official project would supersede all state and local projects in the named fields.[27] It was expected that procedures and forms governing Federal One would be in the mails the week of September 16.[28] There was again delay, however, and *Supplement No. 1 to Bulletin No. 29,* which was the definitive statement with regard to procedure for Federal One, was not issued until September 30.

On the previous day Hopkins, anticipating the issuance of *Supplement No. 1,* wrote a letter of general instructions to the state administrators:

We have set up in the Division of Professional and Service Projects national projects in the fields of Writing, Plastic Arts, Music and the Theatre. Because of the particular professional and technical requirements in these fields, we wish to give a large measure of direction to these projects from Washington and shall of course, expect to have the fullest cooperation and aid from all of the State Administrations and Regional Representatives. The following persons have been appointed Directors of these projects: Mrs. Hallie Flanagan, Director of National Drama Project; Nikolai Sokoloff, Director of National Music Project; Holger Cahill, Director of National Art Project; and Henry Alsberg, Director of National Writers' Project.

The Directors of these projects are authorized to select project units within the states which they wish to include in the national project. You are directed to given them and the members of their staffs continuous advice, suggestions and aid regarding professional personnel and projects that have heretofore been in operation or have been organized for operation. The decision as to those units to be included in the national project rests with its National Director or his designated representative.

With your advice appointments will be made of certain persons required in your State or region for the direction of these national projects and you will receive direction from time to time as to expenditures, facilities, and staff required by these persons. Funds will be provided for this purpose within limitations set in Washington. Such direction will come from me or, in my place and stead, from Jacob Baker, Assistant Administrator. It is intended that the State and Regional Directors so far as possible shall be supplied staffs from your regular organization and I expect that no individual directions in this regard will be required from here but that they, with you, can come to full agreement on personnel and facilities that are required.

Accounting, purchasing and disbursing procedure will be carried forward through the same channels as for the other projects in the Works Progress Administration. Specific direction on those heads will come to the persons responsible for these functions.[29]

This letter, together with the pertinent part of Bulletin No. 29, quoted above, Jacob Baker's letter of August 2 (WP-7), and *Supplement No. 1 to Bulletin No. 29*, which will be examined later, created the fundamental structure of Federal One, and uncovered, although it did not examine, the basic administrative problems that the establishment of Federal One raised. An analysis of these problems is attempted in the chapters that follow.

1. Memorandum, Baker to Hopkins, December 21, 1934, FERA Files.
2. *Ibid.*
3. Memorandum, Baker (to Hopkins?), March 20, 1935, FERA Files.
4. Memorandum, Baker to Hopkins, March 20, 1935, FERA Files.
5. Notes on Conference in Mr. Baker's Office, February 21, 1935, FERA Files.
6. Digest of Staff Conference, April 13, 1935, FERA Files.
7. Memorandum, Baker to Howard B. Myers, March 13, 1935, FERA Files.
8. Letter, Baker to C. R. Keys, Regional Engineer, San Francisco, March 28, 1935, FERA Files.
9. U.S. Congress. House. Committee on Appropriations. 74th Cong., 1st Sess. (1935), *Hearings of a Subcommittee . . . on Emergency Relief Appropriation*, p. 35.
10. U.S. Congress. Senate. Committee on Appropriations. 74th Cong., 1st Sess. (1935), *Hearings of a Subcommittee . . . on Emergency Relief Appropriation*, p. 90.
11. *Ibid.*, p. 101.
12. U.S. Congress. Senate. Committee on Appropriations. 75th Cong., 1st Sess. (1935), *Supplemental Hearings of a Subcommittee . . . on Emergency Relief Appropriation*, p. 17.
13. Letter, Baker to Fay Kennedy, May 6, 1935, FERA Files.
14. Letter, Baker to John Thompson, Lincoln Symphony Band, Lincoln, Nebraska, May 13, 1935, FERA Files.
15. Digest of Staff Conference, Mr. Baker's Office, May 22, 1935, FERA Files.
16. Letter WD-30, FERA, May 3, 1935.
17. Letter, Baker to Fay Kennedy, May 6, 1935, FERA Files.

18. Letter, Baker to Buckner, May 6, 1935, FERA Files.

19. Letter WD-33, FERA, June 1, 1935.

20. *Proceedings,* Conference of State Administrators, WPA, June 17-19, 1935 (Mayflower Hotel, Washington, D.C.), Minutes of Meeting of Group No. 4, June 19, 1935, p. 1.

21. *Ibid.,* Minutes of Meeting of Group No. 3, June 18-19, 1935, pp. 20-21.

22. *Ibid.,* p. 21.

23. *Ibid.,* Minutes of Meeting of Group No. 5, June 18-19, 1935, pp. 18-19.

24. Memorandum, Abt to McClure, July 11, 1935, WPA Files.

25. Letter WP-7, WPA, August 2, 1935.

26. *Professional and Service Projects, Bulletin No. 29, W.P.A.,* September 4, 1935, Section 7.

27. Telegram, Hopkins to All State Administrators, September 12, 1935, WPA Files.

28. *Report on Progress of the W.P.A.,* September 16, 1935.

29. Letter WPA-60, WPA, September 29, 1935.

# 9

## A Problem in Contradiction

In a federal agency that maintains a field staff, the problem of decentralization is paramount. Centralization of direction, which is essential if national unity of purpose is to be secured, must be reconciled with decentralization of operations, which is necessary if regional and local diversification in action is to be achieved. Students of administration have observed and named the two principal ways in which federal agencies attempt this reconciliation. The first is called decentralization by specialty, and involves the extension of each of the divisions of the central staff into the field independently of the others. Several lines of command issue from the central office, and co-ordination of the agency's total activities is attempted—if at all—only on the federal level. Although no precise rules can be formulated to show under what circumstances this form of decentralization is better than the other, it works well when parts of an agency deal with a different subject matter and serve a different clientele (viz., the Bureau of Internal Revenue and the Bureau of Customs, both in the Treasury Department).

The other method is called decentralization by hierarchy, and duplicates in the field the organization of the central office in its entirety. Each field office mirrors the central office; the line of authority is single, and staff co-ordination of the totality of activities is attempted not only on the federal level but also on the subordinate field levels. Such was the structure of the Works Progress Administration; and since this agency, in all its relations, concerned itself with the same subject matter (work relief) and served the same clientele (persons certified as to

134

need), decentralization by hierarchy was the obvious and correct principle of organization. If each division or section of the WPA had projected itself into the field independently of the others, confusion of operation and duplication of effort would have resulted to such a degree as to make co-ordination at any level virtually impossible.*

But though the organization of the WPA as a whole was based upon the principle of decentralization by hierarchy, the organization of Federal One within the WPA was based upon the principle of decentralization by specialty. The Washington directors of the arts program and their field representatives (both regional and state), although in theory staff members of their respective offices, in reality possessed line command. In short, the WPA attempted within one agency, and with reference to the same subject matter and clientele, decentralization by hierarchy *and* decentralization by specialty. This was an essay in the resolution of contradictories.†

THE INSTRUMENTS OF COMMAND AUTHORITY

The authority that a line officer exercises over the area of his jurisdiction derives from three controls: (1) control of the budget; (2)

---

*The above discussion is indebted to Macmahon, Millett, and Ogden, *The Administration of Federal Work Relief* (Chicago: Public Administration Service, 1941), pp. 244-46.

†The fact that Federal One was organized in a way that contradicted the general organization of the WPA reinforces the interpretation, already suggested, that the structure of Federal One was hastily conceived. Second thought would have revealed the antithesis, as indeed it did—but too late!

Incidentally, the organization of the National Youth Administration was not parallel to that of Federal One. The NYA was established as a *separate* administration by executive order, and Aubrey Williams, the NYA executive director, held a presidential letter of appointment. The connection between NYA and WPA was in the nature of a personal union, in that Aubrey Williams, from 1935 to 1939, was at one and the same time NYA executive director and WPA deputy administrator. In theory, to be sure, Williams was not autonomous—there was an element of vassalage in the relationship. But since he and Hopkins shared a common philosophy, he enjoyed practical independence; he gave final approval to NYA projects, and dispatched over his own signature formal instructions to state NYA offices.

Again, the fact that the WPA, through its divisions of finance and employment, "serviced" the NYA in the states does not imply substantive union. The Treasury Department "serviced" the WPA, but was not part of it.

The *de facto* independence of the NYA was recognized as early as 1936, for the ERA Act of that year gave separate recognition to the NYA in fixing budgetary limitations; its *de jure* independence was achieved when, on July 1, 1939, it became part of the Federal Security Agency, whereas the WPA became part of the newly established Federal Works Agency.

control of personnel; and (3) control of operations. The first two controls are direct and immediate, in that questions of budget and personnel are in the realm of high policy; the administrator may, and does, seek the advice of his staff and subordinate line officers in the determination of these two questions; but the decisions are his own, and the responsibility cannot be delegated. Control of operations, on the other hand, is indirect, and exercised through the staff and subordinate line officers. The administrator delimits the confines within which the staff and subordinate line officers may prosecute operations; but he does not himself make operating decisions within these areas. The administrator, to be sure, is *administratively* responsible for operations, but this responsibility is not direct but indirect. The administrator who directly assumes the conduct of operations is as ill-advised as the administrator who delegates decisions of high policy is irresponsible.*

The three levels of the WPA hierarchy were the federal, the state, and district. The federal and state administrators and the district directors exercised line authority within their respective areas; i.e., they were immediately responsible for decisions regarding budget and personnel and indirectly responsible for operations. Each officer at each level was assisted by a staff, which, although it lacked command authority, advised its chief and the subordinate staffs, if any, with respect to budgetary and personnel recommendations and the direct conduct of operations.

The unorthodox organization of Federal One cut across this structure. Control of budget and personnel, without which control of operations is impossible, was taken from the state administrators and district directors and lodged in staff officers of the national, regional, or state offices. Such controls are the essence of line authority, and without them the state and district officers became irresponsible with respect to Federal One.

CONTROL OF PERSONNEL IN THE STATE
ORGANIZATION OF FEDERAL ONE

The structure of Federal One, since it only gradually evolved in the

---

*This is true except at the lowest level (e.g., the district WPA office) where, if operations are not extensive, the line officer may directly conduct them. Even here, especially if operations are extensive and diverse, the line officer does well to delegate their conduct to subordinates, while he himself retains responsibility for the control of budget and personnel.

mind of the Washington staff, revealed itself *pari passu* to the state and district administrations. Indeed, it was not until October, 1935—when field operations began—that the full significance of the innovation became apparent in the states. Jacob Baker's letter of August 2 (WP-7), announcing the establishment of Federal One, gave no indication of a special administrative structure. The statement "Each of these directors will have a staff in Washington and the field to insure the unified planning and execution of the program" seemed to promise orthodoxy. The last paragraph of the letter read:

> You will be notified of the date and procedure of transferring State and local Works Progress Administration Art, Music, Drama and Writers' projects to the four Federal projects. The Federal Directors, or members of their staffs, will call upon you to assist them in making this transfer by supplying such information, recommendations and suggestions as may be necessary. Your cooperation is especially requested in fitting the Federal programs to local requirements.[1]

This paragraph did not appear disturbing at the time, although future events gave it a hidden meaning.

Bulletin No. 29, dated September 4, 1935, was less assuring. With regard to the appointment of personnel, it read:

> The Federal Project Directors, or their representatives, shall advise the State Administrators to appoint State Supervisors and District Assistant Supervisors for the programs of their respective activities whenever, in the judgment of the Federal Project Directors or their representatives, the State or local situation makes technical supervision necessary. Federal Project Directors *may nominate persons* to be appointed to these positions and *all appointees are to be approved by them.* The State Supervisors and District Assistant Supervisors will, following approval by the Federal Project Directors, or their representatives, become members of the staffs of the State Assistant Directors in charge of the Professional and Service Projects Section, and be administratively responsible to the Assistant Directors.[2]

The language here is delicate, but the shading is ominous. "Advise to appoint" may mean more than "advise with reference to appointment," and the qualification of responsibility as *administrative* seems to imply, in addition, an area of independence. The right of nomination by a staff officer was in order, but the prerogative of a veto power implied in the statement *"all appointees are to be approved by them"* might better have been vested in the federal administrator than in a member of his staff.

But whatever ambiguity existed in these earlier communications was dispelled by Hopkins' letter of September 29, 1935 (WPA-60). The "large measure of direction" that "we wish to give to these projects from Washington" is clarified in the context. Appointments in state and regional offices would be made with the *advice* of, but not *by*, the regional representatives and the state administrators. Washington "shall, of course, expect to have the fullest co-operation and aid" from these officers. The state administrators "are directed to give them [the representatives of Federal One] and the members of their staffs continuous advice, suggestions, and aid regarding professional personnel and projects."

Thus the order of administrative providence was inverted, and the state administrators with respect to Federal One became staff officers. As a consequence, the statement in Letter WP-7 (August 2) that "the State Assistant Director in charge of the Professional and Service Projects Section, under the direction of the Director of Projects and Planning and the State Administrator, shall be held responsible for the proper operation of these projects within the State" ceased to have meaning. Responsibility for operations cannot be demanded if the power to select personnel is denied.

CONTROL OF THE BUDGET IN THE STATE
ORGANIZATION OF FEDERAL ONE

The issue of budgetary control was also defined in Hopkins' letter of September 29 (WPA-60). The pertinent passage reads:

> . . . You will receive direction from time to time as to expenditures, facilities, and staff required by these persons. Funds will be provided for this purpose within limitations set in Washington. Such direction will come from me or, in my place and stead, from Jacob Baker, Assistant Administrator. It is intended that the State and Regional Directors so far as possible shall be supplied staffs from your regular organization and I expect that no individual directions in this regard will be required from here but that they, with you, can come to full agreement on personnel and facilities that are required.

Thus the device of earmarking funds from Washington, unsuccessfully attempted by the FERA in the summer and fall of 1934, was again to be tried. But the sting lay not in the Washington limitation but in the fact that the expenditure of earmarked funds, *after* they reached the state office, did not rest within the discretion of the state administrator.

"Direction . . . as to expenditures, facilities, and staff, required by these persons" was to come from Washington. This meant (as the sequel was to show) that the salaries of the state directors of the several arts projects, of their staffs and secretarial help, as well as their expenses for office space and material, were removed from the control of the state administrator. Here again, as with personnel control, control of operations without budgetary control was impossible.

CONTROL OF OPERATIONS IN THE STATE
ORGANIZATION OF FEDERAL ONE

The purpose of the Washington office's assumption of personnel and budgetary control within the states was, of course, to remove operational control from the jurisdiction of the state administrations. The latter followed the former as night follows day, and it was, therefore, with perfect logic that Section 7 of Bulletin No. 29 (dated September 4, 1935) read in part:

> The Preparation of Project Applications, WPA Form 306, will not be necessary for local project units of Works Progress Administration sponsored Federal projects, inasmuch as these projects will be submitted directly for approval and authorization by the Works Progress Administration at Washington.*

Hopkins' letter of September 29 is less devious. The pertinent passage reads:

> The Directors of these projects are authorized to select project units within the states which they wish to include in the national project. . . . The decision as to those units to be included in the national project rests with its National Director or his designated representative.

In short, the state administrators were to have no responsibility for: (1) the appointment of the state directors and their staffs; (2) expenditures, either as to amount or as to object; (3) the selection and approval of projects. A line of authority, parallel to the normal administrative line, ran from the national directors of Federal One through the regional and state offices right down to the districts.

---

*WPA Form 306, Project Application, was submitted by the state administrations to the Washington office in order to secure project approval, and required the *signature* of the state administrator.

SUPPLEMENT NO. 1 TO BULLETIN NO. 29

On September 30, 1935, *Supplement No. 1 to Bulletin No. 29* was issued. This bulletin defined and established procedure for WPA-Sponsored Federal Project Number One (Art, Music, Theater, and Writing).* This supplement confirms and reduces to detail the independence of Federal One from the normal command authority of the state administrators and district directors.

Federal One, unlike the WPA as a whole, was to have four hierarchical levels—the federal, the regional, the state, and the district.† The federal directors stood at the top of the pyramid and had, first of all, authority to appoint regional directors.‡ These regional directors were described as the "representatives" of the federal directors, and possessed from them delegated authority. Second, the federal directors (or, in their stead, the regional directors) had authority to appoint state directors and district supervisors of their respective projects. Section 7 of the *Supplement* reads in part:

> Proper supervision in many places will require that the State or district officer in charge of art, music, theatre, or writing be technically qualified. The Federal Project Directors or their representatives shall request the State Administrator to appoint State Directors and District Supervisors for the programs of their respective activities whenever the State or local situation makes extensive technical supervision necessary. Federal Project Directors may nominate persons to be appointed to these positions and all appointments and conditions of employment, including those of persons now holding such office, are to be approved by them.[3]

*Federal Project Number One, which, though used officially, was a designation of convenience, was composed of four (later five) official projects. An official project was defined in Treasury Regulations No. 1 to mean "an undertaking approved by the President for which a separate official project number has been assigned by the Bureau of the Budget." Art, Music, Theater, Writers', and later the Historical Records Survey, each formed *one* official project. Co-ordination of the activities of these several projects was attempted, except in rare instances, only at the federal level.

†Except the Writers' Project, which omitted the regional level, and thus conformed to the general structure of the WPA. The Writers' Project had no regional directors, but in their stead field representatives, who, like the field representatives of the WPA, were attached to the Washington office.

‡The regions of each of the projects, however, did not coincide with each other or with the regional divisions of the WPA. In the beginning the Theater Project had fourteen regions, the Music Project eleven, and the Art Project ten. The WPA had at this time five regions.

140

The use of phrases like "shall request the State Administrator to appoint" and "may nominate persons to be appointed" merely preserves the formalities. The intent was to give the federal directors and their representatives the power to appoint, and events were to show that, except in a few instances when the state administrators *positively* refused to co-operate, they exercised this power. Thus the state WPA administrators, and with them the district WPA directors, were deprived of control of Federal One personnel in both the state and district offices.

## CONTROL OF PROJECT PERSONNEL IN
## FEDERAL ONE AT THE DISTRICT LEVEL

If the lack of control of staff personnel created in the state and district offices an administrative impasse, the loss of the control of project personnel produced, at the district level, operational chaos. The unit of operations in the WPA was known as a work project, which is defined in Treasury Regulations No. 1 as a "particular job or subdivision of an official project, as designated by an Administrator. It may be a single work relief job or a group of jobs in a particular locality under a project manager. A work project may be identical with an official project or it may be a subdivision or part of an official project for which separate limitations are to be observed through administrative accounts." The purpose of the work project was fiscal control of obligations and expenditures and convenience of management at the operational level. The unit of operations in Federal One was first designated as a work project[4] but later as a project unit.[5] The difference was one of terminology alone.

The first step in the control of project personnel was referral. In establishing a work unit of Federal One, the district supervisors of the arts projects were directed to confer with the local employment office designated by the United States Employment Service and, after conference, "to make informal request by letter to have all registered relief persons with necessary talent referred for interview to the person or committee designated to pass on qualifications."[6] This referral was a matter between the local USES and the district supervisors of the arts projects. The administrative officer—the district WPA director—was by-passed.*

---

*It was necessary, according to the rules of the WPA, that each applicant for

The next step after referral was determination of the qualifications of the referred. Here again, the prerogative lay with the district supervisors of the arts projects, or with an official or committee designated in their place. *Supplement No. 1* reads:

> The analysis of the qualifications of the referred personnel should be in the hands of technically qualified people who draw their authority either (1) through the regional director, or the State Director of Art, Music, Theatre or Writing or some other specially designated person, or (2) directly from the appropriate Federal Director. They are responsible for their technical judgment ultimately to such Federal Director.[7]

This determination of eligibility carried with it the determination of salary classification. The above section continued:

> The individual or committee so authorized shall determine the classification (professional, skilled, intermediate, or unskilled) of each person to be placed in a work project. This determination of skill automatically fixes the monthly salary of the individual.[8]

The district supervisors of the arts projects, having determined who in the locality were eligible and what their qualifications were, were now empowered to determine the kind of project unit to be initiated in that locality:

> Not only must this authorized individual or committee, as described above, pass on the qualifications of referred personnel, but he or they must also determine the exact nature of the work project in which each person who demonstrates his ability could best work. In determining the work projects, two considerations should guide decisions:
> A. The abilities of the referred personnel, and
> B. The need and desires of the community*[9]

Finally, if the personnel thus referred and examined were inadequate, the district supervisors of the arts project were given the right to requisition from the local USES whatever additional personnel of construction, clerical, or domestic type might be necessary and in the absence of qualified relief personnel to employ persons from non-relief sources under the 10 per cent exemption allowable under Executive

project employment be registered at the local USES (or, in its place, the local National Reemployment Service) and be referred by the USES to the WPA district office. The purpose of this requirement was to insure that the names of WPA project employees be available at the local USES office for referral to private employers, when and if they sought workers.

*This caution was salutary, but it will be noticed that in the whole process of project initiation the community, except in so far as it may have been represented on the examining committees, took no part whatsoever.

Order No. 7046, provided that such persons were referred by the USES.[10]

The district supervisors, having canvassed the local situation, were now ready to seek approval of the project units chosen. The procedure for securing such approval was as follows:

> For each work project found desirable by the individual or committee assigning persons to work, a WPA Form 320, Request for Project Approval, should be completely filled out with the advice of the District Supervisor of Projects and Planning and sent to the appropriate State Director of the program (or if there be none, to the State Assistant Director in charge of Professional and Service Projects). (This procedure makes unnecessary WPA Forms 301, 303 and 306.) If in the district there is a person who has been authorized locally to give technical approval to projects of that type, that person should affix his signature before the project request is sent to the State Directors of Art, Music, Theatre or Writing (or if there be none, to the State Assistant Director in charge of Professional and Service Projects.)
>
> When the "Request for Project Approval" is signed by (1) representatives of the Cooperating Sponsor (if any), (2) the appropriate District Supervisor of the program (or if there be none, the District Supervisor of Projects and Planning), (3) the appropriate State Director of the program (or if there be none, the State Assistant Director in charge of Professional and Service Projects), and (4) the person authorized to give technical approval, the work project described therein has met the necessary requirements. In recognition of this the appropriate State Director of the program (or if there be none, the State Assistant Director in charge of Professional and Service Projects) shall request the State Works Progress Administrator, by sending him a signed copy of WPA Form 320, to issue an Advice of Allotment, Treasury Form A-3, which authorizes a district to incur expenditures for a specific project. This should be accompanied by a WPA Form 701, Statement of Allotment Detail, which indicates to the district office the breakdown authorized for the sum stated in the Advice of Allotment. On the Statement of Allotment Detail should be indicated the period of time the allotment is to last.[11]

WPA Form 320, Request for Project Approval, which was devised for the special use of WPA-sponsored federal project units in place of the regular Form 306, required three signatures and three only: the district supervisor; the state director; and the person designated to give technical approval (the federal director or his delegate, who was usually a regional director or field representative). This approval, as an examination of WPA Form 320 indicates, was both administrative and technical. There was no place in the entire process for the approval of the district or state Works Progress administrations. The only caution in the procedure is that the district supervisor should act "with the advice of the District Supervisor of Projects and Planning."*

*In the event that there was no district supervisor of an arts project, the district supervisor of projects and planning was empowered to initiate the proposal and to

After the project unit was thus formally approved, the district supervisor was directed to fill out WPA Form 401 (Requisition for Workers) and to enter thereon the names of persons who had been interviewed and found satisfactory and to send it to the local USES office. This office thereupon used USES Form 325 (Assignment Slip) to make referral of such persons to the district WPA.[12] Thus the district supervisors of the arts projects were permitted to *predesignate* personnel for employment on the arts program—a privilege that was specifically forbidden on other WPA projects; and, as in the preliminary examination of personnel, the district supervisors were entitled to proceed independently of the district WPA director.*

Upon approval of the project units, the budgetary wheels started to turn. Funds for each state, presumably based upon the costs of project units approved or to be approved, were allocated from Washington by the Federal Works Progress administrator upon the request of the federal director of professional and service projects. The initial allocations were made on Treasury Form A-2 (Advice of Project Authorization) and subsequent allocations upon Treasury Form A-2a (Advice of Change in Project Authorization). These forms authorized the state administrator to issue Treasury Form A-3 (Advice of Allotments) for particular project units in his state.

With the form Advice of Project Authorization Washington forwarded to the state administrator a letter from the director of professional and service projects informing him how long the allotted funds were to last and what conditions, if any, attached to the spending of the money. Thus the projects were initiated in the district by the district art supervisors and approved in the state and national offices by the state and national arts directors, respectively; and money was allocated by Washington for their prosecution with conditions as to its spending—all without recourse to the district WPA director or the state WPA administrator.[13]

---

sign WPA Form 320. Similarly, in states where there was no state director of an arts project, the state assistant director in charge of professional and service projects was permitted to sign WPA Form 320. In these cases, however, only administrative and not technical approval was expressed. Likewise, when the state administrator signed Treasury Form A-3 (Advice of Allotment), he too indicated merely administrative approval, and did not assume technical responsibility.

In the entire process, incidentally, this paper (Treasury Form A-3) was the only form that required the attention and signature of the state administrator. The danger of miscarriage here, however, was small. A state administrator, if he chose to defy the procedure, generally preferred to fight in the open rather than merely to obstruct.

*This referral, which was for employment, is to be distinguished from the earlier referral discussed above, which was for a preliminary test of qualifications.

The immediate supervision of the project unit, when approved and in operation, also rested with the district arts supervisors (or the committees that might be set up in their stead); they in turn were technically responsible first to the field representatives and, through them, to the federal directors:

> The directors of Federal projects and the State and district offices, especially the Directors and Supervisors of Art, Music, Theatre and Writing, are responsible for the proper supervision of the work projects. The Federal field advisors and/or regional directors referred to in Section 1 shall not only advise the State officials, but, where possible, the district officials as well. They shall especially attempt to visit and evaluate the work being done on the more prominent work projects.
>
> The immediate technical supervision of the work projects should be performed by a person or persons appointed in the same way as those selected to pass on the qualifications of eligible workers. (See Section 3—Assignment of Workers to Projects). In many cases the two functions of assignment and supervision will be performed by the same person or committee.[14]

Even the discontinuance of a project unit was not within the power of the district WPA director or the state WPA administrator: "Any project which, after having been approved for operation under W.P.A. Sponsored Federal Project Number One, fails to maintain the required standards, may be discontinued upon order of the W.P.A. Administrator at Washington."[15]

Thus, in the initiation and operation of a project unit of Federal One, the district arts supervisors were responsible for: (1) the determination of eligibility of available personnel; (2) the classification of eligibility within the wage groups; (3) the kind of project to be operated in the locality; (4) the predesignation of desired personnel for employment; and (5) the immediate supervision of the project unit. The federal arts directors, or their field representatives, were responsible for: (1) the final approval of the project application; and (2) the overall technical supervision of the project units. The federal WPA administrator, acting on the advice of the federal director of professional and service projects, was responsible for: (1) the allocations of funds to the states for the project units; (2) the conditions attached to the spending of the money; and (3) the decision to discontinue any project unit.

Indeed, the only privilege left with the state and district WPA officials was that of protest:

> . . . When in the opinion of *any* State or district official a project appears not to be desirable for any reason, a letter should be sent to the State Assistant Director in charge of Professional and Service Projects and/or to

145

the Director of Professional and Service Projects at Washington clearly stating the objection.[16]

Accordingly, the passage in Section 7 of the *Supplement*, which made the state arts directors and the district arts supervisors *administratively* responsible to their state and district Works Progress administrations, was meaningless. The passage reads:

> The State Directors and District Supervisors will, following approval by the Federal Project Directors or their representatives, become members of the staffs of the State Assistant Directors in charge of the Professional and Service Section (or of the Assistant District Supervisor in charge of Professional and Service Projects) and be *administratively* responsible to their immediate staff superior.[17]

The state and district WPA administrations, through their divisions of finance and employment, were merely to "service" the project units of the arts program. All else was beyond their jurisdiction.

## OCTOBER STORM

Early in October the deluge came; and although it did not rain continuously for forty days and forty nights, it was early December before the skies began to clear. The storm might have broken earlier if the state administrators had read these letters and procedures more carefully; but they, too, were overwhelmed with the gigantic task of setting in motion the new work-relief program. But in October, when Federal One began the operation of its project units, and field representatives of the federal directors—fortified with roving commissions—began to travel far and wide throughout the land establishing project units and appointing state and local personnel, the state administrators suddenly realized what a lion cub the Washington office had been nursing.

It was in October that actual allocations from Washington to the states began, and by October 15, $3,267,400 had been allocated. On October 8–9, 1935, a conference of regional officials of the several projects was held in Washington and preparations were made to have Federal One well under way by November 1.[18] At the same time, the federal directors began to notify the states of the regional appointments; and the federal directors and their regional representatives began to appoint state directors and district supervisors. The state administrators were informed of these appointments in letters from Jacob Baker.

146

These letters were at first informal; and the following, addressed to the Alabama WPA Administrator, is typical.

October 5, 1935

*Mr. Thad Holt, Administrator*
*Works Progress Administration*
*326 First Street,*
*Montgomery, Alabama*

DEAR MR. HOLT:

Pursuant to Mr. Hopkins' letter to you of September 28th, we are about to inaugurate the Writers' Projects, the chief of which is the American Guide. This will be a Federal publication giving a comprehensive guide to the United States by localities, cities and states. A State Director of Writers' Projects will be appointed in every state, who will direct the field force in the state and act as editor of collected material for a potential state book, which will be a by-product of the Federal project.

Further by-products will be local guides for every locality in which we shall be working. Details of this whole project will be forwarded very shortly, together with a bulletin covering the method of getting up the project in your state. Funds are being allocated to cover the whole operation of the Writers' Projects.

After careful canvass of the field we have selected Miss Myrtle Miles as best qualified to fill the position in your state. Formal notification, together with the amount of salary which this position pays, and other details will be sent to you shortly. Miss Miles' background and experience are as follows:

Well known newspaper and feature writer, has long
been a manager of Women's Bureau of Public Relations,
New York Central, and other publicity work.

Miss Miles will be attached to your staff and, by our personal knowledge of her character, there is every indication that she will readily adapt herself to your organization.

Very truly yours,
JACOB BAKER
Assistant Administrator[19]

It is not difficult to imagine the reaction of the state administrators upon receipt of a letter like this, especially when, as happened upon occasion, the appointee arrived in a state office before the letter of appointment.* They resented: (1) the appointment of a member of their staff by the Washington office without their recommendation and con-

*Apparently, letters of appointment from Washington were sent simultaneously to the state administrators concerned and to the appointees, but the letters addressed to the appointees sometimes arrived before those addressed to the state administrators. The official communications that followed these first informal letters did not differ in any material respect from the foregoing, except that the amount of the salary and the date of entrance upon office were indicated.

sent, and, indeed, in many cases without prior notification of intention or solicitation of advice; and (2) the addition to their administrative payroll of a salary they had no part in fixing.*

Moreover, the regional directors of the Theater and Music projects as well as the field supervisors of the Art Project, though their areas of control exceeded the limits of a particular state, were attached administratively to one state and paid from that state's administrative funds. Thus Jasper Deeter, regional theater director for Pennsylvania and New Jersey, was attached to the staff and administrative payroll of the Pennsylvania office. State administrators naturally objected to paying the salary of a staff member whose area of jurisdiction exceeded theirs. Conversely, other state administrators objected to the trespass upon their domain of an officer who was a member of the staff of a neighboring state.

Almost immediately protests began to arrive at the Washington office by letter, telephone, and telegraph, and for two or three weeks Jacob Baker did little more than attempt to stem the flood. Harry Hopkins, unfortunately, was out of town.†

Perhaps the clearest articulation of the problem appears in the following telephone conversation, which presents the point of view of the state administrator and the dilemma of Baker, who found himself in the uncomfortable position of having to carry through a policy with which he was not in thorough sympathy. The digest of the conversation, dated October 14, reads in part:

Mr. ——: I am in —— today and —— just came down with my mail from ——. Among other things is a copy of a letter dated October 9 written —— by Alsberg and approved by McClure saying "You are hereby authorized. . . ." I don't know how to tie in a thing like that. If you people in Washington are going to run this Writers' Project completely I haven't anything to say about it.

Mr. BAKER: We are, in accordance with Mr. Hopkins' letter of September 29 [WPA-60].

Mr. ——: Hopkins' letter said appointments were going to be in the hands of State Administrators.

*In vain, Baker assured the state administrators that these would be paid by an *addition* to their existing administrative allowance, and consequently would not lessen the amount they were already receiving.

†Since the identity of the state administrators and other officers who made these protests is not pertinent to the argument (for the protests were general), their names are not herein revealed. The documents from which the quotations have been taken repose in the WPA files at the National Archives, Washington, D.C.

Mr. BAKER: It said the reverse; appointments are going to be made here. I recognize your problem clearly and if Harry were here in town I would let him know about some of this. You are not the only person who has called us about this.

Mr. ———: It puts us in a bad spot, having a letter sent to a woman who is not even on our payroll telling her she can approve or disapprove the things I do.

Mr. BAKER: It is confined wholly to the Writers' Projects: you get the money for that separately. I think a letter has gone through to your accounting office setting up some specific money for the Writers' Project. In fact, just before Mr. Hopkins left he got the Directors of the Writers' Project together. He told them "you are in complete charge. What you have to do is to tell the local Works Progress Administrators you want some people. They will also give you some space. Of course, I expect you to cooperate." When you take a bunch like this and tell them that you can readily see I have had a little bit of difficulty keeping them down myself.

Mr. ———: I didn't get that slant at all.

Mr. BAKER: That is the picture. On the other hand, I do not want a situation to come up where you think that is somebody else's show entirely.

Mr. ———: We cannot help but feel that way under these circumstances.

Mr. BAKER: On the other hand, the public press and the way people are going to react, they are not going to make any differentiation between the staff here and there. For that reason I am anxious to place more dependence on the state people. But Mr. Hopkins set it up independently and I am trying to keep a middle course. That is what I want to get at. I am in a tough spot, too.

Mr. ———: Well, here you and I are talking about whether she is the woman to hire and in the meantime she is receiving instructions about what she is to do.

Mr. BAKER: I did not realize she had received that. I am getting a letter off to her addressed in your care. I will have it airmailed tonight. I will read it to you. See if you think this will meet the situation.

Sometimes the appointee lacked tact in approaching the state administrator. A digest of another telephone conversation, also dated October 14, recounts one such instance:

Mr. ———: I have your wire about ———. Here is the situation with her. I talked to her briefly. As far as I am concerned she is her own worst enemy. She got off on the wrong foot with me to start by the little trick things she pulled. She has been doing an awfully lot of talking about how she has been offered this job by Washington, that she usually got what she wanted and she was going to get this job. She tried to see me for a couple of days and could not, and called my secretary and said "it would be too bad if I had to call Washington and tell them I could not get in touch with Mr.

———." I hate to be so small as to hold that against a person, and I am not saying to you that I won't approve her.

Mr. BAKER: I know how you feel. The boys here may have some alternative who would be satisfactory to everybody concerned.

Mr. ———: On the other hand, I am entirely open minded on her. If she were appointed the first thing I would do would be to bring her in and have a good talk with her.

Mr. BAKER: We could also give you some help on that. We could tell her if she were to accomplish her job, even though she had been recommended to us it would be essential that she work in close cooperation with you and your organization.

Mr. ———: I would want an understanding with you that if she did not cooperate we could get somebody else for the job.

Mr. BAKER: I would not burden you with someone who would not cooperate. That was the intention of my telegram,—to give you reassurance. We do not want to unload somebody on you who would not be satisfactory. I will talk to Alsberg and Cronyn and see if they have somebody else to suggest. If not, I will drop a note and tell you. I might also address a letter to ——— and send it to you to give her, together with a letter addressed to you asking you to talk to her and advise her about everything.

Mr. ———: So that she is working for us here and not for Washington.

Mr. BAKER: Of course, all her direction will come out of this office.

Mr. ———: That is all right, but she is going to have to work here with us.

An administrator of a southwestern state was most forthright in declaring that no one could work on his staff without his approval. Part of the digest of the telephone conversation, dated October 11, follows:

Mr. ———: As I understand it, I will try to arrange with your man [Alsberg] for someone to head your writers.

Mr. BAKER: I think they have someone they want to ask you about.

Mr. ———: They offered the position to ———. I have only met her once and we got along very nicely, but there are other people here more fitted. . . .

Mr. BAKER: I will see if they have committed themselves to ———; if not, they can arrange it.

Mr. ———: I have copies of all the telegrams ——— has received. They have committed themselves too far with ———. But I told her that regardless of what Mr. Alsberg wired us she could not come in this office without my approval. . . .

Mr. BAKER: I will tell them and they will probably talk to you about it.

Mr. ———: I can find some other place for ———.

150

Two state administrators in the Middle West were blunt as well as precise in calling Washington's attention to their right to control personnel and the budget in their states. One letter, dated October 15, read in part:

> I would like to have orders come through me to the assistants, rather than through the assistants to me. This I believe will make best for our organization in ———.
>
> Will you please assist me in getting this out, and protecting my administrative payroll until such time as we have need for this division.

The other, dated October 18, was no less frank:

> If I am to be Administrator for the State of ———, and be held responsible for its expense and procedure, and so long as I am attempting to work along the lines laid down by the [federal] Administrator, I cannot see any reason for ignoring me. If this department is to be run independently I want to know that, and if people are to be appointed from Washington without my knowledge I want to be acquainted with that fact. If this is to continue I shall not spend so much time trying to stop ridicule in ———.

The above protests were directed against the method of appointing state directors of the Writers' Project; but objections with regard to the same method as used for the Theater, Music, and Art projects were no less vigorous. The following is a letter of complaint (dated October 18) against the appointment of a state director of the Music Project:

> Since writing the enclosed letter I have received two letters, copies of which are attached. I am interested in taking care of the unemployed in ———. If musicians in this state are unemployed or on relief I shall be only too happy to work along this line, as well as with any other class of people but you must remember that ——— is [not] a densely populated state, and that we have an antagonistic press. I have been running through the clippings and am sorry to inform you we are not getting publicity of the right sort.
>
> The ———, a very dominant press in the state, is running cartoons and are getting ready to enter the campaign against the administration in a big way. They have been attempting for the last thirty days to ridicule things of this sort, and these appointments made from Washington, given to the press, and of which I am later notified.
>
> I do not like such procedure.

In Texas, H. P. Drought, the state administrator, maintained that he had only a few artists on relief and that he could take care of them on the recreational and similar programs. Nothing under heaven could move him; and, in a telephone conversation on October 11, Baker assured Drought that no Art Project would be set up in Texas.

As for the regional directors, who were to be placed on the payroll of the state in which they had headquarters, Baker took pains to assure the state administrations that additional money would be forthcoming for their salaries and expenses. In a telephone conversation with one state administrator, dated October 16, he said, "But they are in addition to the number of people that the State Administrator is authorized to hire. He doesn't need to worry—just put them on on the basis of my letter."

The state administrators were further annoyed by telegrams they received from Washington authorizing them to make expenditures for the expenses of the regional directors. The following telegram, quoted in part and dated October 21, is typical:

THIS IS YOUR AUTHORIZATION TO PROVIDE SUCH EQUIPMENT SUPPLIES AND SERVICE AS REQUESTED BY REGIONAL DIRECTORS WITHIN LIMITS DEEMED REASONABLE BY YOU IN CONSULTATION WITH THEM IN ACCORDANCE WITH MR. HOPKINS LETTER OF SEPTEMBER TWENTY EIGHTH stop THIS AUTHORIZES YOU TO ARRANGE FOR OFFICIAL TELEGRAPH TELEPHONE SERVICE FOR REGIONAL DIRECTORS IN ACCORDANCE WITH REGULAR WPA PROCEDURE stop FRANKED STATIONERY WILL BE SENT DIRECT FROM THIS OFFICE stop THIS AUTHORIZES YOU TO GRANT TRAVEL AUTHORITY FOR EACH REGIONAL DIRECTOR FOR STATES WITHIN HIS REGION AND TO WASHINGTON ON CALL stop YOUR NECESSARY EXPENDITURES IN CONNECTION WITH WORK OF REGIONAL DIRECTORS WILL BE TAKEN CARE OF IN REGULAR FUNDS*

Although the fundamental basis of all the objections was procedural, there were also considerations of personality or point of view that influenced the state administrations. In a Far Western state the man first appointed to head the Writers' Project was *persona non grata* for the reason (among others) that he had recently published an unsympathetic study of Mussolini. Considerations of patronage sometimes arose, although, in general, politics played no significant part in these appointments. In one instance the choice of the Washington office was opposed by a senator who had his own candidate for the position; in another, the state WPA administrator and one of the senators fought each other for the right to name the candidate. In at least one case a private pressure group brought its power to bear upon the appointment. A state administrator, in a telephone conversation with Baker, said, "I have got the —— Federation of Musicians on my neck. They

*Since it was the intention of the Washington office to increase state budgets to meet these added expenses, the use in this telegram of the phrase "regular funds" was misleading. Ambiguities like this, in this and other connections, were frequent, and served further to confuse the state administrators.

say they won't have anything to do with the program at all, but they can get along with ——, if —— lets him alone."

It is not surprising that, on October 16, Baker weakened, partly because of pressure from the states and partly because of his strong feeling for administrative form, and laid down the policy that since the state directors of Writers' Projects were staff members, they must be acceptable to the state administrators. Acting on this policy, Cronyn, deputy director of the Writers' Project in Washington, requested the person who had already been appointed director in a New England state to withdraw, since his name was unacceptable to the state administration.

Despite this definition of policy, however, Baker continued to defend the position of the Washington office. On October 21, in a telegram to a midwestern state administrator, after apologizing for the fact that the state administrator had not been consulted, he added forcibly:

> HOWEVER SINCE THESE FOUR PROJECTS MUST BE RUN ON A NATIONAL AND NOT STATE BASIS MUST ASK YOU TO BEAR WITH ME IF THERE ARE OCCASIONAL FAILURES OF PROPER CONSULTATION SINCE I ASSURE YOU NO INTENDED SLIGHT AND THAT SO FAR AS POSSIBLE SHALL WANT AND VALUE YOUR ADVICE.

On October 23, in a memorandum to a colleague, Baker wrote: "Please advise —— that the National Arts Projects are operated from here. I have written him in considerable detail to that effect but he apparently needs your information as well."

His strongest stand was in Pennsylvania, where the state administrator, Edward N. Jones, strenuously objected to the appointement of Mary Curran as state director of the Art Project. In a memorandum to Lawrence Westbrook, assistant administrator of the WPA in Washington, Baker wrote in no uncertain terms:

> With reference to the telegram received from Mr. Jones, the appointment of Miss Curran has been very thoroughly canvassed with all the interested professional groups concerned. Since Mr. Hopkins has specified that these four arts projects are to be set up on a basis meeting professional approval, that is our first essential. It also is essential that we have the cooperation and acceptance of the State Works Progress Administrator. Sometimes we just cannot get it.
>
> For a variety of reasons, which probably revolve around certain personalities, Mr. Jones did not want to approve Miss Curran although she has done excellent work over a long period of time in connection with the relief program. The State Administrator is directed and not requested to put these

people on in accordance with Mr. Hopkins' letter of September 28, 1935. In a way Pennsylvania is a test case on this. Mr. Hopkins' letter was specific in its authorization to the Directors of these four projects and the Federal Art Director felt so strongly about the matter in Pennsylvania that I decided to accept his recommendations and make this appointment with full knowledge of all the factors.*[20]

The fact was that although Baker was prepared to give ground, the pressure from Hopkins' office did not relent; and the federal administrator, in turn, was confirmed in his attitude by conversations with the federal directors of the arts program, to whom, it seems, he had made unfortunate commitments. In his telephone conversations and other communications with the states, Baker continually emphasized the policy of the Washington office, as defined by Hopkins. In a telephone conversation with the Illinois administrator on October 16, he said: "Mr. Hopkins wants these four national projects run separately from the others."

On occasion, he frankly conceded his dilemma; in a telephone conversation with a state administrator on October 16, his tone was almost plaintive:

> I don't want to get in the same jam as the education people did. I am very anxious to have all you guys in the regular outfit give me all the help you can. . . . Hopkins has set this up and I am trying to control it as much as I can. I am very frank in having to ask you guys to help me out as much as you can out in the field but it is true that Hopkins has told Sokoloff he has the right to appoint his people.

Indeed, if the state administrators could threaten Baker by commenting upon the unfavorable publicity that the arts program was bringing upon the WPA, Baker himself was not above intimidation. In a midwestern state a particularly unpleasant situation arose as to the state administrator's attitude toward both the regional and the state directors of the Music Project. In a telephone conversation on November 7, Baker hinted that if the state administrator did not co-operate, funds

---

*In this instance the state administrator retreated, and the candidate was appointed. However, had the state administrator wished further to obstruct, he could have refused to sign and to issue Treasury Form A-3 (Advice of Allotment), which authorized a district to incur expenditures for a specific project. In the face of such an ultimatum, the federal administrator would have been forced either to withdraw the appointment or to dismiss the state administrator. No such case arose, so far as the records show. It was, to a considerable degree, a game of bluff on both sides. But, had such a decision been necessary, the verdict would have been in favor of the state administrator. No other was politically possible.

for a music project in that state might be withdrawn. The pertinent part
of the dialogue follows:

> Mr. BAKER: You see, my problem is this. The only way I have of dis-
> bursing funds in ——— is through you, and I try to get some joint activity
> between you and the directors of the music program.
>
> Mr. ———: That's perfectly all right about disbursing the funds. That
> can be done any way you want it done.
>
> Mr. BAKER: I want it to be done by you, but the point is, if I can't get
> some joint activity and responsibility there, I just can't put the funds into
> ———. You and I both feel that there has to be a musical program there.
>
> Mr. ———: There has to be.
>
> Mr. BAKER: You see, both you and Dr. Sokoloff have a responsibility in
> this—about 50 per cent—and I still think it would be a very good idea to have
> him come out and talk to you about it. I think I may ask him to do it later.

Evidently, in a telegram subsequently addressed to the state administrator, a more direct threat was made, for in a telephone conversation
later the same day Baker said to Sokoloff: "I just received a telegram
from ———. I think maybe the threat in my telegram that they would
not get money is going to have effect and you won't have to go at all."

In the end, the state director stayed, but the regional director resigned.

Gradually, the Washington WPA administration was forced to take
cognizance of the delicate situation. On October 21 Baker sent the following night letter to all regional and state directors of Federal One:

> RECURRENT COMMENTS AND CRITICISMS FROM OPERATING STATE WORKS
> PROGRESS ADMINISTRATIONS CONVINCES ME THAT DIRECTORS OF THE FOUR NA-
> TIONAL ARTS PROJECTS HAVE NOT FULLY REALIZED NECESSITY OF WORKING
> CLOSELY WITH AND THROUGH GOING ORGANIZATION stop EACH ONE OF US CAN
> ONLY SUCCEED ON THIS JOB BY DEVELOPING EFFECTIVE COOPERATION RATHER
> THAN THE EXERCISE OF AUTHORITY.[21]

Further to calm the administrative waters, Hopkins gave instructions on October 29 that all mail and telegrams dispatched to a state
Works Progress Administration should be addressed to the state Works
Progress administrator and not to a member of his staff. Such communications, however, might be addressed to the attention of a particular
division or staff member.[22]

Baker also gradually came to feel that the federal and regional directors of the Art, Music, and Theater projects were appointing too

many state directors. In states where there were few eligible workers, he suggested that the state Division of Professional and Service Projects administer the program:

> I think we are getting too many State Directors on the National Projects. For instance, in New Mexico there cannot possibly be more than two music project units, both of which I should think could be operated under the state organization. It may be that no State Director will be recommended there, but I use that state as an example in case one is recommended.
>
> I am almost certain that no State Director is needed for the Theatre project, although I think one and perhaps two project units may be set up on that.[23]

### VIOLENTA NON DURANT

One of the basic problems of public administration is to maintain a balance between a decent respect for tradition and a spirit of adventure. If the latter is lacking, routine results; if the former, administrative chaos. Without doubt, the federal directors of Federal One felt as a result of the FERA's experience with its professional program that an art program, national in scope and professional in character, could not be achieved so long as authority rested in the state administrations. Later, looking back upon the events of early Federal One, they maintained that Federal One could never have been started—or, at least, started with such vigor—if the attitude of the Washington office had been less iconoclastic.

But if an attitude of violence toward established administrative tradition was justifiable, the question of degree still remained. The federal nature of the arts program, as a series of WPA-sponsored projects, might have been maintained and, at the same time, courtesy shown the state administrations. The state administrators might well have been consulted with regard to the appointment of state, and even regional, directors who were to become members of their staffs. To be sure, there was the pressure of speed under which all WPA officials, both administrative and technical, in the national, state, and district offices, were working in order to employ upon work relief as many as possible as quickly as possible, in accordance with the President's known desires. But patience is also a virtue, and there is reason to believe that, had negotiation leading to persuasion been used instead of dictation leading to resentment, the critical period of initiation, while it might have lasted longer, would in the end have resulted in a surer foundation.

The state administrations, it must be allowed, represented the layman's attitude toward work relief and, to an even greater degree, toward the arts. Unfortunately, the conduct of those responsible for the initiation of Federal One confirmed them in this attitude when it might have disabused them. The popular concepts that the artist is impractical and, worse than that, that he scorns with Horatian contempt the *profanum vulgus* (among whom are numbered the politicians) were strengthened in the minds of those who after all were the administrative agents through which the program sought realization. Those who seek through the political structure to achieve a socially desirable end should not scorn political methods, and if they do, should not be outraged if they are offered the martyr's crown. In short, in its period of initiation Federal One attempted the politically impossible; for, unlike the social worker, the professional artist had not achieved the conceptual and administrative stature that would have given his attempt to assume public power a reasonable chance of success.

It does not follow that the attempt was not important; if the artist is to achieve eventually a place in public life, premature essays in seeking it are part of his education. But it must be emphasized that if the public needs to be educated in the arts, the artist needs to become disciplined politically and to realize—as it is the business of the politician to realize—that art is one way but not the only way in which a culture expresses itself.

1.  Letter WD-7, WPA, August 2, 1935.
2.  *Professional and Service Projects, Bulletin No. 29, W.P.A.*, September 4, 1935, Section 7.
3.  *W.P.A.–Sponsored Federal Project Number One (Art, Music, Theatre and Writing), Supplement No. 1 to Bulletin No. 29*, September 30, 1935, Section 7.
4.  *Ibid.*, Section 2.
5.  *Ibid.*, "Use of Employees of W.P.A.-Sponsored Federal Project Number One in Providing Leadership for Leisure-Time Community Programs," Appendix A, November 15, 1935.
6.  *Supplement No. 1 to Bulletin No. 29*, September 30, 1935, Section 3.
7.  *Ibid.*
8.  *Ibid.*
9.  *Ibid.*
10.  *Ibid.*
11.  *Ibid.*, Section 6.
12.  *Ibid.*, Section 3.
13.  *Ibid.*, Section 5.
14.  *Ibid.*, Section 7.
15.  *Ibid.*, Section 6.
16.  *Ibid.*, Section 16.

17. *Ibid.*, Section 7.

18. *Report on Progress of the Works Program*, WPA, October 15, 1935.

19. Letter, Baker to Holt, Alabama W.P. Administrator, October 5, 1935, WPA Files.

20. Memorandum, Baker to Westbrook, October 23, 1935, WPA Files.

21. Night Letter, Baker to All Regional and State Directors of the National Arts Projects, October 21, 1935, WPA Files.

22. Memorandum, Hopkins to All Assistant Administrators, October 29, 1935, WPA Files.

23. Memorandum, Baker to McClure, November 22, 1935, WPA Files.

# 10

## The Years of Uneasy Peace

THE COMPROMISE SETTLEMENT OF EARLY 1936

Early in December, 1935, the field representatives of the WPA, after having observed the operation of Federal One in the states for two months, recommended to Washington that the Art, Music, and Theater projects be separated from the WPA administrative structure (presumably as was NYA) and operated entirely on a federal basis.*

This memorandum reads:

> We recommend that the Federal Art, Music, and Drama projects should be operated on a Federal basis from the Washington office, and should only be operated in those centers which thoroughly justify projects of this character on a high standard, for the following reasons:
> (1) The funds themselves are in the nature of a grant for a Federal project.
> (2) Exemptions have been granted to the 90-10 ruling, making it possible in some instances to employ up to 25% non-relief persons.
> (3) Hours of work in conflict with existing hours of work on WPA projects in the State have been established nationally.
> (4) The method of paying salaries and other administrative costs through the states is a cause of complaint on the part of many State Administrators.[1]

Jacob Baker, however, in accordance with the position he had taken from the very beginning, argued that Federal One should be inte-

---

*The Writers' Project, although, like the other three, it offended the state administrators by its method of appointing its state directors, was operated on a state-wide basis in other respects and not on a regional basis. For that reason, presumably, the WPA field representatives felt that it could readily be integrated with the state WPA structure and accordingly omitted it from this recommendation.

159

grated with the state WPA administrative structure. As a result of the conference of the field personnel, Baker wrote a memorandum to Bruce McClure in which he suggested that: (1) the regional organization of the Federal Art, Music, and Theater projects be integrated with the regional structure of the WPA, and that the regional representatives of the arts projects, like the WPA regional representatives, exercise staff duties only and be administratively responsible directly to the Washington office; and (2) that the state directors of the arts projects be staff members of the state administrations and perform staff duties only.[2]

THE STATE CO-ORDINATING PROJECTS

The federal directors, however, were not prepared to make such a concession to orthodoxy, and were able to persuade Harry Hopkins to allow them to adopt a strange device that became known as the co-ordinating project. Its nature was revealed in a telegram, December 20, 1935, from the Washington office to all state administrators. The telegram reads:

IN IMMEDIATE FUTURE WE EXPECT TO TRANSFER TO PROJECT PAYROLLS ALL PERSONS IMMEDIATELY CONNECTED WITH ANY ONE OF THE FOUR NATIONAL PROJECTS IN THE ARTS AND AT PRESENT CARRIED ON STATE ADMINISTRATIVE PAYROLLS stop IN ORDER TO MAKE THIS TRANSFER SMOOTHLY AND TO ALLOW ALL STATES A FAIR SHARE OF PROJECT MONEY FOR THIS SUPERVISORY WORK THE FOLLOWING INFORMATION MUST BE IN THE HANDS OF JACOB BAKER NOT LATER THAN DECEMBER TWENTY SIXTH colon NAMES TITLES SALARIES OF PERSONS CARRIED ON ADMINISTRATIVE PAYROLL FOR EACH OF FOUR PROJECTS stop INCLUDE TRAVEL AND OTHER EXPENSE FOR THESE PERSONS BUT DO NOT INCLUDE SUCH EXPENSE AS CAN REASONABLY BE CONTINUED SUCH AS OFFICE SPACE STATIONERY AND SIMILAR FACILITIES stop NAME AND SALARIES OF SUPERVISORY EMPLOYEES ON EACH PROJECT UNIT PAYROLL stop AIR MAIL REPLY[3]

On January 1, 1936, these new co-ordinating project units were established in accordance with instructions from Hopkins.[4]

The establishment of these co-ordinating project units in the states had two effects. In the first place, the state directors and their staffs were removed from the staffs of the state administrators and the administrative payroll. Without question, the purpose was to emancipate the arts program in the states from staff dependence upon the state administrations and thus to remove the causes of friction between the two. Sec-

160

ond, the money for the salaries and other expenses of Federal One in the states now came from project funds and not from administrative funds. Thus the apparent, though not the real, cost of administration of Federal One was reduced.*

At the same time, the federal directors in Washington and their staffs were organized as national co-ordinating projects.[5] Here, on the federal level, the reason for national co-ordinating projects is not so clear. The purpose could not have been to free the federal directors from the authority of Jacob Baker, for there was no intimation of such an intention anywhere, and, in fact, no such development occurred. It is possible that the desire to avoid the *appearance* of administrative expense in connection with Federal One may have been persuasive—that, and a wish to parallel the state co-ordinating projects with national co-ordinating projects in each of the four projects.†

The personnel of the co-ordinating projects, however, although they were paid from project funds, were regarded in all other respects as though they were administrative employees. They were required to conform to all rules and regulations relating to administrative employees and were entitled to the same leave and other benefits.

The status of these co-ordinating projects was anomalous, and, so far as available evidence goes, without precedent, unless justification is found in the administrative projects of the FERA Emergency Work Program. The state co-ordinating projects, although they removed the arts personnel from staff responsibility to the state administrator, must have remained within the administrative domain of the state administration and, for that matter, within the purview of the state division of professional and service projects. What this responsibility was, if it was not administrative, was never defined, and the degree to which it existed varied from place to place and from time to time. Except for accounting, as between administrative and project funds, the change was more verbal than real, and another instance of the persistence of the idea of word-magic.‡

*It is not here suggested that the main purpose of the state co-ordinating projects was to conceal administrative expense, though the device had that effect, and, indeed, was later criticized on that score.

†The effect of the establishment of national co-ordinating projects, in addition to state co-ordinating projects, was to remove *all* items of administrative expense from the ledger of Federal One. The salary of the personnel and all operating expenses in the co-ordinating projects were paid from project, not administrative, funds.

‡Co-ordinating project units were abolished, effective July 15, 1937 (General Letter No. 144, July 2, 1937, Section 3).

161

Even among students of the WPA's administrative history, the invention of the co-ordinating project unit has created the impression that thereby Federal One was administratively separated from the state administrations. The authors of *The Administration of Federal Work Relief* write: "Therefore, in January, 1936, Federal Project No. 1 was divorced from all connection with state WPA administrations."[6]

This impression, however, is erroneous, as other changes in the administrative structure, initiated at the same time, make abundantly clear.

THE ELIMINATION OF THE COMMAND AUTHORITY
OF THE REGIONAL DIRECTORS

On December 30, 1935, Bulletin No. 37 was issued. This bulletin dealt with the organization of state and district offices and gave instructions intended to tighten administrative control within the respective states. The heads of the state divisions were recognized as staff officers only, acting in an advisory capacity to the state administrators. All orders issued by the Washington office were to be addressed to the state administrator and not to one of his subordinates. Officials and inspectors from the Washington office or from the offices of the field representatives were first to notify the state administrator before conducting any business in the state.[7] Though Federal One is not specifically mentioned in these instructions, neither is it specifically excluded, and it seems likely that the state directors of the arts projects were to be required to exercise the same procedure as the heads of the state divisions.

The next month—January, 1936—Baker proceeded to eliminate the command authority of the regional directors of the Art, Music, and Theater projects. In a memorandum addressed to the federal directors of these two projects, he wrote:

> The period of major promotion of Federal Project No. 1 has passed. We either have the groundwork laid for practically all of the effective work we will do or else it will develop through factors other than our own organization. With this in mind I herewith direct that:
> On and after February 1, 1936 there shall be no persons on your staffs with the title of Regional Director. All such persons shall be transferred to one of the following positions:
> 1. Project Director or Project Representative on state or city wide projects.

2. Regional Advisor. This is particularly applicable to the dollar-a-year people who have been giving attention to more than one state and whose regional advice and help in connection with audience building for touring groups is still desired. Projects in territory for which these Regional Advisors have heretofore been responsible, shall have directly attached to them the necessary supervisory personnel.

3. With the limit of three persons for each of you, you may draw from this regional staff for addition to your national staff in the National Coordinating Project. These persons shall come on that staff with the title of Assistant to the Director of the National Project. In drawing these people in on your National Coordinating Projects their positions in the field shall not be filled so that there shall be no addition to the total number of persons employed in the administration of this project by this step. I shall expect you to use your central staff in such a way as to give you the most efficient representation and that certain persons will give primary attention to specific parts of the country.[8]

On the same day, Baker notified the assistant administrators and field representatives of the WPA of this change[9] and ordered McClure to take the necessary steps to make this memorandum effective.[10] That the action was protested by the federal directors—particularly, by Hallie Flanagan—is sufficient evidence that the step was intended to restrict their freedom and the freedom of their field representatives and to establish firmer control within each state. Despite these objections, Baker proceeded with his action.

In fact, pressure had been exerted upon the federal directors to decrease the number of their regional directors before Baker's final action. Sokoloff, after explaining in detail certain changes he had made or was intending to make in his regional staff, wrote in a memorandum, dated the previous day:

> . . . We began operations with eleven Music Directors and we will have only six by the 15th of February. There are several States where we have not yet appointed State Music Supervisors. The reason for this is that we are still waiting to have the correct report of the case load in these States and to see if the load justifies the appointment of a State Supervisor. If it does not, we shall have music supervisors on the projects and ask the Professional and Service State Directors to be responsible for the business end of the operations.[11]

At the same time, there is evidence that Hopkins, undoubtedly influenced by the representations of his own field men at their December meeting, was prepared to modify his support of the federal directors. This is implied in a memorandum from Baker to Hopkins, dated January 21, 1936.

This memorandum from Dr. Sokoloff indicates that he is moving along toward tightening up his project and in that respect I think sees our problem. This was written before he had received my memorandum that I discussed with you yesterday.[12]

On January 28, 1936, McClure notified Baker that his instructions had been carried out.[13]

In the spring of 1936 a further trend toward conformity was indicated by the issuance of WPA Form 330 (revised) on April 20, 1936. This form replaced WPA Form 320, and, unlike the earlier issue, required the signature of the state assistant director in charge of professional and service projects as evidence of administrative approval of each request for approval of a project unit. Since the state assistant director always acted with the approval of the state administrator, this new form made necessary, in effect, the approval of the state administrator for each project unit of Federal One. Technical approval was given by the representative of the federal director, who was by this time usually the state director or, in states where there was no state director, the state assistant director in charge of professional and service projects.[14] Thus, as Baker observed when he recommended the integration of Federal One in the state organizations, the recognition of the administrative authority of the state administrator implied his control of project initiation and continuance.*

### THE REORGANIZATION OF THE DIVISION
### OF PROFESSIONAL AND SERVICE PROJECTS

The reorganization in the Washington office, which occurred in July, 1936, was foreshadowed in December, 1935, by a change in the states and districts. On December 30, 1935, the women's division and the professional and service division of the state and district offices were combined to form the division of women's and professional projects. It was required that the director in all states and districts be a woman.[15] This change, however, did not affect the national or regional offices, where the two divisions maintained their separate existence.

---

*The Washington office of Federal One, although it no longer controlled directly the personnel and the initiation of projects in the state and district offices, retained control of the budget until the arts program was returned to the states by the ERA Act of 1939. Thus the integration of Federal One with the state organizations was not yet complete.

164

In July, 1936, a similar integration was accomplished in the national office. The Division of Professional and Service Projects (until then under Baker, assisted by McClure) and the women's division (under Mrs. Ellen Woodward) were consolidated into a single women's and professional division under Mrs. Woodward. Both Baker and McClure eventually severed their connections with the WPA, and Mrs. Woodward recruited new personnel. As her administrative assistant, she named Miss Agnes N. Cronin. The division was divided into two parts; that part concerned with non-federal projects was placed under Frank March, and that concerned with federal projects, including Federal One, under Lawrence S. Morris, who entered upon his duties in October, 1936. At the same time Mrs. Woodward was made an assistant administrator of the WPA.[16]

Notice of the new organization and instructions regarding it were issued to the state administrations on August 1, 1936.[17] The appointment of state directors of the Division of Women's and Professional Projects required the approval of the federal administrator.[18] This organization lasted until January, 1939.

Jacob Baker, although for a period after July, 1936, maintaining his connection with the WPA, and returning for a short time at a later date, ceased to influence high policy when he resigned as assistant administrator in July, 1936. For three years (1933–36) he had been the right bower of Harry Hopkins in the elaboration of the work-relief program. Within that program he had, from the beginning, emphasized the needs and rights of the white-collar class. In the development of federal projects in the early ERA, in the institution of Civil Works Service projects in the CWA period, in the ill-fated but courageous attempt to establish a special professional program in the summer of 1934, and, above all, in the initiation of Federal One, he had acted as the loyal and industrious instrument of Hopkins' policy. It was natural, of course, that in the state offices, both during the FERA and the early WPA period, Baker's name should have been connected with programs that were in the main unpopular and that, at times, used methods and procedures that offended. It was, above all, his responsibility to initiate the Federal One program, the structure of which did not evoke his full sympathy; it was his signature that appeared at the bottom of the letters appointing regional and state directors of the arts program—letters that in tone and content aroused the anger of the state administrators; it was from his office that the representatives of Federal One went forth throughout the land to establish project units, sometimes without paying their respects to the state administrations. It was not surprising, therefore, that the state administrations, when they demanded the reorganization of Federal One, centered their attack upon Jacob Baker's office. The appointment of Mrs. Woodward represented a change of fundamental policy with reference to Federal One, and such a change almost always is announced publicly, so to speak, by a change in personnel.

It is perhaps true that Baker, in his administrative relations, was at times not diplomatic and lacked that finesse of approach and expression necessary if one is to command and not to offend. It may be that authority rested too heavily upon him; certainly, he had the courage to express his convictions not only to his chief but also in the environment of the White House. But whatever his shortcomings as an administrator, he was more responsible than any other single person for placing in operation the arts program.

## ELLEN S. WOODWARD

Mrs. Woodward, unlike her predecessor, combined in an unusual degree a political inheritance with a predilection for social work. Her escutcheon was southern, for she was the daughter of a United States senator from Mississippi, W. V. Sullivan, and she married Judge A. V. Woodward of the same state. After the death of her husband, she became active in public life and social work. For two years she served as state legislator (1926–28), and after that as director of the Mississippi State Board of Development (1926–33). At the same time, she served as trustee of the Mississippi State Charity Hospital (1924–29); director of the Children's Home (1928); executive director of the Mississippi Conference of Social Work (1929–30); a member of the executive committee of the Mississippi State Board of Public Welfare; and a member of the White House Conference of Social Welfare (1930–33). Her interest in social welfare was happily joined with a talent for politics. She was a delegate to the Democratic National Convention in 1928 (and again in 1936); and from 1932 to 1934, a member of the Democratic National Committee.

The considerations, both professional and political, that recommended Mrs. Woodward to Harry Hopkins as director of the newly established women's section of the FERA in 1933 need no emphasis. Her southern background and her preoccupation with social betterment won for her connections in the highest circles of women's organizations

166

and, above all, established a community of discourse with Mrs. Roosevelt, which grew as time went on. Mrs. Woodward, as director of women's work, was attached to the FERA Work Division under the authority of Jacob Baker, and, as the professional program increased in importance, rivalry between the two for its control grew. The dichotomy between women's work and professional work was not clear, and, especially after a section for professional projects was created (July, 1934), friction was apparent. The failure to make a clear distinction presented difficulties on both sides: Mrs. Woodward, if she surrendered control of women qualified for professional work, lost the smaller but more impressive part of her clientele; and Baker, if he allowed professional women to remain under Mrs. Woodward's jurisdiction, sacrificed 25 per cent of the professional program. To the problem of definition was added that of personalities, for Baker seemed sometimes less than gallant in his instructions, and Mrs. Woodward, on her part, was not reluctant to use her influence in high places to gain her purpose. In the end, the animus created by the initiation of Federal One was decisive, and Hopkins, by replacing Baker with Mrs. Woodward, resolved both the problem of definition and that of personalities. By combining women's projects and professional projects, the federal administrator created what was in effect a division of non-manual projects, as opposed to the division of operations, which was concerned with construction projects. At the same time, the state administrators were appeased, the White House was pleased, and political connections were established, especially in Congress, which, if they did not in the end save Federal One, were not inconsequential in prolonging its life.

Of the theories of administrative management, there is one that, if not prominent in the textbooks, is common enough in practice. It is the exercise of control, as regards relationships within a staff, through non-definition of responsibility. The subordinate is left in the dark as to the extent of his authority, both with reference to his chief and with reference to his fellow subordinates: at one time he will be told to make decisions of high policy; at another, his duties will hardly transcend those of a messenger boy. If at the same time one subordinate is not clear whether he should work *through*, or *with*, or *without the knowledge of*, another subordinate, a state of staff confusion, as well as a feeling of personal insecurity, results. This method has its advantages for the administrator, who is thus able to claim or disclaim responsibility as occasion requires. It works well, however, only when the administrator is, as Mrs. Woodward was, of such a character that he provokes the full

167

loyalty and confidence of his staff and when the members of his staff, individually, trust one another and recognize the method of staff management under which they work. It was the good fortune of all concerned that such conditions prevailed in the Division of Professional and Service Projects under the leadership of Mrs. Woodward.

Under the new dispensation of July, 1936, Mrs. Woodward was absolutely loyal to the personnel and program of Federal One. Indeed, her closeness to Mrs. Roosevelt permitted her, in periods of crisis, to bring pressure when and where it was effective and, by gentler means, to retain for the program that privileged position it had attempted to achieve by more violent methods under her predecessor. An innate respect for artistic accomplishment joined with a sense of duty that prompted her to defend in public, and especially before Congressional committees, the directors of Federal One and their programs, made her regime (July, 1936–December, 1938) the golden age of the federal arts projects. Without doubt, she enjoyed the kudos that attached to her Medicean role and basked in the borrowed light of artistic recognition. The federal directors on their part recognized her sincerity of purpose and appreciated her genuine enthusiasm. When she left the WPA in December, 1938, to become a member of the Social Security Board, the life of Federal One was—in effect, though not yet officially—ended.*

OPERATING PROCEDURE NO. W-1

The changes by which in January, 1936, the control of state and district personnel, both administrative and project, was transferred from Washington to the state offices, and, with it, the control of project operations (except for the retention of financial control in the Washington office), received procedural form with the issuance on December 14, 1936, of Operating Procedure No. W-1. This superseded *Supplement No. 1 to Bulletin No. 29.* In it the rules governing appointments were laid down.[19] State administrators were no longer *directed* to appoint as state directors the candidates of the federal directors. Rather, they might appoint state directors, on the basis of nominations by the federal

---

*Just as the task of Jacob Baker was to initiate the arts program under difficult circumstances and to fashion for it a secure place in the WPA program, so it was Ellen Woodward's responsibility to retain for the program those privileges without which professional standards could not be maintained and to secure from the President allocations adequate to maintain its coverage. Although the fight was long and against mounting odds, Mrs. Woodward never faltered in courage or vigor.

directors, who in turn must secure the approval of the assistant administrator in charge of the Division of Women's and Professional Projects. Accordingly, though the federal director might nominate, he had no power to appoint, or to compel an appointment of his choice. His authority was checked, first, by the assistant administrator of the women's and professional division, and second, by the state WPA administrator. This, however, merely established procedurely what had been the practice ever since the reforms of January, 1936. There is no instance after December, 1935, in which a state director was appointed against the will, or without the free consent, of a state administrator. The "preliminary clearance" with the state administrator was meant to secure adherence to his wishes.

Moreover, the district supervisors were now to be appointed by the state administrator upon the nomination of the state director of the federal project concerned. This, too, had been the practice since January, 1936. All pretense of administrative authority on the part of state directors was jettisoned, and an attempt made to distinguish between administrative and technical authority.[20] This distinction was substantially the same as the one that exists in any governmental or private organization that distinguishes staff and line. The technical "authority" the state directors exercised was a far cry from the real administrative authority they had enjoyed before January, 1936.

THE DEVICE OF TECHNICAL SERIES

In the next month, January, 1937, an attempt was made to maintain channels of communication between the Washington directors and their state and district offices by the device of two Technical Series: the first, known as Technical Series Letters, for shorter communications; the second, known as Technical Series Circulars, for longer and more detailed statements.[21] If the purpose was to save the *amour propre* of the federal directors, the device was merely a gesture, for the limitations were such as to make the effectiveness of the contents dependent upon the approval of the state administrator. On the other hand, the device had distinct merits, for the communications were addressed directly to the state directors of the particular projects, and not circuitously via the state administrator and the state director of the Division of Professional and Service Projects (as were all communications to technical personnel after the arts program was defederalized in 1939).

169

The informality of this approach to the problem is refreshing, and the use of the method in analogous situations—granted an essential unity of purpose between administrative and technical personnel—would obviate the labyrinthine form "Attentions of" that makes so many official communications problems in pathfinding.

The revised *Handbook of Procedures*, dated April 15, 1937, further clarified (if clarification was still necessary) the conventional position of the federal arts projects within the WPA administrative structure.[22] Thus all ambiguity was removed; and the staff responsibility of the state directors of the arts projects to the state directors of the women's and professional projects (and, in the districts, of the district supervisors of the arts projects to the district supervisor of the women's and professional projects) was stated in unequivocal terms.

Furthermore, the state administrator was given specific authority to close unsatisfactory projects, subject only to the approval of Mrs. Woodward;[23] and finally, on July 2, 1937, the anomalous state Co-ordinating Projects were discontinued.*[24]

With respect to state and district offices, the regime of Mrs. Woodward represents the period of divided control. Control of personnel and control of project operation (which must be distinguished from the actual operation of project units, where the supervision rested with the technical personnel) reverted to the state administrators. At the same time, control of the budget with respect to allotments to the states remained in the Washington office. How this control developed and how it was exercised are subjects that provide an interesting lesson in fiscal strategy, and show that so long as the power of the purse remained in the Washington office, the victory of the state administrators over Federal One was not complete. But Mrs. Woodward's task was not only to maintain this fiscal ascendancy but also to make sure that the preferential treatment, which was deemed essential to the operation of Federal One, was continued. In this she waged a losing but gallant fight, and in the end the project workers of Federal One were required to conform to all the general rules governing project operation in the WPA.

---

*As a result of this order, the state directors of the arts projects became, in effect, project supervisory employees. However, with respect to leave and other benefits, they continued to be treated as administrative employees until the end of Federal One.

1. Recommendation of Field Representatives to Baker, December 12, 1935, WPA Files.

2. Memorandum, Baker to McClure, December 11, 1935, WPA Files.

3. Telegram Serial No. 40, WPA, December 20, 1935.

4. Telegram Serial No. 44, WPA, January 3, 1936.

5. Memorandum, Baker to Bartlett, January 8, 1936, WPA Files.

6. Macmahon, Millet, and Ogden, *op. cit.*, p. 253.

7. *Organization of State and District Offices of the W.P.A.*, Bulletin No. 27 (superseding Bulletins No. 2 and No. 5), December 30, 1935.

8. Memorandum, Baker to Flanagan, Cahill, and Sokoloff, January 21, 1936, WPA Files.

9. Memorandum, Baker to All Assistant Administrators and All Field Representatives, January 21, 1936, WPA Files.

10. Memorandum, Baker to McClure, January 21, 1936 WPA Files.

11. Memorandum, Sokoloff to Baker, January 20, 1936, WPA Files.

12. Memorandum, Baker to Hopkins, January 21, 1936, WPA Files.

13. Memorandum, McClure to Baker, January 28, 1936, WPA Files.

14. Telegram, Serial No. 99, July 18, 1936.

15. *Organization of the State and District Offices of the W.P.A.*, Bulletin No. 37 (superseding Bulletins No. 2 and No. 5), December 30, 1935.

16. Memorandum, Woodward to All Members of Office Staff, July 29, 1936, WPA Files.

17. Handbook of Procedures Letter No. 15, August 1, 1936.

18. *Handbook of Procedures for State and District Works Progress Administrations*, Revised April 15, 1937, Chap. IV, Sec. 1.

19. *Operating Procedure No. W-1*, WPA, December 14, 1936, Section 2.

20. Handbook of Procedures Letter No. 36, WPA, December 14, 1936, Section 2.

21. General Letter No. 108, WPA, January 26, 1937.

22. *Handbook of Procedures for State and District Works Progress Administrations*, Revised, April 15, 1937, Chap. III, Section 1.

23. *Ibid.*, Chap. IX, Section 6.

24. General Letter No. 144, WPA, July 2, 1937, Section 3.

# The Claim for Preference

## THE REASONS FOR PREFERENCE

A consideration of the nature of the case, as well as past experience, recommended special treatment for white-collar workers and, in particular, for those who qualified for the arts program. The kind of supervision required in arts projects was different in nature and extent from that demanded on manual projects, and the experience of the FERA and CWA periods indicated that a sufficient number of qualified supervisors could not be obtained from the relief rolls. In addition, an arts program, it seemed, required a greater number of supervisors in relation to the total number of project workers than a construction program. Project units of the arts program were, as a rule, small; varieties of task and function, both within projects and between projects, were multiform; and the artists themselves, if they were not allergic to discipline, were at least unconventional in their attitude toward routine requirements.

The general rules of the WPA, whether expressed in executive orders or administrative rules, made no provisions for exceptional treatment for arts projects. The rules regarding eligibility for employment, certification, and assignment, the ratio between security and non-security workers, and the hours of work, all were conceived with the manual worker in mind. The WPA could do no other: professional and service projects employed but 10 per cent of all employees; employment on Federal One approximated, even at its height, but 2 per cent of the total. The arts program therefore required preferential treatment. This claim for preference, which existed even in the early FERA and CWA programs, when arts projects were regarded rather as service projects of an educational or recreational type, was reinforced when, under the WPA program, the accent was shifted to professional capacity. Obviously, an arts program that required professional qualifications on the part of its project employees and aimed at accomplishments that would receive professional acclaim necessarily made concessions regarding the nature of the work as well as the psychology of the worker.

## FEDERAL ONE'S CLAIM TO PREFERENCE
## WITH REFERENCE TO NON-RELIEF PERSONNEL

The President's insistence upon the relief nature of the WPA program was fundamental, and throughout the history of the agency he not only never deviated from his purpose but seriously questioned all administrative action on the part of the agency that contradicted, or seemed to contradict, this purpose. He recognized, however, that no work-relief program could be 100 per cent relief, and that project supervisory responsibilities demanded a caliber of training not always obtainable in relief personnel. Accordingly, in Executive Order No. 7046, dated May 20, 1935, the President directed:

> Preference in the employment of workers shall be given to persons from the public relief rolls, and except with the specific authorization of the Works Progress Administration at least 90 per cent of all persons working on a work project shall have been taken from the public relief rolls.[1]

The allowance of 10 per cent non-relief workers was intended to provide adequately for such skilled and supervisory personnel as could not be secured from the local relief rolls.

In October and November, 1935, however, the federal directors of Federal One and their field representatives, going into the localities to establish project units of their respective programs, quickly discovered that for a variety of reasons the local relief rolls supplied them with too few names to warrant the establishment of project units or with personnel insufficiently qualified to undertake supervision. Accordingly, they immediately sought exemption from the 90 per cent relief requirement of Executive Order No. 7046. This exception was given by Administrative Order No. 35, dated November 26, 1935, and signed by Harry Hopkins. The order read:

> 1. The term "project" shall mean *W.P.A. Sponsored Federal Project*

173

*No. 1* for Theatre, Art, Music, and Writing, and *O.P. 12-141* Treasury Relief Art Project.

2. I hereby authorize Jacob Baker to exempt any part, unit or section of a project from the requirement that 90 per cent of all workers employed upon a project shall be taken from the public relief rolls, and to permit the employment on any part, unit or section of any project so exempted of workers, not taken from the public relief rolls, up to a maximum of 25 per cent of the total number of workers employed on such part, unit, or section of a project.

3. The United States Employment Service, or other agency in charge of the placement of workers, is authorized to assign workers not taken from the public relief rolls to a project in accordance with any exemption granted pursuant to Section 2 thereof.*[2]

During the month of December, 1935, Baker, acting on this authorization, issued a series of Adjustment Orders;[3] and these, together with exemptions subsequently granted, removed the major portion of the project units of Federal One from the 10 per cent non-relief limitation.†

Despite the fact that these exemptions were granted to Federal One (and some other federal projects), the *national average* of non-relief to relief personnel remained well below 10 per cent. In December, 1935, for instance, the ratio was 3.4 per cent. This low ratio was possible because the vast majority of project employees belonged to the unskilled class, and in this class the non-relief ratio was 0.2 per cent. On the other hand, within the professional and technical classification 22 per cent of supervisory employees came from the non-relief category.[4] Thus the very low percentage of non-relief workers in the unskilled class allowed the professional, technical, and supervisory classes the luxury of a high percentage. But another reason for the low non-relief percentage in December, 1935, was that Federal One had not yet engaged a large personnel force. The national average increased as employment on Federal One increased, and in May, 1936, 5 per cent came from non-relief sources.[5]

FEDERAL ONE'S CLAIM TO PREFERENCE

WITH REFERENCE TO NON-SECURITY PERSONNEL

The principle of the security wage, adopted in the ERA Act of 1935,

*Registration with the USES was still required of all applicants for WPA work relief.

†This non-relief exemption of 25 per cent did not imply an equal exemption from the wage schedule, i.e., not all those taken from non-relief sources were given non-security wages. Exemption from the security wage never exceeded 10 per cent. WPA Letter No. 22, dated August 13, 1935, was written to remind the state administrators that the monthly earnings schedule applied to project employees whether taken from the relief rolls or not. This warning was repeated in WPA Letter No. 103, issued November 9, 1935.

174

was, as already has been indicated, a compromise between that of the prevailing wage and that of the budget-deficiency calculation. The security wage—which was designed to be a month's payment for a month's work, and not to be calculated on an hourly basis—was set so that in each classification the monthly payment, though it would be less than the prevailing wage for an equal number of hours, would exceed the amount received as direct relief.

Differences in the monthly wage-rate structure of the WPA were based upon three criteria: geographical area, individual skill, and urbanization of county. The whole country was divided into four regions, in each of which wages were established in accordance with the cost *and* standard of living; at the same time, all workers were divided into four classes that were, in descending order: (1) professional and technical, (2) skilled, (3) semiskilled, and (4) unskilled. For each of these classes wages were set in accordance with the skill and training of the worker. Finally, the wage levels within each region were related directly in descending order to the degree of urbanization in each county, based on the following population figures: over 100,000; 50,000 to 100,000; 25,000 to 50,000; 5,000 to 25,000; and under 5,000.*

Under the first schedule of monthly earnings the highest monthly wage that could be paid in the professional and technical classification was ninety-four dollars (in Region I in counties with over 100,000 population according to the 1930 census); the lowest was thirty-nine dollars (in Region IV in counties with under 5,000 population). In the skilled classification the highest wage was eighty-five dollars and the lowest thirty-five dollars. However, in the executive order that established this schedule the Works Progress administrator or his representative was given authority to adjust the rate of earnings for any class of work in a locality by not more than 10 per cent from the monthly earnings shown in the foregoing schedule.[6] On July 31, 1935, Hopkins issued Administrative Order No. 18, which authorized Baker and the several state administrators to make the 10 per cent adjustment.[7] General Hugh C. Johnson, who was then New York City administrator, immediately raised all wages 10 per cent. Thus the highest wage paid to workers in the professional and technical classification became $103.40. Johnson's example was largely followed, especially in the northern states.

Subsequently, by Administrative Order No. 33, dated November 9, 1935, the federal administrator exempted from the schedule of monthly

---

*Since there were four classes of workers, four regions, and five distinctions of rate within each region, the number of different wage rates in the WPA was eighty.

earnings "workers on any projects or portions of projects within any state, up to a maximum of 10 per cent of the total number of workers employed upon all projects within such state."[8] In a covering letter Hopkins explained the reasons for this exemption.

> This Order is issued because of two facts—(1) there has been difficulty in getting from the non-relief rolls the necessary skilled and key personnel for some projects; and (2) we desire that all persons in a given occupation on a project shall work under the same wage and hour arrangements.[9]

This authority to exempt was much more far-reaching than at first sight it appears. Hitherto, an individual project unit might employ 10 per cent non-security personnel. Now, however, the state average and not the project unit was taken as the basis, with the result that particular project units within a state might enjoy a higher than 10 per cent exemption, so long as a statewide average of 10 per cent was maintained. The date of this order, as well as its content, is plausible evidence that it was issued, though not in so many words, out of consideration for the arts program. Indeed, it was this order that made possible the establishment in January, 1936, of the state co-ordinating project units, which were almost entirely staffed with non-security personnel. *

THE PRINCIPLE OF PREVAILING HOURLY RATES

The adoption of the principle of the security wage in the 1935 ERA Act had provoked the determined opposition of organized labor, who saw in it a threat to established union hourly rates. Pressure from this direction prevailed, and in the 1936 ERA Act the payment of prevailing wages was made mandatory by statute. The pertinent clause reads:

> The rates of pay for persons engaged upon projects under the foregoing appropriation shall not be less than the prevailing rates of pay for work of a

---

*Care must be taken to distinguish non-relief personnel from non-security personnel. A non-security worker was a project worker who received higher than the security wage, and it was immaterial in principle whether such a worker was or was not taken from the local relief rolls. Generally, of course, such workers were neither sought nor secured from the relief rolls.

A non-relief worker, on the other hand, was a project worker who was not certified as in need, and it was immaterial in principle whether such a worker received or did not receive security wages. In general, non-relief workers received higher than security wages. For the most part, in practice and by the very nature of the distinction, the majority of non-relief workers were non-security workers, and vice versa.

similar nature as determined by the Works Progress Administration with the approval of the President.[10]

It must not be thought, however, that the adoption of prevailing rates increased the *monthly* salary of project workers. The monthly salary remained as fixed by Executive Order No. 7046, subject to change only (1) by an increase of 10 per cent over the schedule of monthly earnings, and (2) by an exemption of 10 per cent on a statewide basis from the schedule of monthly earnings. The prevailing rate, as adopted in the 1936 act, affected hourly wages *only*.

The result was that the acceptance of the principle of prevailing rates, although not a return to the budget-deficiency principle of the FERA, was largely responsible for the same difficulties. Particularly for workers in the higher wage categories, as was the case with the larger number on Federal One, the working hours had to be reduced in order to make the prevailing hourly rate conform to the monthly security rate. Thus within a given project unit, workers in different categories worked a different number of hours a month; even workers in the same category (e.g., professional and technical) did not work the same number of hours per month if the prevailing hourly rates for each group were not the same. This made it difficult, and at times impossible, to synchronize hours of work of workers on a given project unit. Thus both quality and continuity of supervision suffered, and the proper proportion of skilled to unskilled workers, necessary for efficient operation, was not as readily maintained. Furthermore, the morale that comes from regularity of hours within a working group was lacking, and workers with higher hourly wages and correspondingly shorter hours not infrequently accepted private employment in their leisure time—a practice that aroused the jealousy both of fellow project workers and of those in private employ, who saw in the practice a threat to their own security.

## THE PRESSURE TOWARD CONFORMITY

The early privileges extended to Federal One with respect to non-relief and non-security personnel were under constant attack from July, 1936, to the end of Federal One in 1939. This pressure toward conformity, although it drew strength from complaints from the states and the districts, was exerted principally at the federal level. As will appear in the analysis of budgetary control, the Bureau of the Budget, operating through the White House, and the President himself, because of his insistence upon the relief nature of the program, looked askance at a tendency that, if given full play, would have converted Federal One into an employment program.

As early as July, 1936, the beginning of the next fiscal year—when new official and work project numbers were given for project units operating as part of Federal One—occasion was taken to institute a careful review of exemptions for non-relief employment.[11]

This review harks back to inquiries that were instituted shortly after the beginning of the new fiscal year, which had for their object an examination of the need for the 25 per cent non-relief exemption for Federal One.* This exemption, granted in 1935, had been continued until September 15, 1936,[12] and subsequently was continued until October 1, 1936,[13] and finally until November 1, 1936.[14] These extensions, however, were allowed only to permit the review of non-relief personnel ordered in the letter quoted above.

On November 23, 1936, the impending blow fell. First, the quotas on Federal One were reduced.[15] At the same time, the statewide exemption for non-relief employment was reduced from 25 per cent to 10 per cent, though no limitation was set on non-relief employment on individual project units.[16]

The order was softened to some degree by the provision that state Co-ordinating Project Units, although they were to be included in the state employment quota, were not to be counted in computing the 10 per cent non-relief exemption. This was a substantial concession, for these units were almost without exception staffed 100 per cent with non-relief personnel.[17]

Thus non-relief employment on Federal One, especially in those states that had taken advantage of the 25 per cent exemption, was reduced almost 60 per cent. This was a severe blow to the federal directors of Federal One, and they had fought it bitterly but to no avail.

However, there was one way by which the non-relief personnel could be retained: by causing them to be certified. How extensively this device was used is not clear, but it was quite possible that in many cases individuals who had secured non-relief employment on Federal One were in November, 1936, eligible for certification. To be certified, it was necessary for the non-relief personnel to prove to the local relief offices that they were in need.

*Non-certified is synonymous with non-relief in WPA usage.

178

At the close of January, 1937, a serious shortage of funds embarrassed Federal One, and prompted a further tightening of the reins. On February 20, 1937, Administrative Order No. 52, which reduced non-relief exemptions to 5 per cent, was issued. No exception was made for Federal One. The ruling applied to each work project unit, and could not be averaged over the state or nation as a whole.[18] The same order also reduced exemptions from the schedule of monthly earnings.[19]

At the same time, security and non-security workers were so defined that the distinction between non-security and non-relief no longer existed. All who were paid in accordance with the schedule of monthly earnings were security and certified personnel; all others were non-security and non-certified.[20]

The harshness of Administrative Order No. 52 was mitigated to some extent by Administrative Order No. 57, dated May 8, 1937, which authorized the state administrators to exempt workers from the schedule of monthly earnings ". . . provided that such exemptions shall not exceed ten per cent (10%) of the persons employed upon a project and that at least ninety-five per cent (95%) of the persons employed on all projects within the state shall be paid in accordance with the schedule of monthly earnings."[21] A caution was added that this relaxation was provided to enable state WPA administrators to exempt single projects, and should not be used to nullify the purposes of Administrative Order No. 54.

This order applied to Federal One, although at first rather general exemptions were permitted. On July 12, 1937, however, these exemptions were restricted. The telegram announcing the restrictions read:

THE PROVISIONS OF ADMINISTRATIVE ORDER NUMBER FIFTY SEVEN ARE APPLICABLE TO WPA SPONSORED FEDERAL PROJECT NUMBER ONE AND THEREFORE INSTRUCTIONS CONTAINED THEREIN SHALL BE FOLLOWED WHERE EXEMPTION AUTHORIZATIONS ARE REQUIRED stop EXEMPTIONS PREVIOUSLY AUTHORIZED FOR THIS PROJECT AND EXTENDED BY TELEGRAM UNTIL JULY FIFTEENTH NINETEEN THIRTY SEVEN WILL NOT BE EXTENDED AS A GENERAL EXEMPTION BUT WHERE REQUESTS ARE NECESSARY THEY SHALL BE HANDLED IN ACCORDANCE WITH THE PROVISIONS OF ADMINISTRATIVE ORDER NUMBER FIFTY SEVEN stop EXEMPTIONS REQUESTED UNDER SECTION FOUR OF ADMINISTRATIVE ORDER NUMBER FIFTY SEVEN MAY BE SUBMITTED BY WIRE AND CONFIRMED PROMPTLY BY SUBMITTING WPA FORM FOUR NAUGHT SIX[22]

The effect of this administrative action was described by Harry Hopkins at the Senate hearings in June, 1937.

A basic policy of Works Program operation has always been that at least 90 percent of the workers should be drawn from persons certified as in need

179

of relief, unless unusual circumstances justified exemption from this requirement. At the present time about 90 percent of all Works Program workers are from relief rolls. Throughout the period of operation about 95 percent of the workers on WPA projects have been relief persons and during recent weeks are a result of administrative action directed toward that end, the proportion of workers certified as in need of relief has increased to 96.5 percent.[23]

The privilege of not being counted in the state quota of non-relief workers that state Co-ordinating Project Units enjoyed was withdrawn by an order abolishing such projects as of July 15, 1937. Henceforth the state offices of Federal One were listed as regular work projects.

The fact was that again in May, 1937, as in January of the same year, Federal One suffered budgetary embarrassment. In the latter month employment on Federal One was frozen in accordance with the following telegram:

ALL ADDITIONS TO PROJECT PAYROLLS FEDERAL PROJECTS ONE THROUGH SIX ARE HEREBY STOPPED UNTIL FURTHER NOTICE stop EXCEPTIONS TO THIS ARE AUTHORIZED ONLY IN THE CASE OF REPLACEMENTS WHICH ARE ABSOLUTELY ESSENTIAL TO EFFICIENT PROJECT OPERATION OR IN CASE OF PERSONS WHO HAVE LEFT WPA FOR OTHER EMPLOYMENT WHICH HAS BEEN TERMINATED THROUGH NO FAULT OF THEIR OWN stop REVISED STATE QUOTAS FOR FEDERAL PROJECTS ONE THROUGH SIX YOUR STATE WILL BE FORWARDED TO YOU IN NEAR FUTURE[24]

When quotas were reduced on Federal One, however, workers who were dismissed had the right of assignment to other WPA projects.

When projects of Federal agencies or Federal projects of the Works Progress Administration are terminated or reduced, certified workers on those projects shall have the same status in regard to reassignment as any other WPA workers. Within quota limitations such workers should be transferred to other WPA projects.[25]

The reduced quotas were issued for July 15, 1937, and a new threat to Federal One was seen in the instructions relating to them.

In complying with the employment quotas for July 15, 1937 which have been announced to you, thorough consideration should be given to retaining in operation during the next fiscal year only those projects which are most desirable and best suited to the Works Progress Administration program. The instructions which were embodied in General Letter No. 112, dated February 24, 1937, to govern the conduct of construction projects in the WPA program to June 30, 1937, were of such a nature that it should be possible to attain this objective at this time.

Some of the classes of State WPA projects which should be scrutinized with a view to their possible termination are:

1. Projects on which there is relatively small participation by sponsors, resulting in high man-year cost from Federal funds.

2. Projects which are not susceptible of efficient operation with relief labor at security wages and which therefore require large exemptions.

3. Projects employing such small numbers as to make efficient operation and supervision difficult and expensive.

4. Projects in rural areas where the certified labor load is small and widely distributed.

Consideration should also be given to the possibility of reducing the amount of employment on projects which are at present over-crowded.

The foregoing instructions apply to projects of all types, but are particularly applicable to construction and production projects.[26]

Although Federal One was not specifically mentioned, it was definitely included in the types of projects mentioned in clauses (1), (2), and, to some extent, (3).

Finally, by Administrative Order No. 62, dated June 27, 1938, the adjustment of monthly earnings within the range of 10 per cent was withdrawn so far as the professional and technical wage class was concerned "in those areas in Wage Region I where the population of the largest city within the county or subdivision thereof is 100,000 or over."[27] This had the effect of decreasing the wages of professional and technical workers in New York City from $103.40 to $96.00 a month. Since professional and technical workers predominated on Federal One, and since Federal One was overwhelmingly an urban program and concentrated in New York City, this order was rightly interpreted as a direct challenge to its claim to preference.

FEDERAL ONE'S CLAIM TO PREFERENCE
WITH REFERENCE TO HOURS OF WORK

With respect to WPA no appropriation act before that of 1939 made any statutory provision as to hours of work required of project employees. Executive Order 7046, dated May 20, 1935, merely provided that "for persons employed on a salary basis in accordance with the schedule provided in Part I the maximum hours of work shall be determined by the Works Progress Administrator but shall not be in excess of 8 hours per day and 40 hours per week."

Administrative Order No. 5, dated July 5, 1935, although directing the state administrators to observe the maximum limitations of the above executive order, set no minimum and let the determination of minimum working hours for each project to the state administrations.[28] This was in accord with Arthur Goldschmidt's remarks at the first conference of state administrators:

> The maximum hours have been set at forty per week for work, but nothing has been said of the minimum hours. With this kind of work it is important to realize that they cannot adhere to these rules. For instance a fiddle player can't play forty hours a week. He would be a menace to everyone near and probably go crazy himself. The number of hours per week or month that these people should work should be the number normally and logically expected of this type of people. The hours should be rational hours of work and not follow the rules for maximum of these particular jobs. We may get out a memorandum on this so that you may have something to tell groups that come in. If this memorandum does not come out, use your best judgment.[29]

The first minimum limitation was set on August 8, 1935; professional, educational, and clerical persons, however, were exempted from its provisions.

> The hours of work for any person employed upon a project or projects for two full consecutive semi-monthly pay periods shall aggregate not less than one hundred and twenty hours, except in the case of professional, educational and clerical persons for whom the customary number of hours shall be applicable.[30]

However, perhaps through inadvertence, this order did not express clearly the intention of Baker's staff, as the following memorandum indicates:

> The original intention in discussion of professional projects was that professional workers should work the number of hours customary to the profession in the locality in which the project is in operation. This customary number of hours may be more than 140 or may be less than 120. In consequence, the Administrative Order covering hours of work should have added that on as a separate paragraph.
>
> In the staff meeting where it was discussed that was the expressed intention, but it now appears that the maximum number of hours that professional workers can work is 140, but that they can work any lesser number that is customary. Clerical workers working thirty-five or thirty-nine hours a week in most parts of the country are cut off from part of their normal time.
>
> Consequently, we need a new Administrative Order specifying separately that professional workers may work the customary number of hours.[31]

The intention, therefore, was to allow these classes of workers to work either more or less than the maximum number of hours. The order that Baker requested, however, was never issued, and hours beyond the established maximum, except to make up time lost in the previous pay period, were not allowed.

In November, 1935, minimum hours of 120 a month were established for those on project payrolls receiving a non-security wage, though no minimum was set for security workers.[32]

Special consideration, however, was given to workers on Federal One:

> Persons working under this program should work the customary number of hours. The minimum number of hours suggested for work by musicians or teachers of music is 96 hours per month. This should include the hours spent in rehearsals, performances and teaching. It should not include hours spent in personal preparation or individual practice.
>
> The minimum number of hours suggested for work by artists or teachers of art is 96 hours per month. This should include the hours spent on actual project or in teaching, but should not include the hours spent in personal preparation.
>
> The minimum number of hours suggested for work by actors, teachers of drama, and other specialists of the theatre is 96 hours per month. This should not include hours spent in personal preparation.
>
> The minimum number of hours suggested for work in writing is 120 hours per month.
>
> Other persons engaged on projects who are not classified as artists, musicians or actors should work the minimum number of hours established for the area by the State W.P.A. Administrator.[33]

As early as March, 1936, the special privilege enjoyed by the Art, Music, and Theater projects was withdrawn, and all workers on Federal One were required to work a minimum of 120 hours a month: "Workers on the Federal Art Project, namely, artists, teachers of art, musicians, teachers of music, actors, teachers of drama and other specialists of the theatre, shall be required to work a minimum of 120 hours a month."[34]

So far as Federal One was concerned, the problem of working hours was resolved by the statutory requirement of prevailing wages contained in the ERA Act of 1936. By the simple process of dividing the prevailing hourly wage into the monthly security wage, the number of hours for each profession and class of workers was mathematically determined. In conformity with this new law, the following administrative order was issued on June 22, 1936: "The hours to be worked at the determined hourly rate by any worker shall be sufficient to total the monthly earnings as prescribed but shall not exceed 140 hours per month."[35]

The regulation was repeated in Administrative Order No. 44, dated

July 11, 1936,[36] and remained in effect until July 1, 1939, when the ERA Act of that year abandoned the principle of the hourly prevailing wage.

It will be seen, therefore, that although Federal One made the same general claim to preference in hours of work as in wages and non-security personnel, the aberration from the norm was not so drastic in the former case. Moreover, what privilege was granted—and it was not substantial—became unnecessary with the passage of the 1936 ERA Act. To be sure, other problems were created by the statutory provision of prevailing hourly rates of pay, but that of the *number* of working hours a month was mathematically solved.

### THE ARTS PROGRAM VERSUS THE RELIEF PROGRAM

Federal One's demand for preferential treatment, which, at first successful, was finally denied within approximately two years after its inception, underscores a fundamental antithesis between a professional program and a relief program, at least under the conditions that prevailed during the depression. Throughout its whole history, even in the CWA and the FERA Emergency Work Program, the arts program tended to become a program of employment rather than relief. This was a natural tendency inherent in the subject matter and the availability of trained personnel; it did not result simply from reluctance on the part of the federal directors and their staffs to conform to the general rules of the WPA.

The earlier art programs of the Treasury Department, the PWAP and the TRAP, were superior to the Federal Art Program not because those who directed the earlier programs were better, professionally or administratively, but because they conducted their programs under conditions that were denied to the Federal Art Project. The PWAP was an employment program, and there was no necessity inherent in its concept to employ only those certified for relief. Thus, competence and not destitution was the criterion of personnel selection. In the TRAP, to be sure, certification as to need was required; but it was not demanded of the TRAP that it employ *all* needy artists. Accordingly, Mr. Bruce could select from the relief rolls only those few artists—the TRAP program was purposely kept small—whose superior talents recommended them. On the other hand, Holger Cahill, the director of the Federal Art Project, enjoyed no such luxury. The President, himself, at the very beginning of the WPA had accepted, on behalf of the federal government,

184

responsibility for the employment of *all* employables on the local relief rolls; and, it might be added, he continued to insist that this purpose be carried through—and carried through as quickly as possible. What has just been said with reference to the art program, in the specific sense, is true of the other programs that comprised Federal One. In the Music, Theater, and Writers' projects, as well as in the Art Project, the project worker and not the project was the center of attention.

Under these conditions the federal directors of the arts program, if they had chosen to be consistent, had two alternatives: either they could have emphasized the professional nature of the program to such a degree that only those who passed strict tests were employed; or they could have lowered the standards of acceptance to such a point that all who made any claim to artistry were accepted. Had they chosen the first alternative, two consequences would have resulted: the number of project employees would have been drastically decreased from what it actually was; and the program would have been restricted to a few metropolitan centers where alone adequate personnel of high caliber was obtainable. From the professional point of view, to be sure, both these results were desirable. The difficulty was that the adoption of the policy of high standards of employability would have run counter to the general policy of the WPA as it expressed itself in relation to other categories of workers and, because of this, would have provoked strong protests from professional applicants who were, in 1935, rapidly assuming the organizational form that makes political pressure effective.

Finally—and perhaps, in the end, most important—the White House itself, though not unaware of the prestige that professional accomplishments would bring, was mainly interested in the social service aspects of the experiment. The introduction of urban amenities, both material and cultural, into rural America was one of the basic purposes of the New Deal, and manifested itself in the arts no less than in rural electrification. Such an emphasis—and there was continual pressure from above upon the educational and, to some extent, the recreational, character of the program—required that (1) professional artists be exported from city to countryside (which was difficult under the WPA program, partly because few artists were willing to be exported and partly because certification as to need was a local formality, and consequently provided no national—or even statewide—status for the individual so certified), and that (2) rural programs be devised compatible with the artistic capacity of the countryside.

185

The other alternative was the emphasis of the neighborhood house upon art as a service to the community and as a means whereby the community expressed its ethos. This was, by and large, the approach of the earlier FERA-CWA period, and continued to be that of the educational and recreational projects of the WPA. In the neighborhood house a provincial rather than a cosmopolitan point of view prevailed, and the community rather than the artist was the center of attention. The forms of expression were amateur—amateur dramatics, handicraft, community sings, pageants, and festivals. Such a program demanded only a small core of professional artists for training and direction; the mass of the participants were local citizens who, if they were not artists, found satisfaction in the less-advanced forms of artistic expression. The difficulty of this approach, apart from the fact that it would have involved trespass upon the domain of existing educational and recreational projects, lay in its lack of distinction. Professional artists, to be sure, were required—a bandmaster here, a dramatic director there— but professional projects, in the sense of projects composed entirely or largely of professional artists, were precluded. The symphony orchestra, the ambitious mural, and the new experiments of the art theater were not, for the most part, the media through which art expressed itself, or could express itself, in the smaller community. Prestige would be sacrificed in those circles that mattered most to the artist, even though popular support would be gained in those areas that mattered most to the politician.

The choice, indeed, was difficult, and, perhaps, the arts program met the dilemma best by not resolving it. By attempting both approaches, the federal directors manifested a catholicity of mind, which, if it did not rest upon considerations of logic, showed a commendable tolerance for variety. The difficulty was that as time went on and the rival claims of professional versus amateur art defined themselves, the approval of the *cognoscenti* became more compelling than the applause of the commoner. The directors were inclined to feel that their own standing in the world of art and letters was involved; a "first night" on Broadway provoked a metropolitan acclaim that could not be achieved from a Main Street pageant; an ambitious concert by a symphony orchestra received notices by the music critics, whereas the playing of a local band achieved publicity only in the home-town press. The result was that the WPA arts program found itself staking its reputation upon its artistic accomplishments rather than upon its services to the community.

It would be stupid to argue that the folk arts are fine arts, or that no difference in quality both with respect to subject matter and performer exists between the two. There is room in America for both; not only that—there is need for both. The question in the present discussion is simply whether it was politic and sound to attempt a fine arts program with the personnel available on the relief rolls.

Indeed, the fact that Federal One was forced to demand—and, for a time, achieved—a position of privilege within the WPA indicates clearly enough that the WPA, like any relief program, was almost exclusively directed toward the employment of unskilled labor. The proper demands of artistic endeavor, as the WPA showed, cannot be accommodated to rules and regulations designed for manual labor. To place such a program within such a structure and then to emancipate it from the ordinary controls that hold the structure erect is to create within a single administration a conflict of purpose certain to express itself in administrative confusion and artistic frustration.

1. Executive Order No. 7046, May 20, 1935, Part III (c).
2. Administrative Order No. 35, WPA, November 26, 1935.
3. Adjustment Order No. 12, December 6, 1935; Adjustment Order No. 13, December 6, 1935; Adjustment Order No. 14, December 6, 1935; and Adjustment Order No. 15, December 18, 1935.
4. U.S. Congress. Senate. Committee on Appropriations. 74th Cong. 2d sess. (1936), *Hearings of a Subcommittee . . . on Emergency Relief Appropriations*, Exhibit C, pp. 66-67.
5. U.S. Congress. House. Committee on Appropriations. 74th Cong. 2d sess. (1936), *Hearings of a Subcommittee . . . on Emergency Relief Appropriations*, pp. 98-100.
6. Executive Order No. 7046, May 20, 1935, Regulation No. 1.
7. Administrative Order No. 18, WPA, July 31, 1935.
8. Administrative Order No. 33, WPA, November 9, 1935.
9. Letter WPA-103, WPA, November 9, 1935.
10. Emergency Relief Appropriation Act of 1936, Public No. 739 (H.R. 12624), Title II.
11. General Letter No. 73, WPA, September 3, 1936.
12. Telegram Serial No. 113, WPA, August 29, 1936.
13. Telegram Serial No. 119, WPA, September 15, 1936.
14. Telegram Serial No. 120, WPA, September 29, 1936.
15. General Letter No. 95, WPA, November 23, 1936.
16. *Ibid.*
17. *Ibid.*
18. Administrative Order No. 52, WPA, February 20, 1937.
19. Administrative Order No. 52, WPA, February 20, 1937.
20. Administrative Order No. 52, WPA, February 20, 1937.

21. Administrative Order No. 57, WPA, May 18, 1937.

22. Telegram Serial No. 153, WPA, July 12, 1937.

23. U. S. Congress. Senate. Committee on Appropriations. 75th Cong., 1st sess. (1937), *Hearings of a Subcommittee . . . on Emergency Work Relief*, p. 9.

24. Telegram, Serial No. 146, WPA, May 25, 1937.

25. General Letter No. 133, WPA, May 29, 1937.

26. General Letter No. 134, WPA, June 5, 1937.

27. Administrative Order No. 62, WPA, June 27, 1938.

28. Administrative Order No. 5, WPA, July 5, 1935.

29. Proceedings, Conference of State Administrators, WPA, Minutes of Meeting of Group No. 4, Mayflower Hotel, Washington, D. C., June 18, 1935.

30. Administrative Order No. 13, WPA, August 8, 1935.

31. Memorandum, Baker to Pressman and Robinson, August 21, 1935, WPA Files.

32. WPA Letter No. 103, WPA, November 9, 1935.

33. Supplement No. 1 to Bulletin No. 29, WPA, September 30, 1935, Section 8 (g).

34. Handbook of Procedures for State and District Works Progress Administrations, WPA, March 21, 1936, Chap. VI, Section 27.

35. Administrative Order No. 41, WPA, June 22, 1936.

36. Administrative Order No. 44, WPA, July 11, 1936.

# 12

## Classification and Assignment

THE UNITED STATES EMPLOYMENT SERVICE

The WPA required that all persons seeking work relief be registered with the USES.

> The State Emergency Relief Administrations shall require that all employable persons now receiving emergency relief from public funds be registered with the employment offices designated by the United States Employment Service, in order that such persons may be classified as to occupation and fitness for work, and thus be available for referral to public and private employment.[1]

The duties of the USES were to interview, register, and classify all persons certified as to need and to fill all requisitions for labor (WPA Form 401) received from the WPA. The evidence of registration was USES Form 350 (Identification Card). When the applicant thus referred received assignment, the USES prepared USES Form 325 (Assignment Slip).

Thus no one could be placed on a work project of the WPA unless he was registered with the USES and referred by that agency to the WPA in reply to a requisition. This referral was through job designation and not by name. Frank Persons, director of the National Re-employment Service in 1935, explained this referral as follows:

> Now, when it comes to referral to jobs, we cannot move until we have a written order for a certain number of people of certain qualifications. . . .
> It doesn't need to be said, but we will not fill employers' orders that consist of a list of names. We expect you to refer to us the list of occupations

189

and the number required and we shall select on the basis of their fitness for the jobs.[2]

The purpose of the requirement that relief workers should register with the USES was to have their names available for referral to private employers or to the PWA, both of which enjoyed priority over the WPA in the matter of employment. If a relief worker on the WPA was referred to a private employer or to the PWA (or any other public works project) and received an offer of employment, he was required to accept the offer and to quit the WPA. The WPA was notified of this change in status through USES Form 340 (Notice of Placement).

Thus at the beginning of the WPA, assignment of workers was the responsibility of the USES.[3]

This assignment of workers by the USES was based upon its classification of the work talents of the individual applicants. This classification, however useful it may have been in the unskilled and manual categories, was practically useless when attempted with respect to the professional and technical group, and especially with the arts personnel. The USES classification was not based upon any test or examination but upon forms filled out by the applicant and by personal interviews. Questions were asked concerning education and past experience, and final classification depended almost entirely upon the applicant's own testimony. It is easy to see that, apart from any intention of the applicant to deceive, the information could be readily so selected or so shaded, consciously or unconsciously, that the examiner would be seriously misled. Classification by the USES, therefore, except for the fact that by sheer coincidence it might occasionally uncover a competent applicant for the arts projects, was useless as a satisfactory criterion for acceptance of personnel.

## CLASSIFICATION AND ASSIGNMENT WITHIN THE WPA

But although initial assignment was the responsibility of the USES, reassignment was the prerogative of the WPA.[4] Accordingly, all workers transferred from the state ERA's to the WPA were considered as already assigned. These persons, having been assigned, could then be reassigned by the WPA; i.e., could have their job classification changed. Moreover, once a worker was initially assigned by the USES, the WPA could reassign such a worker either in the light of further knowledge of the individual's capacities or to suit its own needs.

190

The effect of this upon the assignment of workers in Federal One is significant. Officials of Federal One, in seeking workers, had two sources from which to draw. They could requisition workers by job description (violinist, mural painter, etc.) from the USES, or they could comb the files of the WPA labor management division to discover those who, though assigned under a different job classification, had abilities that qualified them for assignment in Federal One. The difficulty with the first method was that, in many localities, workers who were artistically qualified had not registered as such because there were at that time no projects for them. As a result, Federal One did not receive many referrals from the USES. There remained, as possible candidates for employment, those already assigned. In localities where there had been arts projects it was possible to accept those previously employed by the state ERA's and to transfer them en masse to the WPA. In many instances this was done, because in the beginning the need for starting projects quickly was imperative. Again, there was the possibility of going through the rolls of former ERA employees (who had been assigned to WPA in another job classification) and requesting their reassignment to an arts project if their qualifications commended them. The difficulty here was that the act of reassignment was the privilege of WPA's labor management division, and if that division refused or delayed reassignment, as happened in some localities, the workers requested could not be secured. In the end it was found that mass transfer of workers from the ERA's to the WPA was the easiest procedure. Instructions on this score were as follows:

> In order to transfer workers who are employed on a project operating under the State ERA or the State WPA programs, and which project is approved for transfer to W.P.A. *Sponsored Federal Project No. 1*, the person who is to supervise the project shall consult with the Reassignment Office of the District WPA Labor Management Division. The requisition for the transfer shall be made of that office on WPA Form 401. It is not necessary in such transfer to requisition the persons currently at work from the office designated to refer persons to WPA projects, since acceptable workers employed on such projects can be transferred with the project. The assignment will be made on WPA Form 402, Reassignment Slip.[5]

In effect, when this happened, the project, and not the workers individually, was transferred from the state ERA to the WPA. The transfer *en bloc* of arts projects had, in some cases, unfortunate consequences. In the first place, the project workers were not carefully examined as to their attainments (except in so far as they had been tested for ERA as-

191

signment), with the consequence that screening of talent was necessary *after* assignment to the wpa. This examination, if it was attempted with care, resulted in the immediate dismissal of some, sometimes many, project workers for incompetency. The bad feelings, disappointments, recriminations, and charges and countercharges that ensued often wrecked, at least for a time, the morale of the project. If, on the other hand, the problem was approached with delicacy and a humane caution was used in dismissals, incompetent workers were often carried on the project for months, and even for years. In the second place, precisely because the emphasis of the era's in their art programs was different from that of Federal One, competency in the former did not necessarily imply competency in the latter. The era project, indeed, might be transferred, but after transfer it ceased to be the same project; and what were excellent personnel criteria ceased to serve in the new context. Added to this disability was the consciousness of a vested interest in the older project on the part of the era personnel, which sometimes made them reluctant to work along the new lines laid down by the national projects, and uncooperative and sometimes even sullen when pressure from Washington was exerted upon them.

## CLASSIFICATION AND ASSIGNMENT ON FEDERAL ONE

The precise and detailed procedure for the assignment of workers on the projects of Federal One was given in *Supplement No. 1 to Bulletin No. 29:*

> *Assignment of Workers to Projects.* (See Bulletin No. 7, Labor Employment Procedure.) The availability of eligible talent determines what projects can be established, *if any*. In order to determine this, the District Supervisors of Art, Music, Theatre and Writing (or if there be none, the District Supervisor of Projects and Planning) shall, after conference with persons in charge of offices designated by the United States Employment Service, make informal request by letter to that office to have all registered relief persons with necessary talent referred for interview to the person or committee designated to pass on qualifications.
>
> The analysis of the qualifications of the referred personnel should be in the hands of technically qualified people who draw their authority either (1) through the regional director, or the State Director of Art, Music, Theatre or Writing or some other specially designated person, or (2) directly from the appropriate Federal Director. They are responsible for their technical judgment ultimately to such Federal Director. The agent of the Federal Director in a given district may be:

A.  A district official who is recognized (recognition indicated by letter —see next paragraph) as technically qualified. This person may be a District Supervisor of Art, Music, Theatre or Writing.

B.  A designated advisory committee of one or more persons.

C.  An official of the State Works Progress Administration, recognized as technically qualified. This person may be a State Director of Art, Music, Theatre or Writing.

D.  An official of a nearby Works Progress Administration district who has been authorized to give technical advice in other districts in addition to his duties (both technical and administrative) in his own district.

NOTE:  An official here means a supervisory employee whose duties cover activities on more than one work project and who is carried on the administrative payroll.

The authority in a given district for passing upon qualifications of referred persons is granted by the appropriate Federal Project Director, or his representative (i.e., a Regional Director, or a State Director of Art, Music, Theatre or Writing or a specially designated agent) by means of a letter, one copy of which shall go to the District Supervisor of Projects and Planning, and one to the person or committee authorized. The individual or committee so authorized shall determine the classification (professional, skilled, intermediate, or unskilled) of each person to be placed on a work project. This determination of skill automatically fixes the monthly salary of the individual. For salary scale in various parts of the country, see Executive Order No. 7046, dated May 20, 1935. In determination of the classification of each individual, Section 10, Description of Wage Classifications, should serve as a guide.

Persons who do not demonstrate their ability upon examination shall be so advised with the suggestion that they return to the office which referred them and seek reclassification in an allied occupation. In deciding ability, professional background, experience, quality of work performed and present ability to perform work to be assigned should be given major consideration. In considering "writers", the interpretation to be used should not be the narrow technical one, but should include persons of research or academic training and, for the American Guide, persons acceptable as writers to the State Guide Supervisor.[6]

In making the classifications preparatory to assignment, Federal One officials were instructed to follow, so far as possible, the provisions of *Bulletin No. 25, Allocations of Occupations to Wage Classes*. In that bulletin professional and technical classification was thus defined:

Class IV (Professional and Technical)—Professional and technical work requires recognized professional or technical training in a specialized field of employment. It includes professional, scientific, and technical types of employment as well as work of recognized professional grade in the recognized fields of art.[7]

Among the professions classed as skilled (Class III) were editor or

193

checker, senior (research project); musician, junior; and teacher, elementary or junior high. Among professions assigned to Class IV were lawyer, work requiring eligibility to practice; musician, professional; and teacher, senior high school or college.[8]

The description of wage classifications contained in *Supplement No. 1 to Bulletin No. 29* was hardly of the kind to make for precise assignments. The terms were much too general:

> In regard to the determination of wage scales for those who are classified by persons authorized to make assignments, as artists, ac ors, musicians, or writers, the following general principles should be followed:
>
> A.   Professional—Those able to do high grade work *of a creative and/ or interpretive nature.*
>
> B.   Skilled—Those able to do work of recognized merit but of a quality not equivalent to A above.
>
> C.   Intermediate—Those having a limited degree of skill or those who are apprentices.[9]

Instructions were given to follow the provisions of Bulletin No. 25, *Allocation of Occupations to Wage Classes*, but permission was given to depart from this norm and to upgrade occupations when it was to the advantage of Federal One:

> *Description of Wage Classifications.* Insofar as applicable, provisions of Bulletin # 25, Allocation of Occupations to Wage Classes, should be followed in determining the wage scales of persons employed under W.P.A. *Sponsored Federal Project No. 1.* These should be especially followed for occupations found both under the general program and under W.P.A. *Sponsored Federal Project No. 1*, thus avoiding charges of discrimination. However, in cases where an activity under W.P.A. *Sponsored Federal Project No. 1* has the same occupational name as an activity in the general program and yet differs widely from the latter in point of skill and training, a change of wage class for that activity may be made when the particular worker or workers under consideration are duly qualified by experience for the specialized work. Such changes shall be made upon the joint agreement of the person or persons authorized locally to make assignments—(See Section 3— Assignment of Workers to Projects)—and the District Supervisor of Labor Management.[10]

Several items in the above procedures require analysis. In the first place, it is stated in *Supplement No. 1 to Bulletin No. 29* that "the availability of eligible talent determines what projects can be established, *if any.*" This was a salutary caution, but it had meaning only if there existed at the same time a national policy that clearly defined what kinds of projects were desirable. In almost any community *some* type of arts project could be initiated; the question was, what kind of national standard was to prevail as a criterion at the district level. To be sure, the directors of Federal One established, to a degree, national standards that tended to emphasize professional competence. In the beginning, however, when project units were first being established in the localities, the regional, state, and district personnel of Federal One were by no means clear, and certainly not uniform, in their interpretation of national standards. To a certain extent, this was a condition inherent in the process of initiation—the best of projects define themselves in process of development. There was the natural tendency to set up projects wherever possible—a rivalry, so to speak, that expressed itself in computation. But above all, there was the pressure from the high command of the wpa, and even from the White House, to employ as many as possible as quickly as possible. The directors of Federal One, as well as others with a vested interest in this or that aspect of the work-relief program, knew that if they failed to employ their assigned quotas within the designated period, money that was theirs would be transferred to others who could do so. It is fair to say that the principle prevailing in the establishment of project units during the first six months of Federal One's existence was quantitative, not qualitative, and that the project employing the most in the least time best commended itself to the attention of those who decided high policy. This accent upon improvisation, almost as a good in itself, was not conducive to artistic integrity; and the directors of Federal One, although they were the victims of the policy, must be acquitted of responsibility for its formulation. Although they did not sow the wind, they reaped the whirlwind; and on many project units it took time, patience, and a certain hardness of heart to eliminate workers who, if the initial screening had been more careful, would never have been accepted.

The second pertinent observation as to these procedures is that assignment was placed where it properly belonged—at the operational level—and was made the responsibility of technically qualified personnel, who alone were capable of judging artistic talent. A source of friction, however, lay in the fact that the individual or committee empowered to make assignments acted independently of the district supervisor of labor management; consequently, there was little, if any, integration between assignment on Federal One and general assignment at the district level. Indeed, there existed, as it were, a double standard, by virtue of which applicants with the same qualifications received higher occupational rating if assigned to Federal One than if assigned to other work projects. This is manifest in the procedure that permitted upgrading of personnel in Federal One.

Finally, it must be again emphasized that the directions that came from the Washington office with respect to classification did not appreciably assist the local technical committees to make proper assignments. The instruction that "in deciding ability, professional background, experience, quality of work performed, and present ability to perform work to be assigned should be given major consideration" was too general to be of use. This also was true of the definitions of wage classifications contained in Bulletin No. 25 and *Supplement No. 1 to Bulletin No. 29.* Assignment at the operational level, as has been emphasized before, depended almost entirely upon the judgment and concept of purpose of the district supervisors of Federal One and their staffs. The problem, therefore, was the selection of competent supervisory personnel, who would be able to judge the capacity of project workers in relation to the immediate work project unit and in conformity with the purpose and philosophy of the federal directors.

A difficulty that beset the early operation of work project units in the districts was the cumbersome process of referral and assignment through the USES, and then, since the assignment of the USES was not reliable—at least in the higher categories of skill—the reiteration of the process by the district WPA office. Accordingly, on October 20, 1935, Harry Hopkins sent out a telegram substantially changing the assignment procedure.[11] These changes were designed to accelerate the process of assignment. The previous procedure was changed in two particulars: first, the local relief administration assembled the eligible workers at a central place, and the USES personnel were at hand to give identification cards and assignment slips; second, the records work at the place of assembly was made as simple as possible, and as much of it as could be deferred was left to be done later in the USES offices. In effect, this procedure made initial assignment the prerogative of the WPA district office.

A second modification was made on October 30, 1935.[12] On this date Hopkins authorized the WPA regional field representatives to modify the requirement that only persons certified for assignment to work by the USES should be employed on projects. As a result of this privilege, extended to Federal One by the regional field representatives, the officials of Federal One were permitted to place on the project payroll persons not referred to the WPA by the USES. Presumably, such persons registered with the USES after assignment.

The development by which assignment by the USES became a mere formality was not procedurally recognized until February, 1937, when an administrative order made initial assignment the responsibility of the state administrations.[13]

The transfer of the responsibility of assignment from the USES to the WPA, though it moved the process closer to operations, did not entirely solve the problem. At the Senate hearings in February, 1938, Harvey C. Bates, president of the Bricklayers', Masons', and Plasterers' International Union of America, criticized the WPA classification and assignment as making an approach to the problem that did not differ materially from that of the USES:

How is a skilled mechanic who has to be employed on a building project assigned to work under the W.P.A. procedure? The assignment of jobs is done by the Division of Employment of W.P.A. from among workers on relief rolls. A worker certified by the United States Employment Service is referred to the Division of Employment, which furnishes to the Division of Employment his name and relief number. The applicant is then questioned about his experience, training, and ability; and any statement that the applicant may make is accepted for the purposes of his classification. The only test of the worker's continuance on the skilled job to which he is assigned is the judgment of the foreman as to whether or not he is suitably skilled for the purposes of the particular type of work on the project. In many instances the foreman himself may not be a mechanic of sufficient skill to pass valid judgment on the qualifications of mechanics working under him. But even apart from that, high standards of construction performance can hardly be expected under the procedure which relegates to the judgment of the foreman the entire test of the efficiency of the worker's skill and training.

Careful examination of the W.P.A. employment procedure will show that there are no fixed employment requirements with regard to skill on W.P.A. projects. . . .

It is important to know that the individual occupational classification record is the record made by the Division of Employment entirely on the basis of the interview with the applicant, in which he himself states the extent of his skill, ability, training, and experience.

It may be noted that a classification procedure has been established in New York to provide at least some measure of assurance that skilled requirements are met on W.P.A. projects. But even this partial approach to the solution in New York leaves the bulk of the problem untouched there, and leaves the problem wholly unsolved throughout the rest of the country.[14]

What Mr. Bates said with regard to the occupational classes in which he was interested applied equally to the assignment of workers in other categories.

Operating Procedure No. W-1, dated December 14, 1936, established in more detail classification and assignment procedure with respect to Federal One. The pertinent sections of the procedure read:

Section 7. *Approval of Project Personnel.* The State Director of the project is responsible for the approval or disapproval and placement of personnel referred to project units.

The State Director of the Federal Art Project may utilize the services of Advisory Committees to assist him in personnel work.

The State Director of the Federal Theatre Project shall select a classification board (or a person to act as such) to pass on all technical personnel in each community where such personnel are referred to project units. The personnel of the classification board must be approved by the Federal Director or by his representative in the field.

The State Director of the Federal Music Project shall select an audition board to pass on all technical personnel in each community where such personnel are referred to project units. The personnel of the audition board, which should consist of prominent musicians located in the community in which the music project unit operates, must be approved by the Federal Director or a Regional Director.

Section 8. *Duties of Audition and Classification Boards* In addition to the duty of passing on the qualifications of personnel referred to music and theatre project units, as described in section 7, the audition and classification boards shall consult, when deemed advisable, with State and District Divisions of Employment with regard to such matters as classification and rates of pay of musicians and of theatre personnel respectively.

Section 9. *Payment of Audition and Classification Boards* At the option of the Regional Project Director, members of audition and classification boards may be paid not more than $5.00 per session of three hours, and not more than $10.00 for any one day. Pay rolls for these boards are prepared on WPA Form 509 and shall be charged against the project unit or units affected, or against the State Coordinating Project when a new project unit is being established.[15]

The same procedure defined the duties of these boards:

Audition and classification boards or committees, or individuals authorized by the Federal Director concerned, shall have the authority to pass on the qualifications of persons in occupational groups such as actors, musicians, or artists, who are referred to the project units by the State or District Division of Employment or by the local agency designated by the U.S.E.S. Such authorized boards, committees, or individuals shall also make their services available to the State or District Division of Employment on matters such as classification, wage rates, or conditions of employment affecting workers on these projects. Provisions for selection, authorization and payment of these boards, etc. are contained in Operating Procedure No. W-1.[16]

According to these instructions, the use of advisory committees was optional in the Art Project, but the use of classification and audition boards was mandatory in the Theater and Music projects.* The respon-

---

*The Writers' Project is not mentioned in this procedure. At no time, it seems, was a classification board used by that project to assign project personnel.

sibility of the boards was immediate; the responsibility of the state directors was indirect, in that they were responsible for the personnel and performance of the boards. Both the Theater and Music projects lent themselves nicely to the device of tryouts.

THE PROBLEMS OF REASSIGNMENT AND DISMISSAL

The speed with which Federal One was initiated resulted in the employment on the arts projects of many misfits. As time went on and project units took form and moved into operation, the presence of these undesirables became manifest and created a problem that, in many localities, never ceased to plague Federal One. The WPA was not a private enterprise with the single and clear criterion of profit to guide it, and it could not act toward its project personnel with the finality that business sometimes assumes toward its employees. As Harry Hopkins insisted, the project worker and not the project was the primary concern of the agency. Accordingly, the duty of management on the WPA was not to devise the best possible projects but to devise the best projects possible with the available relief personnel. For this reason it was not easy to tell a worker that he did not fit a particular work project, for the worker could reply that the project should be designed to fit him. In the final analysis, of course, the concept was utopian, for only in the perfect state is work so ordered that a perfect relation exists between the capacity of the workers and the needs of the community. In the end the tendency of Federal One was to emphasize the project rather than the project workers and to weed out the least competent in terms of professional standards. This task of continual selection was performed through reassignment and, to a less degree, through dismissal. Classification and audition boards were used not only initially to assign but also, at intervals, to reassign and, upon occasion, to dismiss.*

*It may be argued that the right to work relief did not carry with it the right to work relief on the arts projects; and consequently, dismissal from a particular assignment in the WPA did not involve dismissal from WPA itself. That is true, but the problem was not so simple. Work on Federal One was considered, within the social strata of the WPA, as preferred, and transfer from it to work on another project was reckoned a demotion in wages as well as prestige. For that reason, downgrading within Federal One and dismissal from it were resisted, sometimes in a way that approached violence. The management of Federal One was aware of the eleemosynary nature of the institution, and that consciousness, joined, as it generally was, with natural sympathy toward the problems of the unemployed, prevented them from adopting an attitude that would have improved efficiency but might easily have killed the spirit of the experiment.

199

## THE PROBLEM OF TRAINING AND RETRAINING

So far as possible, the reconciliation of the demands of the project with the capacities of the relief personnel was attempted, not by the straightforward but cold-blooded notice of dismissal, but by the institution of training and retraining on the job. The project personnel on Federal One tended to be either older or younger than the average age of maximum efficiency in their particular callings. If older, they generally needed retraining, both because they had lost something of their aptitude and because methods, to some degree, had changed. If younger, they generally needed training; for as apprentices, they lacked the practical experience that schooling alone cannot give.

In many respects, as will appear in the discussions of the particular projects, the training attempted on Federal One was one of the most valuable contributions of the program to the arts in America. The instruction of music teachers in the techniques of class teaching as opposed to individual teaching and the learning of techniques in the preparation of the Index of American Design were two of many instances in which the work done on Federal One influenced new developments in American art and teaching.

Congress, however, was worried by this development, for it feared that the WPA, by training actors, musicians, and other artists, was adding a burden to an already surfeited labor market. At the Senate hearings in June, 1937, the question of technological unemployment in the theater was discussed, and the following dialogue occurred between the members of the committee and Fred J. Dempsey of the International Alliance of Theatrical Stage Employees:

Senator MC KELLAR. Are many of your folks out of work?

Mr. DEMPSEY. Fifty percent of our organization. I believe that is an absolute fact. I have been in the theatrical business 31 years, and we have probably about a membership of 30,000, and I tell you that 15,000 are not working.

Senator STEIWER. What are the number of unemployed, or rather, what was the number of unemployed at the lowest point of the depression?

Mr. DEMPSEY. At the lowest point of the depression, possibly I would say it went as high as 65 percent.

Senator MC KELLAR. And how much was it in 1929?

Mr. DEMPSEY. One hundred percent employed in 1929. Our legitimate field has gone to smash entirely.

Senator MC KELLAR. Is that due largely to the movies?

Mr. DEMPSEY. Mostly.

Senator MC KELLAR. What is your hope for the future? Is it the thought the Government must provide funds to carry on shows notwithstanding the fact that we all recognize the movies have put the legitimate out of business?[17]

Later in the same conversation the subject is again discussed:

Senator BYRNES. Do you see any hope of this large number securing an opportunity for work?

Mr. DEMPSEY. We can see hope if this project goes through with the appropriation attached to it.

Senator BYRNES. That will help you for a year, but I am looking to the future. Is there any hope unless the Government is going permanently to provide for these shows? How in the world are you going to employ a large number of people heretofore engaged in this business otherwise?

Mr. DEMPSEY. I might add this. How in the name of God are they going to employ people in the textile industry with one man to four looms?

Senator BYRNES. They are employed all over the country and running to capacity.

Mr. DEMPSEY. That may be true to a certain extent, but devices in the theatrical business have not been so systematic.

Senator BYRNES. Do you see any opportunity for the reemployment of a large number of people?

Mr. DEMPSEY. No; I cannot see it.

Senator BYRNES. You do not see it, but you hope it?

Mr. DEMPSEY. I am hoping for the best.

Senator BYRNES. I have great sympathy for you, but I do not see where you are coming out.[18]

At the House hearings in March, 1939, both Mrs. Florence Kerr and Colonel Harrington admitted that the outlook for private employment of musicians and theatrical personnel on the WPA was not encouraging.[19]

The congressmen who raised these questions touched upon—however unconsciously and indirectly—the fundamental problem of the relation between the arts and society. The directors of Federal One, by instituting training and retraining as part of project operation, had in

201

mind primarily the attainment of professional standards by the project personnel. In an oblique way, however, they were expressing an attitude toward art and society that was at variance with the conventional thought of the layman, as revealed in the questions of the congressmen. The latter thought of art as a commodity, which rightly was bought and sold like other commodities; and therefore, they accepted the law of supply and demand as definitive and decisive. The directors of the arts program, on the other hand, considered art as spiritual in essence and therefore, in relation to the human soul, as inexhaustible. Just as the human mind, the more it grows, is the more capable of growth, so the aesthetic experience, far from satisfying the seeker after beauty, creates in him an ever-increasing demand for satisfaction. The discussion of this conflict of attitude, and the application of the problem to the present inquiry, are attempted in a subsequent chapter.

1. Letter A-84, FERA, May 22, 1935.
2. Proceedings, Conference of State Administrators, Works Progress Administration, June 17-19, 1935 (Mayflower Hotel, Washington, D.C.), pp. 48-49.
3. Preliminary Instruction to State Works Progress Administrations. Bulletin No. 7, *Labor Employment Procedure*, June 26, 1935, Section 3.
4. *Ibid.*, Section 7.
5. *Supplement No. 1 to Bulletin No. 29*, WPA-Sponsored Federal Project No. 1, September 30, 1935, Section 3.
6. *Ibid.*
7. Bulletin No. 25, *Allocations of Occupations to Wage Classes*, August 12, 1935, p. 4.
8. *Ibid.*, pp. 9-10.
9. *Supplement No. 1 to Bulletin No. 29*, Section 10.
10. *Ibid.*
11. Night Letter, Hopkins to All Works Progress Administrators, October 20, 1935, WPA Files.
12. Administrative Order No. 29, WPA, October 30, 1935.
13. Administrative Order No. 52, WPA, February 20, 1937.
14. U.S. Congress. Senate. Committee on Appropriations. 75th Cong. 3d Sess. (1937), *Hearings of a Subcommittee . . . on Emergency Relief Appropriation*, pp. 70-71.
15. Operating Procedure No. W-1, WPA, December 14, 1936, Sections 7-9.
16. *Ibid.*, Section 2.
17. U.S. Congress. Senate. Committee on Appropriations. 75th Cong., 1st Sess. (1937), *Hearings of a Subcommittee . . . on Emergency Relief Appropriation*, p. 227.
18. *Ibid.*, p. 228.
19. U.S. Congress. House. Committee on Appropriations. 76th Cong., 1st Sess. (1939), *Hearings of a Subcommittee . . . on Further Additional Relief Appropriation*, p. 162.

# 13

## The President and the Bureau of the Budget

CONGRESSIONAL APPROPRIATIONS

Like all governmental agencies except those corporations for which other provision is made by statute, the Works Progress Administration depended for its existence on congressional appropriations. Its ability to carry on a program of work relief for the needy, and the extent to which it could provide for its clientele, was dependent upon the amount of money, if any, granted to it by Congress. In this ultimate sense Congress was responsible for the inception, continuance, and final liquidation of the program.

The WPA, however, differed from most governmental agencies in that its existence did not derive from a substantive law but from a series of appropriation acts. For this reason the consideration of the WPA's needs came before the appropriation committees of each house and not before permanent or special committees specifically authorized for that purpose. The part of the appropriation committee in each house that conducted the periodic hearings and recommended its findings to the full committee was the subcommittee in charge of deficiency appropriations. Now, it is true that no agency of the government, new or old, can continue its operations unless Congress periodically provides it with funds. In this sense the government itself, and all of its parts, depend upon congressional consent. Nevertheless, a substantive law creates a presumption of permanency that enables an agency to plan its operations over a period longer than that covered by its present appropriation. This sense of security the WPA did not have. It lived from appropriation act to appropriation act and was, so to speak, *in extremis* on the eve of each new act.

This lack of permanence was not due to inadvertence. In the mind of the administration, no less than in congressional thinking, the situation that prompted the creation of the WPA was an emergency. It was hoped in 1935 that the initial appropriation for relief and work relief would provide the impetus to private economic movement that would enable the wheels thereafter to move themselves. That early hope never died, and each succeeding appropriation act was viewed as if it were, or ought to be, the last. In the end, of course, the hope was fulfilled; for the time came when the emergency that created the WPA no longer existed, or rather was subsumed in the higher synthesis of a new emergency—World War II.

## THE PRESIDENT'S RECOMMENDATIONS

The decisions made by the appropriation committees of Congress respecting the amount of money to be appropriated to the WPA were in every case final. In no instance was the sum recommended either increased or decreased by the vote of either house. However, the determination of the amount needed by the WPA was not made by Congress but by the President. In this connection it is necessary to distinguish between constitutional responsibility, which in this instance lay with Congress, and political responsibility, which rested with the President. Congress, to be sure, assumes political responsibility with reference to an appropriation when it chooses to differ substantially with the President's recommendation and writes that difference into an appropriation bill. When, however, Congress substantially accepts the President's budgetary recommendations, then political responsibility rests in the first instance with the administration in office, and only indirectly, and by participation, with Congress. As regards the WPA, it is significant that, of the total amount of money recommended by the President to Congress for the WPA during its lifetime, 97.6 per cent was granted. Without doubt the presidential recommendations were tempered by a nice regard for the attitude of Congress, and especially of the committees on appropriations, which as a whole regarded the WPA as a necessary evil. But, whatever the causes, the fact remains that the political decisions as to the size of the appropriations were made by the President; and in the light of this fact it must be concluded that the amount of money appropriated to the WPA represented substantially the policy of the administration.

The personal role played by the President in the formulation of WPA policy cannot be overemphasized. This role had a statutory basis in that, until the ERA Act of 1938, the money was appropriated directly to the President "to be used in the discretion and under the direction of the President." And throughout the life of the WPA, projects required the personal approval of the President, and money was allocated to them by Presidential Letter. That the President did not consider these obligations an undue burden is amply shown by the personal interest he manifested in every phase of the program and by the personal attention he gave to individual projects and their relation to the general purpose of the agency. This presidential concern for detail pervaded every phase of operations, and not least the arts program. If it may be said that without the enthusiastic support of the President the arts program could not have been initiated, it is no less true that he was not wholly without responsibility for the limitations under which the program operated.

The President, to be sure, did not determine WPA budgetary policy by himself, but in consultation with his advisors. Of these the most important were the administrator of the WPA and the director of the Bureau of the Budget. Both were staff officers of the President, the former to advise him with regard to the needs of the work-relief program, the latter to advise him with reference to the annual budget and the relation of it and its parts to the general state of federal finance. The point of view of each was different. The WPA administrator tended to ask for more, the budget director to argue for less. In the minds of the directors of Federal One, the administrator was the intercessor before the throne; the budget director, the *advocatus diaboli*. In the end, again, the final decision and, with it, the final responsibility rested with the President.

These decisions, of course, were not made *in vacuo* but in relation to the general policy of the government in all its manifestations; and if the WPA administrator could maintain that he knew better the relief needs of the country, the budget director could argue with equal force that he was better aware of the relation of the WPA appropriation to the total annual budget. The final decision represented an adjustment between the WPA's estimate of need and the financial condition of the government as a whole, as seen by the Treasury Department and the Bureau of the Budget. This adjustment was not necessarily a compromise. The President's program of economy was involved, and on more than one occasion he made clear his alertness to the counsels of economic prudence. "The national economy," he said in 1938, "does not today permit the Federal Government to give useful work to all the employable needy unemployed."[1] It was necessary, as he remarked the next year, to keep the program "within the limits of the funds which can reasonably be made available for the purpose."[2] At the very beginning of the program, when the President was asked what factors dictated the appropriation of $4 billion, he replied that these were, first, a desire not to overrun the budget unreasonably and, second, a desire to finance only such projects as could be completed within a year.[3] This solicitude for orthodox finance on the part of the President was not confined to the period of initiation but continued throughout the program. The budgetary confines within which the WPA operated were drawn in the White House.

Although within a narrow margin Congress appropriated what the President requested, it is not so clear that the President always requested what the WPA desired. Here the record is not so candid, for courtesy and usage required that the WPA administrator, once the President had decided upon the amount of the request, defend the presidential decision, both before the congressional committees and in public. The observance of this propriety was not without embarrassment, as when—as sometimes happened—the administrator felt it a duty to defend the presidential request against the arguments of representatives of the unemployed, unions, and other interested groups. Lesser officials did not always feel the constraint that attached to the office of administrator. In January, 1936, a person high in the counsels of the WPA told representatives of the American Association of Social Workers that an appropriation of $4.5 billion should be sought to continue the program. The presidential request was for $1.5 billion. In the Senate hearings of that year, Harry Hopkins, without questioning the President's recommendation, obliquely indicated that the appropriation would provide for 700,000 persons less than the desideratum of $3.5 million.[4] In 1940 at the House hearings Colonel Harrington argued more openly against the presidential request and, in defense of his contention, called the committee's attention to the fact that the business revival, which the President's message had anticipated, had failed to materialize.[5] Howard Hunter was the most forthright of all when in 1941 he stated that the funds recommended would employ only one million of an estimated 2.5 million eligibles.[6] It seems reasonably clear that had the requests of the WPA been followed more closely, the funds recommended by the President to Congress would have been considerably higher.

SUBSTANTIVE PROVISIONS

Although it is against the rules of both houses to insert substantive provisions in an appropriation act, several of the acts affecting the WPA contained such provisions. It was natural that this should happen, for only in the appropriation acts could Congress legislate with respect to the WPA.

The most important substantive clauses, so far as this inquiry is concerned, occurred in the act of 1939. These were:

1.  The abolition of the Theater Project.

2.  The prohibition of any project sponsored solely by the WPA, the effect being to require local sponsorship for the arts program.

3.  The requirement that 25 per cent of total costs be contributed by sponsors.

4.  The requirement that all relief workers who had been continuously employed for more than eighteen months be removed from employment on the WPA. Such workers were eligible for re-employment after the expiration of thirty days only if they were again certified as in need.

5.  The requirement that all receipts and collections, except sponsors' contributions, be covered into the Treasury as miscellaneous receipts. This provision was adopted to stop the practice of the Theater and Music projects to use admission funds to finance certain operating costs.

Although the first, second, and fifth of these provisions were aimed directly at the arts program, the second and third bore more heavily upon it than upon other parts of the WPA program. Indeed, the opinion was current in 1939 that these latter provisions, too, represented an oblique attack upon the arts program. A careful reading of the hearings, however, provides little support for such an interpretation. The committees' conviction that many relief workers were regarding the WPA as a life's career and that the states and localities were not bearing their fair share of the total cost extended to all parts of the program, and did not center on the arts program. Problems of sponsorship, however, and

207

a status of relief personnel peculiar to the arts program made the impact of these provisions more severe in the non-manual categories.

## PRESIDENTIAL ALLOCATIONS

The President's budgetary responsibility began, but did not end, with his recommendation to Congress. In this respect the part that he played in the determination of high policy within the WPA was both personal and immediate. This was particularly true of the arts program, where his interest transcended the formalities. Indeed, it can be said that, in so far as allocations to the arts program were concerned, the President was the administrator of the WPA and the administrator was his deputy.

There was a procedural as well as a personal reason for the President's predominant role. All WPA projects, to be sure, required presidential approval and a Presidential Letter allocating funds before operations could begin. But whereas state, local, and other federal projects were normally proposed by the sponsors, reviewed in the central office, and submitted to the Bureau of the Budget for examination on behalf of the President, in the arts program the project proposals were both initiated and reviewed in the central office. The reason for this was that Federal One, as its official title indicates, was sponsored by the WPA itself. This device was an administrative fiction, for the sponsor was, at the same time, both sponsor and godchild; and the distinction between the two was without any foundation in fact.

Accordingly, project proposals of Federal One were not processed through the Project Control Division but were initiated and elaborated in the Division of Professional and Service Projects, and thence submitted through the administrator directly to the President. Obviously, such proposals involved high policy within the WPA in a manner in which those supported by outside sponsors did not. For this reason the President examined them with more than usual attention. As the program progressed, and Federal One became more and more the object of criticism, the vigilance of the chief executive increased; and in the end, political caution counseled the abandonment of the experiment.

Presidential allocations to Federal One were made *en bloc*, broken down only with reference to the constituent projects—not by states—and designed to cover a variable period that was sometimes six months,

208

sometimes three, and sometimes an even shorter period, especially when there was serious dispute about policy between the administration of Federal One and the White House. Allocations of this kind differed from allocations for construction projects sponsored by localities. These latter, such as for sidewalk construction or repair of sewers, were granted in an amount believed adequate to complete the work. The arts program, however, was continuous by its nature. There was no unit of work whose progress toward completion could be exactly measured. There was no time when it could be said that a theater project unit in Chicago had completed its job, or the New York City WPA Symphony Orchestra had achieved the purpose for which it had been created. Accordingly, Federal One continued to exist not by virtue of an inherent span of life but solely at the pleasure of the President. Indeed, if the WPA was insecure in that it existed only from appropriation act to appropriation act, Federal One was doubly insecure in that it lived only from presidential allocation to presidential allocation. Had funds been allocated to the program on a regular basis, either annually or semiannually, many of the budgetary problems with which the program was beset might have been avoided. At least, the directors of the program would have been able to plan with reasonable confidence and precision. As it was, they never had assurance that their next request for funds would be granted or, if granted, would be in sufficient amount to enable them to continue as before. The conclusion is plausible that this lack of periodicty in allocating to Federal One was a matter of deliberate policy, though in what way it was calculated to further the purposes of the program or to enable the directors of the program to plan rationally is difficult to surmise. It was as though presidential judgment in respect to the program was in a state of permanent suspension.

The procedure by which allocations for Federal One were requested of the President was never routine. Each request was formally presented in writing, but from the very beginning the reasons for it were discussed orally in conference with the President and the administrator. Since these requests were not processed through the WPA Project Control Division and the Bureau of the Budget, copies of all such letters were forwarded to the budget director. The President, in turn, discussed the request with the budget director. These discussions, which were oral, are not a matter of record. Yet in them the thoughts and purposes of the three men most responsible for each decision must have been revealed. Moreover, both before and after the conferences confidential memoranda must have passed back and forth. Presumably, these memoranda rest in the files of the President, the budget director, and WPA administrator, but they have not been available for the present inquiry. Moreover, the part played by Mrs. Roosevelt, if unofficial, was substantial. She often discussed the program and its problems with Mrs. Woodward and Mrs. Kerr, the successive assistant administrators under whose jurisdiction Federal One was placed, and it is commonly believed that on more than one occasion she played the part of intercessor on their behalf. Here the evidence is mainly hearsay. Yet important decisions may have been made over the teacups.

The documentary evidence in the WPA files is the façade behind which are hidden the processes by which decisions were made. Yet, since the decisions at least are a matter of record, the evidence adequately reveals the recurrent budgetary crises that embarrassed the arts program; and reason, even if unaided by documentary evidence, can conjecture the motives that prompted the decisions of the principle actors.

### THE INITIAL ALLOCATIONS

At first the WPA intended to submit the Application for Allotment of Funds (WPA Form No. 307) to cover a period of twelve months. These applications, prepared in July, 1935, envisaged a total employment of 48,425 persons and an expenditure of $53,452,404.75. As finally approved, however, the application was written for six months at an expenditure of $27,315,217. Total employment was estimated at 56,594, at a man-year cost of $978.

Although the President informally approved the project at the close of July and the application was submitted early in August, it was August 29 before formal approval was given. The delay was due to objections raised by the Bureau of the Budget. The acting director, Daniel Bell, questioned first the nationwide allocation, and second, the failure to differentiate in allocation among the four projects.

In a letter addressed to Bell and dated August 10, Jacob Baker argued for the nationwide allocation:

> Because of the fact that the work to be done by eligible persons in the fields of entertainment, music, writing, research (as a basis for such writing), drama and art, is spread all over the nation, and because of the fact that the workers required are in no case residents of the exact places where they will work, and the further fact that they will move from place to place in their

work, it is necessary to set this up on a National, rather than a regional district, or state by state basis.[7]

Baker's contention in this regard finally prevailed. The margin of victory, however, must have been narrow, for on August 25, two days before he approved the nationwide allocations, the President allocated $2,000,000 for the art project on a state-by-state basis.

On the other hand, the Bureau of the Budget was successful in its effort to cause separate allocations to be made for each of the four projects. In support of his plan, Baker had written:

> The reason for putting this in as a single national project without exact differentiation among the several arts is that these professional people, artists and others, frequently function in several fields. To a considerable degree it is intended that they shall function in several fields and it is specifically intended that each one of them shall be given that specific type of work that best fits his skill. . . .
>
> Each of these specifications fits together in units of the project as community interest develops and as we find the most effective use of the people in response to that community interest. For example, writers may write plays to be acted by theatre people with scenery painted by artists and music composed and presented by musicians, all from the relief rolls.[8]

Evidently this argument left both the director of the budget and the President unconvinced, for in the end a separate application was submitted and approved for each of the four projects.

In this initial sparring between Federal One and the Bureau of the Budget, at least the issue was stated even if no decision was indicated. In seeking an allocation undefined as to particular project or state, Baker was arguing for the utmost freedom of budgetary action within Federal One. Bell, on the other hand, was aware, as a result of his training and experience, that budgetary control, which it was his duty to exercise, was in direct relation to detail of apportionment. Accordingly, by requesting detailed designation as to project and state, he sought to limit the discretion of the WPA. There was nothing novel in this argument between a federal agency and the Bureau of the Budget. Every governmental agency seeks budgetary freedom with the same determination with which every budget director endeavors to impose limitations, and equilibrium is achieved only by a nice balance between the two pressures.

On November 15, 1935, the President momentarily shocked Federal One by rescinding $6,700,000 of the sum originally allocated. This rescission was not in the nature of a reprimand but represented an adjustment of funds. Federal One had been unable to move funds into the states and thus to initiate projects as quickly as had been anticipated, and, since the President wished to expedite work-relief employment with the utmost dispatch, the money was transferred to faster-moving projects. In making the rescission, the President indicated that the remaining funds should be adequate to finance Federal One until March 15, 1936.

Authorizations to the states proceeded at a faster pace, and by January 1, 1936, of the $20,615,217 available, $18,268,440 had been authorized. By that time requests for new authorizations were greater than the amount of the unauthorized balance in Federal One accounts. An authorization was simply a permission to obligate funds; it did not connote an expenditure or an obligation. Moreover, these authorizations were in general for a period of six months; and because of the confusion attendant upon the initiation of Federal One and the inability of the federal directors to establish effective local controls at the very beginning, they more often expressed hope that a project would develop than they indicated that a project was in operation. Thus the amounts authorized to the several states in the first six months of operation were subject to considerable variation. Sometimes an authorization to a particular state would be withdrawn entirely and transferred to another state, as when an anticipated project failed to materialize. The fact that nine-tenths of the available funds were authorized on January 1, 1936, did not mean that that money was expended or obligated.

Indeed, it was not until March, as the President had anticipated, that the need for new money became imminent. During that month the finance office of Federal One was occupied in making estimates of need for the remainder of the fiscal year. Here the lack of an adequate reporting and accounting system made prognostication extremely difficult. Moreover, since employment on Federal One was continually increasing, often at an uneven rate, prediction was precarious. As a consequence, five separate estimates were made during the month of March, as follows:

| | |
|---|---|
| March 5 ............... | $3,535,424 |
| March 6 ............... | 3,746,710 |
| March 12 ............. | 3,902,760 |
| March 23 ............. | 5,339,771 |
| March 24 ............. | 4,678,546 |

A Presidential Letter was prepared for signature to the highest of these estimates, that of March 23; but on March 28, although $5,339,771 was indicated as the sum necessary, the finance office expressed its willingness to accept an immediate allocation of $3,500,000. An allocation of this amount was made on April 3, 1936, but the breakdown of the sum among the projects was not the same as that requested by Federal One. The differences were as follows:

|  | REQUESTED | ALLOCATED |
|---|---|---|
| Art | $ 421,669 | $ 450,000 |
| Music | 1,825,236 | 1,700,000 |
| Theater | 1,031,481 | 1,000,000 |
| Writers' | 221,614 | 350,000 |
| Total | $3,500,000 | $3,500,000 |

At this time, Federal One made its second, and last, attempt to secure the money in a lump sum without differentiation among the projects. The try failed.

By June, 1936, these funds were nearing exhaustion, and on June 6 Baker requested an additional allocation as follows:

| Art | $ 163,000 |
|---|---|
| Music | 282,000 |
| Theater | 572,000 |
| Total | $1,017,000 |

The allocation, however, was not made until June 20, and then for approximately half the amount requested, namely:

| Art | $ 93,000 |
|---|---|
| Music | 75,000 |
| Theater | 376,500 |
| Total | $545,500 |

In the meantime the shortage of funds compelled the WPA to discontinue advance payroll encumbrances and to adopt the irregular procedure of encumbering and liquidating simultaneously, i.e., operating on a cash basis. The allocation of June 20 was designed to last two weeks, by which time, it was hoped, the new money from the new appropriation would be available.

When the first allocations were made to Federal One in August, 1935, there was no assurance that the WPA would last beyond the close of the fiscal year 1936. Accordingly, the period that the allocations were designed to cover was fixed at six months, and subsequent allocations for shorter periods were expected to carry the program to the end of June, 1936. These later allocations, as has just been indicated, were made in April and June, 1936.

It became clear, however, long before the end of the fiscal year 1936, that the economic conditions that created the WPA still persisted, and the continuance of the agency was accepted as necessary. The new appropriation was substantially less than the original 1935 appropriation—if calculated for twelve months of full operation—and was approved on June 22, 1935. The administration of the WPA had the choice of prorating this money over a twelve-month period (which would mean a substantial reduction in employment), or of maintaining present employment quotas (which would mean a request, in late winter, for an additional appropriation). The second alternative was chosen.

On this basis Federal One requested an allocation of $12,610,000, apportioned as follows:

| | |
|---|---:|
| Art | $ 1,606,000 |
| Music | 4,512,000 |
| Theater | 3,986,000 |
| Writers' | 1,485,000 |
| H.R.S.* | 1,021,000 |
| Total | $12,610,000 |

This request, which was granted on July 9, 1936, was intended to

*On November 16, 1935, the Historical Records Survey was established as a WPA-sponsored Federal Project under the jurisdiction of the Federal Writers' Project, and on October 15, 1936, it became an independent project within Federal One. *Vide infra*, pp. 761-65.

cover three months of operation, and, presumably, it was hoped that future allocations would be made at quarterly intervals. Expenditures were calculated at the rate of four million dollars a month, the amount that was necessary to employ between 40,000 and 42,000 workers. Since the period of initiation was over and employment on Federal One had become relatively stabilized, regularity was desirable, and with it the maintenance of employment quotas close to the June, 1936, average. On June 30, 1936, employment on Federal One was 44,797, the highest of its history. On July 31, it was 42,716, and did not change drastically during the remaining five months of 1936. Moreover, authorizations to the states were now made on a monthly basis, thus insuring regularity of flow.

Toward the end of September, preparations were made for another request for allocation, since it was seen that funds would be exhausted by October 15. Funds were requested for three months, October, November, December, 1936, as follows:

| | |
|---|---:|
| Art | $ 1,942,000 |
| Music | 4,863,000 |
| Theater | 4,725,000 |
| Writers' | 1,642,000 |
| Total | $13,172,000 |

This request envisaged a 4 per cent increase in expenditures for the second quarter. On October 6, 1936, however, less than two-thirds of this amount was allocated to last for two instead of three months. The allocations were as follows:

| | |
|---|---:|
| Art | $1,113,000 |
| Music | 2,642,000 |
| Theater | 2,697,000 |
| Writers' | 905,000 |
| H.R.S. | 662,000 |
| Total | $8,019,000 |

By November 12, 1936, it was clear that funds would be exhausted about the middle of December. Mrs. Woodward, accordingly, requested funds for two months' operations (December 15, 1936—February 15, 1937) as follows:

| | |
|---|---:|
| Art | $ 810,000 |
| Music | 2,751,000 |
| Theater | 1,974,000 |
| Writers' | 837,000 |
| H.R.S. | 541,000 |
| Total | $6,913,000 |

This request was based on a monthly operating budget of $3.5 million, a reduction of 12.5 per cent. It had now become apparent that the June appropriation would fall far short of the needs of the fiscal year, and preparations were being made to request a supplementary appropriation. In the meantime, it was necessary to exercise caution. Reductions became apparent in December, 1936, when total WPA employment was reduced 11.9 per cent. Federal One, however, was able to secure preferential treatment, and its employment was reduced only 5.4 per cent.

The allocation on December 14, 1936, was for somewhat less than half the amount requested, and designed to last one month (December 15, 1936–January 15, 1937) instead of two months. The allocations were as follows:

| | |
|---|---:|
| Art | $ 365,147 |
| Music | 1,442,293 |
| Theater | 883,633 |
| Writers' | 457,213 |
| H.R.S. | 267,282 |
| Total | $3,415,568 |

Money was being doled out very carefully, for WPA was approaching the bottom of the barrel. New and reduced employment quotas were established on Federal One effective December 15, 1936.[9] At the same time, statewide exemption for non-relief employment was reduced from 25 to 10 per cent.*

On December 22, 1936, it was necessary to ask for funds for the two-week period from January 15, to January 31, 1937. In making this re-

*As early as July, 1936, the non-relief exemption accorded Federal One began to be a matter of concern. Indeed, the exemption was retained from July to December, 1936, only by a series of temporary extension orders. Vide supra, pp. 177-78.

quest, Mrs. Woodward conceded that employment on Federal One was not being reduced at the same rate as on the WPA:

> The present request is predicated on the assumption of reduced employment. Reduced employment quotas were intended to be established as of December 15, 1936. It has, however, been necessary to extend the date for the reduction of employment on these projects and so, you will find that the attached calculations are based upon gradually reduced quotas between the first of December and the fifteenth of January.[10]

The amount requested was granted by the allocation of January 5, 1937, and was as follows:

| | |
|---|---:|
| Art | $ 293,980 |
| Music | 715,381 |
| Theater | 930,793 |
| Writers' | 202,590 |
| H.R.S. | 122,386 |
| Total | $2,265,130 |

This was supplemented by an allocation of $800,000 to the Theater Project (January 28, 1937) and $200,000 to the Art Project (February 4, 1937). On February 9, 1937, Congress granted an additional appropriation of $789 million to the WPA, and the immediate budgetary crisis was over. However, the amount of the appropriation was not sufficient to support operations at the rate of the first six months, and further reductions and economies were foreseen. During this crisis it was necessary to use funds still available from the 1935 appropriation to keep the projects in operation.

In the meantime the finance office of Federal One was preparing its request for an allocation for the three months, February through April, 1937. This request was as follows:

| | |
|---|---:|
| Art | $ 1,792,169 |
| Music | 4,109,745 |
| Theater | 4,075,711 |
| Writers' | 1,324,611 |
| H.R.S. | 829,821 |
| Total | $12,132,057 |

In his memorandum presenting this request to Mrs. Woodward,

Julius Davidson, finance officer of Federal One, wrote: "I do hope that the recent discussion of project costs with Federal Directors will have some effect in the way of a reduction in those costs deemed to be excessive."[11]

The President however refused to allocate funds for three months, and on February 12, 1937, granted but one-fourth of the amount requested for one month's operation. The allocation was:

| | |
|---|---:|
| Art | $ 360,000 |
| Music | 1,350,000 |
| Theater | 600,000 |
| Writers' | 450,000 |
| H.R.S. | 270,000 |
| Total | $3,030,000 |

Davidson's caution about reduced costs might well have been heeded; for although the President at Daniel Bell's suggestion signed the above allocation, the latter's letter to the President protesting against the administration of Federal One was forwarded to Harry Hopkins. Since the letter represents the beginning of a concerted and, except for a brief interval, continuous attack upon Federal One, it deserves quotation in full:

> The attached letter, allocating $3,240,000 for the Federal Art, Music, Theatre, etc. programs for February, has been prepared for your signature at the request of the Works Progress Administration.
>
> Although it is indicated in the fifth column of the attached tabulation that during the period July 1, 1936 to December 31, 1936, almost 75% of the total Federal funds expended on the programs went to persons in need of relief, in many areas a much smaller percentage of the Federal funds expenditures was so used. For instance, only 11.2% of Federal funds expended in the District of Columbia went to those in need of relief. In the Los Angeles area only 59.3% went to relief employees. In Maryland 59.9% went to relief employees. In New Mexico 58.7%, in North Carolina 58.8%, in South Dakota 56.4%, and in Wyoming 59.3% of the Federal expenditures went to these relief employees.
>
> On the other hand, in some areas a substantial part of the Federal expenditures went to relief employees. In Louisiana, Massachusetts, Minnesota, New Jersey, Pennsylvania and Rhode Island, over 80% of the Federal expenditures were so used.
>
> It seems to me that expenditures under these programs might well be substantially curtailed by limiting their operation to those communities where at least 80% of the Federal expenditures will go to persons in need of relief.
>
> A reduction in these expenditures might also be brought about by requiring the submission of a project with a local sponsor for each community.[12]

In this letter Federal One was attacked on two counts: first, that the non-relief expenditures were too high; and second, that it did not confine its operations to those communities in which local sponsorship could be secured.

Hopkins in his reply pointed out to Bell that the use of the District of Columbia as an example of high non-relief costs was unfair, since the national co-ordinating project units of the five projects of Federal One, although their expenses appeared under the District in the Treasury report, were in reality staffed with administrative and supervisory employees of the several nationwide projects. In general, however, Hopkins conceded, at least indirectly, that non-relief expenditures were too high:

> The figures presented in your memorandum are based upon operations through December 31, 1936. The situation will show a decided improvement since December 31, 1936. Attached you will find a copy of wpa General Letter No. 95, dated November 23, 1936, which limits non-certified employment on all wpa-sponsored Federal Projects 1 through 6 to 10%. The January figures reflected the effectiveness of this order. Attached you will also find copy of wpa General Letter 107, dated January 25, 1937, limiting non-labor and superintendence expenditures. The result of this letter will be revealed when the February and March figures are made available.[13]

He also attempted to justify the high non-relief expenditures in the following manner:

> An analysis of persons employed on Federal Projects 1 through 6 clearly indicates very little variation in the average wages paid to certified and non-certified persons, and further, that it is particularly true in connection with Federal Projects 1 through 6 that there is no great difference between certified and non-certified persons in the matter of need.[14]

Hopkins made no reference to the proposition that Federal One should always be locally sponsored.

The fact is that during the first eight months of the fiscal year 1937, at a time when general wpa employment and expenditures were being reduced in conformity with reduced appropriations, Federal One attempted—and succeeded to a considerable degree—to maintain the same rate of expenditures as it enjoyed during the fiscal year 1936, under a larger wpa appropriation. This claim for budgetary preference, and the obvious reluctance of Federal One's officials to conform with the general trend, annoyed Bell and, it must be admitted, caused some anxiety in the White House. Hopkins was aware of this pressure before

November 23, 1936, when General Letter No. 95 was issued. The instructions contained in this letter regarding reduced quotas on Federal One were, if not ignored, at any rate not immediately followed. Indeed, in the second half of this fiscal year, January to June, 1937, while average employment on the WPA as a whole decreased 11.9 per cent, employment on Federal One actually increased 1.1 per cent. When the President forwarded Bell's letter to Hopkins, he was not for the first time acquainting him with the objections of the budget director; rather, he was intimating that he, too, was becoming impatient at Federal One's procrastination. Bell's strictures upon Federal One, though they may have been overdrawn, were not without foundation.

In the same letter in which he answered Bell's complaints, Hopkins requested an allocation of $8,175,000 for two months, March and April, 1937. This request was substantially granted in the allocation of March 8, 1937, to the amount of $8,045,000. This again was on the basis of an average of four million dollars a month.

When in April, 1937, Hopkins requested an additional allocation to carry the program through May and June, he received a letter from the budget director couched in stronger terms. Since this letter indicates the part taken by the President in the negotiations, it is quoted at length:

In accordance with your request, I have recommended that the President approve the allocation of $8,446,333 to your Administration to continue certain nation-wide programs involving the so-called "Federal Projects 1 to 6." The allocation of the funds requested is with the distinct understanding that you personally will look into the matter of revising these programs so that they will meet the President's desires as to the percentage of the Federal funds that will be expended in payments to those certified as in need of relief.

You will recall that in February when you requested an allocation of $3,240,000 to continue these programs through that month, the President referred the letter to you, unsigned, with the indication that the percentage of Federal funds was too low and that projects should be operated only in those communities where at least eighty percent of the Federal expenditures were to go to persons in need of relief. At that time you definitely agreed that the programs would be adjusted to employ the requisite number of relief workers before the March allocation was requested. The President was advised of this agreement on your part. . . .

Before the March allocation was made, your Administration submitted a breakdown of the $655,000,000 which the President had reserved for you from the additional appropriation of $789,000,000. This breakdown indicated that $13,100,000 would be expended on these programs which, I was informed, would carry them through April. No provision was made for the allocation of any funds for them after that month. On this basis I recommended that the President allocate $8,730,000 to complete these programs in accordance with the breakdown of the $655,000,000 approved by Mr. Gill.

Since October 1, 1936 monthly obligations incurred have been as follows:

| October | $4,580,376.57 | January | $4,247,324.35 |
|---------|---------------|---------|---------------|
| November | 4,556,879.05 | February | 3,402,309.39 |
| December | 4,669,400.10 | March | 4,530,454.23 |

From the foregoing table it is indicated that there has been no reduction in expenditure on these projects but, rather, a tendency toward an increase. In March such expenditures were more than in either January or February while for the month ended April 10, 1937, they were, on an obligation basis, $4,607,451.28, or more than in October or November.

I am calling this matter to your personal attention so that these programs may be brought into harmony with the President's previous request.[15]

There are those who think that in this letter Bell was presuming to speak the President's mind; yet, especially in the light of subsequent developments, it is difficult to believe that the points in this communication were raised without the President's knowledge and consent. Indeed, the criticism paralleled that contained in the communication of February 9, 1937, which the President had brought to Hopkins' attention. It was again emphasized that non-relief expenditures were excessive and that programs should be maintained only in those communities in which at least 80 per cent of federal funds were expended for relief wages. Though the question of local sponsorship was not specifically raised, the implication lay between the lines.

Hopkins in his reply, dated May 13, 1936, correctly challenged Bell's use of the Treasury figures. But, more significantly, he conceded the existence of the "President's instructions," and maintained that the program was "now being operated virtually in accordance with the President's instructions." It may be that Daniel Bell provided the fulcrum from which the pressure was exerted, but the pressure itself came from the White House. Hopkins' reply follows:

I have your letter of April 30th, 1937, concerning the allocation of funds for continuing Federally Sponsored wpa Projects 1 through 6, and the President's instructions regarding the operation of these projects.

As I indicated to you in my memorandum of April 28th, I have carried out these instructions to the letter. The number of people working on this program has been reduced by 8,000 during the past seven months. The number of certified relief persons employed on the program has been increased from 81.2% on October 15, to 88.1% on March 15. While the Treasury objective classification for appropriation symbol 265016 only indicates that 77.5% of March expenditures went to relief labors, our records for the actual Federal 1 to 6 program show an expenditure of 79.2% for relief payrolls in the same month. In either case, this ratio has shown a marked increase during the past months and I think it is obvious that, while administrative changes of this nature cannot be made over night, the program is now being operated virtually in accordance with the President's instructions.

With regard to monthly obligations incurred for these projects, I would like to point out again the obvious fact that Treasury accounting figures for any short period are in no way representative of the actual trend of operations on these projects or on any other projects from month to month, and some element of judgment is necessary in the use and interpretation of these figures. With regard to the monthly figures quoted in your letter, they, of course, include not only Federal Projects 1 through 6 but also several miscellaneous nation-wide research projects which have no connection at all with the Federal Arts Programs.

Even though these figures include other expenditures, if you construct simple averages for each of the three-month periods shown, you will note that total obligations during the first three months of this year averaged $540,000 less per month than during the previous quarter.

Two elementary reasons account for the fact that the Treasury records show an increase between February and March. In the first place, funds for the operation of Federal Projects 1 through 5 became depleted in the early part of February, and the allocation of additional funds was delayed so long that it was necessary to discontinue advance payroll encumbrances, and in many areas payrolls were actually suspended. When funds were finally made available, these back payrolls were paid and advance encumbrances restored. As a result the March encumbrance figures reported by the Treasury include liabilities actually incurred in February.

Second, there were twenty-one full working days in February as compared with twenty-five in March. Also, the last day of the Treasury's February accounting period fell on Sunday whereas the end of the March period occurred on Wednesday. This means that in addition to the fact that there was a short work month in February, the accumulated end-of-the-month documents could not be cleared and were recorded in the March figures.[16]

Although the President on April 27, 1937, allocated $7,905,000 for Federal One, $1,875,000 was rescinded by a Presidential Letter dated June 24, 1937. The net allocation, therefore, for May and June was $6,030,000. As a consequence, the monthly average for the allocations for the last five months ($3,420,000) was 12.3 per cent lower than that for the first seven months ($3,900,000). Reduction in allocations, at least, had been achieved.

By the end of the fiscal year 1938, Federal One's claim to budgetary preference had been, in large part, denied. This control, as asserted by the President through the Bureau of the Budget, was reflected in the denial of other claims to preference with respect to operation in the field, which Federal One had been able to assert in the earlier period. On November 23, 1936, the exemption for non-relief personnel was reduced from 25 to 10 per cent, and on February 20, 1937, to 5 per cent.

On the latter date the exemption for non-security workers was reduced from 10 to 5 per cent. To be sure, exceptions to these rulings were, at first, granted rather freely; but on July 12, 1937, the reins were tightened to such a degree that practical conformity of Federal One with the general rules of the WPA was achieved.*

## SENTENCE OF DEATH AND REPRIEVE

But this conformity, both budgetary and regulative, was not enough. Both the President and Congress, especially in view of an apparent revival in business, agreed upon reduced appropriations for the WPA; and in accord with this plan it was decided that for the fiscal year 1938 employment on the WPA, including Federal One, was to be reduced 25 per cent. On Federal One this meant a cut from approximately 37,250 (May, 1937) to 28,500 (July 15, 1937). The request for the allocation for the first six months of the new fiscal year was calculated on the basis of this retrenchment, and amounted to $17,563,228, or a monthly average of $2,927,000.†

The administration of Federal One, therefore, might well have felt at the close of the fiscal year 1937 that, however reluctant and tardy it had shown itself in conforming with the President's expressed desires, its final acceptance of an unprivileged status now assured it of a life of peace thereafter. It was ill prepared, therefore, for the letter the President addressed to Hopkins on July 9, 1937. This communication, which was as abrupt in language as it was final in tone, was in effect a sentence of death upon Federal One. It read:

Your Administration has submitted for my consideration five nationwide programs, aggregating $17,563,228, covering the so-called federal Art, Music, Writers', Drama and Historical Records Projects.

As I do not wish to approve blanket projects for these types of work on a nationwide or statewide basis, I have approved the program for only one-third the amount requested in order to permit the continuation of work under these programs pending the submission of new applications.

*Vide supra, pp. 177-84, for a detailed account of Federal One's loss of these privileges.

†It will be noticed that although the reduction in employment was 23.5 per cent, the reduction in the request for allocation amounted to only 14.4 per cent. The reason for this disparity is that the reduction in personnel was contemplated largely in the lower wage classifications and the lower wage regions. In other words, the reduction, unwanted as it was, was used to raise the average standard of the project personnel, and thus, further to professionalize the program.

I desire to have an application for each type of work in each community only where such projects are justified by existing unemployment conditions.[17]

It is important to observe that the President stated his unwilling-ness to approve these types of projects on a nationwide or *statewide* basis. In this respect, he was prepared in July, 1937, to go further than Congress went in June, 1939, when it returned the arts program to the states. Had the President's decision been final, all arts projects henceforth would have been approved on a *local* basis. Once again, as in the earlier letters of Daniel Bell, the question of non-relief employment looms as decisive, and it is clear that now, whatever may be said of previous pressures, it was the President, not Bell, who had taken the initiative.

The federal directors and their staffs were momentarily demoralized by this decision. They realized only too well that unless the mind of the President could be changed, Federal One was at an end. Accordingly, a letter was hurriedly composed and addressed to the President on July 14, 1937. This letter, since it summarizes the basic arguments for the creation and continuance of Federal One, is quoted in full:

I have received your letter of July 9, 1937 in which you inform me that you do not wish to continue to approve projects for the Federal Art, Music, Writers', Theatre, and Historical Records Programs on a nation-wide basis.

Permit me to state briefly the reasons why those programs should be continued on a nation-wide basis, and why the suggested method of separate allocations by communities would be fatal to the objectives of these programs from the point of view both of artistic achievement and of the relief problem which they present.

Since the Fall of 1935 each of these Federal projects, Art, Music, Writers', Theatre, and Historical Records Survey, has operated as an integrated unit. In each case the project is planned and carried out as a whole, and much of the recognition these programs are receiving today from professional groups and individuals outside the Works Progress Administration is due to the fact that the technical direction, including standards of work, choice of local directors, adherence to policy, etc., has stemmed in a direct line from a central authority in Washington. To give you just one example of how close this contact is between Washington and units in the field, every line of copy produced by the Federal Writers' Project anywhere in the United States is read and edited here under the supervision of Mr. Henry G. Alsberg, Federal Director of this project, before it is released for publication.

Success or failure in solving the very difficult relief problem which the depression has created in the field of the Arts will hang, ultimately, on the ability of these projects to maintain a professional integrity which will command the respect and cooperation of national figures in the world of art, music, theatre, and letters. We have already gone a long way in winning the support of the recognized national associations in the arts, and we could not afford to alienate this support by a change in policy which would invite disorganization of the programs.

Arts projects under state control were attempted prior to 1935. The experiment showed that the results were inevitably disappointing. This is quite understandable if you consider that local administrators scattered throughout the country, however capable in supervising construction and clerical projects, have neither the facilities nor the means to provide themselves with technical advisers of the necessary background and training. For a nation-wide program persons of the calibre of the Federal Directors of these projects can be retained. It was, in fact, because of this previous experience that the present Federal Directors were appointed in 1935 to draw these projects together and raise the quality of their work.

The maintenance of the technical standards which have been set up goes hand in hand with a flexible control over employment and funds. In effect, the very control indicated in the last paragraph of your letter of July 9, is accomplished by this Administration. Units of these projects are established in the states only upon the basis of requests for project approval submitted by State Administrators and closely examined in Washington, before approval is granted, as to technical organization and relief requirements. In the subsequent operation of these projects, no state is permitted to exceed the limitations established on the approved project proposal.

Until the establishment of these projects, millions of Americans had never seen an original painting, witnessed a dramatic performance in the legitimate theatre, or heard any but mechanically reproduced music. Within the past year and a half we have received ample evidence of the creation and steady growth throughout the country of new audiences, which offer the only basis for the future livelihood of these workers, whether in private employment or in a national cultural program. It is not conceivable that a disjointed series of state or local programs, which could not fail to be less professional, could ever accomplish this.

The effect of the control referred to above, already exercised by this Administration, is clearly indicated by the fact that the employment of non-relief workers on these projects has steadily declined from 18.8% last October to 11.8% during May. As a result of recent administrative action this downward trend is expected to continue. I might also point out that a year ago an average of approximately 70% of Federal funds expended on these projects went into wages for certified workers, while our most recent figures show this to be approximately 80% at the present time.

To sum up the above: The successful operation of these projects depends upon a flexible control of technical organization and the shifting, when necessary, of employment quotas and funds from state to state. In the field of the Arts, allocation of funds by states does not imply a closer conformity to the existing unemployment conditions in the various communities. On the contrary, because of constantly changing local conditions, it is essential that this be achieved through nation-wide allocations.[18]

The appendix enclosed with this letter follows:

APPENDIX TO LETTER OF JULY 14, 1937

*TO THE PRESIDENT CONCERNING FEDERAL ARTS PROJECTS*

In my letter I have pointed out the necessity for a flexible control of employment quotas and funds on these projects. I should like to give here a few examples of how this works out in practice.

The Federal Art Project is opening in the South and West a series of community art certers where classes and galleries are maintained. Work done in one state is circulated through others, to their mutual benefit. Plans and funds for this activity, which is receiving enthusiastic local support in every community where it has been undertaken, cannot be determined on the basis of any one state alone.

The Index of American Design, which will present a pictorial record of design in articles in common use in this country from the earliest days, is a single task operating in many states. As the resources of one state in this field are covered, the center of activity shifts to another state.

The Federal Theatre Project is at present working on the problem of touring companies from its best centers through neighboring states, which offer no facilities in this field to their populations. This policy, which the Administration is anxious to see developed, since it is a part of the democratization of cultural opportunities, can only be carried out on the basis of regional groups of states, such as New England, the Northwest, the Southern states, etc.

The Federal Writers' Project is writing the American Guide Series, covering every state in the Union. These volumes are planned to form a unified picture of modern America, and as field work is completed in one state, quota and funds are frequently shifted to another where progress has been less rapid. These transfers of funds, though small, must be made promptly to maintain efficient operation. I have already mentioned in my letter the close editing of these works which is done in Washington.

The problem of the Historical Records Survey is similar. This project is preparing inventories of state, county, and municipal records in every corner of the United States. It is essential that these inventories, which will be placed in the Library of Congress and other libraries for the use of historians, should be compiled and edited on a uniform system throughout the country. As in the case of the Writers' Project funds and quotas are shifted according to the status of the field work.[19]

The length of this letter is enough to reveal the critical situation, for it was an unwritten rule of the WPA that a letter of over one page, single-spaced, should be avoided.

The arguments for Federal One made in the letter were the maintenance of professional standards, flexibility, and effective central control, especially over authorizations of funds to the states. The increase in the ratio of relief expenditures was emphasized by quoting national averages, but the President's contention that each project unit must be locally justified was nowhere answered.

It is significant that Hopkins stressed the recognition that the arts program was receiving from *professional* groups and the necessity of retaining the support of national associations in the arts. Here again the trend toward professionalization is apparent, as opposed to the social-service concept of community regeneration.

The needs for effective central control and for budgetary flexibility were in reality corollaries of the emphasis upon professionalization. National standards, as Hopkins insisted, could not be maintained unless the Washington office controlled authorization of funds to the states, and could increase, decrease, or withhold funds in accordance with the degree of competence that the arts projects in the several states manifested. In short, the criterion of professional standards as employed by Federal One encouraged the flow of funds to metropolitan centers, where they were least needed, and discouraged their flow to the less urban areas, where they were most needed. As a result, Federal One largely lost, if it ever possessed, rural support not only in Congress but also in the country, and that loss spelled its doom. The unexpressed hypothesis of Hopkins' letter, which represented the arguments of the directors of Federal One, was that Federal One existed to serve the art world, not the people. Community art centers, to be sure, represented an exception to this attitude, but they were a late development in the Federal Art Project and represented a by-product of its main emphasis. As for tours in rural areas by companies of the Federal Theater Project, they represented an insignificant portion of the program, both in terms of budget and of personnel. Indeed, it was only as a result of pressure that this project gave serious attention to this aspect of its activity, and then to no avail!*

In the end, conferences were sought with the President and Bell, and the crisis was overcome. The original request was granted by the allocation of August 2, 1937, and no change was made in the organization of Federal One. But if the President's purpose was to frighten Federal One, he eminently succeeded, and thenceforward a chastened attitude toward privilege characterized the direction of the arts program.†

---

*It is not here argued that service to the art world and service to the community at large are in themselves antithetical; without doubt, in a perfect state, the two ideally combine. The question is one of political approach in an imperfect state, and, as has been emphasized before, the artist who chooses to achieve his purpose through the state must act politically, else he perish.

†It was incidental to this crisis that Mrs. Woodward wrote to Mr. Gill complaining about the lack of promptness and periodicity in presidential allocations to Federal One. With considerable justification she wrote: "Allocations in insufficient amounts and repeated delays in making these allocations have caused numerous delayed payrolls and have served materially to hamper the efficient and orderly operations of the various projects. While fully aware of the implications of the President's letter of July 9th, I am hoping that, after the objections to the continuance of these projects as nationwide programs have been overcome, funds for these projects may be allocated more promptly and in larger amounts than heretofore."[20]

In submitting his request for funds for the last six months of the fiscal year, Hopkins in a letter to Bell again took occasion to emphasize Federal One's compliance with the President's wishes; and the cooperative tone of his communication reveals the restraint that now tempered the approach of Federal One to the Bureau of the Budget. The letter read:

> In connection with these applications, I should like to point out that the desire of the President, to approve only those projects in which a substantial portion of Federal funds is to be expended for wages of persons certified as in need, has been particularly stressed by this Administration. Through administrative action and control the percentage of persons certified as in need of relief on these projects has increased from 81.2 percent of the total employed during October, 1936 to 93.2 percent of the total employed during August, 1937. As a result of this increase and also of careful restrictions on expenditures for other than payroll items, the portion of total Federal funds used for the payment of certified persons on these projects has risen from 72 percent during October, 1936 to over 85 percent during August, 1937.
>
> Plans have also been formulated by this Administration to obtain increased sponsorship for the various units of Federal Project Number One. Summer being the dull season for musical and theatrical activities, the carrying out of these plans has necessarily been delayed, but in the next six months we shall be able to secure added local support in the form both of sponsors' contributions and of admissions receipts. The touring of selected units, in order to bring music and drama to communities that lack these cultural advantages, forms, in accordance with the wishes expressed by the President in August, an important part of these plans.[21]

This letter makes it clear that the President approved the August allocation and desisted from his announced intention to defederalize the arts program, on condition that Federal One increase its receipts from sponsors and admission funds. In this connection the President evidently emphasized the encouragement of tours into rural areas. If their purpose was meant to be educational, the stress was well made; but if the President believed, or was led to believe, that the admission funds thence collected would in any significant way lessen the federal cost of the program, he was under a delusion.* As a financial expedient, admission collections were a mirage, as Jacob Baker discovered in 1934 and as the finance office of Federal One realized in 1937. Under these circumstances it is odd that the President should have entertained the idea that touring units could be made self-supporting. It

---

*Vide infra, pp. 278-303, for a discussion of the part played by admission funds in financing the Federal Theater and Music projects.

was not unlikely that he was misled by the genuine but mistaken optimism of the Federal Theater and Music projects personnel, who, as a last resort, grasped at this chance to attain financial respectability for their projects.

## THE FIGHT FOR EQUAL TREATMENT

In submitting the request for $17,199,232 for the second half of the fiscal year 1938, Mrs. Woodward in a letter to Hopkins stressed the reductions already made in the program and expressed the hope that no further reductions would be necessary.

> You will recall that some time prior to the beginning of the present fiscal year I was informed that we must plan a definite reduction in the size of the Nationwide Art Program. I was advised that, although a tentative cut of twenty percent in the cost of the Federal Projects might be accepted as a first step, with further cuts to be contemplated later on, it was far preferable that an immediate cut of twenty-five percent be put into effect on the understanding that no further reduction would be necessary during the balance of the fiscal year. My division acted on the second alternative, and, despite some resistance in the field, a twenty-five percent cut was an accomplished fact by the end of July. In order to carry through these reductions in quota with the least amount of resistance, some commitments had to be made regarding the continuation of newly established quotas for the remainder of the fiscal year, so that further reductions now would be highly embarrassing.[22]

Meanwhile, despite these extenuating circumstances, Bell prepared a recommendation to the President of $16,194,800 for the last six months of the fiscal year 1938. This sum, which was approximately $1,000,000 less than that asked, was allocated by the President on December 10, 1937. Apparently, Bell had reduced the request without consulting the WPA. At any rate, there is no evidence that he sought their advice.

In one sense, this was the cruelest cut of all, for it occurred at a time when national employment was descending into another trough. Moreover, the decrease was definitely aimed at the arts program, and did not affect the rest of the WPA. As a matter of fact, the WPA, succored by a deficiency appropriation of $250 million (approved March 2, 1938), increased its average monthly employment from 1,803,102 in January, 1938, to 2,743,025 in June, 1938, or 52.1 per cent. Within the same interval, Federal One employment increased from 28,029 to 29,636, or only 5.7 per cent. If in the fiscal year 1937 Federal One was fighting to retain its preferential position, in this year (1938) the struggle was for equal treatment.

In the latter part of the fiscal year, Federal One made valiant attempts to secure an additional allocation, but to no avail. On February 28, 1938, Lawrence Morris, Mrs. Woodward's assistant in charge of federal projects, explained the situation and the need in a long memorandum to his superior.[23]

The interesting fact about this letter is that it conceded that Federal One could operate at the current quota practically to the end of the fiscal year. The plea is really for an increased quota to enable the arts projects to increase employment to meet the crisis created by the recession. The request was eminently fair, for Federal One was asking for a percentage of increase much less than that being allowed the WPA as a whole, despite the fact that, at the beginning of the fiscal year 1938, Federal One had decreased employment 25 per cent in accordance with the general policy of the agency

The same emphasis was made by Mrs. Woodward when, on March 3, she forwarded this request to Gill.

> The Federal Arts Projects are now being subjected to the same pressure for increased employment as other projects operated by the Works Progress Administration. If we are not to close our eyes to the needs of the unemployed artists, an increase of 10% of the present quota may be considered only a minimum request.[24]

The request, as forwarded by Aubrey Williams, deputy administrator, to the President, was for $1,369,800, which represented a slight reduction. Williams, though he spoke of a forced reduction in employment of 1,100 persons, placed his major emphasis upon the need of a 10 per cent increase in quota.[25]

The President's reply of March 29, stating his reasons for refusing the above request, is not available. The disappointment in Federal One, however, was so keen that a vigorous letter to the President was drafted for Williams' signature (but never sent), the tone of which was unusual. The first paragraphs of the letter follow:

> Your letter of March 29th, which states the reason for your disapproval of increased allocations to the Federal Arts Projects, has received the most careful study. Please permit me to summarize briefly the reasons that impel me to suggest a reconsideration of your decision.
> These projects now require $375,000 additional to go through the bal-

ance of this fiscal year at the present employment of a little over 28,000 persons, the quota which this administration assured the project workers would be continued for the whole year after they were forced to accept a cut of 25% last July. The failure to receive at least this additional amount of $375,000 will mean further cuts before June 30th, would imply bad faith on the part of this administration, and will have an extremely unfortunate effect upon the morale of all workers on the projects.

The disapproval of an additional $1,000,000 to permit an increase of 10% in employment strikes a note of injustice, because the unemployed have a right to assume that in employing relief persons on projects there will be no discrimination on occupational grounds. The artist has as much a right to a livelihood as the carpenter, the musician as the unskilled laborer.[26]

In the end, discretion prevailed, and Federal One was content to struggle through the rest of the fiscal year 1938 without the additional allocation and, indeed, to finish the year without a reduction in employment. Its resentment, however, over the discrimination that kept its employment practically frozen while employment on WPA as a whole was permitted to increase over 50 per cent was genuine and not without just cause.

### MAN-MONTH COSTS

The pressure applied upon Federal One from 1936 to 1938 by the White House and the Bureau of the Budget was directed against the preferential position that Federal One claimed and enjoyed as a professional program. In particular, the exemptions from the regular rules of the WPA as to non-relief and non-security personnel, and, in 1937, the special consideration given the program's employment quotas, were objects of continuous attack. By the end of the fiscal year 1938 practical conformity in these respects had been imposed. Indeed, in the second half of the fiscal year 1938 positive discrimination was directed against Federal One so far as employment quotas were concerned.

There remained, however, one score on which Federal One was still non-conformist. From the beginning of the WPA, fiscal cost with regard to appropriated federal funds had been reckoned in terms of man-month and man-year costs. The man-month cost of a project was the amount of federal money spent (in both the labor and non-labor categories) to employ one client on work relief for one month. The man-year cost was twelve times the man-month cost. It is clear that, granted the same total expenditures, the lower the man-month cost, the greater the number employed. Since it was the President's desire to employ as many as possible within the limitations of the several appropriations, man-month costs, as a reliable index of the spread of employment, were naturally a matter of concern to him, and watched by him with considerable attention.

The man-month cost on Federal One, as a whole, for the fiscal year 1937, was $99.80. The average wpa man-month cost for the same period was approximately fifty-nine dollars. Thus, Federal One's cost was 69 per cent higher. The cause of the difference was the rate of pay. Of total project personnel on Federal One as of April, 1938, 8.6 per cent were supervisory (non-security); 67.3 per cent belonged to the professional and technical classification, the highest security wage group; 18.7 per cent were rated skilled; and only 5.4 per cent belonged to the intermediate and unskilled groups. Obviously, once it was conceded that actors, artists, musicians, and others were properly classified as professional, no discretion existed within the wpa as to rates of pay. They were mandatory under existing executive orders. It was unfair, therefore, to compare the man-month costs of Federal One with those of the wpa as a whole. The wpa was predominantly an unskilled program, whereas Federal One was predominantly a professional program.

There was another reason why man-month costs on Federal One were high. Employment on the arts program, again because it was a professional program, was concentrated in the metropolitan areas, where in accordance with executive orders higher wages were mandatory.

In the early spring of 1938 pressure was exerted to reduce the man-year costs of the projects under Federal One to not more than $1,000, or a man-month cost of $83.33. This pressure came directly from the Bureau of the Budget, but again the President's hand was seen. At least, he was cognizant of the Bureau's position, and not antagonistic to it. It was immediately recognized in the offices of Federal One that the very existence of the projects was again at stake. The excitement lasted for two months, April and May, 1938, and, though in the end the limitation was not imposed, Federal One was obliged to make certain concessions that reduced the man-month cost in the fiscal year 1939 to $92.06. The finance office of Federal One was especially busy trying to devise ways and means whereby Federal One might be made to conform to the expressed desires of the President. In a memorandum to Aubrey Williams, Mrs. Woodward points out that slightly over two-thirds (67.3%) of the personnel were classified as professional, and then adds:

This is by no means unreasonable for we are either operating professional art programs, or we are operating no art programs worthy of the name. One may arbitrarily say that at least half of the persons now classified as professional should be reduced to skilled. A calculation of the effect from the cost angle alone would show a probable savings of about $2.50 per man-month. Such a saving, while going only a short distance in the direction of saving of $200 per man-year, would at the same time be an act of rank injustice to professional artists, actors, musicians, and writers, and would serve only to demoralize the projects.[27]

At the same time, the finance office of Federal One was instructed to exercise its ingenuity in devising means whereby this reduction in man-month costs might possibly be achieved. A memorandum from Julius Davidson to Lawrence S. Morris indicates some of the steps that were contemplated.[28] Of these, the suggestion that all five projects be combined into one official project and then watered to the extent of some 15,000 to 20,000 additional persons to be employed on the Historical Records Survey is especially interesting. This would have given the administration of Federal One discretion to distribute the allocation as they would see fit. It will be remembered that at the very beginning of Federal One the WPA had attempted without success to persuade the President to allocate the money in this way.

In June the crisis was over. The circumstances of its resolution are not clear, but probably Federal One made certain promises to reduce costs, though not to the extent that the administration had at first demanded. The man-month cost of Federal One in the fiscal year 1938 was $99.36; in the next fiscal year it dropped to $92.06. This decrease was the result of the partial application of some of the devices previously considered. For example, the discretion of state administrators to increase the security wage 10 per cent was made ineffective in many areas, and in some, notably in New York City, modified to 5 per cent. Non-labor costs were reduced, partly because of increased admission collections, but also because of more effective control. Finally, and most important, employment on the Historical Records Survey was increased from 2,987 on June 25, 1938, to 9,309 on November 26 of the same year.

ELECTION YEAR

The collapse of the attempt to make Federal One conform to a man-year cost of not over $1,000 may have been part of a general and

233

remarkable, albeit temporary, change of policy toward Federal One. Suddenly, and apparently without warning, Federal One found itself in favor. On June 10, 1938, the WPA administrator sent the following letter to the President:

> There are being submitted for your consideration through the Bureau of the Budget project applications for five Nation-wide projects under Federal Project Number One to cover operations for a period of eight months, beginning July 1, 1938.
>
> These applications may be briefly summarized as follows:

| PROJECT | EMPLOY-MENT | MAN-YEAR COST | PREVIOUS MAN-YEAR COST | REQUESTED FOR EIGHT MONTHS |
|---|---|---|---|---|
| Federal Art Project | 4,900 | $1,225 | $1,260 | $ 4,001,667 |
| Federal Music Project | 11,500 | 1,135 | 1,152 | 8,701,667 |
| Federal Theater Project | 10,500 | 1,248 | 1,320 | 8,736,000 |
| Federal Writers Project | 4,600 | 1,135 | 1,152 | 3,480,667 |
| Historical Records Survey | 8,100 | 943 | 996 | 5,092,200 |
| Federal Project No. 1 | 39,600 | 1,137 | 1,205 | 30,012,201 |

> You will note from comparisons with previous applications that every effort is being made to conform with requirements recently agreed upon between this Administration and the Bureau of the Budget. The maximum security earnings are set at $100 per month or $1200 per annum, and no project will be operated at a man-year cost in excess of $1250. All five projects will show substantially lower man-year costs as compared with the present operating costs.
>
> I have allowed for a slight expansion in employment on the Art, Music, Theatre, and Writers Projects, which is quite necessary in view of present unemployment conditions. In the case of the Historical Records Survey, I am proposing an increase of about 5,000 persons, because this project is particularly well adapted to pick up the needy white-collar load in the South and West. It is a meritorious project that has received much favorable comment, and it is comparatively low in operating cost.
>
> As funds available from allocations previously made to these projects will have been completely exhausted by June 30, it would be desirable to have additional allocations approved before that time in order to avoid confusion and friction during the transition from the end of the present fiscal year to the beginning of the next.
>
> I look forward to your favorable consideration of these applications.[29]

The increase in employment that this letter requested was by no means "slight." Even if the special plea for the Historical Records Survey is ignored, it amounted to approximately 10,000 persons more than the employment in June, 1938. Between June and November, 1938, Federal One was able to increase its employment from 29,636 to 40,141, or 35.4 per cent. It is true that WPA employment also increased, but in no wise to the same degree. During the same period WPA average employment increased from 2,743,025 (June) to 3,334,594 (November), or 14.3 per cent. It is true, too, that economic conditions continued bad, but pressure for an increase had been just as strong in the latter half of the fiscal year 1938 as it was in the first half of the fiscal year 1939. It is difficult not to conclude that the fact that the congressional elections were scheduled for November, 1938, was persuasive. Indeed, it was in November, 1938, that employment on WPA reached its peak. Certainly, it is remarkable that all pressure from the White House and the Bureau of the Budget was suddenly lifted, and that, in the fiscal year 1939, Federal One was as free from financial worries as previously it had been plagued by them.*

The upward curve of employment on the WPA and Federal One, which reached its peak in November, 1938, began to decline in December, and continued to do so during the remainder of the fiscal year. Federal One's request for an additional allocation in December, 1938, was in conformity with this trend. The amount requested, $17,273,356, was granted without protest or question. The average employment contemplated for these six months was 30,318, but employment never dropped below 32,431 persons.

Only one untoward incident occurred at this time. On all previous occasions when allocations had been made for Federal One, it was allowed to use the unencumbered balances from prior allocations. At this time, however, approval was not given in the form of a supplement to the amount previously approved. Since the sum involved was substantial, $1,700,000, the new administrator, Colonel Francis C. Harrington, wrote to the President on February 4, 1939, as follows:

At this time may I call your attention to a matter involving the financial status of Federal Project Number One which I feel requires correction.

In the applications requesting approval for the operation of this pro-

*It is true that the prospect of the elections, though it may explain the general increase in employment on WPA in the first half of the fiscal year 1939, does not explain—at least, adequately—the special consideration given Federal One, which allowed employment on the arts program to be increased two and a half times as much as employment on the WPA as a whole. The answer to this question, if there is one, does not repose in the files. Perhaps the concentration of Federal One's employment in urban areas, where the greatest voting strength of the Roosevelt administration lay, was taken into consideration. The project workers of Federal One in metropolitan centers were notoriously vocal, especially when they felt themselves neglected, and they might well have raised a noise that, however few made it, would have been heard throughout the land.

gram during the six months' period, January through June 1939, this Administration asked that such approval be given in the form of a supplement to the amount previously approved. It was estimated that the amount requested, $17,273,356 plus the unencumbered balance of approximately $1,700,000 as of December 31, 1938, would be required for the continuation of Federal Project Number One with an employment of 33,500. However, Presidential Letter Number 2655 does not permit the use of the December 31 balance.

I wish again to emphasize that we have just completed a 17 percent reduction on this project in order to bring the quota down to 33,500. If we are to continue to employ this number the use of the unencumbered balance is absolutely necessary. Should this $1,700,000 not be made available, another drastic reduction will be required.[30]

That the failure to include the unencumbered balance was not an oversight is shown by the President's reply:

I have your letter of February 4, 1939 requesting that the unencumbered balance of approximately $1,700,000 of the allotment for Federal Project No. 1 for the first six months of the current fiscal year be continued available for this project during the second half of the fiscal year.

I am willing to approve the use of this unencumbered balance with the understanding that the employment on this project will not at any time hereafter exceed 33,500 persons and that a determined effort be made to effect a substantial reduction in this number prior to the close of the current fiscal year.[31]

The election was over, and with it the belated honeymoon. As a matter of fact, Federal One did not realize how sick it really was, and that preparations were being made for its decent but final interment. In December, 1938, Harry Hopkins had resigned as WPA administrator to become Secretary of Commerce. He was succeeded by Colonel Harrington, who had been assistant administrator of the WPA in charge of the Division of Operations (construction projects). This change at the top was accompanied by other changes in the lower echelons of the Washington staff. In January, 1939, Mrs. Woodward resigned to become a member of the Social Security Board, and was succeeded by Mrs. Florence Kerr, who had been regional director of the Division of Women's and Professional Projects in the Midwest. Before the end of the year four of the five national directors of Federal One (Mr. Cahill of the Arts Project was the only exception) had followed with their resignations. The writing on the wall was visible to all who had eyes to see. The apostolic age was over, and those whose adventurous spirits were unable to endure the monotony of orthodoxy asked permission to withdraw.

CONTROL OF THE BUDGET AND CONTROL OF POLICY

In terms of high policy, "control" is control of the budget. This is true of all organizations and groups, from the imperial power to the humblest family. Planning therefore is fundamentally fiscal planning. The budget *is* the plan expressed in financial terms.

The relation between the plan and the budget may be achieved in one of two ways. In the first case, the plan is logically prior to the budget. The primary concept is that of purpose. The budgets of the armed services in time of war are established in this way. The question is, what budget is necessary so that the enemy will be defeated, not what can be accomplished toward defeating the enemy with a certain limited sum of money.

In the second case, the budget is logically prior to the plan. A plan, to be sure, exists, and indeed is chronologically prior to the budget. But the plan is ultimately defined in terms of the sum of money available for its prosecution. This is the relation between the plan and the budget in times of peace. In the WPA, for instance, the plan was never simply to spend as much money as was necessary to employ all unemployed employables. Such a plan, to be sure, was broached and, for a few months, actually attempted under the CWA. But it would have cost at least three times what the WPA cost, and for that reason was vetoed by the Treasury Department and the administration. The decision to limit WPA employment to those certified as in need was a budgetary decision. The decision to pay security rather than prevailing wages was a budgetary decision. Thus in the last analysis fiscal control of the WPA resided not in the administrator but in the President. The President decided: (1) what appropriation should be requested of Congress; (2) what official projects should be approved for operation; and (3) what sums within the appropriation should be expended upon each official project.

Presidential allocations, therefore, were essentially acts of planning. By deciding how much money to allocate to Federal One, for instance, the President set the boundaries within which Federal One operated and determined to a considerable extent what kind of project Federal One should be. The decision to limit the non-relief exemptions initially granted Federal One was a budgetary decision. The decision to limit the non-security exemptions initially granted Federal One was a budgetary decision. The decision to decrease the man-month cost of Federal One was a budgetary decision. Finally, the several decisions to decrease the amount of funds allocated to Federal One—and, consequently, to reduce employment quotas—were budgetary decisions. All these decisions were made by the President not in an indirect way or in a routine manner but after consultation with the WPA administration, the director of the budget, and other advisers; they represented the considered policy of the national administration.

These budgetary decisions were based upon political considerations. This is said not to condemn but to explain them. The President's responsibility to the American people was political and not, as many within Federal One would have liked to persuade him, artistic. Roosevelt was firmly convinced that, however justified and necessary a work-relief program was, an employment program costing three times as much was beyond the endurance of the national economy. That decision may have been right or wrong; but right or wrong, it was, as it should have been, a political and not an aesthetic decision. Having made it, the President was unwilling to allow one small part of the WPA to be operated as an employment program (which was basically how Federal One wished to operate) while 98 per cent of it was operated as a relief program. There was logic in this contention—and justice, too. If artists could rightly protest that in the establishment of a relief program they should not be the object of discrimination, other workers on the WPA, who formed the large majority of project employees, could equally well protest that in the operation of the relief program artists should not be the recipients of special privilege.

The fact is that many, not only of the personnel of Federal One but also within the high command of the WPA, misread the President's mind. His genuine interest in the arts as an agency of democratic education, which prompted him to encourage the initiation of the program, and his sincere sympathy with the liberal point of view, which made him tolerant of indiscretions that would have tried a less patient man, were interpreted as invitations to engage the federal government in a program that would permanently subsidize professional artists.

The President was as politically wise as his critics were artistically sincere. He saw what they did not see—that public opinion in America would not tolerate an ambitious art program, unconnected with relief, on the part of the federal government. For that reason his admonitions, which, half hidden from the eye, appear here and there in his communications on the subject, were directed toward an emphasis on rural

America and the elaboration of an arts program that would temper its mind to the honest, if untutored, sense of beauty of the common man. He saw, as the *cognoscenti* did not see, that seed planted in the countryside would find deeper root and fuller flower, for those who would bide their time, than that dropped in the garden closes of Greenwich Village.

1. As quoted in the *New York Times*, March 12, 1938.
2. As quoted in the *New York Times*, April 28, 1939.
3. *New York Times*, June 15, 1935.
4. U.S. Congress. Senate. Committee on Appropriations. 74th Cong. 2d sess. (1936), *Hearings of a Subcommittee . . . on First Deficiency Appropriations Bill*, p. 31.
5. U.S. Congress. House. Committee on Appropriations. 76th Cong., 3d sess. (fiscal year 1941), *Hearings of a Subcommittee . . . on Work Relief and Relief*, pp. 401-2.
6. U.S. Congress. House. Committee on Appropriations. 77th Cong. 1st sess. (fiscal year 1942), *Hearings of a Subcommittee . . . on Work Relief and Relief*, pp. 112-13.
7. Letter, Baker to Bell, August 10, 1935, WPA Files.
8. Letter, Baker to Pressman, WPA Files.
9. General Letter No. 95, WPA, November 23, 1936.
10. Memorandum, Woodward to Gill, December 22, 1936, WPA Files.
11. Memorandum, Davidson to Woodward, January 19, 1937, WPA Files.
12. Letter, Bell to the President, February 9, 1937, WPA Files.
13. Letter Hopkins to Bell, March 3, 1937, WPA Files.
14. *Ibid.*
15. Letter, Bell to Hopkins, April 30, 1937, WPA Files.
16. Letter, Hopkins to Bell, May 13, 1937, WPA Files.
17. Letter, the President to Hopkins, July 9, 1937, WPA Files.
18. Letter, Hopkins to the President, July 14, 1937, WPA Files.
19. *Ibid.*
20. Memorandum, Woodward to Gill, July 16, 1937, WPA Files.
21. Letter, Hopkins to Bell, October 28, 1937, WPA Files.
22. Memorandum, Woodward to Hopkins, November 4, 1937, WPA Files.
23. Memorandum, Morris to Woodward, February 28, 1938, WPA Files.
24. Memorandum, Woodward to Gill, March 3, 1938, WPA Files.
25. Letter, Williams to the President, March 18, 1938, WPA Files.
26. Draft, Aubrey Williams to the President, WPA Files.
27. Memorandum, Woodward to Aubrey Williams, April 11, 1938, WPA Files.
28. Memorandum, Davidson to Morris, April 21, 1938, WPA Files.
29. Memorandum, Woodward to Hopkins, April 27, 1938, WPA Files.
30. Letter, Harrington to the President, February 4, 1939, WPA Files.
31. Letter, the President to Harrington, February 16, 1939, WPA Files.

# 14

## Financial Control of Operations

### GOVERNMENT AGENCIES AND FINANCIAL CONTROLS

In government agencies finance plays a dual role. In the first place, as indicated in the previous chapter, it is an instrument of high policy. Congress, the President (acting through the Bureau of the Budget), and to a certain degree the head of the agency design by appropriations, allocations, limitations, and restrictions the budgetary pattern that gives purpose to the agency and, within broad limits, defines its policy. In the case of the arts program of the WPA, it was the President who by the device of allocations played the pilot; and if he did not steer the ship, at least he indicated to the helmsman the general direction of its movement.

But there was an area of discretion within which the agency itself— and in particular, the finance office of Federal One—was free to establish subsidiary controls. This type of control may be called control of operations, to distinguish it from control of policy as exercised at the highest level. In essence it is a service function whereby the agency, through financial procedures, a system of reports, and field inspections, assures itself that its financial responsibilities are being met in accordance with rules and regulations. It usually is best and most economically undertaken at the operational level (in the WPA, at the district office) and best checked at the nearest superior echelon (in the WPA, at the state office). The responsibility of the Washington office ceases when it has established uniform procedures and elaborated a system of reports and field inspections sufficient to secure conformity with general policy. Financial control of this sort involves routine details of accounting, obligating, disbursing, etc., which, if attempted at a high level, deflect the central office from its primary responsibility as to national policy.

## THE TREASURY DEPARTMENT AND THE WPA

In Executive Order No. 7034, promulgated on May 6, 1935, the President made the Treasury Department, through the Office of the Commissioner of Accounts and Deposits, responsible for accounting and disbursement, and, through the Procurement Division, for procurement, in connection with the operations of the WPA. Later, when appropriations were made to the Works Progress Administration and not directly to the President, the several ERA Acts made statutory provision for the continuance of these functions in the Treasury Department. The Treasuary Department was naturally ambitious to demonstrate its ability to undertake this huge responsibility, and the President, on his part, was solicitous that a system of accounts be maintained that would enable him to exercise executive control and provide him with complete current financial information.

As a result of the uniform disbursement system, established in 1933, the Treasury had already set up disbursing offices in the field. In 1935, however, since there existed no accounting or procurement offices outside Washington, it was necessary for the Treasury Department to establish such offices in the field. Accordingly, using the state pattern of the WPA, it set up these offices in each of the states. The department, however, was reluctant to decentralize below the state level. For this reason, since the district office, and not the state office, of the WPA was at the level of operations, the Treasury Department's accounts were not a satisfactory agency of control so far as the WPA's operations were concerned. Obviously, it was necessary for the district manager to know, or to be able to find out immediately, the financial status of projects operating within his district. To obtain a statement from the state office of the Treasury Department usually took time, and when it arrived, it was obsolete. Even if it could be obtained immediately, it did not reflect current operations, for the flow of financial reports from the districts to the state offices of the Treasury Department also took time. Treasury accounting, however helpful it might be as a source of periodic reports to the President and as a check upon financial irregularities, did not serve as a device to control project operations. For this reason it was useless so far as the Works Progress Administration was concerned.*

## THE FINANCE ORGANIZATION OF THE WPA

For its own purposes, therefore, the WPA established its own Division of Finance, the organization of which paralleled that of the WPA as a whole and extended, through the regions and the states, from the national to the district level. To a considerable degree the WPA Division of Finance duplicated the work of the Treasury Department. Its purpose, however, was different; whereas the Treasury Department provided that over-all control that the President deemed salutary, the WPA office of finance, projecting itself into the district offices, where no Treasury branch existed, provided at the lowest level those controls without which project operation might have become fiscally irresponsible.

The WPA finance officers were staff officers serving the several echelons of command. At the top was the WPA director of finance in the Washington office, who headed the Division of Finance—one of the divisions under the assistant administrator in charge of finance, research, and statistics. In each regional office was a chief regional examiner, who was technically responsible to the director of finance in Washington but administratively responsible to the regional director. In each state there was a state director of finance, technically responsible to the chief examiner but administratively responsible to the state administrator; in each district office, a district supervisor of finance, technically responsible to the state director of finance but administratively responsible to the district director. These finance officers were not to engage in project operations but to control them through the imposition of uniform procedures and by providing advice and technical assistance to their respective line officers.

## THE FLOW OF FUNDS FROM THE
## PRESIDENT TO THE PROJECT

By a Presidential Letter of allocation, as already has been indicated, the President moved funds from his jurisdiction to that of the Works

*This account of the relation between the Treasury Department and the WPA is indebted to Macmahon, Millett, and Ogden, op. cit., pp. 359-64.

Progress Administration. The allocation was to a specific project, which might be a local, state, or federal project. The Presidential Letter was addressed to the Secretary of the Treasury, and directed that funds be transferred from the appropriation to the Works Progress Administration for the purpose indicated. Upon receipt of the Presidential Letter an Advice of Allocation (Treasury Form A-1) was prepared in the office of the Commissioner of Accounts and Deposits and addressed to the Works Progress Administrator. This was a certification that the President had made the allocation indicated for the official project or projects enumerated.

Authority over the funds now rested with the administrator, who proceeded to prepare and issue the Advice of Project Authorization (Treasury Form A-2), which was addressed to the Commission of Accounts and Deposits, U.S. Treasury Department, and certified that of the amount allocated, a certain sum was made available for allotment by the state administrator. The state administrator, informed of this authorization, was now entitled to prepare the Advice of Allotment (Treasury Form A-3), which was addressed to the project manager of the individual work project and authorized him to secure supplies, services, or both within the limitations indicated for the purposes shown. The Advice of Allotment was the final step by which money was made available within a district for actual operation. The district office now set up a Project Register (WPA Form 704).

If the project concerned was a local project, the presidential allocation was definitive. If, for instance, the President approved allocation for a paving project in Franklin County, Ohio, then the nature of the project and the amount to be spent upon it was not within the discretion of the WPA administrator, the state administrator, or the district manager. The authorization to the state and the allotment to the district were automatic. In this case, control of policy rested with the President; control of project operations, in the district.*

If the President approved an allocation for a statewide official project, then, though the authorization to the state was not within the discretion of the federal administrator, the state administrator could exercise discretion in allotting funds to districts within the state. If, for

---

*It is to be noted, although the question does not materially affect the present analysis, that, after the early period of initiation, pools of projects were established in each state from which the state administrator was free to choose what projects he wished at the moment to set in operation. He was also entitled to decide whether an official project, state or local, should be operated as one work project unit or broken down into two or more such units.

instance, the President approved a statewide official project for recreational activities within the state of Michigan, the state WPA administrator in Michigan was free to allot the authorized funds among the districts in Michigan as he thought proper. In this case, control of policy within the state rested with the state administrator; control of project operations, however, again resided in the district.

If, however, the President approved an allocation for a federal project (i.e., a nationwide project sponsored by the Works Progress Administration), the authorizations to the states rested within the discretion of the federal administrator. The presidential allocation was in the form of a lump sum—so much, for instance, for the Federal Music Project. How much, if any, of this money should be authorized to each state was decided by the federal administrator. In this case control of policy within the nation rested with the federal administrator; control of project operations, however, resided at the district level.*

It was precisely in this control of authorizations at the national level that the power of the federal directors of the arts program lay. The advices of authorizations, to be sure, were issued over the signature of the federal administrator. Obviously, however, Hopkins did not himself determine the states to receive funds or the amounts to be authorized to each in the arts program. He acted on the advice and recommendation of the federal directors. In this wise, the federal directors actually, though not formally, controlled the flow of money from the national office to the states and thus, in effect, exercised the substance of line authority.† So long as the Washington office retained this authority, the federal directors were, to a degree, sovereign. To be sure, early in 1936 Federal One was forced to surrender control of personnel and project operations within the states and districts; the degree, however, to which they were able, through the exercise of this fiscal control, to influence and indirectly to supervise personnel and project operations within the states and districts was remarkable. The retention of this fiscal control when all other controls were lost served to distinguish Federal One from all other WPA projects, and it was the removal of this control by the ERA Act of 1939 that broke the back of Federal One.

*Vide supra, pp. 134-45, for an account of the unsuccessful attempt of Federal One, at the start of the program, to establish control of project operations at the regional and federal levels instead of at the district level.

†Vide supra, pp. 145-56, for instances in which recalcitrant state administrators who were unsympathetic with the arts program were threatened with a withholding of funds for these projects.

## THE BUDGET AND PROJECT PROPOSALS

There was one other important difference between official state or local projects and a WPA-sponsored federal project. Official state and local projects, for which authorizations were received by the state administrator, were initiated in the states or localities in the form of project proposals (WPA Form 301), which were prepared by the official sponsor. These forms contained an estimate of the amount of federal money needed to complete the job, and the presidential allocation was made in conformity with this application, though not necessarily for the exact amount estimated. Thus the authorizations were in reality answers to applications from the states and localities. Moreover, all local project proposals required the approval of the state administrator before they were forwarded to Washington for further consideration. Thus indirectly, but effectively, the state administrator controlled the kind and number of projects operating in his state through his control of project proposals. In this sense he controlled his operating budget.

In Federal One, on the other hand, work projects—or more properly, project units—were not initiated at the state or local level. The official project was initiated by the Works Progress Administration, which was the official sponsor. The work units, which did not need sponsorship, were initiated by the Request for Project Approval (WPA Form 320), which was filled out by the official representative of the federal director. This form was addressed to the federal director and subject to his approval. When approval was obtained from the federal director, the regional or state director of the program requested the state administrator, by sending him a signed copy of WPA Form 320, to issue an Advice of Allotment (Treasury Form A-3), which authorized a district to incur expenditures for the particular project. This Advice of Allotment was accompanied by the Statement of Allotment Detail for Work Project (WPA Form 701). The state administrator, upon receipt of this request, issued the Advice of Allotment, which enabled the district office to start operations.

In order to enable him to make these allotments to project units, the state administrator received from the federal administrator the Advice of Authorization. This Advice of Authorization, however, was written on the basis of the official project and for statewide operation. Ideally, it should have been for an amount that was the sum of the estimated costs indicated in all project proposals in the state. Actually, however, since the project units could not be put into operation until funds were made available, the Advice of Authorization in the first year of operation preceded the approval of project proposals. The cause of this was the need for speed in initiating work relief. The Advice of Authorization was for an amount that, it was estimated, might be spent within the state on the project; it was not based on actual employment figures or project proposals. Thus in the early days great differences might and did exist between the amount authorized and the sum of the estimated costs in the project proposals at any given time. In general, the authorization was intended to cover all possible project proposals that might be initiated within a state. As a consequence of this confusion, which was perhaps inevitable in a novel and unprecedented program, there was much shifting of funds back and forth between states, until the status of the project in each state became more clearly defined. In some cases authorizations were made in states, and no project proposals approved. In such instances the authorizations were withdrawn.* In other cases original authorizations were found inadequate, whereupon an additional authorization was released by the issuance of the Advice of Change in Project Authorization.

THE FINANCE OFFICE OF FEDERAL ONE

The problem of financial management in Federal One, therefore, was to correlate the authorizations to the states—which were made on a statewide basis and not broken down with reference to project units—with the project proposals, which at first were initiated on a district or local basis. Unless methods could be devised whereby the authorizations to the states would reflect the sum of project proposals within the state, Federal One could exercise no control over the operation of project units.

This was the responsibility of the finance office of Federal One.† Indeed, finance played a distinctive and vital role in the operation of Federal One. In normal government operation, finance is merely a service function, since it is concerned generally with accounting for a spe-

---

*Rescission of authorization, in whole or in part, was accomplished by issuance of Treasury Form A-2a, Advice of Change in Project Authorization.

†The finance office of Federal One existed in Washington alone. In the regions, states, and districts it operated through the regular WPA division of finance, research, and statistics.

246

cific appropriation. In the case of Federal One, however, the importance of finance lay partly in the many discretionary factors involved and partly in the use of financial mechanisms as instrumentalities of control. It became necessary, therefore, at the very beginning of the arts program to assign specific responsibility for financial control. The first person appointed to exercise this responsibility was Solomon D. Ozer. Mr. Ozer was not new to the relief program. He had had considerable experience under the FERA, first in Texas and later in the central office. He came to the arts program from the statistical office, where he had served under Emerson Ross, and brought with him as his assistant, from the same office, Robert Asher. Ozer and Asher spent approximately one year in setting up the finance office of Federal One. In the summer of 1936 Ozer was succeeded by Julius Davidson, who came to the arts program from the field, where he had served as regional examiner attached to the Chicago regional office. The functions of a regional examiner were limited entirely to finance matters because he was responsible only for supervising general WPA finance operations of state and district offices. Although the work of a regional examiner was only remotely related to the duties of a finance officer for the arts program, the connection in this instance was quite important because of the close relationship between the financial operations of Federal One and the responsibilities of the WPA director of finance. Without the co-operation of the WPA director of finance, David Holmes, it would have been practically impossible to overcome many of the obstacles that arose almost daily.

Although Ozer was generally responsible for financial and related controls, his functions were not as clearly defined as those of his successor. As is to be expected in the early operation of a novel program, everyone tended to do everything. Ozer, therefore, found himself involved in preparation of personal instructions, in the approval of project units, in the recommendation of employment quotas, in the authorization of funds, in the attempt to exercise the crude accounting controls that were the only ones available at the time, in program planning, and even in participating in high policy and sitting in council with Jacob Baker, Bruce McClure, the federal directors, and other officials responsible for the initiation of Federal One. Julius Davidson, who succeeded Ozer, served as finance officer of Federal One from the summer of 1936 until its closing on September 30, 1939.*

---

*Even after the end of Federal One, Davidson continued to be concerned with residual problems of the program until he left the agency in December, 1941.

The responsibilities of the finance office of Federal One, as they finally evolved, may be briefly described as (1) the acquisition and use of funds for operation of the program and (2) the establishment of procedures under which such funds were expended. Specifically, the finance office was responsible for the preparation of letters to the President requesting and justifying allocations; the approval of project proposals submitted from the states; the approval of specific limitations of expenditures of funds within the states; the authorization of funds for approved expenditures; the authorization of employment quotas; the accounting for funds expended; and the preparation of reports on funds approved, funds expended, project employment, and related matters.

In addition to appropriated funds, the arts program was authorized to collect admission funds in the case of the Music and Theater projects, and sponsors' funds, either in cash or in kind, in the case of all five projects. Controls had to be exercised on the acquisition and use of these moneys as well as of appropriated funds.

Obviously, it was necessary to elaborate a relatively complex machinery of control in accordance with approved governmental procedures. The specific means of control were based only in part on formal instructional materials. Many of the controls were exercised through various channels of communication, by correspondence, telephone, and telegraph. In addition, Davidson spent a considerable amount of time in the field in personal supervision and consultation with state and regional WPA officials and with state arts program officials. These field visits were, more often than not, specific missions of an emergency nature. It was natural, especially in the period of initiation, that not only officials of Federal One but also the general personnel of the WPA should require advice and counsel in the fiscal management of a program for which no precedents existed.

The organizational pattern into which the finance office fitted was simple enough. The finance officer of Federal One was administratively responsible to Mrs. Woodward (later, to Mrs. Kerr), assistant administrator in charge of women's and professional projects. This responsibility, however, was exercised indirectly through the intervention of Lawrence S. Morris, Mrs. Woodward's executive assistant for the management of federal projects, including Federal One. On the other hand, since it was necessary to maintain liaison with the WPA Division of Finance and to act in accordance with its general procedures, Davidson was technically responsible to David Holmes.*

---

*In view of the amount of detail as well as complexities of its work, the finance

Since in the first year of operation authorizations were not based on project proposals, it is apparent that the central finance office of Federal One exercised no control within the states. An enthusiastic regional or state director might present for approval projects the cost of which might exceed the state's authorization. Then it was necessary for the central office either to increase the authorization or to deny the applications.

The situation this created is exemplified in a memorandum from Frank Y. Cogan to Solomon Ozer, dated January 9, 1936. It reads in part:

> There have been so many extraordinary requests for additional authorizations to the various states under the program of Federal Project No. 1, that we have decided to gather as much basic data as we have conveniently available for the purpose of checking as to whether:
>
> 1. Authorizations to states are sufficient to meet existing needs.
>
> 2. Additional requests for authorizations for some states are not excessive when contemplated with a view of the operation of the entire program.
>
> 3. The proposed coordinating projects may be financed out of available funds without unnecessary disturbance of authorizations of funds already allocated to the states.
>
> You will appreciate, out of your extensive knowledge of the situation, that these figures are in some cases tentative only and that figures on amounts obligated by projects already registered with Business Analyses Section are subject to considerable variation, either above or below the figure given.[1]

From the tables supplied with this memorandum it appears that funds authorized to December 31, 1935, plus authorizations requested between January 1 and January 9, 1936, amounted to $21,523,616, or $908,399 more than total presidental allocations ($20,615,217).

It also appears that the total obligated by registered projects (the sum of all estimated costs appearing in approved project proposals) was $20,233,605, or $1,965,165 more than total authorizations ($18,268,440).

Cogan's memorandum was obviously a first attempt to co-ordinate authorizations with project proposals.

office of Federal One consisted of a small staff. During the last two years of operation there were, in addition to Davidson, a secretary, a statistical clerk, and a typist.

On March 5, 1936, when it became clear that an additional allocation was necessary if the program was to continue until the end of the fiscal year, Ozer, at Baker's suggestion, prepared an estimate of need. In his memorandum Ozer wrote, "We arrived at our man-month cost by dividing January employment into January voucher payments."[2] Man-month costs were then multiplied by anticipated employment to give total monthly costs. This last figure was multiplied by five, the number of months for which the estimate was made (February to June, inclusive, 1936). By this calculation Ozer arrived at an estimated need of $3,535,424.

But within a day, he discovered a miscalculation and explained the error in a memorandum to Whiting:

> Since the figures submitted by the Treasury [voucher payments] really cover not obligations incurred during the month of January, but obligations incurred during the last of December, and do not include the obligations incurred during the last of January, the result of dividing January employment into reports of the Treasury for January was a too low man-month cost, since employment on our Program during this time was rising very rapidly. [3]

The new estimate was for $3,746,710.

Finally, on March 12, a second revision was submitted. In his memorandum Ozer remarked:

> You will note that the major changes in this second revision are caused by an unexpected and sudden increase in the most expensive program which we have—namely, the Theatre Program. In the week and a half prior to the issuance of the order stopping further employment,* this Program increased nearly 1,400.[4]

This second revision called for an allocation of $3,902,760.

When, however, on March 23, 1936, a Presidential Letter was prepared for the President's signature, the amount requested had been still further increased to $5,339,771.

These memorandums indicate the difficulties encountered by the finance office of Federal One in calculating needs in the first year of the program.

Other passages of Ozer's memorandum of March 6, 1936, indicate that perhaps as early as this, the relatively high cost of the arts program was under criticism. In this connection Ozer wrote:

*Telegram Serial No. 60, March 5, 1936.

250

May I call your attention to the fact that this is a highly professional program, and, still further, is concentrated in the large centers of the highest cost zones, New York, for instance, paying professional persons $103 for labor alone. The two most costly parts of the Program are Art and Theatre, which have an unusually high number of [their] personnel in New York City, and practically all the remainder in Zone I, where the labor cost for professional persons is $94. Experience has shown us that in addition to labor costs we must calculate at least 10% for "other than labor." The Music Program, since it has somewhat wider coverage than the others, costs a little less, though it, too, is concentrated in the large centers. Of late, union activity has been forcing an increasing number of people in the field of music into the professional classification. In New York, for instance, we have been forced to accept practically all as professional. The Writers' Program is somewhat less costly, since it has much wider coverage than any of the others.[5]

Among the "other than labor" costs anticipated were traveling expense for touring companies:

Mr. Hopkins has made special requests of the Music and Theatre people, that they travel their companies, in order to educate the people in the more sparsely settled areas. Since it is figured that $3 per diem will be necessary per person on traveling companies, in addition to transportation and other costs, the Federal Directors feel that the estimates here submitted will not be excessive.[6]

It is evident that for purposes of control the finance office lacked: (1) a system of official project fiscal limitations, set up by state, by program, and for a stated period; and (2) a system of financial reports of obligations incurred against these limitations. In the absence of such procedures the finance office was powerless, for funds were authorized in the dark; and as requests came in from the states for additional funds, there was no basis upon which such requests could be denied, at least until the total amount allocated had been authorized. The authorizations themselves were not limitations in any effective sense, for, as the states requested more funds, the authorizations were increased and the prior limitation was removed. In effect, this meant the adjustment of the limitations to what the regional and state directors believed to be their need. In short, the amount authorized to the states at any particular time was not calculated by the finance office on the basis of a comprehensive view of the nationwide needs of the program but simply upon the requests received, one by one, from the states.

It might be thought that if the central finance office was unable to exercise nationwide controls, at least the state WPA finance offices could have exercised statewide controls. To a degree this was true, for money could not be expended within the state beyond the amount of authorization. It was necessary, therefore, that the state finance offices keep accounts adequate to preclude the possibility of incurring illegal obligations. But this was in the nature of merely routine accounting. The same lack of sound procedures that prevented the central finance office from establishing effective nationwide control also hamstrung the state finance offices in the elaboration of effective statewide controls. In theory, to be sure, authorizations were for a six months' period, but in practice a project unit might spend its allotment at a greater or lesser rate, depending upon local circumstances. As a consequence, some project units consumed their funds before the period ended; others were laggard. It depended largely upon the initiative of the state director and the local supervisors. When funds became scarce in a state, the state simply requested an additional authorization. In the beginning, what each state received was what each state requested.

## THE ESTABLISHMENT OF STATEWIDE FINANCIAL
## CONTROL IN THE STATE OFFICES

To a considerable degree, the loose central financial control in the early days of the program came from the inability to predict employment and the consequent irregular and non-final authorizations. A period of exploration was necessary before it became apparent what potentialities for employment on an arts program existed within each state and in each locality. It was natural that false starts should have been made in some areas and possibilities overlooked in others. Indeed, it was not until employment on Federal One became relatively stabilized, as a result of Hopkins telegram of March 5, 1936 (Serial No. 60), that preparations for effective financial control became possible.

The first step was the establishment of periodicity with reference to authorizations to the states. By the late spring of 1936 experience as to employment and costs on Federal One had so accumulated and operation had become relatively so organized that it was possible to authorize funds on a periodic basis. For a brief period this was done bi-monthly, but beginning with July, 1936, it was done on a monthly basis. This was in accordance with Hopkins' telegram dated July 18, 1936.[7]

This telegram established the projects under Federal One as statewide projects; i.e., although they remained *official* nationwide projects, they were considered *as though* they were official statewide projects for purposes of financial control.[*]

---

[*]It was still possible, however, to operate project units on a district basis, so long as the financial control rested in the state office.

Treasury Form A-2d supplemented Treasury Form A-2. The latter, as has already been indicated, was an Advice of Project Authorization, addressed to the state administrator. The former, called the Monthly Operating Release, Advice of State Monthly Budget, released funds from the larger amount for one month's operations.

Concomitantly with the establishment of this control by the WPA finance office, the finance office of Federal One established a similar control, although under a slightly different formality. This was done by the use of the Treasury Forms A-2 and A-2a. The initial authorization for the first month of a new fiscal year was made on Treasury Form A-2, Advice of Project Authorization. Subsequent authorizations for subsequent months were made monthly on Treasury Form A-2a, Advice of Change in Project Authorization. Authorizations were increased monthly by the amount deemed necessary for one month's operations, until at the close of the fiscal year the final authorization indicated the full amount authorized for the entire year.*

The establishment of financial control on the basis of a monthly budget determined by the Washington office enabled the state finance offices in turn to develop devices of control. In the beginning, as has been indicated, the state director of finance had two responsibilities —and only two—with reference to Federal One: (1) he prepared Treasury Form A-3, Advice of Allotment, upon request of the official representative of the federal director and upon receipt of a Project Proposal (WPA Form 320); and (2) he made sure that obligations were not incurred beyond the sum authorized to the official project within the state. Beyond this, he was powerless. In the first place, the sum of the amounts allotted to the districts on the basis of the Forms 320 might, and sometimes did, exceed the state's total authorization. Eventually this led to a request for an additional authorization, or to a reallotment of funds within the state in terms of the prior authorization. In either case, temporary confusion resulted. This was especially true at the beginning, when project proposals were approved by the federal directors or their official representatives without recourse to the state administrators. Second, in the early period the accounts of the project units under Federal One were kept in the district offices, not in the state office. The absence of any proper and regular system of reporting from the district to the state office prevented the state director of finance

---

*Since the purpose of Treasury Form A-2d, as released by the WPA finance office, was the same as that of the Treasury Forms A-2 and A-2a, as released by the finance office of Federal One, the concomitant use of both procedures represented a duplication of effort. This was eventually recognized in early 1938, when the use of Treasury Form A-2d, so far as Federal One was concerned, was abandoned by the WPA finance office.

from knowing at a particular time the financial status of a project unit within his state. Accordingly, a project unit in a district, though the first project proposal was prepared on a six months' basis, might, and sometimes did, expend its total allotment in a lesser period. The state director of finance might have no knowledge of this until he heard a cry of distress; and even when he had such knowledge, he had no power to decrease or regularize the rate of expenditure.

The changes ordered in Hopkins' telegram of July 18, 1936, referred to above, enabled the state director of finance to create proper financial controls. The state administrator, upon receipt of Treasury Form A-2d, Advice of State Monthly Budget, was directed to issue: (1) Treasury Form A-3, Advice of Allotment, which indicated to the district manager what amount he could obligate during that month; and (2) Treasury Form A-3c, which was prepared in the state office and indicated monthly suballotments to each project unit within the state. Thus the state office was able to budget the accounts of Federal One on a monthly basis.

It was possible now to establish proper accounting procedure. This was done by Supplement No. 2 to Handbook of Procedures Letter No. 1, dated July 30, 1936:

> When operating the projects on a state-wide basis, accounts are to be maintained by a unit in the State WPA Office known as the State-wide Project Unit, which unit shall be treated in all respects as an additional district.
> When operating the projects on a district basis, accounts are to be established in district offices with a summary project register account for each official project maintained in the State WPA Office. There should be one summary account for that portion of a project operated in each district and one summary account for each project operated directly by the State Office.
> Where projects are operated on a district basis, one master summary account should be maintained which will accumulate the totals of the individual district summary accounts for each project.
> Entries to the summary accounts shall be made in total of ten-day intervals based on reports submitted by the districts or by the statewide project register unit in the state office. These reports shall consist of totals of the project register accounts.[8]

Thus whether the nationwide project operated on a district basis or a statewide basis, the state finance office always had a picture of the current financial status of the official project within the state. The reports submitted at ten-day intervals by the districts or by the statewide project register unit provided the entries to the summary accounts in the state finance office.

It still remained to correlate the submission of project proposals

(WPA Form 330)* with state accounting procedure. In January, 1937, the first step in this direction was taken. General Letter No. 107, dated January 25, 1937, stated in part:

> The State or Regional Project Directors of WPA Sponsored Federal Projects Nos. 1 and 3 in conjunction with the State Director of Women's and Professional Projects shall prepare as promptly as possible the new applications for project units on WPA Form 330 Revised (printed July 20, 1936). The form shall be filled in completely, including the work project number. Computations should be based on five months' operations beginning February 1, 1937. Actual operations, however, will be subject to the available funds for the purpose.
>
> Applications for individual project units are not to be forwarded to the Works Progress Administration, Washington, D.C. until all the applications for the project units of that division of the Official Project have been prepared; thus all the Requests for the units of the Federal Music Project in the state will be forwarded simultaneously. Furthermore, the six copies of WPA Form 330 Revised for each project unit shall be forwarded.
>
> The Request for Approval of Project Unit, WPA Form 330 Revised, for each project unit of WPA Sponsored Federal Projects Nos. 1 and 3 shall be in the offices of Ellen S. Woodward, Assistant Administrator, Works Progress Administration, Washington, D.C. not later than February 15, 1937. Prompt notification of approval, disapproval, or modifications in each application will be given by the Washington office.
>
> It shall be the responsibility of the State Administrator to see that the amounts approved for each project unit on WPA Form 330 Revised for labor, for superintendence, and for other than labor costs, are not exceeded. The only exception permitted will be minor fluctuations, provided that the proper monthly average is maintained over a three months' period. The Statement of Project Estimate Detail, WPA Form 701, Revised, shall be prepared setting forth the limitations by the three objective classifications, labors, superintendence, and other than labor costs, and shall cover three months' operations. It shall be the duty of the State Director of Finance and Statistics to maintain project register accounts in a manner to indicate the limitations by the threefold classification and to control obligations to such limitations.[9]

The requirement that all Forms 330 should be forwarded simultaneously to the Washington office now permitted that office to aggregate the project proposals for individual work project units into a statewide project proposal. This statewide project proposal necessarily reflected accurately the sum of the costs of the project units. It is to be noted, however, that it was still required that project unit proposals be submitted to the central office, and that there was no requirement for a summary statewide project proposal.†

*WPA Form 320 was superseded by WPA Form 330, first released on November 30, 1935, and subsequently revised on April 20, 1936, July 20, 1936, and June 20, 1938.

†It is significant that in the above letter the state administrator was made responsible for seeing that the amounts approved on each Form 330 were not ex-

The next step was taken on July 2, 1937, by General Letter No. 144, which read in part:

Section 2. *Preparation and Routing of WPA Form 330 Revised.* The State or Regional Directors of wpa Sponsored Federal Project No. 1, in conjunction with State Directors of Women's and Professional Projects, shall prepare and submit as promptly as possible the new applications on wpa Form 330 Revised. The form shall be filled in completely, including the official project number, and all six copies shall be forwarded to the Washington office in accordance with the instructions contained in Operating Procedure No. W-7. One state-wide application for each of the five divisions of wpa Sponsored Federal Project No. 1 shall be submitted, summarizing employment and costs for each official project.

.  .  .  .  .  .  .  .  .  .

Section 4. *Functional Units Under Federal Music and Theatre Projects.* In addition to the state-wide application prepared on wpa Form 330 Revised for each of the five divisions of wpa Sponsored Federal Project No. 1, the State Directors of the Music and Theatre Projects shall prepare applications for functional units to operate as work projects under the official project. The functional units under the Federal Music and Theatre Projects which may be approved for operation as state-wide work projects are set forth in Operating Procedure No. W-1, Revised July 2, 1937.

Applications prepared for functional work project units shall be submitted to the State Director of Women's and Professional Projects for approval, and forwarded to the Division of Women's and Professional Projects at Washington, D.C., for final approval by the Federal Director of the Music or Theatre Project.

In the preparation of applications for the operation of work project units under the Federal Music and Theatre official projects, the sum of the estimated cost and employment for all functional units shall not exceed the amount of such items shown on the state-wide official project application.

A separate project register will be maintained by the Division of Finance and Statistics for each work project unit approved for operation.

Functional work project units will not be established under the Federal Art, Writers' and Historical Records, official projects.[10]

Except for the Music and Theater projects, therefore, only one Form 330 was to be submitted for each state. Any breakdown within the state, either by location or function, was a matter to be decided and recorded by the state administration. In effect, once the authorization to the state was made, the financial control of the money was an affair of the state, and not of the national, office. Even in the case of the Music and Theater projects, in which separate 330's for functional units were permitted in addition to the statewide 330, caution was indicated so

ceeded, and further that the limitations therein on labor, superintendence and other-than-labor costs were observed. Financial control of Federal One, so far as accounting procedure went, was now completely centralized in the state office.

that the sum of the costs of the functional 330's would not exceed the total cost of the statewide project as indicated in the master 330.

On December 9, 1937, by General Letter No. 168, the final step was taken in establishing the official project in each state as the only unit of control so far as the central office was concerned. This letter reads in part:

> One state-wide application [WPA Form 330] summarizing the employment and costs for the official project shall be submitted for each of the five divisions of Federal Project No. 1. . . .
>
> Each approved state-wide project of the Federal Art Project, the Federal Writers' Project, and the Historical Records Survey shall be operated as a single state-wide work project. However, in the case of the Federal Music and Theatre Projects, project units within the limits of the approved state-wide applications may be established by the State Director of the appropriate Federal Project, in cooperation with the State Director of Women's and Professional Projects, along geographic, administrative or functional lines. WPA Forms 330 Revised for such units need not be submitted to the Washington office for approval.[11]

By virtue of this letter, Federal One was controlled by the Washington finance office only in the sense that it controlled authorizations to the states. The funds each state received were earmarked by Washington. Once the authorization reached the state, however, complete financial control of the statewide projects resided in the state administration. In other words, so far as financial control was concerned, the projects under Federal One were, except for earmarking, completely under the supervision of the state administrations.

THE ESTABLISHMENT OF CENTRAL BUDGETARY CONTROL
IN THE WASHINGTON OFFICE

This financial control of project operations within a state by the state finance office, however desirable for purposes of fiscal management, was not meant by the Washington office of Federal One to be ultimate. The federal directors wished to control not only how much money was expended for each project within a state but also the employment quota and the proportion of workers assigned to each project unit by wage classification. The way in which this control was continued by the finance office of Federal One was, if simple in execution, ingenious in concept.

In the first place, budgetary control on the part of the central office depended upon an adequate and regular system of reporting. In the beginning, and until very late in 1936, the finance office of Federal One was obliged to rely entirely upon reports prepared by the Treasury accounting offices. At the request of the WPA, special reports on Treasury Forms SF-1 and SF-2, showing authorizations, encumbrances, and expenditures for each of the nationwide programs under Federal One, were submitted periodically. These reports were broken down by states. They were, however, inadequate for purposes of control. In the first place, they were unreliable, for accounting, when it is divorced completely from operations, is naturally subject to error. Second, they were always late in reaching the WPA, sometimes well over a month after the event. Third, they did not reflect the status of funds as of submittal, because of the necessary lag in receipt of authorization, obligating, and liquidating documents from the WPA. Finally, there was no breakdown in the obligation figures, so that it was impossible to determine labor and other-than-labor costs separately.

By the late fall of 1936 this situation was remedied when the central office of the WPA Division of Finance established a comprehensive financial reporting system with the institution of WPA Form 724. These forms were submitted monthly by each state director of finance and showed obligations by major and minor program class, broken down by two objects of expenditure, labor and non-labor. The earlier Treasury reports were continued as a convenient means of checking the figures in the Forms 724.

Until this reporting system was established, there was little purpose in a careful review of the project proposals (Forms 320 or 330), for unless a reporting system indicated that the money was being expended according to the plan set forth in these forms, a review would be nothing more than a gesture. But with the co-ordination of project proposals with authorizations, and the institution of a reporting system, the elements of control were present.

The project proposals, to be sure, indicated the number of persons to be employed in each class—supervisors, professional and technical, skilled, semiskilled, and unskilled—and broke down non-labor expenditures into three classes: materials and supplies, equipment rentals, and other direct costs.* But these breakdowns were not effective for the simple reason that no provision was made for financial reporting on the basis of them. Moreover, a system of financial reporting that detailed

*This was the breakdown in Form 320. Form 330 required a more detailed breakdown.

expenditures in such a manner would have been useless to the finance office of Federal One because it would have required an amount of clerical work beyond the power of the office to undertake.

It might be thought that the authorization of employment quotas, broken down by states, would have provided the desired control. But though such authorizations were instituted, they were effective only in the sense that they established maximums for each state. There was nothing to prevent a music project in a state, for instance, from employing less than the maximum, and thus to spend more for supervision than was indicated in the application. The central office met this problem by the simple but clever device of establishing a man-month limitation on each project application as it was approved.* This limitation, which was established separately for labor and non-labor expenditures, was easily controlled, because the finance office of Federal One received weekly reports of employment on each program by state. Thus in the end there were three devices by which the central office exercised control. The monthly authorization of funds established a maximum in that category; the monthly authorization of an employment quota established a maximum in that category; the establishment of a man-month limitation insured the desired relationship between employment and costs.†

With a system established under which actual expenditures could be compared with proposed expenditures, the imposition of controls became simply a matter of establishing a proper routine. Financial reports (WPA Form 724) were submitted monthly; employment reports were submitted weekly; project proposals (WPA Form 330) were submitted every six months. The task was to use the financial reports and employment reports to insure that the expenditures in the project proposals were observed for a six months' period. The finance office of Federal One, although conceivably it might have instituted monthly comparisons between monthly obligations and the prorated portion of the approved six months' proposal, rejected this method as impractical. In the first place, the monthly rate of obligations for payrolls was necessarily uneven because of the varying number of days in a month. Second, in regard to non-labor costs, project operations often required a

---

*For a definition of man-month cost, vide supra, pp. 231-33.

†This discussion is concerned only with the controls established over the expenditure of federal money derived from appropriations. There were also sponsors' funds and admission funds, the control of which is treated elsewhere (vide infra, pp. 265-303).

disproportionate amount of funds for a particular month. Accordingly, it was decided that quarterly comparisons would be adequate. If, as a result of such a check, it was discovered that the proper limitations were not being observed by any particular project, the attention of the state administration concerned was directed to the situation by a letter over the signature of the assistant administrator in charge of professional and service projects.

An example of such a letter follows:

An examination has been made of encumbered non-labor costs of the various units of Federal Project Number One operating in your State during the six month period July 1 to December 31, 1938, and these costs have been compared with the limitations established by approved Forms 330.

We find that only the writers project has exceeded the approved amount of non-labor expenditures as is evident from the following:

|  | Approved | Actual |
|---|---|---|
| Non-labor costs | $985 | $1,303 |
| Man-months Employment | 215 | 164 |
| Man-months Non-labor costs | 4.58 | 7.94 |

You will note that this indicates an excess expenditure of about 32% despite the fact that employment averaged about 24% below quota.

Since approved expenditures have been exceeded without prior administrative approval, you are asked for some explanation as well as an assurance that during the current six-month period non-labor costs will be reduced sufficiently to offset the over-expenditure of the previous six months.[12]

If this reminder failed to achieve results, the ultimate sanction lay in directing the state director of finance through finance channels to cease accepting obligations in excess of limitations.

Mrs. Kerr, shortly after she succeeded Mrs. Woodward as assistant administrator in January, 1939, expressed an interest in the manner in which expenditures for Federal One were controlled. In answer to that query Julius Davidson prepared the following memorandum. The document is an excellent summary of the method of control, and particularly valuable because it shows that the controls developed by Federal One were more effective than those used for the WPA as a whole. The memorandum follows:[13]

The following is a brief statement of the general theory and methods of exercising financial control over the various projects under Federal Project Number One.

A comparison of the financial control of local projects and the financial control of our projects offers an instructive approach to the problem. For example, a local project is approved for $750,000 at a man-year cost of $750, or $62.50 a man-month, non-labor cost to be five percent of the total, employment to average 167 for a six month period, making a total of 1,000 man-months. All these figures are entered in one form or another on the project register in the office of the State Director of Finance. However, in maintaining control of operations, no attention need be paid to any of the figures except one, that is the total limitation of $750,000. If, instead of employing 167 persons, 300 persons are employed, if, instead of operating at $750.00 a man-year, the project is operated at $1,000 a man-year, or if non-labor amounts to 10 percent instead of 5 percent, it is not very likely that the matter will come to the attention of either the Treasury Office or the Bureau of the Budget. In the case of local projects, other than the control by one overall limitation, in this instance $750.00, there is only one real control and that is on the basis of the monthly State operating budget for labor and non-labor; and since this State operating budget is in the form of a labor and non-labor man-month cost, there is a measure of control over each project.

How, then, do our projects differ from local projects? The Theatre Project, say, is approved for a six month period with an average employment of 7,900 persons at a man-year cost of $1,248, or $104 a man-month, with non-labor not to exceed 9% of the total. This project is approved on a nationwide basis, and it is our problem to see that the promises implied in our applications are all kept. If our employment is increased to 9,000, we shall definitely run out of funds before the end of six months. If, instead of operating the program with 7,900 persons at $104 a man-month, we choose to employ only 7,000 persons at a man-month cost of $117, I hardly believe that we could "get by with it" even were we desirous of doing so, since we operate under the watchful eye of the Bureau of the Budget assisted by the Treasury offices. It is, therefore, necessary for us to operate our program in such a manner that we not only keep within the total limitations but within the specific limitations for labor and non-labor. Furthermore, it is our clear duty to see that the man-year costs indicated in our applications to the President are not exceeded.

Our applications submitted to the President are based upon five nation-wide projects; in actual day to day operation we have some 200 separate official project units distributed throughout the 48 states. It is our problem, then, so to control the cost of each of the 200 distinct units that at the end of the various accounting periods the operating costs will correspond to the promises we have, in effect, made to the President. The means by which we accomplish the desired results are:

1. WPA Forms 330 as described in Operating Procedure W-1 and W-7.

2. Centralized control of employment quota distribution.

3. Weekly employment reports submitted by state statisticians.

4. Constant analyses of encumbrance reports Forms 724 submitted by the various State Directors of Finance.

Form 330 is a Form that has no standing either with the Bureau of the Budget or with Treasury. It is our own administrative Form of application conceived for the specific purpose of maintaining control of each statewide official project unit. In approving the Forms 330 as submitted by the States, a careful analysis is made both of the financial and of the administrative factors reflected therein. It is important that the total approval given to all

Forms 330 submitted within each nationwide program is consistent with our application Forms 306 submitted to the President.

The normal period covered by Form 330 is six months. However, our procedure requires each State to set up a control so that during each three month period average costs are in accordance with Forms 330 as approved. Therefore, at the end of each three months a comparison is made between Forms 330 as approved and the encumbrance reports as submitted by the States, and excessive costs are brought to the attention of each State Administration in no uncertain terms.

It is by the methods above described that we have succeeded during the past two years in exercising a control over the operation of each of our nationwide projects that I hardly believe is matched by any of the State programs. In a report submitted to Mrs. Woodward on August 39, 1938, I analyzed the operations of the program during the fiscal year ended June 30, 1938. It is unnecessary to repeat the statements in that report. Briefly summarized, we undertook to operate the total Federal Number One Program with an employment aggregating 348,158 man-months, at a total cost of $34,762,450, and an average man-month cost of operation not to exceed $99.85, of which 6.3% was for other than payroll costs. Actually we went through the fiscal year with a total cost of $34,069,692, and employment aggregating 343,107 man-months at a man-month cost of $99.30, with the other than labor cost 5.8% of the total. In other words, with employment averaging about 1½% less than the quota indicated in our applications to the President, the man-month costs averaged about ½% less than the man-month costs indicated in the applications. I believe this is definite evidence of effective control.

The following is a brief summary which conpares the actual man-month costs of operation during the first six months of the current fiscal year with the average man-month costs indicated in Forms 330 and the man-month costs indicated in our applications to the President. These figures leave no doubt about the effectiveness of control.

### COMPARATIVE MAN-MONTH COSTS
#### Six Months Period July 1 – December 31, 1938

| | APPLICATIONS | | ACTUAL |
| | Forms 306 submitted to the President | Forms 330 as Approved | Encumbrances Reported on Forms 724 less adjustments for January Labor |
|---|---|---|---|
| Art | $102.04 | $100.12 | $ 99.56 |
| Music | 94.57 | 93.83 | 92.51 |
| Writers | 94.20 | 91.79 | 91.41 |
| Theatre | 103.97 | 103.90 | 104.00 |
| Records | 78.70 | 75.54 | 74.50 |
| Total | $ 94.70 | $ 92.39 | $ 92.68 |

The proper balance between administrative authority and technical control is a problem that is present in all governmental agencies and in larger private business enterprises. This is especially the case when territorial jurisdiction is involved, as in a government agency that maintains field offices. An exaggerated emphasis upon administrative authority may so localize control that central direction is weakened or destroyed, and too much technical control from the central office may paralyze local initiative. The solution ultimately found by Federal One merits study. After the failure of the initial attempt to place *all* controls in the Washington office, Federal One was able to arrive at a *modus vivendi* with the state office—which, if it left something to be desired, at least approached the ideal. In the first place, no projects or project units could be initiated within a state without the approval of the state WPA administration. Second, control of technical and project personnel was placed in the state and district offices, where it belonged. But once the project or project unit was in being, technical control of its operation was reserved to the Washington office. This reservation was accomplished by the devices elaborated by the finance office of Federal One, which enabled the federal directors: (1) to set a maximum authorization of funds for each state; (2) to set a maximum employment quota for each state; and (3) by the calculation of man-month costs, to maintain the relationship they thought proper among the supervisory, professional and technical, skilled, semiskilled, and unskilled project workers. In doing this, they established the technical standard of each project and project unit.

It was one of the ironies of the experiment that *after* the establishment of this balance, which saved the professional pride of the technical personnnel and, at the same time, preserved the administrative dignity of the politician, it should seem good to Congress to abolish Federal One. By returning the arts program *entirely* to the states, Congress destroyed that central technical control that Federal One had labored so hard to establish.

1. Memorandum, Cogan to Ozer, January 9, 1936, WPA Files.
2. Memorandum, Ozer to Whiting, March 6, 1936, WPA Files.
3. *Ibid.*
4. Memorandum, Ozer to Whiting, March 12, 1936, WPA Files.
5. Memorandum, Ozer to Whiting, March 6, 1936, WPA Files.
6. *Ibid.*
7. Telegram Serial No. 99, WPA, July 18, 1936.
8. Handbook of Procedures Letter No. 1, Supplement No. 2, WPA, July 30, 1936, Section V.
9. General Letter No. 107, WPA, January 25, 1937.
10. General Letter No. 144, WPA, July 2, 1937.
11. General Letter No. 168, WPA, December 9, 1937.
12. Letter, Kerr to Shark, February 1, 1939, WPA Files.
13. Memorandum, Davidson to Kerr, January 24, 1939, WPA Files.

# 15

## Federal One and Sponsorship

### SPONSORSHIP IN THE WPA

Relationship between the Works Progress Administration, as a federal agency, and other governmental agencies (federal, state, and local) was maintained by the device of sponsorship. In the earlier appropriation acts there was no statutory requirement of sponsorship; it owed its existence to administrative rulings.

The first definition of sponsorship was given in Circular No. 1, dated June 15, 1935:

> A "Sponsor" of a Works Progress Administration project is an authorized governmental agency (State, county, city, village, township, etc.) which offers a definite plan and procedure for the employment of persons on relief rolls under the conditions of the Act. . . .
> Unofficial groups may not act as sponsors. Projects may not be sponsored by boards of trade, clubs, societies, churches, orphanages, veterans' organizations, or other private, sectarian, civic, or similar organizations. Such organizations may, however, cooperate unofficially with sponsors in the organization of proper proposals.[1]

Section 9 of the same circular defined sponsors contributions:

> The sponsoring governmental agency is expected to contribute equipment, materials and services to the maximum amount possible. The priority of the project will depend in part on the amount of such contributions and the extent to which they increase the proportion of labor cost to the total Federal funds required for the project.[2]

No non-federal project could be initiated without a sponsor. The act

264

of initiation was the sponsor's preparation of WPA Form 301 (Project Proposal). In it the sponsor indicated what costs he would bear in the matter of labor, equipment, materials, and services. This proposal, after meeting district inspection, was forwarded to the state WPA office, and, if approved, was sent to Washington for final action. Final approval or rejection depended upon, among other considerations, the relative amount of the sponsor's contribution. In theory it was hoped that the sponsor's contribution would cover, or largely cover, non-labor expenditures. The product of the project, if it existed in physical form, was the property of the sponsor.

The reasons that prompted the device of sponsorship were partly fiscal and partly political. In the first place, it was felt not only outside but also inside the WPA that state and local communities, though they could not bear the total cost of relief, should contribute financially, so far as possible, toward the cost of the program. Second, since the sponsor was almost always a non-federal public body, the sponsor's contribution was testimony (1) that the project proposed was desired by the community and (2) that the community was likely to maintain interest until the project was completed.

Sponsors' contributions might be either in the form of cash or of goods and services. In the latter case the contribution was calculated on a cash basis. How far this calculation was inflated by the sponsor is impossible to determine. That there was a tendency to overrate services and equipment in terms of cash is clear. As a result of the 1939 act, by which sponsors' contributions to the extent of at least 25 per cent was required, Colonel Harrington issued precise instructions for the calculation of non-cash contributions.[3] In the preceding four years, since no strict accounting of sponsors' contributions was required, the estimate was largely that of the sponsor or, at most, the result of an agreement between the sponsor and the local WPA. However, no tables are available that distinguish cash and non-cash contributions of sponsors.*

The first statutory provision with respect to sponsorship occurred in the ERA Act of 1937. It read: ". . . No non-Federal project shall be undertaken or prosecuted under this appropriation unless and until the sponsor has made a written agreement to finance such part of the entire cost thereof as is not to be supplied from Federal funds." This provision was directed against the starting of large-scale projects by

*In the beginning, state and district WPA offices were permitted to sponsor state or local projects. This permission, however, was withdrawn early, and there is no evidence that this type of sponsorship was, during its brief life, of any significance.

small allocations—projects that could not be completed without further appropriations in later years. This provision was repeated in subsequent ERA Acts.

It is to be observed that this requirement affected only non-federal projects. There was never any statutory requirement for sponsorship of federal projects, although in the ERA Act of 1938, federal agencies were permitted to accept sponsors' contributions from sponsors of non-federal projects.

> Federal agencies having supervision of projects prosecuted under the appropriations in this title are authorized to receive from sponsors of non-Federal projects contributions in services, materials or money, such money to be deposited with the Treasurer of the United States. Such contributions shall be expended or utilized as agreed upon between the sponsor and the Federal agency.

The decisive provision with respect to sponsorship occurred in the 1939 Act:

> On and after January 1, 1940, in administering the funds appropriated in this section, not to exceed three-fourths of the total cost of all non-Federal projects thereafter approved to be undertaken within any State, Territory, possession, or the District of Columbia, with respect to which any such funds are used, shall be borne by the United States, and not less than one-fourth of such total cost shall be borne by the state and its political subdivisions, or by the Territory, possession, or the District of Columbia, as the case may be. The facts constituting compliance with the requirements of this subsection shall be determined by the Commissioner, and his determinations, made in conformity with rules and regulations prescribed by him, shall be final and conclusive.

It was as a consequence of this requirement that Colonal Harrington established precise rules for the calculation of sponsors' non-cash contributions.

The amount of sponsors' contributions, the ratio of that amount to total expenditures, and the determination of the proper amount, as between projects and between states, were matters of considerable concern to Congress.

SPONSORSHIP IN FEDERAL ONE

In federal projects one through six, the official sponsor was the Works Progress Administration. In federal projects two through six, in addition to the official sponsor, other federal agencies acted as cosponsors. These cosponsors contributed supervision, but made no financial contribution. Indeed, they contributed supervision only in the sense that they provided personnel from their own staffs. These persons, however, were paid from wpa funds, and not from the agency's funds.

In Federal One the wpa, as official sponsor, was the only sponsor. The absence of a cosponsor was, among other reasons, due to the fact that there existed no regular government agency qualified to undertake supervision of an arts program. Thus in effect the Works Progress Administration was responsible not only for relief wages but also for all expenses that would otherwise have been provided by sponsors, i.e., all non-labor costs.

It was thought, however, that there should be some way by which local groups, public, quasi-public, and private non-profit institutions could indicate their support of the program and, if they chose, contribute money or services to its prosecution. For this reason, the device of the co-operating sponsor was elaborated.

The first announcement of the plan of the co-operating sponsor was on September 30, 1935:

> *Cooperating Sponsor.* It is desirable that some public, quasi-public, or non-profit private agency indicate local interest in each work project. This local sponsor will be called the "Cooperating Sponsor." The District Supervisor of Projects and Planning, and the District Supervisors of Art, Music, Theatre and Writing, in cooperation with representatives of the Federal Directors, shall encourage proper agencies to suggest desirable projects for which proper talent is available from the relief rolls. To this end the District Supervisor of Projects and Planning shall circulate to all such agencies wpa Form 320A, Cooperating Sponsor's Project Proposal. On this form the prospective Sponsor may advise that it is willing to aid, either financially or otherwise, in making a project suggested by it of most value to the community. [4]

The same procedure, however, made it clear that the filing of wpa Form 320A placed the body under no obligation to the wpa.

> Copies of wpa Form 320A shall be distributed as widely as possible by the District Supervisors of Art, Music, Theatre and Writing, (or if there be none, by the District Supervisor of Projects and Planning) to public, quasi-public, or non-profit private agencies or institutions which might be interested in acting as cooperating sponsors to some form of activity under this program. The filing of wpa Form 320A does not place the agency or institution under any obligation whatever to the Works Progress Administration.

No directions other than those contained in WPA Form 320A are necessary for filing.[5]

It was hoped, however, that such co-operating sponsors would defray miscellaneous costs, such as travel and rental.

It is desirable that as little as possible of the costs of travel and of the rental of space be charged to the Federal Government. Where the success of a project depends upon extensive expenditures for travel and rental of space, every effort shall be made to have these costs met from sources other than the Federal Government.[6]

Co-operating sponsors could also pay wages.[7] It was the policy of the WPA, however, to pay the wages of all certified employees. The co-operating sponsor might pay the wages of non-certified personnel, who would act in a supervisory position or serve as emergency employees in assignments for which certified personnel was not available. It was hoped that wages thus paid would be higher than the relief scale—or, at least, not lower.[8]

The most complete description of the role of co-operating sponsors was contained in the Handbook, dated March 21, 1936:

An example of the WPA Sponsored project is Federal Project No. 1 covering Music, Art, Theatre, and Writing on a nation-wide basis. Others may be established from time to time. In order to effect better cooperation with existing public, quasi-public, or non-profit private agencies in these fields within the state and to take advantage of such services and assistances that such organizations might offer, a system of cooperating sponsors has been developed. Such cooperating sponsors perform the same functions in connection with work units of these Federal Projects as regular sponsors perform with respect to regular WPA projects. For example, a single work unit may include all persons in a county who are employed at one type of activity under such nation-wide projects and wherein there is one cooperating sponsor. Within the limit of the quota for each state, quasi-public agencies such as Y.M.C.A.'s, Boys' Clubs, Boy and Girl Scouts, Community Clubs, Art Organizations, and other semi-public bodies may propose plans and specifications of desirable work to be done in the field. The proposals are submitted on WPA Form 330. Such cooperating sponsors list on their proposals the services they are prepared to contribute if the plan is approved. These services may take the form of personnel, supervision, equipment, housing facilities, etc.[9]

It was always emphasized, however, that the existence of the co-operating sponsor, although desirable, was not "required" or "mandatory."[10] Co-operating sponsors for the Writers' Project were specifically discouraged. It was felt that in the preparation of guides, freedom

268

of treatment would be best secured if civic organizations were not given a status that, though unofficial, might encourage them to influence the text.*

## THE ROLE OF THE CO-OPERATING SPONSOR
## IN FEDERAL ONE

During the period of federal control the co-operating sponsor played an insignificant part in the operations of the project. The fact that the device was not mandatory inclined those responsible for the initiation of project units to ignore it. When such a sponsor was secured, the matter was generally treated as a mere formality. Indeed, on Federal One there was a general suspicion of co-operating sponsors, induced by the desire of the administrative personnel to be completely independent of outside interference. There is little evidence that such sponsors' pledges were set up on the project register; consequently, there was no urge to liquidate them through reports of contributions received. Indeed, reports of contributions, such as they were, were of a highly sporadic nature, and their very submittal depended largely upon the whims of project supervisors.†

Consequently, it is not surprising that the statistical record of sponsors' contributions is largely without meaning. Indeed, a search of the files fails to reveal any interest in sponsorship before the spring of 1939. At that time Congress began to press vigorously for an increase in sponsors' contributions, and, in addition, for some statutory provision for a definite percentage. As a consequence, during the spring and summer of 1939 the finance office of Federal One was asked to prepare several statistical reports on sponsorship.‡

The great variations between states in reported contributions indicates the haphazard way in which sponsors' contributions were made and reported. Indeed, even after the 1939 Act, although the

*On April 15, 1937, the term "Co-sponsor" was substituted for "Co-operating Sponsor" in Federal One. This change in terminology, however, did not imply a change in meaning.

†The basic forms used for reporting were WPA Form 710 for non-labor contributions and WPA Form 710A for labor contributions. It was the project supervisors' responsibility to prepare these reports and, at the end of each calendar month, to submit them to the division of finance for recording in the project register and compilation of statistical summaries.

‡By administrative definition admission funds collected on the Theater and Music projects were classed as sponsors' contributions.

method of reporting was systematized and tightened, the fact that sponsors' contributions for the arts program were largely non-cash made them suspect. At the House hearings in 1940 Colonel Harrington's answers to congressional inquiries were pertinent:

> Mr. o'NEAL. I want to ask about sponsors' contributions. On page 72 of your statement there is a list of the Art, Music, Writers', and Historical Records projects with the estimated sponsors' contributions, showing an average estimated sponsor's contribution of 13.9. As a matter of fact, what are the sponsors' contributions amounting to? Do you have figures showing what they have actually amounted to in money?

> Colonel HARRINGTON. We have that figure. I would say it was insignificant.

> Mr. o'NEAL. Most of the sponsorship contributions were in kind?

> Colonel HARRINGTON. Yes, sir.

> Mr. o'NEAL. What kind of materials were they?

> Colonel HARRINGTON. I would like to have Mrs. Kerr answer that question.

> Mrs. KERR. Principally space, materials, and technical supervision.

> Mr. o'NEAL. Very little cash enters into it?

> Colonel HARRINGTON. No, sir; sometimes when a community starts a project there is a large amount of cash.

> Mr. o'NEAL. In most cases there is very little cash?

> Mrs. KERR. No sir; I would not say that.

> Mr. o'NEAL. What percentage of the sponsorship contribution is in cash?

> Mrs. KERR. I do not know that.

> Mr. o'NEAL. Can you estimate it?

> Mrs. KERR. No sir.[11]

The fact that no tables were ever made distinguishing cash from non-cash sponsors' contributions makes further analysis impossible.

In connection with cash sponsorship, it should be explained that the receipt of cash from a sponsor did not in itself, according to WPA procedure, constitute sponsorship, for the cash contribution was construed to be in the nature of a trust fund to be devoted to expenditures in behalf of the designated project or projects; the unexpended balance, if any, was to revert to the sponsor. The contribution became actual only as the money was expended and the materials and services received. In other words, a sponsor's pledge was not really liquidated by the contribution of cash, but only by the receipt of materials or services resulting from the expenditure of that cash. There was no way by which the cash receipt could be recorded on the WPA Forms 710 or 710A provided for reporting contributions; the entries on these forms merely indicated the receipt of materials and services in liquidation of a pledge.*

There are two reports, however, that presume to show cash contributions to Federal One; the first, cumulative through December 1, 1938; the second, for the six-month period ending December 31, 1938. The accuracy of these reports, however, is not guaranteed. In his covering letter Julius Davidson wrote: "I do not believe that all of the figures submitted are either complete or accurate, but, at any rate, they give us some idea as to what is happening."[12]

Davidson's figures were obtained from Treasury sources. The tables are reproduced below.

## FEDERAL PROJECT NUMBER ONE

### Cash Contributions from Sponsors
### Cumulative through December 31, 1938

| Project | Cash Contributions | Obligations | Unobligated* |
|---|---|---|---|
| Art | $16,928.34 | $ 9,503.70 | $ 7,424.64 |
| Music | 40,836.18 | 38,237.71 | 2,598.47 |
| Theater | 12,965.05 | 9,557.47 | 3,407.58 |
| H.R.S. | 1,237.25 | 1,049.93 | 187.32 |
| Total | $71,966.82 | $58,348.81 | $13,618.01 |

### Cash Contributions from Sponsors
### for Six-Month Period Ending December 31, 1938

| Project | Cash Contributions | Obligations | Unobligated* |
|---|---|---|---|
| Art | $11,410.57 | $ 6,329.77 | $5,080.80 |
| Music | 13,371.59 | 11,938.42 | 1,433.17 |
| Theater | 10,991.64 | 7,930.46 | 3,061.18 |
| H.R.S. | 49.25 | 5.75 | 43.50 |
| Total | $35,823.05 | $26,204.40 | $9,618.65 |

*Amounts listed here represent excess of receipts over obligations, or excess of obligations over receipts during six-month period.

*The title of Operating Procedure No. F-36, "Sponsors' Pledges Liquidated by Cash," is misleading. This procedure provides that, at the completion of a project, any unexpended balance be returned to the sponsor.

271

With respect to the four projects listed above, it is readily apparent that, even if all cash contributions of sponsors were ultimately liquidated, the percentage of these contributions to total federal funds expended on Federal One remained infinitesimal.

## THE FEDERAL WRITERS' PROJECT AND SPONSORSHIP

Although in the beginning sponsorship did not enter into the scheme of the Writers' Project, which wished to maintain its independence of "booster" organizations, it became apparent within a year that the problem of publication could be most readily met by that device. The system of sponsorship that developed in the Writers' Project, however, was not concerned with contributions in cash or kind, but arose from its special need for a subsidy for publication.

The first important work to be published was the guide to the city of Washington, D.C. Since the work was a government publication, and since by federal legislation the Government Printing Office had a monopoly of all government printing, it wis taken for granted that the GPO would print all the guides. Difficulties, however, soon developed for three reasons. In the first place, the kind of book desired, in the matter of content, format, and illustrations, was alien to the experience of the GPO, and the office, therefore, was unprepared to do a craftsman's job. In the second place, the GPO is notoriously slow in the process of publication, and the Writers' Project, for reasons of public relations, desired speed. In the third place, the GPO provided no proper facilities for publishing and marketing, such as are provided by commercial publishing houses.

To overcome these difficulties, the idea of sponsoring organizations was developed. In some cases these were duly constituted state or local political bodies. In many cases they were unofficial committees of public-spirited citizens who formed ad hoc societies or organizations for the sole purpose of promoting the work of the Writers' Project by subsidizing publication.*

The project's early experience with the GPO suggested the use of these sponsoring committees. It was not long, however, before positive reasons began to suggest themselves to support the contention that private publishing houses were more desirable. Private publishers, unlike

---

*These sponsoring bodies, since they were not official sponsors but co-operating sponsors, could be non-profit private organizations.

the GPO, paid royalties, and, especially when pressure began to be exerted toward the reduction of federal cost, the prospect of large royalties from successful publications loomed as an exciting and obvious solution.

There was also the question of copyright. Since the copyright law provides that no copyright shall subsist in the publications of the federal government, the Writers' Project, as part of an agency of the federal government, could not make contracts for publications with private publishers that would grant the protection of a copyright. This problem was presumably resolved by the use of sponsoring committees that, by agreement with the Writers' Project, were permitted or required to take out a copyright.*

The use of sponsors to subsidize publication was eminently successful. Indeed, by this device this project received substantial contributions, which paid for the cost of printing, advertising, and distributing approximately three hundred titles produced up to December 31, 1938. This subsidy has been estimated as worth about $500,000. Indeed, after the initial experiment in conjunction with the GPO, no costs of publication were met out of appropriated funds.

In the main, this procedure was administered without incident or difficulty, especially when public or quasi-public bodies served as sponsors. In the case of non-profit private groups, however, the device might easily have proved embarrassing. The regulation that permitted such sponsors to receive and to retain in their own possession royalties paid by the publishers was, to say the least, subject to abuse. It is true that it was provided that this money should be used (1) to defray the costs born by the sponsor in subsidizing publication and (2) for the further use of the Writers' Project, if any profit accumulated. There is no evidence of financial irregularity, or any reason to suspect it. At the same time, the method of accounting used by these sponsors was informal and at times, as in the case of the Guild's Committee for Federal Writers' Publications, Inc., of New York City, confusing and inadequate. Under these circumstances, there was not that positive assurance of financial responsibility which the federal government in its fiscal relationships rightly requires.

---

*The use of sponsors for purposes of publication, which was initiated by the Writers' Project, was also used by the Theater Project to publish two volumes of plays. In addition, the Theater Project used the device to "sell" movie rights to plays. A sum of $5,000 was collected on this basis for rights to *One-third of a Nation*.

Indeed, it is surprising that it was not until June, 1939, that the WPA director of finance questioned this procedure and, in a memorandum addressed to Mr. Morris dated June 7, 1939, wrote:

> It has been brought out in recent tabulations prepared at the request of the investigation committee that various sums of moneys covering receipts from Federal Project No. 1 activities are being held by the several co-sponsors of the projects. In most instances, these moneys are being held under an agreement to the effect that funds will be expended to the benefit of the project.
>
> It is my opinion that the Administration is in a very vulnerable position in allowing this money to remain in the hands of the co-sponsors (many of whom may not be legitimate co-sponsors).
>
> It is, therefore, my very definite recommendation that immediate steps be taken by Federal Project No. 1 to see that all such moneys are turned over by the cooperating sponsors to the Federal Works Progress Administration for deposit in the Special Deposit Accounts of the Treasury Disbursing officers.[13]

As the following table indicates,[14] the amount of money received by sponsors as royalty was small, and, if peculation of a petty kind occurred, innocently or deliberately, the sum involved was insignificant.

### FEDERAL WRITERS' PROJECT

ROYALTIES RECEIVED BY SPONSORS AND EXPENDITURES THEREFROM
CUMULATIVE THROUGH DECEMBER 31, 1938

(Since publishers' statements are rendered only semi-annually or annually, only a small part of the royalties or net proceeds would appear prior to December 31, 1938.)

| STATE | ROYALTIES RECEIVED | EXPENDED | BALANCE HELD BY SPONSOR |
|---|---|---|---|
| Delaware | $ 250.00 | . . . | $ 250.00 |
| Louisiana | 500.00 | . . . | 500.00 |
| New York City | 1,200.00 | $358.92 | 841.08 |
| New Jersey | 500.00 | . . . | 500.00 |
| Nebraska | 160.71 | . . . | 160.71 |
| South Dakota | 5.85 | . . . | 5.85 |
| Total | $2,616.56 | $358.92 | $2,257.64 |

Toward the very end of Federal One it seems that the Writers' Project attempted to clear with the General Accounting Office and the Government Printing Office a proposal for direct negotiation with the publishers.[15] Before any change occurred, however, Federal One was abolished, and publication became the direct concern of the new official sponsors, which were agencies of the several state governments. There is no precise record as to the disposal of royalties held at that time by the prior sponsoring agencies. Presumably, they were turned over to the new official sponsors.

## THE FEDERAL ART PROJECT AND SPONSORSHIP

The Federal Art Project, which unlike the Writers' Project was under no necessity to publish, and, unlike the Music and Theater projects, had little, if any, precedent for the collection of admission funds, evolved a procedure for the allocation of works of art that was a model device for encouraging sponsors' contributions. This procedure, which appeared as Operating Procedure No. W-12, is here quoted in full:

PROCEDURE FOR THE LOAN OF WORKS OF ART PRODUCED UNDER THE FEDERAL ART PROJECT OF THE WORKS PROGRESS ADMINISTRATION TO PUBLIC AGENCIES AND INSTITUTIONS, SUPPORTED IN WHOLE OR IN PART BY TAX FUNDS

Section 1. *Policy*   Works of art produced under the Federal Art Project of the Works Progress Administration may be loaned to public agencies or institutions, supported in whole or in part by the tax funds, whose functions do not include the purchase of works of art. No works of art may be loaned which will replace the usual service or activities provided for in the budget of such agencies or institutions.

Section 2. *Requests for Loans of Works of Art*   When requests for loans from eligible institutions are received by the State Art Director and the specific work or works of art are agreed upon, the REQUEST FOR LOANS OF WORKS OF ART, FAP Form 1 Revised, prepared in triplicate, shall be executed. The full name and address of the institution, the delivery instructions, etc. are to be filled in completely. Two copies of the Request shall be signed by the official representative of the institution.

The State or Regional Director of the Federal Art Project shall indicate his approval by signing in the designated space, and shall enter the date on which delivery is promised. The two signed copies shall be sent to the Director of the Federal Art Project, Washington, D.C., who will countersign the Request and return it at once for further attention. His signature constitutes final approval.

Section 3. *Record of Works of Art*   A RECORD CARD, FAP Form 2 Revised, must be made out in the state office of the Federal Art Project on the completion of each painting or piece of sculpture and for each copy of etchings, lithographs, etc., but need not be made for "record photographs," posters, and similar items.

Section I of the Record Card is to be filled out as soon as a work of art has been completed.

Section II is to be filled out when a work of art is loaned to some public office, agency, or institution on a long-term basis.

Section III is to be filled out when a work of art is sent to Washington for national display or circulating exhibitions.

A.   If the work of art is to be assigned to a public office, agency, or institution on a long-term basis, approval of such loan shall be secured from the Director of the Federal Art Project in conformity with the procedure outlined in section 2. Based upon this approval, Section II of FAP Form 2 Revised shall be completed. FAP Form 2 Revised shall then be attached to FAP Forms 1 Revised and 4 Revised, (see section 5 below) and forwarded to Washington for permanent record.

B.   If an institution which has received a work of art on loan desires to be released from the responsibility of custody of the work, the official representative of the institution shall communicate directly with the Director of the Federal Art Project, Washington, D.C. If arrangements for return of the work of art to the state are completed, FAP Form 2 Revised will be returned to the State Director of the Federal Art Project.

C.   When a work of art is sent to Washington for national display or circulating exhibition, FAP Form 2 Revised should be sent to the Washington office of the Federal Art Project, with Sections I and III executed. If the work of art is returned to the state, FAP Form 2 Revised will also be returned, to be retained in the state pending further disposition of the work of art.

It will be noted that the Washington file of Record Cards will not compile an index of all works of art produced under the Federal Art Project; rather, it will be a file of those works forwarded to Washington or placed on loan by the states with Washington approval.

D.   The procedure outlined above will not apply to works of art which are loaned for exhibition purposes which have received the prior approval of the Director of the Federal Art Project. A record of the disposition of works of art loaned for this purpose will be maintained by the use of FAP Form 18 Revised which shall be executed with a list of the works contained in each shipment, and forwarded to the consignee for signature and return to the consignor.

Section 4. *Identification of Works of Art*   AN IDENTIFICATION CARD, FAP Form 3, is to be filled in and firmly affixed to the back of each picture or base of each sculpture. In the case of oil paintings this Card should not be glued to the back of the canvas, but should be glued and tacked to the stretcher. Care should be taken in affixing Identification Cards so that works of art will not be marred or damaged in any way.

A brass tag reading "WPA Federal Art Project" is to be screwed to the lower center of the frame of picture or attached to the base of sculpture. In the case of unframed pictures the corresponding number of the "WPA Federal Art Project" metal tags should be given the institution with complete instructions for affixing to work after framing.

Section 5. *Receipts for Works of Art*   A RECEIPT FOR LOAN OF WORKS OF ART, FAP Form 4 Revised, shall be prepared in triplicate for each item or group of items loaned to any public agency or institution. Upon delivery of the works of art, the official representative of the institution shall sign two copies and retain the third copy for his own record. One signed copy shall remain in the state files, clipped to the duplicate of the REQUEST FOR LOAN, FAP Form 1 Revised. The original of the Recipt, together with the original of the REQUEST FOR LOAN, FAP Form 1 Revised, and RECORD CARD, FAP Form 2 Revised, shall be sent immediately to the Director of the Federal Art Project, Washington, D.C., to be placed in the Federal record files. A central record file of loans of Works of Art is maintained in Washington, D.C.

Samples of the forms required by this procedure are attached, and a supply of each form will be sent upon request to the Director of the Federal Art Project, Federal Works Progress Administration, Washington, D.C.

This operating procedure supersedes Federal Art Project Memorandum of August 28, 1936, signed by Holger Cahill, concerning loan of works of art produced on the Federal Art Project, which is hereby rescinded.[16]

This procedure not only reflects clear thinking on the mechanics of negotiating and exacting loans of works of art but also indicates a proper respect for detail in the matter of identifications, receipts, and records and regard to federal property. But its most important concept was the fiction of a long-term or quasi-permanent loan of federal property to non-federal tax-supported institutions. These institutions, to be sure, were not sponsors in the ordinary sense of the term. They were rather media by which the Art Project conferred the benefit of its products on the general public. Since the works of art created on and by the Art Project were the property of the federal government, they could not be alienated, except through the regular channels of disposition. For this reason the allocation was made in the form of a loan, and a complex system of records was maintained by the Art Project as evidence of the loan. To all intents and purposes, however, the loan was a gift, in the sense that no likelihood existed that the federal government would recall it. Indeed, in the case of certain kinds of products (e.g., murals), return was impossible.

When in 1939 the Federal Art Project was converted into a number of non-federal projects, the same kind of procedure was used to allow official state and local sponsors to allocate works that were now their property to co-operating tax-supported institutions.*

Cosponsors of the art project were expected to make a contribution which, although it was "in consideration of the loan of works of art to eligible agencies," was carefully described as a transaction completely separate from the loan procedure.[17] Thus the suspicion that federal property was being sold was avoided.

As a result of this procedure, and of the technique of salesmanship of the Art Project in soliciting these contributions, Cahill was able to show a higher percentage of sponsors' contributions in relation to total

---

*No problem arose, of course, if, as sometimes happened, the Federal Art Project allocated works of art to federal agencies or if, after 1939, a state official sponsor allocated works to agencies of the state government.

appropriated funds, and a better record for cash contributions than any other project in Federal One.

The Historical Records Survey, although it derived little financial assistance from sponsors' contributions, devised a neat but largely ineffective method for encouraging and handling small cash contributions. Volumes produced on the project were sent to interested institutions with a covering letter like the following:

> We are mailing you under separate cover the *Inventory of the County Archives of Massachusetts, No. 5—Essex County*, a publication of the Massachusetts division of the Historical Records Survey. This edition is limited to 225 copies, intended mainly for the use of public officials, and for deposit in the larger public and university libraries and historical societies.
>
> This volume is not for sale. It is, however, the policy of the Historical Records Survey in line with the general policy of the Works Progress Administration to solicit from prospective cooperating sponsors voluntary contributions which will assist in defraying the material costs of publication such as paper, stencils, and binding. For the above publication these material costs amount to approximately $2.00 per column. Any contribution made by you for more or less than this amount will be used to meet the material cost of future publications of the Historical Records Survey and will facilitate the publication of such volumes at an early date. If, upon examining this work, you find that it merits your support, and if you wish to assist in meeting the publication charges of future volumes, we will gladly accept your contribution in any amount toward that end.[18]

The fact was that the H.R.S., since its man-month costs were always considerably lower than those of the other arts projects, was not under the same pressure to reduce costs, and could afford to be liberal in the disposition of its products.

An inquiry into the collection of admission funds by the Theater and Music projects is properly undertaken here because, by administrative definition, admission funds were deemed to be sponsors' contributions. This was, to be sure, a strain upon language and logic, for only by stretching meaning could an audience at a concert or play be considered a co-operating sponsor in the same way as was a public or quasi-public agency, or a private non-profit organization. There was no contractual relation, even of the most tenuous sort, between the projects and the audience, for the audience was amorphous and had no legal or quasi-legal standing.

Indeed, in the very first days of the wpa, even before Federal One was devised, the assistant counsel of the wpa in answer to a query advised Bruce McClure as follows:

> The question of admission charges for plays, concerts, etc., is not affected by the foregoing distinction [between federal and non-federal projects]. Any project, whether federal or non-federal, may provide for the payment of admission. However, admissions paid upon a federal project would be covered into the general funds of the United States Treasury and will not be available for use by Works Progress Administration. On the other hand, in the case of a non-federal project, a charge of admission and a provision for the use of moneys so collected can be made a part of the project proposal and a condition of the grant of labor and material to the sponsor.[19]

Later, in September, 1935, the same official repeated this interpretation, but suggested a device whereby admission funds might be collected, but not covered into the Treasury as miscellaneous receipts. His latter follows:

> In your memorandum of August 26 to Lee you ask his opinion on charging admission in connection with federal music and drama projects. The point here is that if admission charges are paid over to an agency of the Federal Government, they must immediately be covered into the Treasury as miscellaneous receipts and therefore, are not available to pay the costs incurred in connection with the project.
>
> However, I cannot see any objection to the following arrangement which would permit admission charges to be used to defray a portion of the cost of the project: On federal projects, W.P.A. will pay the salaries of the musicians or actors. A city will agree to make available a theatre, plus lighting equipment, scenery, services of ticket sellers, etc. There would be no reason why the city could not charge admission, with the consent of W.P.A. and use these admission charges to reimburse itself for the use of the theatre, the cost of scenery, etc. If the thing is done in this way, admission charges will never appear as an item of receipts on the books of W.P.A. in connection with the project and the Comptroller will never be able to make objection since the facts will never be brought to his attention and since, moreover, the admission fees will never become federal funds over which he has any kind of control.[20]

Abt's suggestion was not without merit. In fact, it was in this way that, after 1939, admissions were collected on state music projects. In

1935, however, any arrangement that threatened to transfer responsibility from the federal directors to state or local authorities was suspect. The WPA was made the official sponsor of the arts program precisely to avoid official sponsorship by state and lower bodies. It was recognized that official sponsorship conferred authority not only with respect to the process of project initiation but also with respect to prosecution and supervision. For the same reason, the alternative of co-operating sponsors, even though the title conferred no authority, was equally suspect. In the present instance a city or other local subdivision, if it was asked to supply space and some of the personnel for the privilege of collecting the admission receipts, would surely seek some part in the direction of the project. Federal One wished a free hand. Accordingly, in the early part of the program, although co-operating sponsorship was permitted and officially encouraged, the personnel of Federal One, in Washington and in the states, made no serious effort to encourage this type of local support. Local support was welcome only if it could be divorced from local responsibility.

But if the federal directors did not contemplate with satisfaction the handling of admission funds by local agencies, they were no less distressed by the prospect of having this money flow into the miscellaneous receipts of the Treasury, in whose vaults it remained until Congress chose to appropriate it. It was, they were convinced, worth a thought to retain jurisdiction over this money, and to use it, as a supplement to appropriated funds, for the prosecution of the Music and Theater projects.

The invention of the device that the Music and Theater projects collect and expend admission funds was ingenious. Apparently using as an argument the precedent by which certain officers of the armed services and consular officials have petty cash accounts for purposes peculiar to their responsibilities, Federal One proposed and adopted the procedure for business manager—agent cashier. This official had a dual personality, as his title indicates; as business manager he was responsible for the collection of admission funds; as agent cashier he received cash advances from such receipts, and was responsible for an accounting of his expenditures therefrom.*

The considerations that counseled the charging of admissions and

---

*Since the business manager—agent cashier had other duties besides these, an examination of this institution is not attempted here but later; *vide infra*, pp. 293-302. There is no evidence in the WPA files that the Comptroller General ruled, or was asked to rule, upon the legality of the collection and use of admission funds on Federal One. However, by suggesting changes in the procedure for business manager—agent cashier, he obliquely approved the innovation; *vide infra*, p. 298.

the use of the funds thus collected deserve analysis. In the FERA-CWA period, which antedated the WPA, the charging of admissions was recommended by Jacob Baker, partly because he was interested in the co-operative idea and thought it might find realization in the arts as well as in other fields, and partly because he felt under some constraint to make the arts program self-supporting. The scheme that he had in mind, however, was modest, both in respect to the charges (ten to fifty cents), and in respect to the project, which was confined to the community and meant to serve those with artistic interests in it. In short, it represented the application of the principle of the neighborhood house to the community as a whole and was not, in any sense of the word, a commercial venture.

The subsequent decision on the part of the Federal Theater and Music projects of the WPA to charge for admission was made on quite different grounds. The experience with admission charges in the earlier period had shown conclusively that, in so far as the purpose was to pay expenses, the device was woefully inadequate. The fantasy, however, persisted, at least in certain quarters; and more than once during the life of Federal One, especially during fiscal crises, salvation was sought through emphasis upon the financial possibilities of admission collections. Even the President, whether the idea was his own or impressed on him by others, was intrigued by the concept of a commercially successful theater and concert hall, and his continued stress on the importance of admission collections encouraged an emphasis that, at best, was ineffective and, at worst, was positively dangerous.

The management of any symphony orchestra or concert bureau and the promoters of the theater on Broadway could have easily proved, had their opinion been asked, that such a venture as the Theater and Music projects were attempting could not achieve commercial success. Indeed, the finance office of Federal One was always conscious of the chimerical nature of the idea—as well it might have been—since it had statistics that in this instance, at least, did not lie. The Theater Project throughout its existence paid 4.57 per cent of its total expenditures out of money realized through admission funds; the Music Project, 1.00 per cent. Conceivably, had the projects continued, the Theater Project might have realized 5 per cent, and the Music Project 2 per cent (it collected 1.70 per cent in the fiscal year 1939). The best that could have been expected under the most favorable conditions was the payment of a fair proportion of the non-labor expenses of each project.*

---

*It is not that token charges, such as the twenty-five cents collected at the con-

THE CONSEQUENCES OF COMMERCIALISM

The emphasis upon admission receipts had certain unfortunate consequences. In the first place, it was natural that more attention should have been given to metropolitan areas, where such receipts were likely to be substantial, than to less-populated parts of the country. This trend received its full expression in the Theater Project when, in 1936, the federal director moved her headquarters from Washington to New York City and remained there almost to the end of Federal One. In like manner, but to a less degree, the federal director of the Music Project stressed cosmopolitan acclaim by acting as a guest conductor of the better urban WPA symphony orchestras. Statistics confirm this interpretation. In the Federal Theater Project 48.99 per cent of total expenditure was in New York City, and, if Massachusetts, Illinois, and California are added, the percentage was 81.42. In the Music Project, expenditures within the same area amounted to 56.39 per cent. Concern with admission receipts was not, to be sure, the only cause of this concentration, but the influence of a commercial attitude in furthering this tendency cannot be doubted.*

The concentration of expenditures in this restricted area brought with it two further embarrassments. The encroachment of the Theater Project upon Broadway aroused the opposition of the commercial theater, and it must be allowed that, in so far as the federal theater aped the commercial theater, the protests were justified. By charging less than established prices, the federal theater stood on less sure ground than if it had charged no admission at all. Second, by the same concentration Federal One alienated, if it ever possessed, the support of Congress. A congressman, whatever his faults, is attentive to the pressure of his constituents; and in a democratic way of life, it is important that he

certs at the Library of Congress, are undesirable. The purpose there is to discourage the simply curious and the ill-behaved, so that all music lovers may have an opportunity to attend and to enjoy, without distraction, the program. It is true, of course, that the admission charges of federal theater were not as high as those of the commercial theater (the federal theater's top was one dollar, plus tax), and that a generous portion of the seats were reserved, at a lower price, for the many. The point is, however, that the top was not low enough to preclude the charge of commercialism and that the success of the show and, ultimately, of the project came to be judged in terms of admission receipts.

*The degree of disparity is emphasized when comparison is made between the percentage of expenditures in these four states and the percentage of population in this area (20.19) in relation to the total population of continental United States.

should be. The directors of Federal One forgot that in a commonwealth such as ours, the test of a program is not how good it is for the people but what measure of support on the part of the people it can win. The establishment of a public arts program, if such was the purpose of Federal One, was no more dependent upon the approval of the art world than, a hundred years before, the establishment of public education waited upon the support of the ivy-clad colleges of that age. The spirit of school children in Mississippi who traveled long distances without breakfast to study music in the classes instituted by the Music Project was more important, not only socially and politically but also in relation to the artistic future of America, than an exhibition of WPA art in the New York Museum of Modern Art or a musical performance that rivaled in technique the production of a privately subsidized symphony orchestra. The art world, to be sure, has its rightful responsibilities, among which is the maintenance of standards as art and interest in art spread. But the democratization of art and art appreciation is to be achieved not through the art world but through the people, and only by those who, while retaining their respect for professional competence, are willing to risk their reputation among their colleagues by consorting with sinners.

THE GOLDEN GATE EPISODE

The collection of admission funds, as a source of revenue, could have been justified on one ground only, viz., that the money thus collected from the more prosperous areas was to be used, as in current school equalization programs, for the benefit of poorer areas. Except in a few instances—which were inconsequential, relatively speaking—nothing of the sort was attempted. On the contrary, one of the most amazing episodes in the history of Federal One occurred as a result of the transfer of a substantial sum from funds collected in other states to subsidize a theater project unit at the Golden Gate Exposition in San Francisco. That the motive here was prestige, and prestige alone, cannot be doubted.

Admission collections were deposited in a special account of the Treasury Department and credited to each of the projects within each state. However, it was possible to transfer funds within a given project from one state to another, as well as to transfer funds from one project to another. Indeed, this was not only possible but happened quite frequently. The recommendation for such a transfer usually originated with the state director of a particular project who had a plan to use the desired funds. The transfer itself was in the form of a loan, which, it was expected, the borrowing project would repay. Final approval of the transfer was a central-office responsibility. The recommendation came from the national director of the project to the finance officer of Federal One, who in turn requested the WPA director of finance to execute the transfer through the Treasury offices.

A typical experience with respect to a particular situation of this kind is indicated in the following portion of a report on a field visit by the finance officer of Federal One. The report is dated March 6, 1939, and has reference to the Music Project in the state of Virginia.

I discussed with Mr. Pyle and Miss Gartrell the finance status of the Music Project Admission Account with particular attention to the possibility of returning $2,500 received as a loan from New York State. This $2,500 had been borrowed for the purpose of bringing the North Carolina and Virginia orchestra together, on the understanding that in the course of the current fiscal year there would be a possibility of returning this loan out of the proceeds from concerts given in various parts of North Carolina and Virginia. I found that, as of March 1, the orchestra had collected from concerts in Virginia approximately $2,700; expenditures for these concerts amounted to $2,250, leaving a surplus of $450. Concerts in North Carolina had earned $1,000 gross which was just barely sufficient to cover expenditures of $1,000 in connection with those concerts. In other words, only $450 surplus remained towards the repayment of the $2,500 loan. Three engagements have been booked for the month of March which I am told may bring net proceeds of approximately $300.

If the orchestra is to break up at the end of March in accordance with orders already issued, Virginia will not be able to return to New York State more than $750. I am advised in Washington that the orders have been issued to disband the orchestra because (1) the North Carolina Administration wishes its musicians returned, (2) the combined orchestra is not considered technically qualified to undertake the ambitious program that has been planned.

While I do not desire to interfere with matters for technical or administrative determination, I wish to go on record to say that financially the breaking up of the orchestra in the middle of the season is not a sound procedure since there is a possibility during the three months April, May and June of recouping $500 to $1,000 additional. I, therefore, suggest reconsideration of the technical and administrative grounds on which orders have been issued to break up the orchestra. If the orchestra remains together I can give some assurance that the correct financial procedure will be established to prevent any further losses. For example, a procedure which would permit expenditure of only two thirds of the monies collected would be acceptable to the Project and to the State Administration, and at the same time would guarantee the building up of a balance to be applied to the loan.[21]

This memorandum indicates clearly the dependence of a concert unit of the Music Project upon admission receipts. An "ambitious program" was conceived by virtue of which a symphony orchestra, by attaining technical proficiency, would collect enough admission funds to repay a loan. The future of the orchestra was made to depend, to a considerable degree, upon its ability to liquidate its indebtedness. The whole consideration became purely fiscal. What kind of an orchestra the people of Virginia and North Carolina were prepared or able to support, and what services such an orchestra could perform, became matters of secondary consideration—if they were considered at all. If, on the other hand, the transfer had been outright and not in the form of a loan, the technical proficiency of the orchestra in relation to its environment and its services to the peoples of the two states could have been made the primary criteria of its worth.

But the need of poorer states for financial assistance from richer states, which might have justified the above transfer had it been an absolute transfer and not a loan, could not be invoked to explain the Golden Gate episode.

As early as January, 1938, George Creel, commissioner of the Golden Gate International Exposition Commission, approached Ole Ness, regional director of the Federal Theater in the Far West, with a request that the project consider plans for an exhibit in the Federal Building at that exposition. After further meetings and discussions, Alfred Kastner, representing Ness, visited Washington and discussed such plans with the national office of the WPA. The result was a tentative program for participation approved by Creel on June 5, 1938.

This agreement provided for the construction of an Exhibit Building for the Theater Project with Golden Gate International Exhibition funds. On July 21, 1938, however, the Theater Project was informed by the Commission that, because of lack of funds, it would be unable to carry through its construction plans, and accordingly was terminating its agreement with the Federal Theater Project.

It was at this moment that the Federal Theater Project assumed the initiative. J. Howard Miller, deputy director of the Project, was sent to the West Coast to persuade Creel to reconsider his decision. The result was that Creel persuaded Miller to accept a new plan whereby the Commission and the Federal Theater Project, acting jointly, would undertake the construction of a theater unit in the Federal Building, toward which the Theater Project would contribute $65,000. This sum was to be taken from the special deposit accounts of admissions collected by Federal Theater Project units throughout the nation, and was to be transferred to the account of the Exposition Commission. On August 19, 1938, in answer to an inquiry from the WPA, the Acting Comptroller General of the United States expressed his opinion that such a transfer was legal. In a letter dated August 31, 1938, Mrs. Woodward informed Creel that the WPA was prepared to make the desired transfer, and the transfer was subsequently consummated. The building was completed for the opening of the Exhibition on February 18, 1939.

In the meantime preparations were being made for the Federal Theater program at the coming Exposition. On December 1, 1938, Robert C. Schnitzer was appointed supervisor of the unit, and shortly thereafter he submitted a project proposal for its operations. According to the proposal, the general plan of operations was as follows:

1. A unit of 130 persons to supply performers, dancers, writers, clerical, and other operating services to the Exposition.

2. Loan of equipment and personnel from the San Francisco Federal Theater Project to the Golden Gate International Exposition Unit for the duration of the Fair.

3. Loan of equipment and personnel from the Los Angeles Federal Theater Project to the Golden Gate International Exposition Unit for the duration of the Fair.

Performances in the theater were to include marionette and children's plays, the dance, legitimate dramas, musical comedies, and various other productions. An admission was to be charged for these performances in the amount of twenty-five cents for adults and ten cents for children. In addition, twelve films picturing the work of various government departments were to be shown in the Theater Building free of charge.

In addition to performances in the Theater Building, the Federal Theater Project was to have a national exhibit of photographs, theater models, and design and research, and was also to arrange for radio broadcasts from a studio in the same building. The exhibits were to be open to the public free of charge.

Part of the plan was that when the Exposition was over, the complete federal building and all of its equipment (and, in addition, other exhibit buildings that occupied the same wing) would be dismantled and re-erected on a site in San Francisco to serve as a permanent art center, and that the transferred Theater Building would serve as headquarters for the San Francisco unit, and thus save the government rental charges then being paid on the present quarters of the project unit.

Furthermore, it was argued that, on conservative estimates, collections, from which the $65,000 was to be returned to the special deposit accounts from which it was transferred, would total from $150,000 to $200,000 for the life of the Exposition. If the lower estimate is taken and calculations based on a year's duration, this would have meant average daily collections of slightly over $400, or a daily audience of over 1,600, if adults, or 4,000, if children. As a matter of fact, receipts for the first two months of operation totalled $2,200, which constituted a daily average of thirty-six dollars.

But by April, 1939, it was clear that the original investment of $65,000 was not the only issue. The plan had been that the San Francisco and Los Angeles Federal Theater units, personnel, and equipment would be transferred to the Exposition unit. Thus there would be no added expenses, except a few thousand dollars for travel. Actually, however, in addition to the original investment of $65,000, the WPA by April, 1939, had made commitments to the amount of $43,000 for the period ending June 30, 1939. Of this sum, $18,000 covered the cost of transportation and per diem payments of the Los Angeles personnel; $5,000 was expended for extra equipment installed in the theater; $10,000 for ferry charges across the bay; and $10,000 for miscellaneous non-labor items. Thus a total investment of $108,000 was involved. As early as March, 1939, the finance office had attempted to discourage requests for additional funds for the venture, and in April the decision was made that no further funds would be authorized until admission receipts should reach the expenditure figure of $105,000, though it is not clear that adherence to this decision was rigid. At any rate, the statutory provision of the 1939 act, which forbade a theater project, brought the incident to a close.

If the Federal Theater Project had been a commercial concern, advertising its wares—which is precisely what it was in this instance—the expenses might rightly have been charged to public relations. Indeed, when it is remembered that the WPA symphony orchestra of Virginia-North Carolina was embarrassed by its failure to repay a loan of $2,500 from the New York City fund, whereas over $100,000 above the original estimate (including $65,000 from the admission receipt funds from other states) was spent on the Theater Project unit at the Golden Gate Exposition, the movement away from the idea of social service toward professionalism, with all the fanfare of a commercial enterprise, becomes obvious.

## ANALYSIS OF ADMISSION FUND RECEIPTS AND EXPENDITURES

Upon examination, the fact emerges that three states—New York City (which was considered to be a "state" under WPA), California, and Illinois—were responsible for the collection of approximately 80 per cent of the total, and twenty-four other states were responsible for the remaining 20 per cent. On the other hand, Music Project admission collections do not show such marked concentration. The four states with the best showing—California, New York City, Illinois, and Massachusetts—were responsible for 67 per cent of the total collections, with seventeen other states responsible for the remaining 33 per cent.

Over the life of Federal One, which was about three and a half years of actual operation, if one leaves out the first few months of sporadic but growing activity, the following table shows that there was gradual, but by no means spectacular, improvement in the amount of admission collections.

### ADMISSIONS COLLECTED

|  | THEATER | MUSIC |
|---|---|---|
| Period thru June 30, 1937* | $ 849,370.08 | $127,662.01 |
| Fiscal Year Ending June 30, 1938 | 503,676.68 | 158,003.61 |
| Fiscal Year Ending June 30, 1939 | 795,785.05 | 202,953.23 |
| Total | $2,148,831.81 | $488,618.85 |

*Approximately 1½ years of operation.

However, there is no evidence that the projects ever showed any prospect of becoming self-supporting. Indeed, though they approached the goal of paying non-labor costs, they never reached it. The fond hope, so often expressed, that these projects could achieve self-support never had the slightest basis in the experience of the FERA, the CWA, or the WPA.

The relation of admission receipts to project costs makes this clear. The table on page 289 indicates such relationship on the basis of costs from appropriated funds and costs from the sum of appropriated and admission funds.

## FEDERAL THEATER PROJECT

| Period | Expenditures | | | Admission Funds Collected | Admission Funds | |
|---|---|---|---|---|---|---|
| | Federal Funds Expended | Admission Funds Expended | Total Expended | | As a Per Cent of Federal Funds Expended | As a Per Cent of Total Funds Expended |
| Through June 30, 1937 | $23,185,493 | $ 734,546 | $23,920,039 | $ 849,370 | 3.66 | 3.55 |
| Fiscal year 1937-38 | 11,393,481 | 493,449 | 11,886,930 | 503,676 | 4.42 | 4.24 |
| Fiscal year 1938-39 | 10,601,027 | 669,044 | 11,270,071 | 795,785 | 7.51 | 7.06 |
| Total | $45,180,001 | $ 1,897,039 | $47,077,040 | $ 2,148,831 | 4.76 | 4.57 |

## FEDERAL MUSIC PROJECT

| Period | Expenditures | | | Admission Funds Collected | Admission Funds | |
|---|---|---|---|---|---|---|
| | Federal Funds Expended | Admission Funds Expended | Total Expended | | As a Per Cent of Federal Funds Expended | As a Per Cent of Total Funds Expended |
| Through June 30, 1937 | $25,042,858 | $ 109,724 | $25,152,582 | $ 127,662 | .51 | .51 |
| Fiscal year 1937-38 | 11,548,214 | 130,460 | 11,678,674 | 158,003 | 1.37 | 1.35 |
| Fiscal year 1938-39 | 11,777,310 | 172,958 | 11,950,268 | 202,953 | 1.72 | 1.70 |
| Total | $48,368,382 | $ 413,142 | $48,781,524 | $ 488,618 | 1.01 | 1.00 |

The upward curve of admission collections is evident from these tables. Yet a project that throughout its life has collected from the public less than 5 per cent of its cost of operation can hardly be said to show evidence of self-support. Much less can this be said of a project that has collected only 1 per cent of its total cost of operation. Even on the basis of the last and most favorable year, with theater collections accounting for 7 per cent of cost and music collections somewhat less than 2 per cent, the percentage of admission receipts to total costs remains inconsequential.

The picture does not change materially when figures on man-month costs are examined. For the fiscal years 1938 and 1939 the effect of admissions collections and expenditures on man-month cost figures was as follows:

| | THEATER Fiscal Year | | MUSIC Fiscal Year | |
| --- | --- | --- | --- | --- |
| | 1938 | 1939 | 1938 | 1939 |
| Man-month cost, federal funds | $108.6 | $102.9 | $95.1 | $92.7 |
| Man-month cost, admission funds | 4.6 | 6.5 | 1.1 | 1.4 |
| Total man-month | 113.2 | 109.4 | 96.2 | 94.1 |
| Admissions collected per man-month | 4.7 | 7.7 | 1.3 | 1.6 |

Thus far, the figures presented have been designed to show the relation between admissions and costs for each of the two projects as a whole, Naturally, the situation varied among the states. Only two states, California and Illinois, collected 10 per cent or more of the total cost of operations, and one state, Colorado, came close to that ratio. Moreover, the effort to collect admissions necessitated added expenditures, so that what was gained by making the public share in the cost of operation served to increase that cost. Furthermore, Illinois, the one state that led all the others as far as theater admissions were concerned, achieved its unique position through one outstanding production, the Swing Mikado.*

Obviously, the Swing Mikado was in the nature of a "sport" that

---

*From September 25, 1938, the opening date of the Swing Mikado in Chicago, to the closing date in Chicago, February 25, 1939, total admissions collected were $105,284. Thus in the short span of five months the Illinois Theater Project collected on one single production over 25 per cent of the total collected on all its varied productions during a period of three and a half years.

by the laws of probability could not be repeated very often. New York City, on the other hand, shows a much truer picture, for there the collection during the year, despite several apparently successful plays, amounted to less than 5 per cent of the operating cost.

On the Music Project the picture is still less encouraging, for not a single state collected as much as 5 per cent of its cost of operation.

A further study reveals other interesting facts. For the Illinois Theater Project, for example, the figures show a man-month cost from federal funds of $94.30, which is quite normal in view of the schedule of wages for Illinois. However, in order to collect admissions equivalent to $21.90 per man-month, expenditures from such admissions were made to the extent of $18.20 per man-month. In other words, the greater the admissions, the greater the expenditures to collect such admissions. It may be true, as calculated elsewhere in describing the cost of operations, that the reduction in man-year cost during the fiscal year 1939 was in part due to increased admission collections. However, it certainly is not true that all of the admissions collected went to the federal government for reduction in the cost of operation. On the contrary, it may be said that only the smaller part of the seven or eight dollars per man-month collected on the average by the Theater Project during fiscal 1939 served this purpose.

In this connection the cost of the business manager—agent cashiers and the box office treasurers set up to handle the mechanics of collecting and expending admission funds is pertinent. The salaries of these employees, with very few exceptions, were chargeable full-time to project operation. No accurate figures are available on the total number so assigned to the Federal Theater and Music projects, but probably between 400 and 500 employees were needed to handle the cash, make purchases from moneys collected, and perform the necessary clerical and accounting operations involved in the procedure. The total of their salaries alone may well have equaled the $2.5 million that the projects collected during their three and a half years of operation.

The objects of expenditure from admission receipts are indicated in the following table.

EXPENDITURES FROM ADMISSION FUNDS:
PERCENTAGE OF TOTAL FOR EACH CLASS OF EXPENDITURES, JULY-DECEMBER, 1938*

| CLASS | THEATER | MUSIC |
|---|---|---|
| Total | 100.00 | 100.00 |
| Materials and supplies | 36.27 | 26.80 |

EXPENDITURES FROM ADMISSION FUNDS:
PERCENTAGE OF TOTAL FOR EACH CLASS OF EXPENDITURES
JULY-DECEMBER, 1938*—*Continued*

| CLASS | THEATER | MUSIC |
|---|---|---|
| Advertising | 25.96 | 16.59 |
| Rent | 15.44 | 20.59 |
| Travel | 9.96 | 15.74 |
| Taxes | 6.53 | 3.14 |
| Miscellaneous | 4.17 | 7.91 |
| Emergency employment | 1.67 | 9.23 |

*This distribution does not hold precisely true for all periods, but it is reasonably representative.

It is interesting that the two objects of expenditure that were always stressed as necessitating admission charges (viz., advertising and emergency employment) account for scarcely more than 25 per cent of total expenditures. On the other hand, expenditures in the Theater Project for materials, supplies, and rent, and these plus travel in the Music Project, account for over 50 per cent of total expenditures.*

PROHIBITION OF THE USE OF ADMISSION FUNDS
BY THE PROJECTS

Part (b) of Section 13 of the 1939 ERA Act read:

All receipts and collections of Federal agencies by reason of operations in consequence of appropriations made in this joint resolution, except cash contributions of sponsors of projects and amounts credited by revolving funds authorized by this joint resolution, shall be covered into the Treasury as miscellaneous receipts.

Since the operation of a theater project was prohibited by the same law, the question of the use of admission receipts was pertinent now only with reference to the Music Program. In this case arrangements were made whereby the collection of admission charges became the responsibility of the sponsor, and the money itself reckoned as a return for the sponsor's contribution—and, thus, as non-federal money. This arrangement is discussed elsewhere.†

*The expenditure for taxes was necessitated by a ruling of the Commissioner of Internal Revenue, who held that the WPA was not a "religious, educational or charitable organization" within the meaning of the law. His reasoning did not appeal to the WPA officials, but efforts to have the ruling changed were unsuccessful.

†*Vide infra*, pp. 327-29.

The question of the disposition of admission funds already collected and not obligated remained. At first, it was hoped that these balances could be used as before, especially during the difficult transition period from federal to state control. On July 1, 1939, instructions were issued to the effect that "all nonfederal cash received prior to July 1, 1939 from admissions collected . . . shall remain available for obligation and expenditure until further notice except that available balances received as admissions for the Music Project shall be used only for essential advertising and emergency labor."[22] However, on August 25, 1939, the Comptroller General ruled that "any unobligated balance of receipts from such projects must be deposited and covered into the Treasury as required by section 13 (b) with respect to receipts and collections from projects operating under the Federal Emergency Appropriation Act of 1939. Consequently, such accumulated funds may not be transferred for use on state sponsored projects as suggested in the two questions you submit."[23]

Counsel for the WPA believed the decision to be unwarranted, but, for reasons of policy, no serious effort was made to seek reconsideration.

## THE BUSINESS MANAGER–AGENT CASHIER

Since the procedure for business manager–agent cashier was invented, among other reasons, for the purpose of handling admission receipts, its nature may properly be considered in the present context. Hallie Flanagan, in her book on the Federal Theater Project, writes:

> While we should have liked to spend all our time on theatre planning, that was not possible. At least half of every day had to go to administration, for government procedure, particularly at any point where it concerns the spending of public money, is, very rightfully, a labyrinth of protective devices. In the early days none of us working on Federal Theatre fully realized this fact; and our impatience with the delays, the checks and rechecks, the changes and counterchanges must have been maddening to the WPA in Washington, New York and elsewhere. On the other hand, these officials knew nothing of the exigencies of theatre business and could not understand why the handling of the arts projects should differ in any particular from the handling of any other WPA project.[24]

It is true that the financial procedure of the government, as it developed and become fixed in the course of its history, was not adapted to the exigencies of the arts. It was calculated to dismay and confuse the officials of the program, very few of whom had had previous experience in government employ. At times, procedure seemed to encompass them to such a degree that it took on the aspect of a bureaucratic conspiracy to embarrass the program to the point of paralysis.

Government finance officers and their clerks, to be sure, live and act within a routine that has become habitual. They, no less than artists, feel annoyance when their routine is disturbed. Moreover, because of their experience, they are naturally suspicious of those who seek exceptions to the normal procedures. All procedures, particularly finance procedures, derive from experience; and in government, finance procedures are designed to protect the commonwealth. Private enterprise can accept the principle that when the cost of surveillance is greater than the money saved by it, petty peculation is to be tolerated; but government cannot. The reason for this is obvious. Accounting in a profit-making business is cost accounting, and expenses are viewed in relation to gain. Government accounting, on the other hand, is legal accounting. Its purpose is to make certain that encumbrances are made and money expended in accordance with statutory and other limitations upon the funds with which the agency operates. A government cannot countenance illegality, even when the illegality would save the public money.

There is another difference between government and private enterprise in the matter of finance. The primary purpose of business, whatever services it may perform in the process, is to make a profit. Government, on the other hand, undertakes to perform a public service, which, whether profitable or not in accounting terms, is deemed necessary or proper. It is impossible, for instance, to use cost accounting as a criterion of the worth of the public schools, public welfare institutions, or even the protection of the public from harm through the police and fire departments. To be sure, one might argue that these services and others like them are profitable even in the financial sense, but since the profit, however great it may be, is not convertible into cash, there is no device of cost accounting by which a ledger can be kept.

Accordingly, it was not only necessary but also proper that the finances of the arts program should be subject to legal accountability. But, since there were certain exigencies inherent in such a program that could not be met through existing procedure, it was also necessary and proper that new procedures should be invented which, while maintaining legal accountability, would allow the program that flexibility without which operations would be impossible or seriously impeded. Here, though the inertia of established custom was not completely overcome, those responsible for financial operations showed themselves in general open-minded and co-operative. These qualities were nowhere more manifest than in the elaboration of the procedure for the business manager–agent cashier.*

This institution was designed specifically to meet certain problems peculiar to the arts program, and was not available to any other projects of the WPA. Indeed, although in the beginning there was some thought of using it in all the arts projects, in practice its use was initially restricted to the Theater and Music projects. The responsibilities of the business manager–agent cashier were, as the title indicates, twofold. As business manager, the official was designated by the WPA and responsible directly to the state director of finance. At the same time, he was a project employee who was appointed to this post as business manager by the state administrator on recommendation of the state director of the project involved. As business manager, he was responsible for (1) the collection of admissions and (2) the procurement of materials and services. Since a person performing these duties was required to account for his operations, the official, as business manager, also became an accounting officer.†

As agent cashier, the official was a WPA employee designated by the U.S. Treasury Department to handle a cash advance and to account for expenditures therefrom. In this capacity he was directly responsible to the state U.S. Treasury disbursing clerk, and bonded to the U.S. Treasury.

The exigencies counseling this device for the Theater and Music projects were: (1) the handling of cash advances; (2) the collection of

---

*Formal instructions on the procedure for the business manager–agent cashier were first issued on January 11, 1936 as *Supplement 1 to Bulletin #29*, Appendix B, under the title "Financial Procedure for Projects Operating under WPA-sponsored Federal Project No. 1." These instructions were superseded on December 16, 1936, by Operating Procedure No. F-45 issued under the title "Procedure for Business Manager–Agent Cashier."

†The business manager who handled collections and purchases for the arts projects should not be confused with another official often called "Business Manager for Federal Number One." This latter was essentially the administrative co-ordinator in a state for the several programs operating under Federal One. The dual use was unfortunate, but the confusion may be easily clarified if it is understood that when the term was applied to the person handling collections and purchases, it was almost invariably joined with the term applied to his cash disbursing function, namely "agent cashier"; hence the title "business manager–agent cashier." Actually, the person exercising the combined functions was commonly known by those operating the arts projects as the "agent cashier," without the prefactory words "business manager"; seldom, if ever, was he known as "business manager" without the added words "agent cashier."

admission receipts; and (3) the procurement of materials and services that could not be got, or as readily got, through customary governmental channels.

Both the Theater and Music projects—the former more than the latter—undertook tours. Once touring was attempted, the expenses of the company had to be met. The project personnel, consisting of persons in need of relief, were not in an economic position to pay their own expenses and then to seek reimbursement later, as is the normal procedure in the government. Consequently, it was necessary to have at hand a bonded business manager–agent cashier who had ready cash for these expenses.

Second, the business manager–agent cashier was designed to relieve these projects of the necessity of following standard governmental procurement procedures, such as were followed by all other WPA projects. Under standard procedures, requisitions for both materials and services were prepared by the operating projects and submitted to the Treasury Procurement Division for action. To those trained in the theatrical tradition that "the show must go on," such procedures involved delays that made operation extremely hazardous. It might be necessary, especially on the road, to rent a theater or hall at a moment's notice, to purchase a loaf of bread every night for a particular scene in a play,[25] or, because of a breakdown, to buy a part of equipment or a prop immediately. Obviously, it was impossible to meet emergencies like these through normal procedures. Moreover, even if no emergency were involved, the government purchasing agent, accustomed to the purchase of clerical and construction supplies, was not schooled in the discernment necessary for the purchase of theatrical costumes, musical instruments, and artists' supplies.*

Finally, since it was decided to collect admissions to certain concerts and performances, it was necessary to have an official who was responsible for the cash thus collected.

There were two main steps in the process by which this procedure was accepted. In the first place, the WPA officials in charge of Federal One were under the necessity of devising—if not creating—it, and of finding precedents of a kind upon which they might base their plea for

*The procurement authority of the business manager–agent cashier was of two kinds: (1) the authority to obligate the government for purchases that did not immediately involve a cash transaction, which attached to the officer qua business manager; and (2) the authority to make "on the spot" cash purchases with money advanced by the Treasury Department, which attached to the official qua agent cashier.

exception. In the second place, they had the task of securing formal authority to depart from established routine. This story cannot be clearly told. It seems that the initial inspiration was that of Jacob Baker, who discovered precedents in army procedure and that of U.S. consular officials, who keep cash on hand for American travelers in distress. Apparently, after little or no consultation with the General Accounting Office and the U.S. Treasury Department, *Bulletin No. 35, Transportation and Subsistence Allowance for Security Wage Workers, Part II, Group Travel Basis,* was issued on November 7, 1935. The pertinent part of this procedure, which was so general in its requirements that it was sure to provoke objections on the part of the General Accounting Office and the Treasury Department, was as follows:

Sec. 5. *Definition* This procedure applies only to Federal projects and is not on the reimbursable basis. The class of travelers involved will consist entirely of groups traveling from location to location on such projects as traveling theatre companies, where total or partial transportation and/or subsistence may be supplied either by expenditure of receipts resulting from project activities or by the cooperating sponsors. Travel shall always be authorized by the Federal Director in charge of the project for which travel is made. State or Regional Directors should always allow sufficient time in which to obtain the proper authorization.

Sec. 6. *Procedure* The fact that travel expenses may be paid in whole or in part from other than appropriated Federal funds makes it mandatory that some specific arrangement be made whereby such transportation and subsistence expenses may be paid legitimately.

In connection with the group travel contemplated, it will be impossible for transportation and subsistence expenses to be handled on a reimbursement basis. It will, therefore, be necessary for the State or Regional Director of the Federal Project, in cooperation with the State Disbursing Officer in the state in which the projects originate, to appoint a business manager for each traveling troupe. The business manager will act as an agent cashier, and in this dual capacity, will be responsible for the procurement of all necessary essentials and services, and for the payment of all bills as a direct result thereof.

The person selected shall be appointed an agent cashier by the Chief Disbursing Officer and will be bonded (personally paid bond) to the United States Government in an amount satisfactory to that officer.

It will be the responsiblity of the Business Manager—Agent Cashier to account for all receipts resulting from the troupe's activities and all funds advanced to him by the State Disbursing Officer. The manner of such accountability shall be determined by procedure promulgated by the Commissioner of Accounts and Deposits.

The agent cashier will be required to meet the obligations of his troupe primarily from funds received in the way of admission fees as a result of the project's activities, and shall not obligate the funds advanced by the Chief Disbursing Officer unless the receipts of the project are insufficient to meet the project requirements.

Although arrangements covering transportation and subsistence of the individuals of a troupe may or may not be on a per person basis, *it is to be understood* that under no circumstances will an agent cashier be authorized to expend in excess of $3.00 per day per person for the subsistence of his troupe.

The person selected to perform the duties of Business Manager—Agent Cashier of a traveling troupe must be a person of integrity and administrative ability, and the person so designated must be impressed with the responsibility delegated to him.[26]

These instructions were not considered adequate; and subsequently, informal discussions were held between representatives of the WPA Division of Finance and representatives of the General Accounting Office, and, possibly, of the U.S. Treasury Department. As a result, a preliminary draft was made of a procedure that, as amended, subsequently appeared as Appendix B, *Supplement No. 1 to Bulletin No. 29*, under the title "Financial Procedure for Projects Operating under W.P.A. Sponsored Federal Project No. 1," dated January 11, 1936. This preliminary draft was presented to the Comptroller General for informal approval.* In reply, the Comptroller General wrote a letter that, though it indicated neither approval nor disapproval, suggested certain changes in the procedure, and thereby implied approval contingent upon adoption of the suggestions.†

The WPA adopted the changes suggested in the Comptroller General's letter and issued the procedure.

It is significant that the Comptroller General, after making his suggestions for amendment, closes with a promise of continued co-operation:

> However, should any difficulties be encountered in the use of the standard forms provided for such accounting matters, upon request I shall be pleased to assign representative of this office to assist your administration in the preparation of such forms and otherwise assist in the putting into effect of the established accounting procedure applicable in such matters.[27]

This appendix was supplemented on October 3, 1936, by new in-

---

*The Comptroller General was, in effect, asked to give an anticipatory judgment, which, though it bound neither his office nor any other agency of the government, provided reasonable assurance for action.

†The Comptroller General said in effect, "If you make the changes I indicate, I shall not question the legality of expenditures made under this procedure." From the point of view of this study, the changes suggested by the Comptroller General are not important. The letter, as well as discussion of it, appears on pp. 150-57 of the *House Hearings of the Committee on Appropriations on the Further Additional Relief Appropriation* for fiscal year 1939.

structions regarding appointment and responsibilities of these officials. These instructions read:

Section 1. *General* Pending the issuance of detailed instructions relative to Business Manager–Agent Cashiers, the following regulations concerning their appointment and responsibilities are to be observed. Regulations previously issued which are in conflict herewith are hereby superseded.

Section 2. *Appointment* Recommendations for appointment to the positions of Business Manager–Agent Cashier shall be made by the State Director of the Federal Theatre Project or Federal Music Project, as the case may be. Subject to the prior approval of the State Disbursing Clerk and the Chief Disbursing officer of the United States Treasury, and with the approval of the State Administrator, appointment of Business Manager–Agent Cashiers shall be made by the State Director of Finance and Statistics.

Section 3. *Responsibilities* Business Manager–Agent Cashiers shall be responsible to State Disbursing Clerks for the proper handling of and accounting for such cash advances as are made to them by State Disbursing Clerks. Business Manager–Agent Cashiers shall be responsible to project supervisors for such duties as may be assigned to them in connection with project operations. They are responsible to the State Director of Finance and Statistics for all activities in connection with the receipt of admissions and other collections, for all activities as purchasing agents for project units, and for such timekeeping duties as may be assigned to them.

Section 4. *Expenses* The salaries and expenses of Business Manager–Agent cashiers shall be charged to the project units which they serve.[28]

Final procedure for this office appeared as Operating Procedure No. F-45, dated December 16, 1936. The main points in this procedure were as follows:

1. Admissions might be collected for performances of the Theater and Music projects.

2. Forms were prescribed to account for all such collections, and all monies received were to be deposited in special deposit accounts to the credit of the state U.S. Treasury disbursing clerk.

3. Expenditures might be made out of admissions deposited for project purposes and for all objects for which appropriated funds might be used, except that admissions might not be used for payment of regularly assigned WPA workers.

4. Admissions collected might be used for certain objects for which appropriated funds could not be used, namely, for

advertising, for printing not contracted for through the Government Printing Office, and for workers hired on an emergency basis.

5. Procurement authority was given to the business manager–agent cashier, who might make purchases out of any available source of funds: appropriated funds, admission funds, or sponsors funds.

6. An agent cashier might receive a cash advance from the state U.S. Treasury disbursing clerk to be used for emergency expenditures. The agent cashier is accountable to the state U.S. Treasury disbursing clerk for all expenditures from the cash advance. The cash advance is reimbursed through periodic submittal of the prescribed vouchers.

7. The business manager–agent cashier had to be bonded to WPA for all collections and to the state U.S. Treasury disbursing clerk for his cash advance.

From what has been said, it is clear that neither the General Accounting Office nor the Treasury Department was intransigent in its attitude toward the arts program. Their concern was for the use of standard procedures where such were possible, and in other cases, for the writing of procedures that would be adequate to guard the public interest.

Although the device of business manager–agent cashier was invented to meet the exigencies of the Theater and Music projects, there was a temptation to use it for other projects. The written procedures, to be sure, used no language that formally restricted its use to the Theater and Music projects. Indeed, the very first sentence of Appendix B reads, "Admissions may be charged for performances and exhibitions of work projects operating under W.P.A. Sponsored Federal Project No. 1."[29] The use of the world, "exhibitions" must indicate a reference to art exhibits. Even Operating Procedure No. F-45, issued a year later, although it makes specific reference only to the Music and Theater projects and omits all mention of exhibitions, contains no specific prohibition against the use of the procedure in other Federal One projects. In fact, there is clear evidence of sporadic attempts, some of them successful until they were discovered and forbidden by the central office, to apply this special procedure to the Art Project, and even to the Writers' Project and the Historical Records Survey. The Art Project in

New York City, for instance, received permission to use the business manager–agent cashier procedure for the purchase of art supplies. The size of the project seemed to justify the exception. However, Audrey McMahon, who directed the project and also supervised, as regional director, New York State and New Jersey, requested in October, 1938, the extension of the same privilege to those two states. The finance office of Federal One recommended that the request be denied on the ground that procedures already existing provided adequate facilities. The additional exceptions were not granted. Thus, although the need for exception was clearly demonstrable only in the Theater and Music projects, there was a definite tendency to take advantage of it in projects where its use was not justified by special conditions.

Moreover, although for purposes of touring and immediate procurement on the road cash advances were clearly necessary, or at least eminently convenient, there was no justification for the large amounts of some of these advances; the New York City agent cashier for instance, had a cash advance of $15,000. In the early part of the program advances of $10,000 were not usual; normal advances ranged from $3,000 to $5,000. Considerable confusion arose in the use of these funds, and especially in the accounting for them—particularly since those appointed to the office were almost always men who were untrained in bookkeeping and strangers to the severe formalities that encompass the use of federal funds. It is not surprising, therefore, that some cases of considerable peculation occurred; for a time, bonding companies were reluctant to place bonds.

Finally, there arose the practice of making full use of the authority conferred by the procedure. Funds being available, there was the tendency to use them for any and all kinds of equipment, materials, and services, and not to limit their use to the kind of situation for which the exception was originally made.

In the end, of course, these irregularities were eliminated. It was eventually found unnecessary to exercise the full authority permitted by the procedure. It was discovered that the projects could operate efficiently if most purchasing was handled through the normal procurement procedure and the use of the procurement authority of the business manager–agent cashier was limited to cases of genuine emergency and situations for which normal procedure was demonstrably inadequate. Even in these cases experience proved that large advances were unnecessary. A petty cash fund of from $50 to $100 was found everywhere to be sufficient for a stationary company, and $500 to $1,000 for a traveling troupe. There is no evidence that, under these reasonable restrictions, theater or music operations suffered.

## SPECIAL PROCUREMENT PROCEDURE FOR THE
## FEDERAL ART PROJECT

Although the procedure for business manager–agent cashier was permitted on the Art Project only in rare instances, it was clear that this project, like the Theater and Music projects, also had a special procurement problem. Individual artists, for instance, acquire personal preferences with respect to kinds of paint, brushes, and other supplies to which they have become habituated. Standard procurement procedure, however, calls for requisition by non-proprietary specifications. This difficulty was met on November 19, 1937, by the addition of Section 11 to Operating Procedure No. F-1, which permitted under certain conditions proprietary requisitions by the Federal Art Project.[30]

Since the Art Project collected from sponsors a considerable amount of cash contributions, which were deposited with the Treasury in special deposit accounts and intended for purchase of materials and supplies, this same dispensation was applied to purchases from these special deposit accounts. Federal Art Project Letter No. 2, released to the field on August 26, 1938, notified the state WPA administrations of this ruling:

> Attention is called to the provisions of operating Procedure No. F-1 relating to requisition for proprietary articles required by the Federal Art Project. These provisions apply to purchase from co-sponsors funds deposited with the U.S. Treasury as well as those made from Federal funds.[31]

A second form of special dispensation was also given to the Art Project. It was not, however, peculiar to the Art Project but had been granted previously to the WPA Household Service Demonstration projects and to the WPA Nursery School projects. These had experienced difficulty in procuring food supplies, especially fresh vegetables, which could not possibly be handled through the usual channels because of delays involved. The solution was to issue a blanket requisition for purchases of the needed supplies for an amount not exceeding $300. This blanket requisition was in effect a letter of credit that the supervisor used in making purchases directly from vendors. The invoices were accumulated by the supervisor and transmitted through the usual administrative channels to the state U.S. Treasury procurement officer.[32]

302

This technique was exactly suited to the needs of the Federal Art Project, for it was usually impossible to anticipate material and supplies requirements, and, consequently, it was often necessary for the Art Project supervisor, and even the project workers, to expend their own meager cash on purchases at the nearest art supply store. The use of this device, which was generally permitted in an amount not exceeding fifty dollars for any single blanket requisition, solved the problem.

## THE FEDERAL THEATER PROJECT
## AND THE PURCHASE OF ROYALTIES

The Federal Theater Project was permitted to purchase rights to the use of plays through royalty contracts with the authors. When, however, such contracts were made with employees of the Federal Theater Project, suspicion of irregularity was natural. In general, the Theater Project considered the following contracts proper: (1) if the play had been written before the author was employed on the project, even though no copyright had been taken; or (2) if the play was written on the author's own time while he was an employee of the project. In the latter case, unless there was compelling evidence to the contrary, an affidavit by the author that the play was not written on government time was considered adequate evidence. Although it is true that if either of these conditions held, the author was entitled to royalties, there was a wide area for misrepresentation, connivance, and—in the absence of intent to deceive—confusion and misunderstanding. Payments of doubtful legality occurred, and in November, 1938, it was ruled that plays or music or material for radio broadcasts might not be rented when such materials had been written by a project employee during the period of his assignment to the government, even though it had been prepared on the employee's own time; or, under any conditions, where the material was to be used at a location where the worker was actually assigned at the time of its use.

1. Circular No. 1, Preliminary Statement of Information for Sponsors of Works Progress Administration Projects, June 15, 1935, Section 5.

2. *Ibid.*, Section 9.

3. General Letter No. 291, November 1, 1939.

4. *Supplement No. 1 to Bulletin No. 29.* wpa-Sponsored Federal Project No. 1, September 30, 1935, Section 4.

5. *Ibid.*, Section 12.

6. *Ibid.*

7. *Ibid.*

8. *Ibid.*

9. Handbook of Procedures for State and District Works Progress Administrations, March 21, 1936.

10. *Ibid.*, May 15, 1936, Chap. IX, Section 11.

11. U.S. Congress, House. Committee on Appropriations. 76th Cong., 3d sess. (fiscal year 1941), *Hearings of a Subcommittee . . . on Emergency Relief Appropriation*, pp. 590-91.

12. Memorandum, Davidson to Morris, April 4, 1939.

13. Memorandum, Holmes to Morris, June 7, 1939.

14. Memorandum, Davidson to Morris, April 4, 1939.

15. Memorandum, Morris to Holmes, June 10, 1939.

16. Operating Procedure No. W-12, wpa, March 20, 1937.

17. Federal Art Project Letter No. 1, August 22, 1938; Federal Art Project Letter No. 2, August 26, 1938.

18. Letter, Montana State Director of the Writers' Project to Jonesville Public Library, Jonesville, Montana, n.d. (1938), wpa Files.

19. Memorandum, Abt to McClure, July 11, 1937, wpa Files.

20. Memorandum, Abt to McClure, September 3, 1935, wpa Files.

21. Memorandum, Davidson to Morris, March 6, 1939, wpa Files.

22. Telegram Serial No. 228, wpa, July 1, 1939.

23. Letter, Comptroller General to Federal Works Administrator, August 25, 1939, wpa Files.

24. Hallie Flanagan, *Arena* (New York: Duell, Sloan & Pearce, 1940), pp. 52-53.

25. *Ibid.*, p. 34.

26. *Bulletin No. 35. Transportation and Susistence Allowance for Security Wage Workers*, wpa, November 7, 1935. Part II, Group Travel Basis.

27. U.S. Congress. House. Committee on Appropriations. 76th Cong. 1st sess. (1939), *Hearings of a Subcommittee . . . on Further Additional Relief Appropriation*, p. 156.

28. Handbook of Procedures Letter No. 30, wpa, October 3, 1936.

29. *Supplement No. 1 to Bulletin No. 29.* Appendix B, Financial Procedure for Projects Operating under W.P.A. Sponsored Federal Project No. 1, wpa, January 11, 1936.

30. Operating Procedure No. F-1, wpa, Section II, November 19, 1937.

31. Federal Art Project Letter No. 2, wpa, August 26, 1938.

32. *Handbook of Procedures for State and District Works Progress Administrations*, Chap. XX, Section 3 (revised April 15, 1937).

# 16

# The WPA Arts Program under State Control

Although Federal One officially came to an end as a result of a statutory prohibition in the ERA Act of 1939, the sentence of death had been passed well before that not by Congress but by the administration. In this period fundamental changes in personnel occurred within the WPA. On December 24, 1938, Colonel Francis C. Harrington was appointed administrator of the Works Progress Admistration to succeed Harry Hopkins, who resigned to accept the post of Secretary of Commerce. On January 3, 1939, Florence Kerr was appointed assistant administrator in charge of the Division of Women's and Professional Projects. She succeeded Ellen Woodward, who resigned to become a member of the Social Security board. Between January and July, 1939, four of the five federal directors of the projects grouped under Federal One also resigned. They were Nikolai Sokoloff, of the Federal Music Project; Henry Alsberg, of the Federal Writers' Project; Luther Evans, of the Historical Records Survey; and Hallie Flanagan, whose services were terminated when the Federal Theater Project was stopped by congressional enactment. Only Holger Cahill continued as director of the Art Project.

A change in personnel as complete as this, affecting as it did most everyone in high position who had played a major part in the initiation and continuance of Federal One, is to be explained by policy, not by coincidence. The social worker had achieved public power, and, although he was not destined, qua social worker, to remain permanently in public office, the philosophy that had sought expression in the WPA

305

had become part of the accepted attitude of the government toward unemployment. The concept of work relief, however imperfectly articulated in the policy and operation of the WPA; the recognition by the state that a person in need, if unemployed through no fault of his own and able to work, had a right to a job that reasonably fitted his capacity and training; and the admission that, if other sources of employment were not available, it was the duty of the commonwealth itself to provide employment—all these principles represent the achievement of the social worker in the formulation of public policy.

It was not remarkable, therefore, that in December, 1938, a social worker became a politician and an army officer became a social worker. If the government had accepted the legitimacy of social work as a public responsibility, Harry Hopkins, on his part, had served his apprenticeship—and it was an excellent one—in the school of politics. At the end of almost six years as administrator of the several relief agencies of the federal government, Hopkins could accept the post of Secretary of Commerce with the assurance that, even if the attitude of his successor in the WPA was not evangelical, the administrative stability of the new discipline had been so firmly constructed that routine could now continue what fervor had begun.

## FRANCIS C. HARRINGTON

Colonel Francis C. Harrington, who succeeded Hopkins as administrator, was not a newcomer to the WPA at the time of his elevation to the supreme command. In 1933 he had helped to set up the Civilian Conservation Corps. After two years' detail in France he was chosen in 1935 to make a survey of WPA organization and procedure, and, subsequently in the same year, was appointed chief engineer in the Washington office of the agency. In the winter of 1936-37 he was elevated to the position of assistant administrator in charge of operations and project control. He held this post until December, 1938, when he was appointed federal administrator of the WPA.

Colonel Harrington, a graduate of West Point, was an engineer by profession and a career officer in the United States Army by nature and training. Those qualities that distinguish the genuine professional soldier—a sense of discipline, which caused him to administer the agency according to the letter of the law; a consciousness of loyalty to superior authority, which made him attentive to the intent of Congress as well as to statutory language; a sense of responsibility toward his subordinates, which prompted him to defend their policies and conduct before Congress and the public, even when he was unsympathetic toward their aims; and, above all, an appreciation of personal honor, which made his spoken word his bond—all these qualities made the regime of Colonel Harrington as administratively correct and as morally impeccable as it was emotionally uninspired.

As a matter of fact, the age of revelation was over, and the appointment of Harrington was the sign and not the cause of the triumph of organization over inspiration. Moreover, as so often happens when definition succeeds evolution, the acceptance of the new dispensation was dependent upon the rejection of certain gnostic heresies that had flourished in the primitive period. Among these was the concept of a professional arts program as a corollary of the principle of work relief. Indeed, it was not an accident that the man who had been responsible for the manual program of the wpa for four years was now made administrator of the agency, because the concept of work relief that finally prevailed hardly transcended the concept of unskilled labor. To be sure, the non-manual program and an arts program were continued, even to the end of the wpa's existence. But the intensity with which these programs were pursued was relaxed, and, especially with respect to the arts program, an acceptance of continuity rather than a consciousness of a cause was responsible for an attitude that delayed, although it did not prevent, final dissolution.

## THE REORGANIZATION OF THE WOMEN'S AND PROFESSIONAL DIVISION

On January 3, 1939, Florence Kerr was appointed to succeed Mrs. Woodward as assistant administrator in charge of the Division of Women's and Professional Projects. Shortly thereafter, the Division of Recreation Projects and the Division of Education Projects were placed under the supervision of Mrs. Kerr. On February 24, 1939, the Women's and Professional Division was reorganized as the Division of Professional and Service Projects. The functions of the federal co-ordinator of research were placed in this division. It was planned to establish in each state administration a similar division of professional and service projects, but only after analysis and consultation. Margaret Stephenson, who had been assistant to Mrs. Kerr when the latter was regional director in Region 4, was made special assistant to the assistant administrator. Lawrence Morris continued to serve as executive assistant in charge of Federal One. Miss Cronin, who had been administrative assistant to Mrs. Woodward, was transferred in June, 1939, to Region 2, where she acted as chief regional supervisor.

Mrs. Kerr had joined the FERA in July, 1935, as regional director of women's activities in the Middle West. From December, 1935, to January, 1939, she had acted in the same capacity for the WPA, with Chicago as her headquarters. Previously (1932-35), she had lectured throughout the Middle West, presumably on literature, for, from 1922 to 1927 she taught in the English Department of Grinnell College, the alma mater of Harry Hopkins. But even before that, coincidence had brought her twice into the ken of Hopkins: in 1912, when she received her B.A. from Grinnell College, and between 1917 and 1919, when she worked as director of the home service division of the Gulf Division of the American Red Cross.

Colonel Harrington and Mrs. Kerr in 1939 were confronted with a crisis in the relations between Congress and the WPA that was not of their making or, certainly, choosing. In August, 1938, the hearings of the Dies Committee had begun, and it was not long before the activities of Federal One, especially in New York City, were brought to the committee's attention. At the same time, the investigation of the WPA by the Woodrum Committee was in the offing. It was natural, therefore, that an attitude of political caution should have characterized Mrs. Kerr's administration. The informality of Mrs. Woodward's regime, which derived from a cavalier self-assurance on her part as well as from the novelty of the subject matter of her jurisdiction, was succeeded by a more formal attitude toward procedure and toward personal relationships within the staff and between the staff and their chief. In particular, the directors of Federal One felt orphaned by the departure of Mrs. Woodward, and looked upon her successor as a step-mother, who, whatever her efforts, could never become as close to them as their natural mother. It was not that Mrs. Kerr was lacking in a sense of loyalty, for she defended before congressional committees acts and policies that antedated her tenure and persons who were not her own appointees; it was simply that her coming represented a change of policy that, with or without her, was in the circumstances bound to occur, and that nature, with a characteristic sense of propriety, had fitted the person to the situation.

## THE REORGANIZATION ACT OF 1939

Pursuant to the provisions of the Reorganization Act of 1939, the President prepared and transmitted to Congress Reorganization Plan No. 1, approved April 3, 1939. This plan provided that the Works Progress Administration, together with several other agencies, be consolidated into a new agency to be called the Federal Works Administration. Section 301 of the plan read:

> The Works Progress Administration and its functions (except the National Youth Administration and its functions) shall be administered as the Work Projects Administration, with a Commissioner of Work Projects at the head thereof. The Commissioner shall be appointed by the Federal Works Administrator and shall receive a salary at the rate of $10,000 per annum. The Commissioner shall act under the direction and supervision of the Federal Works Administrator.[1]

It was provided that this plan take effect on July 1, 1939.[2] John M. Carmody was appointed administrator of the FWA, and he in turn appointed Harrington as commissioner of the WPA. Harrington immediately designated all existing administrative personnel to continue in office, and all existing rules and regulations were continued in force. The reorganization did not affect the WPA in any substantial way so far as its personnel and operations were concerned. The commissioner, however, was no longer an independent administrator but subordinate to the FWA administrator, and the name of the agency was changed from Works Progress Administration to Work Projects Administration.

The reorganization, so far as it affected the WPA, was another indication that the extraordinary status of the relief activities of the federal government no longer prevailed, and that the administration of work relief, so far as it concerned the federal government, henceforth would be integrated with the regular machinery of the state.

## THE PLAN OF THE ADMINISTRATION
### TO REORGANIZE FEDERAL ONE

On May 23, 1939, Colonel Harrington in his statement before the subcommittee of the House Appropriations Committee gave first public intimation of the administration's change of policy with reference to Federal One:

> A considerable amount of criticism has recently been leveled at the group of projects known as the Federal arts, which include theater, writing, painting, music, and the historical-records survey. I am quite willing to admit that these projects are capable of improvement, although I believe that the criticism of them has been magnified out of due proportion. At the present time the total employment of these projects aggregates 33,500 persons, which is 1.3 percent of the total employment being provided with the funds available to the Works Progress Administration.
>
> In connection with the Federal Arts Projects, it is my intention to proceed with administrative measures to remedy certain defects in their operations which have come to my attention. The measures which I have in mind include the following:
>
> (a) Reduction in the total employment of these projects approximately proportional to the general reduction which is to be made in the W.P.A. program.
>
> (b) The securing of local sponsorship for as many of the projects as possible, thus eliminating their operation as federally sponsored projects. In this connection I would, however, like to say that some of these projects could never have been started except under Federal sponsorship.
>
> (c) Certain changes in personnel and administrative methods. The latter would include the removal of the operating headquarters for all of these projects to the city of Washington, where they will be under the close supervision of the central office.[3]

Harrington thus demonstrated that he was prepared to make the projects conform to the desire of the President and the Bureau of the Budget.

In his letter to the President submitting requests for allocations to Federal One, which was dated June 14, 1939, but prepared on June 1, Harrington made it perfectly clear that the adjustments contemplated were part of a plan already prepared for the reorganization of Federal One. Referring to his previous testimony, the Colonel said:

> In my statement before the House Appropriations Committee on May 23, 1939, I mentioned certain measures which I had in mind regarding the the operation of the Federal Arts Projects. Specifically, these measures have to do with (a) reduction of employment (b) securing of local sponsorship for as many projects as possible, thus eliminating their operation as Federally Sponsored projects, (c) centralizing and strengthening Administrative control in Washington. However, in order to effect these purposes, and particularly to allow for the time necessary to obtain local sponsorship, it is important that an adequate limitation be provided for a transition period of at least six months.

Your letter of February 16, 1939, requested that the employment on Federal Project Number One "will not at any time hereafter exceed 33,500, and that a determined effort be made to effect a substantial reduction in this number prior to the close of the current fiscal year." The employment of these five nationwide projects reached 40,500 during December 1938, and has been maintained at slightly below 33,500 since January. As indicated in the applications now submitted, we are planning to reduce the employment to 28,000 effective shortly after the close of the current fiscal year.

From the attached table of comparative costs it is quite apparent that operating costs of Federal Project Number One during the first six months of the Fiscal Year 1940 will be lower than during any previous comparable six month period.

In making the cut of 5,500 in the overall quota, this Administration is contemplating the first two steps in carrying out the plan for reorganization of these projects:

(1) A cut of 1,000 or more will be applied to the Federal Theatre Project of New York City effective July 1, 1939 in order to bring about a greater degree of decentralization and to increase the efficiency of operation,

(1) A cut of 4,500 will be applied to the Historical Records Survey effective August 1, 1939 as this project will be the easiest to convert into a series of locally sponsored projects.

Regional and state offices are being instructed to study methods for carrying out the remainder of the plan to reorganize these projects.[4]

Memorandums written in June from Lawrence Morris to Florence Kerr and from her to Harrington further confirm this arrangement. Morris mentioned Harrington's intention "of eliminating their operation as federally sponsored projects," and pointed out that limitations must be provided for a transition period of at least half a year.[5] Mrs. Kerr's letter to the commissioner repeated Morris' declaration.[6]

It is not possible to discover how long before the hearings of the House Appropriations Committee the decision to abandon Federal One was made, but it is not unlikely that it occurred during, or shortly after, the beginning of the Woodrum Committee's investigation of WPA, which began on April 11, 1939. The testimony presented before the Dies Committee, which began its hearings in August, 1938, also must have been influential. At any rate, the decision was made well before Congress passed the ERA Act for the fiscal year 1940.

Though the nature and content of the specific conferences that resulted in this decision are not revealed, the general outline of the plan is clear. In return for a reprieve of six months, during which time the arts projects were to be gradually transferred to local sponsorship, the WPA consented to abandon its struggle for the continuance of Federal

One. It is apparent, therefore, that the fundamental decision was made by the administration before Congress acted. Congress refused to grant the six-month reprieve, and thus made the transition, when it occurred, much more awkward than it otherwise would have been. But it is difficult to believe that a further interval of six months would have seriously changed either the history or the nature of Federal One or have provided, as some perhaps thought it might, an opportunity to persuade the administration and Congress to permit its continuance.

The last hours of Federal One were not peaceful. On June 23, 1939, Harold D. Smith, the new director of the Bureau of the Budget, sent two letters to the President.[7] In them he called the President's attention to the fact that in the Relief Bill, as reported by the House, the Theater Project was prohibited, and other projects of Federal One were made dependent upon local sponsorship. He suggested that, in the light of these developments, the President might wish to give special consideration to any allocation requested by Federal One. Harrington, it happened, had requested an additional allocation for the final six months of the fiscal year 1939, in the amount of $16,734,425. The House had legislated against Federal One, but there remained the Senate, and for a time it seemed not unlikely that the upper chamber would at least moderate the House's decision. At any rate, Harrington, as he stated in his letter to the President in answer to the Bureau of the Budget's communication,[8] could only proceed on the basis of the situation as it existed. It was not for him, as it was not for Harold Smith, to anticipate the final action of Congress. In the end, as Smith correctly guessed, the Senate followed the House's lead, and the allocation of June, 1940, although granted, was not used except to liquidate Federal One.*

THE ERA ACT OF 1939

In the ERA Act of 1939, approved June 30, 1939 and providing for the fiscal year 1940, substantial changes were made affecting the operations of the WPA.

In the first place, the Federal Theater Project was abolished. Administrative and supervisory personnel could be carried on the payroll for July, 1939, and project personnel for a period ending not later than September 30, 1939.

*The Bureau of the Budget could afford to be reasonably generous with regard to this final allocation, for even if Congress had relented, the administration had already decided that this allocation should be the last.

Second, the operation after August 31, 1939, of any project sponsored solely by the Work Projects Administration was forbidden. The effect and intent of this clause was to put an end to WPA-Sponsored Federal Project No. 1 as a federal project. The four remaining programs were continued as state programs.

Third, it was required that sponsors contribute at least 25 per cent of the total federal and non-federal cost of the program. The WPA commissioner, however, was given authority to determine the facts constituting compliance with this provision. Subsequently, Colonel Harrington required a *statewide* average of 25 per cent. An individual project, therefore, might operate with a sponsor's contribution of less than 25 per cent. This made possible the continuation of the white-collar program and especially the arts program, although, in general, the state administrators required a relatively high sponsor's contribution on these projects in order not to embarrass their construction program.

Fourth, it was provided that all receipts and collections of the WPA, except cash contributions of sponsors of projects, should be covered into the Treasury as miscellaneous receipts. This outlawed the use of admission funds by the Theater and Music projects.

Fifth, the principle of the prevailing hourly wage was abandoned, and the 1935 principle of a security wage reinstated. It was provided in the act that those engaged on work projects should work not less than 130 hours a month and not more than eight hours in any day and forty hours in any week. This meant that security personnel on the arts projects were required to work the same number of hours as workers on other projects.

Sixth, it was provided that those, excepting veterans, continuously employed by the WPA more than eighteen months should be removed from employment, and not be eligible for re-employment until after the expiration of thirty days. This provision was particularly hard on the arts program, in which were many older persons of long service who had not been able to secure private employment.

At the annual conference of state administrators in July, 1939, Mrs. Kerr commented upon these changes:

> The next radical change in the bill which affects the Professional and Service Division is the transfer to state sponsorship of the other units of Federal Project No. 1, which as you all know is the Fine Arts Project. In this connection, we have been very busy in the Washington office making plans for that transfer in as uniform and orderly a fashion as possible. Project applications for each unit—art, music, writers and historical records survey—are being

prepared in each state, and wherever possible on the basis of statewide sponsorship.

Another important thing to be noted is that all these projects are to be written for a year. In other words, we have the Commissioner's permission to write those projects now and have them averaged into the state program after January 1.

Those projects are going to be written to declare eligible all the activities now maintained by those projects.[9]

General instructions regarding the new arts program were issued on July 31, 1939, as General Letter No. 278. The statement with regard to general policy was encouraging.

Section 1. *General Policy.* Section 25(b) of the Emergency Relief Appropriation Act of 1939 provides that funds will not be available after August 31, 1939, for the operation of projects sponsored solely by the Work Projects Administration. Therefore, the units of WPA sponsored Federal Project Number One will be terminated as WPA sponsored projects not later than August 31, 1939. . . .

The continued development of cultural activities should be continued as a part of each state program. Each State Administrator is requested to cooperate with the State, Regional and Washington staffs, of Federal Project Number One for the continuation of the Art, Music, Writers', and Historical Records Survey activities as statewide projects. Insofar as possible the work now in progress shall be carried on, and new undertakings should be developed which are consistent with good administration and in keeping with the aims and purposes of the nationwide WPA sponsored projects as now constituted. The four programs now under Federal Project Number One will be continued as programs with nationwide scope, each composed of a series of statewide official project units. The securing of sponsorship for existing statewide units shall be effected with the minimum possible interruption to the normal activities of the various programs.[10]

There were now as many official projects as there were states operating projects in one or more of the arts programs. Thus there was a New York State Art Project, a New York State Music Project, a New York State Writers' Project, and a New York State Historical Records Survey Project.

The entire series of projects for the nation as a whole were known as the WPA Arts Program and the various activities as the WPA Art Program, WPA Music Program, WPA Writers' Program, and WPA Historical Records Program. National directors were retained in the Washington office for each of these programs, and they continued to serve on the staff of the Division of Professional and Service Projects. Earl Moore succeeded Nicolai Sokoloff as director of the Music Program; Sargent Child succeeded Luther Evans as director of the Historical Records

Survey Program; and John D. Newsom succeeded Henry Alsberg as director of the Writers' Program. The state directors were now state supervisors and appointed by the state administrator upon recommendation of the Washington director and approval of the assistant commissioner, Division of Professional and Service Projects.[11] Assignment to projects was to be made by the division of employment in accordance with the occupational skills as shown by the records of that division. State supervisors of the several arts programs, however, were privileged to accept or reject these assignments and to determine the nature of the work for which those assigned were fitted.[12]

On January 10, 1940, Operating Procedure No. G-5 was released. This established basic procedure for the operations of the arts program under state control. Professional and service projects were classified as: (1) welfare projects, (2) community service projects, (3) research and records projects.[13] Art, Music and Writing were grouped under community service projects, and the Historical Records Survey under research and records projects. Of community service projects, Operating Procedure No. G-5 said:

> These are projects which aim primarily to assist a public agency in serving the community as a whole through services which are intended to raise the cultural level or to increase the facilities for enjoyment or use of leisure time. These include projects which provide for extending and supplementing library, adult and nursery education, museum, recreational and institutional services, training for conducting these activities, and extension of science and art, and the presentation of public exhibits and musical performances, the creation of books, pamphlets and other literature.[14]

The community service programs were subdivided into:

1. Public activities programs

2. Research and records programs

3. Welfare programs

The Historical Records Survey remained under research and records programs, and Music, Art, and Writing were grouped under public activities programs.*

*At the annual meeting, held at St. Louis in June, 1940, Colonel Harrington raised the question whether the name of the professional and service division should not be changed to community service division. When a vote was taken, the majority were in favor of the change.[15] The change however was not made until February 1, 1941.[16]

## THE ARTS PROGRAM AND NATIONAL DEFENSE

Even before September, 1939, the international situation had begun to exert its influence upon national policy, even with respect to domestic issues. The gradual decrease in appropriations, so apparent from 1939 to the close of the WPA, was in large part due to the unsympathetic attitude of Congress and its desire to diminish expenditures for relief and work relief; at the same time, there was implicit in the thinking of Congress and the administration a sense of foreboding with respect to affairs abroad, and anticipation of a crisis that for a time at least, would relegate relief policy to a subordinate position in national concern. Germany's attack upon Poland in September, 1939, served to heighten the tension, and even those who hoped that the United States would remain a non-participant in the war argued that a program of national defense was imperative. In September, 1939, in the mind of Congress and the administration, the demands of national defense assumed priority over those of unemployment. At first, this shift in emphasis was subtle and largely unexpressed, at least so far as the WPA was concerned. But within a year it was apparent that the WPA would stake its claim to survival not upon its character as a relief organization but rather as a newly devised instrumentality for the furtherance of national defense.

The influence of the tense international situation was indicated as early as May, 1940, when Colonel Harrington issued a memorandum suggesting priority for those projects that would aid the defense program. Shortly thereafter (in June of the same year), Florence Kerr issued a memorandum suggesting the same emphasis on professional and service programs. In particular, she stressed projects concerned with education, recreation, and health as those that would promote national defense.[17]

This emphasis was particularly disadvantageous to the continuance of the arts program, especially in so far as the program pretended to a professional status. The mobilization of the National Guard and the inauguration of conscription in December, 1940, further emphasized the crisis; and in February, 1941, the community service division definitely directed its attention to defense-connected services. By this time projects certified as necessary to national defense were being given priority by the WPA. White-collar projects, in general, did not qualify for such preferred status, and the following lettergram, dispatched by Howard

316

Hunter* and dated February 28, 1941, reveals the effort made to conform the non-manual program to the exigencies of the national emergency:

A GREAT DEAL OF WORK NOW BEING PROSECUTED UNDER REGULARLY APPROVED WPA PROJECTS IN THE COMMUNITY SERVICE DIVISION HAS UNDOUBTED IMPORTANCE AND VALUE FOR DEFENSE PURPOSES, ALTHOUGH IT MAY NOT BE OF A NATURE WHICH REQUIRES CERTIFICATION BY THE ARMY OR NAVY stop IN ADDITION TO THE CATEGORIES ESTABLISHED IN GENERAL LETTER NUMBER THREE TWO TWO AND MY TELEGRAM OF DECEMBER SEVENTH, THE FOLLOWING TYPES OF WORK IN THE COMMUNITY SERVICE PROGRAM HAVE DEFINITE VALUE FOR NATIONAL DEFENSE AND SHALL BE DESIGNATED AS NONCERTIFIED DEFENSE PROJECTS:

1. PROJECTS SPONSORED BY THE ARMY, NAVY, COAST GUARD, NATIONAL GUARD, OR COMPARABLE STATE AGENCY, AND THE COUNCIL OF NATIONAL DEFENSE.

2. PROJECTS, IRRESPECTIVE OF SPONSORSHIP, OPERATING IN OR PROVIDING SERVICES FOR MILITARY CAMPS, CANTONMENTS, TRAINING STATIONS, AND OTHER MILITARY OR NAVAL ESTABLISHMENTS AT THEIR REQUEST stop THIS MAY INVOLVE THE ESTABLISHMENT OF SUCH AN ACTIVITY AS A SEPARATE WORK PROJECT OR REPORTING ON PARTS OF PROJECTS AS INDICATED IN MY TELEGRAM OF DECEMBER SEVENTH

3. ACTIVITIES IN THE FIELDS OF HEALTH AND MEDICAL CARE, NUTRITION, EDUCATION, RECREATION, WELFARE, AND RELATED FIELDS, INCLUDING RESEARCH AND CLERICAL ASSISTANCE, OPERATING IN INDUSTRIAL OR MILITARY DEFENSE AREAS, WHEN THESE ACTIVITIES ARE DESIGNATED BY STATE OR LOCAL DEFENSE COUNCILS AS IMPORTANT TO DEFENSE stop WHERE STATE OR LOCAL DEFENSE COUNCILS HAVE NOT BEEN ESTABLISHED, AND UNTIL SUCH TIME AS THEY ARE ESTABLISHED, THE STATE ADMINISTRATOR IS AUTHORIZED TO SO DESIGNATE ACTIVITIES stop IN ORDER TO EXPEDITE IMMEDIATE REPORTING, PARTICULARLY WITH RESPECT TO EMPLOYMENT AND PENDING A MODIFICATION OF SECTION ONE, SUBSECTION C OF GENERAL LETTER NUMBER THREE TWO TWO, REVISED, THIS WILL BE YOUR AUTHORITY TO DESIGNATE AS NONCERTIFIED DEFENSE PROJECTS ANY PROJECTS OR PARTS THEREOF WHICH FALL WITHIN THE ABOVE CATEGORIES WITHOUT CLEARANCE WITH THIS OFFICE AS NOW PRESCRIBED stop THE FACT THAT CERTIFICATION OF ANY SUCH PROJECTS IS PENDING OR CONTEMPLATED DOES NOT PRECLUDE REPORTING THEM AS NONCERTIFIED PROJECTS PENDING SUCH CERTIFICATION stop PROJECTS, REGARDLESS OF SPONSORSHIP OR LOCATION WHICH IN THE OPINION OF THE STATE ADMINISTRATOR, MAKE SPECIFIC CONTRIBUTION TO THE DEFENSE PROGRAM OTHER THAN THE CATEGORIES ABOVE MENTIONED OR PREVIOUSLY DESIGNATED SHALL BE SUBMITTED TO WASHINGTON FOR DECISION[18]

In July, 1941, the position of the arts program was precarious, but Hunter spoke for its continuance.

In the Community Service Program, I am hoping that Mrs. Kerr will give

---

*Colonel Harrington died in October, 1940, and was succeeded as commissioner of the Work Projects Administration by Howard Hunter.

you in some detail some ideas about priorities, which perhaps in that division are a little more important than in the Operations Division, because of the wider type of work that is carried on. In the main, my policy in that division as to priorities will be to give first priorities to three types of projects: education, recreation, and health. Those will receive priorities in that division.

I have announced, and I want to announce here again today, that I propose to continue the three cultural projects of the WPA in each State: music, art, and writing. The total employment will obviously have to be reduced, and it is possible that small units may have to be shut down, but it is my instruction that those three projects be continued to the best of our ability.[19]

At the same meeting Mrs. Kerr, speaking with an optimism warranted neither by the international situation nor by the changing emphasis within the WPA, remarked:

I think that the bill, as far as the Community Service Division is concerned, is about the same as last year. The Commissioner pointed out to Congress the propriety of reinstating a theater project to be operated in the State programs as are the other cultural projects, and the Congress and the subcommittee refused to consider any such proposition. So we have exactly the same list of projects to operate, as far as the law is concerned, that we had last year. That means that we ought to have about the same type of program, the emphasis being given to certain activities which seem of major importance because of the present situation.[20]

After mentioning the Writers' Program and its accomplishments, Mrs. Kerr continued:

What the music project has done I think is known to all of you, and its importance in a morale program of the present era is also well known and well understood. I have no fears whatever about the support that you will give to the music project everywhere.

The art project also represents, I think, one of the deep cultural values of our nation.

I am very proud and very happy that the Commissioner has seen fit to say to you and to all of us that we are going to remain the custodians of those cultural activities, no matter what other pressures there are.[21]

Sunday, December 7, 1941, was the day of the Japanese attack on Pearl Harbor. The effect of that act upon the non-defense activities of the WPA is indicated in a telegram sent that night.

STATE OF WAR DEMANDS COMPLETE COOPERATION AND EFFECTIVENESS OF WPA stop WAR AND NAVY DEPARTMENTS HAVE REQUESTED ACCELERATION OF WORK ON VITAL PROJCTS AND POSSIBLE DEFERMENT OF OTHERS NOT ESSENTIAL AT THIS TIME stop YOU ARE INSTRUCTED TO CLOSE OFF RAPIDLY AS POSSIBLE ALL CONSTRUCTION PROJECTS OF NONDEFENSE NATURE USING CRITICAL

MATERIALS OR LABOR WHERE THEY CAN BE EFFECTIVELY USED IN DEFENSE ACTIVITY stop WPA EMPLOYMENT QUOTAS ARE SUBJECT TO ADJUSTMENT IF DEFENSE REQUIREMENTS INDICATE stop I HAVE OFFERED SERVICES OF ENTIRE ADMINISTRATIVE STAFF TO WAR AND NAVY DEPARTMENTS FOR ANY LOCAL ASSISTANCE NECESSARY[22]

Although this telegram ordered the cessation of all construction projects of a non-defense nature, the impact of Pearl Harbor upon the non-manual program was equally drastic. On February 13, 1942, integration of the community service program with the war effort was attempted by a reorganization. The Division of Community Service Programs was renamed the Service Division, and subdivided into: (1) the defense, health, and welfare services section; (2) the war services section; and (3) the project services section. The war services section was further subdivided into: (1) recreation; (2) education; (3) cultural services; and (4) clerical services. Art, Music, and Writing were grouped under cultural services, and the Historical Records Survey under clerical services.[23]

By April, 1942, the cultural program practically ceased to exist. Among activities ordered to be discontinued at that time were:

1. Fact-finding, survey, records, and clerical services not included in section 1 [war-connected].

. . . . . . . . . . .

4. Preparation of State pictorial guides; biographical dictionaries; State almanacs; radio scripts not pertinent to defense and books or pamphlets not requested by the Army, Navy, and/or Federal, State and local defense agencies.

5. Recording objects for the Index of American Design; service to museums; craft production; occupational therapy in Art and Music; general exhibitions and informational displays.

6. Creative music activities; collecting, annotating, and recording folk music; music surveys and research activities.

This list is not to be considered as all-inclusive but will serve as a guide. It is intended, however, that all activities which do not directly relate to the war effort shall be discontinued.[24]

At the House hearings in June, 1942, Francis Dryden conceded that the arts program was practically nonexistent:

In the nonconstruction field we have already limited our activity to three important groups of projects: (1) vocational training for defense occupations; (2) projects that will contribute to the health and welfare services of communities; and (3) war service projects requested by war agencies. Peacetime activities, such as art, music, writing, adult education, and research projects have already been largely discontinued.[25]

Well before this, as a matter of fact, the Music, Art, and Writers' programs were able to survive only because they changed their emphasis from professional performance to recreational and educational activities, directed toward defense and war services. Music recordings were sent to the troops, and orchestras played at military posts. The New Jersey WPA Philharmonic Orchestra was particularly active. Guest conductors and guest soloists of reputation often appeared on these programs. The Washington State Art Project made posters to assist in the collection of aluminum, and the art projects in other states performed similar services. The Writers' Projects and the Historical Records Survey in the several states in like manner devoted themselves exclusively to activities that furthered the national defense and the war effort.

Thus although the WPA Arts Program did not officially come to a close until June 30, 1943, when the Work Projects Administration, except for purposes of liquidation, was discontinued, the activities of the program in the field practically ceased six months to a year before that date. The federal directors who held office during the lifetime of Federal One, and others closely connected with them, strongly maintain that the transfer of the federal arts projects to state sponsorship brought about the change in emphasis from professional to educational and recreational stress, and the general deterioration of the program. The fact of decline cannot be doubted; but it remains a question whether the transfer was the sole, or even the major, cause of the decline. It can be said with confidence that, even had Federal One lived beyond 1939, it would have been a war casualty no less than the State Arts Projects that succeeded it. It also would have had to accommodate itself to the national emergency and the war effort; and, it might be added, Federal One would have boasted, as did the Arts Program of 1939-43, of its contribution to the nation in time of crisis. The experience of the WPA Arts Program under state sponsorship, therefore, in the midst of war and war's alarums, does not provide a proper basis of comparison.

This is not to say that the transfer from federal to state control did not bring a deterioration of standards. The emphasis upon professional competence that characterized federal direction from 1935 to 1939 declined and, in the end, disappeared under state control; and, if it be conceded that the professional emphasis was tactically correct in the

320

first place, the change of policy in 1939 was catastrophic in its consequences. In one sense, the willingness of the states, and of cosponsors and co-operating sponsors within the states, to continue the Arts Program after federal sponsorship was withdrawn was a tribute—and a deserved tribute—to the federal directors; on the other hand, the change in emphasis was a rebuke to their appraisal of the situation in 1935, and an indication, if one were needed, that the attempt at professionalism was, in the last analysis, a failure. In the end, what the states wanted was a program rooted in the community and founded upon its needs and its talents—a professional core, to be sure, but an amateur spirit, with the people as participants and not as spectators. This experiment was too short-lived to indicate its worth, for the national emergency intervened before it was well started. But if in 1935 the Washington office had brought to such a program the same vigor and enthusiasm with which it inaugurated its professional program, a good will might have been engendered not only in the states but also in the state WPA administrations that would have served it well in less happy days; in this way, the federal directors, by not demanding professional projects first, might have achieved them in the end.

SPONSORSHIP OF STATE WPA ARTS PROJECTS

When Congress abolished Federal One on June 30, 1939, all but the Theater Project were given two months to effect a transition from federal to state sponsorship. The Theater Project was abolished as of that date and was given merely one month to "liquidate" property and non-certified personnel and three months to "liquidate" certified personnel.[26]

It was natural that the personnel of Federal One, who were carried over from the old to the new regime, both in the national and in the state offices, should attempt to maintain under the state programs the same controls that they exercised under the national program. Having tasted authority, as Herodotus said long ago, they were not content to be ruled by others. The attempt was doomed to early failure, for when they lost control of the purse, they lost that substance of authority without which one cannot command. But the attempt itself is not without interest, and the ease with which it was foiled, instructive.

From July 10 to 12, 1939, an emergency conference was held in Washington, which the regional directors of the arts program attended.

As a result of the considerations raised at this meeting the first general instructions regarding the new arts program were issued. It is not surprising that these instructions reflect the desire for the continuance of central control and the maintenance of existing procedures. The first concern of the technical personnel of the Washington office was with regard to sponsorship. The ERA Act of 1939 contained three definitive provisions on this subject. The first, which had in mind sponsors' contributions, read:

> On and after January 1, 1940, in administering the funds appropriated in this section, not to exceed three-fourths of the total cost of all non-Federal projects thereafter approved to be undertaken within any State, Territory, possession, or the District of Columbia, with respect to which any such funds are used, shall be borne by the United States, and not less than one-fourth of such total cost shall be borne by the State and its political subdivisions, or by the Territory, possession, or the District of Columbia, as the case may be. The facts constituting compliance with the requirements of this subsection shall be determined by the Commissioner, and his determinations, made in conformity with rules and regulations prescribed by him, shall be final and conclusive.[27]

This clause, which required that at least 25 per cent of the total cost of all non-federal projects be borne by the sponsoring agency, applied to the arts projects, since by virtue of the same act these projects now became non-federal.

The second provision respecting sponsorship, contained in the same act, defined more closely the nature of sponsors' contributions:

> No non-Federal project shall be undertaken or prosecuted under appropriations under this joint resolution (except under section 4) unless and until the sponsor has made a written agreement to finance such part of the entire cost thereof as the head of the agency, if the agency administers sponsored projects, determines under the circumstances is an adequate contribution taking into consideration the financial ability of the sponsor. The head of the agency shall prescribe rules and regulations relating to the valuation of contributions in kind by sponsors of projects through furnishing the use of their own facilities and equipment and the services of their own employees, which shall also allow credit only to the extent that the furnishing of such contributions represents a financial burden which is undertaken by the sponsors on account of Work Projects Administration projects, or other sponsored projects.[28]

The third provision of the Act of 1939 respecting sponsorship authorized the WPA to receive sponsors' contributions:

> The various agencies for which appropriations are made in this joint res-

olution are authorized to receive from sponsors of non-Federal projects contributions in services, materials, or money, such money to be deposited with the Treasurer of the United States. Such contributions shall be expended or utilized as agreed upon between the sponsor and such agencies.[29]

In General Letter No. 291, dated November 1, 1939, the administrator ruled that the 25 per cent sponsorship contribution should be calculated on a statewide basis.[30] In sections (4) and (5) of the same letter there appeared a list of eligible and ineligible items in the category of sponsorship contributions.

Further elaboration of these rules was made in a memorandum from the commissioner dated November 24, 1939. It was required that the statewide average of 25 per cent be maintained for a six-month period, January 1–June 30, 1940, and not for each month. Moreover, it was recognized that the same percentage could not be demanded on nonconstruction projects as on construction projects.

> It appears that, in order to average at least 25%, construction projects will, in general, require average sponsors' contributions of 29% and nonconstruction projects 18%. Projects showing lower percentages received from states whose average sponsors' contributions on 1939 Act project applications have been less than 25% will be subjected to special scrutiny, and should, therefore, be accompanied by pertinent explanations or justifications.
>
> The differential in the sponsors' percentage on construction and nonconstruction projects may vary between states, due to the relative volume of construction and non-construction employment. Socially useful projects with low sponsors' contributions which do not require excessive Federal non-labor expenditure should not be discouraged as long as a desirable state-wide average is maintained.*[31]

The difficulty with the 25 per cent sponsorship clause, so far as white-collar projects were concerned, lay in the fact that it could not be observed unless the sponsors assumed part of the labor costs, a procedure against the practice of the wpa. In most white-collar projects, including the arts projects, non-labor costs fell far short of 25 per cent of total cost. Colonel Harrington discussed this problem at the House hearings in March, 1940.

> The 25-percent provision also raises a quite acute problem in connection with nonconstruction projects, especially those of the white-collar type. In

*The only exception to the 25 per cent sponsorship rule was that granted in the era Act, fiscal year 1941, which exempted projects "(1) which have been certified by the Secretary of War and the Secretary of the Navy, respectively, as being important for military or naval purposes, or (2) which authorize necessary temporary measures to avert danger to life, property, or health in the event of disaster or grave emergency caused by flood, storm, fire, earthquake, drought, or similar cause."[32]

this class of work there is usually very little nonlabor cost, the total in many cases being 10 percent or less. Therefore, even if sponsors paid all costs other than certified labor, they would still be far below the required 25 percent.

To meet this general situation it is my suggestion that the control of Federal expenditures among the States be on the basis of a limitation on the amount of Federal funds that may be used for nonlabor purposes in each State. This provision, already in the present act, requires that not more than an average of $6 per man per month shall be spent from Federal funds for nonlabor purposes in any State. Under this provision Federal funds for nonlabor purposes are definitely controlled, and the sponsors must put in whatever is necessary to construct the projects over and above the $6 nonlabor limitation.

This seems to me to achieve the necessary control and yet at the same time enough flexibility in the program to meet the problems of areas with high unemployment and limited resources. Thus in areas having financial difficulties the WPA can operate a sufficient number of projects to provide needed employment, but the projects will be of a character having a relatively low total nonlabor cost. In other areas, where the sponsors can afford it, more expensive types of projects can be operated, with the sponsor putting in the additional funds. In both instances, however, the amount of Federal funds used would be restricted to $6 per man per month, but the amount of sponsors' funds used would vary according to the ability of sponsors to finance projects.

I recommend, therefore, that the 25 percent provision contained in section 1 (d) of the act be eliminated and the $6 nonlabor limitation contained in section 1 (c) be retained.[33]

On this and later occasions, however, Harrington's efforts to persuade Congress to repeal the provision were unsuccessful.

The concern about sponsorship, however, transcended the problems created by this clause, embarrassing as they were, and centered in the very nature of the sponsorship relation under a state program. In the ordinary type of project, state or local, the official sponsor was a public body, legally empowered to prosecute the work and for whom the work was being performed. The personnel of the arts program, unaccustomed to working with official sponsors and believing that state bodies would lack either the inclination or the authority to engage in all the activities of the arts program, evoked an interesting hierarchy of sponsorship.

For each program there was to be in each state an official sponsor, which would be the state government or an agency thereof. This sponsor would be the source of legal authority. Subordinate to the official sponsor would be the cosponsor—a public authority, state or local, that would delegate authority to the official sponsor. This delegation of authority, when the cosponsor was a local body, conferred authority upon the official sponsor to operate in that locality. Finally, on the lowest rung of the ladder, was the co-operating sponsor, a quasi-public or non-profit private agency that would assist the official sponsor and the cosponsors in planning and executing state programs. The procedure was as follows:

> The term Co-sponsors as used in this letter shall refer to public bodies delegating authority to the official sponsors. Cooperating sponsors shall mean any quasi-public or non-profit private agencies who assist sponsors in planning and carrying out the WPA Arts program. The participation of Co-sponsors and Cooperating sponsors in the general activities of local project units or of individual items of work should be encouraged. The provision of Section 6 of Operating Procedure No. G-1, that Co-sponsors of WPA sponsored Federal Project Number One may be quasi-public or non-profit private agencies, shall be construed to apply to cooperating sponsors of state projects initiated in accordance with this General Letter.
>
> Every effort shall be made to secure the maximum possible financial contribution from official sponsors, Co-sponsors and Cooperating sponsors. Anticipated assistance from Sponsors, Co-sponsors and Cooperating sponsors shall be included in the pledges shown in the project applications.
>
> Co-sponsors and Cooperating sponsors shall operate through official sponsors in (1) making contributions and (2) securing allocation of Works of Art.[34]

The difference between the apparent and the real meaning of the language of this procedure shows how precarious it is to write administrative history from formal documents alone. The apparent meaning is that the official sponsor shall serve as the operating sponsor, and that the cosponsor and co-operating sponsor shall assist the official sponsor in fulfilling its responsibilities. The real meaning is that the cosponsor and, better still, the co-operating sponsor shall be the operating sponsors, and that the official sponsor shall serve merely as a formal "dummy" sponsor in whose name the cosponsor and co-operating sponsor shall carry on the project.

The use of the cosponsor and the co-operating sponsor was designed to maintain the system of sponsors' contributions.

With regard to the Art Program, the letter read:

> Financial arrangements relating to the allocation or loan or works of art shall be in accordance with the procedure as outlined in Federal Art Project Letters 1 and 2 dated August 22, 1938, and August 26, 1938, respectively.[35]

With respect to the Music Program, this procedure, although it formally observed the limitations contained in the 1939 Act, forecast a new development whereby admission funds would become and remain the property of sponsors:

> Separate instructions will be issued regarding concert performances for which admission charges are made, the duties of Business Manager–Agent Cashiers, and of bonded Treasurers and the production of Musical comedy, light Chamber and Grand opera. Pending the receipt of such instructions the following policies will be in force:
>
> 1. Where music projects have been producing opera, light opera, etc. as its own activity and not in joint performance with Theatre Project units, such type of performance may continue to be produced by Statewide Music Projects.
> 2. All Admissions collected by the Federal Government from paid performances shall be covered into the U.S. Treasury as miscellaneous receipts.
> 3. Paid admissions collected by lessors or sponsors in accordance with percentage sharing agreements shall be segregated as to Federal and lessors' or sponsors' shares. The lessors' or sponsors' share shall be retained by its agent for uses agreed upon and the Federal share covered into the U.S. Treasury as miscellaneous receipts.
> 4. Contributions in cash shall be deposited in special deposit accounts with the Treasurer of the United States when such contributions are made in connection with free performances of the Music Project, or when such contributions are made in connection with paid performances and are over and above or apart from paid admissions.[36]

For the Writers' Program the official sponsor was expected to effect all arrangements for publication and to handle proceeds from sales or royalties:

> All publications arrangements shall be effected through the official sponsor. The official sponsor shall assume full responsibility for both the cost of publication and for the distribution of the published work, or shall make a contract with a printer or commercial publisher whereby the printer or publisher assumes full responsibility for distribution of the work and relieves the official sponsor from obligation for costs of publication.
>
> Only the official sponsor may handle proceeds from sales of publications, royalties or advance royalties. Further instructions regarding deposition of such proceeds will be issued shortly. Pending such instructions, it is expected that no expenditures out of such proceeds will be incurred by the official sponsor except for costs of publication and distribution of publications.[37]

Though the states were thus carefully instructed to see that only the official sponsor entered into publication agreements and handled the proceeds, such instruction merely meant that everything must be done in the name of the official sponsor, not that the official sponsor must actually perform the functions.

The section that dealt with the Historical Records Survey was similar to the above. Here it was stated: "The sponsor should, in cooperation with co-sponsors and cooperating sponsors accept the responsibility as far as possible for the duplication and distribution of products of the projects."[38]

Thus by the use of cosponsors, and especially by the use of co-operating sponsors, which could be non-profit private associations, the WPA Arts Program secured elasticity and fluidity in the management of sponsors' contributions that, if it had been compelled to negotiate with official sponsors (agencies of a state government) only, it would have lacked.

## THE USE OF ADMISSION FUNDS UNDER
## THE WPA ARTS PROGRAM

Section 13 (b) of the Emergency Relief Appropriation Act of 1939 excepted sponsors' contributions from the provision that all project earnings must be covered into the U.S. Treasury as miscellaneous receipts. For this reason the central office of the WPA made every effort in its new instructions on the operation of the Arts Program to construe all possible cash collections as sponsors' contributions. Accordingly, the instruction on publication procedure and on procedure for allocation of works of art were carefully phrased. The question whether cash contributions to the Art Project were to be covered into miscellaneous receipts arose immediately, and the interpretation of the Treasury was favorable to the WPA. In answer to an inquiry from one of the states, the WPA director of finance wrote:

> Contributions to the Federal Art Project are not to be classified as admission revenue, and may properly be deposited to the Treasury Disbursing Clerk's Special Deposit Account available for expenditure. The Office of the Commissioner of Accounts and Deposits here concurs in the disposition to be made of these contributions, and is today instructing the State Treasury Accountant that such contributions are not to be deposited to Miscellaneous Receipts.[39]

Indeed, it was thought not impossible that admission funds might be classed as sponsors' contributions, and, at first, there was some pressure for such an interpretation. But in view of the plain intent of the statutory language of the 1939 act, the attempt to classify admission funds as federal funds was abandoned. There remained, however, the device of placing authority for the collection of admission funds in the hands of the sponsor or cosponsor. If the moneys thus collected were regarded as the possession of the sponsor, then they never became federal funds and the Treasury or Congress had no jurisdiction over them.

The resolution of this problem was foreshadowed by the remarks of the WPA director of finance at the conference of state administrators held at Chicago, July 12-13, 1939:

> There is another problem involved in the continued operation of those units of Federal Project No. 1 authorized to continue under local sponsorship which I feel will be brought to the fore within the next several weeks, and that is whether or not it would be proper for the sponsors to make the necessary arrangements involving the collection of admissions as the result of the activities of the Federal Music and possibly Art Projects. First, I do not feel that we can ignore the intent of the Congress by establishing a sponsorship arrangement which is not existent in fact. I feel that the sponsors of these projects must be actual sponsors who assume responsibility, and who contribute in a financial manner to the activities of the projects. The question has been asked whether or not under a local sponsorship arrangement it would be within the law to allow the sponsor to collect admissions in connection with our project activity, and I feel the answer to that question is in the affirmative, with the following sponsor arrangement in mind: first, the sponsor must have assumed a financial responsibility in connection with the project operation; second, that the sponsor will agree to make available as future sponsor's contributions on subsequent project production any amounts received as admissions; third, the box office must be manned by employees of the sponsor but that, while the responsibility of collecting admissions is that of the sponsor, the procedures under which such admissions are collected must be approved by the State Director of Finance or his representative for audit purposes. I feel that the aforementioned precautionary steps must be taken in order to protect the Government against the possibility of accruing a profit through its activities to benefit the sponsor.[40]

The final procedure for the collection of admission funds, contained in Operating Procedure No. G-5, followed closely the pattern here drawn by Holmes. It read:

> *Music Projects—Handling of Admission Collections*  Where it is intended that any unit of a Music project will give performances at which paid admissions are collected, an agreement shall be made between the Work Projects Administration and the sponsor under which the sponsor through its agents will handle all admission collections. Such agreements shall be permitted on the following conditions only:
>
> 1. The sponsor shall be the official sponsor of the project or a co-sponsor as defined in section 36, subsection A, item 3, of this Operating Procedure.

2. A financial obligation in connection with the operation of the project shall be assumed by the sponsor. This obligation may be based on assistance from cooperating agencies or organizations as well as on the sponsor's own resources.

3. The collections shall be handled by employees of the sponsor. While the responsibility of collecting admissions is that of the sponsor, the procedure under which such admissions are collected shall be approved by the Work Projects Administration.

4. The sponsor shall agree to make available for future sponsor's contributions in connection with subsequent project operations any amounts received as admissions which are not required for payment of obligations incurred in connection with past or current operations.

5. The sponsor shall agree to make his records, related to sponsorship of the Music project, available to the Work Projects Administration for audit purposes.

Normally, agreements of the type described in this section shall be made only with official sponsors of Music projects. When the official sponsor is limited by statute so that he is not empowered to handle admission funds, or he is otherwise not available for this purpose, he may authorize the Work Projects Administration to make such agreements with eligible co-sponsors. Prior to the execution of such agreements with co-sponsors, written approval shall be obtained from the Director of Finance, Washington, D.C. The request for approval shall be submitted to Washington by the State Administrator in the form of a detailed justification setting forth the reasons why the official sponsor is unable to handle the collections, the geographical area and period of sponsorship by each co-sponsor, and all other pertinent information.

Attached is the form of agreement which shall be made between the Work Projects Administration and the sponsor who undertakes the handling of admission collections. This agreement shall be signed by the authorized agent of the sponsor and by the State Administrator or his authorized representative. A copy of each agreement shall be forwarded to the Director of Finance, Washington, D.C.

Significant modifications in the form of the agreement shall be permitted only with the approval of the Director of Finance, Washington, D.C., and the Assistant Commissioner, Division of Professional and Service Projects, Washington, D.C.

The maximum admission price which will be indicated in section 6c of the agreement shall be in conformity with local conditions, but shall not be in excess of $1.00, exclusive of taxes, except with the prior written approval of the Assistant Commissioner, Division of Professional and Service Projects, Washington, D.C.

State Administrations unable to reach an agreement with the official sponsor and/or co-sponsor on the handling of admission collections, which desire to collect admissions through collection agents of the Work Projects Administration, shall request permission from the Director of Finance, Washington, D.C. supporting this request with a complete justification. Where permission is granted for collection of admissions by collection agents of the Work Projects Administration, all monies collected shall be covered into Treasury as Miscellaneous Receipts.[41]

Under the WPA Arts Program the procedure for the use of sponsors' funds was, *mutatis mutandis*, much the same as that outlined in General Letter 278, and attempted to preserve the essential feature of the procedures of the federal period. The main difference was that allocations of works of art to official sponsors, or, with the consent of the official sponsor, to cosponsors, were now interpreted as transfers of title and not as loans. This was in accord with general WPA procedure whereby the product of a project became the property of the official sponsor, which always was a public body—state, county, or municipal.

With respect to co-operating sponsors, which were non-profit private institutions, works of art might be loaned to them, but no transfer of title was possible. These loans, like those in the federal period, were generally permanent, and this disposition was thus equivalent to final disposal. The work, however, remained the property of the official sponsor and cosponsor, and it is interesting to observe that "murals, architectural sculpture, and other works of art which become a permanent part of a structure are not eligible for loan to nonprofit institutions."[42] As in the federal period, sponsors' contributions were expected of institutions that received allocations or loans of works of art.

On the Writers' Program the publication procedure was also patterned after that of the federal period. Sponsors were classed as official sponsors, cosponsors, and co-operating sponsors. The latter two always acted in the name of the official sponsor, but here again, as in the other programs, the cosponsors and the co-operating sponsors were the operating sponsors. The official sponsor merely conferred legality upon the project. In the Writers' Program a non-profit private agency as co-operating sponsor, with the approval of the official sponsor, made arrangements for publication.[43]

As for the Historical Records Survey, it became distinct from the Arts Program in accordance with the instructions of Operating Procedure No. G-5, and its activities were merged with those of the Research and Records Program.

In addition to its use of admission funds through the device of sponsors' contributions, the Music Program also continued two other practices that were characteristic of the federal period—the use of emergency workers and the use of agent cashiers. The procedure with reference to emergency workers was as follows:

9. *Emergency Labor* In the case of an emergency resulting from the sudden sickness or unavoidable absence of a regular member of the group with no project employees available for replacement, or a group with only major performers or workers but requiring "fill in" or types of workers not readily assignable, it is permissible to employ emergency workers, provided such aid cannot be obtained on a volunteer basis and provided the hiring may not conveniently be done by a sponsor.

Persons employed on an emergency basis shall be paid from sponsors' special deposit funds only, as appropriated funds are not available for payment of persons not regularly assigned to a project. Such payment shall be made under the procedure outlined herein.

(a) *Assignment of Emergency Workers* Before making assignments, the supervisor designated by the State Music Supervisor as the authorized assignment official for such emergency workers shall check with the business manager to determine if funds are available for paying the pay rolls for emergency workers. Sponsors' special deposit funds shall be encumbered before a worker starts to work. Regularly assigned project employees shall not be employed as emergency workers. An appropriate assignment form (WPA Form 402 *shall not* be used for this purpose) should be carefully prepared to indicate the proper reporting date and number of days or hours for which the worker is employed. This form shall be plainly marked "Special Deposit, Sponsors' Funds" and shall not be effective until countersigned by the business manager.

(b) *Rates of Pay* The rates paid emergency employees shall not exceed the prevailing hourly rates in the community. Supervisory employees shall be paid rates that conform with the schedule of rates for regularly assigned supervisory workers.[44]

These instructions are almost identical with those contained in Operating Procedure No. F-45. The principal difference is that the wages of emergency workers, instead of being charged against the admission fund account, were now charged against sponsors' contributions.[*] This was really a distinction without a difference, for sponsors' funds were almost entirely admission funds collected by the sponsor and termed "sponsors' special deposit funds" in the sponsor's transmittal statement.

The use of agent cashiers on the Music Program was another instance of special dispensation. As indicated elsewhere, the business

[*]In the federal period, wages of emergency workers could have been charged against the sponsor's cash account, but this was seldom done because sponsors' cash constituted only a very small portion of sponsors' contributions.

manager–agent cashier performed a variety of duties in the federal period. He was not only a collection and disbursing agent but also a procurement agent and an accountant. With the prohibition in the 1939 Act against the use by the WPA projects of funds collected as a result of project activity, it was no longer considered desirable for the project as such to collect funds, for such funds were necessarily covered into miscellaneous receipts. Therefore, the agent cashier ceased to be a collection agent, except in so far as the person designated as agent cashier handled the admissions collected by the sponsor which the sponsor converted into a sponsor's contribution. Indeed, on occasion the agent cashier did the actual collecting of the admission money, and field officers of the Washington finance office sometimes found them actually manning the box office during concerts. WPA officials were inclined to tolerate this practice, which, after all, was innocent enough, since the agent cashier, in performing such a duty, acted as the agent of the sponsor and not of the WPA.

The disbursing and procurement functions of the agent cashier were now limited to the amount of his cash advance, which was kept exceedingly small and could be obtained only for use in connection with touring units. As an accounting officer, he was required to account for his cash advance and, in addition, to audit the sponsors' admission collections. In short, the business manager–agent cashier of the Arts Program performed a congeries of duties patterned after those that attached to the office in the federal period, but more limited in scope and more qualified in definition. Operating Procedure No. G-5 merely makes this brief statement on agent cashiers: "A cash advance shall be available to agent cashiers only in connection with touring units of Music Projects for the payment of transportation, per diem, subsistence, emergency purchases in the field and the hiring of emergency workers in the field."[*45]

## THE FAILURE OF CENTRAL CONTROL

The elaboration of all these procedures, which represent an effort on the part of the Washington office to retain, as far as possible, the control of the federal period, should not create the impression that the controls were actually exercised. It is true that at the beginning of the new

---

*A more detailed and precise statement of the duties and responsibilities of the agent cashier is contained in Volume IV of the *Manual of Rules and Regulations*, pp. 4.5.103–4.5.106.

regime it was directed that each state should continue to submit the same type of monthly report of financial status and weekly employment report as had been submitted in the federal period.[46] This was to give the central office financial and employment controls over state operation.

This attempt, however, soon failed. Questions were naturally raised as to the necessity and propriety of retaining the financial reporting system in the absence of earmarked authorizations of funds to the states. No justification for the practice could be given, and, accordingly, Supplement No. 1 to General Letter No. 278, dated November 6, 1939, provided that the submittal of these reports should no longer be required. With no statistics upon which to base its control, the Washington office was powerless.

The fact was that, without the earmarking of authorized funds by the central office, financial control, and with it all control, was removed from Washington. The arts projects in the several states became part of each state's pool of projects, and the state administrator was free to choose, or not to choose, to put them in operation. There were no specific allocations, no specific authorizations, no specific budgets, no central office review of financial operations, and no employment quotas. It became simply a matter of submitting the same type of project proposal required of any other project duly sponsored by some state authority, which was reviewed for legality, adequacy, and conformity with administrative criteria for eligibility. Once the project was approved, there were actually no limitations imposed upon the state administrator with respect to its operation. Consequently, the influence and effectiveness of the national directors of the specific programs over program operations in the state were destroyed, for loss of operating control is the natural concomitant of the loss of power over the purse. Whatever supervision the national directors now exercised depended upon their ability to persuade the state administrations of the worth of their advice, and no longer on the control of a nationwide project financed from a nationwide earmarked allocation of funds apportioned to the states through authorizations earmarked by the Washington office.

THE ADEQUACY OF SPONSORSHIP UNDER
THE WPA ARTS PROGRAM

The statutory requirements of the 1939 Act with respect to the amount and nature of sponsors' contributions were: (1) the requirement that 25 per cent of total cost be borne by the sponsor; and (2) the requirement that credit shall be allowed for sponsors' contributions "only to the extent that the furnishing of such contributions represents a financial burden which is undertaken by the sponsors on account of Work Projects Administration projects."[47] Under these two provisions the Arts Program found it very difficult to continue operations. Indeed, it was only because the Washington office was generous in its interpretation of these provisions—particularly of the second—and the state administrations connived at inflated sponsors' contribution reports that the program was able to survive at all. The 25 per cent requirement, to be sure, did not of itself compel the state administrator to obtain that percentage for each project, or even for white-collar projects as a group, but only for all the projects in the state as a whole. Nevertheless, state administrators, especially those who emphasized manual projects, inclined to be severe toward non-manual projects. With respect to the State Arts Projects, some state administrators actually imposed the 25 per cent sponsorship requirement upon such as were operating in the state.

The consequence was that, in those states in which Arts Projects continued to operate, the value of sponsors' contributions were often inflated, sometimes beyond all reason. Florida may be cited as an extreme instance of this tendency. Julius Davidson, the former finance officer of Federal Number One was directed to investigate the sponsors' contribution situation in Florida in the spring of 1941. He presented a report, excerpts from which follow:

### General Findings

According to the latest available report of Sponsors' Contributions for the Florida Community Service Division as a whole, such contributions for the six months period ended December 31, 1940 amounted to 31.5% of the total project costs. Except for Arizona which reports 34.5% contributions for the division, Florida appears to have made the best showing in the Continental United States. Contributions of 25% for our division are not required nor are they feasible. Actually, Florida has obtained excellent support from the communities which is reflected in good sponsorship. However, a correction of reports containing ineligible credits would possibly bring the real figure down closer to 20%, which is really all that should be reasonably required of the division.

And why have these erroneous reports been made? It seemed to me that it was all based on an erroneous policy set by the State Administration requiring each project to obtain a minimum sponsorship of 25%. As we all know, the only statutory requirement is an average of 25% for all non-Federal projects in any State. Some State Administrations, despite this simple requirement and despite statements in our releases, have insisted upon 25% as an average for projects in our division. This is the only case that has come to my notice where the 25% requirement was imposed upon all projects individually. It was, therefore, not at all surprising that projects which cannot normally get even 10% were forced to credit ineligible items so that they might be allowed to continue operating.

*Recommendations*

My recommendations follow quite naturally from my general findings. It is recommended first, that, as long as the State meets the 25% requirement for the group of projects subject to the requirement, projects of the Division of Community Service Programs, which are otherwise desirable and which obtain all the sponsorship they reasonably can obtain, be relieved of the individual 25% requirement; second that all reports on Forms 710 and 710A affecting projects subject to the 25% requirement, beginning with the month of March, 1940, be reviewed and revised to conform with the regulations contained in General Letter No. 291 Revised and with Mr. Hunter's Memorandum of October 25, 1940. I had originally suggested that the revision be made beginning with January 1, 1940, but, since General Letter No. 291 Revised was not released until March 22, 1940, the regulations contained therein cannot very well be made effective for reports prior to March 1940.

These recommendations were discussed with Mr. Schroder, State Administrator, and he readily admitted being rather hard on our projects, and it is my understanding that these recommendations did not appear in anyway unreasonable. These recommendations were further discussed with Mr. MacDougall, Regional Director, who also agreed that they were quite proper.

In concluding this summary, I wish particularly to mention the courtesy and the cooperation received from the State and District staffs in Florida. Although the subject of sponsors' contributions is one which readily lends itself to controversy, all the members of the staff were quite receptive to constructive criticism. Only in the matter of revision and correction of past reports was there some hesitancy, which is understandable, but this recommendation is necessary if we are to fulfill our obligations under the provisions of the Relief Act.[48]

To illustrate one of the techniques of inflating contribution figures, the following extract from the same report is quoted:

At these meetings it was also noted that there was a tendency to establish the validity of items on sponsors' contribution reports by documentation in the form of attached statements from sponsors' representatives aiming to establish the financial burden by resolutions of Boards of County Commissioners and of similar bodies, and by independent appraisals of realtors. It was quite clear that the purpose of all this was to evade a responsibility given to representatives of an operating division, a responsibility which cannot be evaded by a semblance of legality.

Further extracts from the report illustrate the kinds of items included as sponsors' contributions to State Arts Projects:

### Miami Music Project

I noted a number of reports containing a credit of $20.00 per night for use of a bandstand. . . . Another item which poses a problem is a credit of $150.00 per month for fifes and drums supplied to boys in a fife and drum corps. . . . Studio rooms are claimed at 20c per hour. As the rooms are usually half the size of school rooms, if the latter were worth no more than 10c per hour, the former should not be credited at more than 5c per hour.

### Miami Art Project

Among the categories of items for which credit is sought are (a) space in public buildings for exhibits (b) rental values on objects borrowed from various sources for use in connection with the Index of American Design (c) show window space furnished by merchants (d) radio time (e) publicity in newspapers (f) rental values on exhibition paintings.

### Miami Writers Project

Two items of current reports examined are questionable, one for utilities in lieu of space in a school building in the amount of $37.75. . . . When I inquired as to what utilities were used, I was very interested to learn that lights happened not to be available at all. The other item was $31.04 for stack space in a library.

### Jacksonville Music Project

Again I found 20c per classroom hour rate used, and since only studio rooms are used, 5c per hour would be more than sufficient. The largest of the questionable items reported is for the use of uniforms by a high school fife and drum corps. One group of reports for such use totaled over $8000.00. . . . Because of the inclusion of such items I do not believe this project obtains as proper contributions more than half of the 20% reported.

Although responsibility for submitting reports of sponsors' contributions belonged to the operating divisions and not to the division of finance, the latter was authorized under the instructions to refer "those [reports] which appear to be incorrect back to the submitting division for revision."[49]

Only in rare cases did the state finance officers question the reports of contributions. As Davidson remarks in this report, Mr. Bradford, the Florida state director of finance, "was quite sound in his attitude. He has in no way encroached on the province of the operating divisions, but has merely returned questionable reports for further action. Mr. Bradford expressed himself as very skeptical about much of the sponsorship credit claimed and was quite pleased that I intended to survey the situation."

It must be conceded, however, that the inflation of the value of sponsors' contributions, which occurred in connection with the arts program (but which was not confined to that program), however much

336

it may have been an evasion of congressional intent, was pardonable in the circumstances. Congress, for all its restrictions, had not indicated that it desired the cessation of the arts program (the Theater Project excepted), and the WPA administrator, in order to save the white-collar program, and with it the arts program, had ruled that the statutory percentage need not be required of each single project. If in these circumstances certain state administrators chose to exercise their discretion in such a way that, if their rules were strictly followed, the arts program would be destroyed, it is understandable that those in the state who were connected with the arts program should have adopted ways that were devious in their struggle for survival. In fact, the statutory requirement with respect to sponsors' contributions placed a premium upon falsification; the statutory limitation upon non-labor costs provided adequate financial control, from the point of view of Congress, and, at the same time, permitted that flexibility of operation which took into account the different requirements of various kinds of projects.

### THE EIGHTEEN-MONTH RULE

The statutory provision of the 1939 Act which required that all project employees who had been working on the WPA for eighteen consecutive months should be temporarily removed from the rolls worked unusual hardship on the arts program, as well as on the white-collar program in general. With respect to its impact on the non-manual program Mrs. Kerr remarked in July, 1939:

> Now on this matter of the rotation of people, I suppose that this is one of the parts of the bill which, of course, will be discussed in detail by the Employment Division. But again I find that the type of project operated by the Professional and Service Division is going to suffer very heavily by such rotation. I have been told that in certain units it means that 70 percent of the people will go off, and in whole programs 50 and 60 percent of all the present personnel will be dropped. That means that project operation is going to be very, very difficult for those state and district people. I am hoping very much that the suggestion thrown out this morning will be amplified, and that there will be a simplification of the reassignment procedure, and also that full advantages will be taken of the five percent non-relief exemptions.[50]

After a year's operation of the rule Colonel Harrington remarked:

> The operation of the 18-month rule undoubtedly worked considerable hardship on a large number of people because it was necessary to dismiss

337

nearly one-third of those employed on Work Projects Administration during July and August. However, as stated above, at the present time only an average of about 50,000 a month are required to be laid off in accordance with provision of the law.[51]

But there were ways by which the intent of the provision could be avoided, as the following colloquy indicates:

Mr. WOODRUM. The committee has had some information to the effect that the 18-month provision has been made inoperative, in some localities at least, by people resigning with or without knowledge of the W.P.A., after they have been employed, say for 15, 16, or 17 months and then receiving re-employment and starting another 18 months all over again. What can you tell the committee about that?

Colonel HARRINGTON. The principal subterfuge that is being used to avoid the effect of the 18-month lay-off is for a worker who is approaching lay-off to say he has a private job and to go off of our program for a period of 2 to 4 weeks, and then come back and say he has lost his private job; which, under another section of the act gives him preference for reassignment on W.P.A. Then he comes back with this interruption and we have to assign him. Is that correct?

Mr. RAUCH. That has been the principal way; but we require him to furnish a statement of the private employment and then we make very diligent efforts to substantiate whether he has worked, or not.

Colonel HARRINGTON. In other words, we are trying to police it; but I understood you wanted to know what devices they were using, and that has been the principal one?

Mr. RAUCH. That is right.[52]

In the ERA Act, fiscal year 1942, the eighteen-months clause was qualified as follows:

Provided, That such workers shall be removed only in the numbers necessary to provide employment for employable persons with the same or similar job qualifications who have been certified for a period of three months or more as in need of Work Projects Administration project employment and who have not in such period been given employment on work projects.[53]

Apart from this qualification, however, the provision prevailed until the end of the WPA.

1. Reorganization Plan No. 1, approved April 3, 1939, Section 306.

2. Public Resolution No. 26, 76th Cong. (S.J. Res. 138), approved June 7, 1939.

3. U.S. Congress. House. Committee on Appropriations. 76th Cong., 1st sess

(1939), *Hearings of a Subcommittee . . . on Work Relief and Relief for Fiscal Year 1940*, p. 14.

4. Letter, Harrington to the President, June 14, 1939, WPA Files.

5. Memorandum, Morris to Florence Kerr, June 5, 1939, WPA Files.

6. Memorandum, Florence Kerr to Harrington, June 5, 1939, WPA Files.

7. Letter, Smith to the President, June 23, 1939, WPA Files.

8. Letter, Harrington to the President, June 26, 1939, WPA Files.

9. Proceedings, WPA National Meeting, Stevens Hotel, Chicago, July 12-13, 1939, pp. 33-34.

10. General Letter No. 278, WPA, July 31, 1939, Part I, Section 1.

11. *Ibid.*, Section 2.

12. *Ibid.*, Section 5.

13. Operating Procedure No. G-5, WPA, January 10, 1940, Part I, Section 2.

14. *Ibid.*

15. Proceedings, Meeting of the State Administrators, National Directors and Washington Staff of the WPA, St. Louis, Missouri, June 25-27, 1940, pp. 30-31, p. 247.

16. Memorandum, Hunter to All State Work Projects Administrators and Regional Directors, January 22, 1941, WPA Files.

17. Memorandum, Florence Kerr to All Work Projects Administrators, June 5, 1940, WPA Files.

18. Lettergram, Hunter to All State Work Projects Administrators, February 28, 1941, WPA Files.

19. Proceedings, National Meeting of the WPA, July 2-3, 1941, Stevens Hotel, Chicago, Illinois, pp. 11-12.

20. *Ibid.*, p. 146.

21. *Ibid.*, pp. 150-51.

22. Night Telegram, Hunter to All State Work Projects Administrators, December 8, 1941, WPA Files.

23. Service Letter No. 1, WPA, March 12, 1942.

24. Service Letter No. 3, WPA, April 18, 1942.

25. U.S. Congress. House. Committee on Appropriations. 77th Cong., 2d sess., (fiscal year 1943), *Hearings of a Subcommittee . . . on Emergency Relief Appropriation*, p. 142.

26. Emergency Relief Appropriation Act of 1939, Section 29.

27. *Ibid.*

28. *Ibid.*

29. *Ibid.*, Section 13(a).

30. General Letter No. 291, WPA, November 1, 1939.

31. Memorandum, Harrington to All Regional Directors, November 24, 1939.

32. Emergency Relief Appropriation Act, fiscal year 1941.

33. U.S. Congress. House. Committee on Appropriations. 76th Cong., 3d sess. (fiscal year 1941), *Hearings of a Subcommittee . . . on Emergency Relief Appropriation*, pp. 420-21.

34. General Letter No. 278, WPA, July 31, 1939, Section 3.

35. *Ibid.*, Section 8(c).

36. *Ibid.*, Section 9(c).

37. *Ibid.*, Section 10(c).

38. *Ibid.*, Section 11(c).

39. Letter, Holmes to Griffith, July 26, 1939, WPA Files.

40. Minutes of Conference of State Administrators, Chicago, Illinois, July 12-13, 1939.

41. Operating Procedure No. G-5, WPA, January 10, 1940, Section 37.

42. *Ibid.*, Section 32.

43. *Ibid.*, Section 41.

44. *Ibid.*, Section 36.

45. *Ibid.*

46. General Letter No. 278, WPA, July 31, 1939, Section 7.

47. Emergency Relief Appropriation Act of 1939, Sections 1(d) and 11(c).

48. Julius Davidson, "Report of Visit to Florida, April 1-11, 1941," WPA Files.

49. General Letter No. 291, WPA, November 1, 1939.

50. Proceedings, WPA National Meeting, Stevens Hotel, Chicago, July 12-13, 1939.

51. U.S. Congress. House. Committee on Appropriations. 76th Cong., 3d sess. (fiscal year 1941), *Hearings of a Subcommittee . . . on Emergency Relief Appropriation*, p. 439.

52. *Ibid.*, p. 478.

53. Emergency Relief Appropriation Act, fiscal year 1942.

# 17

## The Origins of the Federal Art Project

The Federal Art Project was the dramatic expression of two tendencies in American artistic thought: a greater awareness of art on the part of the American people, and a greater awareness of America on the part of the American artist. These two developments complemented each other and promised, if fostered, to create artistic maturity in the United States. The Federal Art Project was not the cause but the sign of their synthesis. Yet a sign may become in time a cause; and it remains for the future to determine whether the Federal Art Project, having achieved for a time an intimacy between art and the common man, will serve as an inspiration for a more permanent union, once circumstances have emancipated the nation from the bondage of wars and the rumors of war.

America, on the whole, has been too modest with respect to its achievements in the world of art. The declaration of American cultural independence from Europe has long been delayed, if it has at last been made. This cultural bashfulness was natural in a nation that was a child among elders in the European cultural comity, and the preoccupation of the American with the conquest of a physical frontier precluded the leisure that, if it is not the parent of art, fosters the artistic etiquette that makes polite conversation easy.

Yet the potentialities of the American creative genius were always present, and in certain realms have achieved remarkable expression. A people who have created the skyscraper, jazz, and the cinema need not fear the accusation of artistic illiteracy, except from those in whom

341

the remembrance of things past obscures the promise of the present. America, to be sure, has expressed its artistic character in novel ways, peculiar to its environment and history—ways that are beyond the comprehension of the *arbiter elegantiarum* of the Old World.

But these modes, if they lack urbanity, do not lack virility. There is a lustiness about American expression that betokens the age of puberty, but no one can doubt that a man-child is attaining maturity. There is a lack of discipline in America's artistic strivings that is often misunderstood by those who, steeped though they are in the culture of the past, forget that Dionysus, before he became domiciled in Athens, roamed untamed among the Thracian woodlands. There is a lack of delicacy about the American manner that misleads those who, substituting etiquette for courtesy, have locked the conformist in the salon and outlawed the rebel to the garret.

The fact is that America is the *enfant terrible* in the art shop of today, because it is the only nation on the face of the earth that, having created an industrial economy, has attempted to create and, to a considerable degree, succeeded in creating an industrial culture.* This industrial culture, still in its swaddling clothes, has already conquered the industrial world. It is useless to kick against the goad. American jazz has spread beyond the seas, wherever cities and factories are, like an epidemic for whose contagion there is no antidote. The popularity of the American cinema in London, Paris, Shanghai, and Buenos Aires is as incontestable as it is unfathomable by those who would establish a quarantine. London, with that calculating concern for tradition that distinguishes the English upper classes, legislated early against the skyscraper. But such buildings have now become accepted there; and unless the course of history changes abruptly, a skyline such as New York's will eventually become as familiar to Europeans as it now is to Americans.

This new American culture has two fundamental characteristics: it is industrial, and it is proletarian. Nothing like it has ever happened before. Being industrial, it is urban; but it is not urban in the sense that the make-believe culture of Versailles was urban, or in the suburban man-

*Russia has created, or is in process of creating, an industrial economy, but her culture remains classical. In music, the dance, the theater, and in art form, Russia is not revolutionary, but merely modern. Beethoven was as unconventional in his day as Shostakovich is in ours, but both write for the intelligentsia. The Moscow Art Theater is a state-subsidized institution after the manner of the old regime. A change in manner, however superficially radical, must not be mistaken for a change in basic culture. A play about the worker, however sympathetic with his cause, can be as nicely adapted to the demands of the intimate theater as Barrie's *Peter Pan*.

342

ner of the *petit bourgeoisie.* In both of these cases the ugliness of the city is relieved by the artificial cultivation of pastoral and agricultural modes. American culture is urban with a finality and lack of relief from which there is no immediate escape. It is the culture of the factory and the subway; of the department store and Times Square; of the sidewalk and the saloon; even of the bordello and burlesque.*

There is much that is unlovely, if not unholy, in this culture, not merely from the point of view of those who long for the comfortable security of the drawing room but also in the eyes of those who, accepting the new dispensation, are nonetheless aware of the vulgarization of soul that seems almost inherent in the factory system. The conflict is crucial, and the issue is close at hand.

The conflict is not to be resolved by the utter repudiation of the culture of the past. Neither does the solution repose in the minds of those who, accepting industrialism as an instrument of power, reject both the bourgeois culture that preceded the revolution and the proletarian culture that accompanies it. Salvation, if salvation is possible, lies in synthesis.

The remarkable fact about America is that, though it has not achieved this synthesis, it has attempted it with some success. The mighty harbinger of the new world was Walt Whitman, who with a seer's vision foresaw the century of the common man. Edgar Lee Masters and Carl Sandburg—the latter in his epic biography of Lincoln as well as in his poetry—followed in Whitman's footsteps. In our own times a host of new writers have arisen whose breach with Romanticism is complete, not because they have rejected the old forms (although some of them have done so), but because, to paraphrase Aristotle, they have discovered that the American man is an industrial animal.†

This adaptation of literature to the new society was accompanied to a lesser degree by similar changes in the other arts. Steele Mackaye, when he attempted his mammoth civic pageants, caught the spirit of

---

*It is hardly necessary to point out that this industrial culture, wholly urban in character, has crossed the frontiers of the cities and taken possession of the American countryside—even those areas that are economically agricultural and pastoral. The American small town is no less industrialized, so far as the arts are concerned, than the factory city.

†The fact that they write about industrial man does not, of course, of itself make their writing good, any more than the writings of the Romanticists, or, for that matter, of classical Greece, were all good. Mediocrities and fakirs belong to every generation. But by raising industrial society to the level of literary respectability, they have made possible the conversion of belles-lettres to new uses.

American youth and its love for bigness, and tried to discipline it to the Thespian tradition.* Likewise, but by other means, the little-theater movement in the United States, born in a stable on Macdougal Street, was an effort to break the monopoly of the carriage trade and to give the stage back to those who enjoyed it in Shakespeare's time. In *The Emperor Jones*, Eugene O'Neill allegorically transferred the conflicts of industrial society to the jungle. In music, Gershwin and Rodgers tamed "hot jazz," and the former in *Show Boat* and the latter in *Oklahoma!* achieved a medium that promises a synthesis between the music of the streets and the music of the spheres.†

It is this tendency toward an alliance between industrialism and tradition that gives promise of a new cultural order. Tradition, unless it makes peace with the urban worker, will become sterile; and industrial society, unless it is taught a respect for tradition, will become barbaric.

These truths are self-evident in American society today, and it is significant that America, more than any other country, has developed the instruments—public, quasi-public, and private—of a popular culture. These instruments are not those of the academician—the conservative art school, the symphonic or choral society, and the art theater. All these associations perform a necessary function: the maintenance of artistic standards in an age of revolutionary change. But it must be recognized that, like Horatius, they are merely holding the bridge to gain time against disaster. They have not the words of eternal life.

The dynamic elements in American cultural life today are its public schools and colleges, its settlements and neighborhood houses, its playgrounds and civic centers, its adult education groups and labor unions. This is a hard saying for those who love their comfort as much as their art, but Europe has already discovered that the veil of the temple is readily rent by profane hands. The American professional artist, unless he descends from his Olympian security and walks with the sons of Adam, will find that, like his European colleague, he will walk alone to destruction. After all, the common people are not hard to find.

---

*The cultivation of pomp and circumstance, for its own sake, is distinctly American and distinctly urban, and reveals itself most strikingly in college football, which has ceased to be an academic diversion and has become a proletarian spectacle.

†The orchestration of hot jazz would have occurred even if the United States Army had not closed Basin Street in 1917 or Paul Whiteman had not realized the commercial possibilities of the Phrygian mode. Improvisation, which was the essence of early jazz, belonged to the primitive period of the new phenomenon, and its untutored masters could not have been kept permanently in isolation, even by the *cordon sanitaire* that New Orleans maintained around Basin Street.

## THE ARTIST AND THE DEPRESSION

The acceleration of movement, which the twenties had produced in art as in other activities, carried through the first year or two of the depression. As late as February, 1931, Edward Allen Jewell, the art critic of the New York Times, could write of the possibility of a government subsidy without any mention of the economic plight of the artist. Calling attention to the apparent universality of the artistic rebirth, he wrote:

> Without attempting any elaborate inventory at this time, one may mention as outstanding developments within the last few seasons, the creation of the Whitney Museum of American Art. . . . By way of further general art appreciation, the establishment of the Museum of Modern Art . . . the Museum of Living Art, New York University . . . the veritable renascence of opportunity for mural artists—business institutions and schools cooperating to this end; increased activity in the art field, of book publishers, which cannot but mean an increasingly active market; an enthusiastic circulation of traveling exhibitions sponsored by such organizations as the Carnegie Institute of Pittsburgh, the College Art Association, the International Art Centre of Roerich Museum and the American Federation of Art; generous, intelligent and open-minded educational efforts on the part of collectors from coast to coast. . . .
>
> Now and then one looks wistfully in the direction of the government, wondering whether in some way it could not be induced to help in the task of organizing art in America. The American Artists' Professional League . . . is at present earnestly trying to induce the government to give all commissions for official portraits to our own portrait painters. But as a general thing, art has learned that it must not depend upon government help. . . . It seems to boil down, by and large, to individual initiative and private enterprise.[1]

This statement gives credence to the belief that Forbes Watson expressed later in the same year—that the artistic stir of the twenties had been caused more by artists, critics, collectors, and dealers than by an increased aesthetic demand on the part of the people.[2] It may well have been that the Armory Show of 1913 affected the art world more than the Carnegie Corporation's subsidy of art education in the early twenties bestirred the educators. At any rate, the desired liaison between artist and educator had not been accomplished.

In time, of course, artists as a group felt the impact of the depression. The incidence of want naturally bore more heavily upon the younger and less-established members of the profession, although some men of national prominence and more mature years were also affected. As early as April, 1931, art galleries in New York began to hold unemployment fund exhibitions, and, at a later date, artists' organizations, like the Society of Arts and Sciences, attempted to assist some of their members with the limited funds at their disposal.[3]

It was at this point that the artists discovered that the guild, however well it may have expressed solidarity in a craft society, was no substitute in an industrial society for the labor union.* They also became aware of their dependence upon the profiteer. Some dealers and collectors took pity upon their servants and made honest efforts to help them. The majority, however, either removed themselves from the market place or intensified their importation of French art in order to satisfy the vanity of an economically secure clientele.

Two developments resulted from this searching of spirit. The first was a renewed emphasis upon nationalism in art, which now was buttressed by economic as well as artistic considerations. There was an element of chauvinism here, to be sure, which was redolent of the tariff and the embargo. The artists, some of them eminent, who protested against the employment of a Mexican artist to decorate the walls of Radio City, were moved, in part, by other than aesthetic considerations;[4] and the slogan of the American Artists' Professional League, "I am for American Art," was too reminiscent of "Buy British" to be wholly convincing.[5] The American Artists' Guild and the Society of Illustrators demanded that native artists be commissioned to paint official government portraits;[6] and the American Federation of Artists, carrying economic separatism even further, exhorted local communities to support local talent.[7]

But if the spirit of nationalism in art as it developed under the stress of unemployment was not entirely unselfish, it was not without its good effects. In the first place, it served to focus attention upon how little encouragement the professional traffic in art had given American art. The opening of the Whitney Museum of American Art, in 1930, provoked the comment that the Newark Museum had anticipated it in its concern for American art, and that comment bestirred the reflection that the Syracuse Museum of Fine Arts had preceded both.[8] Before that, there was the void. The art season of 1931-32 in New York City was predomi-

---

*This labor weakness of artists (and writers) was in sharp contrast to the labor strength of musicians and actors. The American Federation of Musicians and Actors' Equity, to be sure, had much of the psychology of the guild, but at least they were a tower of strength for their members.

346

nantly American both in the type of exhibition and in the public forum, where artists and critics debated the issue of nationalism in art.

More significant, however, than the emphasis upon nationalism in art was the artist's effort, precipitated by the depression, to find a direct and popular market for his wares. There was a strong element of economic urgency in this development, but implicit in it was a determination to break the claims that bound him to the art dealer. The movement apparently started in Paris, where in December, 1931, an artists' aid committee was formed to trade paintings and sculpture for anything "reasonable."[9] This scheme seems to have been put into effect later at the *Salon des Echanges*, and, by February, 1932, an art salon in New York City was attempting a similar experiment. The Society of Independent Artists adopted the barter plan for its 1932 show.[10]

The use of barter, however, to resolve the crisis was no more successful in art than it was in other commodities, and a more ambitious and promising plan to circumvent the entrepreneur was started in Greenwich Village in January, 1932. There, the front window of a local pharmacy was converted into a gallery. Space was given free, no commissions were charged, and exhibitions were changed every two weeks. Sales were reported to be "considerable."[11]

The idea grew. On April 12, 1932, under the competent leadership of Vernon Porter, needy painters, who were then said to number about 1,000, asked for a permit to display their art in Washington Square, along the lines of exhibitions that had long been held in Paris.[12] The Park Commissioner at first refused to sanction the enterprise, but at length, yielding to the organized pressure of the Artists' Aid Committee, which included many names prominent in art and public life, he relented and issued a permit. Late in May, 1932, the first Washington Square exhibition was opened. Some 185 artists were represented. Prices as low as five and ten dollars were asked, and barter was permitted. A great throng of visitors was attracted, and a festive atmosphere prevailed. The showing, which lasted nine days, was eminently successful. Paintings to the value of $9,716 were sold, with commissions totalling about $3,000 in addition. One artist accumulated $471 in sales; several others were offered employment; and other interesting opportunities were presented as a result of the exhibition.

The idea was contagious, for even department stores, galleries, and other business establishments were surprised and impressed by the demonstration that informality and low prices could attract people who by all the laws of the middle-class tradition were artistically inarticulate. The virus even spread beyond New York City. During July of the same year an outdoor market was opened in the artists' community of Westport, Connecticut, by a number of individuals acting as a co-operative. Chicago provided what a correspondent termed the sensation of the decade. In less than two weeks the number of exhibitors ranging from 56 to 270 sold 4,662 items for a total of over $16,000. In Dallas, Texas, a successful outdoor art festival was organized; similar exhibits were held in Cleveland, Detroit, and Santa Barbara; and subsequently, in Boston, New Orleans, San Francisco, and Los Angeles. News of the movement traveled abroad, and even in far away Rio de Janeiro artists were reported to have formed a co-operative in order to sell their work in the Greenwich Village fashion, with nothing priced over ten dollars.[13]

The establishment of a direct market between the artist and the common man, which was the achievement of the "Village idea" of the early thirties, was the third—and ought to have been the decisive—step in the democratization of American art; for if the revolt of the "Eight" in 1908 made the artist aware of industrial America, and if the Armory Show of 1913 made industrial America aware of art, the Washington Square exhibit attempted to synthesize the awareness of each into a common experience—and, for a moment, succeeded.

The movement, however, was brief. The artist, when he repudiated the middleman, became an economic orphan; for he had not, in his own name, the financial resources to sustain himself in the interval of transition. The public, on its part, for all its enthusiasm, was not able to support the artist in the style to which he had been accustomed. A guardian was needed for both, and the obvious guardian was the commonwealth.

EARLY EFFORTS AT WORK RELIEF FOR ARTISTS

Unfortunately, public bodies—federal, state, and local—were not prepared to intervene during the critical years 1930-33, and the chance to ride the crest of the wave was lost. A subtle change in spirit occurred between 1933 and 1935, which made the timing of the Federal Art Project, when it was initiated in the fall of 1935, just less than perfect.

Artists, like other white-collar workers, suffered from neglect in the early years of the depression. Some communities ignored the existence of the professional classes; others misinterpreted their need. One report stated:

In most cases, of course, the need among this class was for mental relief rather than physical relief. . . .

Recreation was recognized to be the most important single factor in a program of mental relief, and everything possible was done to encourage the extension of recreational facilities in order that the unemployed "white collar" person would have a way of taking his mind from his troubles.[14]

Artists, lacking the organized cohesion of other professional groups, not only were neglected but berated. As late as January, 1933, Henry McBride, the art critic of the New York *Sun*, had a simple solution for their troubles:

A lot of this unpreparedness for life on the part of our artists could be ameliorated if some of these committees now engaged in the task of supplying food and woolen garments to starving painters and sculptors would jot down the stories that these unfortunates tell them, get them printed in a neat and succinct form, and see that they are placed in the hands of parents of cute children that betray an aptitude for drawing. . . .

What is to be done for them? Nothing much physically, I fear, beyond what the aforementioned committees are already doing; but for their souls, I have a specific. It is nothing less than the reminder that for those already at the bottom there is nowhere to go but up. Think that over.[15]

Indeed, it was not until December, 1932, that two programs for unemployed artists were initiated in New York City, the first under public, the second under private, auspices. The public program was inspired by Harry Hopkins, then administrator of the New York State TERA. Hopkins suggested that classes for adults in the fine and applied arts be established by the New York State Education Department at the Central School of Business and Art. The City of New York cooperated with the state by providing the space and assigning the head of a high-school art department to supervise the work. The art teachers, who received fifteen dollars a week, taught students who ranged in age from seventeen to seventy. The students, some of whom were professional artists profiting from the opportunity to go deeper into aspects of the art field, and others who were beginners, were taught twenty-two subjects, ranging from art appreciation to landscape designing.[16]

These classes, which originally employed fifteen artists, became so popular that although it was intended that they should be terminated in May, 1933, they were not only continued but expanded to include thirteen centers in Manhattan, Brooklyn, and the Bronx. The teaching staff soon rose to sixty, and the student body from 150 to 3,500. A modest display of student work was shown at the Art Center in August, 1933;[17] but by April, 1934, the project had so grown in stature that its work was honored by a serious exhibition at the Metropolitan Museum of Art. The work shown included fashion designs, jewelry, sculpture, textile designs, and watches, as well as easel paintings and cartoons. Fifteen prizes were awarded.[18] In June, 1935, the project was serving 8,000 students.[19]

The second program for artists was under the private auspices, first, of the Prosser Committee and then of its successor, the Gibson Committee. Two women prominent in the activities of the College Art Association, Audrey McMahon and Frances Pollak, were primarily responsible for its initiation. In December, 1932, using funds granted them by the Gibson Committee, Mrs. McMahon and Mrs. Pollak made plans to employ artists on public art projects. The modest sum they received was designed only for the payment of artists' wages, and Mrs. McMahon and Mrs. Pollak received no remuneration for their work. Harry Knight, an artist who was with the Gibson Committee, joined them as personnel officer. Space was assigned in the College Art Association quarters, and the employment of artists began immediately. From December, 1932, to August 1, 1933, about a hundred artists were given relief at an expenditure of approximately $20,000.*

Mrs. McMahon supervised the production phase of the program, and Mrs. Pollak devoted herself to art education. The emphasis in this latter element of the program was not so much upon formal instruction as upon art appreciation, as a device to encourage the participation of the general public in the aesthetic experience.

Since the project was modest in size, organization and operations raised few problems. Some of the artists worked on a full-time, others on a part-time, basis. Employment was from month to month. Married men received twenty-five dollars a week, single men eighteen. Work was done only for non-profit institutions, which paid the cost of all necessary material. The quality of the work was approved by distinguished critics as well as by the institutions that benefited from it. The more arresting work in mural painting naturally provoked more comment than the less spectacular experiment in popular art education, but both phases of the program were maintained with a balance that met general approval.[21]

When, in the fall of 1933, the Gibson Committee prepared to dis-

*According to Mrs. McMahon, the following work was accomplished during that period: fifteen churches, schools, and neighborhood houses were decorated with murals; five institutions were completely redecorated; four churches had their statues and paintings restored; two museums were assigned artists who worked "constructively" on their collections; and in twelve neighborhood houses, 750 pupils were instructed in arts and crafts.[20]

continue operations, the project artists demanded a public subsidy; and at a meeting held at the New School for Social Research on October 27, 1933, they were assured of state support by Frederick I. Daniels, executive director of the TERA.[*][22]

The support the project now received from the TERA gave it public status and placed its operations on a more stable and, relatively speaking, a more permanent basis. Among other benefits that the state subsidy conferred was the payment of supervisors' salaries, now that they were recognized as public employees.

In January, 1934, the First Municipal Art Exhibition, sponsored by Mayor Fiorello La Guardia, opened in Rockefeller Center and dramatized the accomplishments of the New York City art project. The credit for the initiation of this exhibition belongs to Edith G. Halpert, director of the Downtown Gallery. Mrs. Halpert broached the idea to the mayor, who promptly gave it official sanction, appeared at its opening, and paid his respects to the artists who had prepared the several "miles of art." The exhibition,[†] under the direction of Holger Cahill, was the sensation of the season, and continued from January to April, 1934. During its first week over 20,000 persons visited it, and $10,000 were spent in purchases.[23]

With the advent of the CWA in November, 1933, it became possible for the New York City Art Project to secure federal support under the Civil Works Service Program, which was instituted specifically to further the employment of white-collar workers. It was not, however, until late January, 1934, that under the direction of Grace Gosselin, an outstanding social service worker, the CWS in New York City authorized the initiation of an art program. The program consisted of two parts: the first involved the employment of 127 art teachers in boys' clubs and settlements; the second, mural and easel paintings to be executed in several high schools. The first was to be directed by Mrs. Pollak, the second by Mrs. McMahon.

[*]It was as a result of this meeting that the first pressure organization designed specifically to secure work relief for artists was formed. This was the Artists' Committee of Action, the precursor of the Artists' Union.

[†]The fact that the exhibition was held at Rockefeller Center, which had recently ordered the destruction of Rivera's murals, caused dissension among artists and their societies. The exhibition was boycotted by the John Reed Club, the American Society of Painters, Sculptors, and Engravers, and men prominent in the art world, like George Biddle and Ralph Pearson. On the other hand, the influential Society of Independent Artists, although it disapproved of the Center's policy, acquiesced in the situation and, lest its own members should suffer, held its annual show as part of the Exhibition.

Early in April, the poster project began. Officially under the Commission of Licenses, and supervised by John H. Weaver, the project leased space in Rockfeller Center, where fifty artists were employed to design posters for city departments and non-commercial institutions.[24] This group constituted the nucleus from which developed, under the Federal Art Project, one of the most oustanding graphic arts programs in the country.

On May 1, 1934, when the cwa, and with it the cws program, came to an end, work relief for artists in New York City became once again the responsibility of the New York TERA, under whose auspices the program was continued until the advent of the Federal Art Project. These activities were divided into mural, poster, and art-teaching projects. The poster project in the course of the next year produced about 10,000 safety posters, made documentary paintings of fish for the Department of Markets, and even attempted murals for city markets. The most significant development within this project, however, was the experimentation attempted in the refinement of the silk-screen process, which was to lead to one of the most outstanding technical achievements of the Federal Art Project.*

In the art-teaching division, under Mrs. Pollak, 156 teachers were employed, 127 of whom held classes in more than fifty social and welfare institutions, where they worked with children of various ages, most of whom had not previously received any art education whatsoever. The method of approach was progressive and experimental, and, as Mrs. Pollak remarked at a meeting of the Progressive Education Association, "only at the children's request are suggestions made as to technique."[25]

But what Edward Allen Jewell called the "waxing mural tide" provided the largest and most sensational part of the program. Murals were feasible, among other reasons, because they attracted substantial financial sponsorship from public and quasi-public institutions. In New York City, murals of every description were attempted, from abstract conceptions to the playful designs created for the Central Park Zoo.[26] Ambitious projects were prosecuted in high schools, hospitals, libraries, and other public places. The walls of rooms of boys' clubs were decorated by the boys themselves, working under the guidance of project artists. The mural phase of the program, which was, as before, under the supervision of Mrs. McMahon, attained a maturity that prompted

*Vide infra, pp. 437-40.

her to declare in a public statement that although relief was still a primary concern, need and competence had been

> assimilated to a point where excuses are no longer required. . . . All the murals executed and in process have been passed by various boards, beginning with those composed of local interests and ending with the City Art Commission. In addition to our own unrelaxed supervision, the teaching activities are constantly scrutinized by such agencies as Brooklyn Museum, College of the City of New York, or the Board of Education, depending on the problem involved.[27]

Indeed, the New York City art project justified itself in terms of accomplishment so well that it escaped the almost universal censure of white-collar projects contained in the Stryker Report.*

Employment varied on the New York City art project in the period between the cessation of the CWA and the inauguration of the WPA largely in relation to the amount of money granted it by the TERA at any particular time. In July, 1934, project employment numbered about 300;[28] in January, 1935, it seems to have maintained that quota; in June, 1935, it had risen to 393, distributed as follows: murals, 159; teaching, 188; posters, 46.[29]

This quota did not begin to exhaust the number of artists seeking relief, or at least employment, in New York City. There were nearly 1,000 artists listed on the state roll of the Public Works of Art Project, of whom the majority, it may be presumed, resided in New York City. The College Art Association had classified more than 1,400 artists in the city as in need of relief.[30] The result of this inadequate coverage was that the needy artists, both those on relief and those seeking it, under the leadership of the Artists' Union and the Artists' Committee of Action, combined to agitate for a city art center. The mayor, whose sympathy with the artists manifested itself throughout the whole period of their extremity, created a Municipal Art Committee, the original purpose of which was to initiate a civic art center. The movement, however, was stillborn, and unfortunately raised hopes that it failed to satisfy.[31] It remained for the Federal Art Project to deal adequately with the relief problems of New York City artists.

---

*Easel painting, which probably represented the major interest of the larger number of artists on relief in New York City, was not developed on the New York City project. The inability to secure adequate sponsorship was, without doubt, a serious impediment. The Woodstock (New York) project, however, which was connected with the artists' colony there and also supervised by Mrs. McMahon, employed twenty-eight artists, mostly in easel work.

THE MEXICAN INFLUENCE

The accent upon mural painting, which provided the predominant emphasis for Mrs. McMahon's New York art project, had just reached America from Mexico. The Mexican *risorgimento*, in turn, had preceded its American acceptance by a decade, for it was in 1922 that a group of young, liberal artists, fresh from the art schools of the Old World, formed in Mexico the Syndicate of Technical Workers, Painters, and Sculptors, and were commissioned by the Ministry of Education to paint frescoes on the walls of government buildings. The new experiment promised to be short-lived, for, within a few months, a change of policy within the Ministry of Education forced the cancellation of all the contracts except Diego Rivera's.

But the Mexican government soon discovered that the "young Turks" were not creating but merely expressing an artistic revolution that was part of the social change Mexico was then experiencing. Gradually in the course of time, the artistic counterrevolution, largely supported by the *Academia* and the conservative press, wore itself thin, and soon the Mexican government was commissioning frescoes for public walls with the same assurance with which Victorian governments once commissioned portraits.

Diego Rivera and José Clemente Orozco soon found themselves at the head of a movement that suddenly acquired international—or at least inter-American—stature, but which, basically, was as Mexican as its young protagonists. The movement was radical, to be sure, and in that sense it had world-wide significance; but it was a protest against capitalism on the part of an agrarian, not an industrial, country.*

In the second place, the Mexican revolutionary school was essentially religious, not material. Moreover, it was not only religious, but

---

*This consideration is basic, if an understanding of Rivera's failure to feel at home in the United States, and of this country's inability to accept him spiritually, is to be achieved. Rivera's protest, as portrayed in his painting, is not simply a protest against *capitalism* but a protest against *industrialism*. It is not merely that he paints the faces of Mexican peasants, not American workers; it is that, as a Mexican, he thinks in terms of an agrarian culture to which industrialism (not just capitalism) is alien, both economically and spiritually. An agrarian culture and capitalism—mostly in the form of foreign money—can live together, as Spain and the whole of Latin America bear witness; but not an agrarian culture and industrialism. Rivera, when he resided in the United States, was always a metic—a resident alien —and it is doubtful if he could ever have become a spiritual citizen of the United States.

354

Catholic and Latin. There is a mystic element in the eyes of Rivera's men and women that cannot escape the sensitive observer, and, beyond that, an asceticism in form and expression that is distinctly Spanish and strongly reminiscent of El Greco. This spiritual affinity between a great Spanish artist (for El Greco plumbed the Spanish soul as no Spaniard has ever done) and a great Mexican artist transcends the limitations of time and space and expresses, above all else, the tragedy of the Fall. In this, as well as in its agrarian spirit, the new Mexican art was indigenous.*

Finally, the Mexican revival was native in the sense that it represented the spiritual fruit of a physical union of the European with the pre-Conquest Aztec and Indian. The Spanish and the English, to be sure, have equally exploited the Indian; but, whereas the English have virtually annihilated the North American native, the Spanish, partly through the influence of the padres and partly because they cultivated a latifundian economy, have assimilated the Mexican native. This difference is important, for it explains why the concept of the primitive in art is authentic in Mexico and merely forms a cult in the United States.†

The move, therefore, to import the Mexican spirit into the United States was a failure, both when it was attempted by radical young intellectuals and when it was essayed, as a kind of tolerant dilettantism, by Dartmouth College, Edsel Ford, and John D. Rockefeller, Jr. But, though the Mexican spirit was alien, the Mexican method as it expressed itself in technique and economy readily acclimatized itself to the American scene.

The mural was, in fact, both an economic and artistic answer to the American artist's dilemma. In the first place, the mural solved the problem of patronage, for, with the multiplication of public buildings (post offices, schools, hospitals, colleges, etc.) in recent times, walls were being provided with a largess equaled only by the number of candidates prepared to decorate them. In the second place, mural

---

*There is an American religious character, too, as well as a Mexican, as is apparent to anyone who studies Grant Wood's "American Gothic." But the faces of these two stern Americans of the frontier are as Calvinist as Rivera's peasants are Catholic. The contrast is between the Protestant spirit of self-reliance and the Catholic concept of dependence. For this reason the American Catholic finds himself amid the alien corn, for he can never wear his religion with that ease and grace that the Latin, from long familiarity and in a sympathetic milieu, has acquired.

†The culture of the United States is a mélange, but of European cultures which, whatever their provincial differences, have a common source. It is not a fusion between a self-conscious and a primitive culture, except in so far as it has through jazz and its derivatives assimilated a native African culture.

painting was not expensive. Blank walls were cheap, if only buildings were designed to provide them, and the painting itself could be made a co-operative enterprise in which high competence was required only on the part of the supervisor. Finally and most significantly, the mural by its very nature created an intimacy between government and art, which far transcended the business relationship that previously prevailed between the Treasury Department and private architects.

It is difficult to express the essence of this intimacy, except perhaps to say that the mural, by its very nature and by the fact that it is an integral part of an institution with a purpose, sets limitations within which the artist must conceive that are not imposed by easel painting, sculpture, and the graphic media. An artist, for example, who accepts a commission to paint a mural in a hospital or a school must, unless he is artistically stupid, choose a subject matter that expresses the purpose of the institution. Thus, by a very natural process and not by any artificial imposition, the concept of social purpose becomes congenial to art. The modern artist is enabled easily and gracefully to express his social purpose through public institutions, just as the medieval craftsman expressed his religious philosophy through the church. The great merit of this relationship is its naturalness. There is no awareness of strain or incongruity between the message and its vehicle.

A corollary of this intimacy between art and government as expressed in the mural was the imperative of technical freedom. The private patron who commissions a portrait or any other work of art, as Rivera discovered, may establish the purpose he wishes the work to express. A public institution, on the other hand, enjoys no such freedom and, indeed, makes itself ridiculous if it attempts to exercise it. A mural in a public institution must, by its nature, express a public purpose. A mural in a public hospital necessarily expresses the relation between medicine and the public, and not merely between medicine and the medical profession. Again, a mural in a public school necessarily expresses a relationship between education and all children, not merely between education and the child whose parents can pay for private schooling. This compulsion is inherent in the medium and, because of it, a latent revolutionary content is present in all sincerely conceived public murals.*

---

*It may be objected that murals were painted in public buildings before the Mexican revolt, and that these earlier allegorical concepts do not express social purpose. The answer is that this earlier mode became a fashion when, as in the old regime in France, public buildings were considered as the private property of the

The artist, through the mural, discovered not only a relationship between himself and the government but also between himself and the public. The public mural is, as its name implies, visible to all who care to look. Its clientele cannot be restricted, either by statute or by property qualification. Accordingly, the artist was constrained to consider, like the newspaper illustrator of fifty years ago, what the public as a whole would understand and appreciate. If this realization resulted in some instances in "painting down," it was, on the whole, salutary. At least, the artist was taught to realize that the esoteric was not necessarily the profound, and that truth could sometimes be expressed otherwise than through allegory. Above all, the artist was forced to think *publicly*, not *privately*, and thus to partake of intellectual and spiritual communion with the many.

## GEORGE BIDDLE AND EDWARD BRUCE

In the early thirties young American artists were making the pilgrimage to Mexico City with the same fervor with which their fathers had sought the Latin Quarter. Among those impressed by the spiritual and economic promise of Rivera's school was George Biddle. A Rittenhouse Square-Groton-Harvard background made Biddle at home among the optimates and, in particular, a friend of the President from the time that both attended Groton. On May 9, 1933, Biddle wrote a letter to Roosevelt that was in a certain sense the occasion that inaugurated the Public Works of Art Project and, after it, the whole arts program of the WPA. The letter read:

DEAR FRANKLIN:

I never doubted your ability and courage; and perhaps that is the reason why I have so delayed in congratulating you on your achievements. The sincerest thing I can say to you is that you have grown and will continue to grow with the demands that America and the world puts on you. I am really proud to have known you at school and college.

There is a matter which I have long considered and which some day might interest your administration. The Mexican artists have produced the greatest national school of mural painting since the Italian Renaissance. Diego Rivera tells me that it was only possible because Obregon allowed Mexican artists to work at plumbers' wages in order to express on the walls of the government buildings the social ideals of the Mexican revolution.

king and were so decorated. It is this incongruity that, persisting long after the legal fiction has been exploded, makes such mural decoration so ridiculous today.

The younger artists of America are conscious as they have never been of the social revolution that our country and civilization are going through; and they would be eager to express these ideals in a permanent art form if they were given the government's co-operation. They would be contributing to and expressing in living monuments the social ideals that you are struggling to achieve. And I am convinced that our mural art with a little impetus can soon result, for the first time in our history, in a vital national expression.

You are too busy at present with more serious problems to give this matter any thought. Perhaps during the summer you will let me drive over from Croton-on-Hudson and pay my respects.[32]

Ten days later, the President replied:

DEAR GEORGE:

It is very delightful to hear from you and I am interested in your suggestion in regard to the expression of modern art through mural paintings. I wish you would have a talk some day with Assistant Secretary of the Treasury Robert, who is in charge of the Public Buildings' work.[33]

The story of what followed is accurately and enthusiastically told in Biddle's autobiography, *An American Artist's Story.* Gathering about him a group of kindred spirits—Henry Varnum Poor, Maurice Sterns, Boardman Robinson, Thomas Benton, and others—Biddle composed a prospectus that he entitled "A Revival of Mural Painting." It was a scheme patterned after the Mexican project of 1922, in which a group of liberal and socially conscious artists would work at mechanics' wages on government walls. The prospectus read in part:

1. A few social-minded, creative artists of the first rank, representing the modern movement, and experienced in mural painting.

2. The assignment to them by the government of public wall space on which to express the social ideals of the government and people.

3. The understanding that in the personal expression and technical execution, the artist be given as complete freedom as possible. Interference would only tend to emasculate his work. The government may exercise the right to assign mural subjects and veto any expression of opinion which it considers embarrassing.[34]

On June 19, 1933, Biddle was in Washington and on June 21 had a conference with Assistant Secretary of the Treasury L. W. Robert and his supervising architect. In the meantime, the President had seen Biddle's memorandum and had referred it to the Fine Arts Commission. The Commission in turn had disapproved the design. After mentioning the "controversy and embarrassment" that already had attended the work of the new school of muralists, who professed "a general faith which the general public does not share," the report continued with the reflection that the new group ignored "the established tradition built up by its pioneers and fostered by the American Academy at Rome—which has brought forth a younger, more liberally minded and murally trained modern talent." On August 6, 1933, the President sent the report to Biddle, with a note which read:

DEAR GEORGE:

The enclosed from the Fine Arts Commission speaks for itself. It does not sound very encouraging for the mural paintings.[35]

Biddle's suggestion had met with more sympathy from Assistant Secretary Robert than from the Fine Arts Commission; and so taking Rexford Tugwell's advice—"If things go wrong get pressure from above. Never go below. You'll get bogged in."[36]—he constituted himself the lobbyist for the group. Among others from whom support was gained were Secretary Perkins, Secretary Ickes, Jerome Frank, Louis McHenry Howe, and Henry T. Hunt, general counsel of the WPA.

In the meantime, a change in the organization of the Treasury Department had occurred. In June, 1933, the President had authorized the creation of a Procurement Division in that department and, in November of that same year, appointed Admiral Christian Joy Peoples as its director. The work of the division was divided into two parts: the branch of supply and the public buildings branch. Among the functions of the latter was placed, by order of the Secretary, "the preparation of drawings, estimates and specifications for public buildings construction, including the taking of proposals and the entering into contracts for such construction."

By November it was decided to inaugurate the CWA with PWA funds. Edward Bruce, an employee of the Treasury Department who was by profession a lawyer and executive and by avocation an artist of established reputation, had already been brought into the conversations. On November 8, 1933, Biddle and Bruce conferred with Secretary Ickes, administrator of the PWA, and with his encouragement a memorandum was drafted by Hunt addressed to Harry Hopkins, administrator of the CWA.

The result of this memorandum, and of subsequent plans and conversations, was the initiation, on December 3, 1933, of the Public Works of Art Project, under a grant from the CWA to the Treasury Department. Assistant Secretary Robert, anticipating the decision, had already appointed Edward Bruce secretary of the Advisory Committee to the Treasury on Fine Art; and the PWAP, when it came into being, was operated under the direction of Edward Bruce and Forbes Watson.*

Edward Bruce had in common with George Biddle that social respectability without which an entrée into the highest levels of official Washington on behalf of a plan as novel and as potentially dissident as was Biddle's would have been impossible, even in the earlier days of the New Deal. They both were artists, and each respected the other; in temperament and political philosophy, however, they differed. Edward Bruce, a corporation lawyer and a business executive before he entered government service, although not reactionary, was politically conservative and a liberal only in the Victorian sense of the term. In art, he was an idealist, but not a social idealist, and, with a catholicity of spirit that reflected the breadth of his aesthetic interests, had carefully refrained from identifying himself either with the extreme conservative or the extreme radical in the world of art.

Thus in 1933 Bruce was not only socially respectable but, unlike Biddle, politically acceptable; and, in the environment of the Washington hierarchy, the latter recommendation was as important as the former. Besides, Bruce was a politician in the sense that he knew the men and methods of Washington. Without his intervention the PWAP would never have been started, and Biddle quite appropriately handed him the torch; in the course of the transfer, however, the plan ceased to be Biddle's, and became Bruce's.

Bruce's philosophy of the relation between art and society is best expressed in a letter he addressed to Mrs. Roosevelt on May 10, 1935, and in which was enclosed a statement "In Support of Project to Employ Artists under the Emergency Relief Appropriation Act of 1935." It considered the role of culture in America historically, pointing out that the nation had hitherto been too much concerned with conquering its physical environment to develop its artistic impulses adequately. Yet, it was only "nations which have produced great works of art [that] have left the world richer because they have lived." America had reached the limit of its physical frontiers; the only ones remaining

---

*Robert represented the Treasury Department on the Advisory Committee to the Treasury on Fine Arts; Mr. Delano, the uncle of the President and chairman of the National Planning Board, became its chairman. Other members of the committee included Charles Moore, Rexford Tugwell, Harry L. Hopkins, and Henry T. Hunt.

were spiritual. There was, therefore, the opportunity not only to encourage a spiritual renascence but also to gain practical benefits as
well. He pointed to the great traffic in Italy that resulted from her art,
and to the fact that the commerce of Paris was firmly linked with her
art resources. However, "no great artistic or spiritual movement has
ever developed without a patron," and in the present instance only the
United States Government could set its artists working.[37]

The difference between the two approaches, as indicated in this
memorandum, is clear enough, if subtle. Biddle's stress upon integrating the subject matter with the social philosophy of the New Deal is
gone. Bruce, on the other hand, although he thought in terms of a larger
subsidy and a wider audience than were traditional, conceived government patronage as essentially the elevation of private patronage to a
higher level. The concept of patronage itself presumes clientage, and
increase in size alone does not betoken, necessarily, a change in purpose. In a word, Bruce still thought of the artist as working *for* the government; Biddle conceived of artists working *with* the government. The
implication of the two prepositions is fundamental.

But though the plan was not Biddle's, it was a *plan*, and had the
merit of being the only kind of plan that in the environment could be
made politically acceptable. Bruce's political approach was a necessary
complement of Biddle's ideological one. Moreover, without unusual
courage and perseverance even Bruce's plan might have miscarried,
for some members of the Fine Arts Commission itself preferred no plan
at all.* Bruce therefore was forced to seek support in high places. Justice Harlan Fiske Stone was particularly helpful, and it is doubtful if
the murals of George Biddle and Maurice Stone would ever have been
executed without his good offices. But two women also were towers of
strength—Mrs. Henry Morgenthau, Jr., and Mrs. Franklin D. Roosevelt.

## THE PRESIDENT AND MRS. ROOSEVELT

In the critical period of the early depression the cause of liberalism,
with which the cause of the arts was so closely entwined, was doubly
blessed, for it had as champions not only the President but also the
President's wife. The decisive influence they both brought to bear upon
events will probably never be adequately revealed, for it lies not in

---

*It was characteristic of Edward Bruce that he appointed to the Advisory Com-
mittee one of the plan's strongest opponents.

statutes or executive orders, or, indeed, principally in the published words of either. Rather, it lies in those casual conversations and executive conferences that never are recorded for posterity and, above all, in that indefinable spirit with which, through gentle innuendo and a nice sense of balance, they steered the ship of state by indirection.

Roosevelt may have been guilty of tactical blunders during his regime, but it is doubtful if history will ever convict him of strategical ineptitude. With a marshal's eye he always distinguished between a major and a minor front, and never allowed the enemy to trick him into a faulty deployment of forces. He was not oblivious of minor fronts, but he used his lesser battalions upon them; and sometimes, when he believed that the occasion required it, he lost a minor battle. The soldiers who fought in these lesser engagements sometimes thought that the war was lost, because they were ordered to withdraw; a few of them, yielding to cynicism, even deserted.

It is in this regard that the President's connection with the arts program must be judged. For all his sympathy for it, the cultivation of the arts by the government during the depression was in his mind a minor issue, not because it was unimportant but because it was less important than mastering the depression as a whole and surviving the international crisis that followed. In the earlier years there were those on the President's staff and among his followers who persuaded him that the welfare of the arts and artists was worthy of his official attention; and the President, with a genuine concern for the cause, allowed them to establish a secondary front. When, in 1939, world events forced him to concentrate his resources against a major attack from without, he left the art front and those who were fighting on it undefended.

On the other hand, if it can be said that the PWAP would never have been initiated had it not been known in official Washington that the President was personally interested in the plans of George Biddle and Edward Bruce, it is equally true that the arts program in its entirety, not only in the beginning but throughout its duration, depended even more upon the active support of Eleanor Roosevelt. The President's wife enjoyed a freedom of word and action that the President, because of his position, could not assume; and it may never be known whether her more candid and forthright espousal of unpopular issues was not, after all, also the master's voice. Here again, one depends upon hearsay and deduction rather than upon the written word and induction; but it is generally agreed by those who ought to know that more than once, when Federal One was in disrepute in the White House, Mrs. Roosevelt interceded on behalf of the prodigal son.

## THE PUBLIC WORKS OF ART PROJECT*

Mrs. Roosevelt addressed the meeting of the advisory committee at which, on December 8, 1933, the Public Works of Art Project was officially opened. Edward Bruce was made director of the project, and Forbes Watson was made technical adviser. Bruce, in his own words, explains the general character and purpose of the program:

> The idea of paying salaries to artists, and allowing them to work in a medium selected by them, to create paintings, prints, sculpture, wood carving, pottery, iron work—allowing them, in fact, complete liberty to express themselves, with the single provision that their work, in the broadest sense, should be appropriate in design and quality for the adornment of public buildings—that idea certainly was a new conception of the relationship between the artist and his client.
>
> The files of the Public Works Project contain many letters by artists written to explain what seems to me a most interesting point in the Government's adventure into the field of art. The artists wrote that the certainty of a regular check gave them a sense of security which enabled them to work without the distraction of financial uncertainty.
>
> This was only one point in the new adventure. Previously the artist carried on his creative efforts under his own solitary guidance. What other people might come to think of his work, what support the public might give him, how quickly he might become well enough known to obtain support, were matters of chance.
>
> On the other hand the receipt of a check from the United States Government meant much more than the amount for which it was drawn. It brought to the artist for the first time in America the realization that he was not a solitary worker. It symbolized a people's interest in his achievement. It gave him a sense of powerful encouragement, which inspired in him both a broader and a more realistic conception. No longer was he, so to speak, talking to himself. No longer was he limited in his appeal to a group of fellow artists or to pleasing a small minority of specialists. Symbolically he had become the spokesman of his community. His statement was unconsciously directed to the understanding of a much larger, less specialized public.
>
> The Public Works of Art Project was an emergency agency, a selective employment plan in which over 3,600 artists participated, producing over 16,000 works in various mediums. It would be folly to maintain that 16,000 masterpieces were produced. However, it is not an exaggeration to say that a sufficient number of vigorous, original works of art were produced to give satisfaction and stimulation to the Government and to all those who had faith in the high civilizing influence of what a disinterested government could accomplish through cooperation with the artists of the country.[38]

For project purposes, the country was divided into sixteen regions,

---

*The PWAP is here examined as an art project specifically; its general significance in the whole development of the government's cultural program has been considered *supra*, pp. 116-17, 184.

each in charge of a volunteer committee that selected and employed artists, and supervised the work in their region.* The collectors of customs in fifteen different sections of the United States and the Treasury disbursing officer in Washington acted as disbursing officers for the project, and accounting was supervised by the accounts division of the supervising architect's office in the Treasury Department.

Employment was rapid. The first artist was engaged on December 9, and within three days the project was in operation. Before the month was out, Bruce was able to present Hopkins with a plan embracing all the regions. By the third of January 1,444 artists and 27 laborers were at work; by February 7 the personnel had increased to 2,294 artists and 168 laborers, with every state in the Union represented.[39] In all, 3,600 artists participated in the program.

The fact that every state was represented in the program is significant, in view of the subsequent failure of the Federal Art Project to achieve similar coverage. The intensity of employment, however, varied. In New England, Massachusetts and Connecticut had thriving projects, but Maine, New Hampshire, Vermont, and Rhode Island lagged. It is not surprising that large projects were developed in New York City, Chicago, California, and Ohio; on the other hand, the strength of the project in such states as Mississippi, Arkansas, Nebraska, and Georgia, where the Federal Art Project failed to develop, is all the more striking.

Jacob Baker's memorandum to Hopkins on the PWAP anticipated employment and wages as follows: 1,500 artists at from thirty-five to forty-five dollars per week; 1,000 assistants at from twenty to thirty dollars per week; 500 laborers at approximately fifteen dollars per week.[40] The PWAP, however, since it was financed with PWA money (through the CWA), necessarily followed the PWA wage structure. For the PWAP this became $15 a week for laborers, $26.50 for artists' assistants, and $42.50 for artists. In New York City the difference between the two higher categories was split, and a uniform $34 a week paid. The PWAP wage structure was patterned upon that of the PWA, which was both higher and less complicated than that of the WPA; and for this reason alone, it avoided many of the labor difficulties that beset Federal One.†

*The regional centers were: Boston, New York City, Philadelphia, Washington, Atlanta, New Orleans, St. Louis, Pittsburgh, Chicago, Cleveland, Denver, Dallas, Santa Fe, Los Angeles, San Francisco, and Portland (Oregon). In the Washington office, Bruce and Watson were assisted by Edward B. Rowan, assistant technical director; Ann Craton, co-ordinator; and Cecil H. Jones, business manager.

†In the light of the number subsequently employed on the Federal Art Project

The program as laid down by this memorandum called for a continuation of work "on state, municipal or other properly commissioned movements of similar nature," such as had already signally appeared in the New York developments in work relief for artists. Under the PWAP the artists were to improve the "craftsmanship of furnishings" of public buildings, embellish federal, state, and municipal buildings and parks, and make pictorial records of such national projects as the Civilian Conservation Corps camps and Boulder Dam.

The PWAP program, therefore, was exclusively a program of production. The public was expected to benefit but not to participate, except in the role of spectator. Art education, even of the formal variety, was not included in the operations of the project. This emphasis was possible because the PWAP was a program for employment, not for relief, as Bruce reminded his regional chairmen in a telegram dated December 17, 1933.[42] For this reason, emphasis in recruiting personnel could be placed upon competence alone.*

The response of the public to the program was generous and enthusiastic. For the most part, sponsorship was readily obtained and, in some instances, spontaneously offered. The citizens of Santa Monica, California, held a mass meeting, and contributed from fifty cents to $100 to raise the $1,000 necessary for the completion of murals for the local library.[43] Texas, where later the WPA administrator refused to allow entrance to the Federal Art Project—because (so he said) there were few, if any, artists in the state—became so enthusiastic for murals that it attracted the attention of the metropolitan press;† and the New Mexico project, which employed a considerable number of Indians in their native aptitudes, attracted national interest.[45]

---

(between 5,000 and 6,000), it is interesting that Baker, in December, 1933, considered 3,000 adequate. In the memorandum to Hopkins, already noted, he wrote: "From a rough survey it is our belief that this list will be sufficiently large to include practically all of the unemployed artists in America, who are capable of doing work of such quality as to make it worthy of permanent record in public buildings."[41]

*It was expected that the PWAP, like the CWA in general, would take half its artists from the relief rolls and half through the USES. It is questionable, however, if this proportion was maintained. The unemployment character of the CWA was predominant, even in the minds of local certifying agencies, and during this period relief status was generally granted with a liberality that did not prevail either before or after the CWA.

†The New York Times reported: "Never has the cult [of artists] had so large and unrestrained an opportunity to express itself. Indeed, there has been such a rush to paint murals on every public wall in Dallas that blank walls are at a premium and . . . [the] Sheriff . . . was forced to announce that the walls of the county jail will not be available."[44]

The artistic merit of the accomplishments naturally varied but, on the whole, was sufficiently sound to attract general, though not universal, approval. Examples of PWAP endeavor were exhibited at the First Municipal Art Exhibition of the City of New York, which Bruce addressed, and shared the approval accorded the show. In April, 1934, a national exhibition of the work was held at the Corcoran Gallery in Washington, D.C., at which about 500 items were displayed. The *Art Digest*, which maintained a sympathetic but objective attitude toward the experiment, stated that the exhibition would represent a "showdown" on the value of PWAP as a producer of art. Later, the same periodical declared, on the basis of the exhibition, that the project had been a success, "realized its investment," given necessary work to artists, and focused the attention of Americans on art.\*[46]

One of the most interesting developments of the PWAP, which had its echoes in the Emergency Work Program of the FERA that followed, was the work done in the CCC. Through a special arrangement made by the President with the director of the Civilian Conservation Corps, a number of PWAP artists were sent to various Emergency Conservation Work camps to portray the life and activities of the young men employed there. Many of these studies were returned to the camps for decorative purposes, or sent to libraries and high schools or to the artist's home town. Their work, consisting of some 200 watercolors, drawings, and oils, was exhibited at the National Museum (the Smithsonian Institution) under the title "Life in the C.C.C." Mrs. Roosevelt opened the show.†

A summary statement of the finances of the PWAP shows that $1,312,177.93 of the total allotment of $1,408,381.00 was disbursed. Of

---

\*As in the New York City TERA project, the mural accomplishments of the PWAP were the most spectacular in the public eye, and so general was the belief that murals constituted the major interest of government that public statements by Forbes Watson and Juliana Force were deemed necessary to dispel the notion that PWAP was confining itself to murals.[47] In a sense the public was right, for many PWAP murals were outstanding, as Bruce and Watson's volume, *Art in Federal Buildings*, amply illustrates. Grant Wood's murals at the Iowa State College at Ames provoked an enthusiastic appreciation in *Fortune* (January, 1935). Other PWAP artists who achieved favorable mention in *Fortune* were Stanley Wood (May, August, 1934) and Richard Jansen (October, 1934).

†After the PWAP was closed, assignments to the CCC camps were continued through the newly created section of painting and sculpture in the Treasury Department. About one hundred artists were assigned for each enrollment period. They received the same status and salary as other CCC workers, but devoted forty hours a week to art work and furnished their own art materials. Their product became government property. The best of it was framed and allocated. Unframed work was transferred to the art section, FERA, for allocation.[48]

the disbursements, 90.29 per cent went for project payroll (artists' wages), 5.27 per cent for administrative payroll, and 4.44 per cent for non-labor costs. The low administrative cost was largely due to the fact that the regional advisory committees served without pay; the low non-labor cost reflects sponsors' contributions.

The PWAP was not without its troubles, and some of the criticism it evoked was bitter. Complaints, however, were less directed against the quality of the work than against certain administrative practices. The employment of such established artists as John Sloan, Joseph Pollet, and William Zorach, who were in no need of work, aroused resentment.[49] In Chicago open favoritism was charged by the art critic C. J. Bulliet;[50] and in New York City unemployed artists several times demonstrated in front of the Whitney Museum (which Juliana Force directed) against what they termed unfairness and favoritism, and with such effect that in the spring of 1934 the museum was prompted to close six weeks earlier than usual.[51]

But these criticisms, whatever their local justification may have been, were not fundamental. As a matter of fact, the PWAP deliberately repudiated the gnostic dialectic of the art world when it avoided the appointment of professional artists and representatives of art societies to the advisory committees. The attack upon Mrs. Force, who was also head of the New York and New Jersey region of the PWAP, came largely from the conservative faction, which was annoyed because professional artists and representative art organizations had not been consulted in the organization of the project.[52] On the other hand, this policy was praised by F. A. Whiting, Jr., who wrote:

> The wise omission of existing professional (and other interested) groups and associations came to seem even wiser as the last weeks of 1933 passed. This was not a time for art politics, long an American cultural blight, to interfere either with the need of the artist or the quality of the work to be done for the Government. Many unbiased citizens were grateful that the project was under way and were willing to wait for reliable information and actual results before being unduly critical.[53]

When, with the termination of the CWA, the PWAP officially came to an end, the FERA allotted it additional funds to conclude its operations gracefully.[54] Ann Craton joined the FERA central office to take charge of the process of liquidation. Works of art produced on the project and not yet allocated were brought to Washington, where they might be allocated to federal agencies. The regional boards, with the advice of

Mrs. Craton, co-operated with state and local officials to facilitate the re-employment of the PWAP artists on the FERA Emergency Work Program.

Forbes Watson summarized the significance of the PWAP in these words:

> Before 1933 . . . we had a large, groping, hungry public which looked to art as a means whereby its cultivation and outlook on life could be broadened. This was a public which, thanks to its idealistic optimism, did not realize the facts about the artist. Suddenly a country which general speaking wanted to be tenderly cultivated without buying was transformed into a country which overnight became the largest purchaser of art in the making that the world has known.[55]

The historical significance of the PWAP lies in the fact that it was the *first* art project subsidized by the federal government on a national scale and, as a federal project, created the precedent upon which rested the whole arts program of the WPA, not only in art in the specific sense but in music, drama, and writing. It was a courageous venture that owed its initiation to George Biddle and the success of its operations to Edward Bruce. But many men and felicitous circumstances co-operated to make it a common achievement of progressive American artists, and the benediction of the White House was upon it.

THE SECTION OF PAINTING AND SCULPTURE

Although the precedent created by the PWAP as a relief and employment program was important, the immediate effect of the experiment was wholly unrelated to relief, except in the sense that the depression created circumstances favorable to its development. Bruce, who was himself a major part of it all, thus describes the philosophy of the section of painting and sculpture:

> It was decided that the time had come when the decoration of public buildings with painting and sculpture should be planned in such a way that artists in every portion of the country would feel the stimulating influence of the Government's recognition of quality and of its desire to secure quality. No longer could the more or less hit or miss system that previously prevailed be continued in the light of what the Government had learned about the needs and potentialities of American artists.
>
> In his Departmental Order, the Secretary of the Treasury stressed two points: first, the acquisition of the best available American art, and, second, the encouragement of those talents which, although known to exist in the country, had not had a reasonable opportunity to bring themselves to the

public attention until after the Government had become a serious client of the artists.

. . . . . . . . .

Up to the time when the Government entered the field of art, painters and sculptors had found it necessary to concentrate in the great financial centers. Roughly speaking, men who were not known in New York, Chicago, San Francisco, or some other great city, found it almost impossible to make a living. The former speculative relationship between the public and the artist made the life of the painter and sculptor a gamble. The star system prevailed in painting and sculpture, if not as obviously at least as effectively as in the case of musicians and actors.

One of the first steps taken by the Treasury Department Art Projects was to initiate a series of competitions which artists could enter anonymously. Indeed they were obliged to enter them anonymously. Mural designs, sculpture models, all were submitted unsigned. The name of the entrant was not disclosed until after the award was made. This method of course was a powerful blow at the star system. For the first time America purchased art on a large scale regardless of the fame of the artists, the purchasing being based entirely on the quality of the work.[56]

The new section was not, as such, concerned with relief, or even with employment as a relief measure. It was simply concerned with the procurement of art for government buildings. The break with the past, however, lay in three important changes: (1) the United States Government, through this section, was now directly responsible for the kind of art in federal buildings (this responsibility had been traditionally that of the architect who held the government contract); (2) the new program was national in scope and continuous in operation (formerly, art embellishment had been incidental to each government construction contract); and (3) the emphasis was upon *American* art and the quality of the product (previously, European modes had predominated, and the stress had been upon the professional reputation of the artist).*

The importance of this work, which was never dramatized as were the PWAP and the Federal Art Project, can be gauged by the fact that by December, 1942, 193 competitions had been conducted; federal buildings in 1,101 cities had been decorated with murals and sculpture; and 13,033 artists had submitted 36,009 designs.

## THE TREASURY RELIEF ART PROJECT

The Treasury Relief Art Project, although operated concurrently with the Federal Art Project from 1935 to 1938, is related historically

*This program also demonstrated the tremendous popularity of the mural, for by far the larger part of the section's awards was for mural decoration.

and administratively to the PWAP and the section of fine arts, rather than to the Federal Art Project; and its story, in brief form, may best be recounted here.

The TRAP was established on July 25, 1935, by a grant of $530,784 allocated to the Treasury Department by the WPA. The fund was administered strictly according to the rules of the WPA, and, as in Federal One, the WPA allowed a 25 per cent non-relief exemption. The work was produced for federal buildings, old or new, that had no money available under the building funds for murals or sculpture. The work thus supplemented that of the section of painting and sculpture, which concerned itself only with new federal buildings.

The employment on the project was kept low, the largest number of artists employed being 356. The criterion of selection was based upon demonstrated competence, and only artists who could meet federal building mural and sculpture standards were eligible; relief certification alone was not enough.

The TRAP worked closely with the section of painting and sculpture and, like it, was under the general direction of Edward Bruce and Forbes Watson. Olin Dows, a young artist who enjoyed the esteem of Bruce and his staff, was made chief of the TRAP and was assisted by Henry La Farge. Three field supervisors served on the project: Alice M. Sharkey of New York City, Elizabeth S. Lane of Boston, and Bernard Roufberg of Los Angeles.

The project was officially closed as of June 30, 1938. The total amount allocated was $771,521, of which $17,091 remained unobligated. The sixteen artists on the payroll on June 30, 1938, were transferred to the Federal Art Project in order that they might complete their assignments. As of June 30, 1938, the project had completed 85 murals, 39 sculptures, and 10,215 easels.*

OTHER CWA ART PROJECTS

Apart from the PWAP (which was a federal project) and the New York City Art Project, which, for purposes of continuity, has already been discussed, the CWA, through Civil Works Service Projects, supported other art projects of lesser moment and of local significance. Murals were freely sponsored in Connecticut, and a mural project was

*Information regarding the organization and operation of the TRAP is contained in the *Annual Reports* of the Treasury Department, 1936-39.

instituted for the library of the University of Kentucky—one artist being assigned, and paid thirty-three dollars for a thirty-hour week. In Berkeley, California, artists painted relief maps and prepared exhibits for public display in museums. New Hampshire created a small project that was to render assistance to the League of New Hampshire Arts and Crafts. The work involved the teaching of block-printing, batik, needlework, and leather work. New Jersey employed an artist to prepare posters, and Virginia attempted a survey of historical portraits. Two educational projects (besides Mrs. Pollak's New York project) are recorded: one in Michigan, which offered opportunities for artists and art teachers; the other in South Dakota, which opened three classes in art.*

### ART PROJECTS UNDER THE FERA
### EMERGENCY WORK PROGRAM

The termination of the CWA (which was a federal program) and with it the termination of the PWAP, at the close of March, 1934, caused a precipitate decline in art activities no less than in other cultural fields. Indeed, in so far as artists had enjoyed greater employment opportunities under the CWA, they were the more seriously affected. Approximately 3,600 artists and helpers had been on the rolls of the PWAP; and if the number employed on the New York City Art Project and the several local projects supported by CWA funds is added, it is probable that the CWA provided work for perhaps 4,000 persons in one or another form of art activity.

Under the FERA Emergency Work Program, which bridged the trough between the CWA and the WPA (April, 1934, through June, 1935), no more than 1,000 persons were employed in art projects.† In the beginning of the Emergency Work Program, the number must have been considerably less. The Washington office of the FERA and the regional committees of the PWAP made valiant efforts, to be sure, to persuade the states to take over the artists left unemployed by the closing

*Information, such as there is, about CWA art activities in the states is contained in the final state reports of the CWA, which repose in the FWA library.

†The official figure given was 952, but, since under the grant-in-aid system of the FERA there was no reporting system that enabled the Washington office accurately to estimate employment on art projects, the figure is at best an approximation:[57] Forbes Watson estimated that there were 1,000 artists supported by FERA funds in January, 1935.

of the PWAP; but a variety of difficulties, some inherent in the grant-in-aid system, others due to the indifference of state relief administrations, made these efforts less than adequate.*

The decline is readily apparent if the employment statistics of individual states and localities are considered. The Illinois Project, which under Mrs. Increase Robinson had been one of the largest PWAP projects, employing over 225 artists, became a project of approximately sixty-five artists. In New York City the art project under Mrs. McMahon and Mrs. Pollak was kept at a quota of approximately three hundred persons, which left little opportunity for the PWAP artists to secure admission to its rolls. In Indiana, employment was cut by 50 per cent. In many rural states (viz., West Virginia, Delaware, Wyoming, North and South Dakota, Nevada, Montana, Virginia, Georgia, Maryland, Tennessee, Mississippi, Missouri, Nebraska, Iowa, Kentucky, Michigan, Minnesota, and Oklahoma) art activities either ceased entirely or became inconsequential.†

But if the termination of the PWAP provoked a reduction in the employment of artists by perhaps three-fourths, the effect was not wholly evil. In the first place, the memory of the PWAP died hard, and the better artists—for the PWAP favored professional competence—continued to exert pressure upon Washington for an expanded art program, modeled, more or less, after it. The growth of artists in political consciousness and especially in awareness of the part that the federal government could and did play in art activities was a major cause in the initiation of the Federal Art Project. In the second place, if the end of the PWAP was unfortunate for the more skilled artist, the transfer of jurisdiction to the states emphasized the interest of communities in less professional activities. Art education, which was alien to the purposes of the PWAP, was given a new impetus, particularly outside New York City, under the Emergency Work Program. This development was particularly conspicuous in Florida. In Ohio, a Radio Junior College, cooperating with the Ohio State University and utilizing its instructors and radio station, was supported by federal funds, and included a course in art for which proficiency examinations could be taken and college credits gained. A new intimacy between the artist and the people developed, which, if homely in its manifestations, was not without

*The causes for the general decline in the professional program under the early Emergency Work Program have already been discussed. *Vide supra*, pp. 68-72.

†On the other hand, Florida, under the direction of Eva Alsman Fuller, expanded its PWAP quota of twenty-five to an FERA quota of 120. But this was the exception that proved the rule.

promise. A young Chicago artist was given the opportunity to paint a mural in one of the rooms of a suburban primary school. The project, which lasted eight weeks, was watched with interest by students, teachers, board of education members, and parent-teacher association members, who paid the thirty dollars necessary to cover costs and traveling expenses. The young man's success secured for him an assignment from the board of education of Des Plaines, Illinois, where he lived in the home of the superintendent of schools while making the preliminary sketches for a mural in the local junior high school.

Craft projects were encouraged, among which the Milwaukee Handicraft Project was unusually distinctive. Elsewhere, artists were employed upon such tasks as the preparation of posters, dioramas, models, lantern slides, etc. An unusual project in Florida attempted the rehabilitation of Key West, which was seeking to recover from a series of physical and economic disasters. A group of artists who had been "discovered" on the PWAP, including Adrian Dornbush, who later supervised the art activities of the Resettlement Administration, were sent to Key West, where, it was reported, they adapted themselves to the community and its problems with remarkable ease and grace. In Georgia considerable local interest was manifested in the restoration of a huge cyclorama depicting the battle of Atlanta. In Nevada, state initiative suggested a project to make a permanent record, through drawings, of Nevada Indian life. In Indiana—such was the influence of the PWAP—a committee headed by Wilbur D. Peat, director of the John Herron Art Institute, was appointed by the Governor's Commission on Unemployment to suggest the names of relief artists who could do creditable work. Each artist was permitted to investigate the need for work in his particular county and to submit sketches to the committee for a proposed task. In Ohio, though there was not a large centralized program, local interest stimulated art activities in several cities. One of the most unusual was the application of art to therapeutics at Longview Hospital in Cincinnati, where courses in art and other cultural subjects were given for schizophrenic patients in classrooms especially renovated for the purpose. The experiment was so successful that it attracted the attention of the FERA in Washington.*

In art activities, as in other professional activities, working proce-

*This account of art activities of the states under the FERA Emergency Work Program is based almost entirely upon reports from the states submitted to the Washington office in answer to a letter from Jacob Baker (Letter WDO-39, July 1, 1935) requesting a review of work relief activities from April 1, 1934, to July 1, 1935.

dures were elaborated by the Washington staff during the Emergency Work Program. The code number for art projects, which were listed under the category F (Public Education, Arts, and Research), was F3, and the specific working procedures were:

F3.1 Specified Commissions for Artists

F3.2 Individual Projects for Artists

F3.3 Community Art Survey

F3.4 Community Art Centers.

Under E (Public Welfare) was listed:

E4.3 Arts and Handicrafts Classes for Recreation.

Other working procedures also involved tasks more or less connected with art. Such were:

F7.3 Museum

F7.6 Architectural Models for Museums

The art activities of the states under the Emergency Work Program, besides emphasizing the interest of communities in other aspects of art than production, served to maintain a certain continuity of personnel over the interval from the PWAP to the Federal Art Project. Mrs. McMahon and Mrs. Pollak in New York City, Mrs. Robinson in Chicago, and Miss Curran in Philadelphia served their respective communities in all three periods.*

*Among others, volunteer advisers to the art projects included Burt Brown Barker, vice president of the University of Oregon, who had been regional director of PWAP in the West, and who assumed a similar role for the Federal Art Project; Ann Craton, an early assistant to Mr. Cahill, had been co-ordinator of PWAP and had supervised its liquidation; Richard C. Morrison, who became the New England regional director, was formerly Massachusetts state director for ERB; Charlotte G. Cooper, Ohio state director under the Federal Art Project, supervised art activities in the FERA period. Outstanding personnel who had been connected with artists' projects before WPA included Stanton MacDonald-Wright, who became head of the Southern California project; Benjamin Knotts, who succeeded Miss Curran as head of the Pennsylvania project; and Francis Robert White, who was appointed state director of the Federal Art Project in Iowa. In addition, many of the artists who later achieved distinction on the Federal Art Project had been employed by state and local FERA projects.

374

1. Edward Allen Jewell, in *New York Times*, February 15, 1931. © 1931 by The New York Times Company. Reprinted by permission.

2. *Ibid.*, October 1, 1931.

3. *Ibid.*, April 9, 1933.

4. *Ibid.*, February 2, 1932.

5. *Ibid.*, July 1, 1932.

6. *Ibid.*, January 18, 1931.

7. *Ibid.*, May 17, 1930.

8. *Ibid.*, March 28, 1930; April 18, 1930.

9. *Ibid.*, December 6, 1931.

10. *Ibid.*, February 2, 1932; March 15, 1932; March 31, 1932.

11. *Ibid.*, January 31, 1932.

12. *Ibid.*, April 13, 1932, *et seqq. passim.*

13. *Ibid.*, October 2, 1932.

14. "A Report of the Activities of the Massachusetts Emergency Committee on Unemployment, October 1931 to April 1932" (FWA Library), p. 60.

15. Henry McBride, as quoted in "Artists in the Bread Line," *Literary Digest*, January 7, 1933.

16. *New York Times*, March 25, 1933.

17. *Art Digest*, August 1, 1933.

18. *New York Times*, April 12, 1934.

19. *Ibid.*, June 21, 1935.

20. Audrey McMahon, "May the Artist Live?", *Parnassus*, October, 1933.

21. *New York Times*, September 14, 1933; October 8, 1933.

22. *Ibid.*, October 28, 1933.

23. *Ibid.*, January 29, 1934; February 14, 15, 18, 20, 27, 28, 1934; March 4, 1934; April 1, 1934.

24. *New York Times*, April 3, 1934.

25. *Ibid.*, November 24, 1935.

26. *Ibid.*, May 19, 1935; August 3, 1936.

27. *Ibid.*, August 19, 1934.

28. *Ibid.*, July 15, 1934.

29. Letter, McMahon to McClure, June 25, 1935, WPA Files.

30. Forbes Watson, "Art and the Government in 1934," *Parnassus*, January, 1935.

31. *New York Times*, January 7, 1934; March 5, 1934; June 26, 1934.

32. As quoted in George Biddle, *An American Artist's Story* (Boston: Little, Brown & Co., 1939), pp. 268-69.

33. As quoted in Biddle, *op. cit.*, p. 269.

34. Biddle, *op. cit.*, p. 270.

35. As quoted in Biddle, *op. cit.*, p. 273.

36. Biddle, *op. cit.*, p. 271.

37. Letter, Bruce to Mrs. Franklin D. Roosevelt, May 10, 1935, WPA Files.

38. Edward Bruce and Forbes Watson, *Mural Designs, 1934-1936* ("Art in Federal Buildings," Vol. I [Washington, D.C.: Art in Federal Buildings, Inc., 1935]), pp. xi-xii.

39. Edward Bruce, "Implications of the Public Works of Art Project," *American Magazine of Art*, March, 1934.

40. Memorandum, Baker to Hopkins, December 20, 1933, CWA Files.

41. *Ibid.*

42. Telegram, Bruce to Regional Chairmen, PWAP, December 17, 1933, CWA Files.

43. *New York Times*, February 23, 1934.

44. *Ibid.*, January 7, 1934.

45. *Ibid.*, January 21, 1934.

46. *Art Digest*, April 15, 1934; May 6, 1934; see also *American Art Annual*, XXXI (1934), 5 ff., and for a critical review of the Corcoran Exhibition by Edward Alden Jewell, *New York Times*, April 24, 1934.

47. *New York Times*, December 22, 1933.

48. Ann Craton, Report, "Public Works of Art Project, Covering its Activities and Liquidation," unpaged, "Emergency Conservation Work Camps," CPA Files.

49. *Art Digest*, April 1, 1934, p. 3.

50. *Ibid.*, April 15, 1934, p. 3.

51. *Ibid.*, April 15, 1934, p. 3; *New York Times*, January 6, 10, 1934.

52. *New York Times*, December 13, 1933.

53. F. A. Whiting, "The Year in Art," *American Art Annual*, XXX (1933), 19-20.

54. Telegram, Hopkins to All State Administrators, FERA, April 26, 1934, CWA Files.

55. Forbes Watson, *American Painting Today* (Washington: American Federation of Arts, 1939), pp. 19-20.

56. Bruce and Watson, *op. cit.*, pp. xi-xii.

57. *The Emergency Work Relief Program of the F.E.R.A.*, April 1, 1934–July 1, 1935, FERA, p. 121.

# 18

## The Organization and Operation of the
## Federal Art Project

HOLGER CAHILL

Jacob Baker's concept of culture as a co-operative enterprise influenced him in his choice of the directors of the four arts projects. He was deeply conscious that in the world of art, in the specific sense, the vested interests of professional artists and their attachments, economic and cultural, to various schools and tendencies made many of them less than catholic in their approach to the problem of art in America in 1935. In particular, he was aware that a schism existed between the "academy" and the younger artists, and that the appointment of a person too closely identified with either faction would offend and possibly alienate the other. As a liberal, Baker leaned toward the rebel, but his political sense warned him that the appointment of a radical, in the artistic if not the political sense, would bring the venture into disrepute with the established artist. On the other hand, he was equally aware that the artist who was in economic straits in the depression was, by and large, the young non-conformist, who would see in the appointment of a conservative the championship of orthodoxy by the state after the European manner.

In approaching Holger Cahill, Baker sought and found the *via media*. Cahill was not an artist in the professional sense, or, indeed, an art critic in the technical sense. He was, rather, an art lover, whose preoccupation with art derived, first, from his concept of art as a form of folk expression and, second, from his conviction that American culture could and should express itself as American in the various artistic media. Born in 1893 and educated at Columbia and the New School for

Social Research, he interested himself early in literature and writing and contributed articles to magazines and newspapers. His first work, *Profane Earth*, was a novel published in 1927; and a later book, *A Yankee Adventurer* (1930), was a romantic biography of an American soldier of fortune in the Far East. His professional connection with art began in 1922, when he joined the staff of the Newark (New Jersey) Museum as adviser in American art. This museum under the directorship of John Cotton Dana had been attempting to bring art, especially American art, into the people's ken and to create intimacy between art and everyday life. Dana had come to Newark in 1902 as head of the Newark Public Library, and had striven through the library and later through the museum to lighten, so to speak, the gloom of the gallery and to divorce art from antiquarianism. Cahill, whose natural tendencies were already in the same direction, was influenced profoundly by Dana's democratic approach. At the museum Cahill assisted in the selection of contemporary American art and organized two exhibitions, "American Primitives" (1930) and "American Folk Sculpture" (1931). It was also during this time that he published *Geo. O. "Pop" Hart* (1928) and *Max Weber* (1930). The untaught genius of Hart, which made him an American primitive, and Weber's academic tendency toward the primitive commended them to Cahill's study. In 1932 Cahill left the Newark Museum to join the staff of the American Museum of Modern Art, New York City, where he served as director of exhibitions until his appointment to the Federal Art Project in the summer of 1935. In 1932 he published his study *American Folk Art*, in which he further emphasized his interest in the American scene and his interpretation of art as a form of folk expression.

Even before his appointment as director of the Federal Art Project, he had expressed his approval of work relief for artists:

> [Government] projects are of the greatest importance. They show that the community is assuming a responsibility toward the artist. Through them there may be a possibility of healing the breach between the artist and the public, a breach which has become distressingly evident in the contemporary period.[1]

The creation of this intimacy between the artist and the people Cahill hoped to achieve by emphasis upon "the importance and pervasiveness of the esthetic experience, the place of the arts as part of the significant life of an organized community, and the necessary unity of the arts with the activities, the objects, and the scenes of everyday life."[2]

Thus there were many qualities in Cahill's character and experience that commended him to Jacob Baker. In the first place, his journalistic training had given him a keen sense, not only of the importance, but also of the delicacy, of public relations, and it was correctly anticipated that he would bring to the project a diplomatic approach that had already served him well in his professional career. In the second place, the fact that he was not himself a creative artist or even a professional art critic was considered in his favor, for it relieved him of allegiances that, in a national venture, might have proved embarrassing. Above all, his proclivity toward popular art not only in the sense of folk art but also as an element of common experience made his approach akin to that of the social worker, who, in the neighborhood house, was attempting through amateur devices to achieve what Cahill was contriving to accomplish in more professional circles. Finally, his experience in administration and organization in connection with museums and exhibitions, joined with a Horatian urbanity of manner, made him adept in his relations with state administrators and their staffs. There was nothing of arrogance or condescension in his conduct, and the ease and informality with which he approached state administrators were the more disarming when it was discovered that he not only played poker but played it well. By all counts, he was the most worldly wise of the directors of Federal One, and his sense of proportion, which made him amenable to compromise, enabled him to resolve crises by anticipation.

### ORGANIZATION OF THE NATIONAL AND REGIONAL OFFICES

Cahill, when he assumed office on August 1, 1935, undertook to create a field staff. The Federal Art Project, like the Music and Theater projects, was first organized on a regional basis, some of the field supervisors being attached to the Washington office, others to the payrolls of state offices within designated regions. Continuity with previous government ventures in work relief for artists was maintained by the employment of Ann Craton as field supervisor. Ann Craton had been closely identified with the PWAP, and after its closing was kept in the Washington office of the FERA to assist in the liquidation of the project and to advise Goldschmidt's section with reference to art projects.* Mildred Holzhauer, another early field supervisor, had worked as assistant to Cahill when he was director (1933-34) of the Municipal Art Ex-

*She remained with the Federal Art Project only during its early organization phase.

hibition, New York City, and at other times she had served on the staff of the College Art Association and as executive director of the Lillienfeld Galleries, New York City, and the Woodstock Art Gallery.*

In January, 1936, Baker directed that all field supervisors who were attached to state offices either should be made assistants to the national director and attached to the Washington office or should become state directors. Accordingly, Mrs. Robinson, Mrs. McMahon, and Robert Morrison were made assistants to the national director, and, at about the same time, Thomas Parker was made assistant director. The other field supervisors were attached to a particular state office, although in some cases they served as advisers for neighboring states.† Likewise, Mrs. Robinson, Mrs. McMahon, and Morrison, although they were attached to the payroll of the central office and held the title of assistant to the national director, continued to reside in their respective states, where they served as state directors and advisers to neighboring states.‡ Finally, there were those, like R. Varnon Hunter, state director for New Mexico, who were simply directors of the project in a particular state, with no regional responsibilities and no attachment to the Washington office staff.

As time went on, a division of labor was achieved in the Washington office. Cahill, quite properly, refrained from identifying himself too closely with one specific part of the program and maintained a catholicity of interest that enabled him to achieve a proper balance between special interests. Miss Holzhauer was given charge of the organization and management of exhibitions, and was assisted in the establishment of this section by Edith G. Halpert, director of the American Folk Art Gallery in New York City, who spent the summer of 1936 in the Washington office. Parker, whose acquaintance with the artistic needs of the South made him intensely aware of the importance of art education, was placed in charge of the development of community art centers and

---

*During the early period the number of field supervisors who served from state offices varied. In October, 1935, there seem to have been nine: Mary Curran (Pennsylvania and West Virginia); Robert C. Morrison (Massachusetts, Connecticut, Vermont, New Hampshire, and Rhode Island); Audrey McMahon (New York and New Jersey); Mrs. Increase Robinson (Illinois, Minnesota, North and South Dakota); C. Law Watkins (District of Columbia, Maryland, and Delaware); Thomas C. Parker (southern and southwestern states); Joseph Danysh (California and Nevada); Burt Brown Barker (Washington, Oregon, Idaho, and Montana); and Donald Bear (Colorado, Utah, Wyoming, Arizona, and New Mexico).

†For instance, Donald Bear is described as state director for Colorado, and adviser to Utah, Wyoming, Arizona, and New Mexico.

‡For instance, Morrison was now described as state director for Illinois, and adviser to Minnesota, South Dakota, and North Dakota.

was assisted in the field by Daniel S. Defenbacher, state director for North Carolina, whose zeal for art education in the South, coupled with his aptitude in creating and maintaining good public relations, made him an excellent agent for the propagandization of a new idea. Finally, when it was decided to inaugurate the Index of American Design on a national scale, Ruth Reeves, a designer of textiles for various well-known institutions, including Rockefeller Center, was brought to Washington as the first national co-ordinator of the project. Later, her title was changed to field expert, and C. Adolph Glassgold, who was a former secretary of the American Union of Decorators and Craftsmen, succeeded her as national co-ordinator. Questions of information and publicity in the national office were handled by Mary Monsell, a former editor of *Art News*.

It is apparent that in the organization of the national office differentiation of function was brought about by emphasis upon those activities capable of national co-ordination, viz., exhibitions, community art centers, and the Index of American Design. Nobody in the Washington office was specifically commissioned to supervise and to co-ordinate creative activities, such as easel painting, sculpture, and the graphic arts. The reason was clear enough. Creative projects, with the possible exception of murals, were largely the work of individuals and not co-operative efforts; they did not lend themselves to national co-ordination; their integrity depended rather upon competent local supervision and direction. Accordingly, it was enough if Cahill and his assistant, Parker, maintained through field inspections and reports a level of local supervision that promoted decent standards.

The personnel of the national office and field staff reveals a pattern of selection. With the exception of Miss Reeves and Mr. Glassgold, both of whom were practicing craftsmen, none was a creative artist. Their interest in art was that of educators, like Mrs. McMahon of the College Art Association; or of patrons like Mrs. Robinson, who had devoted herself to the moral support of young artists in Chicago; or of professional museum administrators, like Robert Morrison of Boston. This emphasis upon art as education was in keeping with Cahill's own training and predilections, and it was natural that the personnel he selected should be in large part the reflection of his own personality. The integration of art as an experience into the life of the community, which was the concept of the neighborhood house raised to a higher and wider level, was fundamental in his thinking; and he rightly conceived that that purpose could be better achieved by those who had already shown their devotion to it than by professional artists, however competent, who thought in terms of the private entrepreneur or the wealthy patron.*

An analysis of the qualifications of the state directors of the Federal Art Project shows the same emphasis toward the educator. Of the twenty-one state directors as of January 30, 1936, twelve were directors of local galleries or museums; four were members of national or local art associations; two were professors of art in universities; one was an editor of an art journal; and only two, Gideon T. Stanton in Louisiana and R. Vernon Hunter of New Mexico, were practicing artists. Obviously, the same considerations prevailed here—the desire to choose a person who was intimately acquainted not only with the artists but also with the art clientele of a community, and who had educational and cultural roots in the locality that would make the initiation of an art project a community venture.

### THE PERIOD OF INITIATION

The organizational pattern and early history of the Federal Art Project followed that of Federal One. In the beginning the field supervisors (or regional directors, as they were sometimes called) were given authority to initiate projects in the states without the approval of the state administrator; but this authority, as in the Theater and Music projects, was taken away in January, 1936. In general, the field supervisors of the Art Project seem to have been more diplomatic in their relations with the state offices than those of the other projects; and it was only in Pennsylvania, where the appointment of Mary Curran was vigorously opposed by the state administrator, that a critical situation developed.†

*Supplement No. 1 to Bulletin No. 29*, dated September 30, 1935, established the general basic procedure for the operation of the projects comprised in Federal One. With regard to the Art Project, it set up the following type of work classification:[3]

---

*Some of Cahill's staff had already proved themselves in connection with the PWAP. Parker had been executive director for Virginia; Mrs. Robinson for Illinois; Barker for Oregon, Washington, Idaho, and Montana; and Miss Curran for eastern Pennsylvania.

†In this case the crisis was resolved in favor of Miss Curran, although the opposition continued; and eventually, because of it and other reasons, Miss Curran resigned. *Vide supra*, pp. 153-54.

1. Mural painting ............................. 1883-(1)
2. Easel paintings: oils, water colors,
   drawings, graphic art ....................... 1883-(2)
3. Sculpture ................................. 1883-(3)
4. Applied arts: posters, signs, etc. ............... 1883-(4)
5. Arts and crafts ............................ 1883-(5)
6. Photography .............................. 1883-(6)
7. Lectures, criticism, and preparation
   of catalogues and pamphlets ................. 1883-(7)
8. Circulating exhibitions of art ................. 1883-(8)
9. Art teaching ............................. 1883-(9)
10. Other ................................... 1883-(0)

The several activities here enumerated derived from the experience and the working procedures elaborated in the FERA period. Two activities not included—community art centers and the Index of American Design—were subsequently initiated.

It was not, however, until the middle of October that Cahill was in a position to send his field supervisors out to approve projects, and not until the end of October that the *Federal Art Project Manual*, which provided the basic procedures for operations, was circulated to the states. The statement of purpose that appears at the beginning of this manual reads:

> The Federal Art Project of the Works Progress Administration will employ persons of training and experience in the art field who are certified to the Works Progress Administration as eligible to participate in the Works Program. The primary objective of the project is the employment of artists who are on the relief rolls. The Federal Art Project will draw at least ninety per cent of its personnel from relief. The project is planned in the belief that among these artists will be found the talent and the skill necessary to carry on an art program which will make contributions of permanent value to the community. Where necessary, artists may be drawn from non-relief sources, but in no case in excess of ten per cent of the total number employed.
>
> The plan of the Federal Art Project provides for the employment of artists in varied enterprises. Through employment of creative artists it is hoped to secure for the public outstanding examples of contemporary American art; through art teaching and recreational art activities to create a broader national art consciousness and work out constructive ways of using leisure time; through services in applied art to aid various campaigns of social value; and through research projects to clarify the native background in the arts. The aim of the project will be to work toward an integration of the arts with the daily life of the community, and an integration of the fine arts and the practical arts.[4]

As of November 1, 1935, a total of 1,499 project workers were employed in eleven states; of these, 1,090, or approximately 78 per cent, were concentrated in New York City.* On November 13, 1935, the employment had increased to 1,893, with 1,129 in New York City, and Massachusetts (which did not appear in the earlier list) second with 156 project workers. By December, 1935, employment had risen to 3,190, and early in 1936 passed beyond 6,000. From that time forward, the rise and fall of employment on the Art Project closely followed the general curve of Federal One.

The ease and speed with which an art project was set up locally depended upon a variety of conditions. In New York City, for instance, where work relief for artists was already flourishing under FERA auspices, it was simple to transfer the project personnel to the WPA, and thus to curtail the period of initiation. The same situation prevailed in Chicago and a few other places, where earlier art projects had been established. But in less metropolitan areas it was necessary to prepare the ground from the very beginning, and, as in the other projects of Federal One, many of the earlier project proposals represented hope rather than accomplishment. Some state directors were discouraged by the requirement of certification, and the state director for South Carolina wrote to Cahill in November, 1939, that under such conditions "I am forced to say that no good work can be expected of this region."[5] In New England, on the other hand, although an adequate number of trained artists were available, they were so geographically scattered that much time was consumed in concentrating them in a few areas for purposes of organization and supervision. Again, especially in the South, Southwest and Rocky Mountain states, there were so few certified applicants that it was difficult to create a nucleus for project operation. In some few cases the state administrator was hostile or indifferent. H. P. Drought of Texas absolutely refused to allow the inauguration of an art project in Texas, and his opposition prevailed.† In Vermont the state administrator was reluctant to approve a project that would require more than 10 per cent non-relief workers. He was inclined to hold that artists, if they were in genuine need, should be

---

*The employment figures were: Alabama, 7; Florida, 57; Illinois, 70; Minnesota, 44; Pennsylvania, 50; New York City, 1,090; New York State, 85; New Jersey, 35; California, 50; Delaware, 3; and Maryland, 8.

†Early in 1939, a unit of the Index of American Design was established in San Antonio, Texas. It employed fifteen persons, and continued in operation for three years. But all other plans for an extension of the Art Project into Texas were unsuccessful.

prepared to accept some other type of work, even manual labor, as an alternative to want.[6] On the other hand, in some states the good will of the state administrator made smooth the path of organization. This was particularly true in Oregon, where the state administrator, E. J. Griffith, actively and enthusiastically supported the art program and made possible, among other things, the construction of Timberline Lodge, a mountain retreat for art and artists designed entirely by the Federal Art Project. In states where the scarcity of artists precluded the appointment of a state director, supervision was undertaken by the professional and service division of the WPA with the advice of an art project director of a neighboring state. In January, 1936, this situation prevailed in Alabama, Arkansas, Iowa, Indiana, Tennessee, and Nebraska.

The penetration of the Federal Art Project into almost all the states was slow, but eventually successful. In January, 1939, Parker wrote: "With the exception of Arkansas, Texas, Georgia, Idaho, Indiana, Nebraska, Nevada, North and South Dakota, and West Virginia, all states now have some form of Art Project activities."[7]

As a matter of fact, every state in the Union at one time or another received funds for art project activities, and before the close of the federal period an Index of American design had been initiated in San Antonio, Texas, a project had been started in South Dakota that experienced a promising growth in the latter period, and a community art center had been established in West Virginia.

The success with which the Federal Art Project eventually, if not always immediately, was able to win favor in almost all states, even those that first showed themselves unsympathetic, derived in large part from its ability and willingness to acommodate its program to the needs and talents of particular localities. Unlike the Writers' Project, which envisaged a guide for every state, the Federal Art Project developed no particular project (except the Index of American Design) that by its very nature required a unit in every state. Accordingly, it was able readily to adapt its program to local needs. Thus it emphasized easel work in Louisiana, the Index of American Design in Missouri, art centers in Florida, sculpture in California, and in areas that could not afford galleries, it encouraged traveling exhibitions. Indeed, although in general the Federal Art Project discouraged handicraft units as beneath its artistic dignity, in New Mexico, where the artistic qualities of handicraft were superior, it not only permitted but fostered their development.

PROJECT PERSONNEL AND EMPLOYMENT

Since the primary object of the Federal Art Project was the employment of artists in need of relief, it was necessary to establish procedures whereby project personnel could be selected on the basis of competence. With reference to the eligibility of personnel the manual reads:

> The availability of talent on the relief rolls indicates what projects may be established. The first step in setting up a project is the determination of the talents and skills of the personnel on relief. In order to determine this, District Art Supervisors, or District Supervisors of Projects and Planning, shall request local offices which have been designated by the United States Employment Service to refer all relief personnel registered as artists, art teachers or craftsmen in the arts to the person or committee authorized to pass on the qualifications of artists. These persons or committees will be named by the Regional or State Art Director. In states where no art directors have been appointed the Federal Director, or his authorized agent, may appoint a local person or committee to interview and classify all people referred by the United States Employment Service.[8]

In the early days of the project, especially on the smaller units, committees of local artists and critics served as volunteer boards to interview applicants, examine their artistic work, and determine their qualifications. In the areas of greater concentration, however, as the project became stabilized, the state director or the local supervisor, or both, usually undertook personally to select the personnel. Indeed, since Cahill was careful to select state directors and local supervisors who were well acquainted in local and state art circles (like Mrs. McMahon in New York City, Mrs. Robinson in Chicago, and Miss Curran in Philadelphia), the task of selecting qualified workers was often best done by the project directors and supervisors.*

In places like New York City, where work relief for artists had been initiated before the WPA, those assigned to the earlier projects were generally transferred en masse, and without examination, to the Federal Art Project. This procedure, although it hastened initiation, was not entirely satisfactory, for the standards of competence established for the

*This method, however, almost invariably led to charges of favoritism. In New York City, Philadelphia, and Chicago, for instance, the directors were accused of allowing considerations of personal friendship, as well as predilection for a particular school or genre of art, to influence their selection of project personnel. Indeed, in Chicago and Philadelphia these accusations became so serious and persistent that they contributed to the decisions of both directors to resign.

earlier projects were not necessarily those that the Federal Art Project desired to prevail. As a consequence, a fair number of applicants whose qualifications were inadequate were admitted, especially in the more metropolitan centers. This created a problem that the Federal Art Project eventually resolved either by creating projects, like the Index of American Design, upon which the less-skilled could be trained to do useful work, or by dismissing them when budgetary considerations forced a reduction in employment.

In the latter case the use of review committees, composed of volunteers who were not connected with the project, sometimes saved the project supervisor from embarrassment. In Minnesota, for instance, when a drastic decrease in the employment quota made necessary a large number of dismissals, the Artists' Union demanded that the state director undertake to rate the artists in terms of competence, and to dismiss the less-skilled. The state director nicely avoided a difficult situation by recourse to an advisory committee, which called upon the artists to submit their best work, whether produced on the project or not, and rated them accordingly. The state director, in turn, retained or dismissed the project workers on the basis of the committee's recommendations.

CLASSIFICATION

The classification of project personnel within the several categories of skill established in Executive Order No. 7046 followed, or was coincident with, the establishment of their eligibility, in terms of artistic competence, for project employment. With reference to this procedure, the *Federal Art Project Manual* states:

> The skill classifications of art project personnel will be made by persons recognized as technically qualified by the Federal Art Director or his representatives. These classifications determine the rates of pay for personnel working on art projects according to the scale set by Executive Order No. 7046. For Artists employed as project supervisors the pay will be in accordance with the usual rates established by the State Works Progress Administration for similar supervisory work. Personnel whose wages are paid by a co-operating sponsor may be paid the co-operating sponsor's usual wage rates. The skill classifications of art project non-supervisory personnel shall be: (A) professional and technical, (B) skilled, (C) intermediate, and (D) unskilled.

*Professional and Technical*

Artists who are experienced in their skill and who are capable of producing creative work of a high standard of excellence are rated as professional. These artists will provide leadership, supervision and training in the various fields of fine and applied art for the artists not classified as professional, and will supply designs for projects. In addition to painters, sculptors and graphic artists, others such as highly skilled craftsmen, photographers, teachers of art, lecturers, and research workers may be placed in this classification.

*Skilled*

Artists able to produce work of recognized merit, but not of a quality equivalent to that of the above classification, and who are qualified by training and experience to take part in any of the various activities of the Federal Art Project, under supervision, are included in this classification. They may be employed on specified commissions in the field of creative art, in arts and crafts, applied art, teaching, and especially in various art activities associated with the recreational field. They may also be employed on individual projects according to the discretion of the person or persons authorized to make assignments of personnel.

*Intermediate*

A group of less skilled and experienced artists, craftsmen and apprentices who need supervision and guidance will be rated as intermediate.

*Unskilled*

This classification will include such personnel as gallery attendants, handyman, messengers, office boys, etc. Classification, wages rates, and hours of work for these unskilled workers, if not already made by the United States Employment Service, will be determined according to the schedule found in WPA Bulletin No. 25.

These classifications will be based upon information furnished by the artists and on the quality of work submitted. Major consideration should be given to professional background, experience, quality of work performed, and present ability to perform work. The classifications will determine not only the skill of the personnel referred by the United States Employment Service, but also the nature of the project in which each person who demonstrates his ability may best work. Every endeavor should be made to have these classifications accurate and fair so that artists may work on projects for which they are best fitted.[9]

It is interesting to observe that "professional" is interpreted in terms of ability to produce objects of professional merit, and not, as on the Theater Project, in terms of previous professional employment. By this definition, Cahill allowed the project a freedom and elasticity in the selection of project personnel that enabled it to employ artists, especially promising young artists, who had not yet been admitted into the professional art world, and thus to encourage the development of unknown talent.

The greatest concentration of employment—naturally enough, since the Federal Art Project was a professional project by definition—was in the highest wage classification. In February, 1937, when total employment on the Art Project stood at 4,753, the percentage employed in the four classes were: (1) professional and technical, 70.8 per cent; (2) skilled, 14.0 per cent; (3) intermediate, 2.3 per cent; and (4) unskilled, 0.5 per cent. The remainder, 12.4 per cent, were non-security personnel serving in a supervisory capacity. Between February, 1937 and March, 1939, the percentage in the highest category decreased slightly (to 66.1 per cent), and the percentages in the other categories correspondingly increased; but the general weighting of the project personnel on the professional side naturally persisted. In the beginning, of all the projects in Federal One, the Art Project had the highest ratio of professional personnel; by 1939, however, its ratio had been surpassed by those of the Music and Theater projects.

The high ratio of professional personnel in the Art Project further caused a concentration of employment in the larger urban areas. Twenty-three selected cities contained 69.8 per cent of all those employed on the Federal Art Project on November 30, 1936. This preponderance tended to increase, rather than decrease, and on July 24, 1937, it stood at 72.3 per cent. The concentration is the more marked if New York City alone is considered. On November 30, 1936, 42.3 per cent of total employment on the Art Project was in New York City; if Chicago is added, practically half (48.4 per cent) of total employment was concentrated in these two metropolitan centers.

There was another consequence of the high ratio of professional personnel. The tests that the applicants passed were almost invariably in productive capacity, and mainly in the realm of creative work. The artists thus chosen were naturally set at productive tasks—easel painting, sculpture, the graphic arts, etc.—with the result that emphasis was upon production, which, proper though it was, lessened in turn the initial emphasis upon community education and participation. The fact is that, in spite of all the protestations made in favor of folk art and crafts as an individual and community participation in the creative act, the Art Project, like the Music and Theater projects, emphasized the maintenance of professional standards of production.

CONTROL THROUGH REPORTS AND FIELD INSPECTIONS

Progress reports were prepared each month by the state directors. These were of two types: the cumulative progress report, which presented a statistical picture of the month's record and achievements, and a more detailed and descriptive report of progress. They provided the basis for the periodical reports prepared by the national office and submitted to the director of the Women's and Professional Division.

These reports, however, unlike the financial reports submitted to the finance office of Federal One, were not instruments of control but rather evaluations directed toward eventual publicity and designed to impress the high command of the WPA, Congress, and the general public with the worth and accomplishments of the project.

Control of operations, on the other hand, was exercised through field inspections. In the Art Project, unlike the Historical Records Survey, this control was fundamentally regional rather than central. The regional advisers (as they were properly called after January, 1936) might be attached to the central office; but they were domiciled in the states, not Washington. Robert Morrison, regional adviser for the New England states, was state director in Massachusetts, and it was from Boston, not Washington, that he exercised technical control over the region. The same situation held with regard to Mrs. McMahon, who acted from New York City, Joseph Danysh in California, and the other regional advisers.*

Cahill and Parker, who were domiciled at the Washington office, also made occasional field inspections. In most instances these were ad hoc journeys, occasioned by a crisis in a particular locality that required the intervention of a central authority, or prompted by considerations of prestige, when, for instance, the opening of an important exhibition was graced by the presence of Washington personnel. On rarer occasions, the national director and his assistant director went on circuit in order to acquire a general knowledge of the current status of operations throughout the country.

In addition, those in the Washington office who held specific responsibilities occasionally found it necessary or salutary to visit the field to superintend their particular concern. Parker, who, in addition to his

---

*The regional advisers, although they used the title of regional director after January, 1936, exercised no such command authority as they had enjoyed in the period of initiation (October to December, 1935). The authority of Morrison over another state director in New England was only as much as Morrison could make it. A state director was technically responsible to the national director and administratively responsible to the state administrator. The regional office did not represent an echelon of command. In Morrison's case, to be sure, since he was by nature a man of authority, and had been mainly responsible for the firm foundation of the project in New England, there was a real exercise of command. For all that, his primacy was one of honor and not of jurisdiction, and in other regions the state directors enjoyed a higher degree of autonomy—and sometimes the fulness thereof.

post as assistant director, was in technical charge of community art centers, naturally had duties that sometimes called him from Washington. In the main, however, so far as community art centers were concerned, Daniel S. Defenbacher, state director for North Carolina, acted as his deputy in the field. Miss Reeves, the first co-ordinator of the Index of American Design, and her successor, Glassgold, spent the major portion of their time away from Washington, since the task of establishing uniform techniques and national standards in the preparation of the Index demanded their personal attention. Finally, the responsibility for exhibitions, which lay upon Miss Holzhauer, was such that it could not be always met from a desk in Washington.

In the Art Project control was more often regional or statewide than national. This was due in part to the nature of the project, for, excepting the Index, there was no type of operation that demanded integration at the national level. It was also due to the personality of Cahill, who, aware of the limitations of a single mind when it attempts to comprehend everything, chose regional advisers and other subordinates who could relieve him of responsibilities.

SPONSORSHIP

The general lack of inclination in the directors of Federal One to encourage sponsorship, partly because sponsorship was not mandatory and partly because they wished to avoid the local control that sponsorship might entail, was not shared by Cahill. In this he showed a keener insight into the value of community support than his colleagues. The statement on sponsorship in the *Federal Art Project Manual* stresses the desirability of local sponsorship, and reads:

It is desirable that some public or quasi-public institution indicate local interest in each project and co-operate with the Works Progress Administration in sponsoring the project. These institutions will be called "co-operating sponsors." Public institutions should be encouraged to submit suggestions as to what art projects would benefit the community, if the proper talent is available from the relief rolls. The District Supervisor of Projects and Planning and the Art Directors and Supervisors shall encourage public agencies to suggest desirable projects for which proper talent is available from the relief rolls. To this end they should circulate to all public or quasi-public agencies which might be interested in becoming co-operating sponsors wpa Form 320A, Co-operating Sponsor's Project Proposal. On this form the prospective sponsor may indicate that it is willing to aid, financially or otherwise, in setting up a project. These co-operating sponsors will usually be public institutions supported in whole or in part by taxes, but they may in some instances be quasi-public or private non-profit organizations which serve the community, provided that works of art produced under the projects remain the property of the Federal Government or some other public agency, and that the services rendered do not replace usual services or activities which should be provided for in the budgets of the co-operating institutions. It is expected that art projects will have co-operating sponsors. However, since the Federal Art Project has been sponsored by the Works Progress Administration, art projects may be set up even when no local public agency is the co-operating sponsor.[10]

The statement that "it is expected that art projects will have co-operating sponsors" was an expression of policy, not merely a pious hope; and Cahill made it clear to his subordinates that, wherever possible, co-operating sponsors should be obtained who would contribute in money, goods, or services to the welfare of the project. To a certain degree the nature of the project made the acquisition of sponsorship easy and, in some cases, necessary. Murals, for instance, could not be placed anywhere; a wall was needed, and, in this case, the wall of a public building—for a mural was by nature permanently allocated to the institution of which it became a physical part. Thus the sponsorship of a school, courthouse, or public library was practically necessary before work on a mural could begin, or, indeed, physical entrée gained within the edifice. Again, in the case of community art centers, it was the studied policy of the Art Project to require a financial guarantee from the community sufficient to insure the continued operation, under ordinary circumstances, of the new institution. The penchant of municipalities and other public institutions for works of sculpture for display in open places also was a profitable source of sponsorship.*

The contributions of sponsors assumed a variety of forms. Sometimes quarters were provided for a project, or material for its operation; travel costs were sometimes paid if a lecture was requested; the salaries of supervisory personnel, especially in the case of murals or other co-operative enterprises, were assumed; and, when community art centers were desired, definite financial obligations were assumed by the sponsoring institution. In the case of sculpture the cost of the material was often substantial, and the project could not be undertaken unless the sponsor was willing to defray that expense. In all cases,

---

*In easel painting and the graphic arts (except posters) sponsorship was not so readily obtained, and these types of work were undertaken, for the most part, without sponsorship and the products subsequently allocated free to such public institutions as were willing to receive them. If no takers appeared, the works were eventually declared expendible and either destroyed or sold at public auction, as is all surplus government property.

however, Cahill, although he appreciated the value of contributions in kind, was aware that, for the most part, sponsorship in cash was the surest and the most impressive indication not only of the sponsor's interest but also of the project's income. For that reason, he encouraged and welcomed, above all other kinds, contributions in the form of money.

This emphasis upon sponsorship established a rapport between the community and the project that was mutually advantageous. The state director for Iowa expressed a conviction shared by his colleagues when he wrote, "Without the voluntary contributions of materials and equipment, labor, technical and professional services and advice, in addition to the sponsoring funds, this project could not have arrived at its present broad scope and potentialities."[11]

Private organizations, although not eligible to receive allocations of works of art, were nonetheless enthusiastic in their support of the project's activities and, upon occasion, served as co-operating sponsors and contributed money, materials, and services. This was particularly true of institutions like the Junior League, which combined a sense of civic pride with a consciousness of social obligation. Indeed, the support the Junior League gave the project was nationwide, and so impressed the central office that in 1938 a form letter was sent to the states requesting information regarding the extent of the League's activities. Their co-operation extended from contributions of cash and equipment to aid of a more personal character. Thus in Arizona they helped gather material for an exhibition and furnishings for a room arranged in period fashion. In Iowa members of the League served as volunteers during the construction of a gallery and sponsored several classes in art. In Montana the president of the local Junior League took the initiative in raising funds for the establishment of the Butte Art Center. But perhaps their greatest contribution was the social prestige that accrued from the association of their name with a project connected with the wpa. As the state director of Montana happily phrased it, their presence "did much to convince the residents of Butte that here at long last was an enterprise that had the backing of all strata of society."[12]

### THE PROBLEM OF COMPETITION

It is characteristic of our economy that almost any activity in which the government engages can be interpreted as competitive with private enterprise. The Federal Art Project did not escape such charges, which arose in the main from two activities: the allocation of works of art to public or quasi-public institutions, and art teaching in or through community art centers.

In accordance with legal opinion and the administrative rulings of the WPA, works of art could be loaned, but title to them could not be transferred, to non-federal public agencies.* These institutions in many instances, as in the case of murals, acted as sponsors of the project and contributed in kind and money toward the expenses of production. In other cases, however, as in easel work, the unsponsored product was simply exhibited, and institutions, if they chose, might express their desire for its allocation. On occasion they might make a token contribution to the project, but in the main the transaction was consummated without payment. In the case of some public institutions, especially museums and galleries, there was anxiety lest works of art produced on the project, which could be had free or for cost, might narrow the market that private producers or dealers enjoyed. For that reason the procedure for loans of works of art was careful to instruct that "no works of art may be loaned which will replace the usual service or activities provided for in the budget of such agencies and institutions."[13]

This policy, however, was more easily expressed than applied. In the period of the depression public agencies, even museums and galleries, could readily claim—and often their claim was sound—that the reduction in their budget temporarily precluded purchasing in the private market. Moreover, schools, courthouses, city halls, libraries, and other public institutions could make a strong case that unless they could commission murals and other works of art at cost, they could not afford them and would not consider their acquisition. In the main, these claims to special consideration were valid, and it would be absurd to maintain that the artist in private practice or the middleman was deprived of any substantial amount of business by reasons of the activity of the Federal Art Project.

Just as the private practitioner and the middleman protested the application of a democratic procedure to the allocation of works of art (surplus works of art not bought and paid for on the private market might better have been destroyed, like surplus commodities), the private teacher and art school objected to the project's democratic approach to art teaching. The more conservative and established societies of artists, and the professional periodicals through which they voiced

---

*The legal and financial aspects of allocation have already been examined. *Vide supra*, pp. 325, 330.

their opinions, were publicly more or less sympathetic with the program of the Art Project, depending upon the number of their members receiving assistance through work relief or as non-certified employees on the project. Individually, however, the members of these organizations protested against both the principle and practice of government support of art.*

Among the charges against the Federal Art Project the most prominent was that it competed in teaching with the private teacher and private art school, especially through its community art centers. In Florida, which had the most ambitious art-center movements of any state, such protests were so violent and so unrelenting that Mrs. Woodward ordered an investigation. The Art Project, like the Music Project, had issued instructions that only students who were unable to pay for private instruction were to be admitted to classes. In an investigation of this sort, therefore, the students at the art center were required to pass a means test, to prove to the project that they or their parents were without means to afford private instruction. The Federal Art Project throughout its life was most solicitious in this regard, and the political considerations that provoked its caution were powerful. Cahill in 1936 was deeply disturbed by charges that the Art Project in New York City, through its instructional activities, had reduced the number of pupils of an art institution by one-third.†

Indeed, the Federal Art Project was not without arguments. In the first place, those who charged it with competition were usually the same persons who claimed incompetence, thus setting themselves

---

*In this connection, the statement of Arthur Freeman Brinkerhoff, president of the Fine Arts Federation of New York, given before the Sirovich Committee in 1938, should be read. Among other things he said: "The federation subscribes generally to the preliminary recitals of the four bills, although, if framing its own statements concerning the matters there covered, it would wish to do so in somewhat different terms. It completely dissents, however, from the claim to be implied from these bills that these forms of Government control of art and artists will be healthy for American art or will in the long run have a cultural effect. On the contrary, the federation believes that these forms of control will in the long run substitute journeyman standards of art for truly artistic standards, mediocre common standards in place of the highest individual standards, regimentation of art work in place of individual talent, and personal and political pull in the award of art jobs in place of free and open competition. This is to sterilize the soil in which art grows and reduce art to the level of either mass employment or political patronage."[14]

†There was no reason in law why students at an art center of the project should have been required to prove destitution in order to secure instruction. They received no relief wages or other compensation from federal funds. It was purely an administrative ruling, and, if there were any logic in it, those who visited exhibitions of the Federal Art Project should also have been required to pass a means test.

astraddle the horns of a dilemma: either the works of art produced on the project were distinctly inferior, in which case competition with professional artists did not exist; or, if competition existed, the works of art were good. In the second place, just as the introduction of free public schools earlier in our history not only did not hurt, but actually and enormously benefited, the private school and college by progressively creating a larger and larger clientele, the application of democratic principles to art education—by producing a greater appreciation of, and demand for, artistic products—might well redound to the benefit of the private artist, entrepreneur, and art school. The field of murals serves to demonstrate this point. Before the initiation of the Federal Art Project, the demand for murals was limited and the cost exorbitant. The project demonstrated that schools, hospitals, libraries, and other public institutions could possess murals at modest cost, and its creation of a demand that has outlived it is one of the most important artistic phenomena of our generation.

### FINANCE

The financial procedures and practices of the Federal Art Project did not differ, except in matters of minor importance, from those elaborated for the operation of Federal One as a whole. In the beginning some confusion was created by the fact that the initial presidential allocation to the project was made under limitation (g) of the FERA Act of 1935. Since the funds under this limitation were defined as loans or grants to the states, it was necessary that they be allocated directly and individually to the several states by Presidential Letter. This initial allocation, made on August 27, 1935, in the amount of $2,000,000, was followed two days later by an allocation to the project of funds under limitation (e) in the amount of $1,152,663. Funds under the (e) limitation were defined as assistance for educational, professional, and clerical persons, and could be allocated federally (i.e., the funds could be allocated by Presidential Letter *en bloc* to a federal project, and subsequently apportioned among the states at the discretion of the Washington office). Since the works of art produced under limitation (g) funds were the property of the several states, whereas those produced under limitation (e) funds were the property of the federal government, it was a fiscal necessity in the early days of the project to keep the two sources distinct. In certain projects (e.g., in New York City) there was a tendency to use the funds allocated under limitation (g) for creative work, which thus could be allocated locally, and to use those allocated under limitation (e) for other expenses of the project.[15] Cahill, although he could not transfer "(g)" funds from state to state, was given jurisdiction over their expenditure and, by instructions and directions, was able in time to integrate their expenditure with that of the "(e)" funds.[16] Within a period of about six months the "(g)" funds were expended, and since all future allocations were made on a federal basis, there was no further fiscal conflict.

Since the Federal Art Project exhibited its products free, no problem arose as to admission funds; and since it could prove no need for substantial deposits of cash to facilitate its operations, the device of business manager–agent cashier was not, except in a few instances, invoked. In the matter of procurement, however, problems arose that, although they were paralleled to some degree in the Music and Theater projects, were basically peculiar to the Art Project.* Before the release of Operating Procedure No. F-1, revised, dated November 19, 1937, which permitted proprietary requisitions by the project, the procurement of artists' supplies by the project presented a real problem. In the early days it was thought that sponsors might purchase art supplies out of their own funds and present them to the project. This device, which was perfectly legal, avoided the standardized procurement procedures of the Treasury Department, and in some cases was used successfully. But it also had its defects. In the first place, the sponsors, for all their good will, did not always observe an artist's discrimination in their selection of material. Second, even if the supplies thus procured were satisfactory, their use was restricted by agreement to the work project unit for which the sponsorship was secured, and the difficulties of other projects that lacked sponsorship remained unresolved. Finally, it was often difficult at the beginning of a work project unit to estimate accurately and specifically the kinds and amounts of supplies necessary for its completion.

For these reasons the Art Project preferred cash contributions, from which the project itself might make purchases as need and occasion directed. Here, however, the difficulty was that once a sponsor made a cash contribution to the project, it was received into the Treasury; and although its use was restricted to the Art Project, the observance of Treasury procurement procedures became mandatory. From the very

*The general question of procurement on the Art Project has been treated *supra*, pp. 302-3.

beginning of the project, complaints were made regarding the slowness and complexity of procurement regulations. In February, 1936, Cahill wrote:

> Many of our state directors are filing complaints with this office regarding their difficulties in obtaining materials and supplies. As a result of the slow procedure in requisitioning materials and supplies, many of the artists have had to purchase these items from their own funds. They have done this in order to be able to produce work and be placed on the payroll. The majority of them will never be reimbursed for these expenditures, and many complaints have already been made to this office on this score.[17]

In some states temporary and local expedients were contrived to avoid these difficulties. In Massachusetts, for instance, the state director for the Art Project was appointed deputy procurement officer, with authority to make single purchases not exceeding twenty-five dollars in amount. When, however, an attempt was made to extend this procedure to Connecticut, the state procurement officer refused on the ground that the project was so small that procurement should present no difficulties. In general, the ease or difficulty with which a project secured proper supplies depended upon the willingness of the state procurement officer of the Treasury to accommodate procedures to the exigencies of the Art Project.

Indeed, Operating Procedure No. F-1 revised, although it relieved the situation to some degree, was so qualified in its language that it was used with difficulty on large projects, such as in New York City. In March, 1938, Julius Davidson, the finance officer of Federal One, investigated the procurement practices of the Art Project in New York City and discovered that sponsors' funds, which should have been deposited into the Treasury, had been used directly and immediately to purchase supplies. The fact that Operating Procedure No. F-1, revised, was not adequate, at least in New York City, is indicated by the suggestions Davidson made in his memorandum to Mrs. Woodward:

> It is necessary, first, that provision be made for the setting up of a general special deposit pooled account into which will be placed all funds turned over to the government for the general use of the Federal Art Project without restrictions, and, in addition, for the setting up of sub-accounts as the occasions arise into which will be placed those contributions which have either a restricted purpose or which carry with them conditions implying the possibility of a refund; second, some modification must be made in the present purchasing procedure which will extend the activities of the purchasing section of the Federal Project Number One to cover a group of exempt items purchased for the Federal Art Project. . . . Treasury Procurement does not have the facilities for ready handling of purchases of this nature.[18]

The procedure for proprietary purchases by the Art Project, as set forth in Section 23 of Operating Procedure No. G-4, dated August 11, 1939, did not substantially change that established by Operating Procedure No. F-1, revised. Indeed, the greater ease with which the problem of procurement was met in the latter days of the project was due less to changes in procedure than to a growth of mutual understanding between procurement officers and art project officials. The latter became more aware of the former's concern with the proper acquisition of, and accounting for, supplies, and the former were gradually educated to understand and to accept the peculiar and, to the lay mind, sometimes incomprehensible preferences of the artist.

### TRANSFER AND LOAN OF PERSONNEL

When Federal One began operations, it was the belief of the federal directors of the several projects that an unprecedented opportunity was presented to carry art from the metropolitan centers to the countryside. This was a natural corollary of the social service concept of art as education and recreation, and presumed an emphasis upon community participation rather than upon professional accomplishment.

This opportunity—and there was such an opportunity—was never realized. The reason was in part that procedural difficulties existed that made the loan and transfer of personnel from state to state cumbersome and awkward; in part, however, the fault lay with the directors of Federal One, especially of the Theater, Music, and Art projects, who failed from the beginning to make a sustained effort to achieve deurbanization and, by their emphasis upon professional acclaim, tended further to increase the concentration of project personnel in metropolitan centers. Indeed, it was not until President Roosevelt in 1938 chided the administration of Federal One for its failure in this regard that the directors of the arts projects were inspired to pay serious attention to the problem—and then it was too late.

In the Art Project, as has already been observed, more than 40 per cent of the personnel was concentrated in New York City, and this ratio did not change appreciably during the federal period. In June, 1938, the New York City project employed 1,617 employees out of a national total of 3,710; and it was obvious then, as it should have been from the beginning, that transfer of some of these urban workers to the less fortunate states was the way to decentralize art in the United States.

The procedural difficulties were real but not insuperable; and if the project had started with the same determination to overcome them as to achieve professional acclaim, it could without doubt have written an epic in the art experience of the American people. The fact is that throughout the life of the project, personnel were transferred and loaned from state to state, but almost invariably with the purpose of meeting administrative and technical problems and not of creating art appreciation in the less populous areas.

In fact, so far as non-certified personnel were concerned, the question was not procedural but administrative. The federal director of the Art Project had as much authority to transfer a non-security employee from one state to another as he had to hire or fire.* The non-certified worker was by definition not on relief, and therefore the problem of certification did not arise. Transfers of this sort, however, when they were made, were purely administrative in purpose. New York City provided directors for two major states, Illinois and Pennsylvania, when, in 1938, reorganization of the projects in these states was necessary. In neither case was the transfer from a metropolitan to a non-metropolitan area. An employee of the New York City project also became a state director for Arizona.†

Technical considerations, as well as administrative reasons, sometimes counseled a transfer of personnel. A western supervisor of the In-

---

*This authority, at least after January, 1936, was not absolute but depended upon the concurrence of the state administrators of the states affected. But it still remained purely an administrative problem, and it is beyond credulity to think that Colonel Somervell, the New York City administrator, would have objected to the transfer of some of the New York City non-security personnel to other areas. The fact is that the objections to this type of transfer came from *within* the Art Project and not from the WPA administration.

†The excuse is given that artists in New York City did not wish to be transferred to the South or West. Undoubtedly, this was true in many cases. But the answer is that a non-certified artist was no different from any other employee of the government, and was subject to orders from his superiors. The fact is that in the Art Project, as in other projects of Federal One, New York City was the tail that wagged the dog.

It is also maintained that the South was allergic to "Yankees" especially if they came from New York City. There is an element of truth in this statement too. But a judicious caution in the selection of the loan personnel could have anticipated the danger of friction; besides, the South was not without a cultural center: New Orleans possessed a flourishing art project, from which kindred souls could have been dispersed throughout Dixie.

As for the trans-Mississippi and Rocky Mountain regions, California, which enjoyed a plethora of professional artists so far as the project was concerned, could have become a fertile source of non-certified personnel for less urban neighboring areas.

In truth, there was a professional pride, which sometimes degenerated into professional jealousy, among the state directors and supervisory personnel of the project with reference to their particular states and projects. This attitude made them reluctant to part with their more competent workers, a natural enough attitude, to be sure, but not one calculated to further decentralization.

dex of American Design, for instance, was sent to Massachusetts to study the techniques developed there, and then was returned to his home state in order that he might introduce them. Again, a talented Vermont artist was sent to New York City to study mural work. These transfers were proper and advantageous, within the purpose for which they were made, but they bore no relation whatever to the oft-repeated program of decentralization.

The transfer or loan of certified workers, on the other hand, raised fundamental procedural difficulties. Certification, like law, was territorial, and a certified worker, when he crossed the frontier of the area in which he was certified, lost his relief status. Other states, in turn, were not anxious to certify non-residents. Florida, for instance, required one-year residence before certification, and in almost all states there were legal or administrative barriers that obstructed the immediate certification of newcomers. Sometimes, if the certified worker was destined for a supervisory appointment, the difficulty could be met by divestiture, as when a relief worker in California formally assumed a non-relief status in order to become state director for Montana.

In general, however, the movement of relief workers from state to state was difficult. In addition to the problem of certification, there was the question of wages and payment of transportation. There were different rates of pay in different regions: should the wages of the transferred worker be those of the state from which he came or those of the state to which he went? In the case of loan personnel, there was the question of jurisdiction: was the person loaned subject to the authority of the state that loaned or the state that borrowed? Who should pay the expenses of travel, the state giving or the state receiving? Many of these questions were petty, and, although they were sometimes the subject of acrimonious debate, a modicum of good will on both sides could resolve them when resolution was seriously desired. They were annoying, however, and created a real hindrance to the transfer and loan of relief personnel.*

TRAINING AND RETRAINING

The Art Project was a professional project in the sense that its primary purpose was to provide employment for artists. It was not, however, inherent in the nature of the project or decreed by statute or ad-

*It must be emphasized again, however, that if art as a vital element in community living were the desideratum, this could have been effectively achieved by the transfer of non-relief personnel, who, when transferred, could have served as supervisors of small art projects in the more rural areas.

ministrative ruling that an applicant, in order to secure employment on the project, must secure the technical rating of professional. From the very beginning, however, the federal director emphasized considerations of professional competence in the selection of project personnel. Even in the early months of initiation, when the pressure was to employ as many as possible as quickly as possible, Cahill tempered his exhortations with cautions against lack of discrimination in choosing personnel. When, early in 1936, the project achieved its maximum employment, and thereafter, in general, waned, reductions in quota were effected for the most part by the release of the artistically less qualified. Apprentices, in general, were not welcome on the project, and a comparable classification, "artist helper," was also rejected. In June, 1938, Thomas Parker wrote to the state director of Montana: "It may be advisable at times to employ junior artists in the skilled classification but I do not feel that this employment should be encouraged due to the fact that, in the majority of the states, there are many applicants who are qualified professionally."[19] Cahill believed that the funds of the National Youth Administration could be more properly spent for such purposes.

Despite his precautions, however, the project found itself with a certain number of artists who were not sufficiently trained or whose skills had been blunted by disuse or misfortune. An attempt was made to care for them in two ways: (1) by the institution of teaching and training courses; and (2) by the elaboration of projects upon which their less-developed talents could be usefully employed.

Art teachers' institutes were held in several sections of the country, especially where competent instruction was available and students could be readily congregated. The largest and best organized of these training centers was in New York City, where a staff of highly competent instructors presented laboratory classes in the technique of drawing and painting, sculpture, etching, lithography, weaving, ceramics, metal crafts, and photography. As the catalogue of the institute described it:

> The artist-teachers have an opportunity to extend their knowledge of the various arts, to learn to do creative work in new media, to attend lectures by authorities, and to have round-table discussions and forums on the problems of child and adult pedagogy. In the modern art gallery jointly used by the Art Teachers' Institute and the Harlem Community Art Center, exhibitions of the work of project artists as well as that of students in the Art Teaching Division are held at regular intervals.[20]

New York City also maintained, for a time, a "Central Studio," which was designed principally for the less competent project workers. Copyists, artists whose work was below standard but capable of improvement, and artists incapable of substantial improvement who could be assigned to tracing from selected books, met here. A voluntary life class and a class in landscape painting were also in the curriculum.[21]

For artists who were not able to take advantage of this formal training, especially in areas not served by such institutes, the project devised a method of training on the job that can best be expressed in the concept of the guild system. Thus the easel painter submitted his work to a supervisor who was usually an artist of competence, and might be a distinguished painter in his own right. If the painting was below a reasonable degree of acceptability, it would be criticized and returned. The opinions of several supervisors might be elicited, and sometimes the project workers themselves, apprehending the co-operative nature of the enterprise and entering into its spirit, criticized one another's work and shared their experiences and discoveries. This was particularly true in the field of the graphic arts, where the very nature of the process encouraged collaboration. In Philadelphia, for instance, where an unusually competent group of graphic artists were on the project, the discovery of the carborundum method of printing was a co-operative achievement. Mural painting, too, was, or could readily be made, a common enterprise, upon which less talented artists could work under the guidance of a competent supervisor without damage to the artistic product and with benefit to themselves.

Without doubt, the guild approach to the problems of artistic training and production was one of the most promising innovations of the project, and both betokened and engendered a spirit of fellowship the lack of which has plagued the world of art in modern times. The concept of the cloistered artist, solitary in his grandeur or penury, was for a time at least displaced by a sense of the aesthetic dependency of artist upon artist, and, to a lesser degree, of the social and economic dependence of all artists upon the community.

This comradeship of master, journeyman, and apprentice, as it were, was nowhere more highly expressed than in the preparation of the Index of American Design. This tremendous research project, although initially inspired by considerations of its own intrinsic merit, was soon recognized as a type of enterprise eminently suitable for the co-operation of skilled and less skilled craftsmen toward a common end. The very nature of the Index, since its essence lay in exact and fine copying, precluded emphasis upon individuality, and compelled the achievement of uniformity in a communion of techniques. It is a tribute to the success of the endeavor that some of the most striking Index plates were produced by individuals who were unable to paint independent works of merit, and, in some cases, were relatively untrained, even in copying, when they were engaged upon the project. There is no doubt but that the collaboration of many, of varying degrees of skill and experience, especially in the graphic arts and on the Index, resulted in the discovery and refinement of processes and techniques (for instance, the silk-screen process), that otherwise might have remained uncharted or relatively undeveloped.

CO-ORDINATING PROJECTS

The Art Project, like the other projects in Federal One, established state co-ordinating projects in January, 1936.* At the same time a national co-ordinating project and two national technical projects were initiated in the Washington office. The national co-ordinating projects included the national director and his staff, numbering, as of April 30, 1937, twenty-six employees. The two national technical projects were: (1) the Index of American Design project, which, as of the same date, numbered seven; and (2) the Exhibitions Project, which also numbered seven. The state co-ordinating projects were abolished, effective July 15, 1937, and at about the same time the administrative personnel in the national office were transferred from the project to the administrative payroll. The national technical projects, however, continued to exist until the abolition of Federal One by Congress in the ERA Act of 1939.

LABOR RELATIONS

Unlike the musicians, who were represented in labor matters by the American Federation of Musicians, and the actors, who brought pressure through Actors' Equity, artists were only in the embryonic stage of labor organization at the beginning of the depression. The impact of the depression, however, though it left the more successful artist—es-

*Vide supra, pp. 160-62.

404

pecially those who held high office in professional societies—both economically and spiritually undisturbed, provoked a revolution in the thought of the younger and less comfortable of the profession. The formation of the John Reed Clubs in 1929, under the aegis of the Communist party, attracted the radical intelligentsia, including artists, and, to a certain degree, won the support of those who were not members of the party, and sometimes not sympathetic with its aims. Later, other organizations of radical and liberal artists, patterned to some extent after the fashion of the John Reed Clubs but by no means limited in membership to those who embraced the Communist point of view, were initiated. The first Artists' Union was formed in 1934, and at about the same time the Artists' Committee of Action was organized to agitate specifically for the creation of art projects for the unemployed. Another similar organization was the Art Students' Council.

The center of activity and the majority of the membership of all these new groups were in New York City; and although in time branches were formed in other cities, the organizations, because of the geographical concentration of their personnel, never achieved dispersion beyond metropolitan confines. Of these groups the largest and most effective was the Artists' Union, which in March, 1935, claimed 1,300 members, most of whom were resident in New York City.

The labor difficulties of the Art Project, like the unions of unemployed or sympathetic artists, were concentrated in a few large cities, and especially in New York City. Naturally, although general policies regarding labor relations were developed in the national office, the responsibility of meeting local crises was largely that of the state director at hand. Indeed, the success or failure of efforts at conciliation was determined for the most part by the attitude and personality of the local administration.

A comparison of the situation in New York City with that in Philadelphia and Chicago illustrates this point. Mrs. Audrey McMahon, the state director in New York City, had been affiliated with the College Art Association and had participated in the development of work relief for artists under the FERA and the New York State TERA. Undoubtedly, experience in this earlier period provided Mrs. McMahon with a novitiate in labor relations, for, as early as December, 1934, she received at her quarters with the College Art Association delegations from the Artists' Union, the John Reed Club of New York City, the Artists' Committee of Action, and the Art Students' Council, while outside the building some one hundred artists demonstrated with banners and slogans.[22]

On this occasion her sense of balance between conflicting responsibilities led her to approve the mass action as a means of influencing public policy, and at the same time warned her against identifying herself personally with the protestants by an endorsement of their program.

Mrs. McMahon was, above all, level-headed, and she recognized that precipitate action might defeat the end it sought too quickly to achieve. In August, 1935, when, during another demonstration, eighty-three picketing artists (who were demanding two weeks' pay that had been delayed during the transfer from the TERA to the WPA) were arrested, Mrs. McMahon's sense of justice prompted her to maintain publicly that they had a right to call attention to their predicament, and she stood ready to appear in court in their behalf.[24]

From the beginning of the WPA Mrs. McMahon was aware that her relations with artists' unions involved more than the Art Project, and included a *modus vivendi* with the WPA administration in New York City. In fact, under General Hugh C. Johnson, the first New York City administrator, she headed the division of labor relations and took the occasion to study the problem of perfecting them. Under later administrators, and especially under Colonel Somervell, she established an *entente cordiale* between the Art Project and the WPA which enabled her to avoid many of the embarrassments that beset the other arts projects in New York City.

In her management of the labor relations of the Art Project, she did not escape crises; no one could. New York City was not only the home of half the artists in the United States, including most of the younger, more militant ones, but during the depression it was the center of a short-lived but intense intellectual revolution. In these circumstances the artists, no less than other professional and labor groups, became not only politically conscious but also physically aggressive. Sometimes delegations of five hundred or more, flooding the building and overflowing the sidewalk, waited upon her; "lie-down" and "sit-down" strikes were frequent, and, on occasion, violence occurred. Petitions, round robins, pamphlets, brochures, and banners were used to impress the project and the public with the plight of the artist.

During all this Mrs. McMahon never lost control of the situation; though she was respectful and attentive toward the grievances of the artists and, for the most part, genuinely sympathetic, she never forgot her administrative dignity. Her patience in negotiation and the essential justice of her decisions (which were never partisan) eventually impressed the dissident artists, and the aura of authority that attached to her, together with her efficiency and dispatch, created an assurance of ultimate satisfaction. In time she was able to establish a set of procedures in dealing with labor that became a model for other units of the Federal Art Project. The project administrations and delegations from the union met once a week. An agenda was drawn up beforehand and submitted to Mrs. McMahon. Besides these weekly conferences, special delegations were occasionally permitted, but only after Mrs. McMahon agreed that the situation warranted a departure from procedure.*

In Philadelphia and Chicago, on the other hand, the labor situation festered until the knife was necessary. Both these projects, like the New York City project, had developed from earlier PWAP and FERA projects into workshops that produced distinguished fine art; and Mrs. Robinson, the Illinois director, and Miss Curran, the Pennsylvania director, had been identified with the earlier period of operation. While Mrs. McMahon was more conscious of the change in purpose in the transition from the PWAP to the WPA, the other two directors attempted to maintain in its integrity the principle of professional accomplishment that characterized Edward Bruce's earlier project. To a considerable degree they were successful in their aim. The Philadelphia project, under Miss Curran, was perhaps the most technically competent in the United States, and a number of sculptors, painters, and especially artists in the graphic media were developed. The Chicago project, under Mrs. Robinson, could point not only to an original school of muralists but also to outstanding artists in other forms who combined to produce a "Chicago style," which made that project the cynosure of artistic eyes throughout the country.

Unfortunately, however, this emphasis upon professional excellence could be achieved only at the expense of project employment. Compared with the New York City project, the Philadelphia and Chicago projects, even considered relatively, were unusually small, the Phila-

---

*At the Woodrum hearings (1939-40) it was charged that Communists were employed on the New York City Art Project. Without doubt, there were some Communists on the project, and, since there was no statutory prohibition at that time against the employment of Communists, the Art Project had no more right to discriminate against them, if they met the qualifiying conditions, that it had to discriminate against Republicans. On the other hand, no evidence was adduced to indicate that the project was controlled by Communists or those sympathetic with the aims of that party.[24]

The same committee was shocked by the discovery by Mr. Burton, one of the committee's investigators, of two albums of nude photographs of professional models, used by the New York City project. The albums were brought to Washington, examined by the committee, and filed as exhibits.[25]

delphia project numbering about one hundred workers, that in Chicago, about two hundred. In both cities the younger artists through their unions protested against discrimination, which in their eyes was of two kinds: discrimination in favor of the more conservative schools of art and discrimination against them as members of the union. The two charges are quite distinct, but they were so entangled in the web of circumstance that it is difficult to indicate where the one begins or the other ends. Certainly, neither the Chicago nor Philadelphia directors had the political sense and aptitude at negotiation that distinguished Mrs. McMahon; and a tendency toward the more conservative in art was, even if it was not meant to be, an act of discrimination against the younger and more militant members of the profession. But the fundamental cause of the tension in both places was the strong emphasis upon professional production, which prevented expansion of activities into other artistic fields and thus curtailed the size of the projects. What the younger artists wanted most, as events were to prove, was employment.

The crisis became acute in Chicago first, and in 1936 George Thorp, a sculptor employed on the New York City project who had already demonstrated administrative capacity, was sent to Chicago to study the situation, and shortly thereafter was appointed state director of Illinois.* He resolved the situation by the simple expedient of increasing employment from 200 to 600 project workers.

In Philadelphia, although the same basic causes of discontent were in evidence from the very inception of the project, a change in administration was not made until the fall of 1938, when Benjamin Knotts, of the New York City project, was appointed acting director of the Pennsylvania project, and later given permanent status. Knotts, like Thorp in Chicago, immediately proceeded to broaden the base of employment by emphasizing educational activities that enabled him to use a larger number of workers of lesser skill. He also attempted to disperse project activities throughout the state, with special attention to Pittsburgh, where little development had occurred. In Philadelphia, as in Chicago, the essence of the complaint was the failure to employ younger and less established artists, and Knotts, like Thorp, relieved the tension by gradually increasing employment on the Philadelphia project from about 100 to about 400 workers.†

*Mrs. Robinson was retained on the Art Project in a regional advisory capacity.

†Kindred difficulties arose in a few other large cities. In Boston a nasty situation developed when the executive secretary of the local Artists' Union was dis-

WAGES AND HOURS OF WORK

In the first year of the WPA, monthly security wages and maximum hours of work (eight hours a day and forty hours a week) were established by Executive Order No. 7046. *Supplement No. 1 to Bulletin No. 29*, however, suggested that ninety-six hours a month be accepted as the minumum for artists and teachers of art. In general, until July 1, 1936, artists worked an average of thirty hours a week.

The ERA Act of 1936, however, provided that prevailing hourly wages be paid all WPA project employees. Since it was necessary for the WPA to maintain the security monthly rate in order to fulfill its employment quotas, the adjustment was made by reducing the number of working hours of those workers whose professional rating entitled them to higher hourly compensation. In New York City, for instance, the work week of artists was decreased from thirty to fifteen hours, a calculation that gave them approximately $1.50 an hour. The Artists' Union demanded a prevailing wage of two dollars an hour, but their demand was never met.

In general, since statutes, executive orders, and administrative rulings from Washington decided wages, hours, and employment quotas, the state directors and local supervisors often found themselves between the sword and the wall. The area within which state and local WPA officials could exercise discretion in these matters was extremely narrow. For a considerable period state administrators could raise or lower established security wages by 10 per cent; state directors could always upgrade or downgrade project personnel, so long as the established ratio was approximately maintained; these privileges, however, were not broad enough to meet serious dissatisfaction, and the project

missed for incompetence; in Baltimore the indifferences of the WPA officials with respect to the Art Project created an impasse that the Artists' Union of Baltimore only gradually and imperfectly relieved. In addition, on many of the project units, as in all establishments, there were differences between individiual workers and their supervisors. Claims and counterclaims led to mutual recrimination, and often the cause of conflict was magnified far beyond its original size. In general, outside the metropolitan centers and especially in a number of western and southern states, labor difficulties were non-existent. State directors in those areas, who received on an average about $1,800 a year, and supervisors, who were paid little more than professional security workers, offered little occasion for resentment and jealousy; and the project workers, by and large, with a sense of common effort that economic equality engendered, were grateful for the encouragment and direction given them by their superiors.

workers knew it. For this reason, pressure was exerted upon state and local officials, not as the causes but as the instruments of policy, with the hope—upon occasion realized—that they, being moved, might move Washington.

## RACE RELATIONS

The problem of race relations on the Federal Art Project was almost exclusively that of the Negro. The administration of the Art Project, like those of the other projects in Federal One, was not only free from prejudice but deeply conscious of its duty to improve race relations and to give the Negro his place in the activities of the project. Cahill, to be sure, was not militant in his liberalism, but he was by no means a time-server; and though he did not welcome embarrassing situations, he could be firm and resolute when faced by them.

The practice of segregation in the South was accepted by the project. But the state directors in the South, as well as the national office, were insistent that equal opportunity, so far as they could achieve it, be given the Negro. Since production of artistic objects could not be emphasized in the South because of the scarcity of competent artists, the Art Project sought fulfilment there through art centers in which the community could use art as a device for education and recreation. In general, wherever such a community art center was opened, the policy was to provide an extension center for Negroes. North Carolina, Alabama, Louisiana, and the District of Columbia were among the areas that achieved outstanding programs of art education for Negroes. Le Moyne College, a Negro educational institution in Tennessee, initiated an academic art program because of the stimulus given by the local art center.*

Florida, however, of all the southern states, achieved the finest results in art education for Negroes. Its eminence was largely the work of Harry Sutton, the supervisor of the Jacksonville Negro Art Center, the largest and most successful of its kind. Sponsored by an outstanding Negro social welfare organization and quartered in the local Mission, this center inaugurated a full program of exhibitions and classes in which local and national leaders of the Federal Art Project took great

---

*The border character of West Virginia was revealed by the fact that, although it refrained from establishing separate centers for Negroes, it apportioned the days of attendance at the single center between the two races.

pride. The other Negro centers throughout the state were largely inspired by the work and special interest of Mr. Sutton; and the state director of Florida, in her final report, thus summarizes her state's distinction in this field:

> Through the art classes for underprivileged Negro children, there was selected, after a reasonable time, typical children's work for a special exhibition, which proceeded to be one of the most acceptable and interest-rousing exhibits emanating from Florida. Florida State College for Women used it in art classes as a study in effects. It was requested and sent to Washington for exhibition in the National Children's Gallery; it was included in the art comments of at least two national magazines. Of far more value than discovering talent among the underprivileged of a racial minority, this experiment gives pause to those concerned with the social advantages of the development of native Negro culture. As a behavior corrective, as an instrument of experimental therapeutics, and as a positive community objective, the project's Negro work in Florida has a definite place in the record.[26]

Whereas art education among the Negroes was emphasized in the South, in northern cities, and especially in New York City, an opportunity presented itself to foster production among Negro artists. In the 1920's the Negro had come of age as an artist in the United States. Most, though not all, eventually found their way to New York City, where, from 1928 to 1933, the Harmon Foundation Exhibitions focused the attention of the cultural world upon their achievements. When the depression came, the Negro artist, no less than others of his race, found himself in even more desperate straits than his white brethren. Under the CWA, courses in adult education instituted in Harlem encouraged Negro artists and contributed toward the formation of the Harlem Art Committee. In co-operation with the College Art Association, this committee, in March, 1935, sponsored an exhibition of 200 canvases, the work of Negro artists, at the 138th Street YWCA.[27] As early as December, 1935, the Harlem Art Committee requested that the Federal Art Project sponsor an art center in Harlem.[28]

It was natural, under the circumstances, that Negro artists should become socially and politically conscious and, in co-operation with the Artists' Union, should form the Harlem Artists' Guild, which became the official pressure group for Negro artists in New York City. Their demands, in general, paralleled those of the Artists' Union, since the problems of unemployed artists were, in large part, common to both races. The Negro group, however, found that special interests, involving real or apparent discrimination, also claimed their attention. Thus, for instance, when the superintendent of the Harlem Hospital (an institution for Negroes) rejected mural sketches by several well-known Harlem artists, which already had been approved by the Municipal Art Commission, the Harlem Artists' Guild, supported by the Artists' Union and the Joint Conference against Discrimination Practices, successfully fought the decision.*

The number of Negro artists employed increased with the life of the project, although it never reached the figure the Harlem Artists' Guild considered appropriate. Although there were practically no Negro artists on the New York City art project when it began in the fall of 1935, there were some 115 workers, including three supervisors, employed in July, 1937.

In the summer of 1937, when drastic decreases in quota were ordered by Washington, a question of principle arose between the Negro artists and the administration of the Federal Art Project in New York City that merits examination. Until that time, Mrs. McMahon had adopted and followed a policy of non-discrimination whereby all applicants were considered and engaged as artists, not as Negroes or whites; accordingly, artists were not listed by race. At this juncture, however, when dismissals were ordered affecting both races, but not as such, the Harlem Artists' Guild, arguing that the Negro merited special consideration, demanded that Negroes be listed as Negroes and that special quotas be established for them. Mrs. McMahon, although she expressed her disagreement with the principle upon which the protest was based, acquiesced in the demand.[30]

The influence of the Federal Art Project upon the Negro artist in New York was profound, and in the summer of 1936 the Harlem Artists' Guild issued a statement that indicates the maturity of thought attained within a year. This statement, which was a repudiation of the leadership of the Harmon Foundation, emphasized that the Negro was now prepared to assume his place as an artist of professional merit, and resented the use of his talents by experimental sociologists. The statement reads in part:

> Harlem Artists Guild, with a view to promoting the best interests of Negro art in America, feels obligated to adopt an attitude of non-cooperation toward the Harmon Foundation in its effort to collect an exhibition of art work done by Negroes to be shown at the Texas Centennial Exposition.
>
> The Guild, comprising a majority of Negro workers in Greater New

*The objection was based on the grounds that the murals contained so much Negro subject matter that, if the racial complexion of Harlem ever changed, they would become inappropriate.[29]

York is convinced that the Harmon Foundation does not serve the best interests of the Negro artists. We feel that the Harmon Foundation's past efforts to advance Negro art have served the opposite purpose by virtue of their coddling rather than professional attitude toward the Negro as an artist. Basic in the ill-direction of the Harmon Foundation's efforts has been the fact that they are not a recognized art agency and, possibly for this reason, have presented Negro Art from the sociological standpoint rather than from the aesthetic. . . .[31]

After earlier experimentation in another location, the Harlem Art Center at 125th Street and Lenox Avenue was opened in December, 1937, under the auspices of a Harlem Citizens Sponsoring Committee, with a ceremony graced by the presence of Mrs. Roosevelt and attended by several hundred Negro and white artists and men of affairs. The 7,200 square feet of space was carefully designed to provide a central gallery flanked by a number of studios equipped for study and practice. Within the next year the Center served 3,141 students. Many more were anxious to enroll, but could not be accommodated. In the same period the Center entertained more than 10,000 guests. By March, 1939, a total of over 70,500 students and guests was reported.

A feature of the institution was that its facilities were available not only to Negroes but to students of any race. It held many unusual exhibitions, and acted as a meeting place for community and project organizations of every kind. Thus it was there that the Art Teachers' Institute of the Federal Art Project of New York City met, and it was there also that the notable exhibition "Art and Psychopathology," jointly sponsored by the Art Project and the Psychiatric Division of Bellevue Hospital, was first held.

But the heart of the Center was its classes, which were in session day and night under the direction of Gwendolyn Bennett, herself a painter. By her zeal and competence, she contributed more than any other individual to the success and prestige of the venture. The reputation of the school attracted many of the most talented younger artists in New York, Negro and white; and as a historian of Negro art has written, they "enjoyed the advantages of . . . a training that was the equal of several professional art schools in New York City."[*][32]

*The experience of the Harlem Art Center shows that professional competence, like happiness, is often best achieved by those who do not seek it for itself alone. The Center was begun with the social service idea of art as a source of community education and recreation, but the fame of its studies became so compelling that in the end it was forced to discourage art as a hobby and to concentrate its discipline upon technical training. This, however, was not a perversion but a sublimation of its original purpose, and is as much a tribute to the people of Harlem as it is to the

413

The national—and indeed, the international—prestige of the Harlem Art Center made its influence powerful even outside New York City. To the Negro who was aware of it, it was a symbol, as nothing else was, of the genius of his race. In Chicago the South Side Community Art Center, which aimed to serve the Negroes in Chicago as the Harlem Art Center served those in New York, was directly inspired by the success of its predecessor, and other Negro groups in other cities were similarly guided by the example of the parent center.*

If the Federal Art Project gave the Negro unusual opportunities in art and art appreciation, the Negro artist on his part contributed to the prestige of the project. Cahill's enthusiasm for the work of Samuel Brown, of the Philadelphia Art Project, seems to have inspired the idea that bore fruit in the New York exhibition "New Horizons in American Art."[33] Other Negro artists of conspicuous talent were developed or discovered on the Federal Art Project not only in New York City, Chicago, and Philadelphia, but also in Massachusetts, Illinois, Ohio, and Delaware.†

The status of other minority groups, so far as the Federal Art Project was concerned, caused little or no difficulty. The Indian, the Mexican, and the Chinese, even in those localities in which they were concentrated, provided so few applicants for project employment that their presence was accepted without comment. As for the Indians, who are not without artistic resources, especially in handicraft, they possessed an alternative to the Federal Art Project in the program of arts and crafts, under the direction of René d'Harnancourt, instituted by the Office of Indian Affairs of the Department of the Interior. There was, to be sure, especially in the South and Middle West, some opposition to

Center. The purpose changed, to be sure, but it was a change of purpose that came from the integration of the professional artist with the genius of the community and thus involved a genuine metamorphosis.

*The decision in 1941 to close the Harlem Art Center was a tragic one. Because of the poverty of its Negro clientele, it was never free from financial difficulties; and the Federal Art Project, on its part, was faced with a constantly falling budget. But the Harlem center certainly deserved a subsidy. On the other hand, the Chicago center, although it was located, as its opening catalogue stated, in "probably the meanest cultural environment in the Chicago area," was set up in a community-owned building, and its program survived the demise of the WPA.

†Dox Thrash is especially worthy of mention because he initiated, while working on the Philadelphia project, the series of experiments that led to the invention of the carborundum process. Negro artists connected with the Federal Art Project are listed, and their work discussed, in James A. Porter, *Modern Negro Art* (New York: Dryden, 1943), and Alain Locke (ed.), *The Negro in Art* (Washington, D. C.: Association in Negro Folk Education, 1940).

the loan or transfer from the East of artists who were Jewish, and the project exercised some caution in this regard.*

## THE ART PROGRAM UNDER STATE CONTROL

When the ERA Act of 1939 forbade projects sponsored solely by the WPA, the national director of the Art Project, like those of the other cultural projects, expected catastrophe. Their pessimism, however, was exaggerated. Control of the budget, to be sure, passed from the national office to the state administrators, who were now in a position to have art programs or not, as they chose, and to continue whatever project activities seemed to them most desirable. The federal director and his staff continued to serve, but in a purely advisory capacity, and to all intents and purposes, except that the money remained federal, the FERA dispensation was restored.

That disaster did not ensue was due to a number of causes. In the first place, the *status quo ante* is never restored; and in this particular case, the four years of operation of the Federal Art Project made the situation in 1939 radically different from what it had been in 1935. Indeed, the fact that art activities continued and in some respects even increased in the period of state control was a tribute to the influence of the Federal Art Project. It is true that the activities emphasized under the later program were not those which the federal director considered primary; but whether the new emphasis upon education and recreation was a step in the right or wrong direction is a question of debate. This much is true: if the federal period revealed the philosophy of the Washington office, the state period no less indicated the desires and preferences of the states and local communities, and to that degree provides a valuable statement of the layman's concept of art's relation to himself.

The transition from federal to state control did not cause a break in continuity. The larger part of the regional and state officials continued in office in the latter period; and even in those cases where changes in administrative personnel occurred, the new officer was almost al-

---

*In this connection the community of Greenville, Mississippi, set an example that merits mention. When they were opening their local art center, they requested the loan of an artist to teach crafts. The regional adviser of the project, in transmitting their request to the Washington office wrote: "He may be Jewish as the community has no prejudice and the committee has said that they would rather have a Jew than a Gentile, in view of the existing world situation, assuming that the man was what they needed."[34]

ways a person who had served in a lesser capacity in the federal period. This continuity of personnel guaranteed, within limits, continuity in policy. Four years of service under national direction had trained the state personnel of the Art Project in the discipline of a national effort and imbued them with its philosophy. In like wise, the state WPA offices and public opinion in the states had been educated by the national office to a degree that the national office, in its modesty, failed to appreciate. Indeed, the national office, in so far as it despaired of the project under state control, passed a vote of no confidence in its own record, for the test of Holger Cahill's program was, in the last analysis, its power to survive without him.

But if continuity in personnel and, to a degree, in policy were maintained after 1939, the emphasis of the program changed. This shift manifested itself principally in the direction of community art centers, and arts and crafts, and away from the production of fine art. On June 30, 1939, there were sixty-six community art centers. During the period of transition from federal to state control, largely because of the eighteen-months clause that resulted in the loss of trained personnel, thirty art centers were closed. In time, however, most art center supervisors were reinstated, new administrative adjustments were made, and the Art Project began its 1939 winter program with sixty art centers. In the following months new art centers and extensions were opened in the South and West, with the result that by June, 1940, twenty-two new centers had been inaugurated. Before the Art Project closed, it had established a record of over one hundred art centers and extensions.

Moreover, there was a fresh effort made to locate art centers in appropriate areas. As a report based on a year's experience with the new situation stated:

> The trend of employment has been in the direction of developing facilities for popular participation in art activity in the rural areas and in the smaller towns which heretofore have not usually been provided with these activities. This is reflected in the increase of employment in community art center activity (the number employed in this field has increased from about 400 in 1939 to about 724 in 1940) and the organization during the past year of art centers in small towns such as Gold Beach, Oregon (pop. 500); Helper, Utah (pop. 2,700); and Provo, Utah (pop. 15,000). . . .[35]

It is not without significance that the 25 per cent sponsorship clause of the 1939 ERA Act encouraged this development. Indeed, from the very beginning of the program for art centers, early in the federal period, the Art Project had insisted upon a local contribution of at least that ratio before it consented to open a center. Thus when the act of 1939 made such a contribution mandatory, the art centers could be continued when other activities of the program, for which similar community support had not been demanded, were forced to close or at least to curtail their activities.

But the continuance and expansion of the art center program are not to be explained solely by its adaptibility to the sponsorship provision. The reason for its favor lay deeper and was rooted in the basic desire of communities, rural as well as urban, to participate in art activities adjusted to their ability to comprehend and perform. In terms of professional competence, these activities were distinctly inferior to those undertaken during the federal period in metropolitan centers. In terms of community participation, however, they encouraged a relationship of intimacy between the professional and the amateur that must be achieved if art is ever to become popular.

This stress upon the development of community art centers was accompanied by a trend toward consolidation of the arts projects in the several states with craft and museum projects. This expansion of interests was expressed in the national office of the Art Program by the appointment to the staff of Adrian Dornbush, as director of arts and crafts. Dornbush had previously served in a similar capacity as director of the special skills division of the Resettlement Administration, and brought to his new position an experience and a philosophy that served well the new development. The Resettlement Administration, in its program of community housing, had used Dornbush's division to promote community recreational and educational activities (involving arts, crafts, music, and other cultural pursuits) as integral parts of community living, and as expressions of the particular genius of each community. His presence on the Art Program enabled the national office to use the professional personnel of the state art projects to raise the technical standards of craft activities. Requests from craft projects for technical aid, which Dornbush had previously received in his earlier capacity, came now to the offices of the Art Project. In addition, he and his assistants made many visits to the field in order to study the operations of existing craft projects and to initiate others. In some cases—notably in Illinois, which boasted many large craft projects—state art project officials contributed direction and supervision. A number of technical projects were strategically placed throughout the country, with the aim of improving the quality of designs, materials, and methods of production. There can be little doubt that the Art Project's services were invaluable in raising the standards of the craft projects when the two activities were joined in the post-federal period.

The integration of the museum program with the art program occurred somewhat later, for it was not until January, 1941, that an official directive placed museum assistance, museum extension, and visual aid projects under a like relationship to the Art Program.[36] The association between the art and the museum programs, like that between the art and the craft programs, was beneficial to both interests.

Museum projects as a whole, because of their undramatic nature, failed to attract public attention and therefore were not an object of concern to the Federal Art Project. Besides, professional art circles felt a contempt for the gloom of the "mausoleum," which prompted the modern artist to shun the institution when he might better have contributed to its illumination. The rehabilitation of museums, valuable though it was, could be judged only by the fresher appearance of the physical structure, the superior quality of the exhibitions, the greater usefulness of catalogues, and the more striking nature of displays—all of interest to visitors, but hardly calculated to focus attention upon the workers responsibile for the transformation. The visual-aids units, usually attached to museums, employed sculptors, artists, photographers, and carvers, as well as handicraft workers, map draftsmen, needlewomen, and clerical and unskilled help. But again, their product was essentially educational—charts, posters, maps, lantern slides, and models. Even dioramas, plates of historical costumes and other categories, miniature furniture, costumed dolls, and craft objects, when prepared for educational purposes, were essentially unspectacular.

But although the work of museums was outside the realm of the fine arts, it involved artistic skills that were constructive if not creative; and it was directed toward an educational end that was secure, though pedestrian. Moreover, museums, whether in metropolitan or small cities, represented an effort on the part of the community to express itself artistically; and however inadequate such essays may have appeared to the creative artist, the community's sincerity was beyond reproach. The museum needed renovation, both physical and spiritual—of that there can be no doubt. Moreover, it needed to be told that antiquarianism was not art and that a cult of the past for its own sake was no better than enslavement to the present. Above all, it needed the intervention of the professional and creative artist who, ousting the caretaker, would let in the sunlight of modern art. This the Federal Art Project was eminently qualified to do, and it is a matter of regret that only after the federal period did the Washington office realize that the museum was an obvious forum for artistic discourse between the professional and the amateur.*

THE ART PROGRAM AND THE WAR

War is at best a necessary evil, and no recital of the contributions of the WPA artists to the war effort can obscure the fact that World War II, like all wars, dissipated the labors of peace. The contribution of the WPA art program, so long as it lasted, to the instrumentalities of armed conflict was substantial. On December 7, 1941, the Art Program, like the rest of the WPA, hastened to place itself at the call of the armed services and the civilian defense agencies, and within a month or so the fine arts activities were entirely discontinued. In February, 1942, the Art Program was integrated with the newly organized war services section of the community service division. The WPA artists were assigned an infinite variety of tasks both in and out of war service. Headquarters, reception rooms, and recreation centers required renovation and refurbishment. Rooms were painted and decorated. Banners were prepared, panels designed and affixed, and curtains, craft objects, and even articles of furniture were produced. Posters announced campaigns for victory gardens, the conservation of essential commodities, and air-raid precautions. Armbands, decorative devices, and illustrated material of every kind were issued by the shops and studios of the state art projects. Thus the Art Program carried on, with the adaptations imposed by the war, what was practically an extension of its community service program.

In September, 1942, a conference was held in Washington between training officers of the army and navy and WPA officials. The meeting resulted in the complete direction of the community service program toward war purposes under the title of technical services. The contribution of the Art Program thereafter lay in the field of visual aids. The purpose of visual aids has been defined as graphically to illustrate "in simple abstract or schematic form an idea, principle or mechanism that would otherwise require lengthy verbal description and blackboard discussion. Actual appearance is always subordinated to produce a

---

*The new emphases of the post-federal period did not betoken abandonment of the earlier program in the five arts. Work in murals, prints, easel work, and similar pursuits continued, though at a slower tempo, at least until the outbreak of war in December, 1941.

clear and simple diagramatic statement."[37] The need of the armed forces for such materials was so great that it provoked the most concentrated efforts of the Art Program; and because the field of visual aids, and particularly the use for which they were now intended, had many novel aspects, the Art Program was able to make many original contributions. Camouflage training charts, demonstrating the principles of protective coloration, required independent research; other charts revealed the basic principles of airplane and ship construction, and the mechanics of arms and ammunition; an ingenious sand table, for which movable models of buildings, bridges, trucks, barges, guns, and other objects were prepared, helped the instructor to explain principles of topographical contour and military maneuver. Most original were the three-dimensional illuminated panels that actively illustrated such scientific phenomena as changes in current, meteorological changes, ignition principles, and the manner in which shells were propelled from a cannon.

Finally, artists (some of them of WPA lineage) serving in or with the various armed services depicted the story of the conflict in various media. Some of them were attached to government service; others acted for private interests—notably the publishers of *Life* and the Abbott Laboratories. These works, although good and honest, were not great, and will be preserved rather as historical memorials than as achievements of high artistic merit. It was the cartoonist Mauldin who caught, like Goya, the irony of the fusion of duty and degradation in the soldier's soul.

1.  Holger Cahill and Alfred H. Barr, Jr. (eds.), *Art in America: A Complete Survey* (New York: Reynal, McClelland, 1935), p. 106.
2.  Holger Cahill, "American Resources in the Arts," n.d.
3.  *Supplement No. 1 to Bulletin No. 29*, WPA, September 30, 1935, Section 9(B).
4.  *Federal Art Project Manual*, October, 1935, p. 1.
5.  Letter, Whitelaw to Cahill, November 9, 1935, FAP Files.
6.  Letter, Rehyer to McClure, December 10, 1935, FAP Files.
7.  Letter, Parker to Louise Upton, Curator, Los Angeles Museum, January 23, 1939, FAP Files.
8.  *Federal Art Project Manual*, October, 1935, pp. 3-4.
9.  *Ibid.*, pp. 4-6.
10. *Ibid.*, pp. 8-9.
11. Letter, White to Cahill, March 9, 1938, FAP Files.
12. Letter, Stevens to Cahill, September 12, 1938, FAP Files.
13. Operating Procedure No. W-12, WPA, March 20, 1937, Section 1.

14. U.S. Congress. House. Committee on Patents. 75th Cong., 3d sess. (1938), *Hearings . . . on a Department of Science, Art, and Literature*, p. 72.

15. Memorandum, Ozer to Asher, March 25, 1936, WPA Files.

16. Telegram, Baker to All State Works Progress Administrators, October 24, 1935, WPA Files; Telegram Serial No. 13, WPA, November 5, 1935; Telegram Serial No. 15, WPA, November 7, 1935.

17. Memorandum, Cahill to Stein, February 7, 1936, FAP Files.

18. Memorandum, Davidson to Woodward, March 17, 1938, FAP Files.

19. Letter, Parker to Stevens, June 1, 1938, FAP Files.

20. "Teachers' Institute, New York" (mimeo), n.d. (1937?), p. 2, FAP Files.

21. Letter, Cornelius to Cahill, June 19, 1936, FAP Files.

22. *New York Times*, December 16, 1934.

23. *Ibid.*, August 16, 1935.

24. U.S. Congress. House. Committee on Appropriations. 76th Cong., 3d sess. (1940), *Hearings of a Subcommittee . . . on Investigation and Study of the Works Progress Administration*, Part 3, pp. 75-76, 260-62.

25. U.S. Congress. House. Committee on Appropriations. 76th Cong., 1st sess. (1939), *Hearings of a Subcommittee . . . on Investigation and Study of the Works Progress Administration*, Part 1, pp. 276-78.

26. Florida Final State Report, Federal Art Project, pp. 16-17, WPA Files.

27. *New York Times*, December 24, 1933; March 18, 1935.

28. Letter, Cahill to E. P. Roberts, Harlem Art Committee, December 13, 1935, FAP Files.

29. *Art Front* (April, 1936), p. 3.

30. Letter, McMahon to Cahill, July 21, FAP Files.

31. *Art Front* (July-August, 1936), p. 4.

32. James A. Porter, *Modern Negro Art* (New York: Dryden, 1943), p. 130.

33. Letter, Cahill to McClure, November 6, 1935, FAP Files.

34. Letter, Robert Armstrong Andrews to Parker, December 14, 1938, FAP Files.

35. "The W.P.A. Art Program, June 30, 1939-June 12, 1940," FAP Files.

36. Professional and Service Letter No. 86, WPA, January 15, 1941.

37. "Summary of Services Rendered to Military, Naval, and O.C.D. Agencies," Illinois War Services Section, WPA, n.d., FAP Files.

# 19

## The Program of the Federal Art Project

THE SCOPE OF THE PROGRAM

The activities of the Federal Art Project may be divided into three types: production of works of art, which never employed less than 50 per cent of the personnel; art education, including the establishment of community art centers, which employed 10 per cent of the personnel in 1936 and, as the popularity of the device increased, 25 per cent in 1939; and art research, the great effort of which was the Index of American Design, which employed approximately 10 per cent of the personnel. Other miscellaneous activities absorbed the remainder of the workers.

That more than half of the artists were engaged in production was due to three main causes: (1) professional artists were principally interested in individual achievement; (2) the assignment policy of the Federal Art Project favored the producer, for the test by virtue of which professional classification was achieved was an appraisal of artistic product by a jury or committee; and (3) the concept that predominated in the earlier part of the program was that the purpose of the project was the maintenance of professional skills among the unemployed and, through that, the maintenance of professional standards in the art world.\*

\*Since the literature of the Federal Art Project during its existence (and much that has been written about it since its close) gives the impression that the principal activity and the major purpose of the project were to relate art to community living, it is important to remember that, at least during the federal period, such an emphasis was not reflected in employment statistics. The mere multiplication of easel paintings, sculptures, and other creative products, undertaken by artists working in the project's workshops or at their homes, was not satisfying a demand on the

The minor attention given to art education and community art centers in the early part of the program was also due to three causes: (1) it was the expressed policy of the Federal Art Project, and stated in so many words, that art education, in the popular as opposed to the technical sense, was more properly the responsibility of education and recreation projects, since it was a non-professional activity; (2) there was no well-established and well-conceived procedure whereby art teachers, as such, who were not professional artists, could achieve professional rating or, in many cases, qualify for project employment;* and (3) the establishment of authority in the Washington office removed from the local communities the initiative in suggesting the type of project that would best fit their circumstances. Indeed, control of finance and operations was concentrated in the Washington office precisely in order to avoid those non-professional art activities that the communities, if left to their own devices, might have favored.

The Index of American Design, perhaps the best known of the project's permanent accomplishments, was a research activity, and was not concerned with production (in the creative sense) nor with art education. Moreover, the Index, as a local project, was projected before

part of the people but a demand on the part of the artist employees. The Federal Art Project did stress art education and popularization more than did the PWAP—for the latter omitted it from its program entirely—but an employment quota for education of between 10 and 25 per cent does not betoken a major emphasis.

It is not argued that the attention paid to production did not have excellent results, but simply that the results were apparent *within* the professional art world and not *between* that world and the people. It might be added, moreover, that the maintenance of professional standards in artistic production did not entirely depend upon the Federal Art Project. For all the depression, there were enough comfortable artists in this country and abroad to defend established traditions in workmanship. No doubt the retention of professional skills by some individuals who otherwise might have lost them and the acquisition of such skills by others who first manifested a natural aptitude on the project were made possible by the emphasis upon production. But unless such an increase in the number of artists is accompanied by an increase in popular demand for their products, the stimulus is likely to be artificial and to cease when the effect of the drug wears off. If a government subsidy for the arts means simply that the government provides the market for the products, then there is, indeed, a change of patron, but not a change of purpose. A government subsidy for the arts—unless we are intending to put Humpty-Dumpty back together again—must mean a government subsidy of the people for whom art exists; and that means an expansion of art education for children and adults, especially those who, according to all the canons of the art world, are artistically illiterate.

*Very few indeed of the administrative personnel of the project—federal, regional, and state—could have qualified for project employment on the basis of professional production. But if there was such a large place for art critics and directors of galleries and museums on the administrative staff, it is difficult to understand why there was such a small place for art teachers on the project payroll.

the establishment of Federal One; and although its possibilities were presently realized by the federal director, no provision was made for it in the earliest listing of activities permissible under the Federal Art Project.

In the following discussion of the Project's program, the various categories of productive activity will be discussed first; then the research activities; and, finally, art education.

## EASEL WORK

The professional emphasis of the project is demonstrated by the fact that easel painters represented by far the largest single class of practicing artists on the project. The Federal Art Project accepted the easel painter for what he was and attempted to turn his talent to new uses in another way. Cahill, whose background was in the field of American folk art, encouraged the depiction of the "American scene," and his persuasion fitted nicely with the emphasis upon cultural nationalism that was current at the time. Many critics have observed that the project "rediscovered America," and in a sense this observation is sound. To most project artists America meant the working man, on the farm or in the city, the factory, the street scene, the tenement, the proletarian beach, and other aspects of industrial culture. Accordingly, the subject matter of their paintings generally followed this pattern.*

The emphasis in easel painting upon the American scene reflected the same stress in mural painting and resulted, within its own limits, in technical freedom for the artist. Many observers and participants have remarked that the artist during his employment on the Federal Art Project enjoyed a freedom of expression that was almost unprecedented in the history of art and utterly refuted the common impression that art and bureaucracy are uncongenial. That the project artist enjoyed such freedom is beyond question and a monument to the artistic integrity of the project and its administration. But the cause of this freedom is likely to be misunderstood. The lack of restraint lay not in statutes or procedures but in the spirit of the national administration as it existed at that time. There was a subtle innuendo in the accent upon the American scene that no more escaped the artist than it escaped the

---

*Traditional subjects were not forbidden. Nudes, to be sure, were discouraged, for reasons of public relations. But many portraits of local celebrities were executed in New England, the South, and the West. Series of portraits, for instance, were prepared for the Universities of Chicago and California.

economist or the political scientist, and it was by this innuendo that direction was given. Social freedom, as opposed to legal freedom, is measured by the area of effective choice at any given time, and the Federal Art Project, by creating a market for other than middle-class subjects, expanded the domain within which the artist might move.*

The primacy of easel painting in the art world of 1935 was indicated by the fact that, whereas other kinds of art activity (the graphic arts, sculpture, etc.) tended to concentrate in particular localities, the easel painter was rather evenly distributed throughout the nation. The easel artist also led in productivity. By 1938 some 15,000 oils and some 27,000 watercolors had been allocated to public or quasi-public institutions. The number of products increased in the later years of the project but not in the same proportion, since the emphasis after 1939 was less upon productivity.

A comprehensive appraisal of the artistic merits of this work is beyond the scope and competence of the present work. Archibald MacLeish, speaking of the Chicago project under Mrs. Robinson, wrote that "a surprising amount of [its work] is very good indeed."[1] But Mrs. Robinson was known for her insistence upon professional competence, and the Chicago project was one of the most unusual in the country. Ralph M. Pearson, on the other hand, criticized the project for what he deemed to be mass production of poor work.[2] That the project conserved the talents of some artists and discovered the talents of others who have achieved a deserved national reputation is clear enough, and is confirmed by the favorable mention that project artists increasingly enjoy in the literature of art. On the other hand, it is scarcely conceivable that of the 42,000 works produced by 1938, the large majority were not mediocre. Indeed, the presence of mediocrity on the project was frankly recognized. In southern California, for instance, a little more than half a year's work resulted in the production of easel paintings that included, according to the state director, MacDonald-Wright, "about three hundred canvasses varying in size from 24" x 30" to 40" x 50" that we cannot let go out to public institutions due to the inferior quality of the work on them";[3] and Holger Cahill, because of this and similar experiences, inquired of the WPA administration the proper procedure for destroying inferior work.[4]

But if easel painting as practiced on the Federal Art Project did not

---

*It is important to remember that it was not government patronage as such that conferred this freedom upon the project artist but the spirit implicit in the Roosevelt administration of those years. Governments may incarcerate as well as emancipate—it all depends on the kind of government.

bring together the artist and the public, it did bring the artists together within their own world, and created a guildlike concern of each with his neighbor's work. Criticisms and suggestions were thus encouraged, and an *esprit de corps*, emphasizing a common purpose, was cultivated. This attitude was fostered by the critical, but kindly, attention that supervisors and project officials gave to the work of their charges. Moreover, project officials often consulted the opinion of committees of experts in the community, and consequently the artist, whose work was under scrutiny, received the benefit of outside professional appraisal. Besides, there were rewards to spur on the project artist. Local projects held occasional exhibits of their best work, and an unusual painting might thus be selected for a regional or national exhibit.

The only serious procedural problem that plagued easel work arose from the very nature of the activity. It was properly recognized by the federal director from the very beginning that easel painters would do their best work at home or in their studios and under those informal conditions congenial to inspiration. On this subject, the manual provided that:

> It should not be necessary for artists to leave their work to make formal appearance before timekeepers. This kind of interruption seriously interferes with creative work and is entirely unreliable as a check on the time the artist has actually worked. Artists employed on individual commissions will submit their own time reports to the person (project supervisor, or person on the Works Progress Administration administrative pay roll) designed to make up the combined time report for the project under which the artist is employed. There will be an automatic time-checking arrangement for artists working on individual commissions based on a tentative estimate of the time necessary to complete these commissions as agreed upon in consultation between the artist and the supervisor in charge of the specific project. Periodical checks on commissions by the project supervisors will indicate whether due progress is being made. Artists working in groups will have their time certified by the person supervising the work.[5]

These instructions, and those of similar content subsequently issued, conflicted with the general timekeeping procedures of the WPA, which were, of course, elaborated with manual labor in mind. In some states and localities, state administrations, either because they lacked imagination or because they welcomed an opportunity to embarrass the project, attempted literally to enforce these general rules. In some instances easel workers were required to "check in" daily; in others, cubicles were installed at headquarters where they were under the constant surveillance of timekeepers. These devices were ridiculous, and were resisted vigorously and, in general, with success by the administration of the Federal Art Project.*

One unusual venture in easel painting occurred on the Federal Art Project. Early in 1937, the Secretary of the Interior requested of the WPA that artists be assigned to paint pictures of the nation's territorial and island possessions. Although the Secretary suggested that artists be sent concurrently to Alaska, the Virgin Islands, Puerto Rico, and Hawaii, Cahill decided to use Alaska alone for the experiment. Twelve project artists were selected from New York City, New York State, Illinois, Massachusetts, and Minnesota. The original intention was to pay them the highest security wage ($103.40 a month) and to require them to work ninety-six hours a month; it was finally decided, however, to give them administrative status and a salary of $135 a month for a thirty-nine hour week.[6] The artists returned with canvases and port-folios that were reported to be of high quality, but the venture was never advertised or the paintings publicly exhibited. The general expenses of the project, including transportation and non-labor costs, were so high that it was thought prudent to avoid the criticism that publicity might evoke.

MURALS

The Federal Art Project shared with the Section of Painting and Sculpture of the Treasury Department and the Treasury Relief Art Project the distinction of dramatizing in America and for Americans the new cult of the mural. Among the three projects there was a division of labor that, although not always rigorously maintained, was in general observed. The Section of Painting and Sculpture confined itself to new federal buildings; the TRAP devoted itself mainly to the decoration of old federal buildings; the Federal Art Project confined itself largely to non-federal public and quasi-public institutions. It differed from the other two in another respect. The Section of Painting

---

*This problem, more than any other connected with the art project, seems to have agitated the minds of both houses of Congress (see, for example, U.S. Congress. House. Committee on Appropriations. 76th Cong., 1st Sess. (1939), *Hearings of a Subcommittee . . . on Investigation and Study of the Works Progress Administration*, pp. 866-68; and Thorp's letter, *ibid.*, pp. 1344-49). That there was some malingering and falsification of time sheets among some nine hundred easel painters goes without question. But no evidence was ever adduced that such practices were characteristic of the project.

and Sculpture, which negotiated on a contractual basis after competition, attracted the more firmly established mural artists, many of whom were not on relief or in need of employment. The TRAP, although it was bound by the same relief requirements as the Federal Art Project, was kept purposely small by Edward Bruce in order to insure competence. It was the responsibility of the Federal Art Project to employ what muralists were left.

Under these conditions the achievement of the project in this medium was high both in quantity and in quality. By January, 1939, approximately 1,150 murals had been proposed. These ranged from projects of modest scope to the fifty-four paneled, 2,400–foot set of murals prepared for the Samuel Tilden High School of Brooklyn, New York, which was entitled "Major Influences in Civilization."

The quality of production was not as uniformly high as in the other two programs. This was to be expected from the limitations under which the project operated, and is in no way a reflection upon its achievements. Indeed, precisely because of its limitations, the project developed from the beginning a larger number of mural artists than its contemporaries and a school of mural painting—the "Chicago School" —that attracted national attention. Moreover, if some of its mural efforts failed to achieve that minimum of technical excellence which warranted approval, in other cases its performance was in no wise inferior to that of the other programs.

The administration of the Federal Art Project was keenly aware that mural painting was not only a novel development, in the technical sense, but also, because of the public place the mural necessarily occupied, a present occasion of controversy. Caution was exercised on both counts. The manual gave instructions that preliminary sketches and designs be approved by the state director, the advisory committee, and the co-operating sponsor before work on a mural was allowed to begin. The manual also advised that the closest co-operation be maintained with committee and sponsor regarding art work, including murals, intended for specified public buildings.[7] Later form letters dispatched from the Washington office emphasized the special care that work in murals demanded. In many of the smaller communities the requirement of sponsor approval of the preliminary sketches was inadequate, for the sponsoring institution was often technically incompetent to pass judgment. In such cases the onus of approval lay wholly upon the project. On the other hand, in metropolitan centers like New York, where active and competent advisory committees were available, the sponsor was often tempted to leave the question of approval entirely to such committees, whose concept of public policy with regard to subject matter was not always identical with that of the sponsor. For these reasons, although most of the unsatisfactory murals were eliminated in preliminary examination, it sometimes happened that labor and material were expended upon efforts that in the end were judged undesirable, either because of lack of quality or because of considerations of public relations.

In time, however, the muralists themselves proved to be their own best critics, for nowhere in the field of the fine arts, as practiced on the project—except perhaps among the workers on the Index of American Design—did the guild spirit manifest itself so well as in the field of the mural. Almost every mural, except the smallest, was by its nature a cooperative enterprise in which the medieval relationship between master artist, journeyman, and apprentice was maintained. The importance of supervision was paramount, and the best results were achieved only when the direction lay in the most competent hands. The guidance that the lesser artists thus received was important in the formation of their own styles and techniques, and the experience they derived from co-operative labor was a social, as well as an educational, discipline. Technical discussion on such subjects as walls, canvas, and colors flourished. The theory of three-dimensional as opposed to flat decoration was debated. The relative merits of fresco as opposed to canvas (which was affixed to the wall) were argued, and the balance of favor was so decisively on the side of the fresco that a veritable revival of this technique was witnessed. The Federal Art Project issued a pamphlet on this subject, which was distributed throughout the states and was in demand among those outside the wpa. In some cases, when mural painting was supervised by distinguished outsiders, project workers received the benefit of contracts that artists outside the project would have paid well to enjoy. Successful muralists were sometimes sent to states other than their own to give local artists instruction in the new techniques.

One of the most influential schools of mural painting to develop on the project was the so-called Chicago School, represented by artists like Edgar Britton and Michael Siporin. This school cultivated a realistic type of design (criticized in some quarters as too photographic); and it emphasized typical American scenes portraying men and women engaged in tasks of social enterprise, such as conservation and reclamation or the mastering of natural forces and human problems. Other styles that attracted attention were the abstract mural, favored by a group in New York City, and the Oriental mode, cultivated in California. Indeed, although in general the project represented common characteristics and techniques, the trend toward local or regional schools was one of the most promising aspects of the program.*

A token of the popularity of the mural and of the general acceptance of the project's standards was the demand on the part of institutions for their installation. Throughout the life of the project requests consistently outran the project's ability to fulfill them, and at the close of the Federal Art Project a backlog of orders had been accumulated that would have occupied its workers for a considerable time.†

SCULPTURE

Sculpture is an expensive form of art activity, whether the burden is borne by artist or patron. This is especially true for the monumental form of sculpture favored by public and private institutions. The Federal Art Project, when it cultivated this medium, was forced, because of the limitations upon its non-labor expenditures, to require a sponsor's contribution that, especially during the depression, was beyond the ability of most institutions to pay. Thus a fountain in San Diego by Donald Hord, one of the best of the California sculptors, called for a sponsorship of about $5,000, which, though nominal for the work, was more than the usual public institution felt itself able to contribute. A monumental statue of St. Francis of Assisi by Beniamino Bufano, the

---

*Among notable accomplishments in mural painting may be mentioned that executed by Tom Loftin Johnson for Washington Hall in the Military Academy at West Point, which required a year's work in research and in the preparation of designs and scale enlargement alone; the decoration of the central hall of the third floor of the New York Public Library—a location that had been long sought by muralists—by Edward Laning with "The Story of the Recorded Word"; the Chicago murals by Edgar Britton and Michael Siporin; the ambitious "Noah and the Ark," done by Dorothy Pucinelli and Helen Forbes for the San Francisco Zoo; and the work done by Emerson Burkhart for the School of Social Administration at Ohio State University in Columbus. In a film entitled "The Making of a Mural" the Project recorded the work of James M. Newell, as he painted a fresco for a New York City high school.

†An unusual experiment, calculated to satisfy this demand, was attempted on the Chicago project. It was suggested that murals be printed in sections on cloth or paper by means of the silk-screen process, and thus multiplied for the simultaneous enjoyment of several institutions. Some experimentation was undertaken, and two sets of copies were actually prepared in quantity, when the closing of the project cut short the venture.

outstanding sculptor in San Francisco of the Federal Art Project, was to have required an investment of more than $12,000 in sponsor's funds. This financial stringency that public institutions felt was in part the effect of the depression; the difficulty, however, in securing sponsorship for sculptural activity also derived from the tradition that, in America at least, restricted sculpture to the commemoration of special occasions. In the years immediately following World War I, American communities both large and small had appropriated funds—some of very substantial size—for memorials in stone and bronze. By 1935 this pressure had been relaxed, and no further occasion had appeared to renew enthusiasm. Moreover, architectural thought in the United States in 1935 had not progressed as far as that in Europe toward the integration of sculpture in the round with the character and purpose of the building it was meant to adorn. Sculpture, whether it was placed in the open or in corridors or niches, was incidental to architectural structure, and sometimes, indeed, out of harmony with it. Such sculptural modes as were favored manifested themselves in low relief as scrolls, arabesques, and other geometrical patterns that were superficially ornamental without being significant. Not only the expense, therefore, but a lack of novelty and the obviously superfluous character of existing sculpture tended to discourage prospective sponsors.

In view of these considerations, the number of sculptors employed on the project (between 400 and 500) was high. Employment, however, was concentrated in the larger cities. Of the sculptors on the project, the largest number (some 180 at the highest point) worked on the New York City project; California employed some seventy-five; Chicago, about fifty.* In addition, in December, 1936, when employment on the project was high, the following states participated in sculptural activities: Florida, 25 sculptors; New Jersey, 23; Oregon, Connecticut, and Ohio, 16 each; Massachusetts, 13. Sculptors scattered in seventeen other states brought total employment at the time to about 500.

Despite the limited demand and high cost, the Federal Art Project produced a goodly number of distinguished works of sculpture. Cahill has listed its achievements in monumental sculpture:

> Among the monumental groups may be mentioned the series of over-life-size figures of warriors carved in stone for the United States Military Academy at West Point, the extensive mural frieze on sports for the Queens-

---

*George Thorp, who succeeded Mrs. Robinson as director of the Illinois project, was himself a sculptor.

bridge Housing development, the 24-foot figure of *Sun Yat Sen* in stone and stainless steel for one of the public parks in San Francisco, and the sculptural decorations for Aquatic Park in the same city, and a series of heroic monuments in Southern California, the monuments of *Father Garces* at Bakersfield, *Juan Bautiste de Anza* at Riverside, the *Guardian of Water* for the Civic Center at San Diego, and the *Muse of Music* for the Hollywood Bowl, which is one of the largest and the most successful sculpture assignments undertaken by the Art Project.[8]

In addition to these products, which were impressive in size as well as in quality, the project's sculptors executed interesting works of more modest dimensions. Five larger than life-sized busts of Civil War generals were installed in Grant's Tomb. A series of busts entitled "Portraits of the Great," and including, among others, studies of Thomas Paine and Lafayette, gave the occasion for radio interviews with the New York City sculptors who had prepared the works. Three of the outstanding project sculptors, Edouard Chassaing and Emanuel Viviano, of Chicago, and Samuel Cashwan, of Detroit, prepared models symbolic of the Works Progress Administration that were selected to be cast in bronze and used as national trophies. A unique discovery of the project was Patrocina Barela, of New Mexico, a former teamster who made carvings in native piñon wood with an untaught genius that aroused the admiration of leading American critics.

The administration of the Federal Art Project was aware that limitations of cost discouraged sponsorship of sculpture, and, for that reason, encouraged work in the less expensive materials. Florida artists worked much in plaster and, at the request of local school boards, prepared sets of low-relief plaques that could be reproduced in quantity and allocated to schools. Again, in Providence, Rhode Island, a statue representing the "Pioneer," made of plaster and covered with a bronze patina, was set up in Roger Williams Park.* In general, however, there was not a heavy traffic in plaster casts or in original plaster concepts; and although small sculpture and wood carvings were decorative and inexpensive, the lack of demand for them by institutions discouraged emphasis.

The sculpture units of the project, more perhaps than other fine arts units, offered legitimate employment to craftsmen who, although they did not merit professional classification, possessed subordinate skills that were necessary and appropriate to the work. The project also

---

*It was suggested that the statue "should last six or eight years, by which time tastes in art may have changed."

used its less skilled personnel in the cleaning, repairing, restoration, and improvement of publicly owned statuary.

The guild influence, deriving from co-operative effort, affected the project's sculptors no less than its other artists. The sculptors exercised a decisive influence upon each other and made technical contributions to the medium. Edouard Chassaing, of the Chicago Project, for example, experimented with poured stone, a variation of the process of poured concrete. Other contributions by Chicago sculptors included glass aggregate surfacing of sculptures and the creation of outdoor sculpture that could be used as clambering devices for children. Sculptors also participated in the art-teaching program of the project.*

## THE GRAPHIC ARTS

The natural affinity between form and content is nowhere more clearly illustrated than in the achievements of the graphic arts section of the Federal Art Project. Indeed, it was not an accident of time or circumstance but a quality inherent in the nature of the medium that made the print the most democratic and the most educational of the project's endeavors in the field of the creative arts. It was here above all that the Federal Art Project achieved that ideal integration of artist with craftsman and of both with the people.

The Index of American Design was, as will be seen, essentially a copying and editing enterprise; it was at once a research project and designed to serve a practical purpose. Yet such was the artistic insight and imagination displayed by the Washington office and the project's supervisors that the venture far transcended a craftsman's accomplishment and revealed, in much of its product, an artistic sensitivity that mere copying could never have attained.

The poster projects, even more than the Index, were directed to practical ends, for the poster, as such, is intended to attract attention

*See Ruth Green Harris and Girolamo Piccoli, *Techniques of Sculpture* (New York: Harper & Bros., 1942), which gives something of the method, with illustrations, fostered by the Federal Art Project. Mr. Piccoli was formerly head of the New York City Art Project, sculpture division.

For photographs showing the variety of style and subject matter in which project sculptors experimented, see *First Annual Exhibition, New York City, 1939, United American Sculptors* (Introduction by Rockwell Kent). All the works therein reproduced were not, of course, by project artists. (The United American Sculptors was a division of the United American Artists, affiliated to the United Office and Professional Workers of America, Local 60, Congress of Industrial Organizations.)

433

to a public message, and form is significant only in so far as it emphasizes the message. Yet here, too, the Federal Art Project, following in the tradition of Toulouse-Lautrec, realized that even the lowly poster, especially if used in a public cause, can achieve a quality of expression that, if it does not necessarily attain the elevation of fine art, rises above the pedestrian. In the Index and the poster the project achieved a union between the practical and the aesthetic that was sincere and not forced, and yet at the same time within the comprehension of the layman.

The print itself, in all its forms, is a democratic vehicle, both because it is within the economic reach of the common man, and because its message or meaning is, almost necessarily, direct and simple. No print is, except by accident, unique, and thus the aristocratic conceit of monopoly, which the oil and watercolor foster, is removed.

By the summer of 1935 printmakers had made their needs known to relief administrators, as a letter written by Audrey McMahon, itemizing the needs of artists on relief in New York City, reveals:

> *Printmakers:* 50 to execute portfolios for educational institutions, for circuit and permanent collections, for framing and use in decorating public buildings where mural and easel paintings are not suitable, etc. An American school of colored lithography to compete with the German and French lithographers can be built up and a very talented and eager group of young people is anxiously waiting to have this opportunity. They are so eager that they offer to buy lithographers presses from their salaries, and a most stimulating project is now on my desk submitted by them.[9]

The administration of the Federal Art Project quickly recognized the possibilities of prints, and a project unit composed of approximately fifty artists was set up in New York City. Other units were in time organized in other states, until the number of workers reached a national total of about 250. This remained approximately the figure for printmakers throughout the life of the project. Most of the prints, however, were produced in a few centers, notably in New York City, Cleveland, Chicago, San Francisco, and Philadelphia. By June, 1940, the project had allocated to public institutions some 95,000 prints representing some 6,000 matrices.

Because of conditions indigenous to the craft, the routine of printmaking on the project was of a democratic and co-operative nature. In New York City the artist usually prepared his sketch or design at home or in the project's print shop. His work was then submitted to the supervisor of the graphic arts division and passed upon by the "subjects and approvals committee," which generally included Mrs. McMahon or an assistant, as well as the supervisors of other projects. Two persons representing the project personnel, and selected from a list submitted by the Artists' Union, were also present, but had no vote. This committee voted upon the selection or rejection of the preliminary design. When sponsorship was involved, prints were also subject to the sponsor's approval.

On February 6, 1936, the Graphic Arts Workshop was officially opened by the New York City project. This was, as Mrs. McMahon pointed out, the first such government-sponsored workshop to be established.[10] A little more than a year later it was ready to open an exhibition that won the complete endorsement of John Taylor Arms, one of America's distinguished printmakers. In his address opening the exhibition, he said:

> To what extent does the present "Exhibition of Fine Prints" by artists of the Graphic Art Division of the Federal Art Project reflect the life and art of today? Admirably. The Project has given to artists of all creeds and tendencies the opportunity to work together, under excellent conditions and, in the case of those of lesser experience, expert guidance. Mutual association has stimulated the exchange of ideas and the widening of personal horizons and has furnished and added most in accomplishment. Individuality has been given free rein, but a standard of execution has been required and achieved. The works shown are deeply and sincerely felt and honestly and, in many cases, beautifully executed. These artists, men and women, are of America today, the product of a national life of vivid and diverse influences, and they have turned for their subjects to those phases of that life which have most poignantly affected them. . . .[11]

Indeed, this universality of interest on the part of the printmaker, which reflected the maxim of the poet Terence, was characteristic of the project; and Holger Cahill himself pointed out, with pardonable pride and considerable justice, that "it would almost be possible to reconstruct a history of our period from the prints produced on the Federal Art Project. The prints give a fresh and vital interpretation of life as it is lived in America today, and give first evidence of new directions."[12]

Carl Zigrosser, curator of prints at the Philadelphia Museum of Art, who made a national survey of the graphic arts work done by the project, considered it one of the greatest of the project's achievements. He also emphasized that, aside from the large number of printmakers who had national reputations before they became attached to the project, an unusually large number of unknown artists were given an opportunity to develop and display their skill.*

## THE CARBORUNDUM PROCESS AND OTHER NEW TECHNIQUES

The Philadelphia graphic arts section, although smaller than New York City's, was equally distinguished, and reflected the Pennsylvania director's high concept of artistic competency. On this project the guild system, which printmaking naturally encourages, manifested itself in the discovery and refinement of a new graphic medium, the so-called carborundum process. Dox Thrash, a Negro artist who had had previously enjoyed but limited opportunities to practice, was responsible for the initiation of a series of experiments, which were subsequently carried forward by him and two other artists on the project, Michael J. Gallagher and Hubert Mesibov. Miss Curran, in her report of the experiment, remarked, "It is not every day that a new process is invented in printmaking," and added:

> The discovery was made by the whole group, each individual adding some contribution to the development of the whole technique. The freedom of the plan, the effort to keep from having water-tight compartments, the sympathetic and experimental attitude of the assistant, Mr. Hood, who criticized the "method" of each print while submitting it to the Director for criticism of the "content," artistically speaking, produced a fine environment for good work.†13

The carborundum print, if expertly executed, possesses a rich tonal quality and a luminosity, which derive from the manipulation of inking.14

---

*A unique collection of Federal Art Project prints is to be found in the Philadelphia Museum of Art department of prints under the curatorship of Mr. Zigrosser. Conscious of the significance that attaches to the pioneer efforts of the Federal Art Project artists, he has made efforts to collect materials that demonstrate the evolution of the various processes, as well as examples of the work of the printmakers themselves.

Other collections of Federal Art Project prints may be studied in the fine arts division of the Library of Congress and in the department of prints of the Metropolitan Museum, New York City, which in 1943 received on permanent loan 1,700 examples of prints in all media.

†The carborundum print was first introduced to the public by the Federal Art Project as a feature of its print exhibition at the National Museum, Washington, D.C., on October 7, 1938. The interest that this innovation aroused on the part of artists and the public encouraged the publication of an article, "Carborundum Tint—A New Print-Maker's Process," in the *Magazine of Art* (November, 1938). The substance of this article was later issued (September 10, 1940) as Art Circular No. 5 of the wpa Technical Series under the title *The Carborundum Print*.

The development of the carborundum etching color process, as a derivative of the carborundum printing process, was the work of Hubert Mesibov, assisted by Michael J. Gallagher.

Among the other processes developed or refined by the project's printmakers were color lithography and color wood-block printing—the work of the New York City project. Four- and five-color lithographs and wood-block prints in three to six colors excited a public interest that had lain dormant for many years. In Cleveland, Kalman Kubinyi, a distinguished graphic artist, president and one of the founders of the Cleveland Print Makers, experimented with the stylotint process, which had been invented earlier by Alexander Von Kubinyi. A portfolio that Mr. Kubinyi prepared, describing the various processes for producing prints and giving an illustration of each, was a successful example of project work. As already indicated, the Chicago project experimented with murals prepared in sections by means of the silk-screen process and which could be manufactured in quantity. The Chicago project was also notable for the work of Max Kahn, who developed the technique of large-figured lithographs that was favored by a group of graphic artists.*

POSTERS AND THE SILK-SCREEN PROCESS

The pedestrian nature of the poster, as such, did not permit the dramatization of this medium to the degree that easel painting, murals, and sculpture admitted. Yet the most striking development in graphic technique occurred on the poster project. The anomaly was more apparent than real, for the very *vulgarisation* of art, which the poster demanded, was a stimulus against monotony, and the urban character of the medium, together with its wide dispersal, encouraged that inventive genius that a wide audience provokes.

The productivity of the poster division was unusual. By May 1, 1940, the poster artists, who usually numbered between four and five hundred, had finished approximately 1,600,000 posters from 30,500 original designs. In New York City they served such agencies as the mayor's Noise Abatement Committee, the Board of Education, the Tene-

---

*The preparation of portfolios illustrating or bearing upon specific themes, although it was mentioned as the primary purpose of Mrs. McMahon's suggestion in June, 1935, was not prominent among the project's activities. A portfolio completed by the New Mexico project contained hand-colored plates dealing with Spanish Colonial themes, and another illustrating Pennsylvania Dutch designs was executed by the Pennsylvania project.

ment House Commission, the Department of Markets, and the Nutrition Service of the Home Relief Bureau. A reason for this fertility was the natural affinity between posters and a public authority. Federal, state, and municipal agencies all had uses for the poster, and the opportunity presented them by sponsorship to avail themselves of this medium at a minimum cost was, especially during the depression, generally and eagerly seized. The effect was mutually beneficial, for, while the artist was made aware of a relationship to government, the public agency in turn was reminded of the uses of art. This joining of the useful with the beautiful was furthered by the policy of the Washington office of the project, which consistently insisted that the poster, humble though its uses, should provide an exercise for imaginative and creative talent. For this reason, the Federal Art Project achieved a distinction in poster-making that no business established merely to prepare utilitarian placards and charts could approach.*

The early poster project, sponsored in New York City by the College Art Association, produced original posters rather than designs adapted to quantitative reproduction. There were several reasons for this. The project itself was a pioneer experiment, and in a way was as ready to produce easels as posters, if easels were what sponsors preferred. In the second place, public bodies had not yet been convinced of the poster's possibilities, and were, therefore, reluctant to make large commitments. Finally, the project tended to be an artist's project rather than a poster-making project, and the experience of commercial artists, who were aware of the primacy of the message over the form, was not solicited.

Months before the inauguration of the Federal Art Project, however, the value of the poster was realized, and the demand for it increased. In April, 1935, the TERA *News Letter* declared:

> The members of the TERA organization will be interested to know that the Safety Division, since it was organized under TERA at the close of CWA activities, has distributed throughout the state approximately 100,000 safety posters. These posters have found their way to not only the largest and most complicated projects, but also to the smallest variety. During the last several weeks, something new in the way of safety posters has been developed, and it will be of further interest to know that not only the subject matter of these original and more elaborate posters has been worked out by members of the

*The poster, like the mural, is an example of the *natural* adaptation of art to public uses. Moreover, the direction of the artist's attention to the public message that he illustrates produces naturally, and not by artificial insemination, a concept of the public weal in the artist's mind.

438

Safety Division, but that the art work and actual printing has been taken care of by members of the Mayor's Poster Project at 570 Lexington Avenue, New York. The Safety Division feels justly proud of these outstanding posters.[15]

The extension of poster-making outside New York City awaited the beginning of the Federal Art Project. Under the impetus provided by federal support of work relief additional projects were set up, notably in Detroit, Chicago, Minneapolis, Cleveland, Boston, St. Paul, and Philadelphia, and a few lesser units were formed in smaller cities.

The New York City project, however, remained not only the largest but the most significant of all, for it achieved that refinement of the use of the silk screen which elevated what had been a craft process of commercial use to the status of a fine art. In this as in so many other developments, the beginnings antedated the cultural program of the WPA; on the other hand, without the support—financial and artistic—of the Federal Art Project the initial experiments might easily have been abortive.

The credit for this technical revolution belongs to Anthony Velonis, a member of the original poster project, and subsequently of the New York City unit of the Federal Art Project. Velonis, as a practicing artist, was aware that the silk-screen process had been used for several decades by commercial houses to prepare simple show cards, college pennants, and other placards that required, for the most part, no more than a crude and simple design. A few individuals, to be sure, had attempted to adapt the process to the production of prints; but since each worked alone and was unaware of the others' experiences, the results, for what they were worth, were merely private *tours de force*.

In the beginning the poster projects preferred the wood block and the lithograph, perhaps largely because they were the techniques traditionally associated with printing as an art. Both on the early poster project and on the Federal Art Project, Velonis was impressed by the colored woodcuts and lithographs produced on the project. Later, when the silk-screen process was introduced on the project, he began to study its possibilities. Demonstrators from supply houses, who were acquainted with existing commercial techniques, were invited to visit the project and to give lessons in the medium. After mastering the elementary process, Velonis and his fellow artists began to experiment with refinements.

Considerable time, and no little patience and pain, were required for the mastery of the technique; and it was relatively late in the federal

439

period before the process itself achieved, as it were, independent status on the project. By 1939, however, tests conducted by supervisors had proved beyond doubt that the process was suitable for fine art printing; and in 1939 the New York City project issued Velonis' brochure, *Technique of the Silk-Screen Process*, followed by a second treatise, entitled, *Methods Other than Profilm.** In the same year Velonis was given charge of a small project devoted entirely to the making of prints by the silk-screen process. The method spread rapidly. By 1940 silk screen accounted for approximately 20 per cent of the prints produced on the project. In the meantime, it was receiving more and more publicity through art publications. An important landmark in the history of the medium was the exhibition of silk-screen prints held at the Weyhe Galleries in New York City under Carl Zigrosser's sponsorship. Accepted by museums and critics as a fine-art medium, and attracting more and more the interest of the art world, the silk-screen process thus made its place in graphic arts in less than a year. A later step was the private organization of artists into a national silk-screen society that holds exhibitions and acts as a clearing house for the prints of its members.†

The commercial exploitation of the silk-screen process as refined by the Federal Art Project, and its use by public institutions to advertise common enterprise, had hardly begun when World War II interrupted the normal development of peaceful pursuits. The versatility of the medium, however (to print on glass, wood, cloth, and almost any solid substance) and the gamut of its artistic gradations (it can be adapted to cheap mass production or to relatively expensive fine-art reproductions) ensures the continuation and variety of its applications.‡

*These two brochures were later reprinted in one volume, and issued by the WPA as *The Silk-Screen Process*, Art Circular No. 6, WPA Technical Series, July 22, 1941.

†Subsequently, the Museum of Modern Art in New York City used the silk-screen process to reproduce modern masterpieces, and with considerable success.

‡The uses to which the process was put are thus described by Velonis: "In spite of the growth of mass-production, printing processes, such as offset, lithography, gravure, four-color copper plate and collatype, the silk-screen process has had a greater proportional growth during the last 5 years than any other modern printing technique. In addition to its basic simplicity, the new technical developments in the process have been successfully applied to new fields and new uses. As a result it is one of the very few handicraft processes that is not only surviving the machine but even displacing it in many instances.

"The silk-screen process was first used in this country about the beginning of the twentieth century. It was first limited to rough and simple show cards. Today,

### THE INDEX OF AMERICAN DESIGN

The *Federal Art Project Manual,* issued in October, 1935, made no mention of an Index of American Design. Yet at that very moment the Index of American Design project, the most ambitious and most important program of research in the field of pictorial representation ever attempted in America, was about to begin operations in New York City, and plans for its inauguration had already been under discussion locally for several months.

The credit not only for the idea that such an index was needed and ought to be attempted but also for the initiation of the program as part of the Federal Art Project belongs to Ruth Reeves, a textile designer of New York City. Miss Reeves describes the episode that was the occasion for the concept. One day early in 1935, she met an artist as he was leaving the Picture Collection of the New York Public Library:

> He had not been able to find in the collection a picture of an American Indian of a certain period which he needed for a mural he was executing. I suggested he try the Museum of National History but warned him that there he would as likely as not find the breeches of the costume he wanted in one case and the shirt and accessories in another, hence his chances to see how the complete costume was actually worn were probably very slim. I bewailed the fact that artists in the United States had never been given anything like the design source publications which Europe, Mexico, China and Japan had for years put before their artists and designers and added that what we artists sorely needed in this country was an American Racinet and Hothenrot.[17]

Miss Reeves discussed the artist's embarrassment with Romana Javitz, the superintendent of the Picture Collection, whom Miss Reeves often consulted for professional reasons. Miss Javitz, whose experience with the problems of design was extensive, prepared a draft of the project at the request of the New York City art project supervisors. These discussions antedated the inauguration of the Federal Art Project, and the New York City art project was then operating under the auspices of the New York State TERA.*

show cards are still being done by silk screen, but the other uses of the process overshadow this one. In the West and in the rural districts most of the car-cards in trolleys, railroad trains and buses are done by silk screen. Department stores are using it more than ever in their sales-promotion material."[16]

*On July 11, 1935, Carl K. Tranum, then senior project supervisor of the New

This draft, "submitted for Miss Ruth Reeves," described the project, which was defined as one "to make an historical, pictorial record of the daily life of the American people." It pointed out the precedent of the records produced in Europe, and in recommending government sponsorship made the arresting observation that governmental work along similar lines in the past had resulted in the best available in the field:

> Government sponsorship of the recording of documentary facts has produced works of rare beauty, both here and abroad. Good local examples are the volumes on the "Wild Flowers of New York," prepared by the University of the State of New York, and the *Annual Reports* of the Forest, Fish and Game Commission of the State of New York. Government sponsorship assures a rigorous standard of selection, based toward a complete record of fact. It avoids influence by such commercial considerations as fad, fashion, or public taste.[20]

The work, Miss Javitz observed, required personnel more than expensive equipment and supplies. Her plan presumed a local project, supplied with an editorial and research staff—Miss Javitz suggested that an editor trained in library methods be appointed to head the project— that would divide the work of copying significant objects into two categories; that of costume and that of dwelling interiors. Once the resources of New York City were exhausted, the project, with "this finished work as guide, . . . [could] branch to other cities until the sources of the entire nation have been tapped to make this record embrace both regional and historical elements."[21]

It was appropriate that the Index should have been first proposed and begun in New York City, for the metropolis possessed two advantages: it contained a large number of artists, including many whose technical qualifications were not of the highest order but whose talents could be properly used in copying; and it contained numerous libraries, museums, and private collections that were abundant in source material.*

York City art project, wrote Miss Javitz as follows: "Thank you very much for the time you devoted to Mr. Kaufman and myself this morning. We both feel more than ever the need for such a project as we discussed. We also feel we are not equipped to write up such a project.

"We would like very much to meet you next Friday morning, if possible, and at that time bring Miss Reeves along. I think the thing we need more than anything else in submitting a comprehensive project is a report on the inadequacy of the present source material. Would you be willing to prepare such a report? I could assign a stenographer and a research worker to assist you in preparing this report.

"I will call you up to find out if Friday is suitable to you for an appointment."[18]

A letter from Mr. Tranum to Miss Javitz, dated July 25, 1935, thanked her for the "project writeup which you so kindly prepared," which was "most satisfactory and I believe will answer every need for which it was intended."[19]

*A plan to record the *santos* of early Spanish-Colonial artists, devised in Santa

Cahill, although he endorsed the plan as part of the New York City project's activities, was at first cautious about approving it on a national scale, and the reasons that gave him pause were sound. In the first place, the Federal Art Project, although it operated nationally, did not, like the Writers' Project, operate a project that was national by its very nature. It was not necessary, for instance, that easel painting or murals or art teaching be carried on in every state. It was enough that such activities be prosecuted in those states in which there was available competent personnel. An Index of *American* Design, on the other hand, implied operations in all, or at least in most, states. This would involve the establishment of a special administrative apparatus and over-all technical co-ordination, for which the Washington office was not, at the moment, prepared. In the second place, there was genuine and justifiable doubt that adequate personnel and competent supervision could be secured in states that, although they were thinly populated, were rich in native design. Finally, the proposed project implied a continuity of activity over at least several years, and it was by no means certain, in October, 1935, that the arts program of the WPA would last longer than six months, or at most a year.*

Indeed, the very farrago of American design appeared to make any attempt to record its evolution chimerical. Design is everywhere and, in America, everywhere different. It is to be found in costumes, furniture, household utensils, textiles, architecture, etc. It changes by locality, sect, and generation. In America, it has been in so constant a state of flux, and derives from such different sources, that the phrases "national dress" or "national architecture" have little, if any, significance. The sheer magnitude of the plan, especially since there was no principle of unity in American design to which deviations could be related, seemed to make its entertainment fantastic.†

---

Fe, New Mexico, had also anticipated the inauguration of the Federal Art Project. This project was duly carried forward to completion under the WPA. However, the New Mexico plan and the Federal Art Project plan were merely coincidental; the element of historical continuity was lacking. Moreover, the New Mexico plan was essentially local in concept, whereas Miss Reeves's was, from the beginning, conceived as national in its coverage.

Other ideas tending in the same direction were bruited about at this time. It is clear that the need for recapturing the artistic past of America was present in many minds.

*Cahill guessed that a plan as ambitious as Miss Reeves's might well require "a space of twenty years or so" for completion.22

†European nations had long since issued comprehensive volumes of national design, and some of the ventures had been state subsidized. But these nations possessed what American lacked—distinctive peasantries, where a respect for tradition and the slow tempo of change had combined to produce relative stability and, to a greater degree than in America, a national or provincial style.

But the enormity of the undertaking, if it was at first sight frightening, was in the end persuasive, for it was soon realized that the attempt could never be made without a degree of subvention that could not be anticipated from private philanthropy. The immediate subsidy that the federal government was at the moment prepared to offer through the WPA provided too present an opportunity to be neglected. Besides, America's interest in its past, hitherto the concern of antiquarians, was now assuming a popular form. Interest in American antiques not only because of their age but also because of their qualities of fashion and design had grown apace in recent years, and had been sedulously fostered by the dealer and the connoisseur. This popular curiosity was at the same time reflected in the literature of the period; books and periodicals gave more and more attention to subjects of antiquarian interest, and the commercial possibilities of older native ware were cultivated by imitation.

Interest, however, soon outran opportunity for research. Apart from museums, none of which aimed at completeness, and books and articles, which for the most part were inadequately illustrated and annotated, there remained only the Picture Collection of the New York Public Library as a source of inquiry. In this collection a large number of pictures of every description are arranged in stacks, classified, and cross-referenced. These pictures may be freely consulted by students, and borrowed on the same terms as books. All pictures have a legitimate place in the collection, foreign as well as domestic; and all kinds of pictures, prints, cartoons, reproductions, photographs, designs, etc., are included.

Despite its magnitude, however, the Picture Collection was not readily adaptable to the uses of the student of American design. In the first place, the collection has been made haphazardly, and has not been winnowed for quality or historical accuracy. In the second place, the catholicity of interest that the collection exhibits makes the search of the inquirer after specifically American design almost labyrinthine. It is not surprising, therefore, that the idea of the Index was provoked by the inability of a student to find in the collection the information he was seeking.

Upon reflection the administration of the Federal Art Project became convinced that the Index might be made to fit the exigencies of the project as nicely as the project seemed to meet the demands of the Index. There were on the project, and especially in New York City, many artists who, although they were not qualified to achieve creative work, were capable of exact copying, or at least could be trained in its techniques. In this way the conflict between the demands of relief and the desire for professional competence could be, in part, resolved; and many project workers could be equipped, if not for a career in the fine arts, at least for commercial employment.

By October, 1935, Miss Reeves had prepared a specimen portfolio and had submitted a plan to the Washington office. Cahill, although by this time convinced of the worth of the project, realized that its magnitude—involving, as it did, major problems of organization, scope, and technique—demanded thorough consideration by the high command of the WPA, particularly by Jacob Baker. At first, Cahill thought of the Index as a subsidiary project, operating "somewhat along the lines of Mr. Alsberg's American Guide Project."[23] It was also thought that, since the Index was a research project, the Writers' Project and the Art Project might profitably co-operate in its persecution. In such a joint effort the latter would provide the illustrations, the former the text.[24] Finally, there was the problem of time. Miss Reeves's original plan was to include the Indian arts, distinctly foreign contributions (those which had not been "Americanized"), and architecture. On December 7, 1935, a meeting of the persons concerned was held in Washington, and another on December 8, in Baltimore, at which these fundamental questions were debated.

By January, 1936, an outline of a national project became discernible. The need of a central technical staff for purposes of supervision and correlation was obvious, and Miss Reeves was appointed supervisor of the Index, with C. Adolph Glassgold (later) as editor. Constance Rourke, a writer in American folklore and folk art, was added as field editor, and a research editor and several other assistants were also employed.

As for the program, Miss Reeves's original proposal was considerably modified. Indian lore was rejected as more properly the concern of the Department of the Interior; it was decided that architecture was already adequately covered in the program of the Historical American Buildings Survey; and "primitive" painting was at first ignored, although later the work done in the Bishop Hill colony in Illinois received the project's attention.

Before the end of January, 1936, a supplement to the *Federal Art Project Manual* was released, in which the purpose and scope of the Index were explained and instructions given regarding the method of work and the submitting and filing of Index plates. This supplement was later amplified and issued as the *Index of American Design Manual* (Art Circular No. 3, November 3, 1938) in the WPA Technical Series.

The purpose and scope of the Index, as finally defined in this manual, is thus described:

> The Index of American Design is a unit of the Federal Art Project of the Works Progress Administration.
>
> The aim of the Index is to compile material for a nation-wide pictorial survey of design in the American decorative, useful and folk arts from their inception to about 1890.
>
> It seeks especially:—
>
> 1. To record material of historical significance which has not heretofore been studied and which, for one reason or another, stands in danger of being lost.
>
> 2. To gather a body of traditional material which may form the basis of an organic development of American design.
>
> 3. To make usable source records of this material accessible to artists, designers, manufacturers, museums, libraries, and art schools.
>
> 4. To give employment to painters, graphic artists, photographers and commercial artists who might not otherwise find employment.
>
> The Index of American Design is preparing a series of accurate illustrations depicting the rise and development of American Design. European nations have long realized the importance of gathering such material. They have prepared collections of plates in color and have published richly illustrated books on their decorative, applied and folk arts, thus placing the full picture of the native arts of design at the disposal of their scholars, creative workers and manufacturers. Familiarity with the roots of their design tradition has given the work of European designers a rich individuality. This quality has attracted American manufacturers to the European design market with a consequent neglect of native American talent.
>
> There is no single comprehensive collection of pictorial data on American design comparable with the great European classics in the field. With compilation of the Index of American Design, typical examples of an indigenous American character will be made available for study. It is hoped that this material will stimulate the artist, designer, and manufacturer of articles of everyday use to build upon American tradition and that it will offer an opportunity for the student, teacher, research worker, and general public to become familiar with this important phase of our culture pattern.
>
> .  .  .  .  .  .  .  .  .  .  .  .
>
> Of the vast array of objects available to the Index of American Design certain aspects are being concentrated upon for reasons of expediency. Typical of the fields from which material is being drawn is the iron work of Maryland and Louisiana; Shaker crafts of New England; Pennsylvania-German crafts; various types of indigenous ceramics; Spanish-American crafts, such as weaving and wood-carving in the Southwest.
>
> In the field of domestic and household arts, subject matter includes furniture, rugs, coverlets, quilts, draperies, textiles, fabrics, household utensils,

446

glassware, ceramics, copper, brass, silver and metal work, ornaments of all types, costumes, objects of personal adornment such as jewelry, and other objects which, because of excellence of design or workmanship, have enriched American life in the past. These subject groupings are neither comprehensive nor definitive; they are merely suggestive of material which is important or typical.

As background material, research workers are gathering much information of general use. For example, a complete list of craftsmen and an exhaustive list of books and articles on American design are being compiled, and specialized studies on New England textile designers, Shaker handicrafts, Spanish-Colonial material, etc., are being made.

Each drawing is accompanied by a data sheet, filled in by research workers and supervisors, which shows the type and material of the object, the date of making and the locality from which it comes, the names of the maker and of the original owner where these are obtainable.[25]

The importance of good public relations was early recognized. The objects that were the concern of the Index lay not only in museums, access to which was needed, but also in the possession of private individuals whose good will it was necessary first to win. In January, 1936, Alexander Williams was appointed publicity director of the Index, and it was his task to clarify its purpose and program and to arouse popular interest in its achievements. Delicacy was often most important when private collectors were approached, for connoisseurs were naturally concerned for the security of their own collections, and particularly apprehensive lest Index plates be used to make forgeries of their unique or rare pieces.

The New York City Index project was originally written up to employ 307 persons, and it was anticipated by the federal director that about 500 project workers would be required if the Index should be extended nationally.[26] Although the later figure remained the maximum for Index employment, which usually ran between four and five hundred, the New York project never attained the original estimate. A much larger number could readily have been employed, both in the metropolis and nationally. The federal director, however, although he accepted the Index as a project upon which artists of lesser ability might be given employment, was reluctant unduly to lower standards and, as the project grew in reputation and accomplishment, inclined more and more to emphasize competence. Moreover, as interest in provincial speciments of American art increased, the tendency was to draw attention from New York City to national needs and opportunities. New York City, of course, always enjoyed the largest employment quota, averaging about 150 workers.

Over 20,000 Index plates, some 7,000 of which are photographic studies, were produced in the course of six years of operation. Of these, more than 7,000 were submitted by the New York City project. Thus in terms of accomplishment, the Index became truly national in scope not in the sense that it covered the nation completely but in the sense that it permanently recorded representative regional manifestations of American folk art.

In the accomplishment of this task, the problem of research was paramount. Since the field was limitless, judicial selection was essential not only as to the kind of object to be represented but also as to the particular object within a class that best represented its class. Economy of time and effort demanded that, before copying was permitted to start, the possessions of a given museum or private collection be adequately and competently surveyed and appraised, and those items be noted that merited inclusion. Moreover, such analyses, unless they were co-ordinated nationally, were unsatisfactory; for it was necessary to determine whether such objects had been copied elsewhere and, if possible, whether they represented the best available specimens. The major part of this task devolved upon Miss Rourke so far as national coordinating was concerned. But much research of this nature was necessarily undertaken in the field, and in November, 1937, of a total staff of 372, the Index employed forty research workers.[27]

The choice of the object to be recorded was merely the first step in research. The object itself required explanation not only as a textual guide to understanding but also as an integral part of the recording itself. The recording artist, no less than the spectator for whom the picture was being drawn, needed to know the nature and purpose of the object. Moreover, knowledge of the function of an object is often important in judging the artistic worth of the design. Thus an object might appear to be a skillet, but it might in fact have been intended for another purpose, or for several purposes. Indeed, in some instances, the precise use of an object could not be satisfactorily ascertained. Finally, it was necessary to fix the object in time and place, to relate it to other kindred objects, and to provide the essential non-artistic historical background against which the object possessed significance.

The extensive and intensive nature of this research can be best realized if it is considered in conjunction with the categories of objects with which the project concerned itself. Among the specific kinds of design recommended for study were: textiles; household utensils; glassware; ceramics; copper, brass, silver, and metal work; ornaments, costumes; and jewelry. Regional varieties were also stressed, such as: glass, blown and pressed, in New England, New Jersey, Ohio, Maryland, and Pennsylvania; a wide assortment of Pennsylvania "Dutch" objects; Shaker material in New England, Zoar material in Ohio, Spanish-American crafts, such as weaving and wood-carving in the Southwest, and Bishop Hill objects in Illinois; and such categories as weather vanes, which might be found in curious and striking design anywhere.

In the early period of the project, the plan to extend Index activities beyond New York City met with difficulties. The Index itself, primarily a research endeavor, did not at first strike the public imagination, as did murals or community art centers. Indeed, financially considered, the Index found local sponsorship difficult, if not impossible, to secure, and was carried, so to speak, by the more popular activities of the Federal Art Project. This initial lack of enthusiasm was not confined to the public; it pervaded the state and local personnel of the project, many of whom were unacquainted with the project as it developed in New York City and dubious of its applicability to local conditions and personnel. The need for apostolic work outside the metropolis became so apparent by the summer of 1936 that Ruth Reeves was relieved of her administrative responsibilities and appointed field expert on the Index. Her technical knowledge and energetic enthusiasm peculiarly equipped her to undertake the tasks of education and propaganda that the Index required. Her first field assignment was in New England, where, in Massachusetts, one of the finest Index groups had already been developed; later she undertook field trips into other parts of the country, seeking out and examining collections, lecturing to the public, and providing technical guidance to local projects.

Miss Reeves's administrative responsibilities were assumed by Glassgold, who was given the title of national co-ordinator of the Index and served in that capacity until August, 1940, when he was succeeded in turn by Benjamin Knotts. Glassgold's regime thus coincided with the project's major period of productive activity, and he was responsible for the orderly administration and procedural regularity of the project as was Miss Reeves for its inspiration and inception.

The technical and administrative problems the Index raised were not inconsequential. In the beginning Miss Reeves had instituted on the New York City project a type of recording she had found employed in a volume on ornament: a "meticulous photographic-*cum*-archeological type of illustration" that brought the object, as it were, immediately before the student in all its details. It was believed that this type of recording would serve a double purpose: (1) it would show the minutiae of the object in reproduction, and (2) so standardize the process of copying that all the plates would, as it were, look like the work of one artist.[28] This technique was fundamental to the work of the Index, the primary purpose of which was not the display of individual genius but rather the utmost fidelity of reproduction. This technique, as developed by Miss Reeves, was revised by Charles O. Cornelius, the first supervisor of the New York City Index project, who adopted a poster-like, textureless pattern that he believed adequate for the purpose and less costly in time. However, when the Index was established nationally, Miss Reeves's technique was found to be the better, and was ultimately used not only in the nation but on the New York City project as well.

Although this technique achieved fidelity in reproduction, however, it did not result in that uniformity of product which was at first thought desirable. Indeed, it was impossible to require of artists mechanical sameness in their execution of plates. In time, and within broad limits, the individual artist was allowed a qualified freedom in execution, which, far from vitiating the total product, explored its possibilities. For example, some artists, emphasized realistic details—the flaws in the antique, the actual texture; others idealized the specimen, adding only those details necessary for authenticity. In general, the artists sought and were urged to achieve journalistically correct interpretation; many plates were executed, however, that critics accounted artistic in their own right. These *tours de force*, as it were, enriched the quality of the Index without detracting from its purpose.

Even a casual examination of the best hand-executed Index plates makes it apparent that the exquisite quality of craftsmanship they exhibit could not have been approached by the camera. There were, of course, objects in which color and texture were so subordinate that photographic reproduction was not only adequate but proper. In this connection, the *Index Manual* read:

> When the object will be recorded more suitably by photography, this method should be used. Such objects as iron stoveplates; silver and other items which are principally "form" and not color fall into this category. Photographs should give an accurate statement of the object recorded, with as little distortion as possible, showing the size and shape, form and texture, in a straightforward manner and against plain backgrounds.[29]

But even within these limits, discrimination was important. It was

450

recognized, for instance, that objects with highly lustrous surfaces appeared to best advantage in photographs; on the other hand, renderings of glass (particularly colored glass), silver, and furniture were generally done best by hand. The contention of some, however, that the whole enterprise could have been best executed by the exclusive use of the camera is not convincing. The essence of many of the objects lay not only in color and texture but also in that indescribable unity of the two that even the most sensitive color photography cannot recapture. The artist's eye, as well as his hand, alone ensured through the use of oils, watercolors, and even blacks and whites, that delicate exactitude which makes imitation an art. The greater coverage that the camera could have encouraged would have been achieved at the cost of quality.

The need of maintaining a national standard in quality of reproduction made competent supervision imperative. Indeed, in so far as the Index failed to achieve national coverage, the fault lay in the lack of trained supervisors. This was especially true in the South, where, despite its wealth of suitable material, the Index was inadequately represented. No Index units were established in Georgia, Alabama, Mississippi, Arkansas, the Carolinas, and Oklahoma; and in Missouri, Texas, and Tennessee, such units as were eventually started were small and late in the history of the project.

The difficulty did not lie entirely or principally in the absence of qualified personnel in these states. To be sure, there were fewer artists who could have been trained for Index work in the South than in northern metropolitan centers. But in most cases there were probably enough to achieve specimen representation. The problem lay in transferring men of supervisory capacity from the better units, where they had become skilled in the necessary techniques, to states where poor, or no, units existed. In this connection it is significant that Missouri and Texas achieved Index units only after competent supervision had been imported. Again, the experience of Louisiana indicates that quality, not size, was the requisite of a good Index unit. Of this project, Glassgold writes:

> The Index unit began with a nucleus of four. Of this group only one artist seemed to have the remotest possibility of even doing commendable work. In two months he had developed a very creditable technique. In six he had not only perfected himself but had brought his three colleagues up almost to his own standard. Today, Louisiana, with nine Index artists, sends us work that ranks with some of the best done on the project.[30]

The very fact that the Index was originally accepted as part of the project's activities because, among other things, it could provide employment for less competent artists, made training, as well as supervision, an essential part of the program. The "guild" system, which, as has already been indicated, developed on other activities of the Federal Art Project, was of the essence in the case of the Index. Sometimes, to be sure, it was difficult to persuade the better artists, who naturally preferred creative work, to transfer to the Index—a project they were inclined to consider beneath the dignity of their professional standing. In the main, however, the Index, as it grew in age, grew also in grace, and eventually an assignment to it was considered to be what in truth it was, an artistic compliment. Although an "Index Training School" seems to have existed for a short period in New York City, artists in general were trained on the job. The very nature of the task and the necessity for relative uniformity fostered consultation and co-operation, and encouraged the better artists to counsel the less capable.

In the beginning the standard of accomplishment was very uneven. Many plates were submitted that, for reasons of technique or accuracy, were judged unacceptable. These defective plates were critically examined by Glassgold, who made detailed comment upon the causes of failure and specific suggestions for improvement. The better plates were not only praised but also sent as exemplars to less qualified units. The experience and innovations of outstanding projects, such as those in New York City, Massachusetts, and Pennsylvania, were used as a source of recommendations to other projects. At times, supervisors and workers on the less qualified units were loaned to the better units, where they remained for a period of study and work, and subsequently brought home to their own project the fruit of their training. Conversely, outstanding Index artists were sometimes temporarily transferred to weaker units, where they were able to demonstrate their superior skill by actually rendering plates of objects indigenous to the locale. New York City furnished the largest number of loan artists, but other states were also able to provide instructors, particularly for the rendering of material in categories they had mastered. Massachusetts, for example, not only loaned artists to Kentucky and Virginia but to New York as well. As further aid to project workers, the *Index of American Design Manual* in its revised form gave detailed instructions on the proper methods for rendering different types of objects, and a large part of the official correspondence relating to Index work was concerned with the technical problems facing the individual units.

If the public was slow to appreciate the significance of the venture, the multiplication of plates and the extraordinary interest that the press and magazines began to exhibit toward the project eventually made the Index the most widely discussed and best-known activity of the Federal Art Project. It is interesting to observe that all, or almost all, the objects represented in the Index had been available for inspection—many of them in museums open to the public—long before the Index itself was conceived. The difficulty was, however, that they were considered more from the point of view of antiquity than design, and were not accompanied by a historical and artistic commentary that related them to American life and manners. The ultimate value of the Index—and it will surely remain as the finest legacy of the Federal Art Project to America—lies in its combination of artistry with research, and its direction of both toward the integration of national artistic experience.

The success that attended early local exhibitions of Index plates encouraged the national office to essay, in July, 1936, a showing in Washington, D.C. Department stores and merchandising associations were quick to grasp the commercial possibilities of the Index, and in November, 1936, the Marshall Field store in Chicago sponsored an exhibition of over 1,000 plates—the first of a series of similar enterprises that culminated, in 1938, in a national exhibition, which was organized and highly publicized by the Associated Merchandising Corporation.

As interest in the Index rose, it became necessary for the national office to discriminate more carefully among the applications for display materials. As Glassgold reported in September, 1937:

> So great a call has come to us for exhibition of Index plates that our supply cannot keep pace with the demand. The importance of the Index . . . is regularly impressed upon us by requests for Index shows from all over the country. These come from museums, art societies, libraries, historical associations, universities and other cultural organizations.
>
> As I said the limited material available makes it impossible for us to comply with more than a fraction of the requests. If it were possible to have a few of our best plates duplicated by some graphic process this would, as you see, enable us to multiply the number of exhibitions.[31]

Coincident with this growth in recognition, there occurred an improvement in quality of production that must have sorely tempted the national office to destroy inferior plates and to replace them with new and improved renderings. Yet Glassgold never lost sight of the fact that the primary purpose of the project was research—a recording of design materials for posterity. In stating this policy, the national co-ordinator observed:

> As newer and better work comes in the old and poorer plates are sifted and set aside. These are not being returned at this time to be done over

again, because there is sufficient material still extant to keep our units constantly occupied for some time to come. Bad plates of worthwhile objects will be returned at such a time when we have organized the various portfolios, which we trust will eventually be published. To my mind it would be at this moment inefficient and wasteful to return old bad plates when many of our units still need technical improvement. . . . We should let the process of improvement continue for some time yet and wait until our portfolios have been organized before returning plates for redoing—plates that at one time seemed creditable but now seem poor because our standards are higher and work generally is superior than in the past.[32]

But the Index of American Design did more than record the "usable past"; it popularized, as museums and art associations had never done, American folk art. This was an art that to a large extent had become forgotten, or, if remembered, known only among small circles of connoisseurs. The Index brought together and correlated in unprecedented form and volume heterogeneous materials, the sum of which was greater than its parts, and the pattern of which was single, although its manifestations were manifold. The Index taught the nation that the work of the hands that built America was guided by an eye not impervious to beauty, and that what had been considered curios for the delectation of collectors or the exploitation of dealers were in reality the material deposit of the artistic genius of the common man. The concern of Holger Cahill in American folk art was realized in the Index of American Design.

America's awareness of its own artistic heritage, however, awaits the publication of the Index. The plates themselves, almost all of them unique, were first allocated to the Metropolitan Museum of Art in New York City, in May, 1942, under an arrangement that stipulated that it should carry on activities such as the organization of the plates, exhibitions, and a publication program.[33] Benjamin Knotts, as curator of the Index, initiated an ambitious program. He made efforts to locate such additional Index material as might still be available in the states. The plates were processed, prepared for ready reference and quick service, and protected in specially designed boxes. An Index file that was itself a repository of valuable information relating to American design was undertaken.

After almost a year's experience, the Metropolitan Museum reported considerable activity in relation to the Index. Two brochures were issued: one, *Emblems of Unity and Freedom*, contained forty-five sepia reproductions of Index plates; the other, *I Remember That*, was a picture book of Index drawings that showed American interiors of the latter part of the nineteenth century. In addition, the Museum included four Index drawings in its Christmas card series. Color-slide experiments were continued under the museum's auspices. Exhibitions, some of which excited much attention and comment, were conducted in the Museum and nationally, and such services as loaning plates to magazines for reproduction, supplying information to designers and others, and aiding them in the search for specific pictorial material were continued.[34]

Although it was generally agreed that the Metropolitan Museum of Art was an appropriate repository and was conscientiously performing its duty to preserve and use the Index, it was finally decided, largely because the Index material was almost entirely federal property, that the National Gallery, Washington, D.C., was more legally qualified to serve as the permanent home for the Index; and in the latter part of 1944, the Index plates were transferred from New York City to Washington.

Through lectures, loans, and other devices, the National Gallery continued to carry forward the work begun by the Metropolitan Museum. It was clear, however, that the exploitation of the Index as a popular vehicle of art education was impossible without publication. Indeed, throughout the life of the project ultimate publication was always before the minds of the national office. In the earlier period, to be sure, the problem of production was primary. As late as March 1937, Cahill wrote:

> Up to the present time the Project has not been concerned with ways and means for the reproduction of portfolios. Our chief concern has been to develop techniques, to record available material and to compile and locate the most important and significant phases of our design. In many fields not being covered by the Index, much valuable material is rapidly disappearing and we have felt that the compilation of this material is more important than hasty reproduction or the development of one or two portfolios. Once the material is recorded and assembled for publication, I am sure that we will have many sponsors to undertake the cost of publication.[35]

In June, 1937, *Fortune* reproduced and published a portfolio of Index plates, with commentary and captions by Archibald MacLeish; and in succeeding years, plates were reproduced in a variety of styles by such periodicals as *House Beautiful, Antiques, Vogue, The Magazine of Art, Design,* and *Woman's Day.* Of these ventures at publication, the technique of *Fortune* established itself as pre-eminent. These issues, however, were private ventures; the Federal Art Project itself was not yet prepared to face the problem of publication.* The enormous expense that publication of the entire Index would involve was recognized as a deterrent, and what plans were eventually made were in terms of limited portfolios devoted to particular subjects or locales. Early in 1940, a portfolio entitled *Folk Art of Rural Pennsylvania,* containing Pennsylvania Dutch designs, was prepared by the silk-screen process and issued in an edition of several hundred copies. This venture was one result of the efforts of Benjamin Knotts, who was then director of the Pennsylvania project, to establish relations between the project and state educational agencies. The designs were rendered in flat colors, and no attempt was made to reproduce the texture of the material as it appeared in the original plates; but the collection was given wide approval as an educational device, and circulated among Art Project directors for their inspection. That same year, the Southern California Art Project issued a brochure, *Carved Ornamentation of the California Mission Period.* Its cover was in color, the text multilithed, and the pamphlet included two pages of halftones and a number of black-and-white illustrations. The national office studied the publication with interest and requested information from the state office regarding the methods used to prepare the booklet, its cost, and other details. In 1941 the same project issued a portfolio, *Mission Motifs,* which, like the Pennsylvania Dutch collection, was silk-screened; the national office, inspired by this issue, sent a form letter to the states recommending that sponsors be sought to finance the issuance of further portfolios of Index plates by means of the silk-screen process.

These limited experiments, however, were terminated by the outbreak of war in December, 1941, which transformed the arts program from a cultural to a defense project. Before that interruption, however, the national office had engaged in discussions directed toward publication. In 1939 extensive efforts were made, through correspondence with printing firms, to estimate minimum terms for publishing portfolios of design material that would satisfy the standards of reproduction set by the national office. At the same time, a grant from the American Council of Learned Societies enabled the Project to enter seriously into the work of preparing a series of color film strips of Index plates under such

---

*In 1938 a portfolio of Spanish-American *bultos* and *retablos* was prepared and circulated by the New Mexico project. The edition of some 200 copies was printed in line woodblock and hand-colored, and distributed apparently without the imprimatur of the federal director and certainly without his approbation of the finished product. The technique of this publication was inferior, and the issue seems to have been recalled, although some copies still survive in public libraries and elsewhere.

headings as "Cultural, Regional, Communal or Ethnic Groups," "Woodcarving," "Playthings," "Glassware," "Costume," and "Miscellaneous." It was planned to devote a number of strips to each category and to issue lecture notes. Co-operation was sought with the American Documentation Institute of the Department of Agriculture, through its Biblio-Film Service, in the preparation of these color strips. So successful appeared to be the experiments made with microfilm that plans and catalogues were prepared for the projected series. It appears, however, that only one strip of forty frames entitled "Typical Examples of American Design" was completed, and this was not released.

The most ambitious of all proposals to issue the Index portfolios was that instituted by the Federal Art Project in co-operation with the Committee on Art and Culture of the Progressive Education Association. The original memorandum, dated December, 1938, envisaged a series of folios that were to be released quarterly on a subscription basis. Each folio was to contain between twenty and thirty plates, half of them in full color, the rest in black and white appropriate to the character of the object, in accordance with usual Index procedure. The plates were to be approximately 11 inches by 14 inches, and a textual introduction was to be included with each collection. The aim was to make the publication self-supporting after an initial grant to cover the first folios and a subscription list had been obtained. Although efforts to launch this enterprise continued late into 1940, nothing was accomplished.

In August, 1940, Glassgold, whose regime spanned the period of the greatest productive achievement of the project, resigned; he was succeeded by Benjamin Knotts, who assumed the title of assistant to the director, in charge of the Index of American Design. Knotts had been director of the Pennsylvania Art Project, as successor to Miss Curran, and, before that, services project supervisor on the New York City project. The incidence of war, some sixteen months after his appointment, made Knotts's tenure short; and the termination of national control over the arts projects, effected by the ERA Act of 1939, raised problems different from those of his predecessor. In particular, since each state now operated a separate official art project under non-federal sponsorship, the products of state activities were no longer the property of the federal government but belonged to the states. The problem was complicated by the fact that, at the time of transfer from federal to state sponsorship, many completed or nearly completed plates were still in state offices, some being held for reference, reworking, or exhibitions. Knotts's

457

major task, therefore, was to recapture this material, most of which belonged to the federal government. Despite his efforts, many plates were never forwarded to Washington.[36] During his tenure in the national office, and later, as curator of the Index at the Metropolitan Museum, he also attempted—and with some success—to persuade state sponsors to allocate material completed under state sponsorship to the national collection.

PHOTOGRAPHY AND FILMS

Among the achievements listed by the Federal Art Project in September, 1938, were 355,126 photographs. These photographs were, for the most part, for the record, and consisted of straightforward photographs of project works of art. The use of photography on the Index of American Design—although perhaps more attention was given here to artistic effects than in the mere recording of project activities—was also essentially concerned with integrity of reproduction rather than with the use of the camera as an aesthetic device. The use of photography as an art, as opposed to mere craftsmanship, was practiced significantly only in San Francisco, Florida, and New York City.

The New York photographic project was under the direction of a distinguished student of the camera, Bernice Abbott. It performed the service of preparing camera studies for sponsors and recording the accomplishments of other projects of the WPA. It also conducted classes in photography, and the ambitious character of its program is seen in the announcement of courses given in 1940-41 in fourteen settlement houses and schools.[37]

In addition to these services, however, the New York City photographic unit engaged in creative and artistic work. The theme of the project's endeavor was "changing New York," and the treatment emphasized not only the city's physical history but also the changes in its inhabitants, such as the differences between immigrants of the first and second generations and the shifting of populations within the city limits. *Changing New York*, edited by Miss Abbott, with captions by the art critic Elizabeth McCausland and an introduction by Mrs. McMahon, was issued by a commercial film in 1939 and immediately accepted as an important addition to the literature of photography.[38]

The San Francisco photographic project produced a photomural measuring six by thirty-three feet, which was approved by the San

458

Francisco Art Commission for installation in the Assessor's Office. Its theme was "the modern city, framed by the architectural elements of the pre-fire era."[39] It was composed of six panels representing Industry, Construction, Business, Residence, Commerce, and Recreation. On the Florida project a photographer of merit, Florence Randall, prepared a portfolio of photographs of Seminole Indians, which was not only artistically successful but also ethnologically valuable.[40]

Motion pictures, either for production or distribution, interested the Federal Art Project chiefly as vehicles for art education. The film program was prosecuted by two units, one a subdivision of the New York City photography project, the other located in Los Angeles. The chief work of these units was to act as clearing houses for educational films that could be shown in the art centers of the project.

Perhaps the best known of the project's original films was *The Making of a Mural*. This was sponsored by the College Art Association, and copies were circulated to tax-supported agencies. The most popular of the motion pictures produced by the Los Angeles project was entitled *The Making of a Mosaic*.

When, in the spring of 1938, the information section of the WPA discontinued making films, the New York City art project was requested to take over the work. But though it released several films—including *From Hand to Mouth*, which visualized the causes and prevention of bacillary dysentery, and *Sculpture for Today*, which recorded with detail and imagination the processes and techniques that went into the making of sculpture—the project never assumed a function comparable to that formerly performed by the information section of the WPA.*

## TECHNICAL SERIES

The need for a technical laboratory that would concern itself with the practical questions confronting artists and craftsmen was first recognized under the emergency program by the Resettlement Administration, which, on August 1, 1935, established a special skills division.

---

*Other applied arts were cultivated on the Federal Art Project. Among them, the making of maps and diagrams was extensively prosecuted, and by 1939 some 39,000 had been prepared. The artistic touch the project successfully applied to this work differentiated its products from those of commercial firms and appealed to boards of education and other public bodies. Other avocations of the project were the construction of over 1,000 dioramas and models, some 15,000 lantern slides, and various types of visual aids.

This division, headed by Adrian Dornbush, employed artists, designers, and technicians, and concerned itself principally with the decorative aspects of building and embellishing the housing projects. It tested materials, estimated costs, did research of a technical nature, and executed models and designs.[41]

The need for an elaborate technical staff on the Federal Art Project was not at first recognized, but by the end of 1935 the New York City project, the most complex and demanding of all the units, possessed a technical staff of twenty-four. Ten technicians prepared panels and walls for murals; five were engaged in restoring and retouching works of art for sponsors; three attended to supplies and two to framing pictures; one was required to make estimates on current projects, and another to make routine chemical analyses.

It remained, however, for the Massachusetts project to inaugurate an ambitious technical program. The instigation derived from the impossibility of purchasing artists' materials by specification in Massachusetts, a situation that forced the project to analyze the composition of paints and other supplies for satisfactory substitutes. Sponsored by the Fogg Museum and under the supervision of Rutherford Gettens, its consulting chemist, a group of Federal Art Project workers directed by Frank Sterner began a series of analyses that were quickly broadened to include such topics as the effect of heat, light, and humidity on works done in various media, the drying time of different pigments, and the relative values of paints under varying conditions.[42]

In two years of work the Massachusetts Federal Art Project Paint Testing and Research Laboratory, as it was officially called, amassed considerable information relating to the quality of artists' oil paints. The head of the National Bureau of Standards of the Department of Commerce was thereupon invited to visit Boston and examine the work that had been accomplished. As a result of his enthusiasm, the laboratory co-operated with the Bureau of Standards in the preparation of a tentative draft of a proposed commercial standard for artists' oil paints.[43] A preliminary meeting of paint manufacturers was held on April 14, 1939, in Boston, the outcome of which was a series of negotiations extending over the better part of a year. On February 9, 1940, a general conference on artists' oil paints was held at the Museum of Modern Art in New York City to consider the commercial standard proposed by the Massachusetts unit. It was attended by the representatives of outstanding business houses in the field, and committees were appointed to settle such questions as remained.[44] As amended, the proposed standard, the first of its kind, was released by the Bureau of Standards.*

During this time the New York City technical unit had increased its work appreciably. As the Restoration, Installation, and Technical Service Division, directed by Raphael Doktor, it restored paintings, installed permanent murals, prepared portable murals for shifting locales, and conducted a testing laboratory. It developed a casein-resin emulsion for painting that allowed slower drying time than casein and was a superior permanent resin. It also devised a new process for adhering canvas to walls for mural purposes, an account of which was issued as a brochure by the New York City project and became a standard government specification.

In September, 1938, Dornbush submitted to Mrs. Woodward, at the request of the several divisions of the WPA and the NYA, a "Prospectus of Program of the Technical Services Laboratory," which was designed to operate from October 1, 1938, to April 1, 1939. It covered substantially the work that Dornbush and his staff had done for the Resettlement Administration, except that it was planned to include the technical requirements of the various WPA projects.†

## THE DESIGN LABORATORY

In October, 1935, the Federal Art Project opened its "Design Laboratory" in New York City. This was an ambitious attempt to develop a school for design technique and experimental studies in crafts production. Its program had been prepared by the art critic Ralph Pearson. Sponsored by a formidable array of advisers, it opened its doors with ample headquarters and staff, and with equipment purchased with money granted by the General Education Board.[45] The purpose of the Design Laboratory, as the New York City supervisor explained, was to create

. . . a free adult school for the teaching of creative design in industrial and graphic arts. Its purpose is not to duplicate existing art schools but to offer

*An exhibition of the work of the Massachusetts Laboratory was held by the Fogg Museum in May, 1940.

†This program was approved in General Letter No. 209, dated November 19, 1938. Dornbush remained head of the Technical Services Laboratory until September, 1939—his tenure having been extended—when he joined the Federal Art Project as director of crafts.

461

a unique curriculum in the co-ordination of all the arts to those amateurs, teachers and professionals who cannot otherwise afford to pay for it. The laboratory method will be used as a basis for all procedure.[46]

After a successful course during the first winter of operation, a seven weeks' summer session was held especially for high school and college students. The second winter term was open to "students slightly older, young men and women who have finished their academic education and are ready to begin their professional training."[47]

During the succeeding year the Design Laboratory continued its successful career, and acquired such prestige that professional artists were glad to donate their services as teachers and consultants to the project. Unhappily, in 1937, when the Federal Art Project, like the other projects in Federal One, was forced to retrench, the Design Laboratory was abandoned.*

The relationship between the Design Laboratory and crafts projects is obvious. When the arts program was placed under state control in 1939, the crafts activities were greatly increased. This caused an increase in the number and activities of state technical laboratories. In June, 1940, Cahill observed:

> One of the developments during the past year has been the establishment of technical laboratories on the various state projects to service their units and other W.P.A. projects. These state technical laboratories, combining the resources of the best artist designers in each state, have been instrumental in providing qualified leadership for the art program, the craft program, and for other W.P.A. projects needing technical and design services.[48]

At that time, technical projects had already been set up—besides those in Massachusetts and New York City—in Illinois, Florida, Ohio, Michigan, Iowa, New Jersey, and Wisconsin; and others were being planned in North Carolina, Missouri, and Oregon. Outstanding among these was the Illinois Craft Project, which was instituted in 1939 to organize the activities of nine separate craft shops.†

---

*The place the laboratory had achieved in the minds not only of the project workers but also of its friends and supporters is indicated by the fact that after the withdrawal of federal support, the program was continued as an independent venture of a co-operative nature under the auspices of the Federation of Architects, Engineers, Chemists, and Technicians. After several years of operation, however, financial embarrassment caused its eventual abandonment.

†These were: Decatur (toys); Champagne (weaving and metal); Petersburg (reproduction of authentic early American furniture); Quincy (furniture); East St. Louis (metal shop); Shawneetown (furniture and weaving); Jacksonville (weaving); Canton (toys and furniture); and Chicago (woodwork and weaving).

462

The Illinois project comprised a large organization, the Chicago unit alone employing 600 workers. Many of these were unskilled, and therefore required close supervision and the paradigms provided by technical research in design and method. Authorities in the various fields of craftwork were consulted, methods were formulated, and a design workshop was established "to service the various shops throughout the state with object and pattern designs and work drawings."[49]

## ART EDUCATION IN THE UNITED STATES

The report entitled "The Place of the Arts in American Life," prepared in 1924 for the Carnegie Foundation, reveals the low estate of art education in American life in the first quarter of the present century. The report concluded that art education could be readily acquired in only a few states—Pennsylvania, New York, Wisconsin, Ohio, and California—and in only a relatively few communities within those states. Only settlement houses had attempted to make art a normal part of community activity. Of these, only one in four offered courses in art, and their natural tendency was to emphasize crafts above the fine arts. The status of art museums offered no greater promise. If, by 1930, most museums were offering courses in art and art appreciation, these courses were often perfunctory, and the teaching personnel lacked professional standing.[50]

The picture, however, was not wholly without relief. In the first decade of the twentieth century the first children's museum, that in Brooklyn, was opened in a building provided by the municipality. Within the next twenty years others like it were opened in several localities. The activities of these children's museums were manifold and included not only art and art appreciation but also other activities, such as music and dramatics.

On the other hand, art centers, in the sense of institutions devoted to community education rather than to professional training, were practically unknown before the depression. The exceptions were the Little Gallery in Cedar Rapids, Iowa, which was an experiment sponsored by the American Federation of Arts, and the Westchester County Center at White Plains, New York, which used money appropriated for recreational activities to foster participation in art, music, and dramatics.[51] Indeed, it was not until the New York City art project developed

463

its teaching program under the direction of Frances Pollak that classes of a truly popular nature were initiated. But even Mrs. Pollak's project, through no fault of hers, fell far short of community coverage.

This New York City project, happily, was the occasion for a development more influential than any other single cause in the subsequent growth of art centers. On May 9, 1934, a public meeting was held under the auspices of the Artists' Committee of Action. An audience of some five hundred heard an address by John Dewey, after which a resolution was approved calling for a municipal art center.[52] In the course of the next year the "civic art center" became a slogan of artists agitating for an expansion of government aid to the needy.

Two other developments contributed to the growth of the idea. *Art Front*, a magazine sponsored jointly by the Artists' Union and the Artists' Committee of Action, made a municipal art gallery and center one of its basic demands, and in the issue of February, 1935, presented a remarkable set of plans for such a center. Second, among the Working Procedures devised during the Emergency Work Program of the FERA was one for "Community Art Centers." However, apart from a children's museum project, sponsored by the Birmingham, Alabama, board of education,[53] little was accomplished before the inauguration of Federal One.

## COMMUNITY ART CENTERS

The credit for the initiation of the art center movement as part of the Federal Art Project, as well as a large part of the credit for its successful prosecution, belongs to Daniel S. Defenbacher. Defenbacher, already identified with art activities in the South, was appointed state supervisor in North Carolina, and before the end of December, 1935, had established three art centers there. All three had galleries, to which were brought exhibitions from private, state, and national collections. Gallery talks were presented, demonstrations of art media given, and art classes for children and adults held. In February, 1936, attendance at these classes in Asheville numbered 350 students. Cahill was not slow to appreciate the promise of Defenbacher's innovation and appointed Thomas Parker, of the Washington staff, director of the art center program. Defenbacher, still retaining the directorship of the North Carolina project, was made Parker's assistant, and subsequently traveled throughout the country on mission in support of the idea.

At first, attention was directed to the South, where the need for art centers was most apparent; and early in 1936 Cahill sent Parker on field trips into the South, where he helped to establish art centers and galleries. By December, 1936, there were twenty-five art centers in the South and West.*[54]

In this brief period, about one million children and adults, in the aggregate, were reported to have visited and participated in the activities of these centers. In Florida, particularly, the movement flourished. There, a veritable chain of galleries crossed the state from Key West to Jacksonville. An interesting development on the Florida project was the use of WPA labor to construct new buildings in several places to house the art centers.

Thus encouraged, the Washington office began to advocate the establishment of art centers wherever feasible. In Arizona, particularly, where creative work never developed appreciably, this recommendation bore fruit. By November, 1937, the Arizona project had opened fifty art centers; by January, 1939, sixty-two; by May, 1940 (after the transfer from federal to state control), eighty; and before the program ended, more than one hundred.

In June, 1936, a tentative program for art centers was drafted by Parker,[55] and, in the next year, a manual was prepared by Parker and Defenbacher. This pamphlet, *Federal Sponsored Community Art Centers*, issued in October, 1937, as Art Circular No. 1 in the WPA Technical Series, was more than a compilation of instructions and suggestions. It also declared its philosophy of the relation between art and the community:

> In the arts, as in many other phases of American life, there has been in our time a development of professionalism without a corresponding development of community participation. The art center program should be directed not only toward building larger audiences for the arts, but also toward guiding and encouraging group activity and group expression leading to more complete community sharing in the experience of art. It should help to further the application of art principles in the selection of articles of everyday use as well as in community and home planning. The project, so far as its personnel and facilities will allow, should endeavor to provide a center for local cultural activities in the visual arts and in related fields.[56]

The control that the national office maintained over these local centers was nicely balanced. Local needs and desires were not only rec-

*The states in which centers were established included: Virginia, Tennessee, North and South Carolina, Florida, Alabama, Arizona, Oklahoma, Illinois, Utah, New Mexico, Wyoming, and District of Columbia, and New York City. In several of these states extension galleries, which were smaller units receiving direction from the major art centers, were also started.

ognized but even encouraged to achieve spontaneous expression; at the same time errors due to local inexperience were carefully corrected or avoided. It was required, for instance, that, so far as possible, art centers be located close to the center of the city, so that their benefits would be available to the average citizen. Decoration and renovation were largely supervised from Washington, with the result that the centers, although they respected local styles, achieved a distinctive appearance. This was particularly true of new buildings specially constructed by the WPA for the purpose. Street entrances and display windows were adorned to attract visitors. Within, the motif was unpretentious, but modern, and the neutral walls and indirect lighting provided a background at once appropriate and not distracting. Rooms were so arranged that gallery activities would not interfere with classes or meetings. Bulletin boards and circulars reminded the visitor that the art center belonged to him, and that the attendants were at his service.

The aim of the Federal Art Project was the use of the centers to their fullest capacity, by children and adults, as individuals and in organized groups. Moreover, the community was encouraged to consider the art center as the proper place for community activities. Hence, although art naturally formed the basis for center programs, the national office sponsored lecturers of "general educational and cultural subjects" from time to time, in order to encourage community interest.[57]

The heart of the community art center was its educational program, as manifested in its classes. At the very beginning of the program, Defenbacher stated principles that were to guide such instruction:

> The school program has been designed to offer recreational art classes for anyone who cares to avail themselves of competent guidance. The atmosphere is exceptionally democratic, with the greatest possible freedom for individual expression. Beginning and advanced students work under the same conditions, instructors keep their criticism to individual problems rather than to class curriculum.[58]

The teaching program of the Federal Art Project as elaborated in the community art centers, far from causing a lowering of standards, encouraged a competence related to the age and experience of the student. That the project was not indifferent to standards is shown by its compilation of the *Bibliography on Art and Art Teaching,* issued in June, 1938,[59] which was designed to provide the teacher with instructional aids for students of all ages and competence. Moreover, teachers' institutes were held in various sections of the country, and periodic inquiries and field trips were directed from the national office.

For adult students a distinction was made between "guild" and "open" classes, since experience soon demonstrated that two types of students applied for instruction: those who already possessed some foundation in the subject, and those who attended classes as a leisure-time diversion. The guild classes were usually restricted to those who had attained a certain level of competence; instruction was of a definite and progressive nature; attendance was considered obligatory (there were usually two classes a week); students were assigned to well-defined projects, and were required to study other media than those of their primary interest. The seriousness with which the project approached the guild class is indicated in Cahill's own words:

> The work of the guild should be established on a basis of four terms of three months each per year. A student must enroll for three terms a year and should not work at the art center for more than two years. It is assumed that within two years the art center will have fulfilled its function in giving the student a grasp of his subject. If a student chooses to go on with his study, he should enroll in a private school or with an individual teacher.[60]

Open classes, on the other hand, were designed for the amateur. Larger classes than in guild teaching were permitted; each class was so organized that it was complete in itself; and attendance was not compulsory. Thus, in a very real sense, the whole community was welcomed to the center.

The quality as well as the nature of the instruction varied among the centers. As the director of the Florida project reported, each art center had a history of its own. Miami emphasized sculpture and ceramics; Key West, oil and watercolor; Daytona Beach, child instruction; Tampa, visual aids; and Pensacola, "social activities pursuant to cultural study."*[61]

But the glory of the centers lay in their children's classes, for if art instruction meant a leisure time activity to most adults, to children it represented a primary and, as the project soon discovered, a necessary form of expression. Moreover, adults for all their enthusiasm remained visitors or, at best, guests of the center; but children, with that simple spontaneity that distinguishes their character, immediately made the

---

*One of the most unusual classes conducted by the Florida project was held within the walls of the Raiford State Prison. The men selected for the experiment were chosen on the grounds of aptitude or past experience, and the aim was to affect their outlook as well as their skill. Of the seven original members of the class, all quickly obtained employment upon release, two of them in the commercial art field. Prison classes were discontinued after the disruption of the fine arts program in favor of war work.[62]

center their home. The popularity of the centers with children is revealed by statistics. In New York City in 1937, for example, 28,000 children were reached in settlements, community houses, service clubs, and hospitals, as well as art centers, as compared with 6,000 adults. A similar proportion held for the rest of the country. The children's interest is further indicated by their concern with the centers' fortunes, and the diligence with which they solicited funds for sponsorship.

The children's classes were the heart of the centers' programs. The freshness of their creations, their extremes of realism and phantasy, and even the aberrations of an undisciplined imagination aroused an interest and appreciation among adults such as the self-conscious primitivism of the reflective artist had not been able to engender.

The instruction in the classes was directed toward making the child's contact with art an enjoyable experience and an adventure in self-expression. Copying was not permitted in children's classes, and aid was given only when the child requested it. Yet, this acceptance of modern progressive principles by the project was tempered by a realization of their limitations. The object of these classes was not to develop artists but to provide the child with an aesthetic experience. If, as sometimes happened, a child was discovered to possess unusual aptitude, the project was prepared to admit him to more formal classes where he would be taught the traditional disciplines.

The standard of creative production in the children's classes was unusual. Exhibitions held by the centers invariably attracted not only fond parents but the public at large—and in the end, the serious attention of critics. Showings of children's art produced at the centers were held in many of the major American galleries. At the exhibition of federal art at the Museum of Modern Art, "New Horizons in American Art," the creations of children provoked more attention than any other part of the showing, and the Museum of Modern Art itself paid the project the compliment of placing in its permanent collection several of the offerings.

The project was always assured of a crowded schedule for its children's classes. At the center in Phoenix, Arizona, for instance, there were children's classes every day. In this city of 60,000, some 400 girls and boys were enrolled. At first they were given cheap paints, which proved unsatisfactory, and then large jars of poster paint, which they dispatched with enthusiasm. Striking experiments, as in many other art centers of the project, were made with murals, usually on paper over a cardboard base. A small gallery was set aside for the children alone, and members of their group were assigned to care for it. There was a radio program each week in which the children participated. They discussed their paintings and formed the immediate audience for the radio speaker, who reviewed the work of the Art Center, told stories of great artists, and provided other instruction and entertainment. It was the experience of the Arizona director that there was no need to adapt the program to various audiences; it interested the adults fully as much as the children. As in other states, school teachers came to observe the conduct of the children's classes and to learn their methods.[63]

Among the several children's museums established by the project, the most outstanding was the Children's Gallery of Washington, D.C., which represented the accumulated experience of art classes held by the project in the settlements, public schools, and community centers of the nation's capital. This gallery reached, in the aggregate, about three thousand children monthly from six to sixteen years of age, and included a pre-kindergarten group. Its program reached into the public schools and elsewhere; it offered classes and held exhibitions on such themes as "Humor in Children's Art" and "Toys throughout the Ages." In time this gallery achieved wide fame; many visitors from out of town were attracted to it, and its exhibitions were eagerly sought by other communities.*

It is descriptive of the character of the movement, as well as a tribute to the artistic sensibility of rural America, that the art centers were confined almost entirely to the South and the West. In New England there were no art centers, with the possible exception of the Parish Art Center in Orleans, Cape Cod, which was sponsored by a religious body. Art classes were held in New England, principally in Boston, where some twenty institutions were served, but the concept of the art center as a community venture did not prevail. New Hampshire and Vermont indicated no art teaching in their final state reports.

In New York City, although the art center as a community enterprise did not exist (the very size of the metropolis precluded any such experiment, at least on the friendly basis that a rural community fostered), art teaching centers as neighborhood ventures achieved remarkable development. The art teaching division of the New York

---

*Upon the closing of the WPA Art Program the institution was incorporated as the Children's Museum of Washington, D.C., and given the loan by the District of a building and grounds, the "Villa Rosa," where an ambitious program patterned upon its earlier experience was continued until 1945, when the villa was sold to a private party.

City project, which grew from the earlier FERA project so ably super-vised by Mrs. Pollak, established centers in each borough.* In these centers an aggregate total of some 30,000 children and adults, in the proportion of four to one, were served each week. The character of the borough centers approximated that of the rural centers in that the teachers were interested not only in instruction but also in establish-ing cordial relations with their pupils, and in building the enterprise upon a community foundation.†

As in the rural centers, the borough centers in New York City taught both adults and children. In their adult classes, however, they were less inclined to emphasize art as recreation. This discouragement of art as a hobby was natural in the circumstances, for the centers soon discovered that the instruction of serious students more than exhausted their resources. In the children's classes, on the other hand, the prin-ciples already established by Mrs. Pollak continued to prevail, and an easy informality, which liberated rather than confined the youthful imagination, was encouraged.

Among the achievements of the New York City art teaching divi-sion was its experiment in art therapy among the mentally defective. It appears that the credit for the initiation of this type of instruction be-longs to the relief agencies of Hamilton County, Ohio, during the FERA period. In 1934-35, before the inauguration of Federal One, ERA proj-ects in art and music co-operated in initiating experiments in occupa-tional therapy with "lower type" patients of the Longview Hospital. An unused basement was renovated and decorated, and rooms were pre-pared for five classes. Subsequently, "higher type" patients were also included. The experiment seemed to be successful enough to warrant further consideration. All the students appeared to enjoy the work, and those who tended toward physical violence were relaxed in class. Mo-tion pictures of the project's activities were made and sent to Washing-ton.[65]

The therapeutic work of the New York City project at Bellevue Hos-pital was more ambitious and comprehensive. Experiments were con-ducted with children, adolescents, and adults. The original purpose of

---

*The unique history of the Harlem Art Center, which, for obvious reasons was a community venture in a sense in which the other borough centers were not, is narrated elsewhere (vide supra, pp. 413-14).

†When, in the summer of 1938, it appeared that the Queensborough Art Center might be forced to close, its pupils, forming a Queensborough Art Center Students' League, protested against the contemplated decision with an esprit de corps that would have done honor to a smaller community.[64]

the instruction was, as at the Longview Hospital, to afford the patients psychological release. It was soon discovered, however, that the drawings of the patients offered keys—some of them startlingly accurate—of their own mental disorders. Thus cause and cure were at once suggested. During 1938 a selection of the paintings of Bellevue patients was exhibited in New York City, and immediately captured the attention of the country's press. Feature articles appeared in magazines, and conferences, which included doctors and psychiatrists, were held. The use of art as a therapeutic agent for mental disorders, although much room for technical improvement remained, became professionally acceptable.[66]

The sponsor of an art center differed essentially from that of other project enterprises. The function of such a sponsor, or sponsoring agency, was not merely to give approval, as with the Index of American Design, or to make contributions of money or materials, as with easel projects, or to make loans of possessions and pay attending railway expenses, as in the case of exhibitions. The sponsor of an art center could, in the first place, never be a single person and rarely even one agency. As a *community* enterprise, it was necessary for an art center to receive the approval of individuals and groups that together represented the whole community. Usually, the initial sum of money required to begin an art center was higher than that needed for other project work—at a minimum, $1,500 to $3,000. It was also required that maintenance be assured, and that gallery and classroom space and other necessities be provided before operations were permitted to begin. Above all, the project demanded evidence of a sense of responsibility on the part of the sponsoring group. As Cahill wrote in March, 1938:

> We are not interested in starting centers unless the community is willing and shows potential resources to carry on an art center of consequence, no matter how small it may be. We are not trying to start temporary art centers solely for the education of under-privileged people. It is our intention to start only active centers which will develop permanent jobs for artists and art workers and, through this, to develop broad community participation.[67]

Sponsorship by a single organization was usually discouraged, especially if that organization was an art society, for experience showed that such groups were often more interested in their own development than in a community enterprise. Again, a single sponsoring agency, although it might with propriety make appeals to the community, did not itself represent the community. For these reasons, the Washington administration recommended: (1) the establishment of a steering committee to take the initiative in stimulating interest and collecting funds; and (2) once the funds were collected, the creation of a sponsoring committee, representative of the community as a whole and of its several parts.[68]

Many methods were used to arouse interest and acquire funds. Parent-teacher associations were approached; women's clubs, men's clubs, and labor unions were acquainted with the proposal. Community leaders in business and cultural pursuits were solicited for financial contributions, and were encouraged to explain the need for an art center to others and to lend prestige to the work. City councils, chambers of commerce, and American Legion units were asked to allocate sums of money to the center, to provide quarters for work, and to cooperate in many other ways. Benefits, card parties, and buffets helped to inspire local enthusiasm and also to raise money. The school children, who were the greatest gainers by the establishment of an art center, were organized to contribute and solicit small contributions in a way that had dramatic and intimate appeal.

The purpose of this achievement of community support was not the good of the Federal Art Project, the temporary nature of which was never overlooked, but the conversion of the community to the belief that a community art center was necessary to its well-being. As Defenbacher remarked in discussing a center that depended too completely upon the project:

> If the Federal Art Project and the Works Progress Administration continue to take all the burden of operation, we will never teach the [sponsoring] Association its function. We will also find that as responsibilities occur, [the center] will slip out from under them and we will find that instead of having a group of people interested in the operation of an active art center, we will have a group of people interested only in "art." If this attitude prevails when the Federal Art Project must withdraw its support, the art center will go to seed because no one is interested or trained in its operation.[69]

For this reason a sense of financial responsibility was impressed upon the sponsoring group. In other activities the project preferred to have sponsors donate money for artistic enterprises, which could then be turned over to the Treasury Department and placed in a special deposit account for general as well as specific uses. In the case of the art centers, however, since the ultimate aim was to resign all duties to the local committees, the project caused special regulations to be approved whereby financial matters became the sole responsibility of those committees, which deposited the contributions in a local bank. The spending of the money, which in no case was in the actual possession of project officials, gave the sponsoring committee a knowledge of the art center's requirements, experience in budgetary planning, and, above all, a consciousness of proprietorship that begat an acceptance of accountability.

By fiscal reckoning, sponsorship of community art centers was most gratifying. By March, 1939, over $360,000 in cash, kind, and services, had been contributed to fifty-eight art centers. On the other hand, the success of the project in preparing the community to assume sole responsibility for the centers was less apparent. The outbreak of war, to be sure, made a proper appraisal impossible, for it forced not only the project but also the communities to concentrate their energies upon other ends. Yet it remained a fact, war or no war, that the federal government, through the Federal Art Project, was contributing the major share of the expenses of the centers. Moreover, the project was staffing the centers with workers paid relief wages, which were, even at the professional level, distinctly below the prevailing rate for work of that kind. The ability of a community, therefore, to assume the sole support of a center was fundamentally an economic question: Was the community willing and able to assume the financial burden? In some cases, community budgets undoubtedly did not permit such expansion; in others, added expenses of this sort, for all the project's teaching, were deemed a luxury.

In a few instances, however, the project's policy was vindicated. Notably among these was the Salt Lake City Art Center. From the very beginning of this center, in 1938, community participation had been broad and deep. The Utah Legislature, as well as the Art Institute of Salt Lake City, appropriated money for its development. Moreover, the center was not solely an art center but also housed the other art projects, and so strong was its influence that it became a mother house, as it were, that provided the charters for associate art centers in other Utah communities, like Provo, Helper, and Price. When the federal government withdrew its support, the center was officially adopted by the state of Utah, which made provision for its director and some of its employees. Thus the center was enabled to continue its work.*

*In a few other places art centers survived both the war and the withdrawal of federal funds. In Sioux City, Iowa, the center became a public gallery, and in New Smyrna, Florida, it was continued under local public auspices. In the main, how-

To the layman it appears that the art center movement, as it manifested itself in New York City and rural America, and as it expressed itself not only in its teaching activities but also in its sensibility to community needs and desires, was easily the most valuable and most promising activity of the Federal Art Project. Professional art in the United States must cease to be merely metropolitan, not only geographically but also psychologically, and become American. To do this the artist must make an act of faith in the common man, and renounce, once and for all, the heresy that art is a monopoly of the middle class. As Cyril Connolly, speaking of England, wrote:

> When we restore the arts then to Europe, we can do one of two things: we can attempt to restore to bourgeois civilization sufficient order and stability to enable the cream of art to come to the top, or we can develop a civilization which will permit a new art to arise. If we adopt the second course instead of trying to put back the nineteenth century Humpty-Dumpty on the wall, then we must radically change our attitude to art here: we must give art a place in our conception of the meaning of life and the artist a place in our conception of the meaning of the State which they have never known before.[71]

## GALLERIES AND EXHIBITIONS

The connection between community art centers on the one hand and galleries and exhibitions on the other was, in the operation of the Federal Art Project, very intimate. It was not merely that the art centers provided galleries at which exhibits might be shown; the relationship lay still deeper, for it rested upon the atmosphere, created by the art center, in which the exhibit was presented to the community. Indeed, it was not until the art center had habituated the community to art that the exhibition program of the Federal Art Project achieved its full development.

Since the first task of the project was the organization of work for artists on relief, the exhibition program was naturally slow in starting. The earliest exhibits seem to have been prepared locally and spontaneously, partly to call public attention to project activities and partly to provide showings from which allocations could be made. The New York City project was the first to establish a gallery, which opened on

ever, the movement was a war casualty. In this connection a former state director of the project writes: "The communities now would love to have their centers back but not as a *transitory* thing peopled by *relief*, . . . [but rather] by permanent government employees on a long-range program with the thought of the program being supported more and more by the community till it took over the center completely."[70]

December 27, 1935. In the South and West galleries became to appear as parts of the community art centers, or, at times, as the first step in the direction of creating such centers.*

It was not until April, 1936, when a form letter was circulated to the states on the subject of exhibitions, that showings on a national scale began to be planned. This letter stated that "the public must be made more fully cognizant of the accomplishments of the Federal Art Project," and that a series of national and circulating exhibitions was being organized. Directors were instructed to set aside for this purpose and for allocations 25 per cent of such work "as would fall into the category of exhibit material." Instructions about matting, mounting, framing, and shipping were promised as shortly forthcoming from Washington. It was suggested that works suitable for national exhibitions and already allocated to public institutions be borrowed and sent with others to Washington for the exhibitions division to examine.[72]

The national exhibitions program of the project was inaugurated by the showing entitled "New Horizons in American Art," held at the Museum of Modern Art in New York City in the fall of 1936. This exhibition, which dramatically introduced the Federal Art Project not only to the art critic but also to the metropolitan public, manifested the national character of the project as well as the catholicity of interest with which the problem of art in America was being approached.

The organization of the exhibitions section of the national office was largely the work of Mildred Holzhauer, who was assisted in the summer of 1936 by Edith G. Halpert. Both Miss Holzhauer and Mrs. Halpert were aware that the organization of an exhibition in New York City, however exacting and however important in the establishment of good relations with the professional art world, was less important than the establishment of a chain of exhibitions across the country. This point of view was emphasized by Daniel Defenbacher, who, in October, 1936, made a trip through Wyoming, Utah, Arizona, New Mexico, and Oklahoma with the specific aim of organizing art galleries as part of community art centers. With twenty-two galleries in operation in the Southeast, and with an estimated sixteen more about to open, he pointed out:

> If we are going to have a fully organized gallery program, it is going to be necessary for the Exhibition section to be prepared to supply continuous exhibitions to all of these galleries. It seems to me that with the national

*In general, the Federal Art Project was reluctant to open simply a "picture gallery"; for the most part, it demanded integration of the gallery into a community art program. "Extension galleries," however, were permitted in those localities in which no other art activity was found feasible.

scope of federal-operated galleries, the supply of exhibitions to these galleries should take preference over allocations and over exhibition loans to non-project agencies.[73]

At "Studio House," the exhibitions section of the Washington office, plans for these continuous, circulating exhibitions were drawn up. The task was not easy. The proper arrangement of an exhibition, when it is offered in the traditional way and directed toward the approval of the connoisseur, is difficult enough, and requires a taste and training that can be acquired only by experience and study. But the adjustment of showings to audiences whose tastes were uncultivated, or, if cultivated, unknown, raised a new and far more serious problem for which no precedents existed.

The method was necessarily one of trial and error. It was soon discovered, for instance, that the unsophisticated spectator more readily appreciated conservative art. The project accepted this situation, and, although its art was predominantly modern, continued generally to introduce itself to a new community with as conservative an approach as possible. It was also discovered that the smaller the community, the greater its pride in its local talent. Here again the project, not without some misgivings but with no ill effects, at first permitted, and at length encouraged, the showing of local creations.

Ingenuity was often manifest, and indeed at times imperative, in the arrangement of showings. One director, for instance, contrasted the parlor of the 1890's, completely furnished and decorated à la mode and hung with pictures of the period, with a modern living room adorned with modern art. It was found, too, that the text of the captions accompanying the objects displayed often was influential in determining the reaction of the audience; the kind of publicity with which the exhibition was anticipated sometimes settled the fate of a showing before the date of opening; and the manner of arrangement, no less than the courtesy and understanding of the attendants, frequently created either a meeting of minds or an atmosphere of suspicion and resentment between the project and its clientele. Experience showed, for instance, that exhibitions held in buildings devoted primarily to other purposes, particularly libraries, were unprofitable, and that extension galleries, although they legitimately served areas unable to support a community art center, could be spread so diffusely, as in Tennessee, that the benefits were dissipated.

In a number of instances, in order to instruct employees in the proper techniques, informal "institutes" were held at which common problems were discussed and individual experiences shared. From these conferences and from its general experience, the exhibitions section of the Washington office was enabled to compose and issue a guide to exhibitions, which was designed to serve the project staff.*[74]

By September, 1937, the program of country-wide exhibitions was well under way and, indeed, was so successful that galleries and museums unconnected with the Federal Art Project began to request the loan of works for showing which they themselves were now proud to sponsor. These institutions included, among others, the Museum of the City of New York, the Los Angeles Museum, the Detroit Institute of Art, the Chicago Art Institute, and the Pennsylvania Museum of Fine Arts.†

In August, 1938, the Federal Art Project reported that it had, since January, 1936, circulated 228 exhibitions to its art centers and other places, had presented 1,116 individual showings, and had included in these exhibits some 8,000 works of art.[77]

The increasing popularity of the project's exhibits at length brought it international attention, and in 1938 a large part of its production was included in an exhibit entitled "Three Hundred Years of American Art" and displayed at the Jeu de Paume Musée in Paris. But perhaps the most representative selection of the project's works were offered in an imposing fashion at San Francisco's De Young Memorial Museum in the spring of 1939.

The years 1939 and 1940 were made notable so far as exhibitions were concerned by the opportunities for display provided by the world's fairs of San Francisco and New York. In one sense the co-operation given by the Art Project to these two enterprises was an exercise in publicity and public relations. But beyond that, the fairs not only offered opportunities for exhibitions of project work, they permitted the national office to present, as it were, the project itself. In San Francisco

---

*Although the project properly considered exhibitions as part of the curriculum of the community art centers, circumstances sometimes prompted the support of galleries as independent institutions. If such galleries were carefully initiated and managed, with due attention to the level of the community's understanding, the venture was fruitful. In Wyoming, for instance, where the project failed to find sufficient workers to institute a technical program, galleries alone were cultivated. In 1935, when the project started, there was not a single professional art gallery in Wyoming; in 1938, after three years of effort on the part of the project, there were not only several galleries, but also an interest and enthusiasm for them on the part of the general public that amazed visitors from the Washington office.[75]

†All the expenses of these exhibitions, including packing and shipping, were paid by the participating institutions, and the Washington office predicted that in 1938 some $200,000 dollars would be so spent.[76]

a booth in the Federal Building, appropriately decorated, formed the background for "a dozen examples which range from copper plaques to tempera, oils, and glass mosaics." It was in the Art in Action Section of the Exposition's Palace of Fine Arts, however, that the Northern California Art Project made its important contribution. On the floor of the room project workers wove tapestries, drew and printed lithographs, and prepared sculpture. In another place, demonstrations were given of fresco making and color binding, and examples shown of ceramic and granite sculpture by project artists.

On one wall of the building Diego Rivera directed a group of workers in the preparation of a large fresco, the theme of which was "Art of the Americas." On the opposite wall workers in mosaic attracted crowds with their version of "Modern Science." Other exhibits to which the project contributed included a 100-foot relief map of the Far West in the Court of the Hall of Western States. The variety of the project's contributions to the fair testified to its versatility as well as to its usefulness.[78]

Impressive as was the demonstration made at Treasure Island, it was the New York World's Fair that enabled the project to spread its wings to their full span. The federal director obtained a leave of absence in order to assume personal charge of the "exhibition of Contemporary American Art," which included twenty-five galleries in a centrally located building. Although WPA artists were represented by murals and other decorations elsewhere, particularly in the building of the Federal Works Agency, it was at the Contemporary Art Building, as it was called in 1939, that the main exhibition was installed. A formidable committee selected 1,200 art works, in the main by project artists, from among 25,000. Oils, sculpture, and prints were shown in styles ranging from the abstract to the romantic. In the course of a season, two million persons were reported as having attended the exhibition.*

In 1940, by agreement between the WPA and the New York World's Fair, the exhibition—renamed "American Art Today" and housed in twenty galleries—became an adjunct of the New York City Art Project, and thus came under the direct supervision of Mrs. McMahon and her staff. The community center motif was predominant; demonstrations were provided, educational features introduced, and special events added to give variety and entertainment.

*The National Art Society published a list catalogue of the 1939 Exhibition, with an introduction by Holger Cahill, under the title, "American Art Today."

The final achievement of the extensive and unremitting labors of the exhibitions section of the project was the creation of National Art Week, which, in 1940 and 1941, was responsible for the grestest mass display of art ever attempted in the United States. The American Artists Professional League had for a number of seasons sponsored "American Art Week." Commendable as it was, this event had served art circles more than the general public. Now, gratified by "the rapidly developing interest in American art in recent years, a development in which the government art programs have played an important part," the President of the United States asked federal agencies supporting active art programs to plan a nationwide program of observance of art and, on September 5, 1940, requested Francis Henry Taylor, director of the Metropolitan Museum of Art, to form and head a National Council. The President himself acted as sponsor for the event, and Mrs. Roosevelt, as honorary chairman. Mrs. Florence Kerr assumed the post of chairman of the Committee of Federal Agencies for Art Week.[79]

Efforts were made throughout the nation to promote participation and co-operation in this event. Not only every section of the country was asked to participate, but department stores and furniture establishments no less than art associations and professional societies were solicited for space, advertising, and other assistance. The Federal Art Project itself, in its offices, workshops, and community art centers, furnished the larger part of the active workers who succeeded in presenting 1,600 exhibitions during the last week of November, 1940. An estimated five million persons viewed some 15,000 objects of art and craftsmanship.

The principal aim of Art Week was to encourage the purchase of American art. Sales were estimated at approximately $100,000 for the entire country. The value of the experiment as a demonstration of American art and as a means of public education was so apparent that Art Week was held for a second time in 1941. In this year, sales were greater than before, and it was possible to observe cumulative effects of the experiment upon public and artist alike. Unfortunately, the war prevented a continuation of the program.

1. "Unemployed Arts," unsigned, *Fortune*, May, 1937, p. 171.
2. Ralph M. Pearson, *Experiencing American Pictures* (New York: Harper & Bros., 1943), pp. 57 ff.
3. Letter, L. Macdonald-Wright to Cahill, June 12, 1936, FAP Files.
4. Memorandum, Cogan to Holmes, July 9, 1936, FAP Files.

5. *Federal Art Project Manual*, wpa, pp. 22-23.

6. Memoranda, Cahill to Holmes, April 16, 1937; Davidson to Holmes, April 23, 1937; Woodward to Niles, May 17, 1937; fap Files.

7. *Federal Art Project Manual*, pp. 10, 22.

8. "Report on Accomplishments of the wpa Art Program," enclosed in memorandum, Cahill to Triggs, June 18, 1940, fap Files.

9. Letter, McMahon to McClure, June 25, 1935, fap Files.

10. Letter, McMahon to Cahill, February 3, 1936, fap Files.

11. John Taylor Arms, "Prints in the Life of Today," *Graphic Arts Exhibition*, New York, March 30, 1937.

12. "Report on the First Three Years' Accomplishments of the Federal Art Project," p. 6, contained in memorandum, Cahill to Woodward, Setpember 21, 1938, fap Files.

13. "Report of the Federal Art Project in Pennsylvania, October, 1935—July, 1938, under the Direction of Mary Curran," p. 4, fap Files.

14. *The Carborundum Print*, Art Circular No. 5, wpa Technical Series, September 10, 1940, pp. 1-2.

15. New York State tera *News Letter*, April 30, 1935.

16. *The Silk-Screen Process*, Art Circular No. 6, wpa Technical Series, July 22, 1941, p. 4.

17. Letter, Ruth Reeves to Harold W. Landin, June 18, 1943. Files of the American Council of Learned Societies, Washington, D.C.

18. Letter, Tranum to Javitz, July 11, 1935, acls Files.

19. Letter, Tranum to Javitz, July 25, 1935, acls Files.

20. Memorandum, Javitz to Tranum, July, 1935, acls Files.

21. *Ibid.*

22. Letter, Cahill to Reeves, August 22, 1935, fap Files.

23. Memorandum, Cahill to Baker, October 22, 1935, fap Files.

24. Memorandum, Cahill to McClure, August 27, 1935, fap Files.

25. *Index of American Design Manual*, Art Circular No. 3, wpa Technical Series, November 3, 1938, pp. 1-3.

26. Memorandum, Cahill to McClure, August 27, 1935, fap Files.

27. Memorandum, Glassgold to Parker, November 24, 1937, fap Files.

28. Letter, Reeves to Landin, June 18, 1943, acls Files.

29. *Index of American Design Manual*, p. 11.

30. Letter, Glassgold to Robinson, August 9, 1937, fap Files.

31. Letter, Glassgold to Danysh, September 29, 1937, fap Files.

32. Memorandum, Glassgold to Parker, August 17, 1938, fap Files.

33. Contract between the Work Projects Administration and the Metropolitan Museum of Art, May 3, 1942, fap Files.

34. "A Report on the W.P.A. Index of American Design from the Time of Its Allocation to the Metropolitan Museum of Art, May, 1942," Horace H. F. Jayne, Vice Director, the Metropolitan Museum of Art, to Kerr, February 27, 1943, wpa Files.

35. Letter, Cahill to Helen Kay, March 30, 1937, fap Files.

36. Letter, Knotts to Filler, July 9, 1943, acls Files.

37. Release of September 3, 1940, Department of Information, wpa.

38. Elizabeth McCausland, *Changing New York*, ed. Berenice Abbott (New York: Dutton, 1939).

39. Memorandum, Parker to Woodward, October 14, 1937, fap Files.

40. Letter, Cahill to James F. Birchfield, December 13, 1938, FAP Files.

41. Resettlement Administration, *First Annual Report* (Washington, D. C., 1936), pp. 89 ff.; Adrian Dornbush, *Outline of Organization and Work of the Special Skills Division*, Special Service Section, Resettlement Administration, n.d.

42. *Federal Art in New England, 1933-1937*, pp. 14 ff., FAP Files.

43. Memorandum, Parker to Morris, April 8, 1939, FAP Files.

44. *Condensed Record of General Conference on Artists' Oil Paints*, February 9, 1940, FAP Files.

45. Letter, Cahill to Pearson, January 15, 1938; letter, Louis Bonney to Cahill, January 15, 1936, FAP Files.

46. Frances M. Pollak to Cahill, October 22, 1935, FAP Files.

47. "Unique W.P.A. School Expands Course," release for August 19, 1936, WPA Department of Information, p. 2.

48. "Report on Accomplishments of the W.P.A. Art Program," Cahill to Triggs, June 18, 1940, p. 6, FAP Files.

49. "Illinois—Final State Report, W.P.A. Art Program," pp. 1-3, WPA Files.

50. A. G. Pelikan, "Free Art Classes for Grade Children," *American Magazine of Art*, September, 1930, pp. 518 ff.

51. *New York Times*, January 11, 1931.

52. *Ibid.*, May 9, 10, 1934.

53. Memorandum, Parker to Cahill, March 9, 1936, FAP Files.

54. Memorandum, Cahill to Woodward, December 10, 1936, FAP Files.

55. Parker to Mrs. Dot Kennan, June 4, 1936, FAP Files.

56. *Federal Sponsored Community Art Centers*, Art Circular No. 1, WPA Technical Series, October 8, 1937, pp. 2-5.

57. Letter, Cahill to the College Art Association, October 14, 1937, FAP Files.

58. Daniel S. Defenbacher, "Report on the Winston-Salem Art Center," April 15, 1936, pp. 7-8, FAP Files.

59. *Bibliography on Art and Art Teaching*, Art Circular No. 2, WPA Technical Series, June, 1938.

60. Cahill to Donald Goodall, Director, Utah Art Center, December 13, 1938.

61. "Florida—Final State Report, W.P.A. Art Program," p. 1, WPA Files.

62. *Ibid.*, p. 16.

63. Letter, Curtis to Filler, June 15, 1943, ACLS Files.

64. Letter, Harry Kronenburg and Other Students to Harry Hopkins, June 1, 1938, WPA Files.

65. *A Brief History of the Organization and Policies of the Hamilton County Emergency Schools from 1933 to 1935*, p. 22, FERA Files.

66. *Art and Psychopathology*, an exhibition jointly sponsored by the psychiatric division, Bellevue Hospital, and the Federal Art Project, Harlem Community Art Center, October 24–November 10, 1938, FAP Files; W. Frederick Searle, "Art Classes with Mental Patients," *Mental Hygiene*, January, 1943, pp. 63-39.

67. Letter, Cahill to Fuller, March 7, 1938, FAP Files.

68. *Federal Sponsored Community Art Centers*, pp. 6-9.

69. Letter, Cahill to Frank L. Stevens, State Director, Montana, February 25, 1938, FAP Files.

70. Letter, R. B. Inverarity to Landin, September 16, 1943, ACLS Files.

71. Cyril Connolly, "England and the Arts," *Harper's Magazine*, July, 1945, p. 89.

72. Letter, Cahill to State Directors, April 7, 1936, FAP Files.

73.  Letter, Defenbacher to E. F. Crofut, Assistant Director of Exhibitions, November 5, 1936, FAP Files.

74.  Memorandum, Morris to Mrs. Charley Tidd Cole, November 17, 1936; *Federal Art Project Exhibitions, Purposes, Functions, Techniques,* n. d., FAP Files.

75.  E. E. Lowry, "A Review of the Federal Art Galleries in Wyoming," March 3, 1938, FAP Files.

76.  Memorandum, Parker to Morris, September 7, 1937, FAP Files.

77.  Letter, Parker to Riddick, August 24, 1938, FAP Files.

78.  *W.P.A. at Treasure Island, 1939-1940,* Works Progress Administration, Northern California, WPA Files.

79.  *Art Week,* National Report, November 25–December 1, 1940, n.d., pp. 1-2.

# 20

## The Origins of the Federal Theater Project

At the beginning of the depression there were three kinds of theater in the United States: the professional theater, which was confined almost exclusively to New York City and, whatever its merits, was at the mercy of a limited metropolitan clientele; the art or experimental theater, cultivated with few exceptions by the colleges and universities, which sought, by the cultivation of philosophic playwrights like Ibsen and O'Neill and by the introduction of novel techniques, to achieve a stage that was currently significant; and the amateur theater, developed by social service, the high school, and recreational agencies of the community, to the end that the theater, as an experience and not merely as a spectacle, be enjoyed by all.

The initial impact of the depression was first felt by the professional theater. The play producers on Broadway, like the producers of other commodities, closed their businesses and dismissed their employees when profitable operation became impossible. The professional actor, like other professionals, faced unemployment; and belonging to a well-organized union—Actors' Equity—he was in a position to bring organized pressure upon the body politic.*

Indeed, even before the crash of 1929 the economic status of the ac-

---

*Undoubtedly, the advent of the cinema, even before the depression, affected the economic status of the professional theater; but its effect upon the professional actor has generally been exaggerated. Indeed, Hollywood expanded rather than contracted the opportunities of the professional actor for employment, and, if a few disdained the new medium, the many sought and quickly found greener pastures.

483

tor, except perhaps of the few eminent performers, was not enviable. Alfred L. Bernheim estimated that in the prosperous season of 1928-29 some 6,000 actors in dramatic or musical performances in New York City averaged but 14.6 weeks of employment a year.[1] Robert Littell in the same year concluded that even with a salary of $200 a week, an actor would probably earn only about $1,000 a year.[2] Willson Whitman, using Equity's statistics for that same successful year, carried the analysis further. She found that 79 per cent of Equity's employed members worked less than nine weeks of the year, 40 per cent only three and one-half weeks, and 30 per cent of its 8,000 members were unemployed. Then she turned to *Billboard* calculations for the year 1937 to report that actors seeking engagements in the commercial field were "at liberty" 46.88 weeks per year.[3]

A condition that was naturally unhealthy became even more grave with the depression. In the season of 1931-32 every Shubert theater in Chicago was dark for an entire week in March; of the 253 companies playing in or near New York City, 213 had closed by the middle of May; two-thirds of the legitimate theaters in New York City were closed for the larger part of the year; by the end of July only six were open on Broadway. Of the members of Actors' Equity (representing 98 per cent of all professional actors), 50 per cent less were employed in 1931 than in 1929. A similar decrease had affected theatrical musicians' employment, and stagehands were in no less serious a plight. Since the motion-picture industry was affected by the same recession in employment, the professional actor who was jettisoned by Broadway was not rescued by Hollywood.

In the beginning the problem of relief for unemployed professional actors was met haphazardly and without recourse to public assistance. The Actors' Fund, founded in the eighties, was the oldest organization for the relief of theater people. Its special concern was care for those who were incapacitated by illness or by age, or were otherwise unemployable. During the theater's prosperous years only a minority of actors had paid the annual dues of two dollars. Fortunately, Daniel Frohman, its president since 1903, had augmented its income by an aggressive program. By arrangement with Actors' Equity, a special benefit matinee for the fund was given in the twentieth week of every play's run. Proceeds from investments, some of which were made possible by generous bequests and by benefits, enabled the fund to extend about fourteen thousand weeks of aid to individual actors during the depression years.

In December, 1931, resourceful theater people organized the Actors' Dinner Club, which operated with a volunteer staff. Famous

Broadway personalities gave generously of their time; they took part in the nightly floor shows and appeared as guests whenever possible so that, by their presence, they might encourage the curious to rub elbows with the great of the theater. Outsiders paid a dollar for their dinner, and each dollar also provided dinner for a needy actor. Unemployed actors could secure tickets from various organizations, such as the welfare agencies of churches and clubs as well as Actors' Equity and Chorus Equity. Producers and managers co-operated by submitting lists of all possible openings, and these were read aloud at the Dinner Club several times each evening.

A year later, theater patrons and their friends recruited a volunteer staff to operate the Stage Relief Fund. Indomitable workers arranged many benefits and solicited every sort of donation, with generous response from within and without the ranks. Home relief and medical and dental care were provided. Later, a clothing division and a quartermaster's division were added and supported by donations. In addition to preserving the health and courage of unfortunate but able professionals, this fund constructively planned to create employment for its clients. The plan was to give new playwrights, directors, and actors opportunities to produce hitherto unproduced plays. Free theater space was arranged, and talent-seeking producers were encouraged to attend performances. Seasoned actors, directors, and dramatists were urgently invited to advise and direct the performances. The staff persuaded theatrical unions that an indulgent attitude about wages, hours, and the number of stage hands would be to the ultimate advantage of their members.

Another effort to create employment was sponsored by Actors' Equity through the so-called National Players. The plan was to prepare condensed versions of good legitimate plays and to book these productions with motion-picture chains across the country. An experiment with the scheme in Detroit seemed to justify its operation. The difficulty arose when the motion-picture chains insisted upon so many concessions that Equity, convinced that the terms thus imposed would seriously endanger the artistic value of the productions and the working conditions of its members, withdrew its sponsorship.

## THE THEATER CODE OF 1933

While the professional actors were exhausting their limited means and attempting through self-help and the aid of friends to weather the storm, the producers in the profit-making theater were persuading the

National Industrial Recovery Administration that they, like other industries, both deserved and needed the aid of a code of fair competition. Representatives of every branch of the enterprise worked with unprecedented unity to prepare "The Code for Fair Competition for the Legitimate Full Length Theatre and Theatrical Musicians," which in August, 1933, was approved by the President.*

At the preliminary hearings such statistical information as was available was presented. The League of New York Theaters reported that the number of producing concerns and the number of productions were reduced by 50 per cent between 1928 and 1933. From a reputed 1928 total of twenty-five thousand employees, it claimed a reduction by 1933 to four thousand. The International Alliance of Theatrical Stage Employees submitted reports of conditions in fifty-one cities—practically all the cities in the country that had legitimate shows in 1933; according to these reports, 6,010 stage hands were currently employed at an average yearly wage of $681.

Because the NIRA was short-lived and in the main ineffective, the code need not be closely examined. Toward the close of 1934, shortly before a decision of the Supreme Court ended the life of the NIRA, Actors' Equity took stock of the situation and concluded that code regulations were being so widely ignored that abandonment was indicated. In its assay of the experiment it listed as permanent gains only three provisions: the establishment of limited rehearsal time, rehearsal pay, and a minimum wage-scale based upon admissions. At about the same time Brock Pemberton, summarizing the year's theatrical progress, said that the code's efforts to put an end to the "cut-rate malady," the "two-for-one," and the "forty-cent throwaway" had been completely ineffective.[4]

The failure of the code to resuscitate the legitimate theater business derived in part from the unwillingness or inability of the members to observe its provisions; but it was not, in the main, an indictment of the business. The theater code, like other codes of the NIRA, was predicated upon the proximate advance of economy recovery; when recession occurred, the code collapsed, and the producer no less than the actor was left at the mercy of circumstances.

---

*Because of special conditions of relative insignificance, repertory shows, tabloids, show boats, tent shows, and similar organizations were exempted from the provisions of the code.

As the depression deepened, it became clear that professional actors could not maintain themselves in a condition free from want. The assistance of organized charity, private or public, was needed.

Accordingly, in 1933, the Entertainment Committee of the Stage Relief Fund sponsored two small but relatively successful projects. The first of these operated as the Barter Theater. In New York City thirty needy actors, actresses, and stage workers formed a stock company under the direction of Robert Porterfield. The committee procured donations of most of the necessary properties and arranged for reduced royalties. Martha Washington College in Abingdon, Virginia, gave the use of its theater for thirteen summer weeks. Living quarters were provided in a near-by inn, co-operatively run. The thirty-cent admission fee could be paid in food or in money. The company reported happy work, health, and maintenance, if not affluence, and a high degree of artistic accomplishment. The experiment was so successful that it was extended through a second summer.

The other project was the first work-relief project for actors to be supported by public funds. In Nassau County, New York, fourteen entirely destitute resident actors formed a stock company, the Playground Players. This group persuaded the director of recreation of the Emergency Relief Bureau of the Nassau County Committee for Adult Education, a branch of the New York State Board of Education, to pay its members forty cents an hour to produce plays. The Stage Relief Fund recognized the project as providing what it considered the only adequate kind of relief for theater people. It loaned the company fifty dollars and procured a royalty-free play from the Century Play Company. The workers built and painted the scenery. In June, 1933, the company gave its first performance and, subsequently, played in nearly every town in the county, usually in schoolhouses, charging thirty-five cents admission. Because salaries, averaging nineteen dollars a week, were paid by state funds, the loan was soon repaid. All receipts thereafter—about four thousand dollars in one season—went toward financing local charities.

Late in 1933, Antoinette Perry of the Stage Relief Society communicated with interested officials in the FERA in Washington. In a letter to Mrs. Woodward she reported the operation of these two projects and announced that the Stage Relief Society had received 2,233 applications for aid in 1933. As a remedy, she submitted "A Proposed Plan to Give Employment to the Allied Workers of the Theatre." A national board of representatives of professional theatrical groups was to have headquarters in New York City; in addition, there were to be three regional centers. Each state, with its own touring company and director, would be guided by national policy as determined by the board, and its activities co-ordinated by the regional offices. It was estimated that at least three thousand workers would be employed under this plan.[5]

Eva Le Gallienne, founder and director of the Civic Repertory Theater, also was consulted. Her approach to the subject was from a totally different point of view. She believed that only high production standards maintained by sound dramatic education for theater workers, together with low admissions, would create a permanently healthy American theater, and that only such a theater could compete with the growing appeal of the cinema. When in Washington conferences she heard talk about hundreds of touring companies giving hundreds of plays everywhere, she stated her conviction that hasty handling of the problem on a mass employment basis would lead only to a more desperate situation for actors and to oblivion for the living drama in the United States. Her organization employed about one hundred people and gave free education to fifty students each year; she asked that the government "protect" it, meaning protection against financial failure. A government subsidy of $90,000 a year would, she calculated enable her enterprise, with its thirty-five completely equipped touring productions, to operate without a deficit.[6]

Miss Le Gallienne's scheme was impossible, for despite its name her Civic Repertory Theater was a private enterprise, and FERA funds could not be used to support other than public organizations. In addition, her strong emphasis upon professional standards ran counter to the influential point of view of Jacob Baker and the Washington staff, who were thinking in terms of the social service philosophy.

### THEATER PROJECTS UNDER THE CWA AND THE FERA

The creation of the CWA in November, 1933, which through the CWS allotted funds for white-collar unemployed, gave a new and wider opportunity to assist actors in distress. In late December, 1933, Mrs. Charles H. Sabin, newly appointed chairman of the advisory committee on women's work of the New York State Civil Works Administration, appointed Emily Holt, associate counsel for Actors' Equity Association, to serve on her committee. Very shortly, Mrs. Holt headed a drama committee; there was little time left in which to make theater workers eligible for employment under the Civil Works Service program, and, if they were not so employed, there was little hope of any quick help for them. It was necessary that projects be approved and in operation by the fifteenth of January. Simplicity was the keynote; no possible controversial feature that might delay approval was permitted. The Dramatics Department of the New York CWA had been working on similar plans; it promptly and actively supported the proposal of Mrs. Holt's committee and wrote it up in simple form, as shown below.

## CIVIL WORKS SERVICE BUREAU
## CITY OF NEW YORK

NAME OF PROJECT:  THEATRICAL UNITS AS–206

CO-OPERATING SPONSOR: Board of Education

| Occupation | Persons Working | Days Working | Rate per Hour | Hours per wk. | Rate per wk. | Amount |
|---|---|---|---|---|---|---|
| Supervisors | 2 | 34 | | | $35.00 | $ 476 |
| Professional actors | 45 | 34 | | | 30.00 | 9,180 |
| Professional actors | 60 | 34 | | | 27.50 | 11,220 |
| Professional actors | 45 | + | | | 25.00 | 7,650 |

The above is composed of 5 companies of 20 actors and 5 companies of 10 actors.

| TOTAL | 152 | | | | | $28,526 |
|---|---|---|---|---|---|---|
| CONTINGENCIES | | | | | | — |
| None | | | | | | — |
| OTHER THAN PERSONAL SERVICE | | | | | | — |
| GRAND TOTAL | | | | | | $28,526 |

DESCRIPTION

Organization of small theatrical units to present classical and well known dramatic works (without royalties) in public institutions such as schools, hospitals, museums, etc., to be offered to public free of charge with cooperation of Actors' Equity Association.

Actors' Equity co-operated not only by waiving salary regulations and other union requirements but also by donating space and the services of its staff for the casting of plays. Twelve plays were selected of sufficient variety to provide for many types of actors. Every hurdle was cleared, and by the evening of January fifteenth, 150 actors had been selected from throngs of applicants and assigned to productions; some units began rehearsals on the sixteenth.

Since the appropriation of $25,000 was to be used exclusively to pay salaries, it was necessary to secure all non-labor costs elsewhere. Once more, friends of the theater came to its support; properties and space for rehearsal and for auditions were donated; funds were raised for such expenses as lighting and even make-up and carfare. By the time the initial appropriation expired, the project had so commended itself that an additional appropriation was granted.

Thus begun under the CWA program, the New York City program of work-relief for actors was expanded and continued into the FERA period (April 1, 1934, to June 30, 1935) under the direction of New York State's TERA. The program was almost exclusively recreational and educational. Performances were usually for underprivileged groups and for students; free performances were given for relief workers. The usual assignment was to direct recreation-center dramatic groups and to teach adult education and recreation dramatic courses. Twenty-seven instructors were thus assigned and paid with relief funds to train and rehabilitate unemployed young professionals at a school operated under the supervision of the University of the State of New York. The school solicited quarters and money to pay utility charges. It conducted classes for over a year with an average attendance of 1,000 students a week.

Another of the popular early activities of the Works Division of the New York City Public Welfare Department was the operation of portable theaters. These were built according to designs worked out by Cleon Throckmorton. The sides of a truck body were so constructed that they could be lowered to form a stage twenty by thirty feet with a height of thirteen feet. Simple sets, elaborately planned to make possible various productions, were provided; extremely successful amplifying systems were installed. By late summer, 1934, five trucks were giving performances in the parks of the city. Audiences were estimated to include as many as 30,000 people.

Another early activity, developed first in New York and later adopted throughout the country, was the provision of professional and amateur dramatic performances for the CCC camps. Resident dramatic directors, appointed from relief rolls, carried on amateur projects; the camps usually had, or contrived to construct, some sort of stage in their recreation halls. In addition, professional companies of about fifteen members traveled among the camps with their own costumes and properties.*

Other activities in New York City included storytelling and classes in public speaking, conducted in recreation centers by professional actors; marionette performances in all five boroughs; and the setting up of stages in play streets in the less-favored neighborhoods. By April, 1935, the dramatic activities of New York City's work-relief projects employed about 1,000 actors, technicians, and property men.

Next to New York City, Los Angeles County, California, had the largest number employed in dramatic activities in the CWA and FERA period. Sixteen acting companies provided free cultural recreation for thousands, as well as rehabilitating 691 workers, some of whom worked full-time and others only part-time. Types of production and performing units varied, but the general concept of the program was similar to that of New York. In San Francisco there were a radio unit and a Negro group.

In 1934 the Massachusetts Emergency Relief Administration developed in Greater Boston a drama and music division that attained flourishing proportions. Fostering and developing amateur artistic talent was the major concern of a program that was enthusiastically sponsored by local planning committees. In 1935, when the works division relinquished direction of these projects, there were seventeen community theaters in the Boston area alone. In addition, a Yiddish unit, a Negro unit, an Italian unit, a Theater of the Air, a Tent Theater, and dancing classes furnished employment for many; professionals taught all branches of dramatic art; costumes and properties were made at the workshops of the Civic Theater.†

Further comments about the Negro unit in Boston add to the im-

---

*This activity was later taken over by the Federal Theater Project, and will be more thoroughly discussed in that connection. *Vide infra*, pp. 558-60.

†A significant note bearing on the artistic merit of the ERA dramatic programs, which was regarded as inexcusably low by the later Federal Theater Project, is supplied by a statement accompanying the announcement of a third original play produced by the Boston Negro Unit: "The selection of another "original" to follow *Genesis* and *Weary Traveler*, which were both written by members of the Negro cast, is not, according to the Director of the Group, because professional actors and singers employed on E.R.A. projects fancy themselves as playwrights. Presentation of original plays is forced upon the Negro group by the fact that there is no provision under E.R.A. regulations for the payment of play royalties. The Negro Theatre is so recent a development in America that many splendid plays which we are anxious to give are still protected by copyright."[7]

pression that it resourcefully overcame the lack of production funds and the limitations imposed by the casting problem. Thus it achieved an original flavor that was widely popular. The director reported that, since most of his cast were college graduates, one of his most serious problems was teaching them to speak as Negroes are supposed to speak. Announced plans included a production of *Macbeth* in modern dress and of *Othello* with a Negro cast—the part of the Moor to be played by a white actor![8]

The emphasis upon the theater as an educational and recreational device was, as has already been indicated, prominent in the Middle West, and, in the period preceding the WPA, manifested itself most significantly in the work-relief program of Minnesota. The CWA in Minnesota inaugurated recreational and leisure-time programs with a threefold aim:

> . . . To provide employment for trained and experienced workers in the fields of recreation, dramatics, art, music, handicrafts and general community leadership; to provide worth while programs of leisure time activities which would contribute to the upbuilding of community spirit and morale; and to create an increased interest in and demand for healthful recreation and character building agencies so that there would be a carry-over in this direction long after C.W.A. and relief work is abolished.[9]

The CWA state office acted merely as a central clearinghouse to assist communities in programs fitted to their particular local needs. Eight of the eighty-seven counties operated dramatic programs; play contests and pageantry stimulated community participation; puppet projects were developed for educational use in libraries and schools, and for mental therapy in state hospitals, as well as for general popular entertainment.*

---

*It was in Minnesota that the only co-operative venture in the theater was attempted. Jacob Baker's interest in co-operatives as a solution to the economic crisis caused him to recommend the experiment. With the advice and approval of the Minnesota ERA and the regional adviser of the FERA the American Art Theater of Minneapolis, under the direction of Robert Breen and Wilma Davis, was incorporated as a self-help co-operative. This company, composed of thirty destitute actors and stagehands, planned to travel in its own specially designed truck with adequate properties and to perform in cities and small communities. It requested $12,000 for equipment and operating costs during rehearsal and the first few weeks, after which it was hoped that the venture would be self-supporting. The self-help co-operative division of the FERA in Washington alloted to the state $6,400 for non-labor costs, and the works division of the state ERA set up a professional project with a fund of $5,000 to carry salaries and early operating costs. Under the name of the Oxford Players, the company toured eleven weeks. Each week brought the financial reckoning closer, and, in the second month of its life, an additional grant of $5,000 was

Chicago, in spite of size and great need, seems to have been laggard in the matter of relief projects for theatrical workers. In the summer of 1935, it reported that about one hundred members of allied professions were being given employment in the educational field and six hundred as musicians, vaudeville performers, and stagehands in dramatic productions. Many parks in the city had outdoor stages. Records, however, reveal little detail and no significant contribution.

This survey of the use of work relief in support of dramatic activities during the CWA and FERA periods reveals that the predominant emphasis was educational and recreational. The cause of this tendency lay in the public character of the sponsorship. Under the FERA it was necessary that a project be sponsored by a state or local public agency, and it is apparent that only recreational and educational public agencies, like state or municipal boards of education or recreation, were legally empowered and properly equipped to sponsor dramatic activities. The state and local character of the sponsorship, therefore, determined the nature of the program.

Because the emphasis was recreational and educational, and thus reflected the social service theory of dramatics, the activities themselves stressed amateur rather than professional performance. From the point of view of the professional theater, which was to have more prominent expression in the period of the Federal Theater Project, the spectacles thus achieved were unworthy. The accomplishment, however, must be judged in terms of the purpose—the benefit of dramatic activity upon the performer rather than the effect of the performer upon the spectator. In addition, through public agencies of education and recreation the professional actor was being brought into touch with public purpose in these two areas, and thus his activities were integrated with those of the body politic.

THE WASHINGTON OFFICE

The establishment of the CWA, which temporarily federalized the administration of work relief, allowed the inauguration of federal projects. In the domain of art, in the specific sense, the PWAP was established by the Washington office. No comparable project, however, was attempted for the relief of actors, and the theater project in New York

sought and secured from the FERA. The venture finally collapsed, and the company was ordered to return to its base at Minneapolis.

City was the only work-relief project specifically designed for actors attempted in the CWA period. A nationwide federal theater project, however, was contemplated at this time. On February 6, 1934, Arthur Hanna of the Washington CWA office wrote:

> It seems very likely that there will be a National theatre program to operate for a few months this Spring. The exact form of this project is very indefinite at the moment but it would seem that the cheapest way to set up a number of units for the employment of actors, would be to establish stock companies in centers where there are now no "living actors" appearing.
>
> Whatever plan is established now, will be considered as a sample program and if it proves feasible, we hope it will be greatly enlarged.[10]

Even before that, Hanna had written to Emily Holt, of the Actors' Equity Association: "We are all interested in making the theatre movement a national project with Federal supervision if such can possibly be done when and if the Civil Works Administration has an increased allotment of funds."[11]

The provision of the Act of February 15, 1934, however, which prohibited federal projects, made further planning in this direction impossible, and the subsequent Works Division of the FERA was forced to be content to encourage such state and local projects as appealed to the various communities. As has already been indicated, these projects, except in a few places like New York City and Boston, were rarely theatrical projects as such, but rather educational and recreational projects in whose programs dramatic activities were included.

In the course of the Emergency Work Program of the FERA, however, working procedures for theatrical projects, as for the other arts projects, were elaborated. These were:

F6. 1. Organizing Theatrical Companies

F6. 2. Workshop and Theater for Marionettes and Puppets

F6. 3. Portable Theater

F6. 4. Dramatic Centers

1. Alfred L. Bernheim, *The Business of the Theatre* (New York: Actors' Equity Association, 1932), p. 125.

2. "Too Many Actors," *Literary Digest*, January 19, 1929.

3. Willson Whitman, *Bread and Circuses* (New York: Oxford University Press, 1937), p. 107.

4.  *New York Times*, December 30, 1934.
5.  Letter, Perry to Woodward, December 2, 1933, FERA Files.
6.  Letter, Eva Le Gallienne to Mrs. Roosevelt, January, 1934, FERA Files.
7.  Massachusetts Emergency Relief Administration, *Calendar, ERA. Shows, Concerts and Broadcasts*, No. 11 (March 19, 1935).
8.  *Ibid.*, No. 14, April 7, 1935.
9.  *Review of C.W.A. Activities in Minnesota*, FWA Library.
10.  Letter, Hanna to Rachel Crothers, February 5, 1934, CWA Files.
11.  Letter, Hanna to Emily Holt, January 23, 1934, CWA Files.

# 21

## The Organization and Operation of the Federal Theater Project

THE EMERGENCY OF A NATIONAL PLAN

The concept of a national theatrical project or series of projects the purpose of which would be to bring the theater to non-metropolitan areas and especially to rural districts had long occupied the minds of President and Mrs. Roosevelt; and the affinity of this concept with the philosophy of social service recommended it to the relief agencies of the federal government. Directly after the establishment of the CWA, Mr. Roosevelt had asked Harry Hopkins to explore the possibilities of a theatrical project that, though a book system, would seek to provide musical and dramatic entertainment for small and remote communities. He repeatedly emphasized this educational and recreational purpose both before and after the beginning of the WPA, and, in December, 1934, he reminded Hopkins of his earlier request for such a plan. Hopkins in turn delegated to Jacob Baker the specific assignment of formulating it.[1]

Baker, when he took this assignment, was not without suggestions. Beginning in January, 1934, and inspired largely by the initiation of the New York City theatrical project on January 15 of that year, the Washington office of the CWA—and after it, the FERA—had been flooded with a deluge of suggestions for work relief for actors from every kind and condition of man and organization. These plans varied from the commonplace to the fantastic, from modest subsidies for a small stock company to huge outlays employing thousands of men. Broadway producers, singly and in groups, submitted their suggestions, little-theater groups pleaded on their own behalf; marionette operators, summer theatricals, manufacturers of portable stages, all sought aid. Trade and union groups within the theatrical profession exposed their rivalries in their competition for support.

Among the early outstanding plans was that of Herman Gantvoort, a Broadway producer who had been associated with Victor Herbert and in the ten years prior to 1934 had produced eight plays on Broadway. In essence, the plan was for the government to establish a fund of one million dollars to form a National Theater Organization.[2] The plan, as initially presented, had the approval of, among others, Eddie Dowling, Brock Pemberton, Arthur Hopkins, and George M. Cohan.

On March 25, 1934, Cohan sent a telegram to Harry Hopkins in support of the plan. Arthur Hanna wrote in reply:

> We received some time ago a copy of Mr. Gantvoort's proposal for the National Theatre Organization. As this proposed project is essentially for the re-financing of business, we regret that this Administration cannot adopt it as it does not fit into our present relief program.[3]

The Washington office of the CWA was correct in its interpretation of Gantvoort's plan. It was, in essence, a subsidy for producers.

Gantvoort and his friends were persistent, however, and from February, 1934, to June, 1935, his plan was kept before the attention of the Washington CWA and FERA offices. The Act of February 15, 1934, which outlawed federal projects and enacted the liquidation of the CWA, caused a contraction in relief expenditures that made further consideration of the plan futile. Finally, on August 31, 1934, in a letter to Gantvoort, Baker summarily disposed of the plan in the following words: "This will simply confirm in writing what I told you several times in conversation, that the Federal Emergency Relief Administration is not a lending agency and cannot lend money to business enterprises."[4]

Another early plan was that suggested by George M. Gatts, representative of the National Dramatic Stock Association. Entitled "A Plan Proposed to Relieve Unemployment among Actors, Stage Employees, Musicians, Scenic Artists and Other Allied Theatrical Workers," dated January 11, 1934, it was addressed to Aubrey Williams. The plan read in part:

> Conceding the wide spread unemployment existing in the legitimate branch of the theatrical business this plan would provide employment for the so-called middle class of theatrical worker among whom distress is the greatest. It is proposed to install throughout the country a chain of perma-

nently located dramatic companies presenting plays on a weekly change basis. During 1929 and 1930 over two hundred of such companies were successfully operating in the United States. Today that number has dwindled to twenty or thirty companies; thus, in practically every city with a population of over one hundred thousand there is available first class, fully equipt theatres now dark which would welcome the installation of such organizations.[5]

Gatts himself came to Washington early in January, 1934, and remained there some time in order to press his plan. Again, however, the prohibition of federal projects in the Act of February 15, 1934, created a stumbling block. Moreover, Gatts's plan, like Gantvoort's, was essentially a device to help the managers, and therefore could not be initiated under the statutory limitations and rules of the CWA or the FERA.*

While the producers and managers were soliciting government aid, Actors' Equity was not idle. The first actors' project, established with CWA funds in New York City on January 15, 1934, was largely the result of Equity's pressure and co-operation. As already indicated, twelve companies were thereby established to give performances in schools, hospitals, and other public institutions in the city. This experiment was so successful that arrangements were made to send the companies on tour to CCC camps in New York State. The favorable reception these performances generally received in the camps inspired a plea for the extension of the itinerary outside the state. This problem was one that, in April, 1934, the Washington office of the FERA was considering.[7]

By June, 1934, a plan was under consideration that would employ some fifteen to twenty companies on an eastern circuit for entertainment in CCC camps. In July, 1934, Lester A. Turner, in writing to Mary Inez Ross, suggested an expansion of the camp program to include: (1) lectures and lessons in amateur dramatics to be given at the camps; (2) co-ordination of play presentation in the public schools with courses in history and English; and (3) the creation of a play library in connection with the work in the public schools. Turner believed that in this way amateur dramatics would be encouraged and a relationship established between the theater and public education.[8] The extension of dramatic activities among the CCC camps was, as indicated elsewhere, accomplished.

*Ralph T. Kettering, a Chicago producer of thirty years' experience, proposed a plan for a revival of the road. Instead of permanently located stock companies, such as Gatts suggested, Kettering recommended fifteen traveling companies that would play in fifteen theaters in fifteen cities, one week at a time. He was convinced that, if the government would underwrite his plan to the amount of $500,000, the companies would become self-supporting within ten weeks' time. As Hanna said in his reply to the proposal, "A project for the financing of the theatre is one which this program cannot establish."[6]

By January, 1935, Frank Gillmore, president of Actors' Equity, had elaborated another plan that he summarized in a letter to the President.[9] Gillmore was invited to come to Washington to confer with Jacob Baker. Several conferences were held, as a result of which a comprehensive plan for a national theatrical project was elaborated and assumed final shape by May 15, 1935. It was discovered, however, that this plan, too, involved a subsidy on a commercial basis and was thus ineligible for FERA funds.*

In the spring of 1935, on the eve of the inauguration of the Theater Project, Elmer Rice went to Washington in support of his Theater Alliance, which had been recently incorporated under the laws of New York State. The by-laws of the organization established it as a democratic co-operative, entirely non-profit and, it was hoped, self-sustaining. A nationwide subscription list was to assure its success; its program was to be repertory. Decentralization of the theater was its aim, and its integration with community organizations was desired.

Rice found the plans that the national office of the WPA had in mind for the theater were, if not definite, far advanced. Accordingly, he at once submitted recommendations for a nationwide federal project. He proposed that a government agency should buy or lease a hundred theaters in large communities to be rehabilitated by WPA workers as community art centers. For these theaters, permanent repertory or stock companies should be established, and out-of-town actors in New York should be persuaded to return to their homes and join these groups. He believed existing little-theater organizations should be included, and that eight thousand people could be employed, including musicians, playwrights, composers, and other theatrical workers. The organization would be self-liquidating if the government pooled, on a national level, all revenues and costs. Finally, he stated his conviction that the federal agency must have as director a strong leader with practical knowledge of theater problems.[10]

## THE CHOICE OF A NATIONAL DIRECTOR

Jacob Baker and his staff studied theese various plans. The appropriation that enabled the President to establish the WPA had cleared the way for an arts program, and it was now the opinion of the Washington office that the program should include a theater project. The problem

---

*A group of New York producers revised the plan with the advice of Actors' Equity and William P. Farnsworth, NRA theatrical code director, hoping to make it eligible for an RFC loan, but nothing came of it.

was the choice of a director. Baker was responsible for making such a choice; and if he had been hitherto unaware of the tensions within the theater, he was now well informed. The professional theater, as he saw it, was interested mainly in a subsidy that would enable it to reconstitute itself financially. To choose a director from among its representatives would have been interpreted as favoritism toward one producer as against others. The professional actors, on their part, were well organized, but not united among themselves. Actors' Equity Association represented the legitimate players, but to choose one of their number would alienate the American Federation of Actors, which represented vaudeville, variety, and circus performers. There was left the independent theater, as represented in little theaters, college theaters, and other such organizations. The difficulty here was that of the plans which had been submitted, few came from the independent theater or were concerned with its future. Nonetheless, Baker's final choice was a woman whose name, in the summer of 1935, was unknown on Broadway, and whose connection with the theater was limited to the direction of the Vassar Experimental Theater.

There can be little doubt that, although the choice rested with Baker, the initiative came from above. Hallie Flanagan, like Harry Hopkins, came from Grinnell College, Iowa. As early as February, 1934, Hopkins had solicited the advice of Mrs. Flanagan. In *Arena*, she writes:

> My first intimation that the problem of unemployed theatre workers was of any concern to the government of the United States came in February of 1934 when Mr. Harry Hopkins telephoned me from New York. "We've got a lot of actors on our hands. Suppose you come in to New York and talk it over."
>
> I told Mr. Hopkins that I was sailing the next week to take a theatre job in England. "What kind of a job?" he said. I explained that Mr. Leonard Elmhirst had invited me to direct the theatre at Darlington Hall during my leave as director of the Vassar Experimental Theatre. "I don't know what an American wants to do in an English theatre," Mr. Hopkins said. "But if you're not interested, who would be?" I suggested Edith Isaacs, Eva Le Gallienne, Elmer Rice.[11]

Moreover, the Roosevelts had become acquainted at Hyde Park with Mrs. Flanagan's work at the Vassar Experimental Theater, and contact was established through President MacCracken of Vassar College.

Mrs. Flanagan's commitments prevented her from placing her services at the disposal of Harry Hopkins in February, 1934. It was not

500

until May, 1935, that the Washington office again approached Hallie Flanagan. She writes:

> None of these things were in my mind on May 16, 1935, when, after my return to Poughkeepsie, I received a telephone call from Washington. That being in the pre-government days before the long-distance telephone became a familiar demon, I was excited.
> It was Mr. Jacob Baker. "Mr. Hopkins wants you to come to Washington to talk about the unemployed actors."
> "Mr. Hopkins knows, of course, that my theater here is a non-commercial one, that I'm not connected with the commercial theatre?"
> "Yes, he knows that," said Mr. Baker. "He's conferring with commercial theatre people, too—there are dozens of theatre people down here. Mr. Hopkins wants to see you. Can you come?"12

Mrs. Flanagan came, and, after conferences with Jacob Baker and Harry Hopkins, was introduced to Mrs. Roosevelt. In the light of the future development of the Federal Theater Project, Mrs. Flanagan's account of her conversation with the President's wife is interesting. Mrs. Roosevelt had inquired about the plays presented at Vassar:

> In mentioning these plays, Mrs. Roosevelt asked me if our productions had been expensive to stage. "Your ambitious productions of Shakespeare and other classics as well as modern plays—weren't they staged with little expense? Wouldn't it be possible to do similar productions which would look well without spending much money?" I said that the Vassar Experimental Theatre operated on a small budget, relying scenically chiefly upon light, that we did not pay for labor, and that critical standards were obviously not those of Broadway. There was another thing, she went on to say: the whole question of whether the time had come when America might consider the theatre, as it was considered abroad, a part of education. Probably not, if it were put to a vote in just that way. Probably because of our heritage of Puritanism in its relation to the stage, the theatre would be the last of the arts to be so accepted; however, since Congress had appropriated money to take care of people in need, wasn't there a chance, at least, of trying it?
> As I rose to leave, Mrs. Roosevelt said, "I shall write President Mac-Cracken that I hope you are going to help work it all out."
> I left Mrs. Roosevelt, feeling that a great new social plan was under way and eager to help work it out.13

In the succeeding month negotiations leading to the acceptance by Mrs. Flanagan of the post of director of the Federal Theater Project were initiated. After completing her work at the Vassar summer school, she joined the Washington staff in August, 1935.

Late in July, 1935, Mrs. Flanagan accompanied Harry Hopkins on a trip to Iowa City, Iowa. Her conversation with him, as reported in

*Arena*, again stressed the social service aspect of the relief program in the arts. Hopkins asked:

> What part could art play in this program? Could we, through the power of the theatre, spotlight the tenements and thus help in the plan to build decent houses for all people? Could we, through actors and artists who had themselves known privation, carry music and plays to children in city parks, and art galleries to little towns? Were not happy people at work the greatest bulwark of democracy?[14]

The occasion of Hopkins' address at Iowa City was the laying of the cornerstone of a new University Theater at the University of Iowa, and, since Iowa City was at the moment the meeting place of the National Theater Conference, he took the occasion to announce the appointment of Mrs. Flanagan as director of the Federal Theater Project. It was then that he made the statement, ". . . I am asked whether a theatre subsidized by the government can be kept free from censorship, and I say, yes, it is going to be kept free from censorship. What we want is a free, adult, uncensored theatre."[15]

Mrs. Flanagan, when, in May, 1935, she first examined the many plans that had been suggested to the Washington office, had come to the conclusion that Elmer Rice's plan for community centers was the best; and with this plan in mind, she drew up a rather indefinite scheme in which she advised a slow beginning with employment of some 7,500 persons. She ended her report by stating that "the Government at Washington would not only be caring for the unemployed but recreating a national theatre and building a national culture."[16]

Subsequently, however, Mrs. Flanagan sought the advice of E. C. Mabie of the State University of Iowa, whose emphasis was toward the development of a regional theater. The two, working together, evolved a plan meant to appeal to the non-professional element in the theater. It provided for the employment of 30,650 people in three major fields —regional centers, units in states, and units in existing drama departments of educational institutions. The plan was submitted to Baker, who in turn asked the opinion of Bruce McClure and his staff. The report on it, though it conceded its worthiness, questioned its practicability, and pointed out that a large number on relief rolls were not good actors and that a large number of professional actors, including those in vaudeville and variety, demanded consideration. The report advised the continuation of such ERA projects as were already under way and suggested that thought be given to the advisability of collecting admissions. It viewed the Mabie-Flanagan plan as so ambitious that it would involve administrative and other expenses far beyond the capacities of the WPA.[17]

## THE ESTABLISHMENT OF THE WASHINGTON OFFICE

This was the situation when, on August 27, 1935, Hallie Flanagan took the oath of office as national director of the Federal Theater Project. Mr. Mabie joined her in Washington during September, and her assistant at Vassar, Lester Lang, was added to the Washington Staff of the Theater Project.

By early October the plan of the project had taken form. The various types of work to be attempted were listed in *Supplement No. 1 to Bulletin No. 29* as follows:[18]

A — *Theatre*
1. Theatre Companies—as a separate department of an existing non-profit theater organization
2. Independent Theatre Companies
3. Marionette Theatres
4. Children's Theatres
5. Vaudeville, variety, and circus projects
6. Theatre Companies traveling between camps
7. Teaching of theatre techniques
8. Theatre research and publication
9. Other

The first manual of the project, entitled *Instructions*, is dated October, 1935, and was issued early in that month. The *Instructions* defined the purpose of the project as follows:

> The primary aim of the Federal Theatre Project is the re-employment of theatre workers now on public relief rolls; actors, directors, playwrights, designers, vaudeville artists, stage technicans, and other workers in the theatre field.
>
> The far reaching purpose is the establishment of theatres so vital to community life that they will continue to function after the program of this Federal Project is completed.[19]

A comparison of the second aim with the first is instructive, and points clearly to the conflict between the professional concept of the theater and the social service concept. The primary aim, as stated, emphasizes professional employment, which was centered in the commercial theater and concentrated mostly in New York City. The less immediate aim, as stated, was the integration of the theater with community life, presumably in the less metropolitan communities, where much depended upon the co-operation of the public agencies of the communities. The two aims, if not contradictory, were at least contrary, as the history of the Federal Theater Project was to show.

Part II of the *Instructions* lists the types of projects in more detail than *Supplement No. 1 to Bulletin No. 29*. The first type described is "Theatre companies—as a separate department of an existing nonprofit theatre organization." This represents Mabie's emphasis, and is listed first presumably because it held first place in the minds of the writers of *Instructions*. The text reads:

> Already existing public theatres or non-profit private theatres of proven excellence, wherever possible, will be selected as the centers about which certain Federal Theatre projects will be developed. It is suggested that such theatres cooperate in the forming of separate, supplementary, producing units composed of from twenty to one hundred or more theatre workers from relief lists.
>
> Certain theatres in universities, towns, or cities have already developed a dramatic expression for their individual regions; such theatres may properly cooperate with Federal Theatre units to test plays of native playwrights, to give a classical repertory, or otherwise to supplement their existing production program. It is assumed that such supplementary theatre units will use the stage and technical plant of the fostering theatre organization, except in certain cases in which additional facilities may be required to house properly the expanded program.[20]

The second permissable activity listed is "Independent theatre companies," described as follows:

> Where no such regional theatre is present, or is practicable as a center, new, independent theatre companies may be formed under the Federal Theatre Project; in which case, such a theatre company should have a definite production program which has the possibility of becoming integrated with community life. It is advisable that this theatre organization be requipped with its own technical work shops.[21]

The important parts of this statement, in terms of the original purpose of the project, are: (1) the emphasis upon independent companies as merely supplementary to existing non-profit theater groups; and (2) the stress upon integration with community life. It is clear that the heart of the project was to be the independent theater movement, as represented in the little theater, the community theater, and the university theater. Since none of these groups, except by way of rare exceptions, employed professional actors or aimed at professional competence, the problem presented itself as to how, without a radical change, professional actors, concentrated as they were on Broadway, could be brought physically and spiritually within the ambit of the independent non-profit theater.

## THE REGIONAL DIRECTORS

In the meantime, Mrs. Flanagan had been appointing her regional directors. The list, as it stood on November 9, 1935, was as follows:

1. New York City Region — Elmer Rice, Regional Director; John Askling, Executive Director; New York, New York

2. New York State Region — Philip Barber, Regional Director; George Gatts, Assistant Regional Director; New York, New York

3. New England Region — Hiram Motherwell, Regional Director,* Boston, Massachusetts

4. New Jersey–Pennsylvania Region — Jasper Deeter, Regional Director; Helen Schoeni, Assistant Regional Director; Philadelphia, Pennsylvania

5. Ohio Region (Ohio, West Virginia, Kentucky) — Frederick McConnell, Regional Director; K. Elmo Lowe, Assistant Regional Director; Cleveland, Ohio

6. Virginia–Carolinas Region — Frederick H. Koch, Regional Director, Chapel Hill, North Carolina

7. Southern Region (Alabama, Florida, Georgia, Mississippi, Louisiana, Tennessee) — John McGee, Regional Director, Birmingham, Alabama

8. Central Region (Illinois, Indiana, Michigan, Wisconsin) — Thomas Wood Stevens, Regional Director, Chicago, Illinois

9. Prairie Region (Iowa, Minnesota, Missouri, Kansas, Nebraska, North Dakota, South Dakota) — E. C. Mabie, Regional Director, Iowa City, Iowa

10. Southwestern Region (Arkansas, Oklahoma, Texas) — Charles Meredith, Regional Director, Dallas, Texas

*The original appointee for New England, Charles Coburn, resigned shortly after his appointment and was succeeded by Hiram Motherwell.

| 11. | Northwestern Region (Idaho, Montana, Washington, Oregon, Wyoming) | Glenn Hughes, Regional Director, Seattle, Washington |
|---|---|---|
| 12. | California Region (California, Nevada, Colorado, Utah, Arizona, New Mexico) | Gilmore Brown, Regional Director, Pasadena, California; J. Howard Miller, Assistant Regional Director, Los Angeles, California |
| 13. | District of Columbia Region (Delaware, Maryland) | Director, Federal Theater Project, Washington, D.C. |

The preponderance of representatives of the independent theater in this group is apparent. Brown, McConnell, Deeter, Meredith, and McGee all represented little theaters; Koch, Hughes, and Mabie, as directors of university theaters, reflected the same point of view. Thomas Wood Stevens, who had been with the Carnegie Institute of Pittsburgh, and was at the moment director of the Globe Theatrical Productions in a repertory season at the California-Pacific International Exposition in San Diego, was more interested in the independent than in the profesfessional theater, as was Hiram Motherwell, former editor of *Stage*. Philip Barber had been stage manager for the New York Group Theater. Five of the regional directors—Mabie, Hughes, Koch, Brown, and McConnell—were dollar-a-year men, and Jasper Deeter was to serve only part time, since he was already involved in current commitments with the Hedgerow Theater. Of the twelve regional directors, only Elmer Rice was representative of the legitimate Broadway theater, and he was a playwright, not a producer.

On October 8, 1935, the regional directors met in Washington, where they were addressed by Hallie Flanagan and representatives of the WPA Washington staff. Mrs. Flanagan began by paying her respects to the McLean mansion, where the project was housed, and proceeded to contrast the passing of individual patronage with the new emphasis upon the theater as an agency of democratic education.[22] Lester Lang followed with an analysis of Federal Theater Project procedure; and on the next day Bartlett explained Treasury procedure and Goldschmidt expounded WPA procedure. At the close of the conference one of the regional directors immediately resigned, and others were dissuaded with difficulty from following his example.

The regional directors saw the difference between the word and the act. On becoming aware of the procedural limitations of the program, those who were interested in the non-professional theater realized that the creation of regional theaters, rooted in the desires and character of the non-metropolitan community, required something more than actors whose background was exclusively professional. They were bewildered, and some of them were so discouraged that they were ready, then and there, to break away from the experiment.

## HALLIE FLANAGAN

Mrs. Flanagan had been dedicated to the theater from her college days. After graduation from Grinnell College, Iowa, where, for a time, she was a contemporary of Harry Hopkins, she entered Radcliffe College, and attended the 47 Workshop of George Pierce Baker, whose production assistant she eventually became. When, in 1925, Professor Baker left Harvard for Yale, he presented as his first production in his new position a satirical comedy by Mrs. Flanagan entitled *Incense*. In 1926 Mrs. Flanagan attained the distinction of being the first woman to be awarded a Guggenheim Fellowship, and her assignment was to study new methods of theater production in several European countries. Mrs. Flanagan visited Ireland, England, Norway, Sweden, Denmark, Latvia, France, Czechoslovakia, Germany, Italy, and Russia, and made permanent her experiences and impressions in a book entitled *Shifting Scenes of the Modern European Theatre*, published in 1928. This book was well received by the critics and reveals the author's paramount interest in the art theater, a preoccupation that was to color her direction of the Federal Theater Project.

When she returned from Europe, Mrs. Flanagan joined the faculty of Vassar College, where she became director of the Vassar Experimental Theater. In this position she was able to devote herself to experimentation, and the story of that theater is told by Mrs. Flanagan in *Dynamo*.[23] As an experiment in dynamogeny, which Funk and Wagnalls defines as "the reinforcing effect of sensorial stimuli upon muscular action," she produced, in 1928, Chekhov's *Marriage Proposal* as "a play with three faces"—realistic, expressionistic, and constructivist."[24] As an experiment in the function of the dynameter, "a kind of transformer," she produced Euripides' *Hippolytus*.[25] Finally, as an experiment in the function of the dynamograph, "an instrument for recording . . . the condition of the track . . . the speed of the train . . . the power consumed in hauling," Mrs. Flanagan produced T. S. Eliot's *Murder in the Cathedral*. Alan Porter reviewing the play in the *Vassar Miscellany* wrote:

. . . The mere picture of the chorus will not be forgotten. Their costumes combined remarkably the suggestions of medievalism and poverty; their faces were haunting in the variety of their pathos. Their movements interested and satisfied the eye. . . . This is something which our Vassar Experimental Theatre does superbly well—as far as my experience goes, unmatchably well.[25]

This concept of the primacy of the chorus again emphasizes Mrs. Flanagan's interest in the experimental theater. Indeed, her devotion to the college theater, unlike that of Mr. Arvold and Mr. Koch, derived from the belief that the college stage provides a unique occasion for dramatic experiment.[26] It is important that Mrs. Flanagan's idea of the place and purpose of the theater be understood, for, of all the arts projects, none assumed the personality of its national director so clearly as did the Federal Theater Project.

This stress upon experiment had certain corollaries. In the first place, there was a tendency to stress, if not the spectacular, at least the novel. The history of the Vassar Experimental Theater disclosed this inclination, and it is apparent in the presentation of Chekhov's *Marriage Proposal*, as well as Thornton Wilder's *Our Town*, which attempted a synthesis of stage and film techniques. In the Federal Theater Project the "Living Newspaper" plays, in like manner, strove to achieve on the stage an effect like that presented on the screen by the newsreel. Orson Welles's adaptation of *Macbeth* to a Haitian milieu was essentially a *tour de force*, and the one "smash hit" of the project, Chicago's *Swing Mikado*, was a clever adjustment of the Gilbert and Sullivan operetta to the environment of Negro rhythm.

This love of the novel engendered a correlative impatience with the commonplace. It was natural that Mrs. Flanagan, because of her preoccupation with the art theater, should be concerned with high standards of production; but it was futile for her to seek to achieve at one and the same time the de-urbanization of the American theater and a metropolitan criterion. It is significant that Greater Boston, under the FERA, created and enjoyed a popular and acceptable dramatic program that included both professional and amateur productions, while, under the Federal Theater Project, the same area supported an insignificant program. Mrs. Flanagan's verdict that the Boston FERA dramatic program was substandard may have been true, at least from the point of view of the art theater; but her resolution of the problem—the practical abandonment of dramatic activity in that area—was not calculated to domesticate the theater in the community.

In view of this emphasis, it is not surprising that, in the course of time, the Federal Theater Project became, to all intents and purposes, the New York City Theater Project; and Mrs. Flanagan eventually left Washington and established her headquarters in Mecca. This hegira, more than anything else, betokens the character of the project and dramatically illustrates the political no less than the philosophic causes of its problems.

The Federal Theater Project failed equally to relate itself in any substantial form with the college or high-school theater, or with dramatic activities in public educational and recreational groups. Drama, so far as it was supported by the WPA in civic activities of this kind, was the concern of the recreational and educational divisions of the agency, and beyond the solicitude of the Federal Theater Project.

It is not surprising, therefore, that the regional directors who attended the Washington conference in October, 1935, were confused and disheartened. When they listened to Mrs. Flanagan, they were made to think in terms of a new art theater; when they read the *Instructions*, they were persuaded that a permanent community theater was the aim of the project; and when they listened to the WPA officials explain procedure, they reluctantly concluded that the sole purpose of the project was the employment of professional actors, properly certified for relief. During the life of the project its purpose was never properly clarified.

## THE INITIATION OF THE PROGRAM

Meanwhile, the project was getting under way. It was deemed advisable, at least for a time, to allow FERA projects already in operation to continue. Accordingly, theater projects in New York City, California, Boston, and Chicago were not interrupted.

Gradually, the other projects indicated in the *Instructions* were begun. In order to make use wherever possible of existing dramatic organizations, it was planned to organize supplementary units employing from 20 to 100 people or more from relief rolls, these units to use the plants of the directing agency. Where institutions had made progress in the development of regional and folk drama, it was deemed most desirable that they continue these activities and use Federal Theater units. Where no good organizations existed, independent companies were to be organized with a program definitely aimed at future integration with community life. It was recognized that these organizations would need their own technical workshops.

Marionette units were to be organized, either separately, as a supplement to already existing organizations, or in connection with new companies. It was expected that these units would be especially suitable for providing free performances in public institutions and unusually good media for developing folk drama of local and regional content.

Children's theater companies—adult actors organized to give plays suitable for children—were strongly recommended. They were expected to prove valuable for developing free entertainment. These groups were to be urged to depart from the use of old, worn-out plays and to develop new techniques and materials.

Where none existed, theatrical companies were to be organized to tour the Civilian Conservation Corps camps, and many additional instructors were to be appointed for the camps. Vaudeville, variety, and circus units were to be encouraged. Teaching was to be part of every unit that could justify its inclusion. Federal funds were to be used to pay salaries of instructors in such existing institutions as were able to present evidence that they could not themselves pay for these services but could wisely use them. Especially was this to be done if it seemed probable that such procedure would develop such a demand for instructors that eventually the institution would assume the cost. A research and publications division, closely modeled on the lines of the National Theater Conference Service Bureau was envisaged; it was to have the benefit of co-operation from the staff of the *Theatre Arts Monthly*, which had actively assisted the bureau.

During the month of October, as a result of conferences between the project and Actors' Equity, Mrs. Flanagan arrived at a definition of "professional" that established the character of the project. In its November issue *Equity Magazine* quoted from a letter addressed to the association by Mrs. Flanagan:

> 1. The object of the Federal Theatre Project is the reemployment of *professional* theatre people: actors, designers, stage hands and others who have hitherto made their living in theatrical professions. . . .
> 2. The Federal Theatre Project is designed to reemploy only such members of the theatrical profession as are skilled enough to have a reasonable chance of making a living in the theatre later; thus ensuring a standard of excellence to enable these theatre units to continue after the federal project is completed.[27]

This definition of "professional" as meaning only those who showed

510

evidence of theatrical employment in the past promised to restrict employment on the project to those who were members of theatrical unions: Actors' Equity for the legitimate stage; the American Federation of Actors for vaudeville and variety; and the International Alliance of Theatrical Stage Employees for stagehands and other workers in the theater.

Despite this concession to the professional actor, eager friends of the independent theater throughout the country enthusiastically supported the project as a result of Mrs. Flanagan's exploratory letters and talks. One of her first appointments was that of John McGee, a Grinnell College graduate who had directed the Purdue University Theater and the Birmingham (Alabama) Little Theater. He was assigned to survey the southern region and report what projects could be set up in the various states; later he was appointed regional director for the South; he began work early in September. Informal surveys of the same sort were being made by others who later were to direct the various regions.

As in the Music and Art projects, a regional organization was adopted. The country was divided into thirteen regions, the directors of which have already been enumerated.

Much space was devoted by the press of the nation to the announced plans of the Federal Theater Project. Although leaders in the educational branch were dismayed but not defeated, various legitimate theater figures voiced sentiments ranging from disapproval to profound lack of faith in the possibility of any worthwhile achievements except, perhaps, in the field of temporary employment. Eva Le Gallienne, expressing her conviction that only by presenting the very best theater could the ailing art become desirable to millions, said, "It is a vast mistake to feed the people of the nation upon very malnutritious and downright bad food."[28]

In the first few months of the project's existence, Mrs. Flanagan, like the other directors in Federal One, was under pressure from above to employ as many as possible as quickly as possible. The difficulties, however, due to inadequate information and the lack of co-operation on the part of WPA regional and state officers, sometimes seemed insurmountable. On September 24, 1935, Mrs. Flanagan put her experiences into a candid memorandum addressed to Bruce McClure:

> Two weeks ago at a staff meeting in Mr. Baker's office, he said "Is there any reason why these arts projects can't start next week?" . . .
> 1. The first reason projects cannot start is the failure on the part of the WPA to support the appointments of the Federal Arts directors and to expe-

511

dite such appointments. I had had a slate of six regional theatre directors I wished to appoint in Mr. McClure's office since the week before Labor Day; of six more since September 3. Two only have been approved and these only after they paid their own expenses and waited around for a week.[29]

After explaining that these appointments had been carefully considered and had the approval of competent judges in the American theater, Mrs. Flanagan continued:

> 2. The second reason why projects cannot start is the increasing emphasis on complicated procedure in starting projects. They are now subject to so many checks in states and districts that the whole affair is assuming the proportions of a colossal joke. Any assistant administrator in any State or locality can now negate or hold up indefinitely any project even if such a project has the approval of the Federal Theatre Director and his Regional representative.[30]

Mrs. Flanagan suggested that state WPA administrators be informed that their authority with respect to the Federal Arts Projects was different from that which they exercised over state and local projects, and that they should be instructed merely to expedite projects that met the approval of the federal director. Then she concluded:

> At the present time, the Federal Directors are not directors but are advisors. It is not in such a capacity they were hired, nor is it their intention to continue to function in a position which is at present all responsibility and no power.[31]

The regional directors who attended the October conference went back to their bases to get projects into operation as speedily as possible, with the assurance that clear lines of authority had been established and that WPA offices would co-operate as prescribed in administrative procedures. The directors' first duty, after the proper formalities to establish relations with their administrative superiors in the regions and the states, was to appoint in writing persons or committees professionally qualified to classify the workers whom the proper local employment boards were directed to refer to them at the request of the state administrators.

The reluctance of the state WPA administrators to recognize the line authority of the regional directors finally caused Jacob Baker, in January, 1936, to order the discontinuance of the regional organization in the Music, Theater, and Art projects.* Mrs. Flanagan, because she had

*Vide supra, pp. 162-64.

fewer people on her Washington staff than had the other arts projects, was permitted to retain five of her regional directors as assistants attached to the Washington office. These assistants were John McGee, with responsibility for the southern region; Hiram Motherwell in New England; Thomas Stevens in Chicago, with responsibility also for Illinois; E. Kendell Davis, who had been E. R. Mabie's assistant, stationed in Chicago and responsible for Missouri, Nebraska, and Iowa; and J. Howard Miller who was in charge in California and the West. These men, however, were now merely field advisers attached to the Washington office, and enjoyed no authority within the state WPA administrations. The other men who had been regional directors were either retained as advisers on a dollar-a-year basis or made state directors, as was Jasper Deeter in Pennsylvania. Thus there was no longer an intermediate level between the federal and the state levels.

ORIGINAL AUTHORIZATIONS TO THE STATES

Although very few projects were operating by the middle of November (nearly all were continuations from the FERA period), enough information had been collected for Mrs. Flanagan to give Baker estimates of the financial needs of the various states. Believing that most states had requested more than they needed, she had reduced the figures, and her plans provided for a reserve of $1,635,500 from the Theater Project's allotment of $6,784,036. The reserve would provide for projects in the thirteen states from which she had not, at that time, received applications. Of the southern states, only Texas and Florida were to have allotments. Recommendations as to the duration of the original projects differed; some were to be provided with enough money to operate for six months, but others, either because of too little information or because they definitely were exploratory or continuations of old projects of doubtful value, were to receive funds for only two, three, or four months. New York City was expected to need at least three million dollars for six months—probably more; California would use one million in three months, and Illinois and Massachusetts about a half million each for the same period. The first transfers of funds to the states were made on a one-month basis according to approved projects, but assurance of additional funds was given.[32]

In many states, and to a certain extent in Congress, there was a feeling that every state should have some of this money even though it had

513

few or no unemployed professional theater workers. Small local theatrical organizations were convinced that they contributed sufficiently to the benefit of their communities to merit federal support. From Cheyenne, Wyoming, a little-theater group appealed for enough money to pay a director's salary. To decide the question of eligibility, the regional theater director appealed for advice to the WPA educational adviser, who reported that the continuance of their work would, in fact, benefit the public of Cheyenne and of Laramie County. The national office, however, ruled against it; and indeed, since the group was under private auspices, it had no alternative.

In the early months the inadequacy of the project proposals also retarded initiation. In some cases the proposals were improperly prepared and were sent back by the Washington office for correction; in other cases state and local WPA administrations, because of lack of sympathy or failure to comprehend the requirements, delayed or refused their approval. Since the authorizations to the states were made on the basis of project proposals as first submitted and not as of the date of actual initiation, surpluses were often created in many states. These were often transferred to other states that had been able to begin operations more expeditiously, and needed more funds sooner.

ADMISSION FUNDS

One of the principal problems that confronted the Theater and Music projects was, as has already been indicated, the collection of admissions.* State and local projects, financed through FERA funds, had previously collected admissions; and in Chicago and Peoria, Illinois, for instance, this practice was continued in the early months of the WPA. Since, however, such collections, because they were made on a federal project, were necessarily covered into the miscellaneous receipts of the Treasury Department, the Theater Project did not benefit financially from the practice. In Washington, legal opinion was sought; and as early as October, 1935, the procedure that reached its formal expression in Appendix B to *Supplement No. 1 to Bulletin No. 29*, issued January 11, 1936, was informally approved. On October 22, 1935, Mrs. Flanagan wired her regional directors that, under a new ruling, co-operating sponsors might not collect admissions, but the Federal Theater unit it-

*Vide supra*, pp. 278-93.

self would collect and disburse currently all admission fees through bonded representatives of the U.S. Treasury Department. Such funds, she added, could be used for current expenses, transportation, and equipment.[33]

Confusion and uncertainty, however, continued; and as conversations with the GAO progressed, the fear became prevalent that admission charges might be banned, or—what amounted to the same thing so far as the Theater Project was concerned—might be approved but ordered covered into the miscellaneous receipts of the Treasury Department. In the latter case, the project itself would have no jurisdiction over their disbursement. In December, 1935, Jacob Baker, in answer to Mrs. Flanagan's appeals, dispatched a telegram authorizing immediate collection of admissions under the stipulation that they be deposited to a special deposit account under the direction of the local treasury disbursing officer.[34] A week later, Corrington Gill sent a similar authorization to Elmer Rice in New York City, in which he stated that any responsible project employee could collect and handle funds, but made no reference to disbursements from these funds.[35] Finally, as the day of decision approached, Hallie Flanagan wrote a final memorandum to Jacob Baker, in which she said that all the plans of the project had been made on the presupposition that admission funds would be used to provide adequate operating funds. She insisted that "no people on earth could run shows on ten per cent of labor costs. *We must have admissions.*"

On January 11, 1936, Appendix B to *Supplement No. 1 to Bulletin No. 29* was issued, and the procedure established whereby the project could collect and disburse admission funds.

### THE GENERAL ORGANIZATION OF THE PROJECT

The Federal Theater Project's organization was not uniform throughout its history. When it achieved final form, it consisted of three branches: administrative, service, and special productions. The administrative branch, which was always in theory but not always in fact located in Washington, worked in conjunction with the WPA Washington office in handling procedures, finance, relationship with unions, travel regulations, and records. The service branch, located in New York City, provided various services for each of the project units in the twenty states in which, in 1939, the project was in operation. These services, analyses of which will be later attempted, were: play-reading, for the purpose of compiling lists of recommended plays in various categories; revisions, translations, adaptations, and creation of plays; providing information concerning royalties; negotiating for plays and preparing contracts for their production, and for loan of personnel and equipment; and research. The special productions branch included national radio programs, information and children's theater (the latter in process rather than a completed fact). This branch also included divisions for participation in the World's Fairs at San Francisco and New York.

At the beginning and throughout the program the national director intimately concerned herself with advising and helping not only her field representatives but all the supervisors, directors, and individual workers on the many project units. Much of this advice was in the field of program-planning, and such of it as was concerned with administrative problems was at first taken care of by form letters. Personal visits frequently were made and personal interviews granted—most of this also for the purpose of program and national policy. In the matter of union relations Mrs. Flanagan was most active in New York City, where national union headquarters made decisions on nationwide union policies with respect to their relations with the Federal Theater Project.

The original central office staff was very small, the regional advisers and assistants many. In February, 1936, William P. Farnsworth, who had been executive head of the Legitimate Theater Code Authority, accepted the appointment as assistant national director, replacing Lester Lang. He relieved Mrs. Flanagan of many administrative details. Directors of the art projects had a dual function, and Mrs. Flanagan needed an assistant with Farnsworth's administrative experience and competence.

### THE HEGIRA

In early 1938 the situation in New York City with respect to Federal One became so critical that drastic change was indicated. Colonel Sommervell, the WPA administrator for New York City refused to accept responsibility if he was not given correlative authority, and Harry Hopkins, forced to make a decision, attempted to resolve the situation by making the arts projects in New York City what was in effect a separate state WPA administration.

Preliminary to this change, Mrs. Flanagan, on March 25, 1937, moved her headquarters from Washington to New York City and assumed, in addition to the national directorship, the directorship of the Federal Theater Project in New York City.[36] At the same time Harold Stein, who had previously been attached to the Professional and Service Division of the Washington office, was made administrative officer for all the projects under Federal One in New York City except the Federal Theater Project.[37]

Mrs. Flanagan's autonomy, however, was short-lived, for on July 26, 1937, Paul Edwards, who had been the state WPA administrator in Massachusetts, was given charge of Federal One in New York City in its entirety. Mrs. Woodward's memorandum read:

> This will supersede my memorandum of March 25 to Assistant Administrators and Division Heads, which set forth the organization of Federal Project No. 1 in New York City.
>
> *Mr. Paul Edwards* has been appointed Administrative Officer for Federal Project No. 1 in New York City, effective immediately.
>
> Federal Project No. 1 includes the Federal Art, Music, Theatre, Writers', and Historical Records Survey Projects.
>
> All communications concerning Federal Project No. 1 as a whole or any of its parts in New York City, should be addressed to Mr. Edwards, whose address is the Chanin Building, Lexington Avenue and 42nd Street, New York City.*[38]

Mrs. Flanagan, when she established her headquarters in New York, placed her Washington office in charge of an assistant. For a time it was managed by E. E. McLeish, who had headed an analysis unit responsible for the collection of information and the evaluation of reports from the field. In May, 1937, he was succeeded by J. Howard Miller, who had been state director in California. John McGee and Robert C. Schnitzer in turn directed the Washington office after Mr. Miller.

### ORGANIZATION OF PROJECT UNITS

At first, project units of the Theater Project were organized locally on a functional basis, i.e., a unit for repertory, another for marionettes,

---

*Edwards' authority was unique in that it approximated, if it did not equal, the authority of a state WPA administrator. As a result of his appointment, Federal One in New York City was removed from the jurisdiction of Colonel Somervell and was responsible directly to the national office in Washington. This arrangement in New York City lasted almost to the end of Federal One, in 1939.

another for an experimental company, etc. Moreover, in 1937, when the other projects under Federal One were organized on a statewide basis, the Theater and Music projects were permitted, but not required, to continue the functional organization.

In the early years of the project's operation, Mrs. Flanagan favored the functional plan. In time, however, careful examination of its working created the impression that it was wasteful of both time and money. The New York City project, for instance, with its some 5,000 project workers and its many operating divisions, was initially organized into functional units. In time, the circus, variety, and dance units were combined into one unit from three. In 1937 drastic budgetary pressure caused the elimination of some of the service divisions, and the absorption of their functions into one department. This process of integration, however, was not carried as far as it might have been. The first difficulty was the opposition of supervisors, who were unwilling to surrender the autonomy of their particular units. In a memorandum to Mrs. Woodward, Mrs. Flanagan wrote, "Originally these projects were set up as small units on their own, and what they want is complete autonomy. . . . They must have their own press representatives and so on."[39]

The second difficulty was that Mrs. Flanagan, although she conceded the advantage of a statewide project unit, was reluctant to take the drastic action necessary for reorganization. Indeed, there were instances in which Mrs. Flanagan continued to urge the functional unit; and in a letter of protest, E. Kendall Davis of the Illinois project wrote to the national director:

> We have not prepared such functional applications for the reason that in Illinois the entire Project, including Peoria, is now operated as one unit. All of the stage hands, seamstresses, actors and other employees . . . are considered as members of one large pool, usable anywhere they may be needed. Supervisors, both administrative and technical, are utilized at any point where their services are needed. Any attempt to make a functional breakdown would not only be a misrepresentation of the actual facts but would, we feel, have distinct disadvantages. Such a breakdown would prevent us from utilizing to the full extent the personnel available in the state. The use of separate work projects would require us to establish and set aside separate personnel and separate material costs for each unit, and we would be prevented from transferring both materials and supplies and personnel from one work unit to another. . . .[40]

PROJECT PERSONNEL AND EMPLOYMENT

The problem of employing some 12,000 theatrical workers was intricate beyond imagination. In order that funds might be authorized to the states promptly and adequately, it was necessary to establish the geographical distribution of eligible workers.* The occupational census of March, 1935, had reported that some 5,800 actors were registered on the relief roles in the nation. If this figure had been correct, a total project personnel of 12,000 would not have been excessive. Unfortunately, later surveys indicated that many who registered as theatrical workers had had little or no professional experience in that business. Some were patently amateurs; others interpreted their ambition alone as qualification for employment. Among those with genuinely professional qualifications, some had outlived their appeal, and others had still to make their way. Besides, among the stagehands, electricians, carpenters, and others whose skills are ancillary to the theater, many possessed no actual experience in theatrical work, and could as readily have applied their competence to other than theatrical tasks.

Again, in the early months the state WPA administrations were often less than co-operative. J. W. Dunn, the state director for Oklahoma, wrote to the regional director that the state relief organization was of no help in finding qualified workers; his best means of information was "grapevine telegraph," but many workers proved to be transients, ineligible for relief certification under state regulations.[41] In Indiana the state WPA administrator feared unfavorable publicity and refused to sanction any reclassification of workers on relief rolls, but he willingly co-operated in a survey of such rolls as existed. The Iowa administrator proved even more difficult, for he was convinced that he and his staff were completely competent to administer all branches of work relief, just as they had been doing.

The problem of certification was complicated by the fact that theatrical unions had dissuaded, and indeed forbidden, their members to enroll for relief. This was true, to a greater or less degree, of the IATSE, the AFA, and Actors' Equity Association. For instance, in Kansas City, a regional booking center for professional road shows, the unions themselves had helped their members, and in the opinion of unemployed actors the difference between that kind of compensation and the amount available from relief was so small that certification was not worth the embarrassment it entailed. From that city an actor wrote to Mrs. Flanagan that there were at least ten destitute show people in his own hotel and that he knew fifteen to twenty-five more. If the state WPA officials would post a notice on the bulletin board, he added, he was

---

*The key figure in a theatrical project is the number of actors; other necessary workers are determined by a fairly well established ratio. This ratio in commercial enterprises is approximately sixty to forty; special functions required by government procedure probably made the percentage of actors in the federal theater somewhat lower.

certain that they would receive at least seventy-five applications for theatrical work. According to him, the state officials were not only not interested in, but definitely obstructed, any such activity as a theatrical project in the city.[42]

An official on the Illinois theater project, a professional theatrical man, described the situation in that state in the following words:

> The reclassification is going on at snail pace. We arrived at the assigned place and there were no desks. We found some tables; but there was no ink. We used pencils, but there were none of the small cards. So we went on, ready to fill out the longer forms, but there were no . . . well, there were some applicants.
>
> At the various offices they pretended a full eagerness to cooperate. One of the sections of USES promised to send letters to about two hundred people on their files, but some official stopped them. I am still trying to find out who it was. Another office was to send a list of names and addresses to Carrington but the list presumably did not arrive. So I just whispered to Carrington that I am going to forget the reclassification. Within a half hour Mr. C. had a call from the office to inform him that the list did arrive, *just then*. And they put three people on to send out notices. If the people come in Monday, I'll believe it.[43]

Elmer Rice declared that in New York City the greatest obstacle to the initiation of the project was the aversion of theatrical workers to certification. In order to lessen the humiliation and to encourage application, he had the following form prepared and posted over his signature:

TO ALL APPLICANTS FOR WORK:

> The Federal Theatre Project has been created for the purpose of providing worthwhile employment for professional theatre workers. Please bear in mind that you are not being offered relief or charity but WORK. The interviewers have been instructed to receive you with the same courtesy and consideration that would be extended by any professional employment agency, our object being to set up so high a standard of professional excellence in these projects that they will be able to continue on their own momentum after the Federal Program is completed.
>
> If you have any complaint to make of the way in which your application is handled, please write to me personally and I shall see that an investigation is made.[44]

The failure of many state WPA administrations to assist the Theater Project in finding workers often caused local officials of the project to seek applicants through other than regular channels. The state director in New Jersey, for instance, secured names of unemployed actors from the several unions and sent out letters to them like the following:

> Are you registered with the National Re-employment Service as an Actor? Are you on relief? If you can answer "yes" to the above questions, you are eligible for employment in the National Federal Theatre Project.[45]

One of his project supervisors reported that, using a list of twenty-six applicants, he had made a personal survey and had found four who were eligible. With these and a few others who were reported to be in need he hoped to start a project unit. In other cities, trade papers and union organs helped to publicize the project. This search for project workers reached such proportions that Jacob Baker felt it necessary to remind all field supervisors of Federal One to "make all inquiries as to prospective labor supply through the labor assignment offices of WPA and in no case independently through the National Re-employment Service."[46]

At the same time, informal regional surveys were being made by the regional directors. John McGee, one of Mrs. Flanagan's first appointments, reported, after surveying the South: "It is easily possible to employ from five hundred to one thousand workers in this area within thirty days if the necessary machinery is permitted to be set up."[47]

The bewilderment of state WPA administrators at the number and kinds of jobs in which they might find professional theatrical workers is understandable. For each of the four classifications of workers, the *Instructions* included fantastic lists. It is difficult to understand why watchmen, elevator operators, janitors, messengers, typists, and truck drivers required theatrical experience in order to be eligible for employment. And how would the WPA employment office know that a dressmaker, tailor, or painter would be qualified for show projects? One state WPA administrator wrote causticly that practically everyone on the WPA could qualify for one or another of the jobs listed.

The recruitment of workers was only the initial step. *Supplement No. 1 to Bulletin No. 29* required that competent individuals or committees hold auditions in order to place the workers in their proper classifications before project units were established. This requirement applied only to actors and was not observed in the beginning in Los Angeles, Boston, Chicago, and New York. In these cities those already employed under the respective state ERA's were transferred to the WPA *en bloc* and without further test.

## THE CONFLICT OF PROFESSIONAL VERSUS AMATEUR

All this while, the Theater Project was under constant pressure from the theatrical unions, which insisted: (1) that all non-professionals be excluded from the project, and (2) that professionals be given the highest (i.e., professional) rating. Mrs. Flanagan, yielding to these pressures, and especially to the IATSE, sent a telegram to her regional directors on October 2, 1935 that restricted employment on the project to professionals.[48]

The consequence of this restriction was soon apparent. In the Northwest, for instance, there were many graduates of university dramatic courses who were ready to return to their home communities and to co-operate with professionals in the establishment of theater units. Glenn Hughes of the University of Washington, Seattle, had submitted to the Washington office a plan whereby professionals would be employed as directors, and amateurs as actors or in other capacities, in a series of community theaters in that region. Mr. Hughes, however, when he attended the October conference in Washington, correctly concluded that he could not employ amateurs, even though talented, unless they could present evidence of at least one professional engagement. But Margaret Klem, a field representative of the WPA Professional and Service Division investigating the delay in initiating theater units in the Northwest, reported to Bruce McClure that she had been assured by Harold Stein that, according to the rules of eligibility, anyone who was passed by an audition board as qualified could be assigned if he were on relief rolls.[49] Stein's interpretation, however, was not followed by Mrs. Flanagan.

The pressure of the Washington office to employ workers as fast as possible brought a sensible reply from Mr. Stevens in the Midwest: "We cannot put all our workers on the payroll until companies are working in their theatres. It is quite useless to have janitors, cleaners and ushers, and stage hands on payrolls previous to housing the companies."[50]

CLASSIFICATIONS

The *Instructions* prescribed the following procedure for establishment of audition boards:

> The Regional Director of the Federal Theatre Project will appoint, by issuing a written statement, a person or committee professionally qualified to supervise (or to conduct if necessary) such an analysis in each community within his region. This committee or person so authorized shall determine the classification (Professional, skilled, intermediate, or unskilled) of each theatre worker to be placed in a theatre work project. This determination of skill automatically determines the salary rank of the individual.

Audition boards used the vocational study form provided by the *Instructions*, which classified workers into four grades—as in all professional projects. The professional grade (grade IV) required evidence of the ability to do high grade work of a creative and/or interpretative nature. This provision, however, was loosely interpreted, for not only actors, stage and technical directors, musicians, and playwrights were so classified but also accountants, house managers, box-office managers, librarians, and business managers. Skilled workers (grade III) were vaguely described as those who could do work of recognized merit but of a quality not equivalent to grade IV. The list included assistants for professionals and actors in secondary roles. Intermediate classification (grade II) included "those who have a limited degree of skill and apprentices." Unskilled workers (grade I) were those necessary to the operation of the project, most of whom were house personnel.

The audition boards, however, did not enjoy full freedom in their work. Membership in theatrical unions, such as Actors' Equity, the AFA, and the IATSE, usually carried with it automatic classification in the professional grade, because of the policy established by the national director.

When, in March, 1936, employment on Federal One was frozen by Hopkins' order, the Theater Project was approximately 2,500 workers short of its quota of 12,000 workers. The limitation, however, was liberally interpreted, and, by July 31, 1936, the Theater Project reached a peak employment of 14,010 workers. Distribution of employment within the national quota was entirely at the discretion of the national director. In the summer of 1936, twenty-eight states, New York City, and the District of Columbia operated project units. In the main, distribution of employment followed theatrical geography. Seven southern states had no projects: Georgia, Kentucky, Mississippi, South Carolina, Tennessee, Virginia, and West Virginia. Most of the central, mountain, and northwestern states had no projects: North and South Dakota, Minnesota, Kansas, New Mexico, Arizona, Utah, Wyoming, Montana, Nevada, and Idaho, were all in this class. In the East, Maryland, Vermont, and New Hampshire were omitted.

Five state programs had been terminated by the end of 1937 partly because of drastic cuts ordered in July, 1937, which made it inadvisable to attempt to maintain small and relatively substandard projects. In 1938 there were programs in only twenty states, and that remained the figure to the end. The states that had been closed out during 1937 and 1938 were: Arkansas, Delaware, Indiana, Iowa, Missouri, Nebraska,

Rhode Island, Texas, and Wisconsin. Georgia had been added. Projects that had failed to achieve artistic standards commensurate with the national director's aim were thus eliminated. The recreation and education divisions of the WPA attempted to meet dramatic needs in those states not cultivated by the Theater Project.

## NON-RELIEF AND NON-CERTIFIED PERSONNEL

The Theater Project's claim to preference in regard to the 10 per cent limitation on non-relief workers raised many difficulties. In the beginning, project after project was found to have exceeded its limitation; and by January, 1936, most projects enjoyed an additional concession of 25 per cent. In November, 1936, General Letter No. 95 reduced the statewide exemption from 25 to 10 per cent, although it allowed, within that limitation, individual project units to enjoy a higher percentage of non-relief personnel. Finally, on February 20, 1937, Administrative Order No. 52 reduced non-relief exemptions to 5 per cent and applied the limitation to each project unit.

These limitiations upon non-relief personnel always embarrassed the Federal Theater Project. There were many reasons for this, the principal one being the attitude of the IATSE. This union of stagehands and allied workers not only insisted that its members make no effort to secure certification but also demanded that most of them receive non-security wages, which after February 20, 1937, automatically classified them as non-relief workers. In September, 1937, 6.7 per cent of the 8,818 employees of the project were non-relief; the order of February 20, 1937, would have raised the non-relief percentage to 17.9. Obviously, further exemptions or drastic reorganization of national employment was required. In New York City, in November, 1938, 495, or 11.7 per cent, of the 4,228 employees were non-security, and 635, or 15 per cent, were non-relief.

The insistence of the WPA upon certification created unusual resentment among theater workers, and this resentment was increased when they remembered that under the CWA certification was waived, and that in the professional program of the FERA the rules of certification had been laxly enforced. Especially violent protests came from workers whose own organizations, as long as funds permitted, had assisted them in keeping off the relief rolls. In October, 1936, several units of the Theater Project signed petitions couched in almost identical language and addressed them to the Washington office. That submitted by the New York City Children's Theater unit read in part:

> We have been told many times that we are done with relief—that we have jobs. We exchange work for pay: we do not ask for unearned money. For this reason we believe that reducing us to a relief status constitutes a patent injustice. Moreover, as you must know, submission to a relief questionnaire is universally felt to be degrading and humiliating. . . .
>
> People of the theatre are as a rule in love with their work, in spite of all discouragement; but it is a fact that we are keeping up our hope for the Federal Theatre—and our pride in it—only by sheer determination against an overwhelming conviction that we are not regarded as workers at all, much less as craftsmen.[51]

Those who protested argued that union certification of need be accepted, as was usual under the professional program of the FERA. The workers conceded that some investigation of circumstances was necessary, for they recognized that those of independent means should yield to those in need. But they maintained that records of the various unions to which they belonged would give the necessary facts concerning the workers' economic status. They cited, as a precedent, that the members of the stagehands' union were so certified, and that they constituted a large portion of the 10 per cent non-relief quota. Union records, they insisted, presented the professional history of members; home relief investigation involved public inquiry from previous employers, with resulting irreparable damage to a worker's professional value and reputation. This was not the way, they argued, for the WPA to try to rehabilitate the unemployed.

The form letter prepared in reply to these protests firmly reminded the workers that WPA rules did not permit certification by unions and that no valid authority existed except the local relief bureau. They were assured, however, that the circumstances of the individual and his need for work would most certainly be taken into consideration, within the rules of procedure laid down. Some unions suggested, as an alternative to public investigation, certification by the U.S. Department of Labor. In November, 1936, representatives of these unions met with E. H. Engelhorn, who was at that time acting business manager of New York City Federal Project No. 1. They reported to Frank Gillmore, president of Actors' Equity, that when they cited the stagehands'-union precedent, Mr. Engelhorn replied, "That is different—the stage hands are essential to the theatre." When asked, "Aren't actors essential to the theatre?", he agreed they were but added that the stagehands' union was "more strongly fortified than the actors'. This statement caused everyone to gasp and then to laugh—except Equity members, who were outraged. Gillmore reported to Mrs. Flanagan:

> As I am bound to believe the above is true, it would seem that Mr. Engelhorn is untactful. If the stage hands *do* hold a preferred position, it is hardly judicious to blazon it before the actors who quite naturally feel that they have as much right to consideration, if not more, than other groups. It is true that as an organization Equity has not taken any arbitrary stand, but many of our people are constantly inciting us to do so.[52]

Particularly in the Theater Project, residence, which was required in almost all states as a requisite for certification, was often difficult to establish. The nature of their profession makes many theater workers peripatetic, and they are likely to pursue employment to far places where friends or rumors tell them of opportunities. In New York a senior project supervisor whom Mrs. Flanagan considered indispensable had seven dependents and no income in 1935. In order to live he had gone to Maryland, although New York had always been his home, to find less expensive or perhaps free living with relatives. When she asked for his appointment on the New York City project, it was ruled that as a non-resident he did not qualify.

The position of Actors' Equity Association, like that of the other unions, was that their own members should be given preference in employment. In 1937, when quotas were reduced, this union insisted that none of their members be dismissed until all non-professionals had been let out. Other theatrical unions took comparable stands, and it may be asserted that the unions, as indeed was their function, were interested only in the employment of their members.*

FINANCE

Mrs. Flanagan was never quite aware of the limitations that surround the spending of government money. On several occasions she appealed to Harry Hopkins directly, or through Jacob Baker, for special budgetary concessions. She asked for a national director's fund to enable her to pay more adequate salaries when required to secure outstanding leadership; to make conferences possible by paying travel ex-

*For a full discussion of the problem of non-relief and non-certified personnel as it affected the operation of Federal One in general, *vide supra*, 173-81.

penses of experts; and to enable her to meet emergencies arising because of unavoidably slow procedure in federal disbursement.[53]

In November, 1935, after seeing a showing of *Let Freedom Ring*, she sent a telegram to Baker asking him to confer with the President to inquire if Theater Project funds might not be used to keep the show in operation for another week. The reply, sent by Bruce McClure, read in part:

> Regardless of merit of production, I do not see how Federal money could be used legitimately to subsidize producers or author in the hope of establishing commercial success. That is considered judgment of Baker and myself and is entirely apart from practical considerations involved in project approval, disbursement of funds and final accounting. . . .[54]

She recommended that Hopkins establish an autonomous nationwide vaudeville project under the directorshop of Eddie Dowling when it became apparent that his unwillingness to accept government regulations made it impossible for him to work in the Federal Theater Project.

COSTS

The salaries paid the administrative personnel on the Federal Theater Project were in line with salaries paid by the government generally. Mrs. Flanagan's salary at first was $6,000 a year, and was later raised to $7,200. The salaries of regional directors averaged $3,600 a year, and those of state directors ranged from $2,400 to $3,000.

These salaries were often compared by the federal director with those paid for similar work in the commercial theater. In December, 1935, Mrs. Flanagan, when presenting the roster of her regional and office staff, wrote, "When you consider that a theater director staging a New York professional show is often paid $25,000 for one month's work, I think the array of Theatre talent secured for six months for slightly more than the above sum is impressive."[55]

This comparison, however, limps for several reasons. In the first place, as in the above letter, the comparison is made between the *highest* salaries paid in the professional theater to a few outstanding men and the average salary paid on the Theater Project. In the second place, the weekly or monthly salaries paid on Federal Theater, although small compared with commercial salaries, were generally adequate, if considered on an annual basis. The continuity of salaries in the commercial theater is notoriously insecure, and employment often lasts but for a few weeks or a few months at most. Salaries on the Theater Project, on the other hand, were paid regularly throughout the year, and the actor's income within the lifetime of the project was practically guaranteed.*

Supervisors on individual project units were paid from $1,200 to $2,400 a year. These salaries were rather low in view of the duties involved, but the number of supervisors deemed necessary made these costs high. Mrs. Flanagan's insistence upon novel and experimental production was also influential in raising supervisory costs. As George Kondolf, state director for Illinois, wrote, with reference to the Chicago unit:

> Please remember . . . we must expect to pay more in Chicago, for the first rate personnel we need to direct and produce our practically exclusively new play program than would have to be paid in New York or California, because of the obvious advantages those key theatrical centers can offer producers, directors or other productive talent who are merely on the spot. . . . And also that a program of new plays obviously calls for considerably more and better direction and supervision than a "reproduction" and revival program. I don't feel I need amplify.[56]

Another factor in increasing costs that must be kept in mind in estimating salaries is that the administrative personnel received travel and per diem allowances when away from their assigned posts. This affected mostly the administrative officers in the higher positions, and often materially raised actual compensation. Mrs. Flanagan, for instance, during the extended period of her stay in New York City, was officially attached to the Washington office and thus received a per diem allowance that substantially increased her salary.

The wages of the project personnel, although they were set by executive order, were materially affected by the pressure of unions and by the weakness of the Washington office in resisting that pressure. The theatrical unions insisted upon, and succeeded in securing, a nationwide maximum of ninety-six working hours a month. Moreover, the Theater Project, by limiting its performances to five a week, was able to pay actors an hourly wage equivalent to the Equity minimum of twenty-five dollars a week for junior members (skilled) and forty dollars for senior members (professional), since the Equity rate covered eight performances a week. Again theater workers, once they were employed on the project, received their full wages whether they were in

---

*Salaries on the Federal Theater Project, if they were below those paid in the commercial theater, were equal, and often superior, to those paid in the independent theater; and those of the project's employees who were secured from that source actually increased their earnings when they joined the Theater Project.

production or not. There was no differential whatever between playing time and rehearsal time. Hours spent in the greenroom were paid for at the same rate as hours spent on the stage. Thus actors on the Federal Theater Project received in general much more then they had ever received in the commercial theater, and enjoyed at the same time a continuity of employment and a degree of security much greater.

Technical unions, especially the International Alliance of Theatrical and Stage Employees, proved even more difficult than the actors' unions. Early in the project's life the IATSE exerted such pressure that Mrs. Flanagan issued a nationwide order classifying all its members as professional and therefore in the highest security wage bracket. Since, by and large, they refused to submit to relief certification, they were classified as non-relief—a fact that increased inordinately the non-relief load of the project. Moreover, they insisted on hourly rates, which, for the most part, placed them in the non-security classification. Since the number of those receiving non-security wages was limited, the presence of stage crews on the list lessened the opportunity to employ actors in this category. Crew chiefs were rated as supervisory, and received $145 a month in New York City. The IATSE firmly banned split shifts; stage crews were not allowed to work less than eight hours a day, and the eight hours had to be unbroken except for luncheon. For most productions this made necessary two complete set of stage crews and six department heads for each production.

Further to confuse the situation, local unions did not always abide by decisions of national policy. Traveling troupes with their own stage crews were often required to hire local workers, even though they were not needed and not on relief. Occasionally, a director firmly refused to comply with these demands. More often, however, they felt that defiance of the union would not be in accord with the national policy of the Theater Project. The extent to which this policy increased costs is shown in a financial statement sent to Mrs. Flanagan from New York City:

> You will note that our receipts at the permanent theatres are approximately $5,000 a week. Due to the necessity of a double shift in all theatres except the Lafayette, the cost of stage hands for the same period is over $8,000.[57]

### NON-LABOR COSTS

The highest single item of non-labor cost on the Theater Project was for theater rentals. Baker and Hopkins had early been told by Mrs. Flanagan that the League of New York Theaters had offered their houses on terms that would require no outlay of federal funds. In October, however, they were told by her and by Elmer Rice that the New York City project must pay for the rental of five theaters. Baker, who feared the reaction of Treasury officials, instructed Mrs. Flanagan to prepare requisitions, but to do so as quietly as possible and not to submit them at the moment. He added: "We wish to arrive at a meeting of minds on exactly what limits on Federal expenditures for theatre rentals are fair and suitable in the light of all circumstances."[58]

Excessive rentals were often asked and, unfortunately, often paid. This was particularly deplorable because, at the time, the theater business was in distress, and the Theater Project was in a position to conduct profitable negotiations with theater owners. In Los Angeles a theater was rented in the fall of 1936 under peculiar circumstances that were questioned by the WPA finance office. Taylor H. Snow, California administrative assistant, retorted that it was the only Hollywood Theater that fulfilled the specifications: seating capacity, 1,200 persons; stage dimensions, seventy by thirty-five feet and seventy-five feet high. An extremely involved financial history of the theater, which had been dark for two months before the Federal Theater took it over, was submitted to prove that the monthly rent was not excessive, although the previous lease had been executed for less than half the amount on a yearly basis. Mr. Holmes' interrogation may have resulted in the recommendation with which Mr. Snow closed his letter:

> The undersigned feels that on February 1, 1937, the government should exercise its option to cancel the lease and endeavor to make a different lease on lower terms due to the fact that at that time the sublessor will show a profit rather than a loss as he does until March 1, 1937. If the sublessor refuses at that time to reduce rental to the government, the theatre should be given up.[59]

## ADMISSION PRICES

The policy of charging admissions was adopted largely to defray non-labor costs. Hopkins early established the principle that free shows should be given for underprivileged groups and a substantial portion of the seats should be free at all performances. He believed that admissions should be charged only in rare cases, and in the beginning a top price of fifty cents was established, with the majority of seats available at ten and twenty-five cents. Gradually, however, prices rose. At

530

first, they ranged from five cents to forty cents; by the end of 1936 the top price rose to fifty cents, and finally to one dollar, with the provision that some seats always must be available at twenty-five cents. At the time of the last advance, an exception made it possible for companies on tour by special permission from the national director to charge $1.50. One case is on record where, for a single performance, permission was granted to charge two dollars.

On the other hand, a large number of performances were always given free. Children's theater, school plays, and marionette shows usually charged no more than fifteen cents, if they charged at all. Passes for the press were issued in accordance with commercial theater practices; if there was any difference, it was by way of greater largess on the part of the project. In figures concerning a proposed tour of a repertory company to New York City, the weekly income was estimated at $3,600, except for the first week, when complimentary and reduced-price tickets would lower it by $2,600. The Theater Project also followed commercial practices in encouraging attendance through reduced admissions. Promotion experts devised systems very like the "throw-aways" and the "two-for-ones" of Broadway productions. In Los Angeles anyone who applied to the box office for the privilege was allowed to buy a ticket at a fifteen-cent reduction from the printed price. In San Francisco "service passes"—upon which there was a service charge of ten or fifteen cents—were believed to increase revenue. At one time such passes were distributed to WPA workers in every paycheck envelope. Presentation of such a pass and payment of the appropriate charge, which depended upon the seat chosen at the box office, entitled the holder to his choice of seats priced from twenty-five cents to one dollar. He could then get the highest price seat for twenty-five cents. In 1933 it was felt that the use of "paper" had increased to unfortunate proportions in southern California, and an effort was made to curb this tendency. Block selling of tickets was also an accepted and widely used method of increasing admissions receipts. An organization willing to arrange a theater party for a certain performance was allowed a cut rate; this difference was credited in the project reports to valuable services such as promotion and good will.

The question of benefit performances frequently occurred. No government agency ever was permitted to give benefit performances in which all expenses were paid by the government and all collections were turned over to a charitable agency; nor could the private agency pay all non-labor expenses and take the profits. Operating Procedure

F-45 stated that "no collections, even of a voluntary nature, shall be taken during the performance of a project unit unless prior authorization has been granted." During flood emergencies in 1936 and 1937, special authorization was issued to permit Red Cross workers to solicit contributions.

## ROYALTIES

Because of the expense involved, it was contrary to the Federal Theater Project's policy to pay high royalties. In general, it was considered unwise to pay more than fifty dollars a week. A few prominent playwrights authorized production of their plays for a payment of this amount, but such arrangements allowed for multiple production. George Bernard Shaw was one of the first to enter into such an agreement, and he was promised at least fifty weeks a year, or $2,500. Eugene O'Neill's agreement called for a sliding scale—fifty dollars a week for the first three weeks, seventy-five dollars a week for each of the next three weeks, and $100 a week for every week thereafter. This came to be the accepted rate for most well-known plays.

The Dramatists' Guild strenuously objected to these low rates and attempted to establish a percentage rate. They declared that, by paying only fifty dollars, the Federal Theater was demanding special consideration and creating unfair competition with the non-professional theater. The usual rate paid by the latter for popular plays was $200 a week; the Guild claimed that a subsidized theater, charging admissions, should meet that rate.

During the first months delays and actual failures to pay became almost a major scandal. Eventually, the play service bureau was provided with a fund of $40,000 out of which to pay royalties. It negotiated contracts, checked performance reports, and sent checks. This change, however, did not effect complete reform, and endured for only about ten months, after which royalties once more were paid by the project using the play. This demanded long-range planning, because it was necessary to write into the project proposals the amount due for royalties and, before this could be done, to choose the pay to be performed.

Although plays written on the project were in the public domain, royalties were collected for a few of them. The cinema rights to *One-third of a Nation* were purchased for $5,000, and the production rights for *Two a Day* brought in $1,000. Through the establishment of the

Guild's Committee for Federal Writers' Publications, it became possible for funds so secured to be treated as sponsors' funds and used by the projects.

## THE ABOLITION OF THE THEATER PROJECT

Unlike the other arts projects, which were allowed to continue under state and local sponsorship, the Theater Project was abolished by Congressional act in the summer of 1939. The reasons for the discrimination were manifold. In the first place, the theater was most vulnerable to criticism because by its very nature it achieved an immediate and at times spectacular publicity; and the enemies of Federal One, in the press and elsewhere, were quick to take advantage of strategic blunders by the project. It must be conceded, therefore, that, of all the directors of the arts projects, Mrs. Flanagan had the most difficult task. At the same time, it must be emphasized that the very precarious nature of her position imposed upon her obligations and responsibilities beyond those required of her colleagues in the other arts projects. Mrs. Flanagan chose to live dangerously—a choice within her province to make and for which she deserves the praise of those to whom compromise is anathema. On the other hand, it was naïve of her and her supporters to believe that the Theater Project, as an enterprise of the federal government, could continually and spectacularly express a social philosophy opposed to that of a substantial element in Congress and on the committees that held the fate of the WPA in their hands. Had Hesiod's maxim, that the half is more than the whole, been heeded, the Theater Project might have been indeed less heroic, but in the end more enduring.

Three causes, beyond all others, were responsible for the abolition of the project in 1939. They were: (1) the failure of the project to achieve a non-metropolitan character; (2) the productions of the Living Newspaper unit in New York City, especially *Power*; and (3) the episode of *The Swing Mikado*.

The desire of the project for metropolitan acclaim, however artistically excusable, was politically indefensible. Both houses of Congress represent the entire nation, not merely New York City, Chicago, and Los Angeles; and members who came from the less-favored areas resented the concentration of project employment in three urban centers. In the House hearings in 1939, this feeling was indicated in the following colloquium:

Mr. DITTER. Referring to the Theater Project, this statement of the Administrator shows the total cost for the week ended March 4, 1939, as $840,271.53, of which $383,130 was spent in the city of New York alone.

Mrs. KERR. That is the estimated cost for the month of March.

Mr. DITTER. So that pretty nearly fifty per cent of the Theater Project cost applies to the city of New York.

Mrs. KERR. Yes, sir: and about thirty-five per cent of the employees or between 35 and 38 per cent of the employees are there, and the higher wage scale makes up for the difference.

Colonel HARRINGTON. I would like to call attention to the fact that the second largest item is in Southern California, which means Los Angeles, and the third largest item is for Illinois, which means Chicago. That is where these qualified theatre workers are. Although they have come from all over the country, they have been stranded in these large cities.

Mr. DITTER. But of course some of us who have not been that fortunate naturally look at it with some degree of misgiving. While your interjection, Colonel, is probably commendable, it does not relieve those of us who reside in States that are helping to pay the bill.[60]

The productions of the New York unit of the Living Newspaper, and especially *Power*, represented a social philosophy which, though it may have been in accord with that of the New Deal, was contrary to that of the Republican party and the conservative element in the Democratic party. Indeed, the men on the project in New York City responsible for the scripts were, if anything, distinctly to the left of the administration. In *Power*, which was a frank plea for public ownership of the sources of power, the script introduced the remarks of certain senators opposed to public ownership of utilities. These were quoted verbatim from public documents, and thus there was no question of authenticity. That they were quoted with disapproval was obvious from the context of the play. The senators concerned were annoyed, and with them many of their colleagues—even some who disagreed with their position.

In the House hearings in 1938, Aubrey Williams, then deputy administrator of the WPA, was questioned on *Power* by Representative Taber of New York:

Mr. TABER. What about such things as I saw in the paper the other day, where different members of the Senate were held up to ridicule?

Mr. WILLIAMS. Do you mean in the play in New York in the Living Newspaper?

Mr. TABER. Yes.

Mr. WILLIAMS. I haven't seen the play, so I couldn't say.

Mr. TABER. Don't you think that that is entirely improper?

Mr. WILLIAMS. I haven't seen the play, so I don't know whether they held them up to ridicule or not.

Mr. TABER. Don't you think it is rather going pretty far afield for the W.P.A. to sponsor that kind of thing?

Mr. WILLIAMS. As I say, I have never seen the play, so I don't know if it is ridicule.

As far as our putting on a theater is concerned, I think it is perfectly proper for us to employ unemployed artists and actors. I think they have to live the same as others.

Mr. TABER. What about the other thing? Do you think it is proper or don't you to hold them up to ridicule?

Mr. WILLIAMS. I think it is in bad taste to hold anyone up to ridicule at any time.[61]

Later, at the Senate hearings, Williams was more forthright in expressing his opinion of *Power*:

Mr. WILLIAMS. Senator, let me say this: I have looked into that particular play and I have made this statement to the committee in the House and I make it here. I don't care. Any theatre that ridicules anyone is wrong. I think it is unfair and it is not the proper and right thing to do, and I have had Mrs. Flanagan see one of the Senators who was involved to discuss the whole matter with him. She feels very strongly that there is nothing in it that he would object to but the press took some things and distorted them. Of course, my position is that the effect is the same. If he feels that way, that's the important thing here.[62]

Without doubt, the production of *Power* resulted in much pressure upon Congress from sources inimical to the theater project. In addition, many individual congressmen, as congressmen, were offended by the script.*

---

*The question raised by *Power*, and indeed by other like productions, such as *Triple-A Plowed Under, Injunction Granted,* and *One-third of a Nation,* is delicate. It is not merely a matter of censorship. In the several hearings at which the question was discussed, no congressman ever suggested that a *private* producer should be denied the right to produce a play presenting a particular social philosophy, or criticizing the government or members of Congress. The question was whether a governmental agency, supported by public funds, should produce a play presenting a social philosophy with which at least a substantial minority of the population was not in sympathy. Certainly, if a Republican administration operating a theater project should have produced a play extolling private monopoly, those who were opposed to that philosophy would have protested no less vigorously. This is only another way of saying that so long as there exists in a democratic commonwealth a substantial minority opposed to the philosophy of the party in power, an uncensored governmental theater is a precarious undertaking.

The defense, occasionally made at the time, that the Living Newspaper produc-

The episode of *The Swing Mikado* was of a different kind. This play was a Negro jazz version of the Gilbert and Sullivan operetta. It opened at the Great Northern Theater in Chicago on September 25, 1938, and closed there on February 25, 1939. It quickly became by all odds the most successful production essayed by the Theater Project. Its total receipts for 158 performances were $105,284.

Encouraged by its popularity, high officials in the WPA and in the Theater Project decided to bring it to New York City. This decision, which was one of policy, was not unprecedented; indeed, from the beginning of the project the practice of touring the more successful productions had been followed.

A difficulty arose, however, when certain theatrical producers, impressed by the possibilities of the play, were ready to make offers of private employment to the cast. Among these was Erik Charrell of New York City.*

In January, 1939, Mr. Charrell, accompanied by Representative Sol Bloom of New York, conferred in Washington with Florence Kerr, WPA assistant administrator in charge of professional and service projects. At the conference Charrell made what seems in substance to have been the following proposal: (1) he offered to employ the entire *Swing Mikado* company (or as many of them as would accept the offer) on the basis of a standard Equity contract. This contract offered the cast (except for the principals, who were to receive higher wages commensurate with their parts) the minimum Equity wage of approximately forty-five dollars a week and the minimum Equity guarantee of two weeks employment; (2) he made this offer contingent upon a commitment by the WPA that it would not persist in its plan to produce *The Swing Mikado* in New York City.

At the conference Mrs. Kerr seems to have made the following response to Charrell's proposal: (1) Mrs. Kerr (or any official of the WPA) was not permitted to act as an agent for a private producer and to make in his name a proposal of private employment to the members of the cast; (2) Charrell (or any agent of his), however, was free to go to Chicago and make to the cast whatever offers he chose; (3) Mrs. Kerr refused to promise that if Charrell made such offers, the WPA would desist from its plan to bring *The Swing Mikado* to New York City.

tions were objective because they quoted verbatim from sources, is too superficial to merit consideration.

*The essence of the controversy over Mr. Charrell's proposition is contained in the *Hearings of a Subcommittee of the House Committee on Appropriations on Further Additional Appropriation*, 76th Cong., 1st sess. (1939), pp. 218-33.

Charrell considered the conference unsatisfactory, and, although subsequent efforts were made to induce the WPA to assent to his proposals, further negotiations were equally unfruitful; and *The Swing Mikado* was opened in New York City by the WPA on March 1, 1939.

An examination of the evidence would seem to show that Mrs. Kerr's position, although perhaps she observed in every instance the technicalities of the law, was not in accord with the spirit and intent of the several appropriation acts by virtue of which WPA existed. It was the intent of the work-relief program of the WPA to afford appropriate employment to competent workers until they received reasonable offers of private employment; and the last prior appropriation act contained a clause that made it unlawful for the WPA to employ any worker who, having received such an offer, refused it.

The core of the disagreement, therefore, as appears clearly but obliquely in the testimony, lay in the question of whether Charrell's proposed offer was reasonable within the meaning of the act. The WPA, apparently, did not think so. In the first place, Mrs. Kerr tried to impugn Charrell's standing as a producer. Among other things, she said:

> Mr. Chairman, I wanted to clear up that point about the private producers not objecting to the *Swing Mikado* coming on to the city of New York. I think you appreciate that all these names that have been mentioned, all these groups that we have been discussing, are individuals and citizens who wanted to get into the theatre business by the *Swing Mikado* route. When I said that no producer objected to our coming in, I meant those actually in operation in New York City this winter.[63]

Charrell, however, was a recognized theatrical producer, and had offered J. P. Morgan and Company as reference for his financial standing. Mrs. Kerr would seem to be convicted of quibbling, since she arbitrarily defines a producer as one who is here and now producing. The fact that Charrell was not at the moment producing a play in New York City did not remove him from the category of producer.

In the second place, the reasonableness of Charrell's offer was questioned. He was prepared to offer forty-five dollars a week, or approximately $180 a month. The professional performers were receiving from the government $94 a month plus $3 a day for subsistence while on the road. Thus the total monthly compensation of a member of the Chicago cast in New York would amount to approximately $184 a month. That a slight differential existed in favor of the WPA wage is indicated in Mrs. Kerr's testimony:

> As far as I know Mr. Charrell did not make any definite offer to the

workers. Mr. Uhlrich offered $45 a week to the cast, and of course their $94 wage plus the $3 per diem would make just a little differential in favor of what they are receiving from the Government.*[64]

On the subject of wages, Colonel Harrington implied that he did not consider any of these offers "reasonable." In his testimony he said:

> However, in that connection, I feel that we should turn these actors over to any private employer that will offer them reasonable employment, and I stand ready to do that at any time. I feel that I am required to do that under the provisions of the appropriation act. But up to the present time no responsible producer has come forward with an offer to employ that cast. As soon as someone does, we will turn the cast over to them and let them run the show; but they have got to guarantee those people reasonable employment before I am willing to do that.
>
> Mr. WOODRUM. For how long a period?
>
> Colonel HARRINGTON. I would think for not less than a month.[65]

It is difficult to examine the evidence with respect to this episode without coming to the conclusion that Charrell's offer (and indeed Ulrich's and Todd's) was a bona fide offer of employment under terms accepted as fair by theatrical producers and the Actors' Equity Association. Accordingly, it is hard to see what justification the WPA officials had for judging these terms unreasonable.

The fact seems to be that the WPA, having already made certain arrangements to bring the play to New York City, was determined to proceed in accordance with its plan. Mrs. Kerr conceded as much when she said, "We had a production scheduled, and the exigencies of our program operation were such that we felt that we had to go on with our program."[66]

There was also the feeling that WPA, by producing this play at a low admission price ($1.10 as opposed to $3.30 or $4.40), would give many people in New York the opportunity to see what they could not afford at commercial theater prices. Colonel Harrington testified:

> The decision to move "The Mikado" from Chicago to New York was my personal decision. It had played in Chicago under good circumstances. We thought it would do the same thing in New York: that it would provide entertainment in New York at a top price of $1.10 for many people who can-

---

*Ulrich was a Chicago producer who also made an offer of private employment to the cast of *The Swing Mikado*. His plan, like that of Charrell, was to produce the show in New York City. A third producer who also seems to have been prepared to make a like offer was Michael Todd. None of these offers, so far as the evidence goes, differed substantially.

not afford $3.30 and $4.40 to get into the regular theaters in New York. The opening night audience in New York—I was there—was comprised of the type of people that you never see in the Broadway theatres, and I have no doubt that that has continued up to the present time. The show has been playing practically to capacity in New York; and I considered that it was proper to move the show from Chicago to New York to provide entertainment for people there, and it was principally upon that consideration that I based my decision.[67]

It was natural that the Theater Project should take pride in the excellent record of *The Swing Mikado*, and should desire to achieve on Broadway the same success as in Chicago. Likewise, it was commendable that the WPA should strive to offer to the less privileged in New York a play that they could not afford to attend at commercial prices. These considerations, however, do not alter the fact that the WPA was at fault in failing to encourage the cast to accept an offer of private employment, which from all the evidence was made in good faith and on terms accepted by producers and actors alike as standard and reasonable.*

THE FAILURE TO ACHIEVE REINSTATEMENT
OF THE THEATER PROJECT

Prior to the fiscal years 1940 and 1941, efforts were made by the WPA, the Actors' Equity Association, and other interested organizations and individuals to persuade Congress to reinstate the Theater Project under the same conditions as the other continuing arts projects. In both

---

*The hearings at which the *Swing Mikado* episode was investigated occurred in the early months of 1939, and consequently only shortly before the final dissolution of the Theater Project at the close of July, 1939. Without doubt, the failure of the WPA to justify its policy in this instance contributed much to the disrepute of the Theater Project, especially in the minds of the House Committee on Appropriations, before which the hearings were held.

Other charges, besides the three mentioned above, were brought against the Theater Project. There were, for instance, accusations of lax administration, extravagance, and subversive activity. These charges, however, were not made against the Theater Project alone, but against all the projects comprised in Federal One and, indeed, against the WPA as a whole. They do not account, therefore, for the discriminatory legislation that discontinued completely and finally the Theater Project alone. Moreover, the analysis here attempted of the *Swing Mikado* episode, although it does not reflect credit upon the WPA administrative personnel involved, is not intended to acquit of unworthy motives many of those who, for three years, had been seeking evidence that would compromise the Theater Project. The mistake of the Theater Project was to present its enemies with evidence as good as that contained in the *Swing Mikado* episode.

instances the efforts were unavailing. In general, the members of the Senate Committee were more sympathetic (as they had been in 1939); but the House Committee and, particularly, its chairman, Mr. Woodrum of Virginia, were adamant; and in conference the Senate yielded to the House.

In connection with these attempts it is interesting to observe that the plan presented by Actors' Equity Association in 1940 hearkened back to the social service concept of the arts prevalent in the FERA period, and repudiated policy that subordinated that concept to one of experimentation and innovation. The proposal, as presented through Maida Reade, of the Association's committee on unemployment, read in part as follows:

WHAT PLANS DOES EQUITY RECOMMEND FOR THE USE OF
RELIEF MONEY?

When Equity first took hold of relief administration it started with $28,000 a month. It did such an effective and economical job that continually that appropriation from the city and state of New York was increased. In the end they were distributing several times this amount.

In determining what to do, Equity brought together the very best brains in the theater and from their experience they now present the following proposed plans:

1. Equity will recommend the revival of its project successfully carried out by it of presenting plays approved by the teaching staffs in the high schools of the larger cities in connection with the class work in English and history and other studies which may be helped by visual education. No admission fee charged.

2. Equity will recommend the continuance of the very successful project of using the traveling theater to bring drama to large audiences outdoors in summer and in large auditoriums in the winter. Admission fee, if any, nominal.

3. Equity will endeavor to revive its most successful project, unqualifiedly approved by Dr. Fechner, of bringing drama to the Civilian Conservation Corps camps, with full practical instructions to camp members in organizing community theaters back home. No admission charge.

4. Equity will sponsor the organization of groups of dramatists to write plays, not for Broadway but of especial value to educational groups. If local sponsors may be secured, groups of dramatists in the several States will be organized to write plays, visualizing state history and local dramatic events.

5. Equity will not endorse productions to be given in competition with regular commercial productions.

6. Consistent with the above, Equity will assist in testing out new methods of production, aiming to bring good theater to smaller communities, such as rotary stock, repeat stock, etc.

7. Equity will assist in promoting a children's theater project.

8. Equity will assist in promoting projects to improve the technical experience of younger actors.[68]

Again at the House hearings in May, 1941, Howard Hunter, Colonel Harrington's successor as WPA administrator, attempted to persuade the committee to restore theater projects. A note of weariness, however, seems to be evident in his plea. When asked if he wanted the theater project back again, he replied, "I am not particularly keen about it, one way or the other. I think it would be helpful to have some of the theater projects out in the country where the local people want them."[69]

Thus all attempts to revive theater projects were in vain. Anyway, by the summer of 1941 the nation was on the eve of war, and all the arts projects—and with them the whole WPA—were *in articulo mortis*. The Theater Project had achieved at least the honor of a public execution, and had met its end at the height of its fame.

1.  Memorandum, Hopkins to Baker, December 15, 1934, FERA Files.
2.  Enclosure, Letter, W. H. Charlton to Stephen D. Early, February 19, 1934, CWA Files.
3.  Letter, Hanna to Cohan, March 29, 1934, CWA Files.
4.  Letter, Baker to Gantvoort, August 31, 1934, FERA Files.
5.  Enclosure, Letter, Gatts to Aubrey Williams, January 18, 1934, CWA Files.
6.  Letter, Kettering to the President, March 11, 1934, CWA Files; Letter, Hanna to Kettering, March 28, 1934.
7.  Letter, Hanna to Turner, April 18, 1934, FERA Files.
8.  Letter, Turner to Mary Inez Ross, July 20, 1934, FERA Files.
9.  Gillmore to the President, January 14, 1935, FERA Files.
10. Letter, Rice to Hopkins, April 28, 1935, FERA Files.
11. Hallie Flanagan, *Arena*, p. 3.
12. *Ibid.*, p. 7.
13. *Ibid.*, pp. 11-12.
14. *Ibid.*, p. 27.
15. *Ibid.*, p. 28.
16. Memorandum, Flanagan to Baker, May 21, 1935, FTP Files.
17. Memorandum, Ringe and Collier to McClure, July 18, 1935, FTP Files.
18. *Supplement No. 1 to Bulletin No. 29*, September 30, 1935, WPA, Section 9.
19. *Instructions*, Federal Theater Project, October, 1935, WPA, p. 1.
20. *Ibid.*, p. 1.
21. *Ibid.*, p. 2.
22. "Address by Hallie Flanagan," First Meeting of Regional Directors, Federal Theater Project, Washington, D. C., October 8, 1935, FTP Files.
23. Hallie Flanagan, *Dynamo* (New York: Duell, Sloan & Pearce, 1943).

24. *Ibid.*, pp. 25-29.

25. *Ibid.*, pp. 66-67.

26. *Ibid.*, pp. 8-9.

27. *Equity Magazine* (November, 1935), p. 5.

28. As quoted in the *New York Times,* October 28, 1935.

29. Memorandum, Flanagan to McClure, September 24, 1935, FTP Files.

30. *Ibid.*

31. *Ibid.*

32. Memorandum, Flanagan to McClure and Baker, November 14, 1935, FTP Files.

33. Telegram, Flanagan to Regional Directors, October 22, 1935, FTP Files.

34. Telegram, Baker to Flanagan, December 23, 1935, FTP Files.

35. Telegram, Gill to Rice, December 30, 1935, FTP Files.

36. Memorandum, Woodward to Assistant Administrators and Division Heads, March 25, 1937, WPA Files.

37. *Ibid.*

38. Memorandum, Woodward to Assistant Administrators and Division Heads, July 26, 1937, WPA Files.

39. Memorandum, Flanagan to Woodward, March, 1937, FTP Files.

40. Letter, E. Kendall Davis to Flanagan, July 30, 1937, FTP Files.

41. Letter, Dunn to Meredith, December 16, 1935, FTP Files.

42. Letter, Davidson to Flanagan, November 29, 1935, FTP Files.

43. Letter, Gnesin to Flanagan, October 17, 1935, FTP Files.

44. Memorandum, Elmer Rice, November 28, 1935, New York City WPA Administration, FTP Files.

45. Letters, Ely to various theatrical workers, October, 1935, New Jersey WPA Administration, FTP Files.

46. Letter, Baker to All Field Supervisors of Federal One, FTP Files.

47. Letter, McGee to Flanagan, September 27, 1935, FTP Files.

48. Telegram, Flanagan to All Regional Directors, October 2, 1935, FTP Files.

49. Letter, Klem to McClure, November 20, 1935, FTP Files.

50. Letter, Stevens to Lang, January 31, 1936, FTP Files.

51. Letter, Staff of Children's Theatre, New York City, to Hopkins, October 19, 1936, FTP Files.

52. Letter, Gillmore to Flanagan, November 10, 1936, FTP Files.

53. Memorandum, Flanagan to McClure, September 19, 1935, FTP Files.

54. Letter, McClure to Flanagan, November 27, 1935, FTP Files.

55. Memorandum, Flanagan to McClure, December 30, 1935, FTP Files.

56. Letter, Kondolf to Flanagan, August 8, 1937, FTP Files.

57. Letter, Rubinstein to Flanagan, November 10, 1936, FTP Files.

58. Memorandum, Baker to Flanagan, October 26, 1935, FTP Files.

59. Letter, Miller to Fransworth, November 17, 1936, FTP Files.

60. U.S. Congress, House, Committee on Appropriations, 76th Cong., 1st sess. (1939), *Hearings of a Subcommittee . . . on Further Additional Relief Appropriation,* pp. 107-10.

61. U.S. Congress. House. Committee on Appropriations. 75th Cong. 3d sess. (1938), *Hearings of a Subcommittee . . . on Supplemental Relief Appropriation,* pp. 67-68).

62. U.S. Congress, Senate. Committee on Appropriations, 75th Cong. 3d sess.

(1938), *Hearings of a Subcommittee . . . on Supplemental Relief Appropriation*, pp. 43-46.

63. U.S. Congress. House. Committee on Appropriations. 76th Cong., 1st sess. (1939), *Hearings of a Subcommittee . . . on Further Relief Appropriation*, p. 233.

64. *Ibid.*, p. 225.

65. *Ibid.*, p. 147.

66. *Ibid.*, p. 226.

67. *Ibid.*, p. 147.

68. U.S. Congress. House. Committee on Appropriations. 76th Cong., 3d sess. (fiscal year 1941), *Hearings of a Subcommittee . . . on Emergency Relief Appropriation*, pp. 1143-44.

69. U.S. Congress. House. Committee on Appropriations, 77th Cong., 1st sess. (fiscal year 1942), *Hearings of a Subcommittee . . . on Emergency Relief Appropriation*, p. 262.

# 22

## The Program of the Federal Theater Project

THE PLANNING OF PRODUCTION

The national plan of the Federal Theater Project represented the personality and the philosophy of its national director. In her speech at the October conference in 1933, Mrs. Flanagan told her regional directors that they must not attempt to put people back to work in theatrical enterprises that were defunct; to do so would be to attempt to revive a corpse. In making this statement, she must have had in mind the commercial theater, although the workers whom her project was about to employ came almost exclusively from that source. Many of these workers were no longer young, and had been trained in the tradition and habits of the professional stage; a few, perhaps, could learn new ways, but most of them had as profound a loyalty to their profession as Mrs. Flanagan harbored for the new theater that it was her intention to create. It was also a fact that the audiences before which her theater was to perform would be less sophisticated than those who frequented her workshop at Vassar.

Mrs. Flanagan was not unaware that the material with which she was about to work was not the best. In her address in October, 1935, she said:

> We should not be fatuous enough however to think it will all be beer and skittles. If we have 6,000 people on relief we all know that probably 4,000 of them are not of the calibre to experiment. However, we must keep steadily in mind that we do not work with the 6,000 alone. We work also with the 600 whom we may choose to work with them; and with the 300 whom we may choose to direct them; and with as many apprentices as we

544

can absorb from the National Youth Administration, who are ready and willing to pay underprivileged youth from 16-25 for studying with the various art groups.[1]

She assured the regional directors that they were to be safeguarded from the necessity of employing theatrical unemployables by instructions that directed them to return to the certifying agencies any who were incapable of making their living in the theater after the end of the project. By January, 1936, she was able to report to her regional directors that the first purpose of the program, the immediate employment of the actor in need, had been achieved. It was time now, she continued, to work toward the second purpose, quality of performance. Entertainment for under-privileged and public groups was well developed; the next step was to build a program of admission shows at low cost that would create new audiences and thereby a future demand for American drama.

> I am increasingly certain that we need new plays, preferably of authentic regional material; or else old plays done in ways to make them exciting to new audiences. We need experimentation in direction, acting and design: direction that, in the absence of elaborate scenery, fills space so that such scenery is unnecessary; design that places emphasis, not on illusion, but on line and light; acting that manages to achieve eloquence without benefit of Bergdorf-Goodman.[2]

In the same communication she emphasized the opportunities for experiment that the federal program promised to provide:

> For here we are as producers, limited possibly in some respects because we are part of a Federal Program, but at the same time freed federally from other pressures: the pressure to keep casts down and settings limited; the pressure of necessity for frequent public performances; the pressure of cutting our cloth to fit the movies. Here are actors, stage hands, designers, musicians, paid and at our service. Within reason we can do any plays in any ways we wish.[3]

In November, 1935, Mrs. Flanagan established an organ of central control for program planning. This body, at first called the Bureau of Research and Publications, and later otherwise designated, was under the direction of Rosamund Gilder, who, with Edith Isaacs, had earlier developed the Service Bureau of the National Theater Conference. The duties of the project's bureau were practically identical with those of the National Theater Conference, and it was intended that both should act in close co-operation with each other and with the *Theatre Arts Monthly.**

The objectives of the Bureau of Research and Publications briefly stated were:

1. To give immediate information service to federal theater projects everywhere on plays, theater books, scripts, etc.

2. To provide appropriate and constructive work for playwrights on the Federal Theater Project.

3. To carry out certain definite research work which will be of permanent value to the theater.[4]

Information service, further defined, included play catalogues, production information and advice, synopses, and royalty information. In co-operation with the Dramatists' Guild, specialists were to negotiate contracts and a responsible business manager was to handle contracts and payments. Bibliographies and indexes were to be compiled. Almost immediately the publication of a house organ, *Federal Theatre*, described as a bulletin and magazine, was undertaken.

Unemployed playwrights presented a problem because, in general, it was not considered wise to have them write plays that would belong to the government, and on which they could never realize more than the pay they received during the composition. This bureau was to provide suitable work for them and leave them opportunity to do their creative work in their free time.

The bureau's first year saw two directors in office; records include caustic criticisms of its slow response to requests for service, its bad judgment in recommendation of plays, and its general negligence. In May, 1936, Mrs. Flanagan persuaded Colonel Somervell to approve the appointment of Francis Bosworth to head a play-reading department. She believed that by paying the higher salary necessary to retain his services, the bureau would become a forceful guiding influence.

About a year after its inception, the Bureau of Research and Publications was reorganized under the name of the National Play Bureau, with Francis Bosworth promoted to the position of director. A deter-

---

*Miss Gilder, a dramatic critic and author, had been since 1933 editorial secretary of the National Theater Conference, an association of college and university theaters, begun as a subscription organization for all in the amateur theatrical field. The *Theatre Arts Monthly*, which Mrs. Isaacs edited, represented, as its name implies, the emphasis upon the art theater.

546

mined effort was made to shift the emphasis to program guidance. Administration was tightened and duties clarified. But the tendency for expansion continued. A music division was added that cleared music copyrights, read musical plays, and arranged and copied musical scores for use in Federal Theater productions. An ambitious folk-song research project developed in this division, and achieved excellent results. An editorial department was created to achieve uniformity for all publications of the bureau. Audience-survey reports were inaugurated, and a new audience-survey division analyzed these in an attempt to arrive at definite opinions as to audience tastes and reactions.

In a further effort to achieve creative program planning, Mrs. Flanagan proposed the establishment of a play policy board. Hopkins, she said, was prepared to support her judgment in all circumstances, but she could not ask him to support the judgment of those in inferior positions. In her letter to Philip Barber, she made this observation: "We have spent a great amount of money and time on the reading and recommending of scripts which have never been picked up by any of our directors anywhere."[5]

Mrs. Flanagan's idea was that knowledge concerning the regional and local requirements of the various project units should be gathered in the field and that therefrom a central committee with final authority should make decisions. Every project director was expected to make recommendations to his superior, and these recommendations, screened by the state and regional directors, were eventually to reach the central committee. To accomplish this, the Play Policy Board was established early in 1937: it was announced by Mrs. Flanagan in February[6] and its existence made formal by Mrs. Woodward in June of the same year.[7]

The Play Policy Board consisted of the national, the deputy national, and the regional directors, the Chicago and New York City directors, and the editor of *Federal Theatre*, under the chairmanship of Hiram Motherwell, assistant national director. At the same time the National Play Bureau was expected to continue its service functions along already operating lines. An unfortunate amount of duplication resulted from this arrangement. The board, as a national co-ordinating project, in addition to being the final authority on program approvals, was authorized to handle all play contracts, all royalty payments, and all per diem and travel costs for actors on loan and companies on tour. An original allotment of $30,000 was provided for this purpose, and a business manager appointed.

In April, 1937, the Play Policy Board held what was reported as an unusually profitable meeting. Firm general policies were established for the more adequate national co-ordination of programs. At this time, Mrs. Flanagan secured agreement to her long-desired prohibition against stock policy anywhere. The resolution read:

> That weekly stock has no place on the Federal Program and that such companies as are now playing weekly stock shift to a production basis, attempting to give to their various companies material more generally in line with FTP policies than the usual stock plays.[8]

A two-week rehearsal period was suggested as a method to make the transition easier. Resolutions regarding publicity standards and methods also were adopted. A department devoted to technical research was proposed, but the plan was tabled for consideration at the next meeting.

Lists were approved for each region and for a national program, but these lists were not to be considered as limiting the projects to these plays alone. However, no other plays could be produced until approval of the assistant director as well as the Play Policy Board was secured. It was necessary that productions be registered with the board's New York office a sufficient time before the first performance (normally thirty days) to permit the clearance of rental quotations and the drawing of contracts. It was not permitted to draw contracts for plays not thus approved. Concerning choice of plays, this general advice was given:

> In the last analysis, the making of a constructive and challenging program is not a problem of picking one title instead of another but of bringing fresh imagination to the interlocking problems of play choice, production, casting, and promotion, so effectively that the audience will feel that the Federal Theatre is a positive force in the community.[9]

Unfortunately, the new board seems to have been as inadequate as its predecessors. A long letter betraying its failures declared that stricter and more rigorous standards must control recommendations. Readers' reports must be tersely professional and provide definite information as to casting requirements and staging details. One forthright recommendation was worth more than a hundred of the non-committal statements emanating from the playreading department. The letter cited a recent instance as an example of expensively bad judgment. Hiram Motherwell had sent telegrams to the assistant directors urging them to guarantee multiple production of two plays that as a personal favor on the part of their authors had been offered to him at low royalties if multiple production was assured.*[10]

Three regional services bureaus, in the South, the West, and the Far West, patterned after the New York bureau, were established. Of these, the San Francisco bureau undertook the most significant research attempted on the project.

In July, 1937, the need for economy caused the consolidation of the National Play Bureau and the Play Policy Board into the National Service Bureau. Its basic policies and its name remained unchanged until the end of the project in 1939.

Its major departments in 1937 were seven: play department, including playreading, playwriting, and translation; reference department; publication department; technical department; music and vaudeville department; clearance and copyrights department; and loan and travel department.

It seems clear that the National Service Bureau never justified the expense its organization entailed. An exchange of caustic letters between George Gerwing, state director for California, and Emmet Lavery, director of the bureau, indicates some of the difficulties. Mrs. Flanagan supported Emmet Lavery's criticism of certain plays chosen by Mr. Gerwing for Los Angeles production and agreed that in general the choice of plays for this unit had been very bad. Mr. Gerwing explained, not too patiently, "We must confine ourselves to plays easily produced with a standard cast, all of whom are working on limited man-hours. . . . We must produce shows, confined, if possible, to one set and, in almost no case exceeding two-set plays."[11]

He declared flatly that it was the duty of the bureau to provide lists of approved plays meeting these requirements or else to allow him to use his judgment.

As early as 1937, the Washington WPA administration was becoming convinced that the National Service Bureau should be curtailed or closed; and by June, 1939, even before the Federal Theater Project itself was terminated by Congress, the curtailment of the bureau's activities was so drastic as to be tantamount to liquidation.

---

*The plays referred to were *To the Ladies,* by Marc Connelly and *The Farmer Takes a Wife,* by George Kaufman and Marc Connelly.

## THE FEDERAL SUMMER THEATER

Another device of program-planning was the Federal Summer Theater. The Rockefeller Foundation, Vassar College, and the Federal Theater Project co-operated to support this venture; the first with funds, the second with facilities, and the Project itself paid the salaries of the enrollees. The purpose of the experiment was to train a selected group of directors and supervisors in the new theater, with the hope that they would return to their projects with creative energy. Some forty people were drawn from the project units throughout the country and brought to Vassar, where they attended the summer session, lasting for six weeks. To those who directed it, the Federal Summer Theater was deemed a success, and, to be sure, some of those who attended attempted new and different productions when they returned to their projects. There is no indication, however, that the Federal Theater Project as a whole was benefited appreciably by the course.

## CLASSICAL DRAMA (PRE-IBSEN)

Classical drama, since it was free of royalties, had offered one of the best reservoirs of plays for directors in the CWA and FERA periods. Unemployment occurred to the greatest extent in an age group, including both actors and directors, that could most easily produce it; comparatively inexpensive staging was possible if old patterns were followed. Tradition and practice placed both amateur and professional companies on fairly firm ground in this field. The most popular and successful branch of ERB dramatic activities in New York City was the presentation of classical drama in the high schools, where it was co-ordinated with class work and provided entertainment as well.

When the ERB units were taken over by the WPA in August, 1935, these programs were continued without change, and most of them survived the transfer to the Federal Theater Project. The classical repertory unit of the New York City project continued to give free productions in parks, schools, and institutions for many months, many of them with the same casts and sets used under the ERB. Their outstanding productions were: *She Stoops to Conquer, Everyman, The Rivals,* and *A Comedy of Errors.* The Yiddish *King Lear* ran for nearly a year

550

after the inception of the Federal Theater Project.

The commercial theater had set a precedent for tabloid versions of Shakespeare; these were presented by the CCC units under the FERA and the Federal Theater Project. Classical drama was very popular, especially in New York City. In May, 1937, nine hundred audience-survey replies from six New York City theaters were selected at random and analyzed in an effort to arrive at an evaluation of audience tastes. The results indicated an overwhelming vote for Shakespeare, and the comment of the analyst was, ". . . On the whole, the classics . . . including the modern ones . . . seem to be in greatest demand."*

The Federal Theater's emphasis on new techniques and material resulted in a decrease of conventional classical productions and the substitution of unique variations. Several original versions of *The Tragical History of Dr. Faustus* were attempted; of these, the most successful was Orson Welles' adaptation in New York City. Welles also produced a rowdy version of Eugene Marin Labiche's *Un Chapeau de Paille d'Italie*, under the novel title *Horse Eats Hat*. Departing from the pattern in another direction, Robert Schnitzer put on *Julius Caesar* in modern dress. Shakespeare's text was in no way altered, and the staging was good. "Modern dress" was the dress of Italy in 1936—black shirts, fascist salute, and all.†

Other uses of classical drama will be mentioned in the comments concerning various special branches of the project; the Negro theater often turned to Shakespeare, and Yiddish groups also inclined toward the classical.

MODERN CLASSICAL DRAMA

Modern classical drama, stemming from the revolt of Ibsen and Strindberg, was naturally favored by a project that stressed experimental drama. The difficulty, however, was that, with reference to the more recent representatives of this school, royalties were required. Here the two leading contemporaries, George Bernard Shaw and Eugene O'Neill, co-operated with the project by offering their plays at reduced rates.

*The preference for the classics is attested only for New York City, and does not necessarily indicate a national point of view. In California, for instance, comedy and musicals were preferred.

†This play provoked protests from the Italian embassy and Italian groups, which resented the implied attack upon Mussolini's regime.

Eugene O'Neill early expressed confidence that the Federal Theater Project would provide the American theater with leadership of sufficient caliber to free it from its limitations, if the project adhered to its announced policies and aims. At Mrs. Flanagan's request, he agreed to the production of his plays but made the reservation that if he found performances inadequate he would withdraw permission to produce them. Several unfortunate incidents developed during negotiations: promised productions were canceled; the original agreement to pay the sliding scale of royalties was overlooked in subsequent correspondence; and the definite schedule of productions for which O'Neill had asked was never achieved. Many of his plays were produced, but the proposed Eugene O'Neill "cycles" became productions of four consecutive plays in several cities and thirteen single productions.

George Bernard Shaw enthusiastically endorsed the project's program by freely permitting the production of any of his plays at a flat fifty dollars a week royalty. Since he was placing at Mrs. Flanagan's disposal thirty-three full-length plays and fifteen short ones, he anticipated royalties of at least $2,500 a year.[12] When Mrs. Flanagan sent Shaw a note of appreciation and promised him to seek a high degree of skill in these productions,[13] Shaw replied—with a realism in sharp contrast with Mrs. Flanagan's idealism—that he was quite prepared to have his plays murdered![14]

The production of standard plays, classical and modern, formed a relatively small part of the project's total activities. Yet it is likely that if this type of drama had been more emphasized, the project would have achieved a firmer foundation, especially in non-metropolitan areas where the experimental theater was unknown.

## CONTEMPORARY DRAMA

Popular dramatists of the current theater followed Shaw's and O'Neill's example and permitted, under various conditions, the production of their plays. Elmer Rice consented to the production of his plays under a guaranteed royalty of $2,500 a year, at the rate of fifty dollars a week a play. Among his plays produced on the project were *Street Scene, See Naples and Die, Judgment Day, The Left Bank*, and *Counsellor-at-Law*. The tendentious nature of Rice's plays appealed to the more progressive directors, but the records fail to indicate that the fifty-weeks-a-year production schedule was ever attained.

Maxwell Anderson's work was represented by his *Outside Looking In*, *Both Your Houses*, *Saturday's Children*, and *Gods of the Lightning*, which he wrote with Harold Hickerson. The longest run was that of *Gods of the Lightning*, with three weeks; his other plays were given only a few performances each.

The simultaneous opening of twenty-one performances of *It Can't Happen Here*, a dramatization by Sinclair Lewis and J. C. Moffitt of Lewis' novel of the same title, earned wide publicity for the project. Critics acclaimed this multiple production as a great feat, but over-emphasis on meeting the deadline unquestionably affected the quality of many of the productions. The presentation of this play was an act of courage, for the cinema had avoided it. Coming as it did, however, on the eve of a national election, it laid the project open to the charge of propaganda.

## THE LIVING NEWSPAPER

The Living Newspaper productions of the Federal Theater Project became the subject of voluminous comment. This technique, aptly described by Pierre de Rohan, editor of *Federal Theatre*, as a "merger of radio program and topical movies,"[15] was a kind of *March of Time* with a new point of view, that of workers instead of capitalists. It offered several advantages for the project—large casts, inexpensive sets, and employment for playwrights and newspapermen, who could do the research and write the scripts.

Elmer Rice and Mrs. Flanagan very early planned the development of this technique and established a unit in New York City. The first script dealt with Italy's aggression in Ethiopia. It was banned on the eve of its production as inimical to the cause of international amity. Elmer Rice resigned in high dudgeon, and Mrs. Flanagan was genuinely distressed.

The first two Living Newspapers to be staged were *Triple A Plowed Under* and *Highlights of 1935*. The next production, *Injunction Granted*, created a furore. Mrs. Flanagan wrote a sharp rebuke to the producers, saying, among other things, that Philip Barber, the New York director, and William Farnsworth wished to discontinue the unit immediately and permanently. She added:

Phil Barber and Bill Farnsworth were opposed to *Injunction Granted*. I took the responsibility and believed that the things I suggested would be done; that you would clean up the script that I saw and make it objective; keep it from becoming wild-eyed propaganda. . . . You did none of these things, but instead loaded it with extraneous scenes.

The facts that *Injunction Granted* is drawing crowds does not help. Everyone knows that these crowds are being sent by their unions. . . .[16]

The letter closed with the statement that none of the three Living Newspapers so far attempted had achieved high standards of production.

Another Living Newspaper, *Power*, which treated the subject of private versus public ownership of electric sources, raised similar difficulties; and it was only after the most exhaustive checking, rechecking, and reviewing by many people—from Harry Hopkins and Mrs. Flanagan down—that it finally reached the public.

Morris Watson, the producer of the Living Newspaper, resigned in 1937, and Mrs. Flanagan personally undertook the planning and production of the next presentation. Its title was *One-third of a Nation*, and it dealt with the New York City housing problem. The Summer Theater in 1937 devoted its entire session to working on its production. After this preliminary work, it was turned over to the unit that opened it on the New York stage in January, 1938. It was the first Living Newspaper to reach the full stature toward which the project had worked for two years. It was favorably received, and various other cities presented locally adapted versions of the same script.*

### RELIGIOUS DRAMA

Only Gareth Hughes's company in Los Angeles specialized in religious drama. The *Nativity*, in the director's version, was repeated several times, and Dickens' *A Christmas Carol* formed part of every Christmas season program. In other places regular companies similarly planned appropriate plays for the season. *Everyman* was produced several times; other versions of the *Nativity* and *A Christmas Carol* were produced. On a nationwide level, no evidence of a concerted plan or accomplishment in developing religious drama appears in the records.

One religious play produced by the Federal Theater Project de-

---

*The Chicago unit produced *Spirochete*, a history and discussion of syphilis, and this production was sent to other cities. Norwalk, Connecticut, and Cleveland, Ohio, had their own Living Newspapers, which enjoyed limited runs. *One-third of a Nation* was sold to a motion picture producer for $5,000. Random House included three Living Newspaper plays in a collection of six federal theater plays published in 1938.

serves special mention. *Murder in the Cathedral* by T. S. Eliot had been running for some time in London and had been produced by the Yale drama group in this country. Mrs. Flanagan decided to produce it in New York. Halsted Wells handled it with creative and compelling artistry, and critics acclaimed it both for its poetic quality and for its notably impressive production.

### THE NEGRO THEATER

The Theater Project, like the other arts projects under Federal One, made special and praiseworthy efforts in the direction of the encouragement of Negro activities. The Negro, to be sure, had a place on the American stage almost from its inception, but his status was largely determined by the characterizations created by the minstrel show. So far as serious drama was concerned, Negro characters like Uncle Tom, played by white actors, were symbols rather than personalities. In general, in American drama Negroes have been portrayed more as caricatures than as characters.

The first American Negro drama was by Edward Sheldon. Its quality was not high, for the gravity of its theme was spoiled by its melodramatic manner; but it courageously attacked the problem of mutual intolerance between Negro and white. It was not until 1917, however, that Negro players commanded the serious attention of the theatrical world. In that year the Hapgood Players, a Negro company, presented three plays by Ridgely Torrence, the first Negro playwright realistically to portray his fellows. These plays brought both races together in the realm of art, and their performance marks the founding of the American Negro theater.

More than any other playwright, Eugene O'Neill realized the dramatic possibilities of the Negro psychology. His greatest Negro plays, *All God's Chillun Got Wings* and *The Emperor Jones*—although they caused a certain resentment among Negroes because the hero of one is a failure and that of the other a murderer—revealed a rare comprehension and a genuine sympathy.

Paul Green, although he did not cultivate the psychological as obviously as did O'Neill, was no less successful in his delineation of the Negro character. By his exploitation of folklore and his emphasis upon the simple rather than the complex, Green perhaps approached more closely to the Negro psyche than his elder contemporary.

These two men became the leaders of a group in the American theater that found in Negro life and character a fecund source of drama. Their plays treated every phase of Negro activity—urban life, economic status, and folklore. Moreover, by this time the Negro had achieved full stature not only as a source of drama but also as an actor on the stage.

Negro dramatic groups with serious aspirations appeared long before the Federal Theater Project; Harlem had its Lafayette Company and Chicago its Ethiopian Art Theater. The latter group visited New York in 1923 and, among other things, presented a jazzed version of *A Comedy of Errors* that may have provided the inspiration for some of the Federal Theater's versions of Shakespeare's plays. In Cleveland, Ohio, the Gilpin Players did significant and serious work, and many other Negro little-theater groups carried on fruitful activities. In 1930 the founding of the Negro Intercollegiate Dramatic Association marked the entrance of the Negro into the field of the non-professional drama.

It was upon these foundations that the Federal Theater Project built its Negro program. In Harlem, Rose McClendon, a Negro actress, was directing a small struggling, professional company whose members easily qualified for relief certification. Mrs. Flanagan thus describes the first conference regarding its program:

> Our Negro unit was the first unit set up in Federal Theatre (New York City). We met at Rose McClendon's house . . . and discussed how we could best develop as a part of the Federal project, a Negro Theatre. My original conception was . . . that plays, players, designs, and direction should all be by Negroes. However, Rose McClendon and others in the group felt at that time this would be a grave mistake. They pointed out that there never had been any opportunity to develop directorial ability and they consequently asked that John Houseman and Orson Welles be assigned to them for the first Negro play. The choice of this play was also interesting. They did not want a play for or about Negroes, which I admit was somewhat disillusioning to me. Their reasoning, however, was clear. They said they saw no reason why the Negro race should not do the works of the greatest white writers. Consequently we produced *Macbeth* which as you know was a tremendous success.[17]

From the first, the Negro theater in New York City was a complete production unit—theater, workshop, stage crew, lighting department —employing at its peak in May, 1936, five hundred people; in December, 1937, this figure was 253. Most other large cities and several smaller towns also had Negro units—Birmingham, Alabama; Greensboro, Rock

Mount, and Raleigh, North Carolina; and Tampa, Florida. In Buffalo, New York, a Negro marionette unit enjoyed the distinction of being the only one entirely manned by Negroes. The Harlem group acquired a Negro director before the end of its first year; by 1939 the only white people on Negro projects were managers for the Seattle and the Boston units.

Negro leaders unceasingly attempted to get positions of greater influence in the Federal Theater Project; it was not enough, they believed, to have production units under Negro direction. They hoped for a national Negro theater, and felt that it was a serious error not to give them more voice in national direction. In the fall of 1936, a Negro co-ordinator was urged for the project. The objection raised by the National Play Bureau was that this function already belonged to it and that such an appointment would result in duplication of services. The very inadequacy of these services had led to the request. In spite of their efforts and pressure from Harry Hopkins for a stronger Negro branch, Negro activities continued under the control of the National Play Bureau and the Play Policy Board without racial representation.

Under its capable directors, John Houseman and Orson Welles, the Negro unit opened New York City Federal Theater's first legitimate production on February 4, 1936. *Walk Together Chillun,* by a Negro playwright, Frank Wilson, was not a strong opening production. The next production, however, the Negro *Macbeth,* was a remarkable success. The text remained Shakespeare's, but the locale was Haiti and the spirit that of voodooism. This company was one of the first to go on tour; it played in several cities and remained ten days at the Dallas Centennial Exposition.

In addition to *Macbeth,* two other productions created wide comment and won popular approval, *The Swing Mikado* and *Run Little Chillun.* The first of these enjoyed an unusually long run at Chicago. In New York City, where it was later moved, it was indifferently received. *Run Little Chillun* was a musical revue and skillfully used the superb musical gifts of the Negro.

Of Eugene O'Neill's two great plays for Negroes, *The Emperor Jones* and *All God's Chillun,* only the former was produced, and it played only two performances. Bad judgment was used in selection of his other plays; the Harlem unit put on the four one-act plays of the S.S. Glencairn series and drew sharp criticism from one of the Federal Theater's strongest supporters, Brooks Atkinson, for its inept casting.[18]

An equally ill-judged move in Chicago led to further unfortunate results. O'Neill was requested to allow the presentation of an adaptation of *The Hairy Ape* that had been made by Shirley Graham, director of the Negro unit. His agent conveyed the playwright's definite refusal to allow any adaptations of his plays, and added that O'Neill considered such a request stupid and impertinent. O'Neill was reported as saying, "If Negroes cannot act white parts as whites have played Negroes, they should not be in the theatre." His further remarks were summarized as condemning "freak theatre, where white plays are faked into black plays," and he added that "he is entirely fed up with the project."[19]

On the other hand, George Bernard Shaw was much more sanguine about the acting ability of Negroes and credited them with a delicacy of interpretation in sharp contrast with the performance of white actors.[20]

The obstacles that faced the Theater Project in its development of a Negro theater were not easy to overcome. The social and economic position of the Negro made the creation of Negro audiences difficult. In Harlem, where there were no barriers to their attendance, most Negroes preferred the cinema. They regarded the plays in the Negro theater as white men's plays. Their favorites were *Conjur Man Dies* and *The Show Off*, both of which were of indifferent quality. Harlem's lack of support of its own theater was noted by the *Amsterdam News* in respect to the play *Haiti*, an excellent production. The newspaper deplored the fact that scarcely 25 per cent of the attendance at this play consisted of Negroes, although the play itself had been chosen expressly because it was thought to have an appeal to a Negro audience.*[21]

## CIVILIAN CONSERVATION CORPS ENTERTAINMENT

The Federal Theater ccc division began operations as the direct heir to the project that had been operated by the fera. The *Instructions* stated that the plan whereby small dramatic companies went to vari-

---

*It is possible that a patronizing attitude on the part of the project toward the Negro in the theater, however well-intentioned it was and without deliberation, may have antagonized the Negro patron. There was also the tendency to think of the Negro theater and the Negro in the theater as things apart from the normal and requiring special treatment. A Broadway success of the season 1944-45 illustrates a more natural and frank attitude: *Anna Lucasta*, although it was performed with a Negro cast, was written about a Polish family. The actors attempted it as a play, and not as a Negro play.

ous camps within certain corps areas was to be expanded to include camps in every part of the country. Since Mrs. Flanagan was dissatisfied with both the administration and performance of the earlier projects, it was decided to discontinue them pending complete reorganization. Because most of the actors in these companies were members of Actors' Equity, this decision was ill received by the professional acting fraternity.

In March, 1936, Colonel Earle L. House was appointed director of the National Co-ordinating ccc Project under the reorganization plan. He announced comprehensive plans for a new theater program in *Happy Days*, the ccc publication. The country was to be organized in three regions centering in New York, Chicago, and Los Angeles. Traveling companies were to tour within their regional boundaries. Professional stage people who could qualify and who were approved by the Army and by the educational authorities were to be appointed as resident drama instructors. A motion picture division would serve New York State camps with films.[25] The most successful single effort of this project was the production of the *CCC Murder Mystery*, a play written specifically for the project. It seems to have lived up to its description as "a thrilling, entertaining, laugh-provoking mystery story, of, by, and for the boys of ccc."

In the fall of 1936 the Theater Project launched a playwriting contest among the ccc camp enrollees. Since playwriting is one of the most intricate of all art forms, this project represented a high degree of optimism. In the end, from the 350,000 enrollees, 410 manuscripts were submitted. In spite of consistently discouraging reports from play readers, circulated only intramurally, fervid announcements were issued to the public and especially to the ccc boys. It was finally decided that two of the plays were so excellent that two awards should be made instead of one. A year later one of these plays was given a single performance in Massachusetts, and the play department was vainly trying to find a director for the other one.*

---

*It is interesting to observe that in this contest, before any award had been made, the department head wrote that he had read the ten best plays submitted, and that only one was even faintly possible.

In addition to the ccc camp contest, Federal Theater sponsored two others. One was for college students. The response was indifferent, and no play worthy of Broadway production was found. The other was sponsored by the Dramatists' Guild. A prize of $250 was offered, and the Federal Theater guaranteed two weeks of professional production under the conditions of the Guild contract. Of the 378 scripts submitted for consideration, *See How They Run*, written by George Milton Savage of the University of Washington faculty, won first prize. It was given a pre-

The ccc theater program involved the shortest possible tours for small companies. These companies were also permitted to include other institutions in their circuits. Their plays and productions were not experimental or new, but they provided employment for 1,260 actors and other workers in ninety-four companies that appeared in 5,420 performances in thirty-five states. In addition, eighty-five resident drama instructors were provided for camps at a cost of $95,500. The play-script service cost the project $7,670. Wherever possible, camps co-operated by providing transportation. The motion picture service appears to have been inadequately managed, and was discontinued in December, 1936.

The ccc Theater Program was discontinued as a national project in August, 1937, and Colonel House resigned. The work was continued after that date by the states. The dramatic instructors were for the most part taken over by the education and recreation divisions of the wpa. State records indicate that generally the project was satisfactorily managed under state wpa supervision.

## VAUDEVILLE

Vaudeville, perhaps more than any other department of the theater, had declined even before the coming of the depression. The competition of the cinema had been fatal, and induced a change of taste on the part of audiences that discouraged Variety. For this reason, there was probably in the larger centers a greater concentration of unemployed vaudeville actors than of any other type of performer. Their acts, since they generally owned their own properties, could usually be staged for little or no non-labor cost. In the early cwa and fera projects their services were welcome, and they gave many free performances.

When the wpa began, regional and state officials willingly transferred these groups to the new agency. At the inception of the Theater Project, Eddie Dowling, successful actor and producer, council member of the American Federation of Actors, a friend of the President's family, and chairman of the entertainment committee of the national Democratic party, was appointed director of vaudeville with headquarters in New York City. Mrs. Flanagan, aware of the excellent work

miere, followed by twenty-three performances in San Francisco, then later played the author's home city, Seattle. It never reached Broadway.

560

being done in this field in other cities, wished his task to be that of organizing touring musical comedy, vaudeville, and circus companies, and routing them throughout the country.

Because Mr. Dowling found it impossible to accommodate himself to government procedure, he was allowed to delegate his responsibilities to Ralph Whitehead, executive secretary of the AFA. At Baker's request Whitehead received a leave of three months from the AFA in order to devote his full time to this assignment. Although no progress was made toward a national program, as originally outlined, the New York City project was able to initiate vaudeville, musical comedy, and circus performances.

Two methods were used to employ the disproportionate number of unemployed vaudeville actors. The first was the creation of chronological medleys, among which the most successful were *Two-a-Day* and *Follow the Parade*. The former was an attempt to tell the story of vaudeville; the latter consisted of episodes of human interest from the nineties to the present. The second method involved the employment of actors in other than vaudeville activities. In writing to the director of the Massachusetts project, Mrs. Flanagan thus expressed herself on this subject:

> We have found in a great many cases that there is no necessity for vaudevillians to keep on being vaudevillians. From the beginning of the project, we have been retraining vaudevillians in the field of children's theatre, living newspaper and musical revues. . . . Almost half the cast of the Living Newspaper unit in New York City is recruited from the field of vaudeville. Especially are the casts of Yasha Frank's *Hansel and Gretel* and *Pinocchio* drawn from the vaudeville ranks.[22]

Mrs. Flanagan mentioned as other examples of the use of vaudeville actors *Follow the Parade*, *Review of Revues* and *Ready, Aim, Fire*.

Figures that indicate the vaudeville project's relative importance in the program appear in a report covering the first fifteen months. Of the ninety-five units in the country in December, 1936, six were classified as drama vaudeville, fifteen as straight vaudeville, and two as vaudeville-circus. Thus 24 per cent of all project activities involved vaudeville. They cost a total of $2,875,479.95 of which $2,652,631.95 was spent for salaries. Of the free entertainment offered by the project, a great part was also provided by this activity.

On the New York City project, in addition to four vaudeville units, several circus units were maintained. The first Federal Theater production in New York City, October 17, 1935, was a circus performance by a unit transferred from the ERA. In May, 1936, this unit acquired a tent of its own seating 4,000 people, and with it toured the boroughs through the summer months each year thereafter.

## CHILDREN'S THEATER

Under the FERA, vaudeville, marionettes, and the dance, which were developed in close co-operation with children's agencies, recreation leaders, and schools, were the usual types of entertainment provided for children. Under the WPA, however, an attempt was made to produce legitimate professional performances exclusively for children.

An important early production of the New York City children's theater unit was *The Emperor's New Clothes*, which opened in June, 1936, at the Adelphi Theater. Later it was played by seven other projects in the country. In New York children were admitted for five cents if they came in groups of twenty-five, and for fifteen cents in smaller groups. The company played outdoor engagements throughout the city after leaving Broadway.

Another production of the New York unit, *The Revolt of the Beavers*, provoked wide discussion. The play was frankly propagandist, and dealt with the revolt of oppressed beaver workers against their capitalist overlords. Brooks Atkinson, one of the project's best friends, wrote disapprovingly of it:

> Beavers of the world, unite! is its unspoken sense. By uniting and shooting down the chief's company police with revolvers and machine guns concealed in their lunch boxes, the hungry beavers joyfully overthrew their industrial oppressors.[23]

This seems to have been the only notable propaganda effort in the children's theater. *Pinocchio*, like *The Emperor's New Clothes*, was entertainment. The version used was an adaptation by Yasha Frank. He first produced it in Los Angeles, and later it was used by seven other projects. The roster of productions for children, aside from these plays, was limited. In New York and Los Angeles special children's theater units were established at the inception of the program. The Cleveland project, much later, operated its only theater project, The Theater of Youth, exclusively for children. Many smaller projects, unable to establish separate units encouraged their regular units occasionally to give productions for children. Apart from marionettes and vaudeville, about fifty productions in all are recorded.

562

In the meantime, Mrs. Flanagan had not lost sight of her early hope to establish a significant national program of drama for children, and, in December, 1938, she appointed Yasha Frank national consultant for the children's theater. Mr. Frank's point of view, like Mrs. Flanagan's, was that the greatest need for a good program was new material. However, since his appointment was virtually on the eve of the demise of the Theater Project, he had little time to initiate a program.

## COMMUNITY THEATER

The importance that the community theater held in the early thinking of those interested in the establishment of the Federal Theater Project has already been discussed. In the period during which the procedure for Federal One were in process of formulation, however, several influences, the chief among which was pressure exerted by professional unions and societies, brought about a change of emphasis that, if subtle in the beginning, was conclusive in the end. *Appendix A to Supplement No. 1 to Bulletin No. 29* made this new stress clear. It read:

Section 1.  *General Principles.* WPA sponsored Project No. 1 has been established for a two-fold purpose:

  A.  To provide proper employment for unemployed eligible artists, musicians, theatre workers, writers; and

  B.  To provide valuable service to the community.[24]

Community service was placed second and further limited:

There are two ways in which the second of these purposes may be fulfilled by persons engaged in WPA sponsored Project No. 1, namely:

  A.  By producing works or presenting performances which meet professional standards for the benefit of the community; and

  B.  By promoting and conducting among residents of the community such leisure-time activities as will increase their participation in music, art, literature and drama.

Insofar as possible, priority should be given to work in professional pursuits, especially where such is the desire of the eligible workers.[25]

This Appendix outlined the procedure for the initiation of such projects, and was followed by further communications that urged co-operation with community institutions. In spite of these efforts, however, this activity did not flourish. Professional theater workers, on the whole, were unsympathetic toward recreational and educational dramatic programs; this lack of sympathy on the part of the project workers was shared by the national director. The natural reaction to this indifference on the part of those devoted to community drama was, first, disappointment, and then, hostility. Frederick H. Koch, who had been foremost in that field for many years, was quoted in the New York *Herald Tribune* as saying:

> It was our hope that regions of the country lacking in entertainment might have a chance to get professional talent which is concentrated in New York and in California. We were all hoping that talented young actors would be sent to communities where there were no theatres. Then we hoped to send talented theatre workers into communities to start people's theatres.
>
> Suddenly Federal headquarters, wherever it is or whoever it is, decided we might only use unemployed theatre workers who lived in the various regions.[26]

Professor Koch was not entirely correct. It was planned to send professional companies into the regions. Early in the project's history, the Studio Theater was organized in New York City for the purpose of training, or retraining, professional theater workers for positions of leadership in recreation and leisure-time activities. Its personnel was expected to include many of the estimated 40 per cent of professional theater workers who were considered unemployable by commercial enterprises. It was to operate as a producing unit that, after six weeks of intensive laboratory training in every branch of production, would be booked through existing agencies. The whole course was designed to equip people for work in the community drama field, with special emphasis upon directing amateur productions and teaching various phases of dramatic art in tax-supported agencies and to underprivileged groups. It was planned, after a two-week run, to terminate the production and to assign its workers to various localities. Similar programs were conducted in Connecticut for a group of twenty-seven workers; in Chicago, for fifty; in Omaha, for twenty; in St. Louis, for four; and the New York City project proposed to train 317 workers.*

*Manteo, Roanoke Island, North Carolina, operated a unique and valuable community project during the Federal Theater period. Although Federal Theater cannot be given much if any credit for the inception and organization of the project, its story is here told because it illustrates local and regional benefits that can be achieved by communal efforts. For fifty years the people of Manteo and the island had sponsored an annual celebration of the founding of the first English colony in America. On this occasion Paul Green, steeped in North Carolina folk-drama, wrote

In 1936 Herbert S. Price was appointed national consultant on community drama. His background was in the recreational and educational fields, and his first position on the project had been as drama coach at the Studio Theater. In his new office his duty was to act as liaison officer between the Theater Project and other agencies working in related fields—the WPA education and recreation divisions and the FSA resettlement division of the Federal Security Agency.

Because of the opportunity presented by increased quotas in 1938, Price, who had already set up several experimental projects in the South, renewed his efforts to form leisure-time projects on a national scale. The essence of his plan was to move professional workers from New York City into the field. The obstacles to this plan, however, were serious. In the first place, it required co-operation with the recreation and education divisions of the WPA, and these divisions were now disenchanted with the Federal Theater Project; and in the second place, New York City professionals were loathe to leave the metropolis and to associate themselves with amateurs.

In the summer of 1938 Price submitted a report in which he first distinguished between the "precious" little theater operating for its own amusement and to give entertainment to a select group of friends and, on the other hand, the "true" theater of tomorrow representing the ethos of the whole community. He then proceeded to insist that no attempt be made "to imitate the professional theater nor ape the professional actor."[27]

Mrs. Flanagan, however, although she was not unsympathetic to the community theater as such, was largely precluded by the very purpose of her agency from spending any considerable amount of money on amateur community dramatics.

a play, *The Lost Colony*, to commemorate the 350th anniversary of the first settlement.

Frederick Koch and his playmakers collaborated in the production; the historical society sponsored it; the local WPA planned a theater, and CCC enrollees helped to build it; local WPA sewing projects made the 200 costumes; and professionals, loaned from New York City, provided the direction and training of the local participants. Their travel and per diem expenses were paid by the sponsors with the result that the non-labor cost to the Theater Project was negligible. This project was one of the few exceptions to the national director's rule that amateur companies could not be supported by Federal Theater Project funds. During three successive summers about a thousand people a week came to Manteo to see Paul Green's play.

A much less admirable adventure was the one-day pageant in Arkansas during its centennial celebration in 1936. At a cost of $12,500 the Theater Project provided an advisory staff, which was 100 per cent non-relief, to stage a spectacle. Originally, the cost was to be $10,000; but, in order properly to accommodate a presidential visit on that day, $2,500 in addition was needed.

RADIO DIVISION

In March, 1936, the Federal Theater radio division, often called the Federal Theater of the Air, gave its first performance in New York City. It was organized under the direction of Evan Roberts with a staff of writers, directors, production managers, and office workers. Its purpose, in addition to giving employment to the unemployed, was "to produce educational and cultural programs to familiarize the American people with the best in drama, art, science, history, music, and literature."

By virtue of its medium, subjects were chosen that could be concluded in broadcasts of from fifteen minutes to one and a half hours. For some of these series the works of well-known authors, who donated the rights, were chosen. Among others, the "Tish" stories of Mary Roberts Rinehart provided humor, and Paul de Kruif contributed articles on medicine. But the best of these programs was *The Epic of America*. The script was based on James Truslow Adams' book of the same name and was prepared and approved by him. Planned for fourteen half-hour broadcasts, it presented the background and growth of our national culture and provided a most effective vehicle for showing the trends and the philosophy that have accompanied our national maturity. Naturally, educational institutions immediately recognized its value, and many teachers incorporated it into their classwork by means of recordings made in the New York studio.

A program of excellent radio drama was also developed. Shakespeare's plays, Elizabethan dramas, and other classics, as well as the work of contemporary dramatists, were included. By polling the nation's drama critics and, through them, their audiences, a program called "Command Performance" was evolved. It consisted of "the thirteen best plays of all times and of all countries." Many prominent actors and actresses agreed to take leading roles. A high percentage of the plays on the list were recent or current Broadway successes. Theater Guild productions were popular, and four plays by Maxwell Anderson were included.

The ways in which the division serviced the WPA and the other arts projects included: "Backstage Interviews," which consisted of scenes from Federal Theater productions and interviews with Federal Theater directors, broadcast in nineteen fifteen-minute episodes; and the "Symphonic Drama" series, which claimed to be unique because it made music coequal with drama by combining such works as *Don Quixote* and Strauss's tone poem on the same subject, and Ibsen's *Peer Gynt* and Grieg's musical suite interpreting it.

The *Story of the Federal Theatre Radio Division*, the division's own autobiography, reported, "In fact, it is said that the Federal Theatre Radio Division has definitely helped to accelerate the trend of networks toward more intelligent, more cultural broadcasts."

## MARIONETTE THEATER

FERA dramatic projects had made wide use of puppetry, both the hand-manipulated kind (puppets) and the string-operated kind (marionettes). Recreation centers, schools, and institutions had a predilection for this type of dramatic activity, and directors found in them a comparatively inexpensive and easy way both to entertain audiences and to employ theatrical workers and such other artisans as could be used to make the dolls and the theaters. Schools found them valuable as an educational device.

The original plans for the Federal Theater included marionette units. Although the vocational study form prepared for the use of audition boards included a special form for marionette workers, it was soon apparent that actors without experience in this field as well as craftsmen from other fields easily could adjust themselves to this type of work. Project units were established to train and retrain such workers on a large scale. The work imposed less physical strain than legitimate drama and was more elastic in the matter of costume and staging.

The Buffalo Historical Marionettes, of Buffalo, New York, did outstanding work before the WPA and continued its progress under the Federal Theater. This unit had strong community support, and the city of Buffalo contributed an entire building for its use as a workshop. The important idea that grew with this program was that most marionette plays on a nationwide project could be interchangeable; duplication of costs thus could be avoided, especially such costs as material and working space. The Buffalo director, Esther B. Wilhelm, thought in terms of regional centers, so that historical and folk material could be incorporated locally into productions that then could with great advantage be loaned to other regions. In addition to entertainment and education for children, the Buffalo project offered productions for

567

adults. Among the marionette units in Buffalo, the Negro unit was competent and well received.

Remo Bufano, who had been doing work in this field under the FERA, was appointed to direct the New York City unit. This unit was elaborately equipped; the construction section employed stage- and set-builders, technicians, benchworkers, electricians, general craftsmen, property men, and porters. The design department employed designers, model and casting artists, costumers, and artists. A trucking department called for and delivered properties and equipment of eight companies. A playwrights' committee, consisting of director, assistant director, production manager, and senior research workers, was included. Administrative difficulties, however, beset the program, and Bufano resigned in 1937.

Meanwhile, Lawrence Westbrook, assistant administrator for WPA, had entered into negotiations with Tony Sarg. Westbrook believed that Sarg's marionettes could effectively be used to inform the public about the social philosophy of the WPA, and recommended that Sarg be retained as advisor to the Federal Theater in the development of a definite program of plays for this purpose, using plots that would be worked out by the WPA department of information. Mrs. Flanagan accepted the suggestion, and offered Sarg a position as Bufano's assistant, a position that Sarg would not consider. He had expected to direct, not to advise. The result of this, apparently, was a pronounced disaffection on Sarg's part for the entire project. Perhaps as a sequel, the marionette program later was under heavy fire for unfair competition with private industry. After his own resignation Bufano also actively pressed similar charges.[28]

Marionette units in other sections of the country were useful in giving employment to workers from the tent, vaudeville, medicine show, tab, and circus fields. Oklahoma operated a unit called the Vagabond Puppeteers, which toured the state and provided entertainment for underprivileged groups and school children. Los Angeles called its marionette unit the Theater of the Magic Strings.

Mrs. Flanagan says in *Arena* that at one time there were twenty-two units, employing 358 persons, and that they presented one hundred performances a week to average audiences of 400.[29]

THE DANCE

In the relief programs that preceded the WPA the recreation division supervised most dance activities. Quite naturally, these projects tended

568

toward athletic rather than aesthetic expression. Indeed, more than half the enrollment usually consisted of people seeking recreation. The Theater Project of the WPA, however, attempted to raise the dance to the echelon of an artistic performance. Mrs. Flanagan was acutely aware of the close relationship between the art of the dance and the theater.[30]

In March, 1936, a dance project was approved for New York City. Under the guidance of professional choreographers, its purpose was to establish a dance theater in which full-length productions, equal in scope and power to the best in the spoken drama, would be developed. Minimum requirements for admission to audition were three years' training with an accredited school or teacher and two years of professional experience. A professional group was defined as "a group which has appeared in a Broadway theatre and received press criticisms." Only dancers who specialized in ballet or modern interpretative schools were eligible for employment.*

Unfortunately, the New York City project was beset with disturbances, and it became difficult if not impossible to regulate the project either in the matter of program or of size. The dance program was also attacked on the ground that it offered competition to private teachers and schools of the dance. At all events, the dance program was a very small part of the national theater program. The Myra Kinch Dancers in Los Angeles came nearest to achieving professional excellence, and their production, *An American Exodus*, had a long run in Los Angeles and was sent to San Francisco. In New York the *Folk Dances of All Nations* played for about four months.

THEATER FOR THE BLIND

At the Oklahoma School for the Blind in Muskogee the Federal Theater provided a director and a supervisor to train students in dramaturgy. The director, a graduate of the school, was one of the few blind professionals in the country. It was necessary that plays be transcribed into Braille and then memorized. No departure from the usual staging and properties was necessary, and very little in the acting. Blind performers were reported as entirely successful in character interpretation and in speech.

---

*Similar projects were organized in Los Angeles and Chicago; less ambitious programs were developed in Philadelphia, Tampa, Oregon, and Dallas, Texas.

## TRYOUT THEATER

At the outset of the project, Mrs. Flanagan planned a tryout theater, a project she believed would meet government requirements and at the same time stimulate legitimate theater business. The plan provided for commercial production of plays in New York City on a trial basis under the sponsorship of the League of New York Theaters, a non-profit organization of producers and managers. The sponsor was to cover most of the non-labor costs and provide the plays. The administrative director was to be appointed by the league and to work with an advisory committee. The Federal Theater would contribute salaries of workers from relief rolls at the prevailing security wage and such other labor costs as were permitted by regulations. Low admission charges were to prevail, and any surplus after the league had been reimbursed was to be used to further the plan. Any play that showed sufficient promise during its trial run was to be continued commercially by the manager who had originally proposed and produced it; it was hoped that he would use many of the original cast and thus remove from relief rolls some of the needy workers.

Actors' Equity and IATSE firmly opposed the plan because they feared that the managers would be able to exploit workers who would, under such an arrangement, be paid according to Federal Theater regulations. Mrs. Flanagan made various efforts to meet their objections: limiting the number of such units that would be established to three; limiting the number of weeks to three for the tryout; and having no more than 10 per cent of the cast paid by the manager. Opposition continued, however, and the idea was shortly abandoned.

## FOREIGN-LANGUAGE DRAMA: YIDDISH

By far the largest number of productions attempted by any foreign-language group was undertaken by the Yiddish units. In New York, Los Angeles, and Massachusetts, companies that had operated under the FERA were taken over by the Federal Theater and produced all told some forty plays. The play with the longest run was the *Yiddish King Lear*, which opened in December, 1934, and closed in July, 1936. Yiddish groups also joined in the multiple productions of *It Can't Happen*

*Here* in New York and in Los Angeles; in New York the production ran about six months. Another popular play in New York was *We Live and Laugh,* which used impressionistic sets and introduced the modern revue technique to the Yiddish theater.

Probably because they shared, within their own groups and with their audiences, a common language and a common culture, these groups knew precisely what they wanted and what their audiences wanted, and they did a workmanlike job of presenting it. Of all the units, they were the least plagued by personality conflicts, arguments with the directors, and work stoppages.

FOREIGN-LANGUAGE DRAMA: FRENCH, ITALIAN,
GERMAN, AND SPANISH

Los Angeles had the only French unit in the Theater Project. Its productions were, with one exception, works of French dramatists— good, standard plays. The exception was the translation of Lillian Hellman's *The Children's Hour.* The longest run was achieved by *Les Trois Bons Amis,* by Eugene Brieux. Like the Yiddish units, this French unit exhibited good morale and consistent devotion to its task.

Italian units appeared only in Massachusetts and New Jersey, and, of these, only the Massachusetts group performed significant work. This unit had been working under the FERA and continued under the Theater Project with much the same type of work, playing mostly in Boston and its suburbs. Most productions gave only one performance, although one variety show ran for six weeks. Several New Jersey productions ran the better part of a year. These performances, however, were not continuous, and the records do not indicate the precise number of single performances.

The German theater in New York City, which began under the FERA, continued for nearly a year under the Theater Project. The German element in the city had never given strong support to any theater using its own language, and the Federal Theater did not inspire any greater enthusiasm than had earlier commercial attempts. Its first productions aroused opposite reactions in the press. *Der Zerbrochene Krug* was acclaimed as distinguished, but *Die Apostel,* an antiwar play, was criticized as propaganda.

Since the period was that of the rise of Hitler and the Nazi party, the German theater unit was rent asunder by the division between those

571

who supported and those who repudiated the Third Reich. In the end, the conflict became so bitter that it was only resolved by the unit's discontinuance toward the end of its first year.

The only Spanish company played in Tampa, Florida, and drew its workers mostly from Cuban citizens who were made ineligible by the anti-alien ruling of 1937. Among its other productions, this unit played a Spanish version of *It Can't Happen Here*, one of the multiple premieres.

## THEATER MODELS

A unique but limited activity that illustrates well the resourcefulness and versatility of the early project directors—especially those who at the beginning lent their support from the non-professional field— was the construction of theater models and costumes. Glenn Hughes, regional director for the Northwest and head of the drama department of the University of Washington, originated the idea. The university sponsored it and supplied working space. Ten craftsmen from relief rolls were employed to build miniature models of the most famous theaters of all times. Such collections were designed as aids to students of theater construction and costume design, and made valuable exhibits that informed and interested the general public. Later, the Los Angeles project made a similar collection. In both places extensive research was required in order to achieve authenticity.

The collections of theater models went on tour, notably to the Golden Gate Exposition at San Francisco, where the University of Washington collection attracted wide interest. The latter was eventually returned to the university, where it continued to be used by students of the drama department.

## THE CINEMA

At various times two sorts of motion picture projects were considered: promotional films to inform the public about Federal Theater and WPA, and films having general entertainment and educational value. Rental and distribution of commercially produced films was attempted only by the motion picture department of the CCC unit. This department usually supplied projection equipment with the films.

The obstacles in the way of any program of creating motion pictures of the sort distributed by the cinema enterprises were numerous and obvious. The high cost of equipment, exhibition, and distribution would have increased non-labor costs to an unreasonable degree. No temporary year-by-year project possibly could have justified such expense even if WPA regulations had permitted it. If, on the other hand, admissions had been charged, motion picture distributors certainly would have protested unfair competition. Accordingly, the Theater Project wisely decided to refrain from both types of activity.

## MENTAL THERAPY

Although the Federal Theater developed nothing new in the field of mental therapy, its activities in this direction were productive of much good. Marionettes, more than any other type of production, were used to divert, to educate, and to entertain physically and mentally ill people; the making and manipulation of the dolls were particularly successful.

The community drama unit in New York City provided a dramatic coach to carry on experiments at Bellevue Hospital; plays were used that were written and acted by the patients, and, according to authorities in psychiatry, often were the means of bringing to light obscure causes of social maladjustment.

The Federal Theater's contribution was largely one of increased quantity; never before had such service been available to such a degree to prisons, reformatories, and children's hospitals.

## TOURING

It was realized from the beginning that the touring of Federal Theater companies was essential to attain the announced objectives: to decentralize employment; to create nationwide awareness of, and hunger for, living drama; and to entertain underprivileged groups in remote communities. Thousands of places had never known living drama; a new generation, born after the end of the legitimate theater's road system, was reaching maturity without acquaintance with the theater. To be sure, non-professional activities of varying degrees of excellence had become a part of almost every community's life. But it is doubtful if

573

these did or could entirely compensate for the vanished opportunity of seeing professional work. Far too often, these activities affected only the local upper class.

Mrs. Flanagan, however, although she often discussed and sometimes emphasized the need for such an apostolate, early expressed herself as unsympathetic with touring. In her address to the members of the first conference of regional directors, she said:

> All the plans for reviving the road seem to me to be born in this naive faith in resuscitation. Of course a great actress like Katherine Cornell touring the country in Romeo and Juliet will always have an audience; but the population of Oskaloosa, Iowa, or Fort Worth, Texas, is not going to be enraptured, as in days of yore, by a third rate touring company in a mediocre play, just because such a company came from New York. Oskaloosa and Fort Worth have been educated by the cinema and the radio. They know a hawk from a handsaw. They no longer measure art by the distance from which it was imported.[31]

*Bulletin No. 35*, issued November 11, 1936, provided the first procedure for handling group travel. It specified that group travel must always be authorized by the federal director and was to be on a non-reimbursable basis. Travel expenses and/or subsistence were to be paid either from receipts resulting from the group's activities or from contributions made by co-operating sponsors. Every group, therefore, needed to have a business manager–agent cashier who could legitimately handle funds. Subsistence was limited to three dollars a day, but this sum could not be given to a worker to use as he saw fit. If subsistence could be arranged for less, he could not keep the balance for himself. After several revisions of this first procedure, a final procedure (*W-17*) regulating touring was issued on July 5, 1938.[32]

The first experiment in touring was made by Touring Unit Number 1, charged to the New York City project and employing New York City workers. The company gave an advance showing of its production, *Jefferson Davis*, by John McGee, in New York; even Mrs. Flanagan found no kind words to say for it. Nevertheless, it departed for a tour of the South, where its sectional theme was expected to popularize it. Local chapters of the Daughters of the Confederacy sponsored its showing in many cities and towns. The tour was a failure. In addition to the workers' salaries, the experiment cost about $10,000. The venture probably permanently injured the project's touring program in the South.

The experience of the Negro company that played *Macbeth* was more furtunate. This large company played in seven widely separated cities, with Dallas, Texas, as its western terminus. The company was competent and won much good will for the Negro theater and the Federal Theater. A subsequent plan of the company to tour from New York to Boston was finally vetoed after an estimate was submitted that the non-labor cost for two weeks would be $12,000, whereas the greatest possible return would be $5,000.

No improvement either in economy, quality, or frequency of tours, appeared in the next year. Then, in the summer of 1937, the President expressed his concern for the extension of the cultural and educational advantages of the arts projects to less-favored communities. Mr. Morris and Mrs. Woodward communicated the President's wishes to the directors of the arts projects, and Mrs. Flanagan was asked to call the attention of the state directors to the fact that a de-urbanization of the project would create opportunities for workers then on relief rolls to find places for themselves in the economic life of the smaller communities.

Several possibilities for the touring program were investigated. In the belief that educational institutions might prove fertile ground, questionnaires were sent to 591 colleges. Only one-quarter of them replied, and only 8 per cent were definitely interested. The plan to use the colleges was abandoned.

In California an entirely different, but equally exhaustive, investigation was made; this concerned a proposed tour of the Myra Kinch dance group from Los Angeles through some of the western states. An experimental booking trip through northern California and into adjoining states was approved and undertaken by Guy Williams. As a result, Williams concluded that no tour could succeed under existing regulations, and presented a new plan that emphasized the essential requisites of successful touring—accurate planning and guaranteed income. It was recognized, however, that such a plan could not be successfully operated by the Federal Theater because of its continued uncertainty as to funds (federal and sponsors'), cast (any member of which, from the director down, might be claimed by private employment at any time), and quotas.*

The Washington finance office of the WPA, which closely watched

---

*In Illinois a touring company successfully operated intrastate tours in a limited area near Peoria. The territory was, theatrically speaking, primeval, and the company's supervisor strongly urged that only simple plays, simply staged, should be considered.

all non-labor and administrative costs, was especially concerned about tours, for which such costs were often excessive. In Administrative Letter No. 27, dated February 25, 1938, J. Howard Miller issued an order that no tours were to be initiated—not even exploratory steps were to be taken—without approval from Washington. Almost a year later, Administrative Letter No. 31 emphatically reiterated these instructions, and included intrastate touring under the ban. An exception later was made with regard to intrastate spot-bookings, for which complete non-labor guarantees had been secured, and which did not involve absence of personnel from official stations for more than twenty-four hours.

Another serious problem of touring companies was the attitude of the IATSE, and especially its locals. Many disputes occurred with locals about the number of union members that ought to be hired for performances, even when the company carried its own stagehands. Although the unions' national headquarters was not inclined to be unreasonable, the locals often were uninformed or unsympathetic. Moreover, because both Actors' Equity and IATSE regarded tours as commercial ventures, there existed a strong inclination on their part to insist upon commercial rates of pay.

Efforts to establish national control, both in the matter of choice of plays and in the planning of tours, resulted in the appointment, in the spring of 1938, of Evan Roberts as director of tours, subscription, and radio. It was hoped that nationwide tours would emanate from the three largest centers and that a well-balanced repertoire of about six plays would be worked out for each center; units were to be sent only to cities where sponsorship in the form of subscriptions had been arranged and where such subscriptions guaranteed non-labor costs, including travel. By early August, however, Roberts reported that he believed the program could not at that time be carried out. In the first place, although it had been clearly stated, and apparently understood in Washington, that a prerequisite for such a program was expert field promotion, a relatively expensive step, Washington had failed to approve the appointment of the necessary five field experts at salaries of $3,600 each. The second reason was:

> Certain regional representatives still object to outside people coming into their territory. For example, in the South, Mr. [Malcolm] Miller has ruled that no one can come into the South without an invitation. . . . A similar situation exists in Southern California.

The failure of the Washington office to appoint field people and the attitude of the regional WPA directors are circumstances beyond your control and mind.[33]

## LOAN OF PERSONNEL

Another very early effort to decentralize employment of relief workers from the congested metropolitan areas was made by loaning workers to remote projects and to the divisions of recreation and education. This activity, involving as it did almost purely administrative procedures, was handled by the National Service Bureau, or its antecedents, in which a loan and co-ordinating unit was established. It was not until August, 1937, however, that Operating Procedure W-15 formalized the procedure. In Operating Procedure F-45 the financial procedures were covered.

Persons loaned were assigned to the project in the lending state. This assured them the same wages and hours under which the home project operated. The loans were limited to three months; at the end of that time, unless service had been terminated and the loaned worker returned to his home project, permanent transfer could be effected or the loan period extended by mutual consent.

One of the disadvantages of the loan service was that the home project naturally inclined to keep its more desirable workers at home. The result was that some who lacked both skill and circumspection were sent to communities already accustomed to regarding the theater as a questionable enterprise. Embarrassing situations arose on several occasions, and sometimes it was necessary to recall workers. On the other hand, loyalty of an unusual sort was required for the fulfillment of a loan assignment, and only workers who were more interested in the success of the project than in their own advancement (and there were such) achieved results as loan personnel.

## THEATER-BUILDING

Although Mrs. Flanagan persistently hoped that the Federal Theater would be able to build its own theaters, it was not until July, 1938, that she received any encouragement from the WPA. At that time the Washington office approved her appointment of Dwight W. Gibbs as architectural consultant on the national co-ordinating project. His duties were to include planning new buildings and advising in the adaptation of old ones.*

When, in the summer of 1938, the Federal Theater decided to participate in the Golden Gate International Exposition on Treasure Island, San Francisco, Gibbs was given the assignment of planning that part of the WPA building that was to house dramatic production. Admission funds in the sum of $65,000 were borrowed from several projects—Chicago, New York, and Los Angeles contributed the most—to finance the construction, and three areas were planned for theatrical production: the Main Theater, the Sylvan Theater, and the Marionette Theater. The venture, under the direction of R. C. Schnitzer, was established as an independent project with a quota of two hundred persons, half of which were administrative staff and half workers transferred from the Los Angeles project. The largest non-labor item in the project cost was the building fund; as plans took shape in November another large item appeared: $10,000 would be needed to bring the hundred workers from Los Angeles and to maintain them during their stay.

Optimism about early repayment of this enormous non-labor cost was not universal. Ole Ness, a regional director of Federal Theater, reported to Mrs. Flanagan about ten weeks before the scheduled opening:

> Both Mr. Creel and Mr. White are just as enthusiastic as ever, and have no idea that our affairs are chaotic. I have been rather worried about the cost of the whole project, but every time I venture a criticism, Mr. White tells me to forget it, that he will be able to absorb any costs above the $65,000 elsewhere in the Federal Building. This, of course, is confidential.[34]

The fact is that the Golden Gate project possessed all the requirements of a commercial venture of a high order, as well as demanding the services of men technically and administratively experienced in the field; and experts of such caliber were not to be found in the Federal Theater. Indeed, California WPA officials were aware of the weaknesses of the venture, and the approval of Schnitzer's appointment was not given until after he arrived on the scene and pressure had been applied from Washington. The establishment of an independent proj-

---

*In the summer of 1937 the WPA had completed the building of a theater under a project initiated under the FERA. This was a replica of the pre-revolutionary Dock Street Theater, in Charleston, S.C., which had been destroyed by fire. Since the Federal Theater had no project in South Carolina, a local dramatiic group opened the new theater with a production of George Farquhar's *The Recruiting Officer*, the play with which the original Dock Street Theater had opened in 1737.

ect with a 12 per cent administrative cost and 50 per cent non-relief quota was precarious enough in 1938; in early 1939, the heavy quota cuts made it almost impossible to justify.

The Golden Gate dramatic project opened on February 18, 1939. The program included Federal Music Project concerts, performances by the modern dance unit from Los Angeles, documentary films, marionette performances, and children's offerings. Soon, however, the Music Project found the daily transportation to the Island prohibitive in cost and discontinued its participation. In the middle of June, shortly before the close of the Federal Theater Project, a Treasure Island version of the *Swing Mikado* was attempted, and receipts from admission appreciably improved.*

RESEARCH

The original title of the National Service Bureau was the Bureau of Research and Publications. Two considerations encouraged the development of research on the project. The first was the presence upon its rolls of many workers who could not otherwise be employed; and the second was the project's great need for original ideas and adaptations if the national director's ideals were to be attained.

The superiority of the western service bureau has already been indicated. Among its outstanding products were four volumes (in mimeograph form) of studies of American social drama from its beginning to the present, and annals of the Seattle, San Francisco, and Los Angeles theater projects. One of its best works was a history of the Chinese theater in America.†

The music division of the National Service Bureau under the direction of Herbert Halpert conducted research in American music for the playwriting department, and from that activity there developed a folklore and folksong department. The department published Richard Winslow Gordon's *Folksongs of America* as the first item of a proposed educational series for Federal Theater directors, musicians, teachers of music, and community groups. The only completed work of a proposed series of publications from every state was *Folksongs of Missis-*

---

*The Theater Project also made plans to participate, as part of the wpa, in the New York World's Fair, but the brief interval between the opening of the Fair and the closing of the Theater Project allowed little opportunity for developing a program.

†The New York Public Library theater collection possesses most of these works.

*sippi.* All the work of the department was carried on in close co-operation with other Federal One projects, from which was drawn the membership of the Joint Folklore Committee of America. Under this committee's direction a Federal Theater sound truck toured several southeastern states in the spring of 1939 and made important recordings; some were also made in New York state and in New Jersey. Altogether the division is credited with 275 recordings.

## PUBLICATIONS

*Federal Theatre* was the project's first national publication; it appeared in November, 1935, as a mimeographed pamphlet of nine pages. Early in 1936, adequate offset-printing equipment was procured with funds from the Rockefeller grant, and the fourth issue, bearing the date, March, 1936, assumed permanent format. A total of eleven issues were published at irregular intervals, although monthly publication was anticipated. In June, 1937, it was discontinued, together with all WPA periodical publications, by order of Harry Hopkins.[35]

In an effort to secure more frequent and accurate information for and about project supervisors and workers, another series of mimeographed publications, *Semi-monthly News Letters*, was issued in 1936, the first bearing the date, May 20. After the first issue, and for the rest of the year, these letters appeared regularly. They carried lists of openings, press comments, plans, hopes, and personal items.

In October, 1938, the first of six issues of a publication conveying information about foreign theatrical activities appeared. The translations department of the National Service Bureau prepared digests of theater news from all over the world and published them in a magazine that first bore the name *Continental Theatre Bulletin* and, later, *The Theatre Abroad.* The first four numbers were mimeographed; the last two were attractively reproduced by offset.*

## THE PROBLEM OF STANDARDS

In the main, the members of the professional theater were dubious about the ability of the Federal Theater to do competent work with the

---

*The larger projects, both regional and state, published bulletins under a great variety of names, some of them supplements to *Federal Theatre* but most of them of purely local interest and inspiration. Los Angeles experimented with *The Prompter.*

type of actor who was unemployed. Early in the project's history, Sidney Howard wrote to Mrs. Flanagan:

I do feel, however, that by far the greater part of our unemployed actors should be hurried out of acting a quickly as possible . . . and relieved of the constant misery of encouragement in a profession for which they are not qualified.[36]

It was in the less than one-third of the productions that charged admissions that Mrs. Flanagan hoped to create the new theater. Her thinking sometimes betrayed her into forgetfulness of the first purpose of the project—employment. Nearly two years after the inception of the project, she prepared an article in which she said: "The Federal Theatre Project has been established to provide a high type of theatrical entertainment for the people of America." The administration asked her to change that wording with the comment: "While this may be one of the aims of the Federal Theatre Project, certainly the project itself was established to provide employment for needy theatrical people."

Mrs. Flanagan overestimated the intellectual development and aesthetic sensitivity of the audiences that saw her plays. It was because of this lack of comprehension of local conditions that Mrs. Flanagan met opposition from her own assistants and the WPA administrations in the states. The National Service Bureau—under its various names—failed to impose its own standards upon play selection and play production in the localities. It failed because it operated in a vacuum; its personnel were not acquainted with—or indeed, concerned with—the local exigencies that confronted state directors and project supervisors. Those who had the most experience in the field—like Esther Porter, who made several visits to the localities—were convinced that the project supervisor was faced with too many local problems to heed the demands of the central office for new and imaginative productions.

Both in production and in play selection, the local supervisors wished to give people what they wanted. Clarence H. Talbot, the Iowa state director, reported: "The productions which I directed were staged with an eye to appealing to the public since it is the public upon whom we have to depend for financial support of our program."[37]

He added that civic leaders, educators, and prominent residents of his region had expressed approval. Mrs. Flanagan however, considered the standards of his project so mediocre that she ordered its discontinuance.

Perhaps the person who, as completely as anyone, realized the importance of fitting the standards to the capacity of the workers was Gareth Hughes, an actor and director of the old school, whose unit, in Los Angeles, played religious drama and Shakespeare. But when he was approached with an offer to have his group—or such of them as could qualify—go to the San Francisco Exposition, he declined. He knew that most of his actors were not of sufficient caliber to put on a creditable performance at the fair, and he did not wish to hurt sensibilities by breaking up the unit and taking only the best ones. He requested that he be allowed to continue his work in Los Angeles.

Presentation of Maxwell Anderson's *Valley Forge* in New England provides an interesting example of the Federal Theater's policy of attempting to change people's tastes precipitously. Hiram Motherwell decided to produce this play in spite of heavy argument against it by local authorities and the fact that royalties would be expensive ($200 for the first week). Plymouth was prepared for the presentation of a patriotic, historical play; school teachers urged their students to attend. Instead of history as told in their textbooks and in those of their forefathers, they heard the story of a great man's conquest of a stupid oligarchy in spite of corruption and treachery in the Continental Congress. No second performance was allowed in Plymouth, and permission to produce the play in Lexington was refused.

1. Address of Hallie Flanagan, Conference of Regional Directors, Washington, D.C., October 8, 1935, FTP Files.

2. Letter, Flanagan to Regional Directors, January, 1936, FTP Files.

3. *Ibid.*

4. Report of Rosamund Gilder, n.d., FTP Files.

5. Letter, Flanagan to Barber, November 15, 1936, FTP Files.

6. Letter, Flanagan to Regional Directors, February 4, 1937, FTP Files.

7. General Letter No. 138, WPA, June 18, 1937, WPA Files.

8. Transcript of the Proceedings of the Play Policy Board Meeting of the Federal Theater Project, Washington, D.C., April 8-9, 1937, FTP Files.

9. *Ibid.*

10. Letter, Flanagan and others to Motherwell, June 7, 1937, FTP Files.

11. Letter, Gerwing to Flanagan, April 11, 1938, FTP Files.

12. Letter, Shaw to Motherwell, April, 1937, FTP Files.

13. Letter, Flanagan to Shaw, May 7, 1937, FTP Files.

14. Letter, Shaw to Flanagan, May 22, 1937, FTP Files.

15. As quoted in Hallie Flanagan, *Arena*, p. 164.

16. Letter, Flanagan to Watson and Losey, August 20, 1936, FTP Files.

17. Letter, Flanagan to Buck, April 12, 1939, FTP Files.

18. *New York Times*, October 31, 1937.

19. Letter, Madden to Rubinstein, October 19, 1937, FTP Files.

20. Letter, Shaw to Flanagan, May 22, 1937, FTP Files.

21. *Amsterdam News*, June 4, 1937.

22. Letter, Flanagan to Mack, December 11, 1938, FTP Files.

23. *New York Times*, May 21, 1937, p. 19.

24. *Appendix A to Supplement No. 1 to Bulletin No. 29*, WPA, November 16, 1935.

25. *Ibid.*

26. Frederick H. Koch, as quoted in New York *Herald Tribune*, December 15, 1935, Sec. II, Part 1, p. 1.

27. Price, Report to Mrs. Flanagan, July, 1938, FTP Files.

28. Letter, Bufano to Sirovich, January 11, 1938, FTP Files.

29. Hallie Flanagan, *Arena*, p. 429.

30. *New York Times*, January 9, 1936.

31. Hallie Flanagan, "Address," Conference of Regional Directors, Washington, D.C., October 8, 1935, FTP Files.

32. Operating Procedure No. W-17, WPA, July 15, 1938.

33. Report, Roberts to Flanagan, August 3, 1938, FTP Files.

34. Letter, Ness to Flanagan, November 27, 1938, FTP Files.

35. General Letter No. 129, WPA, June 15, 1937.

36. Letter, Howard to Flanagan, October 25, 1935, FTP Files.

37. Letter, Talbot to Ashton, December 6, 1937, FTP Files.

# 23

# The Origins of the Federal Music Project

MUSIC IN AMERICAN LIFE

The universality with which music has been cultivated in the United States contrasts strongly with the limited appeal of the other arts; and although mastership is no less difficult to attain in music than in painting or acting, a tolerable competence in one of the many musical forms can be achieved by the non-professional student. By its very nature, therefore, music is the most democratic of the arts; and although at times the *cognoscenti* have attempted to achieve a monopoly, the people irresistibly continue to create new music and, by an artless but by no means unartistic spontaneity, reassert popular dominion over the invention of Jubal and Orpheus.

The imperatives of a frontier society under which the settlers of America labored did not encourage the cultivation of music as an art. The early colonists, however, were not unaware of the intimate relation between music on the one hand and religion, play, and work on the other; and in the midst of physical hardships they kept their souls brave and their hearts merry with the singing of hymns, ballads, and ditties, from which emerged, as Willem Van de Wall has observed, "the popular song, America's outstanding contribution to the world's repertoire of light music."

This folk music, which developed naturally along regional, occupational, and racial lines, culminated by 1915 in the rise of that most remarkable phenomenon of American music, jazz—aptly called the folk music of the modern city. African in its rhythmic origin and Afro-American in its early development in New Orleans, jazz is a unique de-

584

velopment in musical history and, as such, the original contribution of America to music.

In the course of time the educated classes were cultivating the European modes. By the earlier part of the present century the greater symphony orchestras had been organized, and more recently the string quartet cultivated. This wealthy subsidization of art music naturally led to the development of *virtuosi* and the consequent division between the performer, who was active, and the audience, which remained passive.

On the other hand, the encouragement of art music provoked a definite territorial spread of music's influence and a higher qualitative level of performance. This in turn led to greater music appreciation and in particular encouraged formal music education. This discipline, which at first involved a private teacher and a private pupil, had, by the middle of the nineteenth century, gained entrance into the curriculum of the public school. At first accepted for its disciplinary value, music education and appreciation eventually came to be regarded as an important aesthetic and cultural experience of the school-age child.

At the same time, in music as in the other arts, the settlement house played a prominent part in the popularization of the subject, especially among the less-privileged groups. This integration of music activities within the community led to the elevation of music to the level of community enterprise. In fact, by the time of the depression music in the schools and as a community activity had become a vital influence in the life not only of the participants and their friends but of the community itself.

Thus in the United States art music and folk music have complemented each other and, by a happy union, have brought forth that most typically native and most universally popular of all contemporary musical modes, the American musical comedy.

MUSIC AND THE DEPRESSION

Such was the status of music in America when, at the close of the twenties, the depression began. But even before 1929, unemployment among musicians had become chronic. The reason was largely technological. The phonograph had for years been progressively reducing the demand for "live" music, and, by 1925, the increased use of the radio had caused a further decline in the opportunities for employment.

Finally, in 1928 the sound track for moving picture film appeared, bringing with it the dismissal of pit orchestra men and organists. It had been estimated that between 20,000 and 22,000 professional theater musicians lost their jobs within the next two years. In 1929 it was announced that many theaters had installed "Griffen Reprotones" to substitute for orchestras during intermissions;[1] Oscar Hammerstein expressed his intention to use a sound device instead of an orchestra in a musical production; and the New Jersey State Funeral Directors Association even recommended music by radio for funerals.[2]

The musicians were thrown into panic. Strikes occurred, and violence threatened. A musicians' strike in Cincinnati lasted seven months. Explosions at two theaters in St. Louis, Missouri, were laid by the owners to troubles with the musicians' unions.[3] The unions conducted campaigns to persuade the public of the superior quality of "visible flesh and blood musicians over the canned music that comes with the sound film."[4] The Chicago Federation of Musicians insisted that phonograph operators in radio stations be members of the Musicians Union.[5] The New York City Musicians' Mutual Protective Union planned a parade (which was forbidden) against "talkies."[6] The San Francisco Union filed suit to restrain theaters from the use of sound devices without an orchestra and organist.

Cancellations of contracts harassed the professional musician throughout 1929. Two opera companies suspended their season. Orchestras curtailed their seasons and reduced personnel. Hotels, legitimate theaters, and restaurants dispensed with orchestras. State and local assistance for public music was withdrawn in many localities. Pupil enrollment in music schools and private classes dwindled to nothing. College departments and school boards effected economies in music and art.

The American Federation of Musicians was active from the beginning in its efforts to alleviate the needs of its members. Statistical research had shown how serious the plight of union members had become. In 1929 the federation claimed that 5,000 of its members were out of work due to the "talkies" alone. In 1933 it maintained that of its enrollment of more than 15,000 in Greater New York, 12,000 were unemployed, and that at least two-thirds of its national membership was unemployed. Within a three-year period (1930-33) the New York local distributed some $150,000 in outright relief among its indigent members, but the sum was inadequate to meet the urgent circumstances. In March, 1935, Local 802 of the American Federation of Musicians demanded that broadcasting members collect three dollars tax from hotels and night clubs (those that broadcast performances) for relief. At first the hotels stopped broadcasting, but eventually, they agreed to pay the fine.

Although the American Federation of Musicians declared that it lost none of its members during the depression, it often found that a necessary measure in keeping its members was to make loans for payment of dues. It also adopted various devices of relief, from outright payments for food and shelter to concerts by its unemployed members. The New York City local decided in 1931 to tax all members earning over fifty dollars a week 5 per cent of their earnings. This tax was repealed in May of the same year as unsatisfactory. Subsequently, it was found better to tax all earners, regardless of earning capacity, 1 per cent of their weekly wage. The stagger system was another method of relief. The staggering of employment was a means whereby all musicians in permanent employment were required to give one week's work in four, or one day in seven, to an unemployed colleague.

Private music teachers, no less than performers, had had an increasingly difficult time even before the depression. The inclusion of music in public-school courses narrowed the clientele for private music lessons. As an editorial in the *Musician* for June, 1934, stated:

> It must be confessed that the social changes of the last decade have not worked to the advantage of the music teaching profession. We have seen the tonal art pass gradually from the exclusive precincts of private instruction into the public domain. Public schools, settlement schools, and great foundations have taken over an activity that formerly belonged to the trained individual, who sought his livelihood in a field from which he was gradually being crowded out by forces beyond his control.[7]

No accurate calculation of the extent of unemployment of musicians can be made. The American Federation of Musicians, however, estimated that during the years from 1929 to 1934 approximately 70 per cent of the formerly employed musicians were out of work, and that a large proportion of the remainder was not realizing a decent living from the profession itself.

The general public, however, did not tire of "canned" music nor of music of any kind. On the contrary, as the depression deepened, public interest and participation in music activities increased. Music schools suffered because pupils could not afford to pay for lessons; but free lessons attracted more and more students, and lessons on radio became more popular. In 1930 John Erskine said that the danger threatening music schools in America was not lack of interest in music but lack of money. Even music in industry was becoming recognized. James J. Davis, then Secretary of Labor, was quoted as saying: "Music as an aid to the workman is nowadays pretty much of an accepted fact."[8]

Paradoxically, much of this new interest and enthusiasm was due to the mechanization of music. Olin Downes praised the radio business: "For the first time in the history of the civilized world music has become accessible to the whole community."[9]

Some of the more farsighted music leaders, along with Mr. Downes, saw that mechanization, though undeniably hard on the practicing musician, was not necessarily a bad thing for the future of music. William S. Paley, then president of the Columbia Broadcasting System, thought that radio was accomplishing in a few years in the United States what countries abroad had taken centuries to achieve in the development in popular taste.[10] An editorial in the *New York Times* read:

> The recording of Beethoven's symphonies does not drive people away from the concert halls. While sound pictures are still new, the musicians may be temporarily distressed, but wider distribution should not in the end militate against its sustained popularity when fresh from the orchestra.[11]

Even in the realm of music-teaching the radio began to intrude. Zanzig writes: ". . . Recent experiments in broadcasting introductory lessons in piano and in band instruments give promise of making up in large measure for any decline in amateur singing and playing caused by it."[12]

## EARLY PRIVATE ATTEMPTS AT WORK RELIEF FOR MUSICIANS

This, then, was the confused situation when as early as 1929 the plight of musicians became so desperate that organized efforts were undertaken for their relief. At first, as in the other arts, such attempts were the result of private initiative. In July, 1929, the Judson Radio Program Corporation volunteered to form orchestra units to offset unemployment caused by the use of sound equipment in motion picture theaters.[13] In Chicago (1930) Andree Skalski and an orchestra gave a fifteen-week season in Kimbal Hall to relieve musicians' unemployment.[14] In Denver, musicians and stagehands thrown out of employment by the talkies were to organize, finance, and operate a theater.

Walter Damrosch urged parents to help qualified unemployed musicians by giving children music lessons.[15] The League of Composers set out to aid the needy by the formation of a Composers' Fund.[16] Almost any competition was hailed as unfair to the unemployed musician. Mayor Fiorello La Guardia, supported by the American Federation of Musicians, protested the tours of the United States Navy Band as representing unfair competition to unemployed band players.[17] The Musicians' Mutual Corporation protested against competition by bands of the fire department, police, and sanitation departments, and the letter carriers' band in New York City.

Since, according to the figures of the American Federation of Musicians, New York City was at the time of the depression the home of one-eighth of all the professional musicians in the United States and Canada, New York's problem was proportionately more serious than that of any other city; and consequently, its aid to musicians had more than local significance. At first, attempts at relief were private. The Polyphonic Symphony Orchestra sponsored a fund for musicians in November, 1930. Various organizations gave benefit concerts. Letters to the *New York Times* urged that symphonic concerts be given by the unemployed at nominal admission fees. In 1931 the Juilliard graduate students gave a benefit performance of Handel's *Julius Ceasar*. In December of that year E. C. Rybici urged H. D. Gibson to employ some idle musicians for free concerts in public school buildings. A week later Walter Damrosch headed a committee seeking $300,000 to aid New York's unemployed musicians. Benefit concerts at the Roxy Theater were planned under Erno Rapée, and radio listeners sent in contributions. A few unemployed musicians were deliberately included in the Roxy orchestra.

In January, 1932, the Musicians' Emergency Aid was organized. This body, one of the largest relief organizations sustained by private contributions in the field of the arts, gave assistance through work relief to only those professionals who earned their living by music previous to 1928. In addition to sponsoring an orchestra of 175 men, it directed its efforts toward aiding operatic singers, other vocalists, teachers, and accompanists, both union and non-union. Subsequent to its organization, most relief activities for musicians were under its jurisdiction or allied to it. Among these activities were concerts for the unemployed sponsored by the Brooklyn Free Music Society; concerts by the MacDowell Orchestra of New York, formed in February, 1932, by unemployed musicians to play in schools; benefit concerts by a Musicians'

589

Symphony Orchestra composed of 200 unemployed musicians; and free band concerts in Central and Prospect parks sponsored by New York City churches.*

In upper New York State the Buffalo Symphony Orchestra was formed in 1931. Unemployed musicians were assigned to it by the Mayor's Committee on Unemployment. The formation of this orchestra was a purely local enterprise that carried through the fall and winter of 1931-32. Later, however, it was assisted by the New York State TERA, the CWA, the FERA, and finally the WPA. With the closing of the WPA, this orchestra had so fixed itself in the life of the community that it achieved permanent status as the Buffalo Symphony Orchestra.

As in the other arts, private attempts to assist unemployed musicians, however generous and courageous, were inadequate. In May, 1932, at least 3,000 musicians sought the eighty posts in the Roxy Symphony Orchestra. The *New York Times Index* lists three columns of items under "Unemployment for Musicians" for 1932. In 1930 this subject took up only one-half a column. New York State's official aid to musicians began as a part of the "Emergency Education Plan for White Collar Workers," instituted in December, 1932, by the State Department of Education and financed by funds from the TERA for general unemployment relief. By June, 1933, about twelve music ensemble players who had appealed to the Emergency Work Bureau were giving free concerts in tax-supported institutions.

Under the Emergency Reconstruction Act of 1932 states were permitted to apply to the Reconstruction Finance Corporation for loans for relief and work relief. In a few instances, states that applied for these loans used some of the funds for work relief for musicians. Such a project was the "musicians' project 8047" operated in Los Angeles County, California, from October 6, 1933, to the inception of the CWA in November, 1933. A notable feature of the project was the "rotating list" whereby all the qualified applicants were given a turn at the jobs available, thus spreading the work and, with it, the money. On the project the quota set was 300 man jobs, or a total of approximately 900 musicians on a rotating basis, assuming that the turnover would be 300 per cent.[18] It is interesting that the philosophy of work relief for musicians, which was to receive expression later when the principles of the

*The Musicians' Emergency Aid operated in conjunction with the private relief committees of New York City (the Prosser and Gibson committees). *Vide supra,* pp. 19-20.

Works Progress Administration became fully defined, is clearly stated in the Los Angeles report of project activities. The following paragraph is quoted from this report:

> As the purpose of the project is to give suitable employment to professional musicians who have been assigned to pick and shovel work, only those who have been making a livelihood by music were considered eligible for employment under the project. It was believed by those responsible for the starting of the project that musicians were entirely unsuited for heavy labor, which would not only impair their skill but render valueless their years of training and experience, and would jeopardize their health and morale. By providing them with work relief through musical rehearsals and free public concerts, it was believed that they might be rehabilitated and prepared to resume their places in the musical profession.[19]

The project was organized and supervised by the Los Angeles County Department of Recreation, Camps, and Playgrounds. The average number of hours allowed the musicians as a monthly budget was sixty-four. Under the continuous-work basis of the cwa, they might work almost twice that, or about 120 hours. The rate was fifty cents an hour under the cwa—an increase of ten cents an hour over the previous rate. Except for the administrative services of regular county recreation department employees and incidental expenses, there were no expenditures other than the wages paid the musicians. The musicians provided their own instruments and kept them in repair, libraries were loaned or donated, and the use of rehearsal halls was given gratis.*

For a time, unemployed musicians and their representatives saw in the codes of the nra a possible solution to their troubles, and the files of that agency contain many letters requesting and suggesting codes for musicians. The nra codes, however, were intended for industries and not for the professions. To be sure, it was considered at the time that musicians might benefit by the codes for industries that employed them, such as the theater, moving pictures, hotels, radio, etc. This expectation was in vain, though, according to William Farnsworth, a deputy administrator of the nra, some indirect aid was anticipated:

> I am fully confident that the increased leisure time created by codes will bring a prosperity to the amusement industries that will enable them to make more substantial contributions to the victims of discs, wave length and sound films.[20]

*Forms for reports devised by this project were later revised and used by the wpa Federal Music Project.

## WORK RELIEF FOR MUSICIANS UNDER THE CWA

Under the early FERA, work relief of any kind, much less work relief for musicians, was rare. The inauguration of the CWA program in November, 1933, however, immediately caused an emphasis upon work relief in place of the dole; and the device of federal projects used by the Washington office to spread its policy among the states made possible, as in the Public Works of Art Project, work relief in the arts. Indeed, it was hoped that a federal project for musicians, analagous to the PWAP might be initiated. Arthur Hanna wrote, in answer to a query:

> It was our intention to make employment of musicians a Federal project as was done in the case of American artists on the Public Works of Art Project started under the original allotment funds of the CWA. We are still hopeful that a national program for musicians may be determined in the new relief program. However, the State CWA Administrators and relief administrators have within their power the instituting of orchestras out of funds granted them to answer the local unemployment problem.[21]

Since the CWA funds were by statute available only for public works of construction, the Civil Works Service was invented to provide work relief for white-collar unemployed and was financed at first from FERA funds. Thus music projects within the states and sponsored by state or local public agencies could be encouraged by the Washington office.

It was natural at the time that such projects should for the most part be attached to state and local recreational and educational agencies. An emergency education division had been functioning in many states before the inauguration of the CWA. The activities of these programs fitted in with much of the work in music under the CWA. In the recreational field, directors of play activities supplemented the work of the education division. Actors gave free lessons, as did needy musicians who were employed to teach music. Actors were employed to put on plays for the benefit of the unemployed and those who could not pay regular prices of admission. Needy musicians were engaged in orchestras, bands, and string quartets to give free concerts. Festivals of folk dancing and singing were organized. Activities in community centers were also directed by CWA workers.

The emphasis under the CWA, therefore, was on music as a recreational activity. However, since no instructions concerning the employment of musicians as such were issued to the state administrations,

592

there was no uniformity in the projects, nor did all states feel it necessary to make use of unemployed musicians' special skills. It had not been made clear that projects for musicians could operate as Civil Works Service projects. A letter from Robert S. Stannard, president of the Hartford Musicians' Protective Association, Hartford, Connecticut, to Harry Hopkins, complains that

> . . . the local professional musicians on relief were offered manual labor at the minimum rate of compensation . . . and were advised by local CWA administrators that there exists no provision for employment of musicians in their capacity as such. It is our information that projects for the purpose of securing employment for unemployed musicians as such are sponsored and in effect in various parts of the country by the CWA administration.[22]

Nevertheless, in some states music projects were initiated. In Alabama two counties set up a musical project under women's work with the plan of giving concerts in rural communities; in Colorado bands and orchestras were formed for community concerts; in Connecticut pianists were engaged for dancing classes under educational projects; in Georgia a symphony orchestra was formed with a paid leader; in Illinois leisure-time activity included music appreciation, glee clubs, and orchestras; and in Michigan musical training came under the teachers' work relief program. Music in Maryland was part of a "general adult study" under adult education in the women's division. The report of activities of the Minnesota CWA included these statements:

> CWA did not try to force standard programs on communities. It chose to help them to develop programs necessary to them by means of bulletins, a series of institutes for recreation teachers throughout the state, and by organizing local committees.[23]

Although under the CWA the stress was on music as a recreational activity, experiments were also made in many of the fields of music that the Federal Music Project explored more thoroughly at a later date. In Missouri a study of folklore and traditions was undertaken as part of the statewide recreation project; some musicians were employed to collect material. Paid recreation leaders were made available to the 114 counties of the state in December, 1933, and by June, 1934, all 114 counties employed directors. Selection of the county recreation leaders was left to county relief committees, which were advised to select women with experience in music who were in need of employment. Begun under the CWA, classes in music appreciation in both vocal and instrumental music continued until April, 1934, when 700 persons were enrolled for the courses held in public school buildings at night. Concert, symphony, and dance orchestras, and bands, were formed in many states, among them New York (Buffalo and Rochester), Pennsylvania (Philadelphia and Pittsburgh), California, Colorado, Maryland, Massachusetts, New Jersey, and Virginia. Most of the concerts given were free to the public, although some of the more professional units, such as the Buffalo Orchestra, charged admission at popular prices. Standards of performance varied as widely as did types of activity. Although most of the smaller orchestras were mediocre at best, a few of the larger ones achieved recognition for artistic merit. The City Symphony Orchestra of Philadelphia, which was organized in 1934 as a cwa project, was so favorably received by press and public that the National Broadcasting Company offered the use of its facilities and five coast-to-coast broadcasts were arranged, besides an international program given especially for the Byrd South Polar Expedition in April, 1934.

The cwa hoped, apparently, to give aid to established symphony orchestras. An item on the front page of the *Minneapolis Tribune* gives evidence of this intention:

> Federal aid for unemployed musicians was predicted Sunday night by Representative Ellenbogan, Democrat, Pennsylvania, who said he had received assurances from Harry L. Hopkins, civil works administrator, that 12 symphony orchestras would be selected to receive the aid on a 30-hour week and also that he contemplated the expansion of concert schedules, permitting the orchestras to travel and bring their programs to a larger number of audiences.*24

Opera, unlike symphonic music, was not an object of solicitude in the Washington office of the cwa. Pressure, to be sure, was brought to bear in the form of letters and resolutions, but the magnitude and cost of such an activity gave pause.

When the cwa program was terminated in March, 1934, music projects, such as continued to exist, came under the jurisdiction of the Emergency Work Program of the FERA, established April 1, 1934. The state administrators of the various state emergency relief administrations were not all enthusiastic about white-collar projects, much less music projects, as is observed in a wpa report:

*Among the symphony orchestras asking public aid were the National Symphony Orchestra of Washington, D.C., the Baltimore Symphony, the Richmond (Virginia) Symphony, and the Lincoln (Nebraska) Symphony.

To some extent, in developing these service projects, we have been confronted by a peculiar psychological attitude. Many people of the favored economic groups seem to regard it as desirable that a destitute person shall be disciplined. The discipline they think of is manual labor. They like the idea of putting a destitute musician down in a sewer or putting a child psychologist at the sewing machine.[25]

The extent, however, to which the impetus given by the CWA program maintained itself, especially in music projects, was remarkable.

## MUSIC PROJECTS UNDER THE EMERGENCY WORK PROGRAM OF THE FERA

Under the ERA almost every state had some kind of music project, ranging from one individual teaching music in Mississippi to 1,246 (as of May 16, 1935) in New York City engaged in social music, teaching, and concert performance in bands, orchestras, chamber ensembles, etc. Orchestras were organized in Alabama, Arizona, Colorado, Connecticut, Georgia, Idaho, Illinois, Indiana, Iowa, Kentucky, Louisiana, Maine, Massachusetts, Michigan, Minnesota, Missouri, Nebraska, New Jersey, New York State, North Carolina, Pennsylvania, Rhode Island, South Carolina, and Virginia. Nearly all states had music teaching or leadership in some form and under some division—education, recreation, or women's work. Community sings were very popular, and many musicians were employed as leaders for them. Much of the community music was directed through the leisure time–activities divisions of the several state ERA's.

One of the better projects was in Minnesota. The ERA of that state through its recreation and leisure-time department furnished employment for unemployed professional musicians and persons with musical ability in two ways. The first was to establish projects calling for orchestras of ten to thirty-four musicians. These gave public concerts for entertainment and educational purposes. The second was to engage musicians as leaders and directors of amateur groups, such as bands, orchestras, and drum corps. The personnel of these groups were chiefly children and adults who were unable to pay for training of this sort:

We have a state wide recreational project on which 600 recreation workers are employed. The kind of recreational music activities carried on by these workers varies considerably. They may be called on to conduct a community singing, direct rhythm bands for small children or organize a choral group or organize large bands and orchestras. Personnel of the groups organized by the recreation workers is composed of children and adults who could not afford to pay for training.[26]

Eloquent testimony to the warm reception accorded the FERA program is available in the final reports on its operation and in unsolicited letters of appreciation from most of the states in the union. Typical of rural areas that welcomed the opportunities afforded by a music program was Sublette County, Wyoming. Sublette County is sparsely populated; its territory covers 5,000 square miles; its county seat, Pinedale, is 105 miles from the nearest railway station. Four teachers were employed under the emergency education program to carry on a music project in the county, and various clubs of the community paid their travel expenses as they made regular visits over the county to teach music to school children. The four teachers organized orchestras of children in Pinedale, Big Piney, Danile, and Boulder. The county relief secretary, Ruth Healy, commented on the work done in the following report:

> The music program in Sublette county under the Recreational setup proved very successful. It was advantageous in that it developed talent of youngsters. It also set the community to thinking more of the education of their children and the necessity of proper coordination which the music program was instrumental in bringing about. . . . The schools have not adequate money to furnish music teachers for children. The music program phase of the Recreational Program was a luxury to the people of the county. Whether or not it continues through the present administration, prominent individuals of the county will endeavor to carry on the splendid work started through the Recreational Department of the ERA.[27]

The enthusiasm of the audience was equaled in many cases by that of the musicians. The report from Rhode Island states:

> The morale of the musicians who were taken from pick and shovel jobs, for the most part, had notably changed, most of them simply could not do the heavy work of ditch-digging. Their cooperation with the supervisor, a trained recreational and entertainment director, has been very gratifying. Many of the men have voluntarily given two hours to one for which they have been paid. Especially has this been true of the low budget members.[28]

The same phenomenon was observed in Colorado:

> There is a fine cooperative spirit among our musicians. Those on small budgets gave their time freely to help others to work out larger budgets, and by May 16, (1934) the orchestra had contributed 545 hours of unpaid time to enable such a program to be carried out.[29]

596

A trend toward an emphasis on the American in music was indicated as early as the FERA period. Under a program where musicians were to be employed "as musicians," not as manual laborers, thought was given to what kind of music musicians would play on various types of projects. Walter Piston, a composer and professor of music at Harvard University and a special member of the Massachusetts ERA committee on American music, suggested that the works of American composers, who had hitherto not had an audience, be performed. The Composer's Forum Laboratory developed under the Federal Music Project was essentially in agreement with Mr. Piston's plan for encouraging American composers.

Several states under ERA, through their departments of education, sponsored programs favoring native music. Kentucky and Missouri were interested in folk music. The New Mexico ERA report states that that state had a plan for perpetuating the folk music that had been "handed down from one generation to the next in the Southwest."

Under the FERA almost every state had some kind of music paid for out of federal funds. Even Puerto Rico had music provided by bands and orchestras led by musicians on relief, and the Virgin Islands had music classes under the adult education project. In perhaps a majority of cases the performing units were composed of volunteers, and only the conductor or leader was paid; but there were still many more professional units than under the CWA. In San Francisco the project called the "San Francisco Central Entertainment Project," sponsored by the city and county of San Francisco and supervised by the San Francisco County FERA, employed about 350 persons continuously from May, 1934, to July, 1935, in three groups: symphony and novelty orchestras, which gave 325 public performances; a vaudeville and radio unit, which gave 237 public performances; and a choral and chamber music unit, which gave 55 public performances. The following paragraph is taken from the California report:

> The project has been the means of rehabilitating many instrumentalists so that they could return to private employment, and has been of incalculable value in restoring the morale of the entire group. This applies particularly to the class of older professional singers, for whom employment offers so little. The community has derived a great cultural benefit from the groups' performances, which in all cases have been given without admission charges. Public institutions, such as the veterans and military hospitals, county hospitals and homes, have been benefited thereby. Concerts have been given in many schools over a period of a year and these have been of an instructional nature, talks explanatory of the music being given.[30]

In Florida the history of the Jacksonville Civic Orchestra, begun under the CWA and continued under the FERA and the WPA, was typical of many larger orchestras throughout the country. It employed fifty-two musicians who were on relief rolls. The state report makes the following observation:

> This project is an example of the policy of the Florida ERA to employ all relief clients, in so far as possible, upon projects designed especially to fit their needs and abilities. The relief administration has attempted, in this way, to preserve and to develop, among relief clients, professional and technical training which may enable them, at some time in the future, to secure private employment. This band of musicians, in common with several others which were employed on orchestra projects throughout the state, gave two or three public concerts each week, and was required to meet certain regulations concerning time spent at this work. During the FERA period a total of $17,839.85 has been paid these musicians.[31]

Of all music projects under the pre-WPA program, that of New York City functioned the most smoothly; it was taken over almost intact by the Federal Music Project. The New York City project was unique, not typical. Its program was planned for a vast metropolitan area where the needs of a large percentage (one-eighth) of the nation's musicians were most urgent and where there was scope for an educational program in music. The accomplishment in New York City music activities cannot be compared with that of a sparsely populated area where a few community projects met the need of employment for musicians. The success of the New York City project was due largely to the zeal of its music personnel. Among those working from the beginning was Frances McFarland, to whom belongs the credit for much excellent planning, especially in the field of education.

The Music Advisory Committee of the TERA, of which Mrs. McFarland was chairman, in May, 1933, established definite policies for music activities in connection with the adult education program. It was decided that music activities should at no time enter the competitive field and therefore should be carried on in public institutions and on public property such as parks, etc. It was permitted that music services be given to private agencies for extracurricular activities only; that is, not as part of the regular program of such agencies, for which payment was customarily made. The interest and future of activities of musicians both on and off the payroll was to be considered. The constant purpose of the project was to be constructive work that would bring a return to the taxpayer and rehabilitation to the musician. A plan was developed to establish music centers and provide work for teachers. On October 1, 1933, Mrs. McFarland added forty-four teachers to the payroll and opened centers in three continuation schools and two settlement music schools. The centers offered and continued to offer up to the time of and during the Federal Music Project, instruction in every branch of music. All teaching was class instruction. In January, 1934, a music division was established in New York City under the Civil Works Service of the CWA. Plans were written in project form.

One of the first of the music division projects to be approved under CWS was a music survey of the metropolitan area by boroughs to ascertain what music activities already existed and what music needs should be filled. The music survey conducted employed about eighty-five musicians and ten clerks. Information was obtained from public institutions concerning the nature and extent of such activities already being carried on and the desire for inaugurating music programs or augmenting existing ones. This survey was completed under the TERA in June, 1934, resulting in the development of a definite music program. On July 11, 1934, a project was approved for providing social music to various non-profit institutions. This project gave employment to 104 social music leaders and about twenty other musicians. About 250 centers, such as orphanages, prisons, settlement houses, and young men's and young women's associations, participated. The program included folk singing and dancing, pageants, festivals, rhythm and harmonica bands, singing clubs, games, and operettas throughout the city of New York at a cost of less than eight cents a lesson for each participant.

The New York City music program, which at the close of the CWA numbered some 950 persons, continued to expand and prosper under the encouragement of the Emergency Work Program of the FERA. The problem of management and direction became so complicated that on April 15, 1934, the project was divided into two units, each with its own director. Mr. Baldini was appointed manager of the concert unit, and Mrs. McFarland was named director of the music education unit. When in the fall of 1935 Chalmers Clifton assumed direction of the Federal Music Project in New York City, the number on the project had grown from 950 to about 2,000, of which over 800 were in the music education division. During May, 1935, attendance in classes of musical instruction was estimated at nearly 194,000 (in the aggregate).

The summary of music activities under the FERA Emergency Work Program is thus given:[32]

Symphony orchestras (in 21 states) .......................... 124
Dance orchestras (in 13 states) ............................. 115
Other orchestras (in 23 states) ............................. 268
Aggregate audiences (in 17 states) ................... 10,700,000
Community Sings (in 14 states) ............................ 1,553
People participating (in 13 states) ..................... 368,000
Other music projects (in 17 states) ..................... 14,183

## EARLY PLANS FOR A NATIONAL MUSIC PROJECT

The first carefully worked out plan for a federal project had been submitted as early as December, 1933, by Grace Spofford, former dean of the Curtis Institute of Music. The object of the plan, as stated, was to maintain standards of high musicianship, maintain morale of musicians and the public, knit music into a pattern of adult education, and retrain musicians for new forms of civic and recreational music. The program was to be prosecuted in thirty key centers and called for a division of music to be established in Washington. Work for 9,000 musicians, union and non-union, was to be provided through concerts (band, symphony, string orchestras, string ensembles, woodwind and brass ensembles) in dance orchestras and bands, and in group singing (opera singers or choral groups), recitals, and educational programs. The plan, calling for an audition board, had two features: appreciation of a need to analyze community requirements before instituting programs, and a proposal to retrain teachers for *class* instruction.

Two months later, in February, 1934, Glenn M. Tindall submitted a plan to the Federal Emergency Relief Administration. Under it a director of music projects would select and appoint an advisory committee. The plan called for five types of projects: symphony, music conservation camps, concert bands, recreational music, and opera companies. Music conservation camps (similar to the music conservation camps suggested by Max Rabinoff) were a distinguishing feature in the Tindall plan. Needy musicians were to be lodged in camps and routed throughout the division to give concerts. Tindall estimated that, should all of his projects be adopted, employment would be given to approximately 5,670 people.

The National Federation of Music Clubs also labored long and diligently for a plan to relieve unemployment among musicians and to

600

give an outlet for musical expression. In February, 1934, the federation proposed a nationwide plan to organize projects for unemployed musicians. It was reported as follows:

> The relief projects by which it is hoped not only to find employment for thousands of musicians but to increase facilities for leisure time enjoyment by the general public are being organized through state and local relief boards with members of the Federation of Music Clubs working on the plans.
>
> The Federation plan for emergency relief for musicians is an outgrowth of a conference at the White House attended by Mrs. John A. Jardine, Fargo, N. Dak., president of the National Federation of Music Clubs. Mrs. F. D. Roosevelt and Mrs. Ellen S. Woodward, director of women's work, presided at the meeting which was called by Harry Hopkins, Federal Relief Administrator.
>
> Three main types of projects are being organized in the various States: music programs for public institutions; a program for adult education; and formation of various music groups and ensembles.
>
> Under the plan of organizing music for public institutions we are suggesting programs in hospitals, recreation centers, parks, playgrounds, orphanages, jails, music settlements, libraries and schools. The adult education outline calls for the inclusion of serious music courses in the curricula of State emergency colleges and continuation schools which are being organized now for the unemployed.
>
> Choral groups, string ensembles, orchestras and bands are being formed for presentation in public concerts and to be used in carrying out the music plans for public institutions and the adult education program as part of the musicians emergency relief project.
>
> Activities under the relief program will be administered strictly within non-competitive fields, in justice to musicians maintaining themselves by the profession, Mrs. Jardine emphasized.[33]

Finally, the American Federation of Musicians used their influence to lighten the lot of their colleagues. Letters, telegrams, and resolutions poured into the Washington office from almost every union local. The following telegram from the San Francisco local is typical:

> ON BEHALF OF ALL OUR UNEMPLOYED MUSICIANS SOME OF WHICH HAVE NOT WORKED FOR FOUR YEARS WE IMPLORE AND COURTEOUSLY DEMAND IMMEDIATE ACTION AND THE FULFILMENT OF THE PURPOSE FOR WHICH FUNDS HAVE BEEN APPROPRIATED stop KINDLY WIRE THE UNDERSIGNED IMMEDIATELY THE ACTION TAKEN BY YOU IN ACCORDANCE WITH THIS.[34]

Working procedures for music projects, elaborated during this period, were:

F5. 1 Organizing Symphony Orchestras

F5. 2 Organizing Band Concerts

F5. 3 Organizing Dance Orchestras

F5. 4 Community Music Survey

F5. 5 Music Centers

F5. 6 Organizing Chamber Music Groups

F5. 7 Singers for Group and Solo Program

F5. 8 Opera and Operetta

F5. 9 Visiting Music Teachers for Rural Districts*

1.  *New York Times,* July 9, 1929.
2.  *Ibid.,* December 5, 1939.
3.  *Ibid.,* November 3, 1929.
4.  *Ibid.,* October 22, 1929.
5.  *Ibid.,* March 1, 1929, editorial.
6.  *Ibid.,* March 20, 1929.
7.  Editorial, *The Musician,* June, 1934.
8.  James J. Davis, as quoted in Kenneth S. Clark, *Music in Industry* (New York: National Bureau for the Advancement of Music, 1929), p. 3.
9.  *New York Times,* May 24, 1931.
10.  *Ibid.,* March 15, 1931.
11.  *Ibid.,* October 22, 1929, editorial, p. 28.
12.  Augustus Delafield Zanzig, *Music in American Life* (New York: Oxford University Press, 1932), p. 109.
13.  *New York Times,* July 30, 1929.
14.  *Ibid.,* November 6, 1930.
15.  *Ibid.,* November 17, 1930.
16.  *Ibid.,* April 9, 1933.
17.  *Ibid.,* September 11 and November 30, 1931.
18.  Virgil Dahl, "General Report on Musicians' Project 8047," December 19, 1933, CWA Files.
19.  *Ibid.*
20.  Letter, William Farnsworth to John N. Scelsea, March 12, 1934, NRA Files.
21.  Letter, Arthur Hanna to Robert S. Stannard, March 17, 1934, CWA Files.
22.  Letter, Robert S. Stannard to Hopkins, March 15, 1934, CWA Files.
23.  "Review of C.W.A. Activities in Minnesota," p. 114 (FWA Library).
24.  *Minneapolis Tribune,* February 12, 1934.
25.  "Government Aid During the Depression to Professional, Technical, and Other Service Workers," WPA, May 18, 1936, p. 9.
26.  "Annual Report," Minnesota Emergency Relief Administration, May 1, 1935, p. 8.
27.  "Wyoming: A Review of Work Relief Activities," April, 1934–July, 1935, p. 8, FWA Library.
28.  "Summary of Work Relief Activities," April 1, 1934–July 1, 1935, Rhode Island Emergency Relief Administration, p. 00, FWA Library.

*Under public welfare was listed: (E4. 10) Social and Recreational Music for Children and Adults.

29.  "Summary of Work Relief Activities," April 1, 1934–July 1, 1935, Colorado Emergency Relief Administration, p. 185, FWA Library.

30.  "California: Review of Work Relief Activities from April 1, 1934 to July 1, 1935," p. 00, FWA Library.

31.  "The Emergency Work Program in Florida, April, 1934–June, 1935," p. 30, FWA Library.

32.  *The Emergency Work Relief Program of the F.E.R.A., April 1, 1934–July 1, 1935,* FERA, p. 104.

33.  *The Musician,* February, 1934, p. 17.

34.  Telegram, Musicians' Union, Local 6, San Francisco, to President Roosevelt, April, 1934, CWA Files.

# 24

## The Organization and Operation of the
## Federal Music Project

NIKOLAI SOKOLOFF

The choice of Nikolai Sokoloff as national director of the Federal Music Project was inspired by two considerations: his professional eminence in the world of music; and his record, throughout his career as a conductor, in integrating music with the life of the community. The combination of those two qualities promised an administration that would be at once technically competent and socially desirable.

Of Sokoloff's professional standing, there can be no doubt. Born in Russia in 1886, he played the violin at the age of ten years with the Kiev Municipal Orchestra under the baton of his father. Two years later, he came to the United States, and at the age of thirteen he was awarded a special scholarship at the Yale University School of Music for the study of the violin. After three years' study, he became a member of the Boston Symphony Orchestra. Sokoloff achieved a national reputation in his profession as director of the Cleveland Orchestra, a post he had held for fifteen years before joining the Works Progress Administration. During this period, as conductor of the Cleveland Orchestra and as guest conductor with other orchestras, he had appeared in nearly two hundred cities in the United States, Canada, Cuba, England, and Wales. At the same time, he distinguished himself as a leader in the encouragment of the American artist and composer and, in cooperation with the board of education, brought into existence a comprehensive program for music study and instruction in the Cleveland public schools.

The respect that he commanded in the musical world guaranteed

604

the co-operation and support of professional musicians in the purposes of the program. At the same time, his own high regard for technical competence insured a program in which the emphasis would be upon performance. Consequently, of all the programs under Federal One, the Music Project most directly aimed at, and most nearly approached, a high level of artistry. Sokoloff's acquaintance with personnel in the realm of American music enabled him to choose his assistants with discrimination and with regard to the concern for artistry his own training reflected.

However, this accent upon professionalism during his tenure resulted in less stress upon music in education and in recreation than some whose concern lay in that direction would have liked or expected from Sokoloff's previous record. It was less that the national director disdained or neglected non-orchestral music than that he failed aggressively to encourage it. In those areas, as in New York City, where substantial educational programs had developed before the WPA, such programs not only were continued but also expanded under Sokoloff's regime. On the other hand, in less metropolitan areas, where such programs had not been initiated before the WPA and where, even more than in metropolitan centers, music education was needed, the encouragement of music as an amateur activity was less stressed than it was later when Earl Vincent Moore succeeded Sokoloff. The symphony orchestra naturally was closest to the heart of the first federal director, and the occasion the project afforded him both to develop and direct competent symphonic groups left him less time and perhaps less inclination to spend upon activities that, though lower in the hierarchy of musical performance, were perhaps more intimately concerned with the community's acceptance of a music program.

Sokoloff's preference for orchestral performance also caused him to devote less time to purely administrative duties than the exigencies of his position required. His presence in the field was more apt to be as guest conductor of a WPA symphony orchestra than as administrator of the project; and although his appearances on the podium created an atmosphere of distinction and prestige, his visits to the offices of the WPA state administrators were often less effective. State and local WPA officials, other than those on the arts program, were not, in the main, men with highly developed aesthetic sensibilities, and the natural discomfort they felt in the presence of a musical impressario was not eased by Sokoloff's inability to divest himself of his professional manner. But if there was not the same cordiality between the national director of the Music Project and the state administrators as existed, for example, between Holger Cahill and the state administrators, Sokoloff's innate courtesy and kindliness of manner provoked respect not unmixed with friendliness on the part of the lay administrators, and quieted to a considerable degree the uneasiness of the man of affairs in the presence of the artist.

THE WASHINGTON OFFICE

Since the Music Project operated no national projects as such (like the Index of American Design on the Art Project), there was no need in Washington for a large staff; and throughout its life the Washington staff of the Music Project was the smallest of those under Federal One. In the beginning Sokoloff administered the project without an assistant director, but within the first year William C. Mayfarth was appointed to that position. Mayfarth had been dean of music at Converse College in Spartanburg, South Carolina, and came to the Washington staff from the Federal Music Project staff in Pennsylvania. Those who joined the Washington staff at the beginning of the project were Dorothy Fredenhagen, Alma Sandra Munsell, and Ruth Haller Ottaway. Mrs. Fredenhagen was municipal carilloneur at Albany, New York, where she had devoted her musical talents to settlement-house work. Miss Munsell had been an executive officer of the Musicians' Emergency Fund of New York City; and Mrs. Ottaway was president of the National Federation of Music Clubs and president of the National Women's Council. In 1936 Harry L. Hewes joined the staff and served as head of the music analysis unit.

THE REGIONAL AND STAFF OFFICES

Sokoloff's intention was to establish the project on a regional rather than a state basis. In October, 1935, he wrote to Bruce McClure:

> After studying the entire music project, the most satisfactory and least expensive way of helping me to carry out the plan will be on the basis of having eleven Regional Directors instead of individual State Supervisors. The salaries will vary as per our conversation, between $2600 and $3200 per year for Regional Directors.
> The country has been divided into regions as follows:
>
> 1. New York City

2. Maine, New Hampshire, Vermont, Massachusetts, Rhode Island
3. New York State, Connecticut
4. Pennsylvania, New Jersey, Maryland, Delaware, District of Columbia, West Virginia
5. Virginia, North Carolina, Tennessee, South Carolina, Georgia, Alabama, Florida.
6. Michigan, Ohio, Indiana, Kentucky
7. Wisconsin, Illinois, City of Chicago, Illinois, City of St. Louis, Missouri
8. Oklahoma, Arkansas, Mississippi, Louisiana, Texas
9. North Dakota, South Dakota, Minnesota, Iowa, Nebraska, Kansas, Missouri (omitting St. Louis)
10. North California (San Francisco), Oregon, Washington, Idaho, Montana, Wyoming, Nevada
11. Southern California (Los Angeles), Utah, Colorado, Arizona, New Mexico[1]

The regional directors appointed were: Region 1, Chalmers Clifton (Clifton never possessed the title of regional director, but acted as such in New York City); Region 2, Louis Cornell; Region 3, Lee Pattison; Region 4, Thaddeus Rich; Region 5, LaMar Stringfield; Region 6, Guy Maier; Region 7, Joseph Lay; Region 8, Lucille F. Lyons; Region 9, C. B. Righter; Regions 10 and 11, Bruno David Ussher.

In January, 1936, the regional organization was discontinued. Some of the regional directors resigned; some accepted appointments as state directors; and B. D. Ussher, Louis Cornell, and Thaddeus Rich were attached to the Washington office as assistants to the federal director. Until January, 1936, the appointment of state directors was delegated by Sokoloff to the regional directors, subject to his final approval. Thereafter, Sokoloff became immediately responsible for the appointment of state directors, subject to the approval of the state WPA administrator.

THE GENERAL PLAN OF ORGANIZATION

The plan at the outset of the project and throughout its life embraced three major divisions: the administrative branch, the concert branch, and the music education branch. The administrative branch in Washington worked with the WPA offices there and in the field; handled procedures, finance, union relationships, and travel regulations; determined the administrative and technical organization, function, and

607

scope of the program; set technical requirements and established types and standards of work; budgeted expenditures and distributed state quotas; received and answered monthly activity reports from each project; and gave assistance and advice to the field on all administrative matters.

The concert branch offered services of the performing units in the presentation of public performances in communities and in outlying areas. As of January 15, 1939, the concert division embraced the following units:

| | | |
|---|---|---:|
| 28 | symphony orchestras employing | 1,907 |
| 90 | small orchestras employing | 2,075 |
| 68 | bands employing | 2,114 |
| 55 | dance bands and orchestras employing | 633 |
| 15 | chamber music ensembles employing | 114 |
| 33 | opera and choral units employing | 1,100 |
| 1 | soloists' unit employing | 10 |

When the Federal Music Project was created, a program for the rehabilitation of the music teachers on relief rolls was made a fundamental part of the national plan. Within the organization of the education branch were included various research activities: experiments in music therapy; the teaching and training of persons unable to pay for music study; a broad program of social music; a program for the integration of music with other school studies; institute and normal courses for project teachers; and leadership for community musical activities.

### ASSIGNMENT AND THE PROBLEM OF STANDARDS

Assignment of a work-relief applicant to the Music Project was achieved through auditions. At the very beginning Sokoloff had made it clear that none but professional musicians would be admitted to employment. By "professional" he meant more than a professional practitioner—a person who had once made his living at music or a member of a professional society like the American Federation of Musicians. He meant very simply an applicant who could fulfil the requirements established by the project's local audition board.

To Sokoloff's credit it must be said that during his tenure of the national directorship he honestly maintained this simple and straightforward criterion. It was not easy. Political and professional pressures were brought upon him, not the least of which was that of the American Federation of Musicians, which, without necessarily demanding that *only* its members be employed, certainly insisted that *all* members who applied be employed. As a result of his insistence upon a single, definitive standard, Sokoloff, without doubt, achieved on the Music Project the highest level of individual performance among all the arts projects. It is true that it is easier within an hour's time to judge an instrumentalist's ability on the piano or violin than it is to determine the merit of an actor or a writer. To that degree, the very nature of his project facilitated Sokoloff's design. Yet it was largely due to the national director's refusal to compromise on quality that high professional standards (especially in symphonic performances) were achieved and maintained by the Music Project.

This is not to say that the standards of the local audition boards were at all times and everywhere the same. In general, standards were higher in the larger and more metropolitan centers, where more and better applicants were available, than in the smaller cities and rural areas. Again, the attitude of audition boards changed with changing circumstances. In the beginning the tendency was to establish very high professional standards of performance. It soon became apparent, however, that with such criteria as determinative, so few applicants were being accepted that the primary purpose of the project—the relief of unemployment among musicians—was being frustrated. The natural reaction was likely to follow; and the same board, now under social and humanitarian pressure, would be inclined to accept all who manifested even a tolerable competence. Again, especially when quota reductions were ordered from Washington, auditions—or more properly, re-auditions—were used to separate the less competent from the project.

Such variations in time and place were natural and, under the circumstances, unavoidable. In general, on the Music Project audition boards served as a means for insuring a high standard of individual competence. The question at issue, as the controversy developed between Sokoloff and the AF of M was not so much *what standard* as a *standard for what*. On October 1, 1935, Joseph Weber, president of the AF of M wrote a long letter to Sokoloff in which he raised certain fundamental questions. Excerpts from his letter follow:

> As I understand it, the musical projects should be various and not confined to one class of music, but are to be representative of all, beginning with dance music and jazz and ending in symphony. The classification would include: Symphony orchestras per se, concert orchestras, playing standard

music, etc., chamber-music organizations, military bands, dance music of all kinds, jazz organizations playing dance music.

Now as to setting a standard of examination, it must be kept in mind that more than 80% of the musicians do not need superior musicianship for the purpose of following their profession. By superior musicianship, I mean they need not qualify for positions in symphony orchestras. . . .

The general situation in the musical field being as it is, if musical examinations would be too exacting, it would rob the hungry musician of any opportunity for relief, even though he formerly did make his living, and a fairly good one, by following music as a profession. To further illustrate the real conditions in the employment field of musicians, I will say that I, myself, during my career as a professional musician, was forced to play any sort of engagement in circuses, dances, parades, picnics, hotels, then concert bands, and finally for many years I was with the Cincinnati Symphony Orchestra.

. . . The examinations should be based upon the premise of verities and realities in the music professional field, and therefore, my suggestion to you would be that if a musical project of whatever kind is proposed, the musican under present economic conditions should be permitted to be examined in ensemble and the standard should not be set too high, as the standard of such bands and orchestras in any country, as I have had opportunity to observe and absolutely know, runs through the entire scale from passable to excellent.

I am speaking, as you well know, from a thorough knowledge of the conditions in the musical world, and I am in sympathy with your aims and objects, provided of course same do not finally partake entirely of the nature of an educational campaign for the better compositions in music instead of affording relief to unemployed musicians in the entire musical field.[2]

The logic of Weber's contention was not lost upon Sokoloff, who, on November 16, 1938, wrote to Chalmers Clifton of the New York City project relaxing somewhat the criteria for admission to employment on the project:

All musicians whether union or non-union who receive "A" or "B" ratings in the auditions, shall be classified on project forms and payrolls as professional musicians. All musicians receiving a rating of "C" in the auditions are classified as skilled musicians.[3]

LOCAL ORGANIZATION

In the localities, problems of organization and administration were diverse. Where the American Federation of Musicians was strong, it tried to dominate the project. Its pressures took various forms: (1) to compel the local project to accept all applicants certified by the local AF of M; (2) to achieve the union scale of wages and working hours;

610

(3) to restrict the project to activities not in competition with commercially employed musicians. In New York City in December, 1935, when a strike threatened, Local 802 of the AF of M demanded that musicians receive compensation in conformity with union rates of pay, fulfil fewer services a week, and not be required to broadcast from commercial stations or to give concerts to which admission was charged. Chalmers Clifton, the director of the New York City project, averted a serious situation by making some concessions.

In another set of circumstances the Federal Music Project found itself between the sword and the wall: the New York Philharmonic Orchestra demanded that the local project charge at least a fifty-cent admission to its symphony concerts; the AF of M insisted that all concerts given by the project be free.

In general it may be said that Sokoloff and the state directors who served under him maintained the integrity of the project against all unwarranted demands, and showed themselves neither weak in the face of intimidation nor stubborn when sound policy and equity counseled compromise.

In smaller communities the major problem was likely to be the recruitment of enough competent musicians in the several instruments for an ensemble. The Canton (Ohio) project, which was discontinued on March 21, 1938, illustrates the situation. Guy Maier, the regional director, reported to Theodore Hahn, director in Ohio:

> Here is the general summary of the Canton situations, so that you can have the entire picture at your finger ends.

| | |
|---|---|
| 1—Violin | 1—Sax |
| 1—Piano | 1—Piano-Accordion |
| 1—Bass | 1—Atrocious Trumpet |
| 1—Guitar | 1—Clarinet |
| | 1—Drum |

> Majority of engagements at County Jail, Infirmary, one at Work House, several for P.T.A. meetings (which are restricted), three community centers.[4]

## CO-OPERATION WITH OTHER FEDERAL AGENCIES AND WITH PROFESSIONAL SOCIETIES

The National Federation of Women's Clubs early manifested an interest in the Federal Music Project. Before the beginning of the project itself the Federation, through its president, Ruth Haller Ottaway, exerted pressure upon the FERA in the form of letters and requests for aid to unemployed musicians. Mrs. Ottaway had correspondence with Jacob Baker on the formulation of the program of the Federal Music Project, and was one of the first members of the Washington staff. Because of her influence, the Federation, at its annual conventions, endorsed the work of the Federal Music Project. As a consequence, music clubs in localities were able not only to defend the existence of the project against political criticism but also to provide sponsorship for concerts. The Federal Music Project provided appearances with the major symphony orchestras of the project for the winners of the Federation's contests.

The Library of Congress and the Federal Music Project worked in close co-operation for a wider cultural program in music. Harold Spivacke, chief of the music division of the Library of Congress, was a member of the national committee of the WPA Music Program and a sponsor of one of the units of the District of Columbia music project. Folk song recordings made on the southern expedition by the Federal Music Project were deposited in the folk song archive of the Library of Congress. With the assistance of the WPA the Library of Congress published the *Check-List of Recorded Songs in the English Language* in the archive of American folk songs. The Library of Congress is the depository of the incompleted "Index of American Composers," which was the work of Margaret Kerr and Harry L. Hewes of the Washington office.

The Pan American Union also worked closely with the WPA music program in several capacities. Charles Seeger, who had been a member of the Federal Music Project staff, was appointed chief of the music division of the Pan American Union. The music-copying units of the project supplied the Union with material assistance. On the Philadelphia unit scores of Latin-American compositions were reproduced and deposited in the Fleischer collection of the Free Library of Philadelphia. Charles Seeger and Earl Vincent Moore both appeared on the program of the Conference on Inter-American Relations in the Field of Music in October, 1939. In 1938 Seeger, a member of the music education advisory committee, submitted "A Prosposal" for a music education program.

Relationships with the NYA were at times controversial. During 1940 and 1941 there were questions that arose concerning an orchestra the NYA had organized—the American Youth Orchestra. It was not that the WPA Program objected to the existence of an orchestra in NYA, but that the National Youth Administration took away from WPA many of its workers, both young and old. Indeed, there were occasions when the NYA actually took elderly musicians from the rolls of WPA. These musicians, although they were contributing to the cultural life of their communities where they were, were persuaded to become first-chair men in youth orchestras. The national advisory committee protested this practice of the NYA in duplicating the services of the WPA program.

Theater and music projects combined efforts in operatic productions, musical drama, and on the folk music expedition in the South.

RELATIONS WITH THE NEGRO

The Negro, whose role in the development of American music is acknowledged, was offered new opportunities under the Federal Music Project.

Among Negro composers who rank among contemporary American composers are the following: William Grant Still, Clarence Cameron White, Julian Work, John W. Work, Harry T. Burleigh, Will Marion Cook, E. Nathaniel Dett, Charles Dixon, J. Rosemund Johnson, C. Montrose Thompson, Eva Jesaye, and W. C. Handy. The works of these writers were given repeated performances in all sections of the country by WPA musicians. William Grant Still appeared as a guest conductor with the WPA symphony orchestra in San Diego.

All-Negro casts appeared in Federal Music Project performances of Verdi's opera *Il Trovatore* and Auber's comic opera *Fra Diavolo*, the former in New York City and the latter in Los Angeles. In California, Verdi's *Aida* was given its first two presentations with a real "Ethiopian" chorus when an entire Negro choral unit was introduced.

Well-attended music instruction classes for Negroes were held in New York, Pennsylvania, Ohio, Illinois, Oklahoma, North and South Carolina, Florida, Mississippi, Louisiana, New Mexico, and California. Many choruses and instrumental units were created under trained leadership.

Well-trained Negro musicians were assigned as teachers in the Federal Music Project's educational programs in Florida, Oklahoma, Mississippi, Illinois, New Mexico, and California. Negro musicians held supervisory teaching positions in New York City.

Professional choruses of excellent artistic caliber were found in Oakland, Los Angeles, Chicago, Minneapolis, Boston, and New York; and Negro concert bands and dance orchestras existed in a score of cities including Detroit, Los Angeles, Omaha, New Orleans, Kansas City, Missouri, Kansas City, Kansas, Milwaukee, Toledo, Cleveland, Cincinnati, Chicago, New York, and Richmond.

A joint production of the Federal Theater and Federal Music projects was *Run, Little Chillun,* a musical drama whose cast of 150 played to large audiences in California during 1938 and 1939. The play was written by Hall Johnson, a well-known Negro choral director.

At Chicago the Jubilee Singers specialized in Negro songs and spirituals, and were greatly in demand for all types of bookings.

After the termination of the Theater Project, the large Negro chorus that had participated in the famous *Swing Mikado* was transferred to the Music Project. This group provided the Illinois project's only venture into opera and operetta. During the Negro exposition held at the Chicago Coliseum from July to September, 1940, a feature of the program was the performance of the Negro chorus in Planquette's operetta *The Chimes of Normandy* in a modernized swing version. That same year, selections from several operettas were presented before school assemblies and various other groups.*

THE MUSIC PROGRAM UNDER STATE CONTROL

On September 1, 1939, the Federal Music Project was transferred from federal to state control and renamed the WPA Music Program. Sokoloff, anticipating the transfer and the changes in policy implied, resigned shortly before the cessation of the federal program; after a short interim he was succeeded (August 23, 1939) by Earl Vincent Moore, director of the School of Music at the University of Michigan.

*Among the project's concert units composed entirely of Negro musicians were the following: California: Los Angeles Colored Chorus, Los Angeles Concert Band, Oakland Choral Group. Illinois: Chicago Dixie Orchestra, Chicago Jubilee Singers, Chicago Columbia Concert Band, Herrin Jubilee Singers. Kansas: Kansas City Negro Concert Band. Louisiana: New Orleans Negro Military Band. Massachusetts: Boston Southland Singers, Springfield Colored Novelty Orchestra, Cambridge American Folk Singers. Michigan: Detroit Dance Band. Minnesota: Twin Cities Jubilee Singers. Missouri: Kansas City Colored Orchestra, St. Louis Colored Orchestra. Nebraska: Omaha Negro Unit. New York City: Negro Melody Singers, Negro Art Singers Dance Band, Instrumental Trio. Ohio: Cleveland Choral Group, Toledo Dance Orchestra. Pennsylvania: Philadelphia Lincoln Dance Band, Pittsburgh Colored Dance Band. Virginia: Richmond Colored Concert Orchestra. Wisconsin: Milwaukee Dance Orchestra.

Moore remained in office until June, 1940, when he resigned to resume his academic duties at the university. In August, 1940, George Foster, who had been with the project in one capacity or another almost since its inception in 1935, was appointed deputy director of the WPA Music Program, and under that title was responsible for its administration until the end. Because Foster followed substantially the policies of Earl Moore, his succession was not such a break in continuity as was Moore's succession to Sokoloff.

It is easy to compare the Sokoloff regime (1935-39) with the Moore-Foster regime (1939-43) and, in accordance with one's own preferences, to praise the one and condemn the other. In the earlier period the emphasis was upon technical competence in performance, as manifested primarily in the symphony orchestra. In the latter period, the stress was upon the integration of musical activities, through educational and recreational devices, with the life of the community. To a considerable degree, each of these emphases reflected the character and training of the director who was responsible for it: Sokoloff was a professional musician who, however tolerantly he might view amateur performance, was too conscious of academic canons seriously to concern himself with music as a mere means toward social service; Moore on the other hand, although no less conscious than Sokoloff of the difference between excellence and mediocrity, approached his duties as director primarily as an educator, with a realization of the part played by music in the school, the church, the club, and the general life of the community.

This, however, is merely to say that each director personified, so to speak, the period of his directorship. The whole spirit of the Federal Music Project, when it was initiated in the summer of 1935, was to raise relief projects in the field of music above the level of amateurism that characterized the earlier FERA period. To achieve this purpose, a better choice than Nikolai Sokoloff could hardly have been made. Four years later, for better or worse, the attempt of the professional musician to achieve a position of public power and responsibility had failed. Earl Moore, when he succeeded Sokoloff, had no alternative but to accept and practice the social service philosophy of the arts. The states, which were now responsible for the initiation and type of projects, would suffer no other; and indeed, most of the musicians who remained on the project were incapable of the standard of performance characteristic of the earlier period.

As a matter of fact, early in the period of state control there was considerable question as to whether the project would survive. There were several reasons for this: the problem of procuring state and local sponsorship; the statutory requirement with regard to the disposal of admission receipts; and above all, the eighteen-months rule, which enacted that all project workers who had been employed for eighteen or more months be dismissed. The result of this last clause was that projects throughout the country lost many of their more experienced and better performers. As a consequence, performing units like orchestras, bands, and ensembles, which depended for their quality upon equal competance on the part of all participants, were seriously and sometimes fatally injured.

That the Music Project was able to survive this crisis was due to the morale and loyalty of the project workers and supervisors, and to the inventive energy of the Washington office in seeking and finding new activities.

### SERVICES TO THE ARMED FORCES

In 1940-41 the WPA Music Program provided the Civilian Conservation Corps with music instructors. Activities were jointly undertaken in the form of piano classes, glee clubs, bands, orchestras, and community sings.

It was from experience gained in these activities that the Music Program was able so successfully to prosecute its work with the armed services. In the fall of 1940 there was an expressed need felt for the services of bands to play for service units. WPA served the Army Air Corps with bands. WPA bands played for drill of the newly formed state militia units. By January, 1941, twenty-one of the state music projects were engaged in some form of defense activities. As mobilization grew, there was need of entertainment that in many instances orchestras and bands provided. State music projects were called upon to provide leaders for musical activities in the camps. Calls were answered for both choral leaders and instrumental instructors. By June, 1941, forty-two state music projects were engaged in some form of defense activity, and in some states all civilian music services had been discontinued for services to the armed forces. Of great popularity at this time were the dance bands that devoted full-time schedules to military reservations and the communities surrounding them. Symphony concerts were introduced, and it was discovered that the young recruits were enthusiastic for music of this type as well as that of dance bands. Instructors and coaches from the state project units were employed on the military reservations for educational purposes. Foremost among states furnishing a music service to the armed forces were California, Florida, Massachusetts, Illinois, and Indiana.

A plan was under way to revise the activities of the WPA Music Program so as best to serve the national defense program at the end of 1941. A series of work conferences had been called for the week of December 7, 1941. The United States was attacked at Pearl Harbor at the very time a work conference was to be held. Immediately, Howard Hunter sent a telegram to Secretary Stimson and to Secretary Knox saying that the resources of the Work Projects Administration were completely available to the Army and Navy. At the same time a telegram was sent to all State Work Projects administrators stating that the services of the entire administrative staff of WPA had been offered to the War and Navy departments for any local assistance necessary.

The call to the armed services following Pearl Harbor and the opportunities for employment in defense industries soon deprived the Music Program of most of its musicians; and although the projects in the states were not officially terminated until July, 1943, the program to all intents and purposes came to a close shortly after the declaration of war against the Axis powers.

1. Memorandum, Sokoloff to McClure, October 3, 1935, FMP Files.
2. Letter, Joseph Weber to Sokoloff, October 1, 1935, FMP Files.
3. Letter, Sokoloff to Clifton, November 16, 1935, FMP Files.
4. Letter, Maier to Hahn, April 2, 1938, FMP Files.

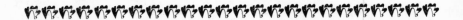

# 25

# The Program of the Federal Music Project

THE GENERAL PLAN

The program contemplated under the Federal Music Project was described in *Supplement No. 1 to Bulletin No. 29* as follows:[1]

*Music*

1. Symphony and concert orchestras
2. Dance orchestras
3. Bands
4. Chamber music ensembles
5. Vocal quartets and ensembles
6. Instrumental and vocal soloists
7. Grand opera, operetta, opera comique, and chamber opera
8. Teaching of music and music appreciation
9. Employment and use of
     Music librarians
     Music copyists
     Music binders
     Piano tuners
     Instrument repairers, etc.
10. Other

This program may be conveniently divided into three parts: performance, education, and research and service.

SYMPHONY ORCHESTRAS

When the Federal Music Project was created as an agency of the WPA to employ, retrain, and rehabilitate musicians on the relief rolls, there were eleven recognized symphony orchestras in the United States. By March, 1938, thirty-four symphony orchestras under the Federal Music Project were employing 2,533 musicians. The home cities of these orchestras were San Bernardino, San Francisco, Oakland, San Diego, Pasadena, and Los Angeles in California; Hartford and Bridgeport in Connecticut; Jacksonville, Florida; Chicago; Lynn, Springfield, and Boston in Massachusetts; Detroit and Grand Rapids in Michigan; St. Paul, Minnesota; Omaha, Nebraska; Manchester, New Hampshire; Newark, New Jersey; Buffalo, Syracuse, and New York City (2) in New York; Winston-Salem, South Carolina; Cincinnati and Cleveland in Ohio; Oklahoma City; Philadelphia; Pittsburgh; Providence, Rhode Island; San Antonio and Dallas in Texas; Richmond, Virginia; and Milwaukee.

At first the musicians, when assigned for audition, were skeptical of the worth of the project. Once they realized, however, that a respect for musical integrity would govern its operation, they responded promptly and with enthusiasm. Of the symphony orchestras thus created, Daniel Gregory Mason, MacDowell Professor of Music at Columbia University, wrote:

> They have vastly deepened qualitatively, as well as broadened quantitatively, our musical public. People either go to these concerts to enjoy music itself, or they stay away. . . . The audiences at N.Y. University's Sunday evening concerts were . . . a revelation. Seventeen hundred people, the capacity of the hall, would be seated half-an-hour before the concert began, hundreds more remained outside, unable to get in. These people gave breathless attention to the music, never coughing or moving restlessly about. They came half-an-hour before the concert began and stayed until it ended. You could see that for them the music was a thing of beauty and deep appeal. . . . To hear and see such audiences filled one with a renewed confidence of our musical destiny.[2]

It is not surprising that a brilliant orchestra performance record should have been set in New York City under the guidance of as able a man as Chalmers Clifton. Musicians were plentiful, and there had been successful music projects there prior to the wPA. Nor is it surprising that in other large metropolitan areas—Chicago, San Francisco, Los Angeles, and Philadelphia—excellent orchestras flourished under the wPA. Those orchestras, however, that were brought into being by the Federal Music Project and kept going by it and after it with standards of real merit in areas where music had not previously been in great demand are the test cases of what a music subsidy can give to the community. The three orchestras whose histories are given below are conspicuous examples.

619

The Oklahoma Orchestra was a creation of the Federal Music Project. The man responsible for its inception and successful continuance was Dean Richardson, state director of the Federal Music Project in Oklahoma. In 1937 the Tulsa Symphony Orchestra had thirty-five musicians, drawn from Oklahoma City as well as Tulsa. Beset by political difficulties in Tulsa, Richardson moved the orchestra to the more congenial environment of Oklahoma City. By the winter season of 1938 the Oklahoma City Symphony Orchestra was an established institution. A "Starlight Series" of concerts was given in the summer of 1938. Victor Alessandor, a graduate of the Eastman School of Music, had been brought to Oklahoma City as conductor. The Oklahoma City Auditorium housed the orchestra. The auditorium was so large that large audiences could be accommodated and low admission prices made possible. In 1939 a series of ten concerts was highly successful. The concerts were given under the sponsorship of the Oklahoma State Symphony Society, an organization that maintained amicable relationships with the Federal Music Project.

When in 1939 control was returned to the state, the University of Oklahoma became the official sponsor of the new state music project and assumed the responsibility for the financial arrangements of all concerts. In 1940 the orchestra again held a "Starlight Series," organized a spring tour, and established an Oklahoma City Junior Symphony Orchestra. When, with the outbreak of the war, the Selective Service Act and private employment began to deplete the ranks of the orchestra so that it became impossible to continue under WPA auspices, the State Symphony Society adopted and nurtured the orphan, and it lives today as a worthy child of the Federal Music Project.

A second example is the Symphony Orchestra of Utah. Although the Utah music project was small—its state symphony before 1940 numbered only twenty-six—every attempt was made to make the orchestra of service not only to Salt Lake City, where it originated, but to the entire state through concerts for the general public and in the schools.

Indeed, it was in its service to the schools that the Utah orchestra (then known as the Utah State Sinfonietta) distinguished itself before 1940. With the enthusiastic co-operation of the state educational system the Sinfonietta developed a music appreciation course that met with much success. Programs in Salt Lake City and in other cities and towns to which the orchestra toured were worked out in connection with boards of education, co-operating sponsors, and the students themselves. Emphasis was placed on study of the simpler forms of music, better acquaintance with certain instruments, and concert and auditorium deportment. Teachers were asked to carry on projects to acquaint students with the appearance and sound of various instruments; instruction through the use of phonograph records was recommended. Programs were actually chosen by students in many instances, all study of music having been done weeks in advance in the schoolroom.

In 1940 Gail Martin, music critic of a Salt Lake City newspaper, formed the Utah State Symphony Orchestra as a section of the Utah State Institute of Fine Arts. During its first year its personnel reached fifty; the following year, seventy-five.

The contributions of sponsors always outweighed those made by the WPA. In addition to the men paid with sponsor funds, sponsorship provided the auditorium rental, publicity, music rental, box office personnel, and the conductor, Hans Henriot. Prominent soloists appeared with the orchestra in programs carefully chosen for audience appeal and featuring many American compositions. With the continuing co-operation of the boards of education, the children's concerts after 1940 were developed into a wider plan. The orchestra thus engendered a desire for music education and a taste for symphonic concerts that has persisted in Utah.

The Utah State Symphony Orchestra continued to function after the demise of the WPA, though many of its members were being called into the armed forces. In 1941 Sir Thomas Beecham was engaged as guest conductor while Hans Henriot served in the military.

Unlike the Oklahoma and Utah orchestras, the Buffalo orchestra had begun under the FERA. The early history of the project under the WPA was unhappy, and, as a result of personal rivalries, the WPA orchestra competed for public support with the Buffalo Philharmonic Orchestra, a private institution. In 1938, however, the two orchestras became one under the WPA Music Project. It enjoyed a successful season both in 1938 and 1939, and several famous soloists—among them Albert Spaulding and Harold Bauer—appeared as guests. When, in 1939, music activities were transferred from federal to state control, the WPA orchestra became the Buffalo Philharmonic Orchestra, entirely supported by private contributions, and many of the musicians secured permanent places in the new enterprise.

OPERA

Because of the high cost of production, opera had been traditionally out of reach of all save a small part of the American people. For this

621

reason an opera project was not viewed as a practical venture for the Federal Music Project. This was unfortunate, since the talent for its production was present, and the desire on the part of the American people was manifest in requests for operatic presentations and attempts to maintain opera in various parts of the country.

In the summer of 1935 interest in the development of opera in English by the Federal Music Project in New York City was keen, and seemed to be possible of fulfilment. Approximately seventy-five singers were chosen from the many on relief for the purpose of forming an opera company. It was soon learned, however, that funds for such an undertaking were not available. This necessitated the giving of opera in concert form. During the fall and winter of that year *Carmen, The Bartered Bride,* and *Samson and Delilah* were readied and presented in Manhattan, Brooklyn, Staten Island, and the Bronx.

A chamber opera company was formed in 1936 from this group, and rehearsals were begun on two short operas, *Abu Hassan,* by Carl Maria von Weber, and *The Princess on the Pea,* by Ernst Toch. Through the courtesy of the Theater Project the Biltmore Theater was loaned to the Music Project for one month, and the Federal Chamber Music Opera Company made its bow to the public on June 9, 1936. The performance was praised by the press and played to capacity for three weeks; it might have run through the summer had it been possible to retain the theater or to secure another one. Later, in November, 1936, the Federal Music Theater was leased; and in April, 1937, two short operas were presented: Pergolesi's *Serva Padrona* and a contrasting modern opera, *Romance of a Robot,* by Frederic Hart. The double bill ran to twenty-one performances.

In the meantime, Offenbach's *Tales of Hoffman* was being rehearsed by the Grand Opera Company, which included all members of the opera group not assigned to the chamber opera. A series of financial difficulties, however, caused this opera to be given only once. By that time Congress had caused a reduction in relief appropriations, which in turn necessitated a 25 per cent cut in personnel and drastic economy in non-labor costs. Further opera productions on this scale were impossible.

In the summer of 1937 and winter of 1937-38 the combined opera groups presented operas in concert form, concerts of opera excerpts, and a number of standard choral works, including the Mozart and Brahms requiems, Beethoven's *Choral Fantasy,* and Bloch's *Israel.*

An effort was made to revive opera in a simplified form in the summer of 1938. Operas were cut to concert length; it was planned to have a commentator carry the story. This plan was approved by the director of the project and the administrative office of Federal One. Skeleton scenery was to be used—drapes, screens, and costumes, the last to be designed and executed by the Federal Theater workshop. The Theater Project was also to loan an expert stage director. *Martha*, by Flotow, was chosen for the first opera. This was to be followed by *Cavalleria Rusticana* and a revival of *The Princess on the Pea*, but the money necessary for screens, lighting, and costumes was not available. The Theater Project could not furnish the expert stage director, and their workshop was reported too crowded to design and make stage equipment. Makeshift scenery was employed. The program was unable to live up to its advance notices. In the end, four performances were given of *Martha, Cavalleria Rusticana,* and *The Princess on the Pea*. There was a deficit of about $1,000. Non-labor costs could not be met by the limited number of performances. Consequently, orders were received canceling all opera productions. It is notable that these operas were rehearsed and produced in six weeks. For *Martha*, opera singers were paid the prevailing wage scale of Local 802, which rate prevented scheduling them for more than forty-five hours a month.

Opera in concert form and repetition of choral repertoire and the oratorio *Elijah*, by Mendelssohn, occupied the group for a time. Finally, on January 16, 1939, the opera chorus was transferred to the concert division.

Outside of New York, opera programs of a sort were presented in Boston, Los Angeles, San Francisco, San Bernardino, Philadelphia, Jacksonville, Buffalo, Cleveland, and Omaha. In general, opera projects were not approved by the central office unless all non-labor costs were assumed by the sponsors.

COMPOSERS

One of the early ambitions of the Federal Music Project was to give encouragement to the American composer. By using funds granted by the American Council on Education in 1935, the federal director commissioned Ernst Bacon of San Francisco, Hilton Rufty of Richmond, and George Antheil of Hollywood to write specific works. Bacon's *County Roads Unpaved*, an orchestral suite, had several performances, and Rufty's *Suite in A*, a piano trio, was expanded into a work for full symphony orchestra. Mr. Antheil, who was to have written a choral work, did not accept the commission.

In 1937 the Music Project, in co-operation with the Columbia Broadcasting System, the Columbia Phonograph Company, and Carl Fisher, Inc., sponsored a contest from which five short choral works were to be selected. The prizes, awarded in March, 1938, went to William Schumann, New York City, for his *Choral Etude*; to A. Loos of Brooklyn for his *Elegy*; to David Diamond of Rochester for his composition *This Is a Garden*; to John Vincent, Jr., of Bowling Green, Kentucky, for his *Three Grecian Songs*; and to Elliot Carter of New York City for his *To Music*. These compositions, sung by the federal madrigal singers of New York, were heard on a coast-to-coast hookup over the Columbia Broadcasting System. The Schumann work, which took first prize, was published by Carl Fischer and recorded by the Columbia Phonograph Company.

It was not until February, 1939, however, that a program for composers was devised as an integral part of the project,[3] and the transfer of the project from federal to state control in the following summer unfortunately precluded any extensive experimentation with this venture.

### THE COMPOSERS' FORUM

The composers' forum laboratory originated on the New York project under Ashley Pettis, and was eagerly supported there from its inception in October, 1935, until its end in 1940.

Techniques developed by the New York City project were copied in other cities, notably Boston, Chicago, and Philadelphia. Los Angeles, too, had a number of orchestral composers' forum laboratory programs that were very well received. Detroit, Milwaukee, and Minneapolis tried a few programs but found that not enough manuscripts were submitted to justify the venture.

In the early days of the program it was proposed to offer the composer, if his works were accepted for performance, an honorarium of ten dollars. This procedure was the subject of much controversy, and in the end the composer was delighted to get a hearing without any financial return. Works in any form could be submitted. It was not always easy, however, to obtain performance for works requiring unusual instrumentation (e.g., the dynaphone) or large voice choirs. The composer submitted his composition to a committee composed of prominent musicians and project administrative heads. If his work was accepted by the committee, it was scheduled for rehearsal, to which the composer was invited. At the rehearsal the composer might conduct, if he so desired, and he might also provide his own artists for the performance of his work.

The composers' forum laboratory was conducted informally. The supervisor of the forum acted as presiding officer and presented the program. After the conclusion of the program the forum was held; questions were invited, and the composer was expected to take the platform and answer questions that the audience might ask concerning his work and contemporary music. George Foster states: "One of the theories behind the public discussion was that it required the composer to do considerable soul-searching before being prepared to take the public platform in defense of his musical deeds."[4] In some instances, unfortunately, criticism descended to the level of heckling. For the most part, however, honest and constructive opinions were offered. In New York the technique of asking the audience to submit questions on slips of paper inserted in the programs was employed. These slips were collected and turned over to the chairman, who could thereby protect the composer from abuse and keep the discussion on a high plane.

The composers' forum was for the most part an exceedingly worthwhile project. From the beginning, part of the philosophy of the music project was to provide encouragement to American composers, to discover and develop new phases of American music and thereby to contribute to the body of American musical culture. Sokoloff encouraged all state directors to be liberal in their programming of American works. Most units of the project were consistent in regularly performing a large number of American compositions.

Transcripts of the forum periods were made in New York City and Boston. Copies are now in the Library of Congress. These records should serve as valuable documents to the future historians of American music. They contain, for example, evaluations of American compositions by the composer himself. Aaron Copland, for one, was asked in a composers' forum laboratory program held on February 24, 1937, the following question: "What according to your own beliefs are the salient characteristics of your own music?" He replied: "The salient characteristics, as I see them, are in the first place a certain massive sense and a certain attempt at quite a large and grandiose effect. Not so much 'effect' but a large and grandiose feeling in the music. The second, is an attempt to get an alive rhythmic vitality in the music. And the third characteristic, I should say, is an attempt to write music which is always logically constructed."

During its lifetime the New York City Forum presented more than 1,000 works by sixty-six composers, some as well known as Roy Harris, others students in music composition in nearby colleges.

In New York City most of the works were chamber music, with an occasional all-orchestra program in Carnegie Hall. In Los Angeles almost all the works were orchestral and were usually presented in all-American programs. In Philadelphia there were chamber music programs and standard orchestra and band programs.

Through a series of forum discussions entitled "Keys to a Contemporary Music," a group of some two hundred teachers of the Federal Music Project availed themselves of the rare opportunity of studying and discussing contemporary music with its composers at special institutes.*

## RADIO PROGRAMS

In the FERA period music services had been extended by means of radio broadcasting. This was done only where broadcasts were not opposed by the American Federation of Musicians. Radio broadcasting continued with the formation of the Federal Music Project.

Previously, radio had been used primarily for the broadcasting of concerts; but from the beginning of the WPA, radio broadcasts went beyond this. In New York City and in some other communities the radio was used as a vehicle for extending the services of the music education units. Lectures on music history, harmony courses, and other subjects were presented over the air with some success. Programs were not generally broadcast in the metropolitan centers because of the competition that would obviously exist with those musicians normally employed by the broadcasting companies. But in the local stations of the smaller cities requests for broadcasting were numerous and from three sources: the local musicians' unions, which felt that the local units were of

*The following colleges and universities were represented in the composers' forum laboratory through participation of members of their faculties: Columbia, Yale, Southwestern College of Memphis, Western Reserve, Eastman School of Music, Vassar, New York University, Hunter College, Danbury School of Music, Harvard School of Music, Juilliard School of Music, Sarah Lawrence College, Smith College, Bennington College, Westminster Choir School, and Dakota Wesleyan University.

such good quality that they should be given the opportunity to be heard over the air; the local stations offering facilities for such broadcasts; and the community itself, which thus expressed its pride in the native talent.

Sokoloff in 1936 initiated a series of recordings for radio transcriptions of fifteen minutes each. The American Federation of Musicians agreed to the making and using of the recordings. The usual program played from the record consisted of ten munutes of music and a three-minute speech on the Federal Music Project.

For over six years recordings were made by symphony orchestras in Los Angeles, New York City, San Francisco, and Boston, Negro choruses in the same cities, and operatic and oratorio choruses in Boston and Los Angeles. Some recordings of dance bands were made in New York City and Boston. By means of the records the WPA informed the public of its federally financed activities, and WPA music services were brought to communities that had no resident project unit.

The Minnesota music project made use of recordings through a series of band clinic programs presented by the Minnesota Symphony Band. These broadcasts consisted of performances of compositions being rehearsed and performed by school bands of all classes throughout Minnesota. Schools were notified in advance so that a period could be set aside while the broadcasts were being given of the band clinic. This program was developed in 1940 and continued throughout the life of the Minnesota music project. New Hampshire had a similar program.

After Pearl Harbor the demands for radio broadcasts by the Music Program were so many that the regulations governing WPA broadcasting were relaxed.

In 1939 the recordings were taken over by the WPA Music Program as part of its educational program. In February, 1941, a technical circular was prepared entitled "The Teaching of Music Appreciation and the Use of W.P.A. Radio Transcriptions." A great many recordings were given to recreation centers and army camps. After 1942 when the need for salvage of old records became acute, most discs were turned over to the procurement division of the United States Treasury.

MUSIC EDUCATION AND TEACHER TRAINING

Before the Federal Music Project began, it was estimated that two-thirds of the 4,000,000 children in the 143,000 rural schools in America were without music instruction in any form. Educators had recognized for a long time that the methods of teaching music in rural schools had not kept pace with other educational trends. Through the teaching of music on the unprecedented scale made possible by the WPA Music Project, there were evolved new texts and techniques. Activities of the project teachers penetrated into the most remote rural regions. On June 30, 1939, there were 102,161 persons enrolled in the project's classes predominantly in rural and small urban communities.

The American countryside once had its own healthy tradition of music covering a century and a half. In the change from an agricultural to an industrial nation the old singing school, the singing convention, and the "singin' gatherin'" dropped out of favor. Reconstruction days were too filled with material advancement to take time for the making of music in friendly assembly. Music became a vicarious experience. There were rewards for the greatest artists of Europe on their visits to America, but the people themselves had little part except as listeners; and the average person of small means had almost no part at all.

Music in America again became a communal art under the program of the Federal Music Project. Some of the spirit of the old singing gathering was recovered. This was notably true in Vermont, New Hampshire, Maine, Virginia, North and South Carolina, Florida, Illinois, Mississippi, and Oklahoma. This stirring-up of musical awareness of the people is one of the important achievements of the Federal Music Project.

By 1936 instruction in music, classes in music appreciation, history, and theory, and leadership for choral and instrumental groups had met a public desire that was unexpected by music leaders. For example, in Oklahoma the music teaching project in 1936 served seventy communities with a total class enrollment of 378,389. Pupils, according to Oklahoma reports, traveled as far as twenty miles at night for group lessons, and singing conventions held in schools or churches drew hundreds of individuals who never before had had music instruction.

In Mississippi, where the WPA music education project was operating in forty counties, there was an enrollment in 1936 of 69,640. The state director reported: "In every community we have found people are intensely interested and that the underprivileged children and adults are eager to take advantage of the opportunity offered by our classes in instruction."[5] This testimony is corroborated by stories related by teachers in the field. One teacher fitted a trailer on her Ford and equipped it with dummy keyboard and Victrola and formed her classes in the rural communities. Five other teachers who were removed from the payroll continued their teaching without compensation.

A narrative report for November, 1936, told of a brisk new trade in secondhand pianos in Mississippi. Purchasers were individuals whose interest in music was aroused by WPA activities. Oklahoma also reported sales of 180 pianos, ten organs, 213 band instruments, 326 string instruments, and 14,458 copies of published music. "These do not represent an expenditure made directly by the Federal Music Project, but they are purchases made by individuals as a result of Music Project activities," wrote the state director.

In Illinois, by 1936, seventy-nine WPA teachers had pupil enrollments of nearly 4,000. In Florida, state reports indicate that teaching projects were flourishing in every community. From South Carolina in 1936 came the plea for "fifty times as many teachers as we have"; and in New Mexico, where, prior to the Federal Music Project, there had been little instruction in the counties, classes enrolled 2,000 persons a week.

A report from Maine states:

> We have only one teacher located in the rural community of Jefferson. These classes . . . at the beginning of the Federal Project program were made up of CCC boys from neighboring camps. The people of the community looked upon the Project as more or less of a joke. Now the project doesn't seem so funny. Those who were loudest in ridicule realize the classes are interesting. Many visit the teacher's big rambling farmhouse where classes are held.[6]

From New Mexico came the following report:

> In Taos County, no music instruction has ever been available. Here an interested class of rural teachers is receiving instruction from an employee who, in turn, visits the rural school herself to give demonstration lessons. Much "appreciation" work is done. The children are taught to tune glasses or bottles to pitch and these are a great help in the rooms where no piano or other instruments are available.[7]

A program for the retraining and rehabilitation of music teachers on relief rolls was made a fundamental part of the initial national plan of the Federal Music Project. Work for teachers fell into various classifications, including: (1) group instruction from simple rhythmic folk dancing and folk-singing games for children who previously had had no instruction in music to courses in advanced theory, counterpoint, composition form and analysis; (2) social music, or community music, the purpose of which was to build music into community life through group participation in enjoyable self-expression and to lay a foundation of cultural interest through music appreciation. Correlated with the social-music program were extension activities connected with welfare houses, public schools, and hospitals.

Lessons given the retrained teachers on the project rolls were intended for those persons who could not afford private instruction, and the classes were drawn almost entirely from the ranks of the underprivileged and those on relief. Efforts were made to avoid competition with the teacher of music who was self-sustaining. In remote communities where there had been no provision for music teaching in the schools, as in certain rural districts in Florida, Mississippi, Oklahoma, and New Mexico, the project classes often embraced whole pupil groups.

A summary compiled at the end of the fiscal year, June 30, 1939, listed 1,197,936 classes held by project teachers with an aggregate pupil attendance of 13,849,919. At one time the Federal Music Project had 6,000 teachers on its rolls, but the administrative cuts in the project rolls, the return of private pupils, and other opportunities for becoming self-sustaining resulted in fewer than 900 having project assignments on August 31, 1939, the date of the close of the Federal Music Project. Teachers on the Federal Music Project were assigned to 410 centers in twenty-two states and the District of Columbia. More than a hundred teachers at the end of the Federal Music Project had found employment in consolidated and township schools.

The President's Advisory Committee on Education prepared a report on education in September, 1937. The paragraph discussing the music education program of the Federal Music Project reads:

> No formal effort has been made to produce the virtuoso, although many highly trained musicians in the cities, temporarily out of employment, have enrolled to advance their art in the teaching of theory and composition. Rather, the stress has rested on training to equip the pupil as an amateur with sufficient skill to afford him the enjoyment that comes from adequate performance and participation in group music, either vocal or instrumental. The emphasis on the teaching of the amateur runs all through the reports of the Project's supervisors and teachers.[8]

Teacher retraining for vocations in music instruction and leadership was seen to be desirable early in the project. Courses in teacher training were established in New York City. Other institute and normal courses were carried on in New Hampshire, Massachusetts, Mississippi, Minnesota, Florida, and California. Well-known educators and musicians donated their services to these institutes.

Steps were taken to bring the teachers of the project into an understanding of new musical trends. Institute discussions were held for groups of twenty. All were encouraged to do personal research in the musical idioms. Institutes devoted to applied theory were held. Alternating demonstrations in piano, violin, and voice, and analysis and discussion of form and content, with actual correlated classroom work, were carried on.

Under the program of social music there were activities in public schools and hospitals, parks and playgrounds, with amateur orchestras and children's rhythm bands, choruses and glee clubs, and amateur operettas. Although such activities passed as "social" music, they can readily be seen to have been of an educational value also.

The character of the accomplishment of the music education unit of the music project in New York City may only be comprehended through the knowledge of its history. This unit did not originate under the WPA. It sprang from the dire necessity of musicians, to be sure; but musicians were hard hit by changing industrial conditions long before the recognized emergency period that eventually affected all groups of artisans.

In September, 1933, Mrs. Frances McFarland, prominent in the music education activities of settlement houses, took the first governmental steps to alleviate the distress that was then widespread among musicians. Under the New York State TERA a group of forty musicians started class instruction in Greenwich House Music School, the Brooklyn Music School Settlement, and in three private school buildings (after school hours). These classes were a part of the adult education program of the TERA. In December, 1933, the state control of the educational program was shifted to the federally controlled CWA. Here it remained until May, 1934, when its operation came under the works division of the FERA. Finally, in July, 1935, it came under WPA as a part of the Federal Music Project. When the Federal Music Program was discontinued in 1939, the New York unit continued under the WPA Music Program.

The diverse character of the public that participated in the educational program of New York City must be studied in connection with the various advantages offered in educational and social music centers, in extracurricular activities, and in the public concerts furnished by the recital bureau.

631

The educational and social-music centers numbered eighteen at the height of accomplishment of the project in 1938. They were located in the boroughs of Manhattan, Bronx, and Brooklyn. The 1938 reports showed an actual weekly attendance of over 15,000. Subjects taught included sight-singing, ear training, harmony, keyboard harmony, theory, composition, form and analysis, counterpoint, orchestration, appreciation, music history, piano, voice, violin, cello, bass, woodwind and brass instruments, percussion, chorus, orchestra, score-reading, chamber music, ensemble, conducting, instrumentation, coaching, diction, acoustics, piano tuning, guitar, mandolin, banjo, languages, teaching methods, practice teaching, music therapy, manuscript writing, drums, bugle, xylophone, harmonica, eurhythmics, creative music, social music, folk dancing, ukulele, solfeggio, accompanying, operettas, and opera-coaching.

The students ranged in age from six to seventy-five years. In certain schools there were both children and adult classes. In Harlem the central Manhattan Music Center had an adult school in the mornings and evenings and children's classes in the afternoons. Other centers such as the school at West Side Vocational High School and Midtown Community Music Center at 93 Park Avenue held adult classes only.

A report from this project gives the following description of activities in such an educational center:

> . . . If one thinks of hordes of people flocking to these free classes for a superficial smattering of musical knowledge, even a cursory visit to these centers would soon shatter this belief. Courses are organized so as to discourage dilettantism. A student coming for a slight knowledge of piano, voice, or violin, soon discovers that he does not "belong." Correlated theoretical subjects are an integral part of the curricula. He must learn to listen, to analyze, even to create, as well as play. The seriousness of the students is their outstanding characteristic.
>
> . . . Students have ample opportunity to bring their work before audiences in the student assemblies, which range from soloists in all instruments and voice to choral and orchestral groups. Recently students from the Central Manhattan School in Harlem gave a concert in the 135th St. YMCA which, in addition to soloists and chorus, had an orchestra of 37 pieces, made up of youths ranging from 8 to 10 to 17 or 18 years of age. The instruments were none too good, but a Brahms Hungarian Dance was performed with an esprit which evoked wild acclaim, and deservedly.
>
> . . . When there was a possibility of Midtown Community Music Center being closed recently, a flood of letters poured in to the administrative offices of the Music Project. A typical letter read: "In these days of distress and depression when all avenues of endeavor have been closed to us, either for reason good or bad, this chance to thus occupy our enforced leisure has

spelled the difference between sanity and the blackest despair. It has maintained our morale and given us strength and hope to carry on until happier times shall once more come back."[9]

Extension activities (primarily social music), conducted in 108 centers, were carried on in conjunction with welfare houses, hospitals, and public schools. The courses and classes embraced the following: accompanying, acoustics, brass and woodwind instruments, chorus, coaching, composition, conducting, counterpoint (free and strict), diction (English, French, German, Italian), dramatization of songs, ear training, form and analysis, fretted instruments, glee and choral clubs, group singing, harmony, instrumental ensemble, instrumentation, keyboard harmony, lecture recitals, music appreciation, music history, music therapy, orchestras, organ, operettas, pageants, percussion instruments, piano, piano accompanying, piano ensemble, piano repertoire, program-making, research, rhythm bands, score-reading, sight-singing, art and folk music, song repertoire, string instruments, theory, and voice.

The social-music groups emphasized music participation. It was believed that children through actual participation, as in the singing games and dances and dramatization of folk songs, developed a keen music appreciation.

Of wide use in the field of music education and indicative of the increased interest in music education on the part of the WPA Music Program were the several circulars published after the Music Program came into being. Of these the first, dated December 12, 1940, was entitled "Organization and Development of a Training Program for Music Education Project Workers." Its purpose was to afford suggestions for the development of a training program that would further the objectives of the program as a whole. These suggestions had been evolved from the experience of states that had developed successful programs. Special attention was given to the training problems of sparsely settled areas. In the preface to this circular, the following statement of the aims of the program was made:

> Both the performer and the private teacher have usually through lack of use become rusty in the teaching of foundation materials. Teaching techniques and the knowledge of study materials have frequently become antiquated. Successful class teaching can only be accomplished when the planning has been based upon the knowledge of group reactions. Thus the W.P.A. teacher must frequently acquire an up-to-date working knowledge of the principles of psychology and education.[10]

Of interest as typical WPA Music Program standards are the following items taken from the circular:

> The W.P.A. Music Education Program operates in the field of democratic group instruction. Its objectives are the development of musical taste, the laying of a broad, well-rounded musical foundation, the stimulation of interest in musical activity and the development of elementary skills, rather than the specialized training of advanced musical techniques. This is a field which is largely noncompetitive and undeveloped and which offers excellent opportunity for the qualified teacher to become self-supporting, since large numbers of students are taught and the cost of individual instruction thereby minimized.
>
> A large proportion of the students enrolled in W.P.A. music education classes have never before had an opportunity to receive musical instruction. Many of them would be uninterested in musical study which had for its objective the development of a high standard of technical performance. The integration of musical activities into the lives of the bulk of the American people requires the development of new teaching techniques and materials.
>
> The successful operation of a W.P.A. Music Education Program therefore demands the organization of a training program which will equip its workers for this challenging opportunity.*[11]

## MUSIC FESTIVALS

Part of the educational program of the project was the stimulation of popular interest in music through the encouragement of music festivals and "music weeks."

In June, 1935, a request for funds to establish national folk festival projects was made to Harry Hopkins by the national folk festival organization. At the same time work in folk music and folk art was being carried on by the resettlement division and by the recreation division of the WPA. The Federal Music Project, although it failed to establish a national program of folk festival activities, assisted and furthered interest in the subject by participating in such folk festivals as occurred and by emphasizing in its program, especially during the several music weeks, the folk songs and folk music of America.

A music festival was carried out on the Kansas project in 1936. It was the combined effort of various relief organizations working in Kansas City. The NYA was responsible for the costuming. The two music

---

*Other circulars issued by the Music Program were: "Music as Recreation," May 29, 1940; "Organization and Operation of Music Education Activities," December 23, 1940; and "The Teaching of Music Appreciation and the Use of WPA Radio Transcriptions," February 21, 1941.

project bands, one Negro, one white, furnished most of the music for the festival. A notable performance during the festival was given by the Negro chorus, a part of the Federal Music Project in Kansas City.

In February, 1939, a nationwide festival of American music was sponsored by the Federal Music Project. The whole history of American music from colonial and revolutionary years to the works of contemporary composers was heard in the three-day festival. Besides the formal programs, special studies were made in more than four hundred project teaching centers, and during Festival Week special concerts of native compositions were presented in the appreciation programs in public and parochial schools.

In May, 1939, it was estimated that 6,000 musicians on the Federal Music Project would participate in the sixteenth annual observance of National Music Week. This was the fourth successive year in which musical resources of the wpa were made available for the nationwide festival.*

WORLD FAIRS

The Federal Music Project was prepared to participate in both the New York and San Francisco world fairs; and despite housing prob-

*The following is a partial list of the activities of the Federal Music Project during this week, and it stands as a tribute to the tremendous vitality of the project:

Some ninety programs were given in New York City during this week. Notable among them was the performance of the madrigal singers in a program of American songs in the shell of the wpa building at the World's Fair. In Kansas City, Kansas, project bands, co-operating with 300 school children, gave a demonstration to show the correlation of music with school activities. In the rural regions of North Carolina, West Florida, Oklahoma, Mississippi, and New Mexico, where thousands of underprivileged children were enrolled in the classes of the project, scores of programs were held.

An abundance of outdoor music was reported from Milwaukee, Omaha, Portland (Ore.), San Francisco, Los Angeles, Peoria, and Decatur (Ill.) during the same week. Seventy special programs were presented in Massachusetts. The Rhode Island Federation of Music Clubs sponsored a concert by the project orchestra of Providence, the program of which was composed entirely of selections from Rhode Island composers. Twenty-four performing units in New Jersey prepared special programs for the week calling for the service of 630 project workers. In Pennsylvania some eighty programs were presented enlisting 526 project workers. Folk and outdoor dances were performed in Pittsburgh. In Baltimore excerpts from "Cairo Madness," written by a native Baltimorean, featured the program. Nine Chicago performing units, numbering 450 musicians, combined for a special festival concert in the Great Northern Theater. Chicago districts at the same time were presented with eighteen programs in public schools, in which the works of American composers predominated. The 1939 Music Week in North Carolina provided twenty-

lems, political antagonisms, and the opposition of unions and other musical organizations, it presented a worthy program at both fairs. At the Golden Gate International Exposition the project presented orchestral offerings and composers' forum laboratories, the latter of especially high musical education value.

At the World's Fair in New York City a more ambitious music education program was prosecuted. Panel discussions on the subject "Music Today and Tomorrow" drew thousands. These were broadcast. Distinguished speakers on the panels included music critics, music educators from universities and music conservatories, Federal Music Project directors, and American composers. Composers' forum laboratories were carried on for the duration of the fair, and presented the works of new and young composers. Institutes in piano and other subjects, music appreciation courses and lectures, and exhibits of the New York City education division and of the entire Federal Music Project were held for those who attended the fair.

FOLK MUSIC

No country in the world, perhaps, has had such a diversity of folk music as America. Some of its sources reside in the taverns and on the greens of "merrie England" and on the highlands of Scotland, to be brought to the American colonies and over the Wilderness Trail to Kentucky and beyond. Other sources were Spain, with its colonial possessions of Cuba and Mexico; the jungles of Africa; and the rituals of planting, harvesting, and war of the American Indian. Busy harbors heard the chanteys of the mariners who sailed the clipper ships around the Horn. Stretches of plain and prairie echoed with the songs of those who drove the stage coaches, felled the forests, steered the canal boats, mined the ore, dug the oil wells, and wagoned goods across the land.

Awareness of this native idiom antedated the inauguration of the Federal Music Project. As early as 1882, a study of American folk music was published in Leipzig by Theodore Baker. By the beginning of the present century many American colleges and universities had established courses in musicology, under which the study of folk music falls, and American folklore societies had been gathering folk songs.

eight programs in eleven communities. Folk music was featured at performances in New Orleans and throughout Mississippi. In Texas both concert and tipica orchestras gave concerts.

636

The folk song, however, is both a hardy and a delicate plant—hardy, since it thrives in a kindly climate, sending forth new shoots, new verses, and new versions as time goes on; and delicate, since it often withers and dies when transplanted from its native soil, the spontaneous singing of the common people. In 1936, therefore, there seemed compelling reason for haste in gathering old songs and melodies (hundreds of which had no written notation) before the persons in whose memories they rested had passed on. So, on December 7, 1938, the co-ordinating committee on living folklore, folk music, and folk arts of the WPA met and changed its name to the joint committee on folk arts. The existence of the committee was the result of numerous conferences among numerous scholars, some employed by the government and some by private agencies. These individuals met in the offices of, and at the suggestion of, the American Council of Learned Societies, whose committee on musicology had for some time carried on research and put forth publications in the field of folk music. Membership of the committee was composed of: Chairman B. A. Botkin, of the Federal Writers' Project; Vice-chairman Charles Seeger, of the Federal Music Project; Herbert Halpert, of the Federal Theater Project; C. Adolph Glassgold, of the Federal Art Project; Ernestine L. Friedman, of the WPA education division; S. B. Child, of the Historical Records Survey; and Nicholas Ray of the WPA recreation division.

In general, the program of the committee, at the suggestion of Chairman Botkin, followed the plan of the folklore studies already set up by the Federal Writers' Project.

In gathering folklore material, there has been found to be a great disparity in the amount of material gathered and in scientific, valid results. Therefore, the folk arts committee decided on recordings as the most reliable means of preservation of folk music. A great deal of sound-recording equipment was needed. A sound truck, on loan from the technical services laboratory, was operated by Herbert Halpert and sent into the southern region on a folk music—gathering expedition under the direction of Botkin. The expedition was jointly sponsored by the folk arts committee and by the Library of Congress, and was a happy plan, indeed. All the actual original recordings made by the Federal Music Project (now in the folk music archive of the Library of Congress) were made by Halpert on this trip through Virginia, North Carolina, Mississippi, Louisiana, Florida, George, and South Carolina.*

*From the southern expedition Halpert brought back 419 twelve-inch acetate re-

637

The southern expedition of the folk arts committee was successful from several points of view. It represented definite accomplishment in obtaining actual records of folk music in the United States, thereby materially adding to national musical culture. It stood as an achievement in co-operation between various parts of the WPA arts program, since the results of the expedition were the combined efforts of the Music Project, the Theater Project, the Writers' Project, and the Historical Records Survey. Finally, it presented a new approach to exploring the folkways of America by bringing together and using oral, popular, and traditional materials expressive of ways of life in a country of heterogeneous cultural heritage.

A second co-operative plan whereby the Federal Music Project made a contribution to the body of American folk music was carried out in conjunction with the department of Hispanic studies of the University of New Mexico. A sheaf of folk songs and tunes derived from Spain, Cuba, and Mexico was gathered, and several brochures were published. Music Project teachers began the collection of New Mexico folk music as soon as projects were set up in that state in 1935. Stencils were cut for words and simple music notation, mimeographed copies were supplied to schools, and singing groups and string orchestras were conducted under project leadership. A notable publication—thoroughly of a co-operative nature, since material gathered was compiled by workers on the Writers' Project, Music Project, and Art Project under the sponsorship of the University of New Mexico and the state superintendent of public instruction of New Mexico—was the "Song and Games Book." Helen Ryan, director of the New Mexico project, assisted by A. L. Campa, professor of folklore at the University of New Mexico, and Edmundo Lasalle of the division of intellectual co-operation of the Pan American Union, checked the manuscript for accuracy and established the authenticity of the games.

Except for the primitive songs and dance lines of the Indians, the folk music of New Mexico, some of it brought to this continent by Coronado 400 years ago, is the oldest folk music in America. "The

cordings that were accessioned by the Library of Congress on September 18, 1939. In addition, 38 twelve-inch aluminum and acetate recordings made for the Art Project, and 10 twelve-inch aluminum and acetate duplicate recordings made by Halpert in New York City are in the folk music archive of the Library of Congress. In all, some 7,000 recordings of folk music, many of which are obtainable on commercial records, are to be found in the folk music archive of the Library of Congress. The Library furnishes a catalogue and list of about two thousand commercial records.

Alabado," a religious song sung by the Penitentes, was discovered to be a direct, though debased, outgrowth of the Gregorian chant. Other forms studied by the Federal Music Project in New Mexico were the "Decima," the "Cuanda," and the "Corrido"—the last a heroic song of epic pretensions.

A study of the old songs brought about an interest in the proper musical instrument to bring out the fullest in tone and meaning of the music, and it was found that the old gut-string guitar of Spanish origin possessed the most desirable quality. Accordingly, a collection of musical arrangements for the guitar to accompany the old songs was completed on the project.

The products and activities of the New Mexico project were of use to various groups during the cuarto-centennial coronado festivals in 1939. Sarah Gertrude Knott, at that time director of national folk festivals, is reported as saying, "There is here in New Mexico a finer integration of music project activities with the life of the people than in any other part of the United States that I have visited."[12] Because of the work of the Music Project in studying and compiling the traditional music, songs, and dances of the Southwest, and the work of project teachers together with the League of Latin American Citizens and with the department of Hispanic studies of the University of New Mexico in collecting and annotating music, the cuarto-centennial festivals were spectacular.*

Mississippi furnished a vast collection of Negro spirituals, work songs, play songs, river songs, hillbilly songs, and fiddler's tunes. Under the direction of Jerome Sage of the Federal Music Project many of these were mimeographed, bound, and supplied to county libraries, state colleges, and other schools throughout the country.† Geographically, however, the field of folk music in Mississippi was inadequately explored. In particular, the Bayou region could not be properly studied because of the natives' reluctance to reveal their songs.

In Oklahoma a project supervisor obtained over three hundred disc recordings of the songs and dance lines of five Indian tribes. These recordings are now in the possession of the State Historical Society of Oklahoma. A portfolio of 400 fiddle tunes was also gathered, and with

---

*Much of the material gathered on the music project in New Mexico was deposited at the University of New Mexico.

†The National Play Bureau of the Federal Theater Project published a volume of "Folk Tunes of Mississippi" in July, 1937. The tunes were collected by Arthur Palmer Hudson and edited by George Herzog for the music research department.

it was compiled a list of instructions for tuning the fiddles. This material is in the possession of the University of Oklahoma.

The work of tipica orchestras under the Federal Music Project attracted wide attention. These were colorful units playing in the folk idiom. Tipica orchestras were organized in San Antonio and El Paso, Texas, and in Los Angeles, California, and presented hundreds of programs that included the lighter music of Latin American writers. Music of these orchestras was preserved on electrically transcribed records; some of the discs of the San Antonio unit form a part of the permanent collection of folk music in the Library of Congress.

Some progress was made in gathering Creole and Acadian songs in Louisiana. Considerable work was also done in gathering spirituals, work songs, play songs, river songs, blues, jubilees, and shouts in North Carolina. North Carolina represented a music project on which co-ordination between racial groups was highly successful. Nell Hunter, a Negro teacher on the project and an able musician, had previously done much work with her people in preserving the old Negro songs in North Carolina, and contributed materially to the work of the project. Negro choirs in New York City and in Los Angeles, organized under the Federal Music Project, made R.C.A. recordings and appeared on several occasions over station WNYC in New York, and made WPA discs in Los Angeles. The city Negro had been said to be somewhat contemptuous of the old songs. However, after successful experiments of broadcasting and recording under the Federal Music Project, many members of the Negro choruses were reported full of enthusiasm to carry on the music of the older generations of their people.

From West Virginia came much folk music, some of which was collected by the Federal Music Project and some under the sponsorship of the national service bureau of the Federal Theater Project. A publication of the folk songs of West Virginia was issued in June, 1939, by the National Service Bureau, under the editorship of Herbert Halpert and George Herzog.

The Federal Music Project was not very active in folk music-gathering in Nebraska, but the Writers' Project there published folk music pamphlets from material gathered for a book on Nebraska folklore. An interesting pamphlet is the one dated June, 1939, which contains a number of pioneer dance calls found in Nebraska.

In Virginia music teaching and appreciation classes in 1937 and 1938 used many of the native songs of the Virginia mountains as class material. Indeed, the mountain community music classes in the state had a larger attendance than those of the more thickly populated districts.

From California the Federal Music Project's folk-music workers brought evidence that in Carmel and Monterey certain of the liturgical chants of the California missions deriving from the Gregorian, and even from the Ambrosian plain song, had been preserved in folk music. A WPA musician, versed in music of the Middle Ages, notated the fragments of the California songs, and in 1938 some of them were sung by modern choirs along the Carmel Coast area. From California came also songs of the Gold Rush days, such as "The Days of Forty-Nine," "Sweet Betsy from Pike," and "The Banks of the Sacramento." These songs were published in San Francisco.

The research library of the Federal Music Project in New York City was the depository of a great many early American songs gathered on the music project in New York. These were put to use in public school activities in New York and elsewhere.

One objection raised to the folk music project rested in the belief that the work could not be professionally or academically done by project teachers. It was discovered, however, that project teachers working within their own territory frequently were able to approach as neighbors those in whom the music resided. Their notations were regarded as a friendly act, and the minstrels were neither abashed nor impelled to show off. It is reasonable to believe that the material obtained by them is as exact as that acquired by musicologists. In the case of the recording expedition of the folk arts committee, there is no doubt as to the authenticity of the results.*

---

*Research in folk music was also carried on under the special-skills division of the Resettlement Administration. This division was set up "as a service division to serve all phases of the Resettlement Administration in the field of Fine and Applied Arts."[13] The activities of the group were various but the work was divided roughly into four functions: arts, crafts, and design activities, and recreational community activities. Under the last, music and drama activities were initiated and supervised in a number of communities. "Choruses, bands, drama groups, etc., were organized and with these groups as nuclei, community productions of all kinds were given; special pageants, Christmas and Easter festivals, minstrel shows, puppet shows, etc."[14] Charles Seeger, who was later an assistant director of the Federal Music Project, was head of this work. "About 1,000 recordings in American folk music were made, preparatory to publishing a book of such music for general school and community use. A manual for the supervisors of community music has been begun."[15] Margaret Valiant, later head of the music division of NYA, was also a member of the staff for music. According to Seeger, some 160 to 170 of the disc recordings are now in the archives of American folk song at the Library of Congress. Nine folk songs were published in pamphlet form, with pen and ink drawings on the front page or cover. It was planned to publish many more of these, and thirteen or four-

MUSIC THERAPY

In the tradition of David and Saul the Federal Music Project under-took experiments in musical therapy. A foundation for the work on the project was laid in New York City by the music education division un-der Frances McFarland. Experiments were begun at Bellevue Hospital in January, 1935. By September of the same year these experiments were under the jurisdiction of the Federal Music Project. Experiments were subsequently undertaken in five more hospitals in New York City, under the supervision of Isabel Parkman.

In Massachusetts' Worcester State Hospital and in Michigan's Eloise Hospital other experiments in music for mental patients were conducted. In Lansing, Michigan, experiments were conducted in co-operation with the public schools to determine whether the completely deaf child could be brought to an appreciation of music and, through appreciation, to a self-expression in music somewhat approximating that of the normal child. In Tulsa, Oklahoma, another experiment with hard-of-hearing children was conducted in the public schools.

An experiment in music for deaf children at Chinchuba Institute for the Deaf in Marrero, Louisiana, was carried out, with some interest-ing findings. Classes for handicapped children were conducted in both Miami, Florida, and Grand Rapids, Michigan, with encouraging re-sults.

Dr. Lauretta Bender, senior psychiatrist, Psychiatric Hospital, Belle-vue, speaking on the Panel Discussion on Music Therapy on March 7, 1937, made the following statement:

> In the case of the Music Project, I have been fully satisfied from the be-ginning that there appears to be a specific value of a different type. It is that specific value which I want to discuss with you because I feel I can offer something significant and because it is a little different from what you have heard. In order to explain it let me re-define music, not as a musician knows it but as a child psychiatrist sees it. I look upon the music work for the chil-dren as offering an integrated pattern or to use the new term, a "Gestalt" of sensory-motor-emotional and social components. If we can succeed in inte-grating the child in these components, we have done an enormous amount towards integrating the personality. It is very clear to me that those children who have benefited most from the music program are those children who

teen were actually set up, but publication was subsequently banned. Some work was done by the music staff in the field of community music in the special skills division.

642

have failed to attain an integrated pattern of behavior through any other medium. So far you have heard that music is stimulating. I don't question that of course. But I would like to emphasize the pattern value of music, the integrating value. I am convinced that this is of particular value to the children who are benefiting the most from our music program.[16]

THE INDEX OF AMERICAN COMPOSERS

The index of American composers, an undertaking of the music analysis unit of the Federal Music Project, never reached completion and was never published. This is much to be regretted, since the published index would have been a definite contribution to American music. The recording of index material was brought to an end in 1940. However, the index in its present form contains much information on American composers and their works.

As worked out by Mrs. Margaret Kerr and Mrs. Harry Hewes, the index is divided into four classifications:

1.  An alphabetical list of composers with biographical information giving date and place of birth, music education, current place of residence (this was valuable as source material and also for the information of conductors and performers who desired to get in touch with the composers); notes and dates on performances, performing units, conductors, and soloists.

2.  An alphabetical list of compositions by form giving date of composition, performance time, and previous performances (where, when, and by whom performed, not necessarily under WPA auspices); data as to whether compositions had been published or were still in manuscript form.

3.  Program notes, excerpts from reviews by reputable critics.

4.  Notes showing derivations of folk tunes, legends, settings, etc.

The card files of the index are now deposited in the music division with the Library of Congress. The information contained on the cards was checked with all known published material and is as accurate as state supervision could make it. When deposited in the Library of Congress, the index included more than 20,000 typed index cards recording some 7,300 compositions by 2,258 native and resident American

643

composers performed by WPA units since 1935. Popular music in the jazz idiom is not included in the index.

Mrs. Kerr compiled "A List of American Orchestral Works Recommended by WPA Music Project Conductors," which was released in July, 1941, in mimeographed book form. The list was made from the recommendations of WPA conductors and for their future use. "Practicability of performance" and "audience acceptability" were the criteria for selection. Compositions are arranged by composer, title, playing time, location of scores and parts, and pertinent press comments. It was not long before this list, originally released only to WPA conductors, was eagerly sought by independent symphony conductors throughout the country, and hundreds of copies were distributed.

MUSIC COPYING

Begun as a necessary service function for the WPA orchestras and music units, music copying soon developed into a larger enterprise having for its purpose the servicing of university and public libraries. As early as 1936-37, there were copying units in all metropolitan areas. The Los Angeles unit not only contributed its services to the performing groups of the project but also to boards of education and public libraries interested in preserving and making available the scores of original American compositions. In the course of this work, project composers and arrangers found it necessary to transpose older scores from the obsolete key in which the archaic instruments were built to the key in which these instruments are built today. Commercial music publishers had not undertaken the task of transposition prior to the work of the project's music copyists.

Among the more outstanding copying units besides Los Angeles were those of Milwaukee and Philadelphia. In Milwaukee, as a result of the project's work for a period of five years (1935-40), the Milwaukee Public Library was enabled to make available to the public more than 2,000 musical scores for symphonies, bands, orchestras, choruses, and other musical groups. In Philadelphia the copying unit worked at the Free Library, copying scores for the E. A. Fleischer Collection under the personal sponsorship of Mr. Fleischer.

Methods of reproduction varied. In Michigan the "line print" was used. In Philadelphia all work, except the duplication of string parts, was done entirely by hand on 100 per cent rag paper. In New York City music was duplicated by a "Pease Machine." In Los Angeles a Wikes Simplex Blueprinter was used at the initial stage, and the Dietzgen Automatic Developing Machine at the second stage. In Milwaukee music was copied directly on zinc plates with a special ink.*

MUSIC ANALYSIS UNIT

The music analysis unit began in 1935 as one of the projects carried on in the District of Columbia. Later in that year, it was taken into the national office in Washington and continued its functions on a broader scale; some of its best work was performed after the Federal Music Project had ended and the WPA Music Program came into existence.

The function of the music analysis unit was to compile statistical reports on operation and outline outstanding project achievement of various kinds. The unit also made press clipping books. These were at first groupings-together of press clippings by state, the clippings having been collected and sent to the Washington office by the states.

The distribution of some scores that had been made on the New York City copying project was accomplished by the analysis unit. There was also a distribution performed by the unit of Latin American scores when these were required for performance in Pan American observances. For example, on May 7, 1940, WPA music bands and orchestras in several cities presented compositions by Latin American composers on the occasion of the fiftieth anniversary of the founding of the Pan American Union.†

A music exchange library, domiciled in Washington, D.C., first suggested in 1936, never came into being. Its purpose would have been to maintain in Washington an index in triplicate of all music in possession of the project. By referral to this index the states could exchange, lend, and rent musical scores, the records of such transactions being kept in the national and regional offices. Without doubt, the operation of such a project would have prevented much wasteful duplication of music purchases and would have permitted more diversified programs throughout the country.

*A compilation dated November 7, 1942, lists 425,556 pages copied and 4,408 pages arranged on projects throughout the country between July 1, 1940, and June 30, 1942, and this includes only two years of six years' active operation.

†The Pan American music made available was distributed for public performance in San Francisco, New York City, Boston, Oklahoma City, Dayton (Ohio), and Philadelphia, Pittsburgh, Reading, Scranton, Upper Darby, Williamsport (all in Pennsylvania).

1. *Supplement No. 1 to Bulletin No. 29*, WPA, Section 9(c).

2. Daniel Gregory Mason to Lawrence Gilman, in New York *Herald Tribune*, April 12, 1936.

3. Letter, Sokoloff to All State Directors, February 24, 1939, FMP Files.

4. George Foster, "Record of Program Operation and Accomplishment; the Federal Music Project, 1935-1939; the WPA Music Program, 1939-1943," June 30, 1943, FWA Library, p. 323.

5. Mississippi Music Project, "State Reports," 1936, FMP Files.

6. Maine Music Project, "State Reports," March, 1937, FMP Files.

7. New Mexico Music Project, "State Reports," March, 1937, FMP Files.

8. "Report of the President's Advisory Committee on Education," September, 1937 (Washington, D.C.: Government Printing Office).

9. "New York City Music Project Education Report," March, 1937, FMP Files.

10. "Organization and Development of a Training Program for Music Education Project Workers," WPA Technical Series, Community Service Circular No. 11, Music Program Circular No. 1, December 12, 1940, WPA, Preface.

11. *Ibid.*

12. "New Mexico: Narrative Report," October, 1939, FMP Files.

13. "Outline of Organization and Work," Special Skills Division, Resettlement Administration, n.d., p. 9.

14. *Ibid.*

15. *Ibid.*

16. "Panel Discussion on Music Therapy," March 7, 1937, FMP Files.

# 26

## The Origins of the Federal Writers' Project

### THE MATURITY OF AMERICAN LETTERS

American literature, no less than American music, art, and theater, came of age in the period of the depression; and the Federal Writers' Project, like the other projects in Federal One, expressed this new maturity. American letters, in the period between the beginning of the century and World War I, had repudiated the urbane tradition of the nineteenth century and cultivated in its place an attitude of realism and naturalism that exposed, or threatened to expose, the skeleton that lay behind the whited sepulcher. Disillusionment followed in the wake of World War I, and in the decade from 1919 to 1929 material prosperity only deepened the doubt of the American intellectual in the integrity of the national tradition.

It is a tribute to the American character and to the insight of American men of letters into that character that the decade of the depression (1929-39), far from causing doubt to degenerate into despair, revived or re-created a national faith through the strange alchemy of tribulation. Unlike the earlier faith, it was founded upon want, not comfort; it sought its material not in the annals of the leisure class but in the yet unwritten chronicles of the workers. It gave up European models and fashioned its philosophy, and to no small extent its style, within a less rigid native matrix, which gave form to the cast of thought and at the same time was formed by it.

This new nationalism—for such it was—betokened that period in the life of a nation when it has matured sufficiently to be conscious of its own youth, and to seek to recapture or at least to record the experiences of its childhood. Such an age came upon ancient Greece at the time of Pericles and upon ancient Rome in the days of Augustus. There is a period when a nation, like a man, becomes conscious of itself and by virtue of that consciousness assertive of its individuality. America had always possessed a character; it was not until the depression, however, that America recognized that character and, having recognized it, Narcissus-like embraced it.

The lineaments, as they gradually revealed themselves to those who sought them in the thirties, were manifold. It was discovered that the American nature, although it is predominantly Anglo-Saxon—in the sense that its language and literature derive from English roots—is not exclusively so. The presence of other elements in the American blood stream was recognized: the Negro, the Jew, the Irish, and peoples from the diverse parts of continental Europe. It was seen, too, that these many peoples—some in a greater degree than others—had impressed America with their several personalities and, if they had rarely occupied the seats of power in the counsels of national policy and economy, had made dynamic contributions to the formation of the national ethos. Indeed, the national minorities, as they are called, had provided the United States with precisely those elements that differentiate it from England and every other European nation: a sense of freedom from cultural traditions with a concomitant faculty for innovation and experiment; an ease of manner that, if it sacrifices formal etiquette, emphasizes natural courtesy; and an acceptance of diversity in language, religion, and other mores, not only as a fact but as a good.

This discovery that the American character was a new phenomenon accompanied the realization that the American land mass was a new continent. This consciousness of geographical newness was not that of the explorer, who penetrates virgin territory but is unaware of its character, but rather that of the philosopher, who reflects upon a conquered continent and finds in it and in himself the meaning of the conquest. The facility of transportation brought by the automobile contributed much to this awakening; but the discovery itself far transcended the mechanics that made it easy, embracing not only the mountains, plains, lakes, and rivers that shape the physical contour of the land but also all the peoples of the nation's diverse regions, and seeing in the very diversity the promise of true unity. In becoming conscious of itself, America became conscious of its parts—and the difference among them—and realized that the fabric of the Union was a coat of many colors. If all were Americans, Americans were not all the same, and the oneness of their loyalty was coupled with a multiplicity in their modes of expressing it.

This new patriotism, which by its very nature was a repudiation of chauvinism and was particular only as an instance of the universal, expressed itself vertically as well as horizontally, and recognized fully and without qualification, for the first time, that the source of the nation's labor was also the source of its song and story. The folk—the common people—in their folklore, folk music, and folk art, became an object not only of interest but also of cultivation; and the Homeric artlessness of their expression contrasted with the Virgilian finish of an older style charmed those who had become impatient with the niceties of studied language. The Negro, in the urban North no less than in the rural South; the sharecropper in Arkansas; the steelworker in Pittsburgh; the automobile worker in Detroit; the Irish ward politician; the tenement dweller of the metropolis and the dirt farmer of submarginal land: all these became objects not merely of treatment—for their lot had been discussed in earlier American literature—but of sympathy; and in that sympathetic approach they were seen not as hewers of wood and drawers of water but as human souls who were fashioning, much more than those who profited from their labor, the new spirit of America.

## THE AMERICAN WRITER AND THE DEPRESSION

It was not merely coincidental that this new and deeper consciousness of the character of America developed at a time of severe economic crisis. Adversity is the tamer of men, and the American writer, when he became conscious of himself and his colleagues in the years of want, was made aware at the same time of the community of nature he shared with his fellow citizens. The concept of the writer as the spectator of events yielded by the very force of circumstances to the concept of the writer as participant in, and indeed victim of, his environment. This realization of partnership in a community came more slowly to writers than to the practitioners of the other arts. By its very nature, music, though it may be cultivated in isolation, engenders comradeship, and in many of its forms, both popular and artistic, requires the co-operation of many toward a common end. In the theater, too, the actor rarely acts alone but in the company of his fellows; and even in the medium of the monologue, the act demands an audience, and the rapport between the two, which is the essence of the theater, creates a community of thought and feeling that transcends the individual. Even the artist, most like the writer in his traditional preference for solitary activity, had in the decade preceding the depression discovered in the mural an opportunity for co-operative enterprise.

Only the writer, like a god or a beast, continued to live alone—and liked it. For this reason he entered the depression unarmed. The musician wore the device of the American Federation of Musicians; the actor's cause was championed by Actors' Equity and the AFA; the artist, if he lacked a union, at least had professional societies to plead his case; but the writer lacked the corporate strength that an organization, professional or labor, contributes to a movement.

## PRESSURE FROM NEWSPAPERMEN

Under these circumstances it is not surprising that projects for writers as such developed later than those designed to help other professional classes. Indeed, when the question was first raised, the Washington office of the FERA was inclined to prefer direct relief for writers on the ground that it "provides them with a subsistence and gives them plenty of time to do their writing."[1] This point of view was founded on the individualistic notion that writers should work for and by themselves, and that the idea of writers working together toward a common project was alien to the craft.

There was, however, one exception to this lack of organization among writers. Newspapermen had recently formed a union, and it was for men in that profession that pressure was first brought upon Washington for writers' projects. On August 23, 1934, Hugh Harlan wrote to Harry Hopkins that a newspaper writers' project (under the sponsorship of the Professional, Technical, and Women's Work Division of the Los Angeles County SERA) had been established and was in operation, and inquired: "Why can't this thing be established upon a national scale?" Harlan saw this as an opportunity to "employ the services of trained observers and interpreters of the American scene."[2] The Los Angeles project employed some fifty editors, reporters, feature writers, and newspaper photographers and artists under Harlan's supervision. According to him, the work consisted not of news writing or editorial writing but of "ferreting out pertinent information concerning subjects . . . to be handled impartially." The data were on subjects ranging from "reforestation in Southern California" to "purpose and significance of the FERA." Harlan also rewrote FERA reports and prepared lectures on the FERA.[3]

Earlier, in May, 1934, when Harlan had corresponded with Hopkins concerning his newly proposed project, Jacob Baker replied:

> The question has been raised from a good many sources and we are concerned with the development of suitable projects for writers along with all the other white collar folks. . . .
>
> A good many writers, of course, have been drawn into projects that require reporting and recording of facts and information. No projects have been developed thus far for actual publication of newly written material.[4]

On the problem of publication, an interesting difference of opinion developed between Baker and Harlan. According to the former:

> The difficulty about writers' projects is that the larger part of the expense seems to be that of publication, paper material, printing and binding. . . . We are not justified in spending more than ten or fifteen per cent of the total cost of a project upon other than labor cost.[5]

On the other hand, Harlan maintained:

> Under normal conditions the cost of research work is at least twice as much as the cost of publication. Hence it is that many business and semi-public organizations find it impossible to produce research works that, in many cases, are of vital importance to their functioning.[6]

From this observation proceeded the suggestion (of considerable interest in view of later forms of sponsorship) that these organizations "supply funds for the publication of the research findings."[7]

Throughout the next twelve months Harlan continued his pressure for a national writers' project, and on June 19, 1935, in a letter to Hopkins, renewed his plea for such an undertaking. He was informed by Arthur Goldschmidt:

> A project for the employment of newspapermen and other writers is under consideration, but has not been developed in all its phases up to the present time. We appreciate your sustained interest in the program for newspapermen and we are keeping your proposal at hand to be given further consideration in the development of the program for writers.[8]

Other newspaper projects were suggested. As early as January 4, 1934, R. E. Reed of Rockland, Maine, proposed to Hopkins, then ad-

651

ministrator of the CWA, that newspapermen be employed to contribute columns to daily and weekly papers on CWA activities and accomplishments.[9] Earlier, a more general project, for the rewriting in popular language of the reports, bulletins, and monographs of federal agencies, had been suggested by Bruno Lasker of New York City.[10] In February, 1934, Francis Bonn, president of the Newspaper Guild of Rochester, New York, proposed a Rochester–Monroe County CWA weekly newspaper under the direction of the CWA publicity department. In his letter he referred to "a CWA newswriters' project under way in New York City, employing, we are informed, 110 men and women. This project was proposed by our national Guild and approved by both the local and state CWA administrations."[11] He also quoted "a recent announcement by President Roosevelt that he [Roosevelt] favored C. W.A. projects employing the 'forgotten newspaperman.'"

## THE ADOPTION OF REPORTING PROJECTS

The result of this pressure on the part of newspapermen was the establishment of reporting projects. These projects were authorized by Hopkins in his letter dated September 7, 1935, and addressed to all state administrators.[12]

Their purpose was to prepare information for use by the Division of Research, Statistics, and Records in the semimonthly narrative reports on the Works Progress Administration. It was originally intended that narrative reports should be prepared by the assistant to the administrator in each state to supplement the statistical and engineering reports. Accordingly, these reporting projects were welcomed by the state administrators because the latter's public relations staffs would thus be relieved of the work.

Reporting projects were described as "writers' projects for the employment of unemployed writers and photographers to describe the various relief activities." The personnel consisted of writers, photographers, and clerical persons on a ratio of one stenographer or typist to two writers and one photographer to ten or twelve writers. Writers were expected to prepare human interest material ("material of an unusual or human interest nature such as would be prepared by a newspaper reporter or magazine writer")[13] or, if desired by the state administrator, to do the entire work of preparing the reports in close co-operation with, and under the general editorial supervision of, the person responsible for preparing the semimonthly narrative reports. In the same way, photographers worked under the general supervision of the photographer of the state administration, using their own laboratory facilities or one central laboratory for project photographers in the WPA headquarters. Reporting projects thus served as a continuation and specialization of the earlier FERA newspaper writers' projects along the lines of public information on the WPA.

These projects served not only as a link between earlier and later relief projects for writers but also as a medium for organizing the Federal Writers' Project. As national director of the Project and (until his resignation on January 31, 1936) assistant director of the Division of Research and editor of reports, Henry G. Alsberg maintained a close relationship between reporting and Guide projects.* Likewise, until his resignation on January 31, 1936, Reed Harris, assistant director of the Federal Writers' Project, was also executive editor of the special reports and photo section. Also employed in this section was George W. Cronyn, associate director of the Federal Writers' Project. All three were a living link between reporting and Guide projects, and helped to recruit personnel for the Federal Writers' Project. During September, 1935, requests went forth from Washington for suggested names of potential editors with "encyclopedic training," "a good sense of proportion, both in condensing and rewriting copy," and "a keen eye for factual accuracy."[14]

## PRESSURE FROM OTHER WRITERS' ORGANIZATIONS

One expression of the increased social consciousness of writers in the early years of the depression was the growth of writers' organizations. The oldest craft or professional organization of writers in the United States is the Authors' League of America (incorporated in 1912), which, through its component guilds (the Authors' Guild, the Dramatists' Guild, and the Radio Writers' Guild) and the affiliated Screen Writers' Guild, aims to "promote and protect the general professional interests of all creators of literary, dramatic, or musical material," including adequate copyright legislation, fair dealings with editors, publishers, producers, agents, etc., better working conditions and payment, equitable adjustment of disputes, and minimum contracts, and to disseminate information on all these matters.

*For the Guide, *vide infra*, pp. 693-96.

On February 28, 1934, following preliminary conversations between Luise Sillcox and Arthur Hanna, the Authors' League (Marc Connelly, president; Luise Sillcox, secretary and treasurer), drew up a "Suggestion for CWA Employment of Writers," proposing a "survey of varying aspects of everyday life as it is lived in all parts of the United States." In many ways this proposal approximated some of the aims and methods of the American Guide. Though stressing "social usefulness," it took into consideration the "variety of talents, abilities, and limitations of the five hundred writers throughout the country it hopes to put to work."

> For instance, an indefinite number of writers trained to the work (free lance magazine and newspaper writers, certain short story writers and novelists) would receive assignments to write a complete hour to hour account of a single day in the life of a man, woman, or child in a community in which the writer lives.
>
> It can be seen how other classes of writers can be assigned work contributable to the survey. An historian would be assigned to consider the purely historical aspects of his community; another writer would be given an opportunity to comment on ethnological aspects of the development of his community, or any other, or any group of communities if his professional background warranted such an assignment. It is obvious such a compendium would prove of enormous value in the future.[15]

The material was to be assigned, assembled, and edited under the guidance of a voluntary editorial board, with four regional committees of volunteers appointed by the Authors' League to pass upon qualifications and need of applicants and to appoint regional volunteer editorial boards, which in turn would appoint ten assistant supervisors to carry out the detail work in the regions. The projects were to employ in addition to the supervisory and clerical force from 250 to 500 writers for a minimum period of ten weeks. The board of directors of the Authors' League Fund (a separately incorporated benevolent and welfare organization for needy writers) would contribute $1,500 "for necessary overhead expenses for registration and supervision of this project," and would try to raise additional funds if necessary. No provisions were made for publication.

At the same time unemployed writers, like unemployed artists and other white-collar workers, had organized their own protective association, the Unemployed Writers Association. On February 28, 1934, Robert Whitcomb, secretary of the new organization, sent the following forceful letter to Julius Stone, the CWA director of federal projects:

> The unemployed writers of New York City do not intend to continue under the semi-starvation condition meted out to them, particularly while

the painters of pictures, some of them, receive adequate treatment from the government. We have written to the President, outlining our treatment both from you and from the CWA authorities in New York, which has been one of referral back and forth. At first you informed us that you were thinking of something for writers—should Congress appropriate the money. In Washington I learned that you were thinking of nothing definite, and that Congress appropriates the money Mr. Hopkins asks for. I whereupon informed Mr. Hanna that the Unemployed Writers Association thereupon demanded that Mr. Hopkins ask Congress for money to help us. Since then every demand we have made upon you has been answered with a request for our project, but that project is now before you in outline. The only reply we have had from you about the project is that you have received it and there is no immediate possibility for a new national project, referring us back to the city and state.

We are going to see Colonel Delamater again on March 5, in a body. We are continuing our registration and classification of writers. Saturday night we will elect our delegation to Washington.

We are tired of being referred elsewhere. If the government does not intent to formulate some policy regarding the class of intellectual known as a writer, who is trained for nothing else in the present economic emergency, then the writer must organize and conduct a fight to better his condition.[16]

By August, 1934, the Unemployed Writers' Association, now combined with the Writers' Union, had developed a number of specific projects, ranging from the employment of unemployed creative writers in their own homes to a New York City project for twenty-five writers to "do research on the subject of unemployment and the writing profession." This proposed study had six divisions: (1) writers and their organizations; (2) publishers as industrial employers; (3) historical relation of writer and publishers, methods of payment, copyright, etc.; (4) unemployment statistics; (5) comparative methods of relief; (6) summary. In a letter of September 6, 1934, to Arthur Goldschmidt describing the latter project, Whitcomb classified the members of his organization in three groups: (1) practicing writers; (2) writers now working on other projects; and (3) "unemployed writers either on Home Relief or in a state of nervous prostration and starvation." Regarding the method of selection of applicants, he proposed the following "definition of a writer" as a criterion: "One who has earned a living as such, been published in major periodicals or who can produce satisfactory manuscripts." As to publication, it was proposed that the "work of those chosen be weeded out for publication by the Government Printing Office or other public presses; and that these publications be distributed free to libraries and other public institutions. The work of selection of writers and their works, we suggest, should be done by a committee of writers and critics."[17]

The pressure for writers' projects thus organized in 1934 by the

Authors' League, the Unemployed Writers' Association, and the Writers' Union, was given a new impetus in 1935 by the union of twenty-three organizations, including the Writers' Union, into a Conference of Professional, Cultural, and White Collar Workers, whose first meeting, held in New York City, endorsed the following program:

1. Expansion of work program to give employment to all workers in their special crafts.

2. Union rates of pay where unions exist; prevailing rates where no unions exist, but in no case less than $21 per week. The hours of work shall not exceed thirty.

3. The financing of these measures shall not be at the expense of the working and consuming population, but at the expense of the Government.

4. No discrimination on account of race, sex, political or religious belief.

5. Freedom to organize and bargain collectively.

6. Abolition of Pauper's Oath as basis for getting job.

7. Enactment of genuine unemployment and social insurance measure.

These proposals were the basis for a call issued by the group for a mass meeting to be held at the Washington Irving High School, New York City, on March 14, 1935:

THE PROFESSIONAL, CULTURAL,

AND WHITE COLLAR WORKER

IS DISPOSSESSED!

NO PROVISION HAS BEEN MADE FOR HIM IN THE NEW

FEDERAL WORKS PROGRAM

There are many professional, cultural, and white collar organizations. They have until now worked separately. United, working together for common economic interests, they would not be the first to experience unemployment, they would not be excluded from the Public Works Program.

WORKERS, employed and unemployed! All professional, cultural and white collar organizations! We must unite our forces! We must have jobs for the half million office and professional workers in New York still without work! We must reject the $50 per month wage plan!

OUR only weapon is solid organization. That is why we call the mass meeting—to insure every worker a job at a decent wage.

## THE GENESIS OF THE AMERICAN GUIDE PROJECT

The ideas that emanated from the suggestions offered by newspapermen and writers' organizations contributed in a general way to the development of the central concept of the Federal Writers' Project, the elaboration of an American Guide. Among them, however, were a few suggestions that contributed more directly to the inspiration.

On April 9, 1935, Livingstone H. Elder of New York City wrote to Senator Royal S. Copeland:

> At this time last year I brought to your attention a proposal for the use of P.W.A. funds which you were kind enough to refer to Secretary Ickes. Although it was not deemed eligible for a project at that time, I am still confident that it would surely be an excellent suggestion for the recent work relief appropriation.
>
> Briefly, the idea is to employ a white collar group of historic and artistic background in the preparation of a complete, reliable, stimulating guide book for the whole United States. None of the publishing houses capable of preparing such a volume or series of volumes are willing to attempt it, although there is no question as to the increasing demand for something of this sort more recent than the 1914 Baedeker Guide Book.
>
> I would welcome the opportunity for explaining in detail such a non-competitive self-liquidating project to Mr. Hopkins.[18]

On April 22 Arthur Goldschmidt replied:

> Your letter of April 9th to Senator Royal S. Copeland suggesting the preparation of an American Guide book has been referred to this Administration for reply.
>
> A detailed plan for the preparation of a guide book similar to the Baedeker has been drawn up. It is suggested that this project be prosecuted for the employment of writers, newspaper men and map makers who are on the relief rolls or eligible for relief.
>
> However, since authority for the conduct of the new Work Program has not yet been delegated it is impossible for this Administration to comment on what projects that program will include.
>
> We are keeping this project and a copy of your letter in our files for transmittal to the Administration whose responsibility the new program for professional and clerical persons will be.
>
> Thank you for your expression of interest in the relief program.[19]

Still another germ of the Guide project was contained in a proposal of an official directory of points of interest made on August 1, 1934, by

Henry S. Curtis, of Ann Arbor, Michigan, director of the FERA recreational survey of Washentaw County. This proposal, transmitted to Goldschmidt by Lewis R. Alderman of the United States Office of Education, called for "a sort of public Baedeker, which would point out to the curious traveler the points of real travel value in each state and county," and which "would be a great asset to our educational systems and would also we well worth while commercially." The important idea here was the adaptation of Baedeker to an automobile age. On this subject Curtis wrote:

> Many foreign countries have travel bureaus. Probably the people of America travel more by auto than all the rest of the world put together but there is no directory to show us what is worth seeing on the social, industrial or historical side. It would look like a good project for the FERA to get out such a travel guide at this time for each state and the nation. To make our people know America is to build the foundations of patriotism. The expense would be justified by that alone. But such a directory would serve no less to stimulate travel from foreign lands and make the real America known to the world. Why not an official guide to America, that recognizes highways as well as railroads? America spends today seven billion dollars a year on travel, would not a travel bureau to give these billions intelligent direction be worth while?[20]

The American Guide had the benefit not only of many suggestions that contributed to its genesis but also of an actual precedent in *The Connecticut Guide*, in which the "idea of a guide book was first tried out." A project of the State Planning Board initiated under the CWA and completed with FERA funds, compiled by Edgar L. Heermance and published by the Emergency Relief Commission at Hartford in May, 1935, this 320-page book was produced by eleven relief workers and about 1,000 volunteers. Although it served as "an illustration of how the work can be carried out," its value for the American Guide was negative rather than positive. Henry Alsberg wrote: "While we have much admiration for this guide book, it has been realized that the publication was assembled by voluntary workers and needs considerable revision and a number of additions. Certain types of information that we are including in the American Guide have not been included in The Connecticut Guide."[21]

THE ESTABLISHMENT OF THE PRECEDENCE OF THE AMERICAN GUIDE
OVER OTHER WRITERS' PROJECTS

In setting up writers' projects, state directors were authorized "to approve or disapprove, on the basis of their fitness as units of the Federal Writers' Projects, projects calling for the employment of writers and persons of related abilities." In effect this gave precedence to the Guide over all other existing projects. This was a necessary step in the transition from decentralized FERA and CWA writers' projects to the nationwide WPA-sponsored Federal Writers' Project. It was also the first test of the principle of a central control that would at the same time recognize and encourage local initiative and responsibility. Although most states readily co-operated in the "larger purposes and broader aims" of the Guide in the interest of employing the largest number of writers in all categories on projects that would yield the greatest public benefit, it was inevitable that in some instances friction should develop and that in such cases the Washington office should intervene. Thus in New Mexico the translation project was threatened with closure if allowed to interfere seriously with the other main projects. As late as January 6, 1936, Alsberg wrote to Mary B. Perry, state director for New Mexico:

> I am rather alarmed by the number of writers apparently at work, the amount of material that apparently is being turned out on that undertaking, and the very little information I have about any work being done on the American Guide. However valuable the Translation Project may be, the Guide and Reporting Projects take precedence."[22]

The most serious situation, however, developed in California. In that state the administration had continued from the FERA a number of research projects for writers, such as the "Compilation of Bibliographies and Biographies of California Literature and Authors from Pre–Gold Rush Period to 1935"; "Italians of San Francisco, Their Adjustments and Acculturation"; "History of Labor Movement in Bay Area"; "History of Migratory Labor in California"; and "Study of California Folklore and Indians." The products of these projects, supervised by Paul Radin and Hugh Harlan, "have been universally praised," according to a report on the "Status of Federal Writers' Projects throughout the Country," issued late in 1935; and "Italians of San Francisco, Their Adjustments and Acculturation," Parts I and II, were described by George Cronyn as "splendid monographs which deserve publication."[23] Yet on December 7, 1935, it became necessary for George Cronyn to wire Paul Radin to "terminate at once all projects other than American Guide." Alsberg sent a similar wire to Hugh Harlan, rejecting the project proposal for a central literary project of eighty-six people and four supervisors. The difficulty that led to these summary instructions arose from the fact that both Radin and Harlan were so attached to the writers' projects they themselves had started and supervised that they were reluctant to discontinue them, even in view of the Washington office's insistence upon priority for the Guide. On January 2, 1936, Alsberg wrote to Max Radin that he would have been willing to allow Paul Radin to complete such FERA writers' projects as could be done with a small staff, but that the latter was "unwilling to subordinate his own preferences to the program which has been laid down for us."[24] Paul Radin was presently dismissed.

Similar drastic action was taken in Los Angeles. In December, 1935, Cronyn was sent to California to resolve the impasse. In Los Angeles he dismissed Harlan and three assistants, and appointed Le Roi Gant as acting district supervisor. Various local organizations protested Cronyn's "arbitrary and unjust" action and asked for the reinstatement of the four and a guarantee of job security to the project for the duration of the WPA.* As a result of the protest, Cronyn was recalled to Washington and Maurice Howe, state director of the Writers' Project in Utah, was sent to California to take charge of the "minor reorganization that had to be made."[25] In Los Angeles, Harlan was reinstated; and in San Francisco, Paul Radin was made research editor, and James Hopper succeeded him as state director.†

It seems that the writers on the California project were under the impression that the American Guide was "supposed to be an unimportant project to be used as a stop-gap until worthwhile projects were found." Moreover, Paul Radin may well have felt that the guide could be written by a few people and the rest could be engaged in other research. But in the main, the friction as it developed in California and a few other states pointed to the problem of federal versus state control. Those states that had on their own developed writers' projects before the inauguration of the Guide were unsympathetic to federal suggestion and so attached to their own inventions that only drastic procedure caused them finally to abandon the earlier programs.

THE FERA WORKING PROCEDURES FOR WRITERS

During the FERA period, as a result of the agency's own experi-

---

*These organizations were the Northern Newspaper Guild at San Francisco, the Interprofessional Association, San Diego Chapter, and the Central Labor Council of Alameda County at Oakland.

†George Cronyn, when he summarily dismissed Harlan, neglected to investigate his antecedents. Harlan was an alumnus of Grinnell College and a friend of Harry Hopkins, to whom he successfully appealed his dismissal.

660

ence and suggestions from the states and individuals, the Washington office developed five distinct working procedures for writers. These were:

F8.1. Individual Projects for Writers.
F8.2. Specified Commissions for Writers.
F8.3. Preparation of Iconographies.
F8.4. Survey to Collect Testimony of Ex-Slaves.
F8.5. Collecting Folklore.

"Individual Projects for Writers" differed from "Specified Commissions for Writers." Under the former, writers were to execute projects on "subjects of their own selection," including creative work, to be done in their own workrooms, and the completed works were to be the property of the state or local ERA and to be available to the public. However, unless the works were used within a reasonable length of time by the ERA, ownership might revert to the author; or "an agreement may be entered into with the writer whereby if works are sold the local relief administration is reimbursed to cover fully or partially the budgetary allowance made to the writer." In the case of specified commissions, on the other hand, writers were to work on special assignments, such as the arrangement and classification of information and research drawn from particular fields, under the supervision of a sponsoring agency, such as departments of education, libraries, or other public agencies. Here the emphasis was on research, including "creative research," and the completed work was the property of the state FERA and/or to be used by the sponsoring agency and made available to the public.

The preparation of iconographies came nearest to serving local and community needs and to anticipating certain phases of the Guide Project and Historical Records Survey. An iconography is defined as a "compilation of pictures, broadsides, handbills, and all the other original source material that describes the events, attitudes, and customs of a given place or region or group," together with descriptive comment and an index of source material. Here the emphasis was on historical and local material, such as the development of a city, community, era, region, or industry. These iconographies were intended for public use in schools, libraries, and so on, but no provisions were made for publication. Another kind of historical data to be collected from primary sources included folklore and the testimonies of ex-slaves, the purpose here being (1) to provide material of interest to historians, students, and the general public, and (2) to encourage community interest in such materials.

1. Letter, Goldschmidt to Clement Wood, November 16, 1934, FERA Files.
2. Letter, Hugh Harlan to Hopkins, August 23, 1934, FERA Files.
3. Letter, Virgil Dahl to Hopkins, July 2, 1934, FERA Files.
4. Letter, Jacob Baker to Hugh Harlan, May 12, 1934, FERA Files.
5. *Ibid.*
6. Letter, Hugh Harlan to Jacob Baker, May 24, 1934, FERA Files.
7. *Ibid.*
8. Letter, Goldschmidt to Hugh Harlan, June 24, 1935, FERA Files.
9. Letter, R. E. Reed to Hopkins, January 4, 1934, CWA Files.
10. Letter, Bruno Lasker to Julius F. Stone, Jr., December 22, 1933, FERA Files.
11. Letter, Francis Bonn to Hopkins, February 24, 1934, FERA Files.
12. Letter WPA-38, WPA, September 7, 1935.
13. "Instructions for Setting Up Reporting Projects," Alsberg to all state directors, FWP Files.
14. Letter, Cronyn to Van Olinda, September 3, 1935, FWP Files.
15. "Suggestion for CWA Employment of Writers," submitted by Authors' League, February 28, 1934, CWA Files.
16. Letter, Whitcomb to Stone, February 28, 1934, CWA Files.
17. Letter, Whitcomb to Goldschmidt, September 6, 1934, FERA Files .
18. Letter, Elder to Copeland, April 9, 1935, FERA Files.
19. Letter, Goldschmidt to Elder, April 22, 1935, FERA Files.
20. Letter, Henry S. Curtis to the FERA, August 1, 1934, FERA Files.
21. Letter, Alsberg to Redding, November 22, 1935, FWP Files.
22. Letter, Alsberg to Perry, January 6, 1936, FWP Files.
23. Memorandum, Cronyn to Baker, October 14, 1935, FWP Files.
24. Letter, Alsberg to Max Radin, January 2, 1936, FWP Files.
25. Memorandum, Baker to Hopkins, January, 1936, FWP Files.

# 27

## The Organization and Operation of the Federal Writers' Project

HENRY G. ALSBERG

The director of the Writers' Project, unlike the other directors in Federal One, came from the ranks of those who had already identified themselves with the Federal Emergency Relief Administration. Henry G. Alsberg, a friend of Jacob Baker, joined the FERA in the early spring of 1934 and subsequently became supervisor of reports. His duties were those of receiving information about relief and work-relief activities from the states and of disseminating information from the Washington office to the states. His previous experience as a newspaperman and correspondent qualified him for literary and editorial tasks, and his genuine and consistent interest in social reform commended him to the favor of the Washington staff of the FERA.

Alsberg, although his occupation was that of a journalist, had acquired a background of study and experience that endowed him with a catholicity of mind and a tolerance of attitude. He attended Columbia College of Columbia University and subsequently the Columbia Law School, and was awarded the degrees of Bachelor of Arts and Bachelor of Laws. After leaving Columbia, he spent one year at Harvard as a graduate student of literature. He then practiced law for three and one-half years in New York City. But Alsberg's gifts were literary rather than legal, and he abandoned the law to become an editorial writer for the New York *Evening Post*. After serving with the *Post* for some five years, he became secretary to the American ambassador to Turkey in 1916.

The life of a correspondent appealed to Alsberg, and he remained

663

in Europe as such during the troublous times of the German and Russian revolutions. Subsequently, he went to Mexico in the same capacity, where he stayed until he was asked to serve as director of the Joint Distribution Company, which was concerned with the relief of famine in Russia. Alsberg, whose consistently liberal philosophy had made him sympathetic with the Russian experiment, was shocked during his stay in Russia and afterward by what seemed to him a Thermidorean reaction within the Bolshevik party and the suppression of civil liberties that followed upon it. Consequently, upon his return to the United States he organized meetings of protest and wrote articles aimed at exposing the non-liberal attitude of the Russian regime. He thus made himself a *persona non grata* to the Communist party in the United States, and, indeed, was subsequently refused passports to the Soviet Union.

After his return to the United States he became interested in the theater, and, in particular, in the Provincetown Theater, of which he served as director for two years. It was during this period that he adapted the Yiddish play *The Dybbuk* for the American stage, and his version was produced on Broadway, where it became one of the most successful plays of the twenties and ran for two years.

Leaving the Provincetown Theater, Alsberg returned to journalism and represented various American newspapers and magazines in Europe and North Africa. Between his foreign assignments he lectured in the United States. Early in 1934, he became connected with the FERA, and in August, 1935, was appointed national director of the Federal Writers' Project.

It was natural that Alsberg, with his background, training, and experience, should interest himself in the status of writers during the depression and, particularly as a member of the Washington staff of the FERA, in the development of projects designed to employ needy newspapermen and other writers. Indeed, although he was not connected with the section of professional and non-manual projects, within whose province the concern for such projects lay, he worked closely with Goldschmidt in the examination and evaluation of such proposals for the employment of writers as reached the Washington office. There is evidence that as early as January, 1934, the nucleus of the concept of an American Guide was already in being in Alsberg's office; and as the new work program developed within the Executive and Congress, the concept grew and took form. When it became necessary to secure a national director for the Writers' Project, Alsberg's name naturally presented itself to the mind of Jacob Baker.

But if Alsberg enjoyed a certain priority among the possible candidates for the position by virtue of his presence in the office and the time and labor he had already spent upon the development of the project, the reasons that prompted Baker's choice were not solely those of friendship and accommodation. Alsberg had that cast of liberalism which Baker sought in all the directors of Federal One, and if his training was not in the field of social service, the adaptation of his thinking to the philosophy of the social worker was merely a matter of environment. His experiences abroad in the early postwar years, though they failed to shake his faith in a new and better order, subtly narrowed its ambit; and he saw in America and its native institutions a promise of that leadership toward reform which Europe and Asia had already abdicated. Consequently, he conceived of the Guide not as a revised Baedeker but as a discovery of the roots from which America had grown and a signpost of America's potentialities for the future. In a word, the Guide was to be an appreciation of America and a revelation of the democratic tradition, which, though it had never ceased to exist, had been obscured by an alien film. Emphasis upon folklore; the speech and mores of the common people; stress upon the contributions of minorities, like the American Negro, to the creation of a genuinely native culture; and an accent upon regional, sectional, and local characteristics that in their variety formed a manifold unity that only a decent respect for each could preserve—these were the principles that guided the thought of Henry Alsberg as he approached the creation of an American Guide.

But Alsberg's liberalism, although it was as sincere as his approach was direct, was more intellectual than practical. That power to implement thought by action and policy by procedure, which is the unique gift of the competent administrator, was not possessed in its fullness by Alsberg. His natural tendency was to act as editor rather than administrator, and his preoccupation with creative composition left him less time for the demands of national supervision than the exigencies of the project required. This reluctance on the part of the writer to forsake his pen was coupled with that lack of worldly wisdom that is the cross of those who excel in philosophic speculation. If Alsberg was the least concerned with self of all the directors in Federal One, he was also the most completely naive; and his failure to distinguish between friend and foe left him in the end naked before his enemies.

THE WASHINGTON OFFICE

When the national office of the Federal Writers' Project was set up in Washington in the summer of 1935, it had as an administrative nucleus a director (Henry Alsberg) and an assistant director (Reed Harris), both on the payroll of the Special Reports and Photo Section, Division of Research, Statistics, and Records. Originally, it probably was not intended to create a large technical staff; the Federal Art, Music, and Theater projects had only small administrative staffs in Washington. Gradually, however, the national office of the Federal Writers' Project attracted to itself more administrative workers and editors, recruited partly from the Special Reports and Photo Section (Arnold Serwer, Charles D. Wood), partly from the outside (Leonard Abbott, Waldo R. Browne, George Cronyn, Joseph Gaer, and Katherine Kellock), and partly from the state offices (Kathryn Cordell), until at its height the technical staff numbered as many as seventy or eighty persons.*

There were special reasons why the Writers' Project needed, or seemed to need, a large central technical staff. In the summer of 1939, when the technical staff was abolished, these reasons were summarized in a letter to Florence Kerr:

> On the Writers' Project, the national technical staff has been charged with responsibility for the maintenance of literary and technical standards which meet the exacting requirements of leading national publishers. This includes editorial review for style, completeness and accuracy of material, typographical styling, making of maps, selection of illustrations and format, details of sponsorship and contracts and publishers.
>
> Locally-sponsored projects, in the absence of national supervision and co-ordination, are not equipped to handle all these details. If this responsibility is now thrown without warning upon such tiny local units, which up to this time have relied entirely on the national staff for this work, chaos will result and the quality of performance, in many places, will deteriorate to the level of local booster literature, as even the administrators of WPA have admitted. . . .
>
> It is important that the national administrative officials of the Works Progress Administration should find ways whereby a national staff is maintained to uphold the professional standards and cultural significance of the arts program. . . .[1]

The function of the National Technical Project was fourfold: (1) editorial; (2) technical; (3) research; and (4) co-ordinating. Primarily, as a liaison between the state and the sponsor, on the one hand, and the publisher, on the other, the National Technical Project served as a publication office. As such, its duties were to undertake all tasks connected

---

*In January, 1936, the Washington staff of the Writers' Project, like the national staffs of the other arts projects, was organized as a national co-ordinating project and paid from project funds. This co-ordinating project was also known as the National Technical Project.

with the making of the guides except actual publication. These functions included planning the contents and treatment; preparing instructions on the gathering, organization, and writing of the field data; reading, checking, and approving copy; typography, maps, and illustrations; contracts, printing schedules, and proofreading. For this purpose it was necessary to maintain a staff not only of editors but also of research workers and technical experts in such special fields as art, architecture, folklore, labor, racial groups, Negro affairs, etc., whose combined responsibility was to set and maintain uniform national standards of accuracy, form, and style.

The Washington office of the Writers' Project, therefore, was primarily an editorial office rather than an administrative office. Apart from the clerical personnel, even those whose duties were defined as administrative were assigned editorial responsibilities, and in many cases these editorial duties consumed the major portion of the individual's time and effort.

Alsberg's immediate assistant in the beginning, Reed Harris, came over with his chief from the Section of Special Reports of the FERA. As assistant director of the Writers' Project, Harris, according to a memorandum by Alsberg, "takes care of the administrative details and, in addition, occasionally handles rewriting and editing."[2] Harris' training and experience were journalistic. Before he joined the FERA he had spent six years in newspaper work, including employment on a college paper (Columbia University's *Daily Spectator*), a country weekly, a small city daily, and the *New York Times* and the New York *Journal*. He had written one book, *King Football*, and had ghostwritten two others; he also had contributed to a number of periodicals. Harris was entitled to sign letters from the Washington office in Alsberg's absence.

In August, 1935, George Cronyn was engaged by the Washington office as associate director of the Federal Writers' Project. Although, like Alsberg, he had had a varied career, most of his postcollegiate life had been devoted to editorial and kindred tasks. He had studied at the University of Montana and at Columbia University, and had taught English for one year at the former institution. Among Cronyn's nonliterary activities was work as a rancher in the Southwest, as an applegrower in the Northwest, and as a plumber. He had purposely cultivated a catholicity of experience in order to fit himself for the profession of novelist, and before joining the project had published two novels, *The Fool of Venus* and *Fortune and Men's Eyes*, as well as an anthology of American Indian songs entitled *The Path of the Rainbow*.

As a journalist, Cronyn had been business manager of the magazine *Story*, an editor of *System, A Magazine of Business*, an associate editor of the *New Standard Encyclopedia*, and a contributing editor to the *Columbia Encyclopedia*. Cronyn's sense of practicality and concern for detail contrasted strongly with Alsberg's preference for creative writing, and, although in the beginning he acted in fact as a deputy director and signed correspondence, his position in the central office was for the most part that of general editorial manager.

Alsberg, Harris, and Cronyn exercised general editorial supervision, in addition to their administrative responsibilities. Among those of the editorial staff with specific responsibilities was, first of all, Katherine Kellock. Mrs. Kellock's importance lay not only in the fact that she was editor of the tours section of the Guide but also in the fact that she contributed more than any other single individual to the detailed elaboration of the plan for the American Guide. Her mind had long been agitated by the need for a new American Guide to supplant the old Baedeker, and, before coming to Washington, she had suggested such a venture to publishing houses and had elaborated a complete plan for such a book for a leading publisher. Her twin concepts—that the tours should be adjusted to the exigencies of the automobile and that the text should be interpretive rather than descriptive—laid the foundation for the philosophy that guided the project's greatest achievement. Among her other occupations, Mrs. Kellock had worked with Lillian Wald of the Henry Street Settlement in New York City, and to her solicitude for social service was added the equipment of a scholar. Among her contributions to scholarship are between thirty and forty biographies in the *Dictionary of American Biography*.

Of its four functions—editorial, technical, research, and co-ordination—the national office was weakest in co-ordination. Since it was necessary that all outgoing correspondence pass over Alsberg's desk, the national director, in theory, reviewed all editorial comment. But as national director, Alsberg had little time to follow the work of each state closely, and his review served chiefly to keep him informed, rather than to guide the others. For that reason the final editorial review was lodged in the heads of the various departments, subject to the final approval of the managing or co-ordinating editor (successively, George Cronyn, Harold Coy, and Gorham B. Munson).

The departmental organization of the national office was such, however, as to make for piecemeal editing. The three main departments corresponded to the three main divisions of the guide: essays, cities, and tours. To overcome the defects of departmentalization, the system of state editorships was established in the Washington office providing one editor for each state. But each state editor was responsible only for the essays or cities or tours in his state; none saw the book as a whole. The tours editors were expected to read the essays for their states, but there was no check on cross references between tours and cities and tours and essays. As a member of the essays section later stated:

> When I came, they were getting out the guide books in three sections—cities, tours, and essays. I was in the essay section. For practical purposes, you never even saw the other parts of the book. It was surprising the books were as good as they were. . . .[3]

THE FLOW OF COPY

Manuscripts from the states, when they arrived in the Washington office, were routed first to the checker, whose duty, as his name implies, was to note the arrival of the copy and to maintain cognizance of its whereabouts while it was in the national office. The checker, in short, was responsible for the physical safety of the manuscript. From the checker the manuscript passed to the reviewer (Alsberg, Cronyn, or Harris), whose function at this point was merely to examine the manuscript cursorily in order to be aware of the general flow of material to the central office. From the reviewer the manuscript passed back through the checker to the state editor. From the state editor the copy passed, always through the checker, to the general editor; from the general editor to the field editor; finally, when the manuscript treated a particular subject (e.g., folklore), for which there was a specialist in the national office, it was routed to him.*

The procedures in the essays department and the tours department were analogous to those in the cities department. The multiple reading of each manuscript in each department was intended to insure expert checking and, as a consequence, accuracy and literary style. But the resultant division of authority, and the conflict and confusion that derived from it, made necessary some device for the collation of comment and the resolution of differences. In the first four years of the project this

---

*The duties of these several editors are described in detail in "Method of Handling State Copy," Memorandum, Reed Harris to All Editors, May 4, 1936, FWP Files.

responsibility, so far as it was exercised, was assumed by the person (the field editor or the head of the department) who prepared the letter accompanying the manuscript back to the editorial office in the state under consideration.

Eventually, however, it was realized that this type of co-ordination was not enough, and in 1939 it was decided to assign to each state a co-ordinating editor whose responsibility it was to see the particular state guide through to completion. One of the staff who was given such a responsibility remarked upon the superiority of this over the previous procedure:

> In 1939 they started as an experiment appointing a person as a co-ordinating editor. I was the first. I had Arizona. When the essays and tours were finished they came to me. I was startled to see how much overlap there was. You put points of interest in the cities section and also in the tours.[4]

Besides the lack of co-ordination and division of authority, another defect of the national office was the absence of final authority. In theory, Alsberg was in command in the Washington office, but his administrative responsibilities often left him little time for the details of editing. Consequently, editorial supervision devolved upon George Cronyn—until he came into conflict with Alsberg and was relieved of his authority. Many have testified to the excellence of Cronyn's criticism. Stella Hanau observes:

> . . . He read the cities completely and the essays completely, and made suggestions and criticisms. You had to show him the stuff and he sent it back with his memorandum. You were not bound to change your work according to it, however. But his suggestions were very good. He was very valuable—he was a clever fellow and he knew the country. Very often if you wrote an essay that wasn't right he would say, "Why don't you start with this?" or "You can't leave out the abalone in the fishing industry." As far as the technical set-up went he was very much off to one side. I gathered that he gradually had less and less power. I think that before my time he had all the power that went with his position and gradually it became less and less.[5]

Cronyn himself was loath to assume the final authority, since, in his opinion, such authority resided in the states. He wrote:

> In regard to "final authority" no one in this organization can be granted such power. I do not myself exercise it, nor does any one else. I must feel free to modify and delete many items of criticism that I feel are unwise as a part of our general policy. Especially, in connection with every comment, from archeology to tours, phrases implying reproof or condescension have

been and will be modified. We will continue to offer advice but will not issue orders, except in a general way.[6]

In the fall of 1935 the necessary and difficult task of selecting and appointing state directors was undertaken *pari passu* with that of establishing the national office. The problem of finding competent state directors was not easy. There was first of all, as in the whole works program, the demand for speed; second, the procedure under which state directors on Federal One were officially appointed and approved was complicated and cumbersome; finally, the salaries offered were not calculated to attract men who possessed in happy combination the required technical and administrative qualifications.

Even before the project was authorized on September 28, Henry Alsberg wrote to key persons in writing, publishing, and education, as well as in the wpa, for suggestions of likely candidates. Names were also submitted by such organizations as the Authors' League of America, and by Hopkins, Baker, and other federal officials. The correspondence of this period brings out some of the problems involved. Thus on September 20, 1935, Alsberg wrote to Eric Branham, of the New York State wpa administration, asking him to recommend as New York state director

> some one . . . of unusual calibre, an editor or writer of recognized standing in the community, who will command co-operation on all hands. This person must at the same time have a certain amount of executive experience.
>
> I think by consulting prominent newspaper men in Albany, Buffalo, and Rochester, and the professors of literature and history in some of the important up-state universities, and the presidents of the various historical societies, you might be able to get the names of some suitable people.[7]

To Lawrence Joseph Henderson and to Felix Frankfurter, Alsberg wrote on October 8, 1935:

> We feel that Massachusetts is not only an important state in itself but that any appointment we make, unless it is above criticism might arouse unfavorable comment. One of the horns of our dilemma is that we cannot pay a really decent salary—probably only $3200 in Massachusetts. In a number of states we have secured the services of very able people for considerably less than this. It is astonishing how many people whose names are in *Who's Who* will take a job of this sort because of present depression conditions.[8]

On September 12, 1935, Cronyn wrote to Robert Morss Lovett:

> At this moment we are collecting names of persons with both writing and administrative ability to serve as state supervisors. The person would not have to be on relief. A knowledge of the state is required, and residence in the state of Illinois will be necessary, as no travel from another state to the state where the person would take his job can be paid by the government.[9]

A survey of the qualifications of the state directors indicates that they were, in the main, sought in three walks of life: (1) college teachers; (2) free-lance writers; and (3) newspapermen. In general, in the choice of the directors, professional qualifications in the fields of writing, history, or science, and knowledge of the state, including acquaintance with state organizations and leaders, were placed above administrative ability and experience. Here as elsewhere in the program, conflict between the technical and administrative functions gave rise to considerable difficulty and controversy.

On the one hand, there were those who insisted that writers and scholars were incapable of directing a project.[10] On the other hand, there were those who felt that, since the making of a guidebook was primarily a literary task, only those with humanistic or journalistic training and reputation were capable of understanding the problems involved, of creating the proper atmosphere for work, and of inspiring public confidence. At the same time, it was recognized that the supervision of a guide project, as an endeavor in collective research and writing, called for more organizational ability than writing a novel or a poem, and that newspaper or magazine editorial experience, even more than administrative experience, was a valuable asset in a state director.

In the end, the reconciliation of administrative with technical ability was best achieved not by seeking both qualities in the same person but by delegation of one or the other responsibility. The success of Lyle Saxon, a writer of reputation who was state director of Louisiana, lay chiefly in the fact that he possessed the good sense to appoint an assistant director who was capable of dealing with administrative detail. Conversely, it was sometimes necessary to bulwark directors with administrative talent but without technical ability with editors who relieved them of their literary responsibilities. An example of this occurred in Pennsylvania, where Logan B. Sisson, the state director, was relieved of his editorial responsibilities and Paul Comly French was appointed associate director of the project in the state and made executive editor of the Guide. Thus the imperatives of editorial work on the Guide soon made it clear that, in some states at least, separate personnel were required for administrative and technical duties. Indeed, as

672

the work on the Guide progressed, it became increasingly evident that the strength or weakness of a state project lay in its editorial direction and that the assistant state supervisor, associate director, or executive editor of the Guide, if not the director himself, must be a practicing writer and editor who could do much of the writing and rewriting himself. In Massachusetts, for example, the assistant state supervisor (by November, 1935), was Merle Colby, author of three novels (*All Ye People*, 1931; *New Road*, 1933; and *Brown Rifle*, 1934) and later in charge of the Alaska Guide. In Montana it was the poet Grace Stone Coates, and in South Carolina, the poetess Louise J. DuBose (Nancy Telfair).

The tendency to relieve the state director of technical responsibilities marked in higher relief his administrative duties. Among these requirements was diplomatic aptitude, especially in dealing with the state WPA administrators and their staffs. The initial gaucherie with which state directors were introduced to the state WPA administrators alienated many of the latter, and demanded thereafter on the part of the director a greater attention to personal sensibilities than otherwise might have been necessary. Moreover, state WPA administrators, although not all congenitally opposed to writers' projects as such (since there were writers' projects in some states before the WPA), were suspicious of a national writers' project under the direction of the Washington office. On the subject of this relationship between the project and the state administration opinions varied. The regional director for the South, W. T. Couch, expressed his opinion thus:

> The Writers' Project was the stepchild of the State WPA Administrators. If any one of the Administrators in the eight states with which I had to do as Regional Director was at all interested in the state guide, I did not see any evidence of this interest. On the contrary, I saw evidence everywhere that the Writers' Project was regarded by the State Administrators as a New Deal whim—something that a few crackpots in Washington wanted, but that didn't amount to anything, something that would be dropped at the first opportunity, and the people employed on it put to work on jobs not quite so useless. A few subordinate regional and state officials were interested and could be counted on, but they did not have much power and were unable to move their superiors. . . . That good guide books were finally produced and published is little short of miraculous.[11]

The central office of the Writers' Project was more aware than those of the other arts projects of the necessity of good political and public relations, as the following report indicates:

> We feel that the Writers' Projects, but especially the American Guide, are generally very popular. So far with a very few exceptions State Admin-

istrators have welcomed our plan to compile sufficient material for a guide for every state and for guides for the larger cities. That seems to be the inducement which brings us almost universal cooperation.

In conclusion I wish to say that we have been under comparatively little pressure to make political appointments. Pretty nearly all the recommendations originating with State Administrators have been of people of real professional standing. Also most of the Senators and Congressmen recommending candidates for State Supervisorships have actually recommended fairly able people. In most instances where we have not acted on congressional or senatorial recommendations because the persons recommended were not of the highest caliber there have been practically no protests when the facts were properly explained.[12]

During the first year of the project's existence several state directors were either removed from the agency entirely or relegated to an inferior position. These changes indicated that the national office, if it exercised insufficient control over the original appointments either because of pressure for speed from above or because of political interference, was able later to exercise adequate control through removal or demotion. One state director was dismissed three days after his appointment "for inebriation"; another for "frequent, unauthorized absences from his position."

Less drastic action, however, was generally preferred. In some states, state directors were relieved of their administrative duties and made research editors in the state offices. This happened in the case of Paul Radin in northern California, Karl Singewald in Maryland, and Roland P. Gray in New York State. In still other cases the state director was allowed to keep the shadow, but deprived of the substance, of his authority. The device of reducing such a director to faineance is nicely illustrated by the attempted resolution of the Arkansas situation:

> If some arrangement could be worked out whereby Mrs. Babcock could be shown the desirability of her creating good will for the Guide throughout Arkansas and speaking perhaps before Women's Clubs, Service Clubs, etc., while the actual efficient work is directed either by Mrs. Cordell or by a new person working with her, the Arkansas Guide could be considerably advanced. This would not involve any change in her status as State Director. It might perhaps be shown her that her standing as one of the literary Big Four of Arkansas makes it eminently desirable that she contact and address various organizations in the state.[13]

In West Virginia the state director was assigned duties that effectively removed him from both administrative and editorial control of the project.[14]

THE FIELD SUPERVISORS

The field supervisors or field representatives, as they were called indifferently, served as liaison officers between the national office and the state offices. In the first weeks of the project's existence, the field representative's responsibility was crucial, for it was largely through him, acting as representative of the national office, that projects were initiated, directors appointed, and workers assigned. During the life of the project the field representative carried out in the states the policies, pleasant and unpleasant, of the central office; he investigated crisis, effected dismissals, and reduced quotas; in the technical realm he gave editorial and literary direction in research and composition, advised in relation to the securing of sponsorship, and instructed with regard to the task of publication. These field representatives included some of the most capable and intelligent members of the Washington and state staffs—Jay DuVon, T. J. Edmonds, J. Harry Gable, Joseph Gaer, Maurice Howe, Katherine Kellock, Edward A. Kennard, Clair Laning, Darel McConkey, Wallace Miller, Lawrence S. Morris, and Roderick Seidenberg.

At times the field representatives were assigned on a regional basis; more often, however, they were subject to instructions that might carry them to any part of the country. In the fall of 1935, for instance, Mr. McConkey was responsible for the Southeast; Mr. Morris, for the Middle West; and Mr. Gaer, for the Far West. Subsequently, both Mr. Morris and Mr. Gaer were assigned to New England, where Mr. Gaer was instrumental in achieving the completion of the New England guides.

Besides the field representatives, properly so called, all Washington directors and editors, including Alsberg and Cronyn, made periodic surveys of the field; and in addition, state directors and editors were occasionally commissioned as acting field representatives and given specific assignments. Thus in December, 1935, after Cronyn's settlement of the California crisis was reversed, Maurice Howe of Utah was dispatched to the West Coast to reorganize the projects in San Francisco and Los Angeles. In 1936 Jay DuVon of Iowa served as acting field representative in that area; in March and April, 1936, T. J. Edmonds of Oregon acted as a special investigator in Seattle and San

Francisco, where changes in state directorships were contemplated. All three later served for a time as regular field representatives. Occasionally, a Washington editor represented the national office on a special mission, as when, in March, 1936, Roderick Seidenberg conferred with acting administrator Paul Edwards and other interested parties in the state administration, Harvard University, and the Massachusetts Historical Society, to secure the transfer of Clifford K. Shipton from the post of state director of the Massachusetts Writers' Project to regional supervisor of the Historical Records Survey. Finally, toward the end of the project, especially in the weaker state offices, Washington editors were sometimes assigned to a state office for from one to several months in order to complete the work on the state guide. In such cases they served, to all intents and purposes, as resident members of the state editorial office.

The field representatives' responsibility in carrying out in the field the instructions of the Washington office was balanced by an equal responsibility to inform the central office of the situations and problems peculiar to the states within their jurisdiction. In the Writers' Project, as in all administrations operating in the field, there was a tendency to be summary, if not arrogant, in relations with the state offices, and it was the duty of the field representatives to counteract this by representing the view of the state offices. The field representatives were in a peculiarly favorable position to do this, for they were acquainted with the vagaries of both offices, and reconciled, in their own thinking, the necessity of national standards, which were the concern of Washington, with a proper respect for local differences in personnel and policy. Under such conditions it is not surprising that at times the field representatives exceeded their authority and acted with a directness that the situation demanded but that administrative procedure did not justify. Such an assumption of command authority on the part of the field representatives was not always happy; if the Washington office failed to support the solution of its representatives, as sometimes happened, friction and embarrassment resulted. In the main, however, circumspection prevailed, and the diplomacy and tact the field representatives exhibited in the dealings with contrary tendencies, both within states and between states and the national office, contributed significantly to the success of the project.

THE DEVELOPMENT OF REGIONAL DIRECTORS AND
REGIONAL EDITORIAL OFFICES

After some three years of project operation, the office of regional director was devised. This office must be carefully distinguished from that of field supervisor, which existed from the beginning of the project. Both the field supervisor and the regional director were representatives of the national office, and held what administrative and technical authority was theirs by virtue of delegation from Henry Alsberg. In theory, neither officer held command authority, though both sometimes exercised it. But whereas the earlier field representative was generally attached to the national office, from which he held a roving commission, the later regional director was attached to a state office and assigned duties, editorial and administrative, within a carefully defined region.

The considerations that led to the establishment of regional offices were twofold. In the first place, experience had taught the Washington office that its assumption of editorial responsibility for all states placed upon it a technical burden that was beyond its power to sustain. The regional office, therefore, represented an attempt to decentralize editorial responsibility, and was devised in 1938, in view of the probable end of the project, to accelerate the completion of the state guides.

In the second place, the regional office represented the revival of a concept that was in Alsberg's mind at the very commencement of the project. The original idea of the Guide was that of a work in five regional volumes, which were to be written, presumably by the Washington staff, out of material supplied by the several state projects. In the beginning it was expected that all material from the states would be in the Washington office by May 15, 1936, at the latest, at which time the central staff would undertake the task of regional organization in the composition. This estimate was badly awry, and it became clear even before the deadline that the required material would not be at hand. At the same time, there was pressure from above upon the Writers' Project to show results in the form of publication. For these reasons the concept of five regional guides was abandoned in favor of a guide for each state.

The new regional organization, however, although it was immediately inspired by the logjam of editorial work in the central office, was more deeply rooted in this concept of regional cultures, and was intended, in addition to its administrative purpose, to encourage the development of a regional program. In the mind of the Washington office, this regional program was to include (1) regional guides and (2) the cultivation of other regional material of a literary nature.*

*Although it was originally intended to establish regional offices in all or most regions, only four such offices were established. The regional directors of these offices were, in the order of their appointment, John T. Frederick (Region 4, Illinois,

Unfortunately, the attempt to write regional guides was stillborn. The transfer of the project from national to state control in the summer of 1939, less than a year after the establishment of the regional organization, was a primary cause of the miscarriage. After 1939 state WPA administrators objected to the presence on their staff of men with responsibilities outside the state, and, since all decisions of policy now rested with the former, their determination was decisive. The only regional guide for which an outline was made seems to have been the New England guide. Work on it did not progress beyond this stage, although a recreation guide, *Here's New England*, was published in 1939.

Of the regional directors of the Federal Writers' Project, the one who came nearest to realizing the regional ideal was W. T. Couch. As director of the University of North Carolina Press since 1932 and editor of *Culture in the South* (1934), Couch was admirably qualified not only for the position of regional director, which he held in 1938 and 1939, but also for the role of regional interpreter—a role that, as publisher, he had definitely made his own.

Couch's great contribution to southern regional portraiture was the development of the "life history" technique from that of a scientific case history to that of a literary and documentary narrative. To be sure, life histories had previously been recorded from pioneers and ex-slaves, as well as from folklore informants. Couch, however, by covering many groups—"tenant farmers, farm owners, textile and other factory workers, persons in service occupations in towns and cities (such as bell hops, waitresses, messenger boys, clerks in five and ten cent stores, soda jerks), and persons in miscellaneous occupations such as lumbering, mining, turpentining, and fishing"—achieved a cross-section of southern life that, if ever integrated, would become panoramic in its coverage. This life-history technique, begun under his direction by the writers' project in North Carolina, gradually spread to other states in Region 5 and even Region 6, until it became one of the major activities of the southern states next to the state guides, and resulted in the collection of thousands of life histories. One volume of such histories, *These Are Our Lives*, was published by the University of North Carolina Press in 1939.[15] In addition, several manuscripts were completed, or almost completed, among them *Big Ivy* and *Tobacco People*.

Indiana, Michigan, Missouri, and Ohio), Frank Manuel (Region 1, New England), W. T. Couch (Region 5, Alabama, Florida, Georgia, Kentucky, North and South Carolina, and Tennessee), and Lyle Saxon (Region 6, Arkansas, Louisiana, Mississippi, Oklahoma, and Texas).

Couch's success with this novel program is a tribute not only to his own imaginative and executive gifts but also to the intellectual atmosphere and regional emphasis that distinguish the campus of his university. His ability to achieve results also derived from the prestige he enjoyed as director of the university's press and the facility with which the uses of the project could be converted to the uses of the press. Naturally, he was very conscious of his own primacy in the initiation and elaboration of the experiment and extremely sensitive to direction from the national office. Thus when Benjamin Botkin, the national folklore editor, requested likely folklore material for inclusion in a contemplated book, "American Folk Stuff," he wrote in a very forthright manner:

> I have definite plans and the plans I have are workable if no one interferes with them and if I am permitted to carry them to completion. These plans will be wrecked if any one is permitted to come into this region and select any material he cares to have, without reference to our plans and if I am not permitted to go into Southern states outside of Region 5 and I am not given full co-operation in getting material in these states. I am very much worried for fear we shall not be able to carry our plans to completion because I am having to explain everything to everybody and there is not time enough for me to do this. I simply cannot get around to it.[16]

Couch also resented the tenuous nature of his authority in regional affairs, especially with reference to administrative matters. In connection with difficulties in Tennessee, he wrote to the national director:

> I am not willing to continue as Regional Director of the Federal Writers' Project unless definite measures are taken to correct this situation and to prevent such occurrences in the future. The real difficulty is that I do not have authority commensurate with my responsibility. Worse yet, I do not know where to turn to find the authority necessary to clear the Tennessee situation, or to find out that it cannot be cleared.[17]

The shifting of the editorial and supervisory load from the national to the regional offices proved most effective in those states in which the state guides were still in progress. In such cases the regional director was free to move editors from state to state as necessity required, or, better still, to bring the state editors into the regional office, where they undertook the task of final editing under the personal direction, of the regional director. This decentralization of editorial responsibility was both more economical and more effective than the previous arrangement whereby the Washington office concentrated in its own hands all editorial supervision.

679

The regional method was most effectively employed in Regions 4 and 6. In the former, John T. Frederick, editor, teacher, and critic, conducted his office like a large editorial workshop; in the latter, Lyle Saxon, dean of Louisiana writers, represented the culture of the South at its best. In general, the regional director exercised an influence commensurate with his literary status and the maturity of his personality.

The regional office also provided the opportunity and incentive for the inauguaration of regional conferences such as that held in Chicago, under Mr. Frederick's direction, in 1939. National, regional, and state directors and editors were brought together to meet one another and discuss new projects and common problems. Outside speakers were introduced as well as representatives of other projects, to give the benefit of fresh points of view. Above all, the regional conference enabled state directors, who might otherwise never have met, to meet and exchange ideas with one another as well as with national and regional personnel. In this way, experience was shared within an area wide enough to exhibit diversity, but not so extended that the problems of each were not the problems of all.

### THE PROBLEM OF PROJECT PERSONNEL

In a commercial venture for the purpose of writing and publishing guides to the several states, the obvious administrative procedure on the part of the central and controlling corporation would have been the delegation of full editorial responsibility to groups of writers in each state, each group under the supervision of a competent and well-paid director. The central office would have devised the initial plan, outlined the procedure, and exercised a continuous general guidance toward the minimum uniformity that a series needs.

The Federal Writers' Project, however, was in no position to enjoy the luxury of such a rational plan. The salaries it could afford to offer its state directors (ranging from $1,800 to $3,800, and averaging closer to the lower figure) were not calculated, even in the depth of the depression, to attract men of superior literary and managerial ability. It is true, indeed, that a few men of outstanding talent were persuaded to serve on the project; in the main, however, the state directors represented, at best, adequacy. Moreover, the difficulties of these state directors, faced with a research task that would have demanded the full faculties of an outstanding and experienced writer and administrator, was complicated by the fact that they were asked to fulfil their assignments through the employment of relief personnel.

Beginning in August, 1935, relief rolls were combed for available personnel. Regional and state officials of the WPA and its professional and service division were enlisted in the work by the Washington office of the Federal Writers' Project. One of the first questions to be raised was the definition of a writer. The extension of the term was interpreted broadly. In September, 1935, Alsberg wrote:

> As to . . . the lists of eligible writers and research people on relief rolls—I think it would help us a great deal if we would get these lists directly from the states because the compilation here has not been complete as yet. Such lists should not only include writers and research people but also librarians, architects, reporters, editors, lawyers, and others whose classification indicates education that would make them useful to us. We are now even including insurance salesmen of whom there are a great number everywhere.[18]

Prospective applicants who wrote to Washington for information concerning employment on writers' projects were advised in one of two veins, depending on whether they were certified for relief or not. In the former case, a reply like the following was sent:

> Since you are on relief, I assume that your name is on the United States Employment Service files. I would suggest that you make sure you are properly classified as a writer so that when local projects are organized you will receive consideration.[19]

If the applicant was merely unemployed, but not certified for relief, he was usually advised as follows:

> Since the American Guide Book program was announced, we have had many letters from well qualified writers in urgent need of employment who are not, however, on the relief rolls.
>
> It is not really a question of a technicality being invoked to prevent assistance to a writer who needs work and has proven his abilities. The program of writers' projects and the American Guide Book was conceived as an answer to the urgent question, e.g., what work could be found for nonmanual and professional men already on the relief rolls? Naturally, it is our hope to find some solution for accomplished, needy writers not on the relief rolls.
>
> I would suggest that you file an application with the State Re-employment Service, at 417-420 Scarborough Building, Post Office Box 957, Austin. Mr. Byron Mitchell is the Director. Then, when the Guide Book work is organized in Texas, if there is an insufficient number of qualified writers

available from the relief rolls, your name will be given the consideration it deserves.[20]

Thus at the outset the Writers' Project straddled the horns of a dilemma: the duty, on the one hand, of filling quotas from an unevenly distributed and unevenly qualified supply of unemployed persons certified for relief; and, on the other hand, the pressure to employ needy writers not on relief. The attempted solution of the dilemma, the 10 (and later 25) per cent non-relief exemption, was not wholly satisfactory, not only because it was not always adequate to supply deficiencies but also because it was an indirect admission of the fundamental weakness of the attempt to perform a highly technical task with untrained or partly trained personnel.

As a result, it soon became necessary for the Writers' Project to refute charges that it gave employment to all *but* writers:

> Of course we have not employed people whose principal occupation was that of chief plumber, mechanic, or other unrelated fields. If any one has made that statement, then it has been on the basis of half-truth. It is true that some of the people who had successful careers as newspapermen, free-lance writers, etc., came to us from temporary jobs of various kinds which ranged from one end of the employment list to the other. Their experience records, however, showed that their principal work and principal means of support had been writing in one form or another. This included advertising-copy writers, historians, writers on religious subjects, writers of pulp fiction, newspapermen, lawyers who had principally been engaged in preparing briefs for other lawyers, etc.[21]

In theory, project workers were selected in accordance with the following general principle:

> The method involved in the selection of personnel for the Federal Writers' Project has been first to take professional writers from the relief rolls. Professional writers are any persons who have earned their living as writers, whether newspaper or otherwise. This definition covers the newspaper reporter, the fiction writer, the poet, and even the advertising copywriter. As soon as the list of these professional writers was exhausted, other lists were drawn on for persons who had research and writing abilities indicated by their past training, so that they would be useful in the work of preparing the American Guide and the American Guide Series. Certain specialists were appointed without reference to these two categories since we needed architectural experts, map draftsmen, etc. A definite proportion of the people also had to be clerical and administrative.
>
> The provision under which the project was set up does not make it mandatory that persons actually do writing for their compensation, because if such a strict limitation were placed on the work, it would be impossible to employ clerks, draftsmen, stenographers, etc. Project workers are expected

to do whatever tasks are assigned to them in connection with the accomplishment of the objectives laid down for this program. The chief objective has been the completion of guide books and the work naturally has involved research, editing, coordination of material, indexing, and checking in addition to straight writing.

The proportion of newspaper workers naturally varies from state to state. If there had been a large number of qualified newspaper persons on the relief rolls at the time our project was set up, undoubtedly the proportion of newspaper workers would have been much higher.

Costs of various kinds are held to certain percentages by this office and Minnesota like other states must stay within these percentages. We do not feel that we should compare the Minnesota project with those in other states as to "coming up to standard." Standards must vary to a degree, as far as work accomplished is concerned, from state to state because the quality of personnel available varies. We naturally expect better work from the New York City project than from others because there is a greater supply of professional writers available there for the project.[22]

In practice, however, as the above letter obliquely concedes, many limitations and obstacles were encountered. Except for those applicants who had published books or articles, there was little or no criterion upon which a judgment of their capacity could be based, and, even in the case of those with published works, it is doubtful that those who undertook to assign examined the contents of their writings. Here, as elsewhere on the program, the deceptive notion that classification insures proper assignment prevailed, with the result that many were engaged who met the formal requirements but lacked the abilities that those requirements presupposed. Moreover, in the absence of a sufficient number of writers of professional standing, it was necessary to recruit persons from occupations with which writing is incidentally, and not necessarily, connected, such as teachers, lawyers, and even simply college graduates.

To be sure, the Presidential Letter that created the arts program encouraged a broad interpretation of the term *writer* by including along with writers proper a number of related occupations, and placing the emphasis on "professional workers" and on "accumulation" and "preparation" of "material" rather than on professional writing. Thus the letter provided for:

Employment of writers, editors, historians, research workers, art critics, architects, archeologists, map draftsmen, geologists and other professional workers for the preparation of material for an American Guide and the accumulation of new research material on matters of local, historical, art, and scientific interest in the United States; preparation of material for a complete encyclopaedia of government functions and periodical publications in Washington.[23]

*Supplement No. 1 to Bulletin No. 29* further stressed the need for a generous definition: "In considering 'writers' the interpretation to be used should not be the narrow technical one, but should include persons of research or academic training and, for the American Guide, persons acceptable as writers to the State Guide Supervisor."[24]

The same supplement, however, was not unaware of the temptation to employ indifferent personnel, and provided means whereby a locality with less-qualified personnel might be fortified:

> Its [the Guide's] national scope and special character makes the project different from others.
> It cannot be entirely dependent on the availability of qualified relief personnel in the particular community.
> Where qualified persons are not available in the districts others may be called into the District, through the U.S. Employment Service.[25]

The "national scope and special character" of the American Guide lay simply in the fact that it called for a guide in every state, whether or not there were qualified writers on relief in that state. Accordingly, the Writers' Project, unlike the other arts projects, set itself the difficult task of fitting the people to the program instead of the program to the people—a task that resulted in many anomalies and compromises.

In addition to the unevenness of distribution and quality of available personnel and of the resulting standards of performance (factors that also affected the other arts projects), a further limitation imposed upon the Writers' Project was the lack of precedent for work relief for writers:

> Without putting in any alibis, it must be realized that, with the exception of California, there were practically no writers' projects of any account in the States under FERA, so that everywhere a new technique and organization had to be established for this type of undertaking. Another difficulty encountered was the fact that many writers who could not hope to get relief jobs on Writers' projects because there were none, have had themselves classified under some other occupation. Added to this was the further fact that in many jurisdictions Relief Administrations and, even now, Works Progress Administrations, have been unwilling to classify an applicant for a job as a writer. Therefore, our new directors have had to comb the lists over again to find writers. Had it not been for the excellent co-operation of the State Administrations they would not have been able to have put many projects into operation; especially as a number of them had had no experience whatsoever in FERA or WPA organization work.[26]

But perhaps the most embarrassing claim was that of unemployed writers who could not qualify for local relief certification:

In most of the large cities we have been facing the problem of what to do about writers who managed to keep off the relief rolls up to June 1st. Many of these people, who have applied for jobs, state that they now have exhausted their resources and do not see why they should be penalized for having managed to keep self-dependent so long. To cite one instance: The Philadelphia Newspaper Guild has managed to support fifty-two of its destitute members out of its funds until quite recently. Now these funds have been exhausted and the organization asks us to give these writers jobs on our projects. This is a typical case. The same situation exists in New York, Boston, Cleveland, Chicago, etc.[27]

The Authors' League of America was particularly agitated over this phase of the situation, and, in October, 1935, its president addressed a sharp letter to Harry Hopkins:

As President of the Authors' League Fund, I can say to you that the WPA has not done one single thing for our people, who are the needy professional writers of the United States. The means test, together with the stupid arrangement by which each state has been given a certain amount of money regardless of whether that state has writers or not, has defeated your purpose and our hope. As you must know, writers are largely grouped in various centers. As a consequence, three-quarters of the states are utterly unable to find writers to fill their quotas, while in a city like New York, the quota is utterly inadequate to take care of the professional writers who are desperately in need of work.

About all that you have done is to destroy the Fund's own ability to take care of our own people. Voluntary contributions have fallen off to almost nothing because everybody believes implicitly that the WPA has taken over the entire burden.

Let me say to you again, as I have said to you in the past, that the whole task of administration in connection with the writers has been turned over, almost entirely, to people who know nothing whatsoever about writing or writers, and as a result, the people that you are now taking care of are either the rankest amateurs or else men and women whose only connection with the profession is the impudent assertion that they are writers.[28]

In replying to Creel on December 20, 1935, Alsberg cited his own efforts to use and expand the non-relief quota for the benefit of members of the Authors' League and the Newspaper Guild in cities like New York and Philadelphia. Elsewhere, he answered the charges of incompetence of the Project's personnel by listing the literary qualifications and achievements of state directors, and indicating the steps being taken to correct certain inevitable errors:

It is true that under pressure of getting as many people as possible to work at the earliest possible moment our directors were unable to be as careful in their selection as might have been desirable. Unquestionably, a number of people from the relief rolls of lesser qualifications were taken on

685

at the beginning. The situation is gradually being corrected. Those that are less competent to do the work are being shifted to other projects and more competent people are being taken on.[29]

The problems of large and thinly populated states with a dearth of writers were, if somewhat different, just as pressing as those of larger cities in which writers were concentrated. The state director of Texas candidly revealed in a letter to Alsberg the difficulties that arose from a dearth of qualified personnel. Texas, to be sure, presented an unusual problem in that coverage of the state involved distances not readily conceived by the alien; yet, on the whole, the situation in Texas was duplicated in rural areas generally, even in those of states like Massachusetts and New York.

At the other extreme lay the "state" of New York City, where, as Alsberg wrote to the Massachusetts director, there were "too many applicants."[30] Orrick Johns, the first director of the writers' project in New York City, writes in his autobiography a sensitive and spirited account of the first year and a half of the project's life:

> We began work on the WPA newspaper project in September, 1935, with one supervisor and ten assistants. The ten were chosen from recommendations of the Newspaper Guild, the Authors' League and the New York Writers' Union. We faced the task of interviewing hundreds of unclassified people who declared they were writers. Office space was scarce, so we sent to the old 69th Regiment Armory on Lexington Avenue and 26th street. In that draughty arena, where our staff looked the pygmies they felt, the unemployed writers filed past and related their sorry tales. To most of them we could hold out no hope of employment. There were dozens of applications for every job provided. Writers were hired in two classes: legmen at $21.67 a week and "editors" at $23.86 a week.
>
> Records of long unemployment, of jobs on vanished publications and claims of hidden creative talent predominated. Official orders said, "Get to work." There was no time to check on skills and reliability. Most of the people we selected could show newspaper experience; and our business, to start with, was reporting the WPA projects.[31]

Texas and New York City represented extremes. Other state offices lay somewhere between the two. It is clear enough, however, that the material for the guides when it arrived at the state offices was rough in form and imposed upon the state editorial staffs a task in composition and editing that in many cases exceeded their capacity. The failure of the state offices to achieve a finished product threw upon the national office an editorial and literary burden, which, although it was within the ability of the national staff to assume, overtaxed their strength and diverted their attention from administrative concerns.

## THE WPA WRITERS' PROGRAM UNDER STATE CONTROL

The end of Federal One at the close of August, 1939, meant that the authority of the national office of the Writers' Project, like that of the arts projects, was reduced to that of advice to the state offices. In effect, there was no longer one Writers' Project but as many projects as there were state offices, each independent of the others. John D. Newsom, who became the national director of the project upon Alsberg's resignation in the spring of 1939, expressed the position of the Washington office as follows:

> The National staff of the WPA Writers' Program functions as follows: Reads manuscripts for style and policy. Acts in advisory capacity to projects in the states and District of Columbia. Suggests nationwide publications such as the Encyclopedia Series; History of Grazing, Place Name Series, state picture books, and recreational pamphlets. Issues technical manuals to provide uniform methodology in research compilation, and preparation of material so that publications of any series will be standard in format and table of contents.[32]

Under the new program each state project operated on a statewide basis, and was required to have a state body as official sponsor (since the Works Progress Administration no longer acted as official federal sponsor). The official state sponsors might be individuals (governors, secretaries of state, state librarians, etc.) or bodies (state departments of education, state universities, etc.). These state sponsors were official but inactive, and merely served as the source of legal authority. The active sponsors were the so-called co-sponsors (state or local public bodies) or, more often, the co-operating sponsors (quasi-public or non-profit private agencies).*

Newsom conceived, and rightly, the completion of the Guide series as his major responsibility. After 1939, therefore, the emphasis was not upon innovation but upon consummation. To be sure, in those states where the state guide had already been finished, other auxiliary and subsidiary projects (like local guides, folklore studies, etc.) were prosecuted; but here again the stress was upon continuation of operation rather than the elaboration of new projects. Such new projects as were initiated were those which appealed to the several states (which now

*Vide supra, pp.

687

possessed ultimate authority) as immediately useful. Among these were picture books, recreational booklets, children's stories, school texts, etc. Some of these products, especially those in the educational field, were not without worth; the grand design of the federal period, however, was abandoned, and the panoramic concept of America reinterpreted gave way to the idea of the immediately and narrowly useful.

## THE WPA WRITERS' PROGRAM AND THE WAR

This change in emphasis in the Writers' Program, as in the other arts programs, was immediately due to the transfer of the arts projects from federal to state control. It was not long, however, before the emergency created by the international situation forced the redirection of the program in the interest of national defense. As has already been indicated, Colonel Harrington, as early as May, 1940, suggested priority for those projects that would aid the defense program; and in June of the same year Florence Kerr requested a similar emphasis in the professional and service program.

The Writers' Program, no less than the other arts programs, hastened to adapt itself to the new situation. As early as September, 1939, on the very morrow of the German invasion of Poland, Newsom wrote to Mrs. Kerr.

> In case of National Emergency I believe that the Work Projects Administration Writers' Program, acting in conjunction with the state-wide Writers' Projects, is in a position to render the following services:
>
> 1. Survey and report upon racial minority groups with particular reference to their geographic distribution and degree of integration.
>
> 2. Gather information on a county-wide basis (in collaboration with the Historical Records Survey) as to distribution of population, crops, timber, and mineral resources.
>
> 3. Prepare detailed description of highways and connecting routes; of airport facilities; of other means of transportation. (Railroads and bus depots, etc.)
>
> 4. Prepare maps of special areas.
>
> 5. Prepare special copy for posters, broadsheets, etc.
>
> 6. Prepare and disseminate information relative to conservation of food and other resources.
>
> 7. Prepare scenarios and continuities; also radio information service.
>
> 8. Undertake informational and survey work for government and other agencies.

9. Assist in gathering information for use in preparation of releases for magazines and newspapers.

10. Prepare military histories of states.[33]

A year later, an effort was made to evaluate the Writers' Program—not only what was being attempted, but also what had already been accomplished—in terms of national defense:

> The Writers' Program can perform a defense service which no other existing apparatus can undertake. It can supply cultural content to patriotism. The books of the Writers' Program have provided a realistic basis for patriotic feeling: they reveal the multitudinous life of America that rolls out behind the flag. By creating a sense of community growth, the American Guide Series has tended to counteract impulses arising from blind personal interest. We have placed before the people an accumulation of cultural experience specifically American. Awareness of a unified tradition is the most powerful stimulus to integrated action. Patriotism cannot be deeply founded upon ritual and symbol alone.
>
> The Writers' Program can . . . popularize a knowledge of those community backgrounds which are referred to in all present-day discussions of American values . . . the books of the Writers' Program have done much to make America conscious of the early settlers as living ancestors, and of the country today as the accomplishments of the efforts of generations. . . .
>
> The Writers' Program will bring out a series of 46 uniform State reference books acquainting the people with practical and cultural facts about their communities; numerous volumes portraying the rise of cities and towns, their personalities and intimate lives, and what native and immigrant groups have contributed to them; stories of men at work in the fields and factories, giving a dramatic picture of skills, processes, and backgrounds; dictionaries of the biographies of men and women distinguished in their localities; books dealing with influences as diverse as grazing in the West and architecture in rural Kansas; illustrated volumes, monographs, brochures describing handicrafts in New Hampshire, fiestas in New Mexico, old cattle trails, river shipping, folk songs in Virginia, Tarheel tales, legends of Indians, turpentine and fishing in Florida, tobacco people in North Carolina, Negroes in Little Rock; a nation-wide series of picture books displaying through words and photographs the distinctive features and beauties of each of the States.
>
> These works . . . are sure to create a strong, perhaps because indirect, effect upon the attitudes of people in time of emergency.[34]

When, therefore, in December, 1941, Japan attacked Pearl Harbor, the Writers' Program was ready both psychologically and administratively to further the war effort. On December 12, 1941, Newsom wrote:

> . . . The Writers' Program can be of immediate assistance in the present war emergency by
>
> (1) explaining and interpreting national policies to local communities of

many different types, through trained personnel residing in these communities and intimately acquainted with local attitudes and problems, and by

(2) providing a continuous flow of information from the "grass roots" to Washington on all matters that must be considered if national policies are to be intelligently shaped and adjusted to fit particular local situations.[35]

By February, 1942, the plans of the Writers' Program for aiding in the prosecution of the war had taken form. In that month Stella B. Hanau wrote to George F. Willison of the Washington office:

> Writers' Program will take following direction: 1) Assistance to national, regional, state and local defense organizations, governmental agencies, and defense projects by making available to them the services of trained writers, editors, and research workers.[36]

It was suggested that these activities be prosecuted under such agencies as Civilian Defense, Armed Forces, Government Units, and Civic Organizations; and that the services to be rendered include

> . . . pamphlets, flyers, bulletins, informational releases, feature articles, dramatic skits, pageants, recreational and other directories, service men's guides, histories and descriptions of ethnic and language groups, dictionaries of technical terms, captions for exhibits, picture books and collections of photographs for exhibit purposes, elementary readers and curriculum material, health almanacs, agricultural and home garden bulletins, "how to do" information, background and source material on current problems, etc. . . .
>
> (2) Compilation of data and contribution of manuscripts to significant program publications. . . .[37]

With regard to projects of a non-defense character, the Writers' Program was advised:

> (1) Limit completion of work in progress to those important books which are almost finished and under contract to publishers, or for which publication is assured.
>
> (2) Curtail county histories, local guides. . . .[38]

Finally, the state offices were directed to suspend or discontinue publications that "do not directly build morale or promote the public welfare."[39]

The defense publications of the Program, known as the "National Defense Series," included guides to military and naval areas, as well as guides to service academies, and a series of State Health almanacs. The *Foreign Language Press*, published by the New York City Project, was of particular value to a number of federal agencies, including the

War Department, the Navy Department, the Department of Justice, and the Office of Facts and Figures. Pamphlets were prepared listing educational films important for war work; the New York City Project wrote pamphlets designed to assist various municipal departments in meeting emergencies. Booklets on aviation, mechanics, radio, and military histories, radio scripts, and general publications stressing the nature and advantages of American democracy were also issued.

The experience of the Writers' Program after 1939 was so colored by the imminence and then the impact of war that a fair comparison between the periods of federal and state control is difficult. It is tempting to believe that the kinds of activity that the states devised after 1939 were precisely those which they would have prosecuted in 1935, had the choice then been theirs. Certainly the several states, each acting according to its own provincial needs and desires, would not have achieved a national synthesis such as the Guides manifested. On the other hand, the state in the nation in 1939 was not what it was in 1935; by the later date work relief was subtly but surely yielding to war services, and the freedom to devise cultural programs, which the states would have possessed in 1935, was now circumscribed by the necessity to further national defense.

1. Memorandum, Local 1, United Federal Workers of America to Kerr, August 4, 1939, FWP Files.

2. Memorandum, Alsberg to Westbrook, January 25, 1936, FWP Files.

3. "Transcript of Conference at Home of B. A. Botkin, June 6, 1943," ACLS Files.

4. *Ibid.*

5. *Ibid.*

6. Memorandum, Cronyn to E. M. Williams, January 8, 1937, FWP Files.

7. Letter, Alsberg to Eric Branham, September 20, 1935, FWP Files.

8. Letters, Alsberg to Henderson and Frankfurter, October 8, 1935, FWP Files.

9. Letter, Cronyn to Lovett, September 12, 1935, FWP Files.

10. Letter, Earl Minderman to Mildred Thrasher, January 27, 1940, FWP Files.

11. Letter, W. T. Couch to Harold W. Landin, June 7, 1943, ACLS Files.

12. "Status of Federal Writers' Projects throughout the Country," n.d. (October, 1935?), FWP Files.

13. Letter, Alsberg to Floyd Sharp, April 4, 1936, WPA Files.

14. Letter, Darel McConkey to L. W. Burns, Mrs. Eva Wilson Crane, and James C. Herbert, March 1, 1936, FWP Files.

15. Federal Writers' Project, WPA, *These Are Our Lives* (Chapel Hill: University of North Carolina Press, 1939), Preface.

16. Letter, Couch to William R. McDaniel, April 17, 1939, FWP Files.

17. Letter, Couch to Alsberg, October 29, 1938, FWP Files.

18. Letter, Alsberg to Margaret C. Klem, September 18, 1935, FWP Files.
19. Letter, Alsberg to Patrick A. Morgan, September 17, 1935, FWP Files.
20. Letter, Alsberg to Harold Preece, October 7, 1935, FWP Files.
21. Letter, Harris to Blair Bolles, December 6, 1937, FWP Files.
22. Letter, Alsberg to Arnold E. Severeid, February 23, 1937, FWP Files.
23. Presidential Letter No. 321, August 29, 1935.
24. *Supplement No. 1 to Bulletin No. 29*, WPA, September 30, 1935, Section 3.
25. *Ibid.*, Section 11.
26. "Status of Federal Writers' Projects throughout the Country," n.d. (October, 1935?), FWP Files.
27. *Ibid.*
28. Letter, George Creel to Hopkins, December 14, 1935, FWP Files.
29. Memorandum, Alsberg to Baker, December 24, 1935, FWP Files.
30. Letter, Alsberg to Shipton, November 15, 1935, FWP Files.
31. Orrick Jones, *Times of Our Lives, the Story of My Father and Myself* (New York: Stackpole Sons, 1937), pp. 341-50.
32. Memorandum, Newsom to Triggs, March 1, 1940, FWP Files.
33. Memorandum, Newsom to Kerr, September 9, 1939, FWP Files.
34. Memorandum, Greene to Brummett, September 12, 1940, FWP Files.
35. Memorandum, Newsom to Walter Kiplinger, December 12, 1941, FWP Files.
36. Memorandum, Stella B. Hanau to Willison, February 7, 1942, FWP Files.
37. *Ibid.*
38. *Ibid.*
39. *Ibid.*

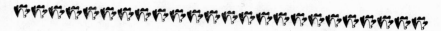

# 28

# The Program of the Federal Writers' Project

The core of the program of the Federal Writers' Project was the American Guide. According to the American Guide Manual, "The American Guide is a Federal Writers' Project sponsored by the WPA."[1] The word *guide* here denotes an activity rather than a product. In the original plan the American Guide was contemplated as one of several projects. As the Guide became the principal project activity, the *s* in *projects* was omitted, and the Federal Writers' Project came to stand for an organization rather than an activity. In time other activities than the Guide were undertaken by the Writers' Project, although the Guide always maintained its primacy. At the same time, the American Guide, originally conceived as a five-volume guide with each volume devoted to a separate region, was displaced by the American Guide Series, which consisted of state and local guides. The original American Guide, either as a single volume or as a five-volume regional set, never progressed beyond the conceptual stage.

The origin of the American Guide may be traced to the *Connecticut Guide* and, ultimately, to Baedeker, though, as has been indicated above, the idea of American guidebooks as a relief project seems to have occurred independently to several persons in 1934 and 1935. About the development of the American Guide from a mere Baedeker into a series of state encyclopedias, we have little information.

With reference to the inspiration of the American Guide, Reed Harris wrote:

No one individual can be credited with originating the idea of the guide.

693

However, the guide idea was originated before this Project was begun. Under the FERA a guide was prepared in the State of Connecticut by relief workers. The idea had been put into effect by Mr. Jacob Baker, then Assistant Administrator, but he was influenced by the ideas of Mr. Alsberg, Mr. George W. Cronyn (Editorial Consultant of the Federal Writers' Project) and Mrs. Katherine Kellock (Tour Editor of the Federal Writers' Project at present). I cannot properly speak for Mrs. Woodward or even for Mr. Alsberg as to what they think is the guide's chief virtue. I can say, however, that Mr. Alsberg feels that it is making an important contribution to our contemporary culture. We both feel that it is bringing about a sort of rediscovery of America not only by the people who use the books but by the many writers who have participated in the preparation of them. Already some novels and short stories and articles have been prepared by workers of the Project or formerly of the Project indicating a new interest in all the nooks and crannies of the country.[2]

The concept of the Guide's purpose differed within the project. Alsberg regarded it as primarily cultural and indeed creative, whereas Cronyn was more inclined to look at it from the point of view of an encyclopedist. Harris seems to have acted as a balance between these two emphases.

Alsberg's idea of the purpose was expressed on various occasions. In a letter dated April 3, 1937, he wrote:

> We are all surprised by the high literary quality, color, and interest there is in these guides that are nearing completion. A great deal of creative effort has gone into them, both into the essays and into the material of the cities and tours. I think there has been a rather false assumption by many people that these guides consist entirely of dull hack work. There is a good deal of dull technical detail, but the actual body of the job is, in most cases, very well done and colorful.[3]

Again, in testifying before the Sirovich Committee in February, 1938, Alsberg said:

> Of course, I also want to correct or dissipate the impression that these guidebooks have no creative side to them. They have. We demand that color and imagination and vividness be used in the descriptions. The first third of the book usually consists of essays on art, literature, history, industry, commerce, and all of the cultural background, the folklore of the State. And merely because a man does not write a novel does not brand him as a "hack." It is perhaps more difficult, for instance, to write an interesting and beautifully done essay than a novel. Even within the framework of the tours, I insist that interest and vividness be preserved. The tour form is a difficult form; it is like a sonnet; but, if you can learn it, you can be more interesting in the description of a tour than in any novel. I have told that to our writers—that there is no reason why they cannot use their creative abilities, even on these guidebooks.[4]

694

He was equally emphatic regarding the cultural significance of the guides:

> We in America have concentrated so actively on the exploitation of our natural resources for industrial and agricultural purposes that until recently, when technological unemployment created the problem and the opportunity, we have not thought it worth while to spare the time to chart our cultural, scenic, archeological, or even industrial and commercial facilities. Scattered throughout the large territory of the United States are hundreds of communities with distinctive features and with special values, but for lack of knowledge of them scholars and educators, tourists and merchants, sportsmen and recreation hunters have ignored the natural and cultural advantages of the United States in favor of the carefully exploited features of similar nature in foreign countries.[5]

The cultural value lay, Alsberg believed, in the evocation of local atmosphere and color:

> Unlike the usual commercial guide book publishers, the Federal Writers' Projects have been able to follow a method which allows definite local color and feeling to penetrate into the guides—material has actually been collected locally, on the spot, by Guide workers who are native to the location and catch its real spirit. This local material has been assembled in state editorial offices and rearranged and rewritten somewhat, but there has been constant attention to the problem of catching and keeping the local color.[6]

Cronyn on the other hand, was less imaginative than his chief. He possessed to an unusual degree the editorial gift of using works like bricks to build a structure, provided that the concept of the structure was presented to him. But he lacked the gift for imaginative writing as distinguished from correct composition. Undoubtedly, his editorial work with the *Columbia Encyclopedia* gave him this concentration on detail. But quite apart from differences of nature, Cronyn differed with Alsberg on questions of basic policy. In the first place, he was not impressed by the director's plan for regional guides, partly because he felt that the regions as established—except perhaps New England and the Old South—did not represent cultural unities, and partly because he doubted the suitability of the region as an administrative unit. His presentation of the case in July and August, 1935, persuaded Alsberg to choose the state rather than the region as the administrative unit; but it was not until several months had passed that Alsberg abandoned his idea of regional guides. In general, Cronyn had a keener concept of administrative procedure than did the national director and also a more practical understanding of the difficulties, both editorial and administrative, that were likely to arise. Alsberg may well have interpreted his cautions as an indication of lack of enthusiasm. At any rate, relations between the two became less cordial, and Cronyn was shortly deprived of his administrative authority and served thenceforth in an editorial capacity.

In the end Cronyn was justified, for the director's plan—that regional guides should be written first, and state and local guides later—did not achieve fulfilment. As the project developed, the very exigencies of the program and the very nature of the machinery through which the program operated made it expedient to publish first local and state guides. The regional guides were never published; but if time and opportunity had allowed, they would have come last.

Local guides were published first for the simple reason that they were finished first. Moreover, from the point of view of public relations, local and state guides were preferable to regional guides. State lines may be imaginary, but a state government is not; moreover, states, since they are political sovereignties, provide an object of loyalty that regions do not. By promising each state a guide, and by persuading not only each state administration but also other organizations based on state or local boundaries that the guide would benefit them commercially as well as culturally, the national office of the Writers' Project was able, for the most part, to secure support and sponsorship.

### CREATIVE WORK

From first to last the Federal Writers' Project was under pressure from writers and writers' organizations to employ project workers in creative work. Indeed, in the FERA period a working procedure, "Individual Projects for Writers," permitted "writers to execute individual projects on subjects of their own selection." If any commissions for creative writing were given to individuals, no evidence of them or of products resulting from them appears in the files. These projects, as contemplated in the FERA period, seem to have been conceived as fellowships, and provided that an advisory committee of competent judges approve the applicant's qualifications, subject, and plan of work.

Katherine Kellock has indicated how the idea of creative work as a principal activity suggested itself and was abandoned early in the program:

As the Works Progress Administration took shape, friends of the arts,

696

especially in the influential metropolitan areas, began to dream dreams and see visions. Having heard of genius starving, and holding a low opinion of entrepeneurs in the arts fields, they seized on the new work program as the solution to the Latin Quarter's perpetual problem of finding the means for food and shelter—and also an unfailing patron. Almost every worthwhile artist could qualify for work relief, they assured one another, and soon the federal government would be fathering and producing the masterpieces— dramas, pictures, novels, operas, epic poems—a crude commercial world had scorned.

The champions of an arts program reached a sympathetic ear in Washington and were told to draw up projects. It was not long, however, before they learned that all programs had to be passed by a control board uninterested in art for art's sake and well aware that even the federal projects would have to have local approval. The writing of novels, plays, and poetry as a major activity of a writers' project was ruled out almost immediately. Hundreds of plans were rejected before the guide program was reluctantly submitted. The chief comfort the champions of the arts could find in the plan was that the guides might be largely essays in which brilliant staffs could turn a blinding searchlight on America; it was a minor consolation that the program was not so rigid as not to leave quiet niches in which at least a few geniuses could be sheltered; and finally, it was remembered that, thanks to the A.F. of L. unions' demands for an hourly pay rate for their members in line with union scales, all project hours would be short, and employees would have ample time in which to write fiction and poetry.[7]

When the WPA was established, projects for individuals who wished to undertake creative work of a solitary nature were rejected. A typical reply to such a request, many of which were made, follows:

> There is no provision in the Federal Writers' Projects, as approved by the President, for subsidizing writers to do creative writing. It is the general opinion here that the projects which we have set up, the chief of which is the American Guide, will provide a security wage for writers and still give them plenty of leisure to do their own creative work. The writers on the Federal Projects work only thirty hours a week. Their assignments are not very difficult—gathering data and writing articles for the Guide, between 1200 and 2000 words weekly. Any experienced author can turn out his stint in very short order and without exhausting himself to such an extent that his energy for creative writing will be diminished.*[8]

But if projects for creative writing as such were outlawed, the central office was not without sympathy for those who talents lay in that direction. A consideration of public relations counseled caution, as Jacob Baker perceived, for the subsidization of poets and novelists

---

*As the letter states, there was no authority for a subsidy as such. On the other hand, there was nothing in the Presidential Letter to prevent the Writers' Project from allowing, if it so chose, a writer in its employ to compose poetry or create a novel. This kind of activity was ruled out as a matter of policy and not by reason of superior administration limitations. The determination to give priority to the guides precluded projects for individuals.

might well have offended a rather general demand that those on relief be subject to discipline. In a speech in 1936 Baker said:

> The federal government as an employer starts not with work which it wishes to have done, but with workers, who have certain abilities. It will not do to confine our employment to construction jobs if that will leave unemployed all the white collar workers on the relief rolls. . . .
>
> To many people of the favored economic groups it seems desirable that a destitute person shall be disciplined. The discipline they think of is manual labor. They like the idea of putting a musician who is broke down in a sewer or putting a child psychologist at a sewing machine. This brutal attitude of manual discipline which is abroad in the Western world is a prime ingredient of Fascism and Nazism. Fortunately, it has not thus far controlled our work program but it is becoming more articulate and its spread from business to politics may have to be reckoned with seriously.[9]

The co-operative effort that the Guide demanded served as a kind of white-collar discipline. The individual was subordinated to the group, and the creative concept to that of the socially useful. At the same time certain discretionary powers and privileges were granted to the more creative-minded state directors and project workers. It was important, however, that this freedom not be abused. Cronyn wrote to a state director, less amenable to discipline than most, as follows:

> Referring to the statement in your letter of October 20, State directors are given *certain* discretionary powers but these powers are limited and definitely so, and have been from the beginning, just as our powers here are discretionary to a certain degree but are definitely limited.
>
> We have tried to combine considerable allowance for variations in States with the necessity for having books of a definite standard of quality and of uniform makeup and organization. To have done anything else would have reduced this whole project to complete chaos.
>
> Realizing the particular difficulties and circumstances in Idaho, we gave you greater leeway in the arrangement of your material and treatment than we have given any other State director in the country. But it seems to me you have been under a misapprehension as to the fundamental character of this work in that you have treated your share of it as a personal and private enterprise. This matter I pointed out before and will have to repeat—that the project, financed by public money, cannot, and must not, be taken as merely the vehicle of expression for an individual creative writer, no matter how high his standing.[10]

Within certain limitations, however, creative writing was allowed and even encouraged; but to avoid abuse, such assignments were made only with the approval of the national director. The general procedure is thus expressed by Alsberg:

698

As to No. 15 on this list, please note that creative writing, as a proposal of work, should not, for reasons of office routine, be advertised among workers, lest too many ask to be thus employed. No. 15 should apply in special cases, to persons of merit based on known scholarship or record of authorship, who would pursue a creative task of definite prospective value if their subsistence were paid them. It would be well to consult this office before granting periodical payment in such a case. Please report who are already working on this basis.[11]

The number so assigned, however, was very limited, as the following letter indicates:

Mr. Alsberg received recently a letter written January 5th to Miss Mary Siegrist, one of the writers on your staff. Miss Siegrist asks for reassignment to the creative writing group.

Since Miss Siegrist is apparently an established writer with a definite record of published material, chiefly poetry, Mr. Alsberg feels that she should be considered in case the creative writers group is ever expanded. Mr. Alsberg has explained to Miss Siegrist that there is very little chance of such a development.[12]

It was decided early in the project's life, nonetheless, to publish a magazine as an outlet for creative work done on the project. For this reason, the project was combed for writers with the appropriate talent. Alsberg wrote a memorandum to Reed Harris, who evidently was to supervise the venture, in which the outline of the program is adumbrated:

I have looked over the work of the four writers who have applied for creative writing jobs on your force—Fanya Foss, Israel Sandrof, Helen Neville, and Philip Sterling.

I think Fanya Foss the most promising of the lot, I distinctly recommend that she be put at creative writing. Sandrof comes next, although I do not think his work nearly as original or interesting. I think he also should be put at creative writing. I don't care much about Helen Neville's prose, and her poetry—although I am not a judge of poetry—seems to me rather imitative and commonplace. However, I think she should get a job at creative writing, as well. Philip Sterling seems to me nothing but a person engaged in pamphleteering of a rather third rate type.

We have decided to make Karl Schriftgiesser editor of our magazine.

Might I keep Sandrof's specimens of writing for consideration as contributions to the magazine? I am keeping Neville's CORRUPTED HEART, POEM, EPITAPH FOR A SELFISH WOMAN, MAN ALL TO BODY GONE, POEM, TIMES EMBRACE, as none of these seems to have yet been published. Would it be possible for Fanya Foss to write something for the first issue? I am returning the magazines in which her work appears, also those of Helen Neville's poems which apparently have been published. The fragments of her novel I am also returning, as I do not consider them particularly available for our proposed publication. I am also returning Philip Sterling's clippings.[13]

This program never materialized. However, in 1937 the Viking Press published *American Stuff*, an anthology of prose and verse by members of the Federal Writers' Project (with sixteen prints by the Federal Art Project). The publication was sponsored by the Guild's Committee for Federal Writers' Publications, Inc. In his foreword to this volume, Alsberg nicely states the problem:

The Federal Writers' Project has been faced with peculiar difficulties in bringing its creative work before the public. Musicians can and do reach a vast audience through a variety of media: symphony orchestras, string quartets, choruses, bands, music dramas. Actors appear in plays; and the influence of the Federal Theatre, exemplified in a series of plays which have been boldly and intelligently chosen, resourcefully produced, and vigorously acted, has already made a very deep dent in the traditional and rather desiccated Broadway stage. The Federal Artists, through their exhibitions and mural displays, have acquainted millions with the vitality and power of contemporary American art.

The Writers' Project, unfortunately, has been handicapped in several directions. It has produced a considerable number of publications—in August, 1937, these totaled more than five million words—which have been on the whole favorably reviewed and welcomed by a large public, local and national. But these publications have been semi-utilitarian in character—guide books for the most part, in which the creative element is present only incidentally. These guide books are unique, the project believes, in that they attempt to organize a broad cultural picture of the American scene, past and present—its folkways, its social, political, and industrial economy, side by side with the more usual scenic and historic features. In this form, which sets rather rigid limitations, the creative writer functions with difficulty; but he has been responsible for a good deal of the originality, color, vividness, and humor evident in the guide books. However, our workshops have produced as yet no one publication, national in scope, devoted to work of a purely creative character.

Various explanations may be advanced for this failure. There is plenty of first-rate talent among our writers and this talent demands an outlet. Unfortunately a writer's work does nobody any good until it is published. But the Federal Government provides no facilities or funds for publication of Federal Writers' manuscripts except, to a very limited extent, in the case of a few of the National Guide Series. All state and local guide books are published at the expense of sponsors. Why could not such sponsors be found for creative work as well? The answer is that states and cities and towns are directly interested in their local guides. Sponsors are willing to invest money in such books because they are reasonably assured that sales will reimburse them. One such local guide has already run through sixteen thousand copies; another, a large city guide, sold ten thousand copies before publication. The Washington, District of Columbia, volume bids fair to exhaust an edition of eight thousand copies three months after publication date. But in the case of an anthology of prose and verse, such as the present collection, someone must be found to undertake the risk. The same statement applies as to the possibility of publishing longer manuscripts: novels, plays, books on history, sociology, political economy.

In this connection we are faced with a further, almost insurmountable obstacle. All manuscripts produced on project time become government property. Quite naturally, very few of our writers care to risk a possible best-seller as a contribution to the United States Treasury. The top security wage of one hundred and three dollars and fifty cents a month would scarcely compensate a writer for a best-seller, or a successful Broadway play, or even the motion-picture rights to a mediocre product in these categories. Consequently, most of our personnel have done creative work only in their leisure time; and while there have been a good many novels, plays, and miscellaneous manuscripts published by members of the staff—the project shelves are crowded with autographed copies of these works—they have contributed little, and that only indirectly, to the reputation of the project. Except for books turned out by a group or by individuals at work on definite undertakings planned and directed by members of the staffs, work usually of a more or less utilitarian character, we cannot hope to get long and important manuscripts in the creative field.

There remains only the possibility of procuring verse, short stories, essays, and excerpts from unpublished novels. Here again the logical outlet for this type of work has been closed to us. For more than a year and a half we have tried to initiate a national magazine, but complications of one sort or another have choked off this enterprise in spite of an insistent and overwhelming demand by staff members all over the country. Manuscripts, often accompanied by letters of protest, have piled up in our Washington offices. In many states, the project workers have turned to on their own time and produced local magazines, usually with begged or borrowed equipment. Some of these, notably a magazine sponsored by the very talented California group, have been well received by the local press. But the general public hears little of this; and the impression persists that our writers are incapable of producing anything but guides and the other less creative types of publications.

Finally, as a desperate remedy the National Director of the project called for contributions of off-time work, to be published if and when a sponsor willing to gamble on an anthology could be found. Hundreds of manuscripts flowed in from all parts of the country; but many of our best writers, discouraged by false alarms too often repeated, failed to take the call seriously and sent nothing or only material shopworn with rejections. The general quality, however, was surprisingly high; and, what was even more interesting, we found that the average unemployed writer was concerned not with the remote aspects and far islands of existence, but with the realities of the American here-and-now. This has been true of the Art Project contributions as well. Apparently these young artists and writers are preoccupied with life as they have known it, with what they have seen and felt, with the tough sledding which constitutes American experience for millions of people today.

In this book the reader will find comparatively little to remind him of the classics, little echo of the higher aestheticism or the delicate attenuations of emotion. This is the American scene to the life, very often as it appears from the roadside ditch, the poverty-stricken tenement or shack, the relief station. The style is sometimes crude, the technique often perhaps inexpert or diffuse; but there is sincerity in it, a solid passionate feeling for the life of the less prosperous millions.[14]

As a sequel to *American Stuff* a number of magazines published special issues devoted to Writers' Project off-time work. Among these were *Poetry*, the *New Republic*, the *Nation*, the *New Masses*, and the *Frontier*. The most notable special issue was that of *Direction*, Vol. I, No. 3, 1938, which appeared after negotiations with two other magazines, *Story Magazine* and the *American Quarterly*, had failed. The success of the issue was attested by the fact that 5,000 copies were sold in two months. The introduction by the editors of *Direction* and the editorial, "Literature without Money," by Harold Rosenberg, Writers' Project editor of the issue, emphasized the twofold value of the experiment as (1) testimony of the cultural significance of the Writers' Project and (2) representative of the stimulation that the project provided for creative writing. With regard to the first point, the editors of *Direction* wrote:

> There could be no more eloquent testimony to the cultural significance of the WPA than the fact that, for the first time in American history, a magazine can present material maintaining such a high degree of excellence which was made possible by government employment. Men and women whose economic position would have stunted and warped their creative faculties have been enabled to achieve a means of expression. The full promise of the Federal Writers' Project has not yet been envisioned; now it can but suggest a new life, a new age in American letters. Out of it may emerge a true people's literature. In the fight for democracy the American people are slowly forging a cultural front. Here is its vanguard.[15]

As to the second point, Mr. Rosenberg wrote:

> The Federal Writers' undertook to alleviate the financial unemployment of writers by providing them with paid work. To the creative writer this was but half a solution. While he might now continue to perfect his art in his spare time, the continued exhaustion of independent literary enterprise provided little opportunity for new beginnings.
> Endowment of the producers of letters and the endowment of literary conscience-publications were thus seen to be a single need—the need of literature to reproduce itself constantly under conditions free of economic constraint.
> The anthology *American Stuff* presented a collection of the off-time writings of the Federal Writers. Now once more—through the sponsorship of the Guild's Committee for Federal Writers' Publications, Inc., and the generous support of the publishers of *Direction*—the Federal Writers offer their spare time work to the public.
> The present selection differs from earlier little magazine issues in that it came into being not as the result of a theoretical or esthetic grouping, but through an economic predicament. But if the employment of all its contributors on Federal Project No. 1 does not confer upon them an esthetic unity,

it does immerse them in a common social experience from which a special literary emphasis may well arise. In some contributors a new attentiveness to and consciousness of the people and problems of America are already visible. Others achieve their value within more familiar modes. We trust that the means will be found to present further collections in the future so that the direction in which their thought is moving may become explicit. In any case, all are exercising literary skill on a level which justifies broad communication and response.[16]

Following this issue of *Direction*, plans were set up for an "American Stuff" magazine to be sponsored by the Guild's Committee and to be edited from Washington with the assistance of a board of editors representing "about ten of the most important points in America," including California, Iowa, Illinois, Arizona, Michigan, Ohio, Georgia, Louisiana, Pennsylvania, Massachusetts, and New York. The magazine was to be self-supporting and was to contain contributions by writers outside the project as well as off-time writing by project workers.[17] Although considerable material was collected, the magazine was never published.

Under the head of creative and semi-creative work are also to be included a number of special, local, and miscellaneous productions (some of which, of course, never reached the publication stage), such as almanacs (notably, *Almanac for New Yorkers*, 1937, 1938, and 1939), plays, radio plays, and pageants, and collections of local tales, legends, life histories, and interviews (especially, *These Are Our Lives* and *God Bless the Devil!*).

An example of off-time creative work made possible by the project is seen in *Bowleg Bill*, by Jeremiah Digges (Josef Berger). In the acknowledgment Berger writes:

> For the opportunity to work which has made this book possible, acknowledgment is due the Federal Writers' Project, Works Progress Administration for the State of Massachusetts. The book was written as an "off-time" work, over a period in which employment and subsistence were provided the writer, through fulfilment of regular assignments as a member of the Project. Thus, for the chance to support a family and concurrently carry to completion a work which might otherwise have been impossible, this acknowledgment is made.[18]

In an indirect way creative writing was also stimulated by a variety of lesser devices, such as encouraging project workers to submit scripts to the Federal Theater Project, constructively criticizing manuscripts submitted to the Washington office, and encouraging project workers to try for prizes and awards. Among these were the $500 prize awarded by *Story Magazine* to Richard Wright in 1938 for the best manuscript submitted by a WPA worker, and the Guggenheim fellowships awarded to Richard Wright, Sterling A. Brown, Josef Berger (Jeremiah Digges), Jack Conroy, Kenneth Patchen, and Kenneth Fearing.*

### FOLKLORE STUDIES

Among the working procedures of the FERA was one (WDO-21, F8.5) that provided for the collection and study of folklore. When in 1935 the concept of the Guide became primary, the emphasis upon folklore was not slighted, for a proper consideration of that subject was deemed an integral part of the Guide treatment. Moreover, in the first year of the Federal Writers' Project several proposals for folklore projects were submitted by Roland P. Gray, Joseph Gaer, Mrs. Nina Otero-Warren, and Jean Thomas. From June 25, 1936, to October 23, 1937 (with a ninety-day furlough beginning July 24, 1937), John A. Lomax, honorary curator of the archive of American folk song in the Library of Congress, was national advisor on folklore and folkways, on the payroll of the Historical Records Survey. He was succeeded by Benjamin A. Botkin (on leave from the University of Oklahoma) as folklore consultant from May 2, 1938, to July 31, 1938, and folklore editor from August 1, 1938, to August 31, 1939.

On March 12, 1936, the national office issued its first formal instructions on folklore collection. The emphasis here was on collecting folklore for use in the state guides, and hence on local customs and place lore:

*This creative activity, as has already been emphasized, owed most to the sympathetic and consistent encouragement of the national director. Cronyn, on the other hand, was unimpressed by the creative accomplishments of the project. It is true, to be sure, that, among those who were assigned creative tasks, some—and, indeed, some from whom much was expected—abused the privilege and, if they worked, worked for themselves rather than for the project. This sort of malingering, however, occurs universally on all sorts of jobs, and not least on fellowships, and the Writers' Project cannot be justly criticized because it suffered from an endemic malady.

On the other hand, Cronyn was attracted by the "primitive" character of some of the copy that found its way into the central office from local offices, and thought specimens of it worthy of preservation. His suggestion was not followed. As a matter of fact, much of the primitive stuff never moved beyond the state offices, the staffs of which were reluctant to send to Washington material whose quality did not meet the standards set by primers on grammar and composition.

704

An introductory essay will cover the field as a whole; in a state having large groups with different racial origins it may be necessary to subdivide the introductory essay to cover the topic for each large group. The bulk of the material will be used in connection with the sectional descriptions or place descriptions.

For the purposes of the State Guides folk customs are more important than folklore because they can be tied to one place, one section or one subject. . . .[19]

Because "the American Guide is being compiled primarily to introduce Americans to their own rich culture," the living rather than the nostalgic values of folklore were stressed. Of the two classes of folklorists, the antiquarians and those who might be termed the "contemporanians," the Writers' Project folklore collectors were more akin to the latter: " . . . They recognize the European origins of American culture but are interested in the mutations and developments wrought by transfer to a new and pioneer land."[20]

At the same time, workers were to employ scientific methods, including the "exact source of information," accurate and objective recording of interviews, and notes on variants and origins. The material was broken down in "divisions" under two heads: folk customs and folk tales.

The primacy of the Guide in the plan of the central office was responsible for the concept of folklore as tangential to the main project. It was not long, however, before the possibility of a folklore study in its own right presented itself. On July 27, 1936, further supplementary instructions were issued, which, in addition to adding "superstitions" to the categories already elaborated, subordinated the primary use of this material for the state guides to the idea of a "collection of national folklore": "In any case items gathered now will be a serviceable mine for folklorists and students of American life."[21]

On August 4, 1936, a sample guidebook essay, "Oklahoma Folklore and Folk Customs," was presented for the help of the state offices.*[22] It was followed eight days later by a letter from Alsberg that explained the central office's increasing concern for folklore:

I have recently sent you for the second time somewhat detailed instructions for the collection and assembling of material for the folklore and folk custom section of the Guide. In sending you the instructions and the sample article herewith enclosed, I wish to point out again that continuing the

*An earlier sample, "Iowa Folkways," was distributed on May 22, 1936, as part of *Supplementary Instructions No. 10 to the American Guide Manual, Appendix B.*

work of making as full a collection of folk material as possible in each State is important. There is in prospect the probability of our making a collection of national folklore. While use for the State Guide is the immediate consideration in covering the field, items too abundant for inclusion, except as summarized in an introductory essay or worked into place descriptions, will have great future value. Such an opportunity to collect this material may never recur.

In this kind of work, moreover, field employees can make a really effective contribution. Their local connections should give them invaluable knowledge of sources. Please bear in mind that this is a subject in which original investigation waits to be done.

I wish, therefore, to ask you to impress your district officials with the importance of having their field workers follow closely the outline in Supplementary Instructions No. 9-A. Each field worker should use the Instructions as a guide. Request should be made for each type of folk material mentioned, so as to be sure that every noteworthy item from each State is included. It is difficult to tell any field worker precisely when and through what sources he may discover interesting material. However, the suggestions made in the Instructions, based on actual field experience, I hope may be found useful and productive.

Especial care should be taken to see that the field worker gives the source of each item collected, whether from actual interview or from print—the time, place, person (giving age), book or periodical. Material sent in by field workers should be copied exactly as presented, and collected at the State office. It will, of course, be handled for use in the State Guide as the editor thinks advisable. But the original items as collected are the important source material of which future use will be made.

We have found that a number of State Directors have tried to limit material collected to that typical of their States. This, of course, is an impossible standard. While treatment in the State Guide will try to present the most individual features of material found in that State, collection is to be made of all kinds of material. Evaluation, conclusions as to the spread of customs and tales can be made only on a national basis.

The copy of the article from Oklahoma illustrates in general the scope and treatment of the Guide articles. It is not complete, covering only part of the State's material. It offers, however, a noteworthy example of how entertaining folklore may be. Naturally, wide variation from this sample my be expected.

Mr. John A. Lomax is now serving as our special consultant on folklore. He will read all material sent to the Washington office and assist with comment and suggestion. We shall want to see all field copy on this subject. We ask that you send in copies of whatever is now available, and that in the future material be sent in at regular intervals.[23]

From the material collected thus far it became evident that the Federal Writers' Project provided an exceptional and unique opportunity for a large-scale nationwide folklore collection. One desideratum of such a collection—familiarity with local sources and resources—was admirably fulfilled by the conditions of the Writers' Project, which permitted both extensive and intensive coverage of the field. Over against this advantage it was necessary to meet the limitations of an emergency organization—lack of technical training and supervision, instability of personnel, imperfect distribution of workers, improper facilities for handling and storing materials, duplication of effort, changes of policy, and sudden termination of projects. It was inevitable that the flavor of amateurism should pervade much of this work; on the other hand, there was the element of humanization in the influence of cooperation upon the worker and in his attitude toward folklore.

The need of training, therefore, was obvious. Further supplementary instructions issued October 21, 1936, caution workers against copying already published material: "Primarily we wish our material collected from *persons* and not from books."[24]

In the same instructions, it was also pointed out that certain kinds of material are not folklore: e.g., popular poems, anecdotes of historical persons, reminiscences of old people "unless they deal with supernatural forces or have connection with present-day customs," and biographies of celebrities.

On the same day further instructions provided a questionnaire, which the state director for Oregon had sent out to his field workers. This was revised and supplemented by John Lomax. The questionnaire itself is interesting, and the questions follow:

1. Are there any Indian legends which tell stories of your community? What are they? Give the exact location of the scene of the story.

2. Are there any geographic features, canyons, mountains, peaks, headlands, etc., named for Indian legends? What are they?

3. Are there recognized such things as wishing seats, wishing wells, swamps or quicksands with sinister properties, localities with beneficent qualities, proposal rocks or lands, etc.?

4. Are there any stories concerned with animals or animal life, or the relation between human beings and animals, which are native to your community?

5. Are there any special festivals celebrated at special times of the year designed to insure good luck, good crops, good weather, etc.? Describe them.

6. Can you discover any local songs or ballads, sung or commonly used by any group of people or passed down in any particular family? Copy them or get them by word of mouth.

7. Are there special fairs or market days, particularly if they are significant as related to local products or local life or industry? Describe them.

8. Is there a particular kind of costume common to a sect or group worn in your district? Describe it. How did it originate?

9. Are there special customs relating to particular days in the year, such as Fourth of July Hallowe'en, Christmas, etc.? Describe them.

10. Are there special customs observed at the birth of a child, upon the death of a person, at marriages?

11. Are there community gatherings such as quilting, singing schools, etc.? Describe them.

12. Are there any peculiarities of table service or dining routine, such as serving the husband first, serving of bread by the father, etc.?

13. Are there religious customs, such as public denunciation of wrongdoing, Easter services, blessing of crops or of rivers, camp meetings? Describe them.

14. Are there rodeos, joustings, log-rolling contests? Are there localized ghost stories, witch stories, etc.?[25]

## The addenda, as prepared by Lomax, follow:

1. Are there any words, phrases, or expressions peculiar to your section, such as dialect, slang, unusual "graces" at table, drinking toasts, short rhymes, dance calls, "play party" songs, etc.?

2. Are there any of the so-called "Tall Tales," where the story teller gets the effect either through exaggeration or understatement, stories that are not in print but that are passed around by "word of mouth"?

3. Are there any jokes, anecdotes, about some local character or unusual person of the present or past that are passed around by the campfire or where two or three good fellows meet together?

4. Are there any unusual epitaphs in old graveyards, or signs about abandoned mines or starved-out towns, or painted on way-side stones?

5. Are there any persons in your community who are believed to possess power to see into the future? Tell some of the current stories about such persons.[26]

In spite of the emphasis on sources, many workers continued to copy material from books. This was true especially in New York City, where collections of secondary material, *Look Behind You* and *The Folklore of the Metropolis*, were compiled by Manly Wade Wellman and Frank Shay. In Wisconsin, under the direction of Charles Brown, the folklore unit amassed a great bulk of material, including Old World lore, amounting almost to an encyclopedia, but of little value because it was secondhand. On the products of this unit, Alsberg observed:

> It rather saddens me, as a matter of fact, to see such beautifully bound books on Folklore coming out of Wisconsin with so little worthwhile reading matter in them. Unless much better material can be turned out by this

Folklore Unit than has been the case in the past, I think it would be a good idea to disband it and put the workers on other tasks.[27]

Likewise, in the New England states, during the year 1936-37, little original work seems to have been done except in Connecticut and Maine—and even in these states the value of the material was impaired because informants were not identified.

The relative inactivity of the northeastern states may be explained partly on the ground that they are predominantly urban, and the folklore sense is deficient in cities generally. Indeed, even in the rural areas of New England, written tradition predominates over oral. An additional cause of the neglect, however, was the natural inclination of Lomax, who was a Texan, to emphasize the South and, in particular, his own interest in Negro folk song, especially in connection with his southern recording trips for the Library of Congress. It was obviously necessary, before much could be achieved in folklore endeavor in the Northeast and even in the Middle West, to develop a program for the collection of urban and industrial lore. This was the aim of the reorganized folklore studies established in conjunction with the social-ethnic studies in 1938.

## THE EMPHASIS UPON URBAN AND INDUSTRIAL FOLKLORE

The Writers' Project section on folklore was reorganized in September, 1938, under the direction of Benjamin A. Botkin. Botkin's training and predilections caused him to favor two emphases: (1) the use of *oral* sources and (2) urban and industrial sources.

The *Manual for Folklore Studies*, issued in September, 1938, stressed the collection of material from oral sources, with reference to the background of the community and the life of the informant. To this end, the interviewing technique was elaborated with detailed instructions on methods of locating and handling informants, interviewing, and recording and submitting data, and forms were provided for interviews and personal histories:

> The working unit is the full unedited field notes for each interview, together with the personal history of the informant, submitted on the regular forms, which are to be duplicated in the state office.[28]

By this time, moreover, since some of the state guides had been completed and others were approaching completion, it was contemplated that folklore volumes for each state and a national volume, entitled "American Folk Stuff," might profitably be initiated. Accordingly, the manual envisaged such a plan.* Such works as were subsequently published or planned for publication illustrate the new emphasis on regional and occupational groupings as a basis for folklore study. In 1929 Botkin had written in the introduction to *Folk-Say, A Regional Miscellany*, ". . . There is not one folk but many folk groups —as many as there are regional cultures or racial or occupational groups within a region."[29]

Again, in a paper on "wpa and Folklore Research: Bread and Song" (read before the Popular Literature Section of the Modern Language Association of America, December 30, 1938), reviewing the folklore program of the Federal Writers' Project, Botkin revealed his emphasis upon urban life:

> An inventory of the 355,000 words of New York City folklore copy collected by a staff of 27 workers in 88 working days from September through December, 1938, reveals in its titles and texts the predominance of industrial and occupational interests in the folklore of the metropolis. The childhood level of playing at work and at being grown up becomes the adolescent and adult level of work and amusement—the epic of construction, excavation, and wrecking (subways, skyscrapers, bridges), transportation (taxi, bus, subway), shipping (railroads, trucking, longshore and maritime industry), the needle trades (garments, fur, hats), the white collar professions and retail trades (department stores, peddling, markets), and the symphony of New York night life—dance halls, night clubs, honky tonks. . . .
>
> . . . In New England a regional collection is investigating the lives and lore of Connecticut clockmakers and munitions workers, Rhode Island fishermen and French-Canadian textile workers, Maine clam diggers, Vermont Welsh slate workers and Italian granite workers, and a half-dozen additional nationality and occupational types of Massachusetts. . . . Tales of railroading, brickmaking, and steel mills from Chicago; tales of the Oklahoma oilfields; tales of the Montana and Arizona copper mines; tales of Southern textile mill workers and service occupations.
>
> Meanwhile, we are not neglecting the lore of the more strictly rural folk, past and present—folk songs of the Cumberlands from Virginia; life histories and lore of the Southern tenant-farmer, of the Conchs and Latin colony of Florida; negro spirituals and play-party songs from Alabama and South Carolina; Louisiana Voodoo and Creole lore; stories and songs of the Creole pioneers of Indiana; Spanish-American folk songs from New Mexico; old timers' and tall tales from Iowa, Idaho, and Washington.[30]

*Examples of state publications that appeared are: *Idaho Lore* (1939), *God Bless the Devil!: Liars' Bench Tales*, (1940), *South Carolina Folk Tales: Stories of Animals and Supernatural Beings* (1941), and *A Bundle of Troubles and Other Tarheel Tales* (1943). Other studies planned but not published included "Chase the White Horse" (New York City), "Chicago Industrial Lore," and "Living Lore in New England."

Although the collection of folklore was intended to be especially useful to folklorists as well as to the guides, its interest for the general public was also emphasized. Accordingly, in presenting the material to the reader, human and literary values, rather than antiquarian and academic ones, were stressed. The national volume, "American Folk Stuff," was designed as a "collection of readable tales," consisting of folk-way or oral literature: "All stories must be narrated as told by an informant or as they might be told orally with all the flavor of talk and all the native art of casual narrative belonging to the natural story-teller."[31]

At the same time, it was deemed desirable that these stories be related to living in America:

> All types and forms of folk story-telling and all minority groups—ethnic, regional, and occupational—are to be represented for two reasons: first, to give a comprehensive picture of the composite America—how it lives and works and plays—as seen through its folk story–tellers; second: by the richness of material and the variety of forms to prove that the art of story-telling is still alive and that story-telling is an art.
>
> Avoid the fragmentary and trivial. Stories need not be long but they should be significant of ways of living and character and should have human as well as local interest. To avoid these faults it might be stated, as a general principle, that all material must have group reference, that is, it must relate to group activities, to regions or neighborhoods, and express or affect group attitudes.[32]

Under the supervision of Alfred Hartog and, after him, of Nicholas Wirth, the living-lore unit of the New York City project, organized in August, 1938, began operations in October of the same year. The plan was to do studies of a cross-section of contemporary New York City folklore by occupational groups (the idea was in part suggested by the *Lexicon of Trade Jargon*), correlated with nationalities and neighborhoods. Many of the writers who joined the unit had been members of the creative writing and the racial groups units, and were attracted by the opportunities to use folklore for both sociological and literary purposes. The sociological purpose that had become dominant by January, 1939, was suggested in a comment on "I'm a Might-Have-Been" in the magazine, *Direction*.

> In "Good Morning America" Carl Sandburg announces the arrival of a code . . . language, lingo, slang . . . the proverbs of a people. The New York Federal Writers' Project has a work in progress which attempts to record this code, and so far as possible, provide a key to its significance. *I'm A Might-Have-Been* is a fragment from this work in progress.
>
> It is customary to think that "folkways" and "folk attitudes" together

711

with their corresponding pattern of folk fantasy emerge, develop and find expression only in the isolation of homogeneous rural communities. There is already an immense body of evidence indicating that urban industrial life creates its own types of "isolation" and "homogeneity" and consequently evolves its own "folkways" and its own fantasy patterns. These find expression in the stories and anecdotes as well as in the general rhythm and figures of urban speech. The chief "isolating" factor in urban industrial life, and the one which fuses large groups of city-dwellers into closely-knit homogeneous groups is *occupation*. The book being prepared by the Federal Writers' Project, will, on completion, be at least a partial record of the developing folk attitudes and fantasy patterns of a number of urban occupational groups.*

*I'm A Might-Have-Been*, however, is part of a section of the book which deals with a group, which paradoxically (and regretably) owes its homogeneity to the fact that it is excluded from the occupational "communities" through unemployment. Bewilderment, cynicism, resentment, philosophical resignation, utter uncertainty are the main characteristics of the thought and speech of this group. Theirs is a profound and disturbing commentary on the social maladjustments responsible for their existence.[33]

Hyde Partnow in "I'm a Might-Have-Been" records the maundering of one of the unemployed. The specimen, which is truly Petronian in its style and content, deserves quotation:

> I admit it, I'm a hog. In other words human. I enjoy women and a pair of doughnuts like anybody else. Say tomorrer I wake up I'm covered in communism, say I can go and get what I want by asking—I want six wives. You maybe want 24 suits and him, they gotta give him twelve yachts,—otherwise he's miserable. We're nuts, we're all deprived so long we went nuts. Plain hogs. It's chemical, you can't do nothing. We're 90% water, $H_2O$, and 10% other things—sodium helium oxygen hydrogen potassium phosphorus calcium and so forth. At the same time in this kinda world 2 plus 2 makes 5. Now. Look at me. I look like a dirt monkey. True? I'm among the world of missing men. I'm so insignificant if they sent out a radio call for me a hundred years nobody would find me. Economically I'm collapsed, I could write my whole will on a postage stamp, not a single coin of the realm you'll find in my pocket, I ain't got enough real estate to put in a flower pot. Tell me, then, why should I sing my country tis of thee or welcome sweet springtime I greet you in song? *And yet*, my friend, you can never tell the way you stand by the way you're sitting down. Listen to what I'm gonna say to you now, carefully—the bacteriologist of today was himself a bacteria in primeval times. Sh! Don't talk. Think that over. . . .
>
> Myself, I'm a might-have-been. I could tell you something else—I'm a genius and so forth, after all, you're a stranger to me. But it ain't what you call yourself, you can say you're Jesus and you ain't even St. Patrick. True? Well, I got lost inside a sweat shop like a fly in winter time. You go into it a man and you come out cockeyed hunchbacked knockneed pigeontoed

*The work to which reference is made is "Chase the White Horse," so called from a children's game of that name (*vide supra*, p. 710n.).

flatchested—you're a washrag and a walking prospect for the undertaker. You gotta put a mark on your feet to know right from left. The gray matter and the different parts of the cerebellum are deflated. So I am fired. The boss said he gotta make sacrifices he started with *me*. *Before*, I was lost, after I was still worse. I had bicycles in my brain. I was asking myself always: am I coming from or going to? Here I was free, the whole day in the air, in the sun, but still I was groping, the park was the same as the shop.

One swallow don't make a summer. When you're alone you can bark at the moon like a boogie dog, you can go sit down on the ground and open up your mouth you'll catch mosquitoes, that's all. A chain is strong like its weakest link and that was *me*. I don't say I didn't let off a lotta hot air in them trying times, it's a free country. I lived by my own oxygen. But also—we got a check and balance system here, there ain't no dictatorship, nobody gets away with murder, you can manifest yourself, true, you can express yourself, but the other guy can check up on you if he wants to.

Well, I got plenty checking up but *in the end* I was a citizen of the world. I didn't bow down to the dollar, I was international, a progressive. I followed the head, you understand, the others followed the rear end, they were retro-gressive. You find some people in this day and age they like to be both. If they're down in the Battery they're up in the Bronx too, these budweisers, these political fakers. They claim if you're in a steam room at the highest temperature you're freezing and if you go into a frigidaire you're hot. Why does ice smoke? They tell you: because it went crazy with the frost. They're always arguing: if it's hot as it's warm while it's freezing it should be cold you think it's gonna be hot? Bah! I wouldn't stoop myself so low. The average man should think twice before he speaks and then—shut up.

Which reminds me—ain't it time for me too? Here I'm riding a whole cavalry of ideas and I ain't got enough to buy doughnuts. If I had my life to live over again I'd choose an existence of plenty. But, for the present, it's my opinion the government should take us over, otherwise it's better for us to shut our eyes, the undertaker downtown got a special this week.

Which means this, this whole spiel. It's an explosion, I mean an explanation, of one thing—I got cursed with a social consciousness and how much I would like to do something about it I can't. Brain I got plenty, but the will power of a Chinese Eskimo.[34]

Partnow, at the folklore craft session of the Third American Writers' Congress, explained his literary method of "creative listening."

The streets are full of people, some of them talking. You walk into a park and sit down on a bench. What do you listen for among the afternoon voices?

Next to you sits a kid, he continues. You perceive him picking you out by secret signs, but you say nothing. Nor does he. Then you hear: "Can you spare a cigarette?" In a few minutes he's spilling his heart. Why? . . . Another case. A smashup in the street. A crowd collects, looks, a man talks. About accidents, life, sudden death. He looks around for somebody to talk to. He spots you. For a few minutes he talks out to anybody. Then, little by little, his eye begins returning to you. Then he's talking to you only. Why? . . . Or a man, drunk for the moment, is stumbling along the sidewalk. He goes for you, attaches himself, talks. You give him your ear. He keeps talking, won't let you go . . . Why?

Well, other things considered, maybe it's because you're a good listener. You give them plenty of time, you never laugh at the wrong time, you leave yourself out and, for the time being, you're willing to give in to them and, sitting or standing, look *out*, see, hear and—be silent. They may talk to you for hours. All the time you feel that tomorrow you may not see them again, or tomorrow they may die—that's the way you listen.

We, on the folklore work, listen that way. One of our writers goes out with a shorthand pad, another with a typewriter. Both get lots of good folk-say.

I, myself, go out most of the time without any of the writer's firearms but my ears. After a while you get so sharp even your mother begins sounding like folk-say. Then you're all right, you're beginning to hear things.

Each time I listen I know I'm watching a more or less submerged person coming to the top. All I know is he's living in hard times, he's enduring change and violence and conflict, and he's got notions and ways of looking at these things that are his own and yet not wholly his own, because they are also his folks'.

In the course of a few hours I may be listening to as many words as go into a short novel. I can't use them all or half, or half of that. "I help myself to material and immaterial," as Walt Whitman has said, "And fly the flight of the fluid and swallowing soul," but all the time I'm selecting.

This selecting process ends when I record what I've heard on my typewriter. What I attempt to do is: 1, build up a unique person; 2, relate that person to the group in which I found him, or in which he found himself; 3, use his own idiom and lyric.

It's a tough job and I do it by trying hard to leave myself out of it. I do it by trying hard to leave out of it what was not this person's. I only know that if I listen long enough I'll be able to put down what I never could put down myself in my words or any words I could possibly get out of myself.

I only know the best of today's writing must be "in the present, it is this earth today." It is the life of one man or one woman today—the average man of today, any man. I only know that to write well today you've got to go out to the people and hear what they're saying, and in so doing believe as Walt Whitman did, that "not till the sun excludes you do I exclude you." And this, I believe, is what we on the folklore project are trying to do.[35]

Partnow's "creative listening," although it departs from folklore proper, is a good example of an experiment that perhaps came nearer than anything else to combining the guidebook interpretation of America with the interests of the creative writer. The value of this living lore was twofold: (1) it accumulated a vast body of source material —sayings, anecdotes, jests, allusions, wisecracks—that comes under the head of folk stuff and Americana; and (2) it trained writers to record what they heard as well as what they saw, with an ear for characteristic speech rhythms and the vernacular.

In Chicago the folklore unit was established by Botkin in December, 1938, and operated under the supervision of Nelson Algren. This unit investigated the lore of the packing house, steel mill, auto plant, post office, etc. After a visit to the New York City project, Algren declared at a staff meeting on July 13, 1939:

> . . . We are interested in a contemporary folklore which differs widely from the conventional idea of the tall story. That is, the document which substitutes dialog for just a sort of literary pattern is the most contemporary form of folk literature and will probably have a significance in the future that would almost be termed "proletarian literature" for some years to come. They are the same thing.[36]

The Chicago project developed a species of industrial or occupational tall tale that differs from the "conventional tall tale" in its contemporary and sociological coloring. It is the tall tale transplanted from the country to the city, with freaks of machinery replacing freaks of nature and with the work hero supplanting the frontier wastrel. The strong-man tradition, however, survives in the conception of the biggest and best man on the job. Unlike the usual occupational lore, which is of an esoteric character and told within the group, these tall tales have a general interest, both for what they tell us of the occupation and for their humor.*

In New England the emphasis in the folklore studies was upon life histories, with workers in each state interviewing "ideal informants" in the various occupational, ethnic, and regional groups. "Living Lore in New England," or "Yankee Folk," which was never published, differed from *These Are Our Lives*, the southern collection edited by W. T. Couch, in that it was more folkloristic than sociological, and the unit of organization was a group of interviews rather than the single interview. The idea of recording life histories grew out of the folklore interview as follows:

> If the informant is judged worthy of recording, either before or after submitting the preliminary information to the Folklore Editor, a life history should be obtained, as indicated in Form A of the *Manual for Folklore Studies*. Whenever the life history has sufficient interest and value and the

---

*Although the national collection, "A Tall Chance of Work," was never published, some of the best of the Chicago industrial tales, by Jack Conroy and Nelson Algren, appear in *A Treasury of American Folklore*: "The Sissy from the Hardscrabble County Rock Quarries," "The Demon Bricksetter from Williamson County," "The Boomer Fireman's Fast Sooner Hound," "Greedy-Gut Gus, the Car Toad," "Hank, the Free Wheeler," "Slappy Hooper, World's Biggest, Fastest, Bestest, Sign Painter," "The Type Louse," and "The High Divers."[37]

informant can be made to talk freely, the entire narrative may be recorded in the first person. Sometimes the interview will be interspersed with bits of folklore material which should be inserted in the proper place, as they occur to the informant. Otherwise, the folklore material and personal histories should be kept separate. . . .

Informants should be interviewed not only for their life histories but for their knowledge of folk activities and gatherings, such as dances, games, revivals, and occupational customs. Descriptions of these customs should include methods of playing games, accounts of food and dress habits, and typical characters and incidents.

Even when there is no special folklore content, the life histories have folklore value in their speech (idioms, comparisons, localisms, etc.) and allusions.[38]

The plan for "Living Lore" in New England was worked out in collaboration with Frank Manuel, the New England regional director:[39]

We would divide the New England area into three main regions:

    a.  Coastal and Islands

    b.  River valleys and valley towns

    c.  Hills and hill towns

In these three main regions we would look for about twenty outstanding types. For example:

1. The Portuguese fisherman
2. The Swedish loggerman
3. The Jewish garment maker
4. The Slav brass worker
5. The French Canadian textile worker
6. The Maine potato worker
7. The Italian shoe worker
8. The Irish truck driver
9. The Yankee inn keeper
10. The Vermont dairy farmer
11. The Connecticut clock maker
12. The Connecticut tobacco worker

THE JOINT COMMITTEE ON FOLK ARTS

In a review of *A Treasury of American Folklore*, John A. Loma wrote:

When the American Folklore Society met in its annual session at Yale in December, 1937, Henry Alsberg, at that time head of the Federal Writers'

Project, requested the Society to select some competent person to come to Washington on a salary paid by the Project, and evaluate the collection of American folklore assembled through the work of thousands of collectors of the Writers' Project throughout the United States. He suggested also that this person should recommend procedural changes necessary in making further collections inclusive and authoritative. On the following day the Executive Committee of the Folklore Society by formal resolution declined to look into the merits of the Writers' Project collection on the ground that no one who is not a scientifically-trained folklorist can collect dependable folklore. Presumably the collector must go out among the people dressed in cap and gown. Other reporters are not to be trusted. The Writers' Projects did not meet the Society's standard. They were outside the pale. Henry Alsberg went back to Washington crestfallen and humiliated, but finally he found Ben Botkin to put in charge of his folklore collection. Now, seven years after the pronouncement at the Yale meeting, Ben Botkin, President of this same Folklore Society, confesses in his Introduction to the "Treasury of American Folklore" that many of his most vital items came from the collections made by the Federal Writers' Project, now permanently deposited in the Library of Congress. In other words he brands as top-of-the-heap folklore what his very recent predecessors openly sneered at.[40]

Alsberg later confessed that all he achieved at this session was a lukewarm resolution to the effect that the Writers' Project folklore materials could be put to much better use. Alsberg had also conferred with Percy Long at the Christmas meeting of the Modern Language Association of America in Chicago regarding a grant, but to no avail. Alsberg explained the antagonism of the American Folklore Society on the grounds that the project had been enjoying more newspaper publicity than the society and that professional folklorists were skeptical of an unorthodox folklorist like John Lomax, whose scholarship they questioned.

By the next year, however, the American Folklore Society had reversed its position. At the 1938 meeting, the executive council passed the following resolution:

> The Council of the American Folklore Society notes with interest the organization of a Joint Committee on Folk Arts of the Federal Writers' Project under the direction of a trained folklorist, Dr. Botkin, and wishes to express its willingness to co-operate in the activities of the Joint Committee.[41]

Botkin lost no time in seeking the advice of his professional colleagues. Copies of the *Manual for Folklore Studies* were sent to George Herzog, Louise Pound, the late Reed Smith, and Stith Thompson, who all responded with endorsements and constructive criticism. In his first field trip to the South, Botkin met Dr. Smith, who

. . . expressed the keen interest of the Southeastern Folklore Society and the Modern Language Association of America in the folklore studies of the Federal Writers' Project. The chief problem is to make the materials accessible to the public through a central Archive in the Library of Congress and through local and regional depositories; and the main idea is to get the stuff before it dies and let the chips fall as they may.[42]

Later endorsements of the program were secured from the Southeastern Folklore Society and the Folklore Council of the University of South Carolina. In his Foreword to *South Carolina Folk Tales: Stories of Animals and Supernatural Beings*, compiled by workers of the Writers' Program of the Work Projects Administration in the state of South Carolina (1941), Dr. Smith paid tribute to the work of the project:

As the result of five and a half years' work by the Writers' Project, which covered practically every county in this State, a gratifyingly large and interesting body of folklore of all kinds has been accumulated. In all, the collection runs to more than 2,600 typewritten pages. . . .

With a far-sighted spirit of service and co-operation, in addition to the originals filed in the Library of Congress, the Writers' Project has deposited with the University of South Carolina a copy of this material which so intimately concerns the past traditions and the unwritten folk culture of this state. The collection is to be stored in the South Caroliniana branch of the University Library, where it can be readily and freely consulted by all interested persons.[43]

This reciprocity of effort and interest between the Writers' Project and the several societies of folklorists, which was sedulously cultivated by Botkin, illustrates the importance of correct public relations in this, as in other phases of the arts program.

Meanwhile, in Washington and New York City steps had been taken to bring together the folklore, folk music, and folk arts experts within the WPA, for the purpose of exchanging information and ideas relating to materials of research and their collection, organization, preservation, and utilization. Informal discussions had taken place between Nicholas Ray (dramatic supervisor of the recreation division), Charles Seeger (assistant to the director of the Federal Music Project), Herbert Halpert (director of the folk song department of the National Service Bureau, Federal Theater Project) and Benjamin Botkin; and between them and outside agencies represented by Donald H. Daugherty of the American Council of Learned Societies, George Herzog of the department of anthropology, Columbia University, and Harold Spivacke of the music division of the Library of Congress. In a memorandum recording the discussions, Botkin wrote:

All are agreed on the immediate need of co-ordinating folklore research within the Works Progress Administration and of integrating it with the work of other government and private research agencies in the field. Such co-operation would minimize wasted or misdirected effort and loss or neglect of valuable materials resulting from ignorance of sources, improper handling, termination of projects, and inadequate facilities for preservation and distribution.[44]

These discussions had their origin in a meeting called by Daugherty in June, 1938, to consider the questions of whether material gathered by the various emergency agencies of the government might be of value to research in American culture, and how this material could best be preserved and made available to scholars.

The process by which the Joint Committee on Folk Arts of the WPA was finally constituted is described in the minutes of its first meeting:

Meanwhile, at a conference called in New Orleans, October 24th and 25th, by Mrs. Blanche M. Ralston, Regional Director, Women's and Professional Projects, and attended by National and Regional officers of the Arts Projects, a report upon the activities of the Washington group created so much interest that a subcommittee was designated to discuss the setting up of a bureau or office in Region III, for the collection, preservation, study, distribution, and utilization of folk arts materials. This committee met October 26th in the Regional offices in New Orleans under the temporary chairmanship of Mr. Josef Lentz, Regional Director, Federal Theatre Project. Mr. J. Howard Miller, Deputy Director, Federal Theatre Project, agreed to assign a number of workers under supervision of Mr. Robert Russell of the Theatre Project to constitute in New Orleans a central bureau of information and coordination of the work in Region III.

On November 10th, in Washington, Mrs. Ralston invited a number of project directors and the members of their staffs working with folk arts materials to meet with Mr. Morris in her office for further discussion of the coordination of the Federal Theatre's bureau in New Orleans and the Washington group. A memorandum outlining the plans of the Washington group was presented, and the set-up, objectives and function of a coordinating committee were approved in principle. Dr. B. A. Botkin was elected Chairman of the Committee and Mr. Charles Seeger, Vice-Chairman.[45]

Gradually, the committee was enlarged to include representatives of the Historical Records Survey (Sargent B. Child), the Federal Art Project (C. Adolph Glassgold), the education division (Ernestine L. Friedmann), the technical services laboratory (Greta M. Franke), and the National Youth Administration (Grace Falke).

Perhaps the most important activity of the Joint Committee was the southern recording expedition, which grew out of the interest of the Library of Congress in continuing the joint folk song recording work previously undertaken with John Lomax while he was with the Historical Records Survey.

The southern recording expedition was planned and executed as a joint project of the Federal Music, Federal Theater, and Federal Writers' projects, with Herbert Halpert as field supervisor (driving a Federal Theater sound truck) and with the Joint Committee pooling the knowledge and advice of seven projects and divisions in planning the itinerary. Charles Seeger and Benjamin Botkin drew up an elaborate schedule, listing the places to be visited, sources of information, intermediaries, informants, and materials available. The trip lasted three and a half months (from March to June, 1939) and extended through Virginia, North Carolina, Tennessee, Alabama, Mississippi, Florida, and Georgia. Besides the 419 records, the originals of which are on deposit in the Library of Congress, the expedition afforded valuable experience in utilizing the personnel of the WPA as a kind of intelligence service for collecting data, stimulated the whole program of folklore interviewing and literary recording on the Writers' Project, and furthered co-operation among the fine arts projects.*

SLAVE NARRATIVES

Closely related to the folklore studies, but cultivated in their own right, were the interviews with former slaves under the supervision of the folklore editor. These were initiated in the FERA period through a proposal submitted to Harry Hopkins by Lawrence D. Reddick, head of the department of history in the Kentucky State Industrial College at Frankfort.[46] The proposal called for a project "to study the needs and collect the testimony of ex-slaves." Reddick's interest, consistent with his profession, was historical, and he commented: "Historians are unanimous in the conclusion that the picture of slavery and the Reconstruction will never be complete until we get the view as presented through the slave himself."[47]

---

*Among these other co-operative projects promoted and participated in by the Joint Committee were: the compilation of a Mississippi folk song book by the Mississippi Writers' and Music projects, based on the southern recording expedition; the preparation of a school folk song book sponsored by the Virginia State Department of Education; a recording expedition of the Florida Joint Committee on Folk Arts, under the joint sponsorship of the WPA and the Library of Congress, with Alton C. Morris of the University of Florida as consultant; and the preparation of a book of Spanish-American children's game songs by the Writers', Music, and Art projects of New Mexico.

This original plan commended itself to the FERA as a device for the work-relief employment of Negroes in the South, and called for a staff of twelve Negro college graduates to conduct the interviews in the six states of the Ohio River Valley for a period of six months; it was initiated in 1935 in Kentucky and Indiana and was extended by the WPA to cover not only the Ohio Valley but the entire South and Kansas and Missouri.

The work on slave narratives was encouraged by Lomax, whose interest in the Negro in the South has already been indicated; and the project was practically complete when, in 1938, Botkin succeeded Lomax. The first of the WPA slave narratives were recorded in Florida, Georgia, and South Carolina in 1936. In the beginning, and perhaps because Reddick's historical emphasis still prevailed, the interest lay in the context rather than in the form and diction of the narratives, and the tendency of the interviewer was to record the story in the third person. In time, however, it was recognized that the stories had literary as well as historical qualities, and interviewers were instructed to record the narrative, so far as possible, in the words and style of the narrator. The concept of a historical questionnaire, however, still persisted, as instructions issued by Lomax in April, 1937, indicate. These instructions were accompanied by a questionnaire to guide the interviewer. The purpose and method of work were thus expressed:

> The main purpose of these detailed and homely questions is to get the Negro interested in talking about the days of slavery. If he will talk freely, he should be encouraged to say what he pleases without reference to the question. It should be remembered that the Federal Writers' Project is not interested in taking sides on any question. The worker should not censor any material collected, regardless of its nature.
>
> It will not be necessary, indeed, it will probably be a mistake, to ask every person all of the questions. Any incidents or facts he can recall should be written down as nearly as possible just as he says them, but do not use dialect spelling so complicated that it may confuse the reader.
>
> A second visit, a few days after the first one, is important, so that the worker may gather all the worthwhile recollections that the first talk has aroused.[48]

The questions covered the following subjects: place and date of birth; parents' names and origin; brothers' and sisters' names; recollections or stories of grandparents; life in the quarters; kind of work; money earned, if any, and how, and what was purchased with it; food and cooking; clothing; owner and his family; the big house; overseer or driver and poor white neighbors; size of plantation and number of slaves; daily schedule; punishments; slave sales and auctions; education; religion; runaway slaves; trouble between blacks and whites; patrollers; leisure-time activities; holidays, weddings, funerals; games, songs, stories, superstitions; health, medicine and folk cures; the Civil War; the Yankees; news of freedom; the first year of freedom; the Ku Klux and night riders; marriage and children; opinions concerning Negro and white leaders; attitude toward slavery and the church.

Additional instructions issued later in 1937 advised greater discretion in approaching informants and greater selectivity in the choice of informants. Additional questions bore on the following points: what the slaves expected of freedom and what they got; attitude toward Reconstruction; the influence of secret organizations; experience in voting and holding office; life since 1864; attitude toward the younger generation and the present; slave uprisings; the Nat Turner Rebellion; songs of the period.[49]

The problem of recording dialect was one of the most difficult, and Sterling A. Brown, editor of Negro affairs in the Washington office of the Federal Writers' Project, issued a memorandum for the guidance of the workers. Brown emphasized that "truth to idiom be paramount and exact truth to pronunciation secondary."[50]

In 1939, when the Writers' Project passed from federal to state control, the unpublished manuscripts of the slave narratives passed into the hands of the Library of Congress project, established on October 17, 1939. The narratives were thus prepared under Botkin's supervision for deposit in the Library. The manuscripts (and photographs) were arranged by states, and alphabetically by informants within each state, listing informants and illustrations and collating them in seventeen volumes and thirty-three parts.*

A large number of additional narratives received from the state projects after the 1939 transfer are on file in the WPA storage collection in the Library of Congress. Other narratives rest in specially designated depositories in the states.†

*These volumes and parts are: Volume I, Alabama Narratives; Volume II (Parts 1-7), Arkansas Narratives; Volume III, Florida Narratives; Volume IV (Parts 1-4), Georgia Narratives; Volume V, Indiana Narratives; Volume VI, Kansas Narratives; Volume VII, Kentucky Narratives; Volume VIII, Maryland Narratives; Volume IX,, Mississippi Narratives; Volume X, Missouri Narratives; Volume XI (Parts 1-2), North Carolina Narratives; Volume XII, Ohio Narratives; Volume XIII, Oklahoma Narratives; Volume XIV (Parts 1-4), South Carolina Narratives; Volume XV, Tennessee Narratives; Volume XVI (Parts 1-4), Texas Narratives; Volume XVII, Virginia Narratives.

†The following WPA slave narratives have been published: *The Negro in Vir-*

Botkin published a selection of these narratives in 1944, from which the following, entitled "Leonard Allen," is taken as a specimen:

I was skeered of Marse Jordan, an' all of de grown niggahs was too 'cept Leonard an' Burrus Allen. Dem niggahs wasn't skeered of nothin'. If de debil hese'f had come an' shook er stick at dem dey'd hit him back. Leonard was er big black buck niggah; he was de bigges' niggah I ever seed, an' Burrus was near 'bout as big, an' dey 'spised Marse Jordan wuss'n pizen.

I was sort of skeered of Mis' Polly too [Author's note: Hereafter referred to as "Mis' Sally."]. When Marse Jordan wasn' 'roun' she was sweet an' kind, but when he was 'round', she was er yes suh, yes suh woman. Everythin' he tole her to do she done. He made her slap Mammy one time kaze when she passed his coffee she spilled some in de saucer. Mis' Sally hit Mammy easy, but Marse Jordan say: "Hit her, Sally, hit de black bitch like she 'zerve to be hit." Den Mis' Sally draw back her hand an' hit Mammy in de face, pow, den she went back to her place at de table an' play like she eatin' her breakfas'. Den when Marse Jordan leave she come in de kitchen an' put her arms 'roun' Mammy an' cry, an' Mammy pat her on de back an' she cry too. I loved Mis' Sally when Marse Jordan wasn' 'roun'.

Marse Jordan's two sons went to de war; dey went all dressed up in dey fightin' clothes. Young Marse Jordan was jus' like Mis' Sally but Marse Gregory was like Marse Jordan, even to de bully way he walk. Young Marse Jordan never come back from de war, but 'twould take more den er bullet to kill Marse Gregory; he too mean to die anyhow kaze de debil didn't want him an' de Lawd wouldn' have him.

One day Marse Gregory come home on er furlo'. He think he look pretty wid his sword clankin' an' his boots shining'. He was er colonel, lootenent er somethin'. He was struttin' 'round' de yard showin' off, when Leonard Allen say under his breth, "Look at dat God damn sojer. He fightin' to keep us niggahs from bein' free."

'Bout dat time Marse Jordan come up. He look at Leonard an' say; "What you' mumblin' 'bout?"

Dat big Leonard wasn't skeered. He say, "I say, 'Look at dat God damn sojer. He fightin' to keep us niggahs from bein' free.'"

Marsh Jordan's face begun to swell. It turned so red dat de blood near 'bout bust out. He turned to pappy an' tole him to go an' bring him his shot gun. When pappy come back Mis' Sally come wid him. De tears was streamin' down her face. She run up to Marse Jordan an' caught his arm. Ole Marse flung her off an' took de gun from pappy. He leveled it on Leonard an' tole him to pull his shirt open. Leonard opened his shirt an' stood dare big as er black giant sneerin' at Ole Marse.

Den Mis' Sally run up again an' stood 'tween dat gun an' Leonard.

Ole Marse yell to pappy an' tole him to take dat woman out of de way, but nobody ain't moved to touch Mis' Sally, an' she didn' move neither, she jus' stood dere facin' Ole Marse. Den Ole Marse let down de gun. He

ginia (New York: Hastings House, 1940) contains excerpts from the Virginia narratives; Drums and Shadows, Survival Studies among the Georgia Coastal Negroes (Athens: University of Georgia Press, 1940) contains Georgia narratives; and Elizabeth Lomax's article, "Slaves," in Direction, Vol. I, No. 3, 1938, pp. 85-90, incorporates excerpts from three interviews.

reached over an' slapped Mis' Sally down, den picked up de gun an' shot er hole in Leonard's ches' big as yo' fis'. Den he took up Mis' Sally an' toted her in de house. But I was so skeered dat I run an' hid in de stable loft, an' even wid my eyes shut I could see Leonard layin' on de groun' wid dat bloody hole in his ches' an' dat sneer on his black mouf.[51]

### SOCIAL-ETHNIC STUDIES

In April, 1938, Morton W. Royse was appointed consultant on labor and social groups; and between him and Botkin, who became folklore consultant a month later, there immediately arose a community of interest that happily led to the correlation of the two fields. The nature of the co-operation between the two units is thus expressed:

As a major part of its immediate program, the Federal Writers' Project is planning two series of cultural studies—the social-ethnic studies and the folklore studies.

In both the social-ethnic and the folklore studies the approach is functional. The studies will be organized around nationality groups, communities, and regions. The emphasis is on ways of living and cultural diversity with special reference to population distribution and change.

In correlating the work of the two series, the following connections and distinctions should be observed:

1. The social-ethnic studies deal with the whole life of a group or community, including cultural backgrounds and activities; the folklore studies deal with a body of lore in relation to the life of a group or community.

2. The social-ethnic studies involve special and separate treatments of nationality groups; the folklore studies fit native and imported traditions into the diversified American pattern.

3. Supervisors in the two series should be encouraged to familiarize themselves with the methods and materials of both the social-ethnic and the folklore studies, since in many cases the work will be carried on by the same staff.

4. The preparation of both series calls for:
   a. The gathering of field data, including selected interviews, personal histories, and documentary material;
   b. A staff of field workers drawn from the group or community being studied, having the advantage of familiarity with local conditions, inhabitants, and organizations;
   c. Full co-operation with consultants drawn from the ranks of State writers, historians, folklorists, anthropologists, sociologists, economists, etc., and with historical and folklore societies, foreign-language organizations, etc.[52]

In addition to closely related subject matter and the problem of training untrained or semitrained workers to collect field data, there was the common problem of reorienting the project to treat both folk-lore and social-ethnic materials as cultural data. Earlier project pub-lications on nationality groups, like *The Armenians in Massachusetts* (1937) and *The Italians of New York* (1938), were written largely from the point of view of "contributions" and "leaders." In substituting the term "social-ethnic" for "racial," the stress was placed upon the cultural or functional approach, which studies society as a totality of interrelationships or a pattern of social behavior and emphasizes par-ticipation and acculturation. In a discussion of the problems of cultural groups at the 1939 meeting of the American Historical Association in Washington, D.C., Royse, with Caroline F. Ware and Joseph S. Rou-cek, expressed the philosophy of the Federal Writers' Project with ref-erence to contributions vs. participation:

> The concept of immigrant "contributions" implies that the culture of old-American groups constitutes "American civilization" and that bits of immigrant culture are added to it. The experience of the directors of the Federal Writers' Project casts doubts on this approach. In setting up a series of social-ethnic studies, they first attempted to use the "contributions" ap-proach. After trying it out for several months in different places, they aban-doned it. In their study of North Dakota, for example, they found it quite inapplicable, for all the people in North Dakota were recent immigrants from somewhere—Europe or the Eastern United States.
>
> The idea of "contributions" of immigrants in North Dakota raised the question of "contributions to what?" The same difficulty arose in eastern communities in which the greater majority of the population belongs to re-cent immigrant groups. Immigrants and the children of immigrants are the American people. Their culture *is* American culture, not merely a contribu-tion to American culture. The Federal Writers' Project abandoned the "con-tribution" approach and focused its attention on "participation" in various aspects of the life of the communities in which ethnic groups are living.[53]

The social-ethnic program, like the folklore program, was an ambi-tious and vital one. Both were integral and basic parts of the portrait of America that was the work of the Writers' Project. But for a number of reasons the results fell short of expectations. At the root of the trouble was the matter of personnel. Each of the programs required careful supervision in the field. In order to secure or provide proper supervi-sion Royse spent most of his time traveling, with the result that ma-terial accumulated faster and in greater quantity than it could be edited and organized. Moreover, the social-ethnic studies suffered from the fact that Royse's gifts lay in collection and field supervision rather than in editing and writing—a limitation he sought to guard against in the state offices:

Experience in many State Offices has demonstrated that only when planning, research, and writing are unified, in the hands of one person, can the aimless gathering of material be avoided, a real story be told, and the writer become an author rather than a rewriter and editor. Credit should be given to him as well as to the staff.[54]

Another difficulty encountered by both the social-ethnic and the folklore studies was the fact that they necessarily played a minor role in a program the main purpose of which was the preparation of guides. In the hierarchy of values social-ethnic and folklore studies were classed as collateral publications, and thus lower in the scale than the auxiliary publications, which were city and county guides. As a result, they were apt to be slighted and even resented by state and regional directors, who looked askance upon large-scale, long-term collecting projects calling for special techniques and not immediately convertible into publications. As long as Alsberg was national director, he encouraged the cultural program because his own sympathies lay in that direction. But his successor, John D. Newson, who became national director in the spring of 1939, stressed immediate results, and was distrustful of research projects of an investigative nature.

Especially in the South, the social-ethnic studies met with resistance from the regional director, W. T. Couch, who regarded the social-ethnic studies as foreign to the South and as an interference in local option and autonomy, and insisted upon preference for his own life-history project, with which in a sense the other studies seemed to compete: "According to Couch, Royse's Manual should be revised for the South, where the immigration is older and the attitudes of foreign groups have become thoroughly American."[55]

Couch's insistence upon his technical authority in the southern region is indicated by the following letter:

I have just received a copy of a letter from Miss Miles to Dr. Royse, indicating that instructions were being given to the Alabama staff without my knowing about these instructions.

The consequence of such procedure inevitably is confusion.

I suggest that you send me copies of all communications that go to State Directors in this region. Before any communications are sent, general approval of the study to be made ought to be given there and if my services are to be effective I ought to know at least that is being done.

Obviously confusion and contradictory instructions cannot be avoided until details of this kind are properly handled.[56]

His preference for the life history studies over the social-ethnic studies reveals itself in the following regional instructions:

The life histories and the social-ethnic studies are two different jobs and should not be confused. For the present it has been decided to delay work in the South on the social-ethnic studies and to concentrate on the life histories.[57]

Social-ethnic studies fell into three classes: (1) intensive studies of single groups (nationalities or occupations); (2) cross-sectional studies of whole communities; and (3) extensive studies of larger areas (regions). In addition, these special studies were to contribute data to a one-volume nationwide survey, *Composite America*. In all, 161 studies were undertaken.

From their distribution it appears that the social-ethnic studies received most attention in urban and industrial areas, especially in the Northeast and Middle West, where the immigrant population was larger, more recent, more culturally and socially conscious, and better represented on the projects.

The nature of these studies may be gathered from the following titles (by states) from a list of March 25, 1939, showing their distribution. At that date, some of these studies were tentative, some in progress, and some (represented by italics) already published:

ALABAMA

Silverhill; Swedish farming community (tentative).

Cajans. Impoverished group in pine barrens (tentative).

NEW YORK

Foreign-language Press study.

Irish of New York.

Jews of New York.

*Landsmanschaften.* Jewish study (published, 1938).

Schenectady social-ethnic study.

Mineville; iron mine community.

Rome; copper town.

*Italians of New York* (published in English, 1938; in Italian, 1939).

Spanish-speaking study.

WISCONSIN

Stoughton; community study of Norwegian town.

Monroe; cheese town—includes study of New Glarus (Swiss town unchanged in character after four generations).

Milwaukee; folk study of life of the town; showing decline of Germanism and immigration of Poles, Czechs, Mexicans, and Negroes.

Menominee Indian Reservation; co-operative community, with lumbering and milling as the main industry, and subsistence farming as an adjunct.

Study of rural German community.
Wisconsin Stump-land (regional) study.
Study of a Polish village.

In addition the following nationwide studies were initiated:

Lithuanians (from Chicago office)
Hungarians (from Philadelphia office)
Greeks (from New York City office)
Poles
Russians
Ukrainians
Czechs

The specific subject-matter of the social-ethnic studies was broken down as follows:

a. Old World backgrounds.
b. Migration and settlement.
c. Geographical distribution.
d. Labor relations.
e. Living standards.
f. Adjustment and adaptation.
g. Organized life.
h. The foreign-language press.
i. Group relations and attitudes.
j. Folkways and expression.
k. Second generation problems.

Each of these topics was further broken down internally to guide the field investigator and the writer.

NEGRO STUDIES

The Negro Studies of the Federal Writers' Project originated in the twofold desire to give employment to needy Negro writers and to depict the role of the Negro in American life. The two motives went hand in hand, since, as was often stated in justification of employing Negroes on state projects, "such information [on the Negro] can be more effectively secured by qualified Negro writers."[58] Complaints of discrimination began to reach the national office soon after the setting up of the project. Partly because of the pressure of public opinion and partly because of a sincere desire to give the Negro representation in both the guides and their writing, the national office took steps to appoint an editor on Negro affairs:

> Mr. Alsberg and I are both extremely desirous of getting the Negro Project on the American Guide in operation. We both attended a special banquet given at Howard University on November 22, at which about fifteen representatives of various cultural interests were present.
>
> We have a specific plan, namely, the inclusion in the Guide of a section to be called "Negro Culture in America." This would be an abridged treatment of a much more comprehensive survey of the historic and cultural past of the Negroes in America and their present condition and culture. Such a survey has never been undertaken before. We contemplate the possibility of the unabridged material being eventually published in some form or other.
>
> In assembling this material we have in mind the employment of groups of Negroes who have been assigned to American Guide work in various centers combined with Negro studies of the National Youth Administration and directed by Negro specialists and leaders wherever such groups are in operation. In connection with this plan we have proposed a National Negro Council which would further supplement the work done by research people and special writers.
>
> . . . . . . . . . . . . . .
>
> A feasible procedure here I believe would be to combine our own group of non-relief workers with the Youth Administration students at Howard and place the group at Howard University where a good library would be accessible and also the advice and assistance of such men as Mr. Sterling Brown, Dr. Locke and others who were at the banquet and much interested in the whole program.[59]

In the spring of 1936 Sterling A. Brown, of the department of English, Howard University, was appointed editor of Negro affairs. A native of Washington, D.C., Brown had taught at Virginia Seminary, Fisk University, and Lincoln University (Missouri), had conducted a book page in *Opportunity, Journal of Negro Life,* and was the author of a volume of poems, *Southern Road* (1932), and two books of criticism, *The Negro in American Fiction* (1938) and *Negro Poetry and Drama* (1938). He had a wide acquaintance among Negro writers and professionals and a broad understanding of, and deep insight into, Negro culture and problems. In planning his work on the project he sought the advice of Negro and white experts on Negro affairs in Washington and the co-operation and assistance of Negro colleges and universities, where many of the state Negro projects were set up (e.g., Hampton Institute, Virginia, and Dillard University, Louisiana). In Washington he gradually built up a staff that included Eugene Holmes, also of Howard University, Ulysses Lee, Bernard Braxton, and Glaucia B. Roberts.

The office of Negro affairs served in both an advisory and an editorial capacity. It advised on all matters involving Negro personnel and the treatment of the Negro in project publications, and it edited the guide essays on the Negro and planned and directed special national and local Negro books. In this work it co-operated especially with the folklore and social-ethnic studies. A typical guide essay on the Negro (that in *North Carolina: A Guide to the Old North State*) treated of population figures and distribution, history before and since emancipation, health and public welfare, the Negro farmer, occupations and town life, education, and customary racial distinctions and discriminations. To the tours and points of interest the office of Negro affairs contributed items on Negro towns and sections, including housing conditions and accommodations, Negro theaters, schools, and institutions of higher learning, historic Negro houses and monuments, and important Negro events.*

These studies were undertaken with sympathy and understanding, not merely because they were directed by Negroes but also because the personnel of the Washington office of the Federal Writers' Project, from Alsberg down, were men of liberal leanings to whom such an attitude was congenial. On the other hand, every effort was made to present an accurate and complete picture, and bias was discouraged, from whichever side it appeared. The guiding principles of the Negro studies are best expressed in instructions that accompanied the tentative outline for "The Portrait of the Negro as American." They read:

> The Negro in America has been greatly written about, but most frequently as a separate entity, as a problem, not as a participant. Largely neglected in broad historical considerations, or receiving specialized attention from social scientists, the Negro has too seldom been revealed as an integral part of American life. Many Negro historians have attempted to counter the neglect, but the result has been overemphasis, and, still "separateness." Where white historians find few or no Negroes and too little important par-

*In addition to the Negro material that appeared as an integral part of the guides, special state and local studies on the Negro were undertaken and published. These were, by state: Arkansas: *Survey of Negroes in Little Rock and North Little Rock* (1941); Georgia: *Drums and Shadows: Negro Survival Studies* (1941); Illinois: *Calvalcade of the American Negro* (1940); Nebraska: *The Negroes of Nebraska* (1940); Virginia: *The Negro in Virginia* (1940). Also, two collections of Negro folklore were published: *South Carolina Folk Tales* (1941) and *A Bundle of Troubles and Other Tarheel Tales* (1943). Other Negro books brought to various degrees of completion but never published include "The Negro in New York City" (drawn heavily upon by Roi Ottley, New York City Negro editor, in his *New World A-Coming*), "The Negro in Oklahoma," "Portrait of the Negro as American," "Go Down Moses: The Negro's Struggle for Freedom" (originally "The Underground Railroad"), and "A Selected Bibliography of Negro Materials."

ticipation, Negro historians find too many and too much. This racial basis is understandable, but it does not produce the accurate picture of the Negro in American social history at which *The Portrait of the Negro as American* aims.

The composite portrait of the American Negro, set squarely against the background of America, will be an essay in social history and biography, not an exercise in race glorification. While I feel that the record of the Negro in America, if accurately presented, will be highly creditable, the propelling force behind the book is not race pride but a wish to see the truth told. Like all portraits, this one must be selective, but it will result from long acquaintance with and study of the subject.

Much in the book will be fairly new to the American public—to Negro readers as well as to white. No such work as yet exists. Instead of a thesis to be proved or a cause advanced, a portrait is to be created. The emphasis will be biographical. Dramatic material abounds; to mention a few items: Esteban guiding Spanish explorers, York with Lewis and Clark, Jim Beckwourth ruling over the Creeks with big lies and big deeds, John Chavis teaching the classics to slaveholders' sons, Denmark Vesey plotting at Charleston, Harriet Tubman leading the slaves out of "Egypt," Frederick Douglas being mobbed in Illinois, Madison Washington leading the "mutiny" on the *Creole*, John Brown's Negro comrades at Harpers Ferry. Reconstruction legislators, Booker Washington founding Tuskegee, Negro soldiers at Boston Common, Bunker Hill, with Perry on Lake Erie, at Fort Wagner, Petersburg crater, San Juan Hill, in France. In the contemporary scene there will be not only such newsworthies as Joe Louis, Father Divine, Bojangles Robinson and the Scottsboro boys but also the less known: sharecroppers, factory workers, students, business men—all of those who make up the mosaic of Negro life in America.

But if the spirit of the Washington office was liberal, that of some of the state offices—not all of them in the South—was less generous. Indeed, the work of Negroes on the Federal Writers' Project proceeded under the handicap of a constant fight for existence in the face of discrimination and threats of dismissal. From Charleston came a report that a Negro project of four persons, started several months after the setting up of the local Writers' Project on December 1, 1935, had been eliminated by July 8, 1937, in order to absorb a cut in quota. Two members of the project wrote to the President:

> We know that it is not your will that we are "last to be hired and first to be fired," but as Father of all Americans you should be consulted, where injustices are concerned. Work to us has the same meaning as to any other persons, and without it we perish as others do.[60]

In this spirit the Conference on Immediate Human Needs in 1939 passed the following "Resolution on Expansion of Negro Art Projects":

> Since it is a generally acknowledged fact that 80% of our Negro population suffers unemployment, and that private industry holds but slight hope

of employment for the Negro workers in the arts, this Conference goes on record as supporting the campaign of the Negro Arts Committee to expand project employment opportunities for Negro art workers, and projects for enriching the American cultural scene through the study and planned use of Negro art.

To this end, this Conference further endorses the Conference on Education and Culture being held in Harlem on April 1st and 2nd, 1939, by the Negro Arts Committee, for the extension of the rights of the Negro people to participate in the art life of America.[61]

In the same spirit Alsberg put pressure upon state directors in the South to employ Negro workers. The following is a specimen of many such letters he wrote:

> I think, if you still have room in your quota, you should employ some Negroes. It is important that the Negro race should be represented among our workers. Certainly they could be put to collecting information about the Negro population. I think you should, perhaps, consult with representatives of some Negro organizations in Florida in this connection. If there are none such, then you might get in touch with Mr. Walter White, Secretary of the National Association for the Advancement of Colored People, 69 Fifth Avenue, New York City. He may be able to put you in touch with a representative of his organization in Florida.[62]

LOCAL GUIDES

In the beginning of the Federal Writers' Project, although there was no provision for the publication of any guide except the American Guide, the gathering of material for local publications was foreseen:

> A copy of the data which is gathered will be left in each community, and it is probable that after the publication of the American Guide this material will be released to local public libraries or similar organizations in the various communities, so that it may be available for the publication of local guides.[63]

Local and special publications—or auxiliary and collateral publications—were inherent in the guide program inasmuch as more material was gathered than could be used in the guides. Moreover, the folklore, social-ethnic, and Negro studies, besides contributing to the guides, provided materials for local and special publications that were demanded by the cultural diversity that fed these studies.

> The plans for collateral publications are not yet formulated, but the localities are calling for books on such matters as folklore, Indian research,

732

geological or botanical studies, etc. A vast amount of material which cannot be squeezed in the American Guide has been produced with great care and labor, and we hope that the collateral volumes will be published locally and possibly nationally to make this mass of research available to the public. It would be a great cultural loss if this plan could not be followed.[64]

The local and special publications, since they were by-products, tend to be obscured by the main products (the state guides) and ignored in appraising the achievements and estimating the cost of the Writers' Project. Thus, figuring on the basis of the guidebook word-age alone, adverse critics of the project arrived at a fantastically high cost per word. Cronyn replied to one such critic:

> I think I made it plain to you that the American Guide was engaged in producing as by-products hundreds of local guides as well as forty-eight state books. The wordage, therefore, includes the more expanded writing; and the almost incalculable returns to localities, cities, and states may be measured against the total cost of the project.[65]

Moreover, the morale value of these publications was significant. Undertaken for the most part when the state guides were finished or approaching completion, they maintained the spirit and occupied the time of the project workers. This antidote to relaxation was not wholly effective in all states. In some states the drop in morale, consequent upon the completion of the state guides, was persistent; in other states, where state guides were not completed until late in the project's life, auxiliary and collateral publications were never seriously undertaken; in many states, however, these lesser works, although they represent no grand design like the Guide, are not without merit, and in some cases are of considerable worth.

INDEX INVENTORIES AND ENCYCLOPEDIAS (FACT BOOKS)

A convenient and practical basis for special publications was furnished by the index inventories of manuscripts that the states were first asked to prepare on October 21, 1937, and again in connection with the preliminary work on the state encyclopedias, later called "fact books," inaugurated August 12, 1938. The index (on 5 x 8 cards, stating title of manuscript, author, date completed, length, whether complete or incomplete, edited or unedited, contents, source, consultant, and reliability) was meant to serve a twofold purpose:

. . . First, it will give us the preliminary estimate of all the work that has been done (throughout the country) by the Federal Writers' Project; second, it will give each state director an indication of how much material is on hand for the encyclopedia, how much of it still needs rechecking and final verification, and how much is still to be gathered.[66]

The American Encyclopedia Series itself was stillborn, except for one volume, *The Idaho Encyclopedia*, which, like the Idaho Guide, anticipated procedure. The failure of the encyclopedia project may be attributed to the fact that, coming after the state guides, to which it was intended to be sequential, it was anticlimactic. Indeed, as a "purely factual portrayal of the state"—dealing with facts rather than with people—the encyclopedia was little less than a rehash of the guide, without the imaginative appeal of the latter and with all the attributes of hack work of which the guides were sometimes accused but which they succeeded in transcending. Primarily, the encyclopedia failed because it was too obviously conceived and planned as "made work" in order to absorb surplus materials and personnel.*

### OTHER LOCAL PRODUCTS

Other local publications of more modest concept included many types of books both fertile in idea and successful in execution. Among the types attempted were tour books (other than state and local guides) such as the *Intracoastal Highway* and *Route Number One*, trade jargon, children's books, small county histories, zoo books, adult education pamphlets, and almanacs.

### PRODUCTION PROBLEMS AND TECHNIQUES

The production problems and techniques of the Federal Writers' Project grew out of the two objectives of the program: "In setting up the Federal Writers' Project, two considerations were basic. First the necessity of projects sufficiently broad in scope to employ all categories

---

*The origin of the idea of such "fact books" and the real purpose that prompted their initiation are perhaps revealed in a letter written as early as August, 1936: "Some difficulty has been experienced in finding work suitable for some of the less talented people on the project in Georgia. Too much time has been taken by administrative people to instruct the various workers in what they are to do. In order to relieve that situation, I suggested that a beginning be made, only in a very small way, toward compiling material that might be eventually used in the State Encyclopedia. This will not in any way interfere with the present program, but will serve to provide work for people of limited ability."[67]

of writers; and secondly, the selection of activities from which the greatest public benefit would result."[68]

It is generally conceded that the project succeeded better in achieving the second objective than it did the first; and that only because a few qualified workers carried the load of the many less-qualified ones. If the project had set itself a task of less magnitude and complexity, and one more pedestrian, like that of the Historical Records Survey, it would have been able to fit the task to the workers. As it was, the Writers' Project was compelled to fit the workers to the task—a job of training, retraining, and supervision for which the project had neither time nor the capacity.

The Guide was selected as the activity that would be of "greatest public benefit" because it was believed that nothing could be of greater public benefit than helping a country to know and understand itself. The idea was magnificent, and the execution only a little less so because of the conditions and limitations under which the project operated. In the first place, the Guide was a professional task for which few of the available writers on relief were fitted. "The preparation of a State Guide is a task comparable in complexity to the preparation of a volume of an encyclopedia or a volume of such a set as the Dictionary of American Biography," as Reed Harris reminded Lawrence S. Morris in answering the complaint of Thomas H. Moodie, WPA administrator for North Dakota, who wrote that "taking two years to complete the State Guide in North Dakota is indefensible."

> Even with a staff of outstanding excellence, the publishers who put out the Dictionary of American Biography took more than 10 years to complete that particular set of volumes. Any publisher of reference volumes of the general type of our guides would inform Mr. Moodie, should he inquire, that two years is not by any means a long time to spend in preparing such a book. As a matter of fact, I believe that he could obtain a statement from the sponsor of the State Guide, the Superintendent of the State Historical Society, that the work has been done with considerable efficiency and as rapidly as could be expected with the limited hours of the relief work schedule.[69]

The first of the state guides (Idaho, the District of Columbia, and the New England states) were published in 1937; the last of the guides (Oklahoma), in 1941.

One of the paradoxes of guide production was that although uniform standards were set by the Washington office, these standards were modified in practice by the greatest conceivable disparity in qualifications, quotas, distribution, and productivity of workers. In the matter of qualifications, as soon as it became obvious that there were not enough writers on relief to suffice, the term "writer" was broadened to include "teachers, librarians, college graduates, and other persons of enough intelligence to gather information."[70] In the same vein, Reed Harris wrote:

> As for classification of workers, Mr. Alsberg feels that we would be able to use a wide variety of skills, including persons with training as insurance salesmen, clergymen, teachers, librarians, and almost any other occupation that involves an understanding of the English language, and some training in observation and the preparation of records.[71]

The writers themselves were a most heterogeneous group:

> We are not prejudiced in favor of any particular school or type of writing, and you will find that the major part of the four thousand writers already employed taken from the relief rolls is made up of persons who have made a living in the past at some form of writing, but not any particular sort. We have already employed newspaper men, advertising copy writers, 'pulp' fiction writers, magazine article writers, novelists, critics, and in fact almost every known variety of writers. Most of these fields are even represented here on our central staff.[72]

Some idea of the range of variations may be gained by comparing allocations of funds, employment figures, and production figures for a selected number of states. From this table it appears that states with a small number of workers turned out almost as much copy for the state guide as states with a large number.

| State* | Allocation† | Number of Workers‡ | Number of Words Submitted‡ |
|---|---|---|---|
| South Dakota ... | $ 11,900 | 28 | 180,000 |
| North Dakota ... | 14,700 | 42 | 125,000 |
| Nebraska ....... | 31,400 | 70 | 320,000 |
| Minnesota ...... | 69,250 | 74 | 186,000 |
| Oklahoma ...... | 36,700 | 94 | 270,000 |
| Wisconsin ...... | 47,950 | 95 | 98,761 |
| Kentucky ....... | 34,950 | 98 | 130,000 |
| Indiana ........ | 82,650 | 110 | 190,000 |
| Missouri ........ | 56,015 | 132 | 73,430 |
| Kansas ......... | 56,000 | 142 | 110,000 |
| Ohio .......... | 164,500 | 281 | 187,000 |
| Illinois ......... | 146,200 | 308 | 326,000 |
| Pennsylvania .... | 236,250 | 340 | 188,000 |

*In order of number of workers.
†As of March 15, 1936.
‡As of August 12, 1936.

Without taking into account other factors, such as the quality of the copy and the supervision, the figures seem to indicate that there was little correlation between the size of the project and its production.

Even these figures, however, do not adequately tell the story. For example, in view of all the variables and intangibles, any attempt to estimate the cost of a guide per word or on any other fixed basis would be quixotic:

> I find that we cannot, for several reasons, make any estimate of the total cost of preparing a guide. During the time that they are preparing and editing a state guide our project workers assemble material totaling millions of words. This material may be used in a dozen publications after the guide is out, and all of it is to be turned over to Historical Societies or other public bodies where it will be available for all time. Of course it may be possible to give the exact cost of a project from the time it was started to the day that the guide book goes to press. However, it would be impossible to estimate how much energy went into guidebook making and how much went into gathering other material, and of course it is impossible to estimate the value of the guide in relation to the other work of the Project. You can see how different our work is from that of those Projects which build court houses.[73]

Most variable and intangible of all was the human factor. The following list of "Backgrounds of representative men and women" in the quota of 190 for the Massachusetts Writers' Project represents an unusually good selection of personnel:[74]

Lawyer and one-time magazine publisher

Editor of a foreign language newspaper in one of the largest Massachusetts cities

Superintendent of schools in a district of China, who has also been editor of a house organ, a publicity director, and author of a book

Author of five published volumes; his biography is included in *Who's Who in America*

Editor of a woman's magazine of large national circulation

Doctor of medicine, practising since 1925, who has published a medical treatise

Two present members of city school committees

Author of numerous detective stories; his biography is in *Who's Who in America*

Managing editor of a scientific journal

Author of a history of a foreign country, later editor of a foreign language paper in the United States

Poet of reputation, whose work has been published in book form and has appeared in leading magazines of the "quality group"

Foreign correspondent who has published three books

Principal of an industrial school

Author of four novels

City editor of the leading newspaper in a Massachusetts city

Principal of a school in Japan

Publicity director of a large charitable institution

Associate editor of a well-known historical periodical

Editor of a trade paper

Three members of the Christian ministry, who served their churches from nine to over twenty years

On the other hand, the Virginia project presents quite a different picture. In the early days the director was the state historian, and, presumably because of other duties, had failed to give adequate time to the project. Of fifty-eight on the project in 1937, eleven had non-relief status, of whom eight were supervisors. Two of the supervisors had published books. The assistant director was a former telegraph operator. Another was an elderly man who had written advertisements for a department store; another had worked a short time on a rural paper. As late as March, 1937, the project had published nothing, and only one essay, that on architecture, had been accepted by the Washington office as suitable for the state guide. Later, even that essay was found to be full of inaccuracies.

The work on the guides fell roughly into two parts: (1) field work, or the gathering of factual material; and (2) editing and writing. Naturally, every fieldworker was compelled to do some editing (in writing his field notes up into the field continuity and revising and condensing the latter into field editorial copy); and every editor was compelled to do some research in connection with checking. But roughly, the division of labor demanded research in the field and editing and writing in the state office.

In theory the workers with more competence and experience, who were rated as professional, were assigned to the editing and writing; and those with less competence and experience, who were rated as skilled, were assigned to field work:

Professional Workers include those who are technically writers or authors; who have made writing their profession or have contributed articles, stories, or reports to publications; journalists and editorial workers; historians, research workers, art and literary critics, architects, archeologists, map draftsmen, geologists, and other specialists in fields covered by the Guide.

Newspapermen on evidence of competency or experience will be classified as Professional Workers. Also included are graduates of institutions, who have been educated in sociology, economics, civic planning, or any other category of cultural subject included in the Guide field of investigation. Commercial or industrial professional workers may be considered eligible.

*Skilled Workers* include draftsmen, assistants in cartography, field research, library or documentary research, and other assistants in the above categories; also secretarial personnel.[75]

In principle, however, Alsberg was opposed to the strict separation of research and writing. In 1937 he wrote to a state director:

> Some time ago I received from your office a proposed project entitled "Manual for National Journalistic Survey."
>
> I should not like to approve this survey. For one thing, the proponents merely want the manuscripts proposed and then filed in the Library of Congress—in other words, buried. Our aim, on the contrary, is to produce the type of manuscript which will find an outlet through a sponsor and publisher.
>
> Moreover, I think that the research that would have to be done on this sub-project is beyond the capabilities of most of the field workers—accuracy, discrimination, and instinct for what is important and interesting. In the second place, I doubt whether we have enough writers and editors to rewrite and edit the material. Aside from that, I have very little confidence in one set of people doing the research and another set doing the writing. If a work of value is to be turned out, research people must be directed by some one in charge who plans the work and sees that it is properly carried out.
>
> I think we have so many possibilities for other projects that we need not feel compelled to undertake this sort of vague and heavy research work.[76]

But, when he reflected upon his experience as director of the project, Alsberg came to a different conclusion: "Experience has taught that the mass of material written and accumulated by field workers, most of whom are relief people, must of necessity be rewritten and condensed into state guide copy. This is a job which must be done in the State Office."[77]

Even in 1935, he wrote in the same vein to a state director:

> I think you will have to be satisfied with the people actually available, even if they are not all technically writers. The dozen people who have already been put on the project by you and are bona fide writers will have to do the editing and rewriting of the material collected by the less qualified people. After all, you do not need a professional writer to collect the data necessary for the compilation of a guide to Vermont.[78]

The effects of this separation of research and writing were felt all along the line. For one thing, it put an immense responsibility and work load upon the editors in the state and national offices, who spent valuable time in checking and criticizing inaccurate and poorly observed or interpreted data. Darel McConkey thus commented on field copy:

> I conferred with Miss Hellams, State Editor. I also read a number of manuscripts which had been turned in. Seventeen manuscripts in all from the Columbia District Office have been turned over to the State Office. The total wordage on them is 9,733. Nine scripts have come into the State Office from Charleston, South Carolina, having a total wordage of 4,460. Generally speaking, the copy was fair but much in need of editing. The practice of giving references to sources seems to be generally followed. At this time and later in the District Office (in the back of the City Health Building) when I read unedited material, the principal lacks seemed to be a failure to give derivatives of place names and, more particularly, failure on the part of writers to approach their material with a point of view of fresh childlike interest. An example of this: As I rode in a taxi to the hotel I saw a statue labelled Gonzales. It seemed strange for a little American town and I wondered; when I read the articles on statues of Columbia, I learned that he was a former editor of a Columbia newspaper who was killed by a former lieutenant governor. From Mrs. Louise J. DuBose, Columbia District Supervisor, I learned that he was a Cuban expatriate, and that his brother, now very old, still edits the same paper. Another instance: a young man had just finished an essay on an Aiken, South Carolina, fox-hunt. He said it was a "drag." I had to ask him what a drag was and learned that it was a scent dragged along the trail and this scent the dogs followed in a foxless fox hunt, accompanied by the elite on horseback; nor did the story relate how far the concourse was from Aiken, how one might get there, how one might enter horses, whether spectators could watch, nor what the admission charge is. These are typical examples of the objections that might very well be raised to the material now completed.[79]

As a consequence, checking for accuracy became one of the main tasks of the national office.[80] One effect of this checking on the part of the central office was to destroy the confidence of the state editors in their own work:

> Because no confidence is placed in the statements we make, we have become careless in making them. How loud grows that cry from the force-fed host of indifference—"Well let it go, Washington will catch it, anyway." We check and re-check, and check again, everything we write for a commercial publisher, because we know he has confidence in us, and our statements, if open to question, would embarrass him. But there is hardly an item in the Guide Book copy that has been accepted as authoritative, no matter how carefully we may have checked it. And so our instinct naturally is to be less careful.[81]

Although freshness of approach was one of the requirements of field work, "accuracy, discrimination, and instinct for what is important and interesting," as Alsberg wrote to a state director, were "beyond the capabilities of most of the field workers." Moreover, for lack of time, original research was not encouraged except as a by-product:

> We certainly do not intend to do original historic research in obtaining material for the Guide. As a matter of fact, however, a good deal of such work is being done by our workers and quite a little new material is being turned up. Naturally, if you put an intelligent person in a library to look up a certain subject, or in a court house to look through records, he or she may come on something interesting and new which has not yet been exploited in any published work. Any such material we turn up is, of couse, merely a by-product of the project.[82]

The result was that much that was called research was merely the copying of secondary material, such as was found in books, periodicals, etc. Robert C. Binkley, whose interest in the Writers' Project was only less than his concern with the Historical Records Survey, was aware of this tendency, and wrote, "Do not rehash or popularize material already available in print."

> Concretely, this would mean that they would work as far as possible from archives, old newspapers, and manuscripts, in preparation of local histories. Most "county histories" are notoriously shallow. The Federal Writers would do nothing of value if they rewrite material from county histories. They should be warned specifically, "Keep away from the county histories." They should seek to avoid as much as possible the inclusion in their own writings of material that already is available in book form. Let them go to the original sources. Better bring to light a series of interesting facts hitherto unknown than to make a rearrangement of known material.*[83]

Much of the original investigation was undertaken and accomplished by the so-called volunteer associates—people in communities of under 10,000 population, where the project generally had no representative, who agreed to supply data to the district supervisor gratis. This plan had been successful in the making of the FERA *Connecticut Guide*, the material for which was compiled chiefly by volunteers. The device, although it was not cultivated as extensively as perhaps it might have been by the Writers' Project, was not ignored, and had the advantage not only of securing more thorough coverage but also of enlisting community support and interest.†

---

*In this connection, it should be noted that the Writers' Project undertook and accomplished a significant amount of original research in its folklore, social-ethnic, and life history activities. An important discovery, shared by the Writers' Project and the Historical Records Survey, was that of the Morman diaries in Utah, which Vardis Fisher subsequently used in his *Children of God*.

†There was no intellectual snobbishness about the Federal Writers' Project. The

The help of local authorities, as well as of local amateurs, was solicited. The purpose here was partly prestige (as in the formation of state advisory committees, comprised of the governor and leading citizens), and partly technical assistance (as in the solicitation of aid from state historical and archival societies, and other bodies of a similar nature). The *American Guide Manual* stated:

> The authenticity of factual material in the Guide must be unquestioned. Whenever an editor doubts the accuracy of a statement contained in a field report, the matter should be checked from other sources. A local historian or specialist may supply information that is open to question or incomplete. Besides consulting whatever records may be available, the Local Field Worker should go to other persons of standing to check data, especially to members of the Local Advisory Committee.[84]

Again, in writing to a state director, Alsberg advised:

> Your letter of December 2nd raised the point as to how we expect to check the facts contained in the copy of our field workers.
> The plan which we have already inaugurated in many cities is to appoint a committee of outstanding citizens who will assist the local writers of the American Guide in selecting subjects and by checking their statements before their articles are submitted to their State Directors.
> We are happy to be able to say that in every center that we have heard from, people like yourself have been good enough to volunteer their services for this work of checking. Without this service of the committees, it would be quite impossible for any human being to pass on the articles in volume. Through this checking by committees, we will be able to bring to bear on every statement the best local opinion, and that should insure us a very high standard of accuracy.[85]

The final step in the process was the actual writing. Alsberg wrote:

> Both in the matter of Handbook of Government and in this Racial Group Sub-project the manner of writing and interpreting is as important as the actual research work. I don't know, of course, whether you have individuals able to do a swell job on these proposed books. Unless the writing is excellent and interesting, the manuscripts will certainly not find a publisher.
> You will understand, of course, that none of what I have written is in the nature of a criticism. But I do feel that more "wordages" mean nothing. There is danger, if there is no stock-taking, that a number of these sub-projects will run along without jelling into something concrete and usable. Also, I feel that unless the material is put in final shape by single competent indi-

whole experiment was predicated on the assumption that a person of average intelligence with an understanding of the English language, an acuteness of observation, and some training in records work could become a reasonably good writer and amateur historian.

742

viduals, the product will not be very good. You and I know that the final writing must be done by one or two persons with a flair for presenting the subject in proper shape, of course with plenty of assistance. Books on government or on racial groups in New York cannot be written co-operatively, although the material and preliminary work can be so done.[86]

In its conception of writing as a collective rather than an individual operation, the Writers' Project stressed certain new and basic principles. One was co-operation, both in "large collective sub-projects in which by means of the vast research man-power available, the FWP can accomplish what no private author or publisher could afford to undertake"; and in "smaller collective sub-projects, in which one or two talented writers are given skilled research assistance of a type never before available to them." In each case the problem was somewhat different. In the former the problem was the "making of a balanced and harmonious manuscript out of the contributions of thirty to fifty writers," so that "by frequent conferences and a guiding editorial board, results such as *New York Panorama . . .* have been achieved." In the latter the "imagination and interpretative ability of the writer is given full play, while at the same time he is stimulated by the endless amount of raw material made available by the research workers. (The New York project alone has 28 million words of classified and indexed field notes in its files.)"[87]

The experience of the Writers' Project demonstrated that although writing cannot be co-operative in the same sense and to the same degree as research, it can be a group activity in the sense not of some mystical act of "communal composition" but of successive improvements and additions by the "collaboration of many hands and many minds." From the first field notes to the final copy, this was a steady process of criticism, revision, and rewriting, involving copyreading for the mechanics of grammar and form (based on the *Government Style Manual*), cutting (the "ability to condense without losing the substance of an article and to rearrange material wherever logic and proportion justify it"), and improving the style and organization to "conform to the character of the subjects." The whole was a problem in directing multiple efforts toward a single end.

To accomplish this it was necessary to establish high and uniform standards based upon a strong central editorial organization and policy. Cronyn wrote:

Now for this Federal publication we are setting a standard and uniform method of treatment and style of writing which we will insist upon in all

743

cases. This is indicated in the Guide Manual, both in the questionnaire section and the examples given at the end of the Manual, but actually we will have to gradually discipline all State Directors in the precise method and literary treatment which we demand for the Federal work.

Very few people are adaptable to this editorial work. It will be distinctly different from any and all publicity, no matter how excellent, which has appeared or is appearing for commercial or other purposes.[88]

It was contended that the Washington office was in a uniquely favorable position to write final copy:

Even though our Washington office may not be wholly familiar with all aspects of every State, we have here considerable facilities for obtaining a clear picture of each State, and through the examination of hundreds of manuscripts have formed standards of comparison which will be of great service to State editors.[89]

In cutting copy, state offices often took the easier, rather than the better, way. Cronyn complained to the state director in Massachusetts:

In examining some of the revised copy that has come in to us, I am rather dismayed to discover that your editors apparently have an unprofessional point of view toward the question of cutting copy to fit word quotas. It is too simple a process merely to delete whole paragraphs or pages that sometimes contain a kernel of important fact. The cutting should be done paragraph by paragraph by eliminating unnecessary statements and words and literary flourishes in order to preserve essentials.

Sometimes a paragraph yields only one fact and a page may have three or four of importance but if whole blocks of copy are cut those previous bits, of course, are lost, and therefore the information is correspondingly inadequate.[90]

The establishment and enforcement of national standards by the Washington office were not without their risks and penalties. There was a tendency to substitute routine for creative approach and a bureaucratic authority for an appreciation of local color and variations. The states, especially those in which the better men were employed, often and bitterly complained that Washington was forcing them into a strait jacket:

We feel that in the matters of rewriting and editing, the efforts of the State office thus far virtually have been wasted. We think we would have saved time, money, and the lowering of morale by simply forwarding the source material to Washington and allowing it to be put in final form there. The Guide Book—to which we have chiefly devoted our time—is not ours. There is hardly a sentence in it that has not been changed from one to a dozen times.

744

We have wondered, frequently just what the New England Guides would have been like if the Southwestern groups had been published first; whether or not they would have been crowded into a mold, into which even the almighty could not make them fit. We have wondered why we must use simple declarative sentences (and that is what they are, even when connected interminably by semicolons) when the most feeble impulse in our brains demands something else—why after years of evolving from the "I see the man" stage, we were forced to return to it. We have written nothing of our own; we have simply digested a book of form telegrams, from which we select as the need arises. When we see an oil well or a statue, or come across some interesting item of history we flip the pages of our inhibition-bound experience until we find some sentence into which our thought will fit, or almost. It may be that in so doing we will have to say (for instance) that so and so died young instead of "he died early in life." But that is the way it is wanted; and after all, it isn't our book.

We have come to know how the six hundred must have felt when they marched into the valley of death. All of our literary training may have taught us that interest and originality should never be sacrificed for brevity and simplicity, but we have learned to follow orders no matter how wrong we know them to be. We have not developed our talents; we have simply become cogs in a machine, the like of which is not to be found in private industry.[91]

A less violent but perhaps more penetrating criticism of the Washington office is contained in a field supervisor's letter:

To generalize (and this applies to the H.R.S. as well as to the Guide), I find among the Western states a continual disposition to criticize the Washington offices on the ground that they are judged by Eastern standards and that the peculiarities of their states are not appreciated. To some extent I think that this is true; although I recognize that other factors enter in which contribute to this impression. I find too the related complaint that local color is edited out. There is a certain strong pride in state and individuality here in the West. Long ago Mrs. Cassidy emphasized to me her plans for giving strong individuality to every tour or locality. Santee once told me that his aim was to make his guide actually *smell* of Arizona. Crane complained that his predecessors in Montana were not Montanans and did not know the state; and that his aim was to make the Guide reek of Montana. The very task of working on the Guide strengthens this local pride and patriotism; so that there is everywhere apparent a discontent against criticism which they claim tends to emasculate this individuality and rob the tours and essays of color. I do not know how true this is; for I have not had the time or background or experience to judge; but I am reporting this condition as a fact.[92]

Another frequent source of irritation to the state offices was the tone of many comments from Washington. The Washington office was aware of this and warned against it:

Mr. Alsberg, just before leaving for New England yesterday, asked me to make sure that all letters and editorial comments sent out in the future

745

are phrased with more care than has been the case in the past. A number of the letters that have been sent out in the past on tours and tour copy have sounded as if we were posing as little tin gods. There has been a definite school-teacherish method of expression used. We must avoid this in order to get the best work out of our state offices.

In looking through certain editorial comments and letters in the past few days, I have noticed that quite often such phrases as the following have been used:

"We told you on January 11th. . . . "
"This must be rewritten entirely immediately."
"Send us immediately. . . . "
"You will have to do this right away."

This sort of phraseology is very poor. It immediately antagonizes the reader. It makes every line of your letter, or editorial letter, sound like a slap. There are very few times when it is necessary to use this type of language in dealing with state directors. It must be assumed that they are intelligent human beings, and in many cases they have long experience in the writing and editorial fields, and that they will not stand for being treated like school children.

At Mr. Alsberg's suggestion, I will stop all letters and editorial comments from going out which contain language of this kind, in the future.[93]

Over a year later, however, Alsberg felt it necessary to issue a similar caution:

I wish to pass on to the editorial staff a word about the complaints which have come to me from various state officers.

In several cases, state staffs have taken offense at facetious comments made in editorial reports or on the margin of returned manuscripts. These comments, while infrequent, are invariably treasured in state files to be pulled out and shown to the visitor from Washington as an example of our wrong-minded and unsympathetic attitude toward their literary efforts. Moreover, they provide a convenient alibi for discounting Washington's really constructive criticism.

For the sake of good working relations, we are asked to be particularly careful to avoid sarcasm, wisecracks or invidious observations reflecting on the ability of state writers. Of course, this is not meant to curb in any way criticism of an objective and impersonal kind.

Also to be avoided if we are to escape the charge of being pedantic is the practice of sending typed editorial comments calling for minute changes in copy, such as the insertion of hyphens, change in capitalization, the use of a synonym, etc. Small changes like this should be made directly on the manuscript.[94]

But the most substantial charge made by the state offices against the Washington office was inconsistency, in that contradictory procedures and conflicting orders were continually issued. This charge was well founded; on the other hand, the Washington office, especially in the beginning, was *in statu pupillari*, and improved as it learned.

Other causes of confusion also existed, as Cronyn pointed out:

> If it seems confusing to receiving conflicting orders, you may be sure that it is far from simple here where any one order involves hundreds of instances, and we have had the experience of having to countermand first instructions after advice from above or from some divisions. As an example of the type of thing we have run into, the Guide manual had to be read and passed upon by thirty-seven people, and that manual is only one of dozens of like instances and details of the work here.[95]

On the other hand, the editorial staff in Washington was not without cause for annoyance:

> . . . I do not feel that the Massachusetts office is justified in leaving so much straight copyreading for incorrect syntax, misuse of words, etc., to this office. Someone has to do it somewhere, and it naturally should be done at the source before it comes to us for criticism. This burden of unnecessary corrections is getting on our copyreaders' nerves and is going a long way to increase a personal underestimation they have of the Boston office, which ought not exist at all. Sloppy copy throws the writer of it on the horns of the well-known dilemma; he is either doing his best, or he isn't. If he is doing his best it indicts his efficiency as a writer; if not it convicts him of a carelessness and indifference that is gumming the whole works. With that feeling fermenting in the copyreading staff, they naturally make acrid comments.[96]

### RELIEF VERSUS QUALITY

Henry G. Alsberg combined in a remarkable degree a genuine sympathy for the plight of writers in need of relief with a lofty concept of writing as an art and as a vehicle for the expression of the national character. For that reason the Guides are, and always will remain, a monument to his magnanimity and professional integrity.

The conceptual possibility, however, of combining in one mind relief and belles-lettres is no assurance that the same synthesis is possible in action. A society on relief is not a society at its best, and there was much in the productions of the Writers' Project that was hackwork; there was also much that was inspired. The Guides, the folklore studies, the life histories, and the social-ethnic program, all these held up the mirror to America; and if the glass reflected, along with the lakes and oceans, mountains and valleys, cities and highways, rich and poor, black and white, the Project itself, and all its faults and virtues, the image was so much the more authentic and complete.

747

1. *American Guide Manual*, WPA, p. 4.

2. Letter, Harris to Blair Bolles, December 6, 1937, FWP Files.

3. Letter, Alsberg to James Hopper, April 3, 1937, FWP Files.

4. U.S. Congress. House. 75th Cong., 3d sess. (1938), *Hearings before the Committee on Patents on H.J. Res. 79 (Department of Science, Art and Literature)*, p. 141.

5. Henry G. Alsberg, "The American Guide," FWP Files.

6. Henry G. Alsberg, "Notes on the Federal Writers' Projects with Special Reference to the American Guide," September 17, 1936, FWP Files.

7. Katherine Kellock, "The WPA Writers: Portraitists of the United States," *American Scholar*, Vol. IX, No. 4 (Autumn, 1940), pp. 477-78.

8. Letter, Alsberg to Ethel B. Kelly, January 6, 1936, FWP Files.

9. Jacob Baker, "The Relationship of the Federal Work Program to Unemployment," April 15, 1936, WPA Files.

10. Letter, Cronyn to Vardis Fisher, October 22, 1936, FWP Files.

11. Letter, Alsberg to Bert James Loewenberg, August 1, 1936, FWP Files.

12. Letter, Harris to Travis Hoke, January 14, 1936, FWP Files.

13. Memorandum, Alsberg to Harris, October 5, 1936, FWP Files.

14. Federal Writers' Project, *American Stuff* (New York: Viking Press, 1937), Foreword by Henry Alsberg.

15. *Direction*, Vol. I, No. 3 (1938), p. 2.

16. *Ibid.*, p. 10.

17. Letter, Alsberg to All State Directors, FWP, March 26, 1938, FWP Files.

18. Josef Berger, *Bowleg Bill* (New York: Viking Press, 1938), p. 5.

19. Instructions No. 9 to the *American Guide Manual, Part A*, WPA, March 12, 1936.

20. *Ibid.*

21. Supplementary Instructions No. 9-A to the *American Guide Manual*, WPA, July 27, 1936.

22. Supplementary Instructions No. 9-C to the *American Guide Manual*, WPA, August 4, 1936.

23. Letter, Alsberg to Charles Ernest White, August 12, 1936, FWP Files.

24. Supplementary Instructions No. 16 to the *American Guide Manual*, WPA, October 21, 1936.

25. Supplementary Instructions No. 9-D to the *American Guide Manual*, WPA, October 31, 1936.

26. *Ibid.*

27. Letter, Alsberg to John J. Lyons, December 4, 1937, FWP Files.

28. *Manual for Folklore Studies*, WPA, September, 1938.

29. Benjamin A. Botkin, *Folk-Say: A Regional Miscellany* (Norman, Okla. Oklahoma Folk-Lore Society, 1929), p. 12.

30. Benjamin A. Botkin, "WPA and Folklore Research: Bread and Song," *Southern Folklore Quarterly* (March, 1939), pp. 7-14.

31. Letters, Alsberg to All State Directors, December 1, 1938, and February 15, 1939, FWP Files.

32. *Ibid.*

33. David Silver, Introduction to "I'm a Might-Have-Been," *Direction*, April-May, 1939.

34. Hyde Partnow, "I'm a Might-Have-Been," *Direction*, May-June, 1939, p. 14.

35. Hyde Partnow, *Fighting Words*, ed. Donald Ogden Stewart (New York: Harcourt, Brace & Co., 1940), pp. 7-9.

36. "Transcript of Staff Conference," FWP, July 13, 1939, FWP Files.

37. Benjamin A. Botkin, *A Treasury of American Folklore* (New York: Crown, 1944), pp. 529-52.

38. Supplement to the Manual for Folklore Studies, FWP, n.d. (1938?), FWP Files.

39. Memorandum on "Living Lore in New England," Botkin to Manuel, August 8, 1938, FWP Files.

40. John A. Lomax, review of *A Treasury of American Folklore* in *Saturday Review of Literature*, July 1, 1944, p. 19. Copyright 1944 The Saturday Review Associates, Inc.

41. Letter, Ruth Benedict to Botkin, January 4, 1939, FWP Files.

42. Memorandum, Botkin to Alsberg, November 14, 1938, FWP Files.

43. Federal Writers' Project, *South Carolina Folk Tales: Stories of Animals and Supernatural Beings* (Columbia, S.C.: University of South Carolina, 1941), Introduction by Reed Smith, p. ix.

44. B. A. Botkin, "Memorandum on Co-operative Folklore and Folk Song Research," October 20, 1938, FWP Files.

45. "Minutes," First Meeting, Joint Committee on Folk Arts, WPA, December 23, 1938.

46. Letter, Lawrence D. Reddick to Hopkins, June 14, 1934, FERA Files.

47. *Ibid.*

48. Supplementary Instructions No. 9-E to the *American Guide Manual*, WPA., April 22, 1937.

49. Memorandum to All State Directors, July 30, 1937, FWP Files.

50. Memorandum, "Notes by an editor on dialect usage in accounts by interviews with ex-slaves," Sterling A. Brown, June 20, 1937, FWP Files.

51. Benjamin A. Botkin, "The Slave as His Own Interpreter," *Library of Congress Quarterly Journal of Current Acquisitions*, Vol. II, No. 1 (November, 1944), pp. 49-50.

52. *Manual for Folklore Studies* and *Manual for Social-Ethnic Studies*, WPA, September, 1938.

53. Caroline F. Ware (ed.), *The Cultural Approach to History* (New York: Columbia University Press, 1940), p. 87.

54. *Manual for Social-Ethnic Studies*, WPA, September, 1938, p. 12.

55. Memorandum, Botkin to Alsberg, November 14, 1938, FWP Files.

56. Letter, Couch to Alsberg, June 1, 1939, FWP Files.

57. Memorandum, Couch to State Directors in the South, December 8, 1939, FWP Files.

58. Letter, Forrester B. Washington to Henry G. Alsberg, January 9, 1936, FWP Files.

59. Memorandum, Cronyn to Baker, November 30, 1935, FWP Files.

60. Letter, Laura D. Middleton and Augustus Ladson to the President, July 8, 1937, WPA Files.

61. "Representation and Resolutions of the Conference on Immediate Human Needs," held at the Russell Sage Foundation Building, March 11, 1939, under the sponsorship of the United Labor and Citizens' Committees, FWP Files.

62. Letter, Alsberg to Carita Doggett Corse, December 10, 1935, FWP Files.

63. Letter, Alsberg to C. J. Nuttall, December 12, 1935, FWP Files.

64. Letter, Alsberg to Grace Overmeyer, June 7, 1936, FWP Files.

65. Letter, Cronyn to T. J. Hamilton, January 27, 1936, FWP Files.

66. Letter, Alsberg to All State Directors, August 12, 1938, FWP Files.

67. Letter, Darel McConkey to Alsberg, August 31, 1936, FWP Files.

68. Memorandum, "The American Guide Exhibition," Reed Harris, FWP Files.

69. Memorandum, Harris to Morris, January 14, 1938, FWP Files.

70. Letter, Cronyn to L. S. Hill, October 25, 1935, FWP Files.

71. Letter, Harris to Gay B. Shepperson, October 12, 1935, FWP Files.

72. Letter, Alsberg to Paul Ellsworth Triem, November 26, 1935, FWP Files.

73. Letter, William Cunningham to Dorothy Pratt, April 19, 1938, FWP Files.

74. "A Report on Progress, June 15, 1939," The Federal Writers' Project of Massachusetts, FWP Files.

75. *The American Guide Manual*, WPA, October, 1935, p. 6.

76. Letter, Alsberg to James Hopper, April 19, 1937, FWP Files.

77. Letter, Alsberg to Floyd Sharp, April 14, 1936, FWP Files.

78. Letter, Alsberg to Dana M. Doten, November 14, 1935, FWP Files.

79. Letter, McConkey to Alsberg, December 21, 1935, FWP Files.

80. Memorandum, Alsberg to Woodward, August 24, 1935, FWP Files.

81. Letter, James Thompson to Botkin, May 16, 1939, FWP Files.

82. Letter, Alsberg to Lincoln Colcord, March 7, 1936, FWP Files.

83. Letter, Binkley to Alsberg, June 11, 1936, FWP Files.

84. *The American Guide Manual*, WPA, October, 1935, p. 26.

85. Letter, Alsberg to William B. Browne, December 4, 1935, FWP Files.

86. Letter, Alsberg to Travis Hoke, January 25, 1937, FWP Files.

87. Merle Colby, "Work of the Federal Writers' Project," *Publishers' Weekly*, March 18, 1939.

88. Letter, Cronyn to William P. Fahey, October 22, 1935, FWP Files.

89. Letter, Cronyn to Mabel Ulrich, June 25, 1936, FWP Files.

90. Letter, Cronyn to Ray A. Billington, April 7, 1937, FWP Files.

91. Letter, James Thompson to B. A. Botkin, May 16, 1939, FWP Files.

92. Report of J. M. Scammell, as quoted in letter, Reed to Mary Barret *et al.*, January 26, 1938, FWP Files.

93. Memorandum, Reed Harris to Katherine Kellock *et al.*, February 17, 1937, FWP Files.

94. Memorandum, Alsberg to Members of the Editorial Staff, June 16, 1938, FWP Files.

95. Letter, Cronyn to Vardis Fisher, November 2, 1935, FWP Files.

96. Letter, Edward Barrows to Joseph Gaer, April 27, 1937, FWP Files.

# 29

## The Origins of the Historical Records Survey

HISTORICAL RECORDS PROJECTS IN THE
EARLY FERA AND CWA

A fortuitous but fortunate combination of circumstances in the early 1930's made work-relief projects in the field of archives and historical records both popular and providential. In the first place, the archival discipline had developed to such a point that public officials—federal, state, and local—were aware of the importance of public records and the need for their care and accessibility. Second, archivists, partly because of the pressure they were able to exert through professional societies and partly because some of their number had already achieved public administrative status, were able to recommend to relief officials the advantages of archival projects. Most important of all, such projects recommended themselves almost universally as ideally suited to the employment needs of the white-collar class, especially those in the clerical category. The impression was current that the techniques necessary for this kind of work were so elementary that, under proper supervision, almost anyone with an ability to read and write and intelligent enough to understand simple directions could undertake the task. Thus, it was thought, archival projects could achieve an "assembly line" character that would permit the establishment of large projects with a minimum of supervision and resolve the antithesis between mass unemployment and technical competence that was so apparent in the arts projects.*

*That archival projects generally required less specialized personnel than arts projects is true enough. This emphasis upon simplicity of technique, however, was overdrawn and, where it prevailed unduly, resulted in untrustworthy products. An

751

Perhaps the earliest significant attempt to adapt records work to the exigencies of relief was made in New Orleans in 1931, and possibly in 1930. A report written early in 1932 states that "the New Orleans Welfare Committee has used clerical workers in the various city departments to do filing, sorting, copying, and so on. They have done a particularly good job on the city archives which had had no attention for years because of lack of funds."[1] Mrs. Woodward reported in November, 1933, that in New Orleans 250 women were being used in seventy different city offices repairing and indexing records dating back 200 years. "For the first time in the history of the City, records have been made available for convenient use."[2]

But the two most important projects preceding the inauguration of the Historical Records Survey were those of Alabama and Pennsylvania. The Alabama project, sponsored by the Alabama Department of Archives and History, was initiated with a grant from the RFC and subsequently continued by grants from the CWA and the FERA. Thomas M. Owen, Jr., at that time assistant to the director of the department and most responsible for the project and its administration, reported in 1933 that the activities of the program included: the copying of some 70,000 epitaphs from gravestones in Montgomery County cemeteries; copying of county histories, old diaries, and other miscellaneous material; copying and indexing marriage records of Montgomery and Autauga counties from 1817 to 1919; copying six of twelve volumes of Montgomery County wills; copying 5,000 obituary and marriage notices from Alabama county newspapers; filing more than 25,000 newspaper clippings; indexing out-of-print books; indexing the map collection of the department; card-indexing the commissions issued to state and county officials from 1818 to 1900; making cards of all civil commissions issued to citizens of Alabama from 1818 to 1900; card-indexing all bound records of the department; card-indexing some 122,000 Confederate military records; reorganizing the state archives; rearranging, indexing, and labeling all bound volumes of Alabama newspapers; and arranging the magazine collection so that all numbers were in their proper places.[3]

early archives survey project, begun in Schenectady, New York, in 1933, was abandoned because the workers obtainable from relief were not qualified for the tasks demanded by that particular program. In a sense, as those who became connected with the several archival programs eventually discovered, competent supervision, no less than competent personnel, was as necessary in a records project as in any other technical project. The difficulty was (and therein lay the danger of self-deception) that a shoddy work of art was immediately apparent to the critic, whereas a careless inventory escaped detection unless it was checked by an examination almost as meticulous as the original compilation.

These many and varied tasks were attempted with a relief personnel of modest size. Mrs. Woodward reported in November, 1933, that the Alabama Department of Archives and History was utilizing the services of 132 persons, mostly women, on seventeen different projects concerned with the discovery and recording of historical data.[4]

The Alabama project, although it included tasks of an archival nature, was really a historical project that attempted work well beyond the limits of records administration. Its importance lies in the fact that it was attempted under professional supervision (Owen was ably assisted by other members of the staff of the Alabama Department of Archives and History) and provided an example by which the Washington office of the FERA could instruct and encourage other public bodies to attempt similar projects.

The archival project in Pennsylvania was authorized on December 2, 1933, by the CWA. Its purpose was to conduct a historical survey of Pennsylvania, including state, county, and municipal archives, manuscript material that was not archival, church records, newspapers, and bibliography. The survey was originally directed by the archivist of Pennsylvania, Curtis W. Garrison, and later by John Paul Selsam. Forms were devised for the collection of data on the various types of historical documents, and instructions as to the assembling of the data were furnished. A separate form was prepared for each county office showing the classes of records the workers might expect to find. On this form, workers were required to collect information as to the title of each record series, inclusive dates, quantity, and location. There was also a form for general information on the condition of the records of a county, adequacy of storage facilities, etc.*

The temporary federalization of relief under the CWA late in 1933 made possible the operation of federal projects, one of which was sponsored by the Library of Congress and inaugurated in December, 1933. Its purpose was the preparation of an index of portraits appearing in periodicals. In 1906 the American Library Association had compiled an index of portraits appearing in printed books and periodicals prior to

---

*The projects in Alabama and Pennsylvania were the largest but not the only manifestations of a professional interest on the part of state and local officials in the use of work relief for archival surveys. Theodore C. Blegen, of the Minnesota Historical Society, in discussing accomplishments under the CWA, reported similar work in other states as follows: Colorado, Minnesota, Texas; and on a smaller scale in Kansas, Nebraska, Missouri, Iowa, Idaho, and North Dakota.[5] Among undertakings not mentioned by Dr. Blegen were projects in Schenectady, New York, in Monogalia and Harrison Counties in West Virginia, in Burke County, Georgia, and in Bismarck, North Dakota.

1904, and the present occasion was taken to bring the index to date. The project operated with a staff of from thirty to fifty-one workers, and by March 21, 1934, it had prepared 110,000 index cards at the cost of $10,909.69.

## THE JOINT COMMITTEE'S PROPOSAL FOR A NATIONWIDE SURVEY

It was indicative of the applicability of archival projects to the device of work relief, as developed by the early FERA and the CWA, that in December, 1933, a suggestion for a wider use of historical surveys by Joanna C. Colcord, a professional social worker, coincided with an attempt by professional historians and archivists to initiate a nationwide survey of archives. On December 6, 1933, Miss Colcord, director of the charity organization department of the Russell Sage Foundation, addressed a letter to Jacob Baker pointing out that state historical societies and similar organizations should be called upon for suggestions as to useful public-service projects that might be initiated with federal aid. She suggested such undertakings as copying of disintegrating documents; indexing of Revolutionary War and Civil War pension lists; compiling early vital statistics for preservation, since early town records were being lost in large numbers yearly through fires and neglect; preparing local town and county histories where none existed; copying for state libraries ancient diaries and other historical material in private hands; and copying tombstone inscriptions before they became completely illegible. These types of work were also called to the attention of some one hundred state and local historical societies in a circular letter of the same date, with the idea that these agencies might be instrumental in initiating projects to carry forward such work; and a summary of replies to the circular letter was sent to Julius Stone, then director of federal projects of the CWA, on December 21, 1933.[6]

The inspiration for this inquiry, as Miss Colcord pointed out, was the possibility of initiating federal projects under the auspices of the CWA. The same chance was seized by certain historians and archivists to prepare a nationwide survey of archives. At the annual meeting of the American Historical Association in Columbus, Ohio, in December, 1933, Jean Stephenson, then chairman of the genealogical records committee of the D.A.R., proposed taking advantage of the availability of the unemployed manpower of the country and of federal financial aid in launching a nationwide archival project. At the same time, Francis

S. Philbrick, of the University of Pennsylvania Law School, taking note of the archival survey already begun in Pennsylvania under the direction of Curtis W. Garrison, archivist of Pennsylvania, addressed a letter to Joseph Mayer of the Library of Congress expressing the hope that Mayer might be able "to initiate in Washington some general plan for the preparation of archive inventories and possibly also the preparation of legal history bibliographies."[7] This letter was answered by Corrington Gill, director of the research and statistics division of FERA. He replied:

> In so far as your suggestion pertains to a national project to be undertaken by some department of the Federal Government with Civil Works funds, we believe that in view of the necessity of winding up all projects by February 15th it would be impracticable to attempt at this stage to organize such a project. Should it happen that further funds will become available after February 15th, it is possible that a project of the type you suggest might be sponsored by one of the Federal departments.[8]

Encouraged by this reply, Philbrick, in co-operation with Conyers Read, executive secretary of the American Historical Association, worked out a tentative plan for a national survey of county archives. This plan is outlined in a letter of January 11, 1934, to Robert C. Binkley, chairman of the Joint Committee on Materials for Research of the American Council of Learned Societies and the Social Science Research Council, and professor of history at Western Reserve University, with the hope that he might assist in carrying the plan through to realization. Philbrick addressed similar communications to Theodore C. Pease of the Illinois Historical Society; A. R. Newsome, chairman of the history department, University of North Carolina and secretary of the North Carolina Historical Commission; Solon J. Buck, director of the Western Pennsylvania Historical Society; Wayne C. Coy, director of the California State Historical Society; Lieutenant Colonel J. M. Scammell, of the National Guard Bureau in Washington, and other scholars. Binkley forthwith proposed a conference in Washington to consider the launching of a nationwide archival survey. This was held late in January, and the joint committee further considered the matter at a conference in New York early in February. The executive secretary of the joint committee, T. R. Schellenberg, was directed to draft a proposal for such a project, and the joint committee formed a subcommittee on inventory (the Commission on National Archives Survey) to promote it.*

*The Commission consisted of the following members: Joseph Mayer, Library

On February 12, 1934, this commission addressed a circular letter to archivists, librarians, historians, adjutant generals, and others throughout the country, with a copy of the proposal calling for the employment during an eight-week period of 2,775 workers at a cost of approximately $677,000, on a survey of archives preserved in county offices and other local and state depositories.

A second proposal by the commission provided for either a two-month or twelve-month project. The former called for a national director, state directors, traveling supervisors for groups of counties, one or more workers in each county, and assistants in state directors' offices. The twelve-month project called for the same personnel except that one group of traveling workers for a state (about four in number) would be used in lieu of one or two workers in each county. The results anticipated from the proposed nationwide survey of local archives were: stimulation of local history studies; preservation of local archival materials; and improvement in archival practices of American local government units. The commission was assured of the support of such professional bodies as the following: the joint committee of the American Council of Learned Societies, the American Military History Foundation, the American Library Association, the American Association of Museums, the Office of National Parks, Buildings, and Reservations of the Department of the Interior, the National Guard Bureau, the American Historical Association, and the American Legal History Society.*

This move for the institution of a nationwide survey of records was almost completely under way when Congress, by the statutory limitation that it inserted in the ERA Act of February 15, 1934, prohibited federal projects. The commission and other learned bodies and interested individuals were consequently forced to bring their energy to bear upon the encouragement and initiation of local projects.

RECORDS PROJECTS UNDER THE FERA'S
EMERGENCY WORK PROGRAM

Under the Emergency Work Program of the FERA, instituted in

of Congress; Verne E. Chatelaine, Historian, Office of National Parks, Buildings, and Reservations, Department of the Interior; Curtis W. Garrison, Archivist, State of Pennsylvania; A. R. Newsome; Francis S. Philbrick; Lt. Col. J. M. Scammell; and T. R. Schellenberg.

*This account of the activity of the joint committee owes much to the personal files of Francis S. Philbrick, Philadelphia.

April, 1934, the Work Division, under the director of Jacob Baker, was designated as responsible for the furtherance of professional projects.* Since, with the discontinuance of the CWA, the national office was unable to initiate projects, the staff contented itself with a program of education, hoping to inspire sponsorship of records projects by state and local government. The Section for Professional and Non-manual Projects, under the direction of Arthur Goldschmidt, used the device of "working procedures," which were elaborated on the basis of FERA and CWA experiences and of suggestions, such as those of the joint committee, made by individuals and groups interested in the program. The earliest of these working procedures for historical records projects were circulated among state ERA offices in October, 1934.†[9]

Despite the difficulties that professional projects encountered under the grant-in-aid system of the FERA,‡ the state and local archival and historical projects demonstrated that relief workers, if carefully selected on the basis of their previous training and properly supervised and instructed, could do creditable and useful work in this field. They also showed that professional bodies, cognizant of the need and importance of archival reform, were ready to encourage and promote such projects and to contribute their technical experience and wisdom. Finally, and not least of all, a well-managed project and well-done product attracted the attention and favorable comment of state, county, and local officials, most of whom quickly became aware of the importance not only to themselves but also to their clientele of proper records properly kept and readily accessible.

*Vide supra, p. 67 ff.

†Four working procedures were enclosed with this letter, viz: F2.3 Inventory of State, County and Municipal Archives; F2.4. Inventory of Military Records; F2.5. Inventory of Historical Manuscripts; and F4.1. Classification and Physical Renovation of Records. Three days later a fifth working procedure (F2.6. Legal Research Work) was added.[10]

‡Vide supra, pp. 71-74.

1. "Unemployed Relief Methods," Family Welfare Association of America, Monthly Summary No. 3, Vol. VI, No. 10 (February, 1932).

2. *Proceedings of the Conference on Emergency Needs of Women*, FERA, White House, November 20, 1933, p. 13.

3. Digest of report in letter, J. C. Colcord to Julius Stone, December 21, 1933, CWA Files.

4. *Proceedings of the Conference on Emergency Needs of Women*, FERA, White House, November 20, 1933, p. 14.

5. Theodore C. Blegen, "Aspects of Historical Work under the New Deal," a paper read at the Historical Society Conference of the Mississippi Valley Historical Association, Columbia, Missouri, April 18, 1934. A copy reposes in the files of the Joint Committee on Materials for Research of the American Council of Learned Societies and the Social Science Research Council, "Archives" folder, Library of Congress.

6. Letter with attachments, Colcord to Stone, December 21, 1933, CWA Files.

7. Letter, Philbrick to Mayer, December 18, 1933, CWA Files.

8. Letter, Gill to Philbrick, December 22, 1933, CWA Files.

9. Letter WDO-13, FERA, October 16, 1934.

10. Letter WDO-14, FERA, October 19, 1934.

758

# 30

# The Organization and Operation of the Historical Records Survey

THE INITIATION OF THE HISTORICAL RECORDS SURVEY

The influence of accident or coincidence upon the growth of a historical idea is nicely illustrated by the series of circumstances that eventually led to the appointment of Luther H. Evans as head of the WPA Historical Records Survey. At the close of the academic year 1934–35, Evans was assistant professor of political science at Princeton University. So far as is known, he not only was unconnected with any of the efforts to institute a survey of historical records as a work-relief project but was wholly unaware of them. Late in June, 1935, however, it seems, Harry Hopkins had discussed with Raymond Moley of Columbia University the possibility of a nationwide records survey. Moley, who in turn had become acquainted with Evans through one of the latter's students at Princeton, suggested that he go to Washington and confer with Hopkins on the subject. He accepted the suggestion and after one or two conferences undertook the drafting of detailed plans for a nationwide archival survey. Characteristically, he threw himself into this work without any assurance from the administrator of the WPA that such a project would be approved or that he would be chosen to direct it.

Evans, if he came to Washington unaware of the nature of the earlier records project, possessed the good judgment immediately to avail himself of professional assistance. Fortunately, he enjoyed the friendship of Dr. Binkley, of Western Reserve University, to whom he announced in a confidential telegram, June 29, 1935, that he was investigating the possibilities of a historical project and requested Binkley's suggestions.[1] Binkley immediately advised him by wire to see T. R.

Schellenberg, executive secretary of the joint committee, who was also a member of the National Archives staff. The latter wrote on June 30 outlining the plans, already described, that had been made early in 1934 for a nationwide archival project. The joint committee files were made available to Evans, and with the co-operation of representatives of the National Archives, the American Council of Learned Societies, the Social Science Research Council, the National Park Service, and some officials of the WPA, he began drafting plans for a nationwide project. The speed with which he worked is indicated by the fact that on July 6, less than a week after Binkley's letter, he addressed a memorandum to Hopkins on a project for a survey of state and local archives. This set forth the purpose of the project, outlined its more important aspects, gave a plan of administration, and discussed the amount of money required to finance the undertaking.

On July 23, in a second memorandum more detailed than the first, he discussed the purpose of the project and the work to be undertaken, and proposed the appointment of an advisory committee on surveys of state and local archives to assist him, as the national co-ordinator, in working out detailed plans. Ten persons were suggested as members of the committee. Duties of the national co-ordinator, advisory committee, assistant national co-ordinators, state directors, and executive assistants were also defined. An allotment of $15,480,660, exclusive of the national co-ordinator's salary, was proposed, and details of the estimate were given.

A conference on July 26, attended by R. D. W. Connor, archivist of the United States, Verne E. Chatelaine, chief of the historical division in the branch of research and education of the National Park Service, Department of the Interior, and Jacob Baker, Bruce McClure, and Arthur Goldschmidt of the Washington office of the WPA, resulted in a tentative arrangement for the establishment of two archival projects. One was to be a survey of federal records located in depositories within the United States but outside the District of Columbia, and the other was to be a survey of state and local historical records. The first was to be set up under the co-sponsorship of the National Archives; the second, under that of the National Park Service.

This arrangement was fulfilled in part in the Survey of Federal Archives, which was eventually established under the co-sponsorship of the National Archives as WPA-sponsored Federal Project No. 4, but it was not final with respect to the survey of state and local records. For two months thereafter (August and September, 1935) Evans was afforded the facilities of Chatelaine's office in the National Park Service. Chatelaine's files, which contained important material on earlier projects and project proposals, were made available; and Chatelaine and his assistant, Herman Kahn, worked with Evans in drafting the basic plans of the contemplated survey. The original intention, however, that the National Park Service should act as co-sponsor, was eventually abandoned.

## THE PERIOD OF VASSALAGE

During the period of incubation Evans not only profited from the files and from advice of the joint committee and the National Park Service but also consulted frequently with staff members of the National Archives and of the Library of Congress, particularly in the manuscript and map divisions. Valuable suggestions were also offered by A. R. Newsome, Francis S. Philbrick, and Curtis W. Garrison, all members of the Commission on National Archives Survey; William D. Overman, historian and archivist of the state of Ohio; Alexander Flick, New York State Historian; Robert T. Crane, permanent secretary of the Social Science Research Council; and Waldo G. Leland, secretary of the American Council of Learned Societies.[2]

As a result, when Evans was finally appointed on October 1, 1935, to the technical staff of the Washington office of the WPA as "supervisor of historic projects," plans for the survey of state and local historical records were almost complete except for the manual of technical instructions; and as work on the manual progressed, the project proposal advanced through the devious channels that eventually led to official approval. Finally, on November 16, initial funds were made available to the survey in the amount of $1,195,800 by Presidential Letter No. 1090, dated November 16, 1935. Although the project was described as nationwide, the initial allocation was not made in a lump sum as for the four arts projects that comprised Federal One but broken down into a separate allotment for each state, each allotment identified by a separate official project number. If this arrangement had endured, there would have been no WPA-sponsored federal historical records survey, but instead a series of state projects—co-ordinated, to be sure, by the Washington staff, but initiated and controlled by the states.

By November 16, however, it was decided to administer the project, now called the Historical Records Survey, as a WPA-sponsored federal project, and a new Presidential Letter (No. 1188) rescinded No. 1090 and consolidated in Washington under one official project number the amounts previously allocated individually to each of the states. Moreover, since the venture with the National Park Service was disappointing and the survey had lost a co-sponsor, it was adopted by the WPA as its own federally sponsored child and placed in the immediate care of the Writers' Project.

The administrative decision that brought the H.R.S. within Federal One, at first as a subordinate part of the Writers' Project, was an accident. It was not based upon considerations of consanguinity between the H.R.S. and the four arts projects (the H.R.S., for all its cultural implications, was not an art project) but upon considerations of administrative convenience, which counseled the grouping of all projects sponsored solely by the WPA under one general heading (Federal One). Within Federal One the relationship between the H.R.S. and the Writers' Project was more obvious, although at bottom superficial. It is true that both projects were concerned with writing; but if that had been a principle of union, the whole research program of the WPA might well have been subordinated to the Writers' Project. The Writers' Project, especially in the mind of its director, Henry Alsberg, aimed at creative interpretation of American life; and if the guides and other products of the project did not always or wholly achieve this end, the pedestrian character of much of the project's work was leavened by the romantic approach of the Washington office. The work of the H.R.S. on the other hand, was prosaic and to a considerable degree clerical, and the inventories produced, however much they might provide the inspired writer with material for historical and romantic exercises, were not in themselves imaginative or interpretive. In the end, after 1939, true relationship prevailed, and the H.R.S. was placed where by every principle of kinship it belonged—in the research and record program.

There were other reasons why the Writers' Project did not provide an acceptable domicile for the H.R.S. The subordination of Evans as national supervisor of the survey to Alsberg, the national director of the Writers' Project, was implicit in the arrangement, even if not clearly defined; and friction was increased by the fact that the subjects of concern to the principals were different. Alsberg was not director of both projects but of the Writers' Project only, and a staff relationship that might have been otherwise comfortable was made awkward by the technical independence that Evans both enjoyed and asserted in the Washington office.

The lack of co-ordination between the two projects was even more apparent in the field than in the Washington office. Appendix C to *Supplement No. 1 to Bulletin No. 29*, dated January 10, 1936, which established the rules governing the H.R.S., provided that it should operate with and under the Federal Writers' Project, and should use the existing machinery of that project. Among other things, the Appendix provided that the state directors of the Federal Writers' Project should serve as state supervisors of the Survey, but that, upon authorization from the federal director of the Writers' Project, assistant state supervisors might be appointed with special charge of the survey, to be paid from the sums specifically authorized to the individual states for the survey. In accordance with the procedure used by Federal One, requests for project approval were to be made on WPA Form 330 (later WPA Form 330, Revised), over the signature of the state director of the Writers' Project. Thus Evans, though he was able to assert his technical jurisdication in the Washington office, found himself without a line of staff authority extending into the states, and, as a result, was unable to ensure the execution of his technical directions in the field.

It was not that Alsberg failed or refused to co-operate. From January 4 to 6, 1935, he sent letters to the state directors of the Writers' Project, telling them about the Historical Records Survey, what it hoped to accomplish, and how much money would be allotted for the project in each state. They were asked to make contacts with state librarians, historians, archivists, and historical societies to secure their recommendations and advice before proceeding with the actual initiation of the project within the states. Again in March, 1936, Alsberg and Evans sent out a joint letter instructing workers on the Writers' Project and on the survey to co-operate in the exchange of information that would be mutually helpful. It was under Alsberg's regime that the *Manual of the Survey of Historical Records* was finally completed (January, 1936) and distributed to the states. The first state project unit was organized late in January, and by the end of April projects had been established in every state.*

The fact was that for all his show of co-operation—and it was sincere enough—Alsberg was not by temperament or by virtue of his assigned responsibility interested in the H.R.S.; and this lack of interest

---

*Unlike the Music, Theater, and Art projects, which were authorized to establish work project units along geographic, administrative, or functional lines within the limits of the approved statewide authorization, the Historical Records Survey operated in each state as a single statewide project. In this arrangement it followed the structure of the Writers' Project as it existed in January, 1936.

in the Washington office was reflected in the attitude of indifference in the state offices of the Writers' Project. The primary concern of the Writers' Project was the preparation of the guides; and as it was still in the feverish period of initiation, its technical personnel lacked the time and the inclination to devote itself to the affairs of the H.R.S.

## THE DECLARATION OF INDEPENDENCE

The fundamental incompatibility of the two projects resulted in mutual suspicion and, eventually, in recrimination, especially on the part of the H.R.S., which, smarting under its position as vassal, accused the Writers' Project of asserting a liege lord's claim to temporal support. In reporting on the status of the survey in the middle of August, 1936, Evans wrote:

"The source of most of our troubles in regard to our quota of workers has been the fact that since the middle of April we have had to carry on our payroll several hundred Guide workers. We estimate that the Survey has lost between fifty and one hundred thousand dollars of its funds by carrying writers on its payrolls."[3]

In commenting on the situation in various states, Evans pointed out that in Pennsylvania the assistant state supervisor and the director of the Writers' Project had been unable to co-operate satisfactorily and that, with the consent of the director, full responsibility for managing the survey had been delegated to the assistant state supervisor, with the reservation that the director should sign the project approval (WPA Form 330). He reported further that the same sort of action had been taken in Wisconsin and Illinois.

As more and more instances of trouble were called to his attention by his field supervisors, Evans finally requested a report, state by state, indicating whether the situation in each was (1) disadvantageous to the Historical Records Survey with regard to personnel, costs, etc., (2) fairly or moderately advantageous, or (3) advantageous. With the information in these reports at hand, Evans proposed in September, 1936, separation of the Historical Records Survey from the Writers' Project, and establishment of the survey as Federal Project No. 7.[4]

This memorandum was supplemented by a résumé of the situation as it existed in each state at that time. This protest was submitted to Mrs. Woodward's office without preliminary clearance through Alsberg's office—a violation of procedural form that provoked Alsberg's protests. For several days the situation was tense; but in the end, despite his unorthodox means, Evans won his point. Alsberg, in consideration of the withdrawal of the memorandum from the files, consented to join with Evans in a joint recommendation for the separation of the two projects.

Early in October, 1936, Alsberg and Evans sent out letters to the state directors of the Writers' Project and assistant state supervisors of the H.R.S. notifying them that on October 15 the survey would become an independent project under Federal One, in accordance with the regulation just issued by Mrs. Woodward upon their joint request, and that the assistant state supervisor would automatically become the state director of the survey.* This regulation, however, addressed to all state administrators over Mrs. Woodward's signature, was not finally issued until November 20, 1936.[5]

After separation from the Writers' Project, the survey continued as an independent unit of Federal One until the ERA Act of 1939 abolished projects sponsored solely by the WPA, breaking it down into a series of state and local projects.

## LUTHER H. EVANS

Luther H. Evans was born in Texas in 1902. He manifested, as national supervisor of the H.R.S., those qualities of pertinacity and self-assertiveness that are traditionally associated with his native state. He was academically trained, having received his B.A. degree from the University of Texas in 1923 with a major in political science and a minor in economics, his M.A. in 1924, and his Ph.D. from Stanford University in 1927 with a major in political science and minors in modern European and American history. However, there was nothing in the summer of 1935 to recommend him to Harry Hopkins' attention except Raymond Moley's good offices and his own presence on the scene of action.

Furthermore, his professional career before 1935 gave him no special claim to consideration in the field of archives and archival administration, and he was untried as an administrator. He was a student

---

*In a few states, where such procedure appeared desirable, state directors of the Writers' Project served as directors of the survey, without additional compensation, or an agreement was reached whereby the survey paid the director's salary in one state and the Writers' Project paid it in another.

reader in political science at the University of Texas, 1922-24, and he traveled abroad in the summer of 1924 to study the League of Nations and European governments. Upon his return to the United States in the fall he held the position of instructor in problems of citizenship at Stanford University while studying for his doctorate. He visited Europe again in the summer of 1927 and served as instructor in government at New York University, 1927-28, in political science at Dartmouth, 1928-30, and as assistant professor of politics at Princeton University, 1930-35.

Luther Evans' mind was clear, and his purpose was single; and the very fact that he was a novice among professional archivists inspired him to absorb by hard work and concentrated effort what others had elaborated in the course of years. In this he was helped by the unselfish attitude of the archivists, who, together with scholars in the field of history and allied subjects, co-operated generously in the initiation of the project; and their zeal did not lessen when Evans, who was not one of their number, was appointed supervisor. Indeed, as early as January, 1936, when the project was just beginning, the joint committee sent out a letter to historians, librarians, archivists, political scientists, and scholars in related fields informing them of the launching of the Historical Records Survey, giving the survey its endorsement, and requesting their co-operation in the various states. The letter stated that Evans' point of view coincided with that of archivists and historical experts, and added that "the Joint Committee is glad to give him its full support, and sincerely hopes that you will do the same."[6]

Evans, on his part, observed a respectful and indeed humble attitude toward professional advice. For this reason the public relations of the H.R.S. were not only above reproach but a tower of strength to the project. Throughout the life of the project the annual meetings of the American Historical Association, the American Library Association, the Society of American Archivists, and other professional and scholarly organizations were usually attended by representatives of the survey. For several years a special session of the American Library Association's annual meetings was devoted to the work of the survey, and some of the papers read by members of the project staff at the special sessions were published. In 1940 four papers by members of the survey staff were published in the American Library Association's *Public Documents*. Papers were also frequently read by members of the staff at annual meetings of the Society of American Archivists—a considerable number of the staff were members of this organization—and some were subsequently published in the society's quarterly, the *American Archi-*

*vist.* The political and social, no less than the professional, importance of good public relations was always in Evans' mind, and he assiduously cultivated the good will of the Daughters of the American Revolution and the Daughters of the Confederacy. Jean Stephenson of the D.A.R. offered the assistance and co-operation of the members of her society, particularly of the genealogical records committee. She told Evans that she had worked out plans and forms for such a survey as early as 1932 and that it was intended that work should begin on it in 1936. Copies of the plans, instructions, and forms drawn up were placed at the disposal of the H.R.S. Since such a nationwide survey was now being launched under WPA, she was ready to abandon her plan and lend whatever assistance was possible to the Historical Records Survey.[7] Evans was diligent in seeing that this cordial relationship was not confined to the federal level, and with his encouragement contacts with local chapters of the D.A.R. were made and maintained by the H.R.S. personnel in the states.

The use of advisory committees in the states, however, was not particularly successful. Those who were nominated to these committees were generally occupied with other duties and accepted the invitation as a routine gesture on the part of the project. The state staffs were usually too busy with administrative and technical details to encourage meetings of the committees or to enter into discussions that were inspiring, perhaps, but little related to the immediate needs of the particular project unit. Indeed, such advisory committees as were formed were a gesture toward good public relations, and were accepted as such both by those who created the committees and by those who sat on them. In Louisiana, by way of exception, the state committee gave advice on editorial policy and techniques, and assisted in recruiting technically qualified supervisory personnel and in advancing public relations with local officials through personal contact and publicity. In Indiana a more practical approach to immediate problems was attempted when the state office encouraged the formation of county commissions on public records; these bodies were authorized by act of the general assembly, with power to dispose of old records and plan archival measures for the county.

Although advisory committees, as such, were not generally active in the states, individual members and others interested in the project were generous in giving technical aid and advice. In these cases the relationship between the state director and his staff on the one hand and the interested individuals on the other was usually personal; and these informal friendships, based upon common interests and mutual respect, were more fruitful by far than formal committees.

In the national office, also, although the joint committee, as such, performed indispensable service, especially in the period of initiation, the constant relationship between Evans and a few interested scholars provided that abiding guidance that few committees have the vitality to contribute. Indeed, it was not until 1940 that Sargent B. Child, Evans' successor, acting largely under the prompting of Mrs. Kerr and in conformity with the action of the three arts projects, formed a national advisory committee.

But if Luther Evans was energetic in seeking and securing the good opinion of professional bodies and other groups of standing interested in the program, his attitude toward publicity in general was not without discrimination. A characteristic sense of caution, which made his program the most politically acceptable of the five in Federal One, warned him against the dangers of wholesale releases; and especially at the beginning of the program, when the WPA was being violently attacked by the press, he counseled moderation and enjoined, for the most part, the issue of general releases, lest the H.R.S. be considered another example of "boondoggling."

His demeanor of respectful attention toward professional archivists and learned societies was equaled by his reluctance to admit them to positions of administrative and technical responsibility within the program. The contradiction here was more apparent than real, and the attitude, though it may well have derived in part from a natural sense of professional inferiority, was based upon sound administrative considerations. In the establishment of procedures and the elaboration of technical instructions, Evans recognized the importance of professional advice; in the execution of a program, however, once the procedural and technical lines were established, he insisted upon conformity. The presence of technical experts with professional standing on the staff of the project might, he feared, create tensions arising from their special interests that he, because of his amateur status, would lack the prestige to resolve. At one time he considered asking Grace Lee Nute, a specialist in the field of manuscripts, to direct the manuscripts program; after reflection he changed his mind, because, as he remarked, he wanted the manuscripts program to be his, and not Miss Nute's. His experience in the imprints program confirmed him in this attitude. An expert in the field of imprints was chosen to direct this section of the project. The experiment was unhappy, for the expert, aware of his own eminence in the field, found it difficult to accept instructions from Washington and, in the end, resigned.

Thus the technical personnel of the H.R.S., both in Washington and in the states, was composed of younger men and women. Indeed, almost as a matter of principle, Evans avoided engaging older persons; and many members of the Washington staff, as their personal history statements show, were in their early twenties. This policy enabled him to retain in his own hands strong control over all phases of the program— a control that approached rigidity at times. This lack of elasticity, which in another kind of program might have been fatal, was congenial to the demands of the H.R.S. The very nature of the subject matter made uniformity a virtue once the technical instructions were established, and the area within which discretion and imagination were demanded or desirable on the part of the subordinate personnel was extremely limited.*

Evans' extension of the authoritarian attitude from the technical to the administrative domain was perhaps less happy. In his own office, and with the state project personnel, he attached a high degree of importance to harmonious relations; and by a quality of approachability that made him accessible and sympathetic with the problems and interests of his staff, he developed in his project an *esprit de corps*, which, if it did not derive from a genuine affection for the chief, was based upon a deep respect for his integrity. On the other hand, his action toward state supervisors and other subordinates who gave evidence of disloyalty or incompetence was often drastic and, upon occasion, ruthless. There was considerable turnover in the personnel of the central office during 1936 and 1937, as well as among the state supervisors during Evans' tenure. It is a tribute to his character, however, that his appointees were able in the main to accept discipline with good grace; and even later, those who participated in the program agreed that the first national supervisor was responsible for a program that was well managed administratively and, so far as was possible under the limitations of work relief, technically competent.

In his relations with his own superiors, and especially with the office of the assistant administrator in charge of professional and service projects, Evans maintained an attitude of self-sufficiency that gave the high

---

*It must be conceded, of course, that the salaries the H.R.S. was able to offer subordinate personnel were not in general adequate to attract men of established reputation, and that Evans, even had he been so inclined, could not have brought into the program on a full-time basis men in a position of economic security.

command the impression that he was a competent young man who raised few questions, made still fewer demands, and disposed of problems as they arose with a dispatch and finality that made intervention superfluous. His concept of the primacy of the project as opposed to that of relief was well expressed in his reply to a protest against a reduction in quota addressed to him by the Federal Writers' Project Guild. Although expressing regret at the necessity for the reduction, he reminded the Guild, with a frankness that was disarming, that his chief responsibility was not to take care of the New Jersey relief situation but to plan carefully the work of the H.R.S. on a nationwide basis.[8] This emphasis, although it was not wholly in keeping with the purpose of the WPA, was possible in a project that, unlike the arts projects, was professional only in the sense that it was professionally supervised and therefore could choose, subject to training and guidance, the most promising college graduates of the depression years.

### THE ORGANIZATION OF THE WASHINGTON OFFICE

Although in the earlier days of the project both Sargent B. Child and Howard E. Colgan assisted Evans in the Washington office, it was not until the middle of 1938 that an assistant to the director was officially designated. This was Edythe Weiner, who first came to the project in a technical capacity in February, 1936, upon the recommendation of Raymond Moley. Subsequently, Evans appointed her editor of county archives, in which capacity her development of standard editorial practice was her most significant contribution to the program. Gradually, during 1937, Miss Weiner was assigned administrative responsibilities, and by July, 1938, she was serving as assistant to the national director, in which capacity she continued until October, 1940, when she resigned. Both as editor in charge of the public records unit (which grew out of the county records unit) and as assistant to the national director, Miss Weiner, next to Evans, was most influential in shaping the policies and practices of the Washington office.

When in 1938, she was made assistant to the national director, she was succeeded as editor of the public records unit by Mabel S. Brodie. Miss Brodie continued to apply the basic editorial principles already developed by Miss Weiner and assumed leadership in the compilation of a revised and consolidated manual of instructions for the preparation of inventories of public records, which was finally published in

770

1941. She continued as editor in charge of the public records until the end of 1941, when the technical staff was completely abolished.

Donald A. Thompson, who had been assistant state supervisor of the H.R.S. in Massachusetts, was made editor of the church records unit in August, 1936.* A student of church history at the Meadville Theological school and Harvard, Thompson was a tireless and conscientious worker and well fitted by nature and training for his task. Unfortunately, however, the instructions governing the preparation of church records inventories were never consolidated into a single manual but lay dispersed in various bulletins and hundreds of letters.

Margaret S. Eliot was appointed to the central office staff in the spring of 1937 to assist in the development of the manuscripts program. She had a B.A. degree from Boston University in German and Latin, taught Latin and English, and had done considerable independent research. The manuscripts program was not as well defined as the public records program, was technically difficult, and never developed in a wholly satisfactory manner. This was not Mrs. Elliot's fault, although the lack of consistency in her instructions was sometimes discouraging to state directors.†

## THE FIELD STAFF

The field supervisors of the H.R.S. were from the beginning attached to the central office and not to the regional or state offices; and for this reason the unhappy relations that prevailed in the early days of Fed-

---

*The first editor was Ronald R. Burr, whom Evans had known at Princeton. In December, 1936, when budgetary stringency required the dismissal of one member of the Washington staff, he graciously and generously (since he had no dependents) volunteered to join the H.R.S. staff in Connecticut.

†Among other personnel in the Washington office were: Elizabeth Edwards, a student and teacher of history, who was editor in charge of the federal archives inventory unit; George M. McFarland, with a Ph.D. degree in American history and constitutional law from Princeton, who was given charge of the work on an annotated bibliography of American history; and Douglas C. McMurtrie, who was appointed consultant for the imprints unit.

McMurtrie was a typographical connoisseur with a keen personal interest in imprints. The editorial office of the imprints unit was domiciled in Chicago, and this geographical separation from the national office bestowed a territorial independence upon the Chicago office and made possible an assumption of technical sovereignty by McMurtrie such as was not enjoyed by other technical units of the H.R.S. McMurtrie, however, was an acknowledged expert in the field, and his devotion to the purposes of the unit, even after his separation from it in July, 1941, resulted in the accumulation of a mass of material, which, if it ever assumes published form, will be a valuable contribution to the bibliographical records of the nation.

eral One between the Washington office and the regional and state offices in the Theater, Music, and Art projects did not affect the field administration of the H.R.S. The field supervisors were the personal representatives of the national director, and their task was to extend his personality into the state offices by interpreting instructions and assisting in the organization and operation of project units. Affability of manner, a diplomatic approach, and a sense of proportion, which enabled them to adjust national policies to local differences, were the qualities that contributed most to success in field operations. Those longest and most continuously in field service were Sargent B. Child and Lieutenant Colonel J. M. Scammell. A member of the staff from the very inception of the program, Child possessed not only the appropriate educational training (B.A. from Amherst College and M.A. in history and political science from Columbia University, 1928) but also the charm of manner that his duties demanded. Scammell's experience with military records and his adeptness at diplomacy recommended him.

Three other competent regional supervisors were developed on the project. They were all under thirty years of age when they joined the H.R.S., and it was their excellent records as state directors (John C. L. Andreassen in Louisiana, Dan Lacy in North Carolina, and Robert H. Slover in Oklahoma) that brought them to the attention of Evans, who eventually promoted them to the post of field supervisor. Each had an M.A. in history, and the first two had completed, except for the dissertation, their work for the doctorate.*

The survey never had regional offices. The field supervisors or regional directors operated out of the central office, or from state headquarters in those instances where state directors were appointed as field or regional men. In the early days of the survey a field supervisor or a representative of the central office (including the national director) might visit any state. As the program developed, it became desirable for one person to confine his field supervision to a limited group of states. In 1938 there were five WPA regions—New England and New

---

*Robert C. Binkley of Western Reserve University, although he served as field supervisor only on a part-time basis and for a short period of time, without doubt contributed more than any other single individual not officially connected with the H.R.S., in the initiation, prosecution, and successful completion of the project. He acted as liaison between Evans and the learned world, and the esteem in which he was held by both created an atmosphere of cordial co-operation between the professional and the neophyte that was one of the happiest accomplishments of the survey.

York, the Middle Atlantic States, the South, Middle West, and Far West. In 1939 the number of WPA regions was increased to nine.

The duties of the field supervisor were both administrative and technical. His administrative responsibilities, subject always to the approval of the national director, included: the selection of new state directors when a vacancy occurred, the displacement of unsatisfactory state directors, the resolution of personnel problems within the state offices, and the co-ordination of the activities of the various units within a state project. On the technical side, it was his duty to study thoroughly the distribution of workers as to job classification, location, and work assignment; to examine editorial and administrative controls as they expressed themselves in the states; to answer general and specific editorial questions; and to help solve the problems of the project editors. What the regional supervisor heard, saw, and concluded, he reported, with recommendations, to the national director. If, however, the need for decision or action was urgent, he proceeded on his own initiative, subject to the subsequent approval of the national director. On occasion, a field supervisor authorized the publication of inventories or other material.[9]

The maintenance of administrative courtesy between the H.R.S. and the regional and state offices of the WPA was not difficult, partly because the survey came into existence after the early troublous days of Federal One—and consequently was not connected in the minds of state administrators with unhappy past experiences—and partly because the subject matter of the survey was not of the nature to provoke controversy. In visiting a state, a regional supervisor called first at the state WPA administrative offices, where he conferred with the state director of women's and professional projects and, occasionally, with the state administrator. Thence, he proceeded to the survey offices and, if necessary, conferred further with the state administration officials. The same attention to protocol governed relations with the WPA regional offices. Although the H.R.S. did not maintain representatives at the WPA regional offices, Evans, in July, 1938, ordered his state directors to send to the appropriate state and regional directors of women's and professional projects a copy of each communication addressed to the central office:

> It has proved very helpful to good administration for this office to send the above mentioned persons copies of letters it writes to the project directors. It has been discovered, however, that much of the correspondence is meaningless without the letter to which reply is made, or the letter which

is sent in reply, as the case may be. I realize that it is sometimes necessary to write personal or off-the-record letters. This type of thing should be kept to an absolute minimum, however, as I have discovered that it is almost never necessary to say anything which would be inappropriate for the files.[10]

Copies of reports made to the national director by his field supervisors were also sent to the regional directors of women's and professional projects.

The salaries paid to the central office staff of the survey were lower than those paid for comparable positions in other units of Federal One. Evans was appointed at a salary of $3,600, which later was raised to $4,000, and finally to $5,600. The top salary of other directors in Federal One was $7,200. Child's salary as director was $4,600. Field supervisors or regional directors were paid an average of $3,200. The chief editors or persons in charge of the various phases of the program received salaries of $1,800 and $2,000 until March 1, 1939, when they were reclassified by Civil Service as assistant archivists and their salaries raised to $2,600. The salaries of the assistants to the national director ranged from $1,800 to $3,600.

### THE STATE OFFICES

Appendix C to *Supplement No. 1 to Bulletin No. 29* and the survey manual provided for the organization of state units. A state supervisor (assistant state supervisor, at first) was provided for each state. Of the assistant state supervisors originally appointed, nineteen were the personal choice of Evans or were selected upon the recommendation of professional historians. The appointees in twenty-seven other states were recommended by the state directors or field supervisors of the Federal Writers' Project. One appointment was made on the recommendation of Jacob Baker. After ascertaining the acceptability to the state administrator of each candidate, Alsberg signed a letter of appointment and Baker notified the administrator of the appointment; and in some of the states the state administrators also issued letters of appointment. Of the original appointees, twelve held the degree of doctor of philosophy, and one was a candidate for the degree; nine were professors or instructors, and two of these were deans of state universities; four were state archivists, and one was archivist in a university; one was a librarian emeritus; and four occupied responsible positions in state historical societies. The average salary paid these original appointees was $140 per month. When the H.R.S. became independent of the Writers' Project,

774

the appointment of state directors was made by Evans, subject to the approval of his superior, Mrs. Woodward, and that of the appropriate state administrator. The appointment of district supervisors within a state required the written approval of the appropriate state director.*

Neither Appendix C to *Supplement No. 1 to Bulletin No. 29* nor the manual specified the qualifications to be sought in state supervisors. Operating Procedure No. G-5, however, stated that the state supervisor should be carefully selected, since his duties included both managerial and technical responsibilities. He should be capable of making satisfactory contacts with public officials and other record custodians, persons of academic standing, and the general public. Experience in research, in editing or publication, and academic training in the social sciences were listed as desirable, but other special qualifications might be an adequate substitute in particular cases.[11] In a memorandum of May 14, 1940, written by Sargent Child, the qualifications for state supervisors were listed.[12]

In addition to state supervisors, the original manual provided also for a research editor in the state office, local survey supervisors, and fieldworkers in each state office. As in the case of the Washington office, however, the state staffs developed with the program, and the state organization tended to follow the pattern of the central office.

The organization below the state level also varied. In some states, staffs of limited size were maintained at each district office and controlled operations within the district, subject to state and national direction. Usually, such district staffs concerned themselves primarily with administrative matters, such as requisitioning workers and supplies; preparing for, opening, and closing work at a given location, accounting for property; and checking timekeeping forms.[13]

---

*It was soon discovered that part-time appointments were frequently unsatisfactory. In the first place, proper supervision of the H.R.S. within a state required constant and continual attention. Moreover, part-time appointees, generally men who continued to hold a responsible and well-paying position in addition to their commitment to the survey, either considered the H.R.S. a *divertissement* and neglected it or were contemptuous of its pretensions and offended it. Experiences like these confirmed Evans in his predilection for young and untried talent, and in filling vacancies he tended to promote individuals from the existing project personnel. These young persons were conscious not only that they were being given an opportunity to prove themselves but also that they held their position by the grace of the national director and not by virtue of professional eminence. The result was a determination to justify the confidence of their superior and a loyalty to his person—a combination that in many instances produced excellent results. Turnover among the state directors, however, was fairly heavy; and of the original appointees only two served throughout the life of the survey; Anne K. Gregorie of South Carolina and Eva M. Carnes of West Virginia.

In a few states small editorial offices were established in the district offices, but this practice never proved satisfactory. It was tried in Indiana for a time, but, as the state supervisor commented, it "led to as many interpretations of the technical manual as there were editorial offices, and in 1940 all final editing was concentrated in the state office to guarantee uniformity of editorial output."[14] Georgia likewise experimented with district editorial offices, but abandoned the plan because of the untrustworthiness of the editorial work. Where district offices were maintained, therefore, the duties of the small staffs were almost exclusively administrative. This policy, by virtue of which technical control was concentrated in the state offices, made for reasonable uniformity of practice within a state and at the same time allowed a proper diversity between states when place and circumstance required. At the same time, the collaboration of the limited technical staff allowable in most states prevented that dispersion of talent which would have weakened its effectiveness.

## THE EXERCISE OF CONTROL THROUGH REPORTS

The control of the national office over state and district offices by means of periodic and special inspection visits of the field supervisors was strengthened by a system of reports from the states to the national office. Control of project personnel was first exercised through a labor report, devised as early as February, 1936, which was submitted bimonthly. This called for information as to total number of employees and a breakdown by classifications, man-months, labor cost, new employees, number of workers terminated, number resigned, and number transferred to other projects. This labor report was later supplemented by the county program report,[15] to be submitted at least once a month and required of each county in which work was under way. This report called for such items of information as date county entered, number of workers, number of man-months expended to date, and percentage of work completed in listing various types of records in the county. The county completion report, instituted in April, 1937, called for substantially the same information, with added inquiries regarding the preparation of draft inventories. An effort was made to consolidate these county progress reports with a semimonthly state progress report, announced March 4, 1937, and requiring information (1) regarding the number of counties in which the filling out of HR forms on county records had been 100 per cent completed; (2) the percentage of the total quantity of county records in the state for which HR forms had been filled out; and (3) the percentage of the total quantity of county records in the state for which HR forms had been edited and made ready for the preparation of draft inventories. These precise report forms, supplemented and checked by the reports and inspections of the field supervisors, were valuable to the national office during the period of federal control, when it was necessary for Evans to know in detail the progress and needs of each state in order intelligently to apportion funds and to assign employment quotas. The substitution of narrative reports for these report forms in the later years of the H.R.S. merely indicated procedurally the transition of control from the central to the state offices.

## PROJECT EMPLOYMENT

In the employment, classification, and assignment of personnel the Historical Records Survey was governed by the general rules of the WPA, as well as the special provisions made for Federal One, which have already been discussed.*

When the survey began operations in 1936, all project employees were classified as professional and technical, skilled, intermediate, or unskilled; and these classifications determined their wages. In July of that year the principle of the prevailing hourly wage became a statutory requirement, and occupational classifications were assigned.

In the original scheme of classification only broad and general guiding principles could be observed. Once a worker was appointed, however, he might be reclassified either upward or downward, depending on his performance. Some few state offices, however, encountered difficulty in their attempts to reclassify employees. Indiana reported, for example, that promotions on the project in that state were difficult because the WPA division of employment felt that skills acquired on the project could not be recognized as readily as skills possessed prior to assignment. "Thus, toward the end of the project, some workers were employed at project skills higher than their assignments called for, while other workers transferred from related projects at high classifications were unable to perform survey assignments common to those high ratings. This inability to upgrade after project training was detrimental to project morale."[16]

*Vide supra*, pp. 189-202.

Along with the general descriptions of qualifications, based largely on theory, issued by the Washington office early in the project's history, the considered opinions of supervisory personnel after several years of experience in project operation as to the qualifications that made most for success on a project are deserving of quotation. The Indiana state office reported at the close of the project:

> On the basic field level, workers were needed who could transcribe in good handwriting old and sometimes nearly illegible county records, or who could rearrange county records by series and chronologically within a series, or could fill out the basic forms for inventories of archives, or interview persons to secure information on churches. . . .Prime requisites were a passion for accuracy and an interest in local government and the records it produces. . . . Many aged and physically handicapped workers were used in all field phases, except rearrangement of public records. . . . Higher skills were demanded by the state editorial office.[17]

The Ohio state office reported that various types of white-collar workers could be employed on a project such as the Historical Records Survey, including clerks, typists, secretaries, machine operators (mimeograph and multilith), bookbinders, research workers, editors, writers, timekeepers, and supervisors.[18]

South Carolina recommended that field workers be "100 percent honest and discreet, since public records contain a large element of personal information";[19] and the Vermont state office commented that the best success was achieved with very young workers, just out of school and trained on the job to fit the needs, although handicapped and elderly people could be used to some extent if mentally alert.[20]

The qualifications of workers available to the survey varied geographically. The more urban states had larger numbers of unemployed professional people who could be used profitably in the survey (such as lawyers, writers, historians, teachers, and research workers) than the more rural states. Evans reported in April, 1938, that it had been difficult to find competent personnel in Arkansas for any phase of the survey work, administrative or technical, and that it had not been easy to secure competent certified workers, particularly of supervisory caliber, in Georgia, South Carolina, Nevada, New Mexico, Virginia, Washington, and West Virginia. Less difficulty was encountered in Florida than in most southern states.[21]

Reports on the background of the project personnel indicate the large variety of occupational groups from which the survey could choose its workers and illustrate the impact of the depression on the professional and white-collar classes. A report by the Massachusetts project (Boston *Herald,* June 16, 1939) stated that of the 329 persons working on that project forty-seven were unemployed business executives, twenty-six were formerly newspaper or advertising men, thirty-seven were jobless teachers, thirty-six were members of the Massachusetts bar, and seventeen had been production or office managers. The assistant archivist at Louisiana State University stated in October, 1939, that he had made an analysis of the past work and educational records of fifty persons in supervisory positions on the survey in five states. He discovered that one held the degree of doctor of philosophy, ten the master's degree, nine the bachelor of arts degree, and three the bachelor of law degree. Several had been high school and college instructors. There were also six clerks, five bookkeepers and accountants, two ministers, two social workers, a county treasurer, a credit manager and editor of a business journal, a sports editor, an assistant superintendent of a state tax survey, an army pilot and county attorney, a radio script and free-lance writer, a fur buyer, a bus driver, an actor, a theater manager, and an army sergeant. More than two-thirds were less than forty years of age, and two were over sixty.[22] Of sixteen supervisors on the Illinois project, as of October, 1939, one held a Ph.D. degree; four, bachelor of arts degrees; one, a bachelor of science degree; one, a master of arts degree; one, a bachelor of law degree; two had business college diplomas; one, some university and many years' library training; one, normal-school training; and one, some college work.[23]

The picture, however, was not always so bright as a mere statistical summary of the educational and occupational background of the workers would give one to believe. There was a tendency in some places to use the H.R.S. as a *refugium peccatorum,* and a field supervisor of the Survey, reporting on the personnel in one of the states in December, 1936, wrote, "Here we have to deal with, not only simple psychopathic cases and frustrated females, but hop-heads, homos, and all sorts of screwy people whom the W.P.A. could not get on with and who were transferred to Fisher."[24]

An observer, interested in the project, but not officially connected with it, writes:

> All of us doubtless have had experiences with Survey workers who could provide anti-New Deal cartoonists with materials for fascinating, frenetic compositions. I have seen and heard three Survey courthouse workers asleep in the same room, but my only emotion was gratification because I knew that these particular persons were doing less harm in somnolence than they would

in their waking moments. I have talked with others who were apparently psychopathic, which does not necessarily mean that they were incapable of performing competent archival work. I have seen three courthouse workers—two men and a woman—patiently gazing at a single manuscript volume day after day. Since the woman was facing the back of the volume, from an angle that gave her an upside down view of the writing, one of my stenographic assistants commented in all earnestness that the female worker must be the wife of one of the men and was engaged in checking up on her husband in his working hours. I have talked with dozens of workers who had only a very sketchy idea of the value and ultimate uses of their labors.[25]

In the period of federal control, state employment quotas for project employees and allocations of authorized funds to each state were established by the national director. Early in January, 1936, a table of tentative allocations was prepared by Evans, who computed the apportionment on the basis of each state's population. Subsequently, adjustments were made, taking into account the following factors: (1) the existence of local projects in the same field and of the work already done; (2) the immediate availability of competent supervisory personnel; and (3) the availability of white-collar relief labor. Of the initial allocation to each state 75 per cent was made available to carry the project until May 15, 1936 (Pennsylvania received a smaller percentage because a local project, with an authorization of $68,000, had recently been set up in Philadelphia County). Each state was advised of the amount of money allocated to it for the survey, and then, in accordance with the procedure prescribed in Appendix C to *Supplement 1 to Bulletin No. 29*, requests for funds were made to Washington on wpa Form 320. Upon approval of these forms in Washington, funds were released to the states.*

The national employment quota and the employment quota for each state necessarily followed the amount of funds authorized to the H.R.S. by Presidential Letter and the portion of that amount allocated to each state by the national director. Therefore, once the H.R.S. was fully under way, its national employment curve and, in general, its state employment curve, rose or fell in accordance with the pattern set by Federal One as a whole. There was one notable exception to this conformity: between June and November, 1938, national employment on the H.R.S. rose over 300 per cent, but employment on the four arts projects rose at a much slower rate. The occasion of this lack of conformity was

*The fact that the H.R.S. started late, as compared with other projects in Federal One, saved it from the confusion created by the initial failure to co-ordinate the project applications (wpa Form 320) with the early allocations to the states. *Vide supra*, pp. 245-62.

the attempt of Federal One to conform with the President's instructions to reduce the man-year costs of the arts program to $1,000.*

It was characteristic of Evans, and natural enough in the circumstances, that he should see in the embarrassment of the four arts projects an opportunity to increase his own quota. At the height of the crisis, in memorandums dated May 2 and 3, 1938, he suggested to Mrs. Woodward the addition of 15,000 or 20,000 project employees to the survey to prepare an index of American biography.[26] This idea was apparently not sanctioned, and he later proposed an increase from approximately 3,100 to approximately 10,000. The additional workers were to be utilized in the following ways: 2,000 to accelerate the regular program; 3,000 to prepare indexes to important public records; and 2,000 to index newspapers.[27] Mrs. Woodward had already called to the attention of the deputy administrator of the WPA the comparatively low man-year cost of the H.R.S. "Of the five distinct nationwide units of Federal One," she wrote, "the Survey of Historical Records is the only one which operates at a man-year cost within $1,000."[28] Later, on June 10, 1938, Harry Hopkins recommended to the President that the quota of the Historical Records Survey be increased by 5,000 persons, "because this project is particularly well adapted to pick up the needy white-collar load in the South and West. It is a meritorious project that has received much favorable comment, and it is comparatively low in operating cost."[29] In the end, a quota increase of more than 6,000 was granted, but a comparison of the quota distribution by states for November, 1937, and November, 1938, fails to show that the increase in employment was concentrated in the southern and western states. As a matter of fact, Evans, in a letter to his state directors dated June 1, 1938, informing them that he was requesting an increase in quota, hastened to add, "I have no intention of granting a flat one-third increase to the various states," and made clear his intention to allocate the additional funds, if and when granted, in such a way as to expedite the work of the survey to the best advantage nationally.[30] When the increase in quota was granted, he announced that in distributing this increase among the states he had in mind such considerations as: (1) amount of progress made to date; (2) amount of work remaining to be done; (3) quality of work performed by the administrative and technical staffs; and (4) availability of white-collar workers.†

*The general implications of this crisis have been discussed earlier. *Vide supra,* pp. 231-33.

†A quota increase of this magnitude was not an unmixed blessing so far as technical competence was concerned. Although it allowed the survey to increase its

781

Having played Cinderella in Federal One for three long years, Evans was quite willing to act the part of the fairy godmother and to show to the directors of the four arts projects that the H.R.S., though it might not be an artistic experiment, had modest merits of its own. Moreover, he was in an excellent position to do this, for the H.R.S. was of such a nature that its man-year costs could be kept distinctly lower than those of the four arts projects and well below the maximum limitation of $1,000. The man-year costs of a nationwide project such as those included in Federal One depended in the main upon two factors: (1) the proportion of the workers in the higher wage regions (mostly urban areas) and (2) the proportion of the workers in the higher wage categories. In the Music and Theater projects, and to a degree in the Art and Writers' projects, these proportions militated against a low man-year cost. Because these projects insisted upon professional personnel and because that personnel was concentrated in states with relatively large urban populations where the higher regional wages prevailed, their man-year costs were unusually high; for this reason, they were constantly under attack from the Bureau of the Budget and subject to surveillance by the President's office. The Historical Records Survey, on its part, was under no such pressure. Although persons on relief who were qualified to work on records and kindred tasks were not dispersed evenly throughout the nation, there were almost everywhere enough supervisory and professional applicants to provide the minimum of guidance and training. Besides, Evans never considered his program professional in the sense that its project personnel should be taken exclusively or predominantly from the professional class. The H.R.S. was a professional program only in the sense that its supervision was professional. The subject matter of the project favored Evans' interpretation of professionalism. An archival discipline, to be sure, was required even of the project workers, and it was not so simple or elementary that it could be taught to anyone. An ability to read and write was not enough, and a clerical approach to the demands of the program not only was inadequate but could be positively dangerous. The intellectual discipline that the American arts college attempts to impart and

supervisory and professional personnel, at the same time it retarded production during the period when it was necessary to absorb and train a much greater number of new and less-experienced personnel, and encouraged ventures of a large scale in which size obscured quality.

the scholar's conscience and approach were necessary, and other training and experience rarely compensated for the lack of them. But, given such qualities, the regimen that turned apprentices into archivists was neither so extended nor so exacting that it could not be imparted by competent supervisors in a comparatively short time. At any rate, the project never lacked promising candidates; for in the worst years of the depression, college graduates were being placed upon the labor market at a rate that varied inversely with its ability to absorb them.

Finally, with respect to non-relief and non-security personnel, the H.R.S. never had to seek the degree of exemption that the four arts projects deemed necessary. The differences here, although not so striking, were substantial; and they enabled Evans to avoid the embarrassment attending requests for special consideration.

As a result of the favored position of the H.R.S., which derived from its limited use of professional and supervisory personnel, the man-month and man-year costs of the project were substantially lower than those of any other project in Federal One. In the fiscal year 1939, for instance, the man-month cost of the H.R.S. was $73.65, compared with $91.54 for the Writers' Project (the next lowest) and $102.87 for the Theater Project (the highest). In a sense, such a comparison with the four arts projects is unfair and misleading, for the advantages of the H.R.S. came to it precisely because it was *not* an arts project. At the same time, the administrative location of the H.R.S. within Federal One, accidental and inappropriate though it was, made such a comparison administratively correct, and, as in the spring of 1938, it sometimes occurred to the high command of Federal One that the H.R.S., if it had no artistic pretensions, had its administrative uses.

The concentration of project workers on the H.R.S. in the middle wage classifications allowed that project another advantage not enjoyed to the same degree by the four arts projects. When the ERA Act of 1936 made prevailing hourly wages mandatory, it was necessary for the WPA to correlate the number of working hours a month with the monthly security wage. In general, the higher a project worker's hourly wage (within the same wage classification), the fewer hours a month he worked. This resulted in a staggering of employment, especially in the higher wage groups, which generally adversely affected efficiency of project operation. In the H.R.S. the awkwardness of such an arrangement, for reasons already given, was less pronounced. The spread in monthly working hours (between 120 and 140) was not so great as to preclude proper co-ordination of time schedules, and was considerably less than the spread in the four arts projects.

## FINANCE

The general financial controls, as to man-month costs, and the ratios of non-relief, non-security, and non-labor costs to total costs, which were elaborated and eventually instituted by the finance office of Federal One, have already been analyzed, and need not be considered further.* In the main, the difference in this respect between the H.R.S. and the four arts projects lay in the personality of the directors. Whereas the directors of the arts projects often allowed, and sometimes connived at, the violation of financial limitations by state offices, and thus placed the burden of reproof upon the finance office of Federal One or higher superiors, Evans never hesitated to take summary action against subordinates who were inattentive to instructions. In January, 1938, when informed that several state projects had exceeded their non-labor limitations, he addressed a letter to the state offices that read in part:

> Each director should start keeping careful data on all requisitions submitted, all requisitions filled, all travel vouchers submitted, all travel vouchers paid, light, heat, telephone, telegraph and other non-labor expenditures. These should be totaled at the end of each month, and a copy of each submitted immediately to this office.[31]

State directors who continued to exceed limitations after their attention had been called to the fact sometimes received letters like the following:

> This office is disturbed by your apparent disregard to certain regulations imposed upon you from Washington. I should like to point out at this time that no matter how good a project is technically and administratively, we will not tolerate longer than a certain period such wilful disregard of regulations on the part of a state director. I am further able to inform you that that period has just about expired in the case of Kentucky.[32]

Evans was also able to keep the level of expenditures for administrative and supervisory employees well under the average of the other projects in Federal One. Here he set an example, as it were, by his own

*Vide supra*, pp. 231-33.

salary; and without doubt the more pedestrian nature of his project allowed him to engage subordinates at more modest amounts than those paid on the four arts projects. In a memorandum of June, 1939, on this subject, he remarked:

> High wages to workers and supervisors do not apply to us. Our State Directors receive an average salary of less than $200 per month. There are only 7 persons in the Nation-wide organization who receive more than $2900 per year, or one person out of each thousand.[33]

The highest wage paid a state director, as of January 15, 1938, was $300 (New York City); the lowest, if part-time directors are excluded, $100 (Arizona and Montana). The salaries of directors in a majority of states were raised subsequent to January, 1938; but the average was held at about $200 a month.

## CO-ORDINATING PROJECT UNITS

Although co-ordinating project units were established in the states and in the national office in January, 1936,* it was not until December, 1936, that the H.R.S. adopted the device in the national office and in a limited number of states. The employment on co-ordinating project units as of April 22, 1937, was 183, the number on a unit varying from two in a number of states to twenty in New York City. The average wage of workers on these units was $123.53, and of state directors, $161.01. State co-ordinating projects units were abolished as of June 15, 1937, and the state staffs thereafter became part of the statewide units.

The co-ordinating project unit in the national office (usually called the national technical unit) included almost all members of the staff except the national director, who remained on the administrative payroll. It was not abolished when the state co-ordinating units were discontinued, but lasted until the end of Federal One (August 31, 1939).

## SPONSORSHIP

Since the WPA was the official sponsor of the H.R.S., as it was of the other projects under Federal One, other sponsorship (from co-operat-

*Vide supra, pp. 160-62.

ing sponsors—later called cosponsors) was generally neither sought nor secured. Public and private bodies, to be sure, that were interested in its service contributed space and other services, and a show of sponsors' contributions was made by expressing these services in monetary terms. This conversion, however, was so notoriously inexact and generally so inflated that any attempt at analysis would be fruitless. As for cash contributions to the H.R.S., the total amount received was so infinitesimal compared with total costs that it may be disregarded. In the fall of 1937, when business manager–agent cashiers were riding high on the Theater and Music projects, Evans suggested the use of this device by the H.R.S. and was advised by Davidson that it was unnecessary.[34] Sponsorship on the H.R.S., except as it provided a means to achieve public relations, was of no significance.

THE HISTORICAL RECORDS SURVEY UNDER STATE CONTROL

The statutory provision of the 1939 ERA Act, which prohibited WPA-sponsored projects, although it was a blow to the arts projects, neither surprised nor disappointed Evans. As a matter of fact, with that foresight which often enabled him to anticipate developments and to take them, so to speak, by the forelock, he had not only been preparing for the event some six months before it occurred but even had begun to take the initial formal steps toward the transfer of the H.R.S. to state control. There were reasons, apart from Evans' agility in adjustment, why the transfer bore lightly on the H.R.S. In the first place, the problem of formal state sponsorship was simple. Whereas in 1939 only a few states had agencies empowered by law to undertake the responsibility of sponsorship in the Music and Art projects, almost every state had an official body with archival jurisdiction. In the second place, there was an official cast to the work of the H.R.S. that made it politically respectable, and the musty smell of learning impressed the county clerk. Above all, the ease with which the transition was made (or rather, anticipated) was a high tribute to Evans. The fact that after July, 1939, the state and local projects of the H.R.S. continued to operate efficiently without federal control, and indeed without Luther Evans, was an encomium and not a reproach, for he succeeded in doing what the directors of the arts projects tried not to do—he made himself unnecessary.

On November 30, 1939, Evans resigned as national director to accept an appointment to the Library of Congress, and was succeeded on

March 1, 1940, by Sargent Child.* Child had personal charm and affability, and with the variety and length of his experience on the project in the field and in Washington, and in both administrative and technical domains, he was the obvious choice as second director. His task was to finish what his predecessor had begun, and he was responsible for a program of production that brought it as near completion as was possible in circumstances not conductive to anything unrelated to war work. In particular, he deserves commendation for sending out instructions, on his own responsibility, for the preparation of inventories of H.R.S. files while individuals who knew the files were still available to do the work. Because of his foresight, copies of these inventories for practically all the states are now available in the National Archives, the Library of Congress, and in state depositories.†

## THE LIBRARY OF CONGRESS PROJECT

The abolition of Federal One by act of Congress, effective August 31, 1939, made the continuance of the national technical project unit in the Washington office impossible. Since only state and local projects were now permissible, there was no place for federal project employees; and since the WPA was unwilling to place them on the administrative payroll of the national office, the employees of this unit were, for a few weeks, literally on the streets. The Writers' Project, however, was in the same predicament, and combined with the H.R.S. to initiate a District of Columbia project (the District was a "state" in the WPA) sponsored by the Library of Congress. The project proposal was signed by Herbert Putnam, the librarian, on September 20 and by the President on October 16; and operation began on October 21, 1939. The project offices were in the Annex to the Library of Congress. In theory, the project personnel should have been requisitioned from the District's relief rolls; in practice, the project was a continuation, although on a reduced scale, of the national technical units of the Federal Writers' Project and

*George M. McFarland succeeded Miss Weiner as assistant to the director, and when he resigned, Dan Lacy was appointed to the position, to be followed in turn by Don Farran.

†Child, who resigned in June, 1942, was the last national director of the Historical Records Survey, since by that time the survey had lost its separate identity. After his resignation, Lillian Kessler, former state director in Ohio, was appointed to care for unfinished business; and, when she resigned in the fall of 1942, Cyril E. Paquin, who had been in charge of the inventory of federal archives in California, undertook the task of liquidation.

the H.R.S. It lasted, however, only to August, 1940; thereafter, what limited technical personnel survived were carried on the WPA administrative payroll. By June, 1941, the central office staff had been reduced to twelve; by January 1, 1942, to four. In these circumstances technical supervision by the national office was completely abandoned, and the H.R.S. in the states was practically at an end.*

The statutory provisions of the 1939 ERA Act, which required a 25 per cent sponsorship contribution and the dismissal and removal from the relief rolls of all workers (except veterans) who had been continually employed on the WPA for eighteen months, affected the H.R.S. no less than other white-collar projects. Although it was easy for the H.R.S. to secure formal sponsorship in the states, it was not easy to secure a 25 per cent contribution from the sponsors. Indeed, as in other similar projects, if Colonel Harrington had not interpreted the clause to mean a contribution of 25 per cent on a statewide basis, the continuance of the H.R.S. would have been impossible. In the main the state administrators accepted the intention of this interpretation and allowed the higher contributions obtainable on construction projects to compensate for the lower contributions to the work of the H.R.S. The H.R.S., nonetheless, felt constrained to increase its sponsors' contributions, at least on paper; and even more so than in the federal period, it inflated the worth of space and other services that it received from private and public bodies. Indeed, as indicated before, since 95 per cent of the total funds of the H.R.S. were paid for labor costs, the imposition of the 25 per cent requirement, so far as that program was concerned, was inappropriate.

The eighteen-month rule was also embarrassing. For the most part, those who had been on the project longest were the best trained, and their forced dismissal, all at once, suddenly deprived the project of many of its best workers. It took time to train new workers in the special techniques of the survey, even when they came to the project with the proper background; and a lack of continuity, as well as a slackening of morale, resulted for the requirement. At that, however, the H.R.S. was better situated than the more professional Music Project, where the

*When Federal One was abolished, the H.R.S. became a part of the newly created research and records section of the Community Service Programs, as the Division of Women's and Professional Projects was renamed after February 1, 1941. Early in 1942, the Community Service Programs became the Service Division, and the survey (now losing its identity as a separate unit) was included in the war services section of this division. The position of its central office in the national structure determined the position of state H.R.S. projects in the state structures.

loss of even one key person might wreck the integrity of an orchestra or band.

1. Telegram, Evans to Binkley, June 29, 1935, Joint Committee Files, "Archives" Folder, Library of Congress.

2. The correspondence and documents upon which this account of the initiation of the H.R.S. is based repose, for the most part, in the files of the joint committee, deposited in the Library of Congress.

3. "Report on the Historical Records Survey during the Period July 15 to August 15, 1936," Memorandum, Evans to Keyes, August 15, 1936, H.R.S. Files.

4. "Relations of the Historical Records Survey with the Federal Writers' Project," Memorandum, Evans to Woodward, September 1, 1936, Joint Committee Files, Library of Congress.

5. Handbook of Procedures Letter No. 35, WPA, November 20, 1936.

6. Circular Letter, signed by Binkley, January 10, 1936, Joint Committee and H.R.S. Files.

7. Correspondence between Stephenson and Evans, H.R.S. Files, Box 134, "Dr. Jean Stephenson" Folder.

8. Letter, Evans to Federal Writers' Project Guild, Local No. 6 of the American Writers Union, August 20 ,1936, H.R.S. Files.

9. John C. L. Andreassen, "The National Survey of County Archives," pp. 4-5. Copy in Luther Evans' personal files.

10. H.R.S. Circular Letter No. 54, July 23, 1938, H.R.S. Files.

11. Operating Procedure No. G-5, WPA, January 10, 1940.

12. Memorandum, Child to McCormick, May 14, 1940, H.R.S. Files.

13. "Indiana—Final State Report, H.R.S.," H.R.S., Files, p. 7.

14. *Ibid.*, p. 6.

15. H.R.S. Circular Letter No. 2, November 18, 1936. H.R.S. Files.

16. "Indiana—Final State Report," pp. 13-14.

17. "Indiana—Final State Report," p. 4.

18. "Ohio—Final State Report, H.R.S.," H.R.S. Files.

19. "South Carolina—Final State Report, H.R.S.," H.R.S. Files.

20. "Vermont—Final State Report, H.R.S.," H.R.S. Files, p. 3.

21. Memorandum, Evans to Hopkins, April, 1938, H.R.S. Files.

22. William R. Hogan, "The Historical Records Survey: An Outside View," an address at the Third Annual Meeting of the Society of American Archivists, Annapolis, Maryland, H.R.S. Files.

23. Illinois Progress Report, October 20, 1939, H.R.S. Files.

24. Memorandum, Scammell to Evans, December 18, 1936, H.R.S. Files.

25. Hogan, *op. cit.*, pp. 10-11.

26. "Index of American Biography," Memorandum, Evans to Woodward, May 2, 1938, H.R.S. Files.

27. "Increase in Quota of Historical Records Survey," Memorandum, Evans to Woodward, May 26, 1938, H.R.S. Files.

28. Memorandum, Woodward to Aubrey Williams, April 11, 1938, H.R.S. Files.

29. Letter, Hopkins to the President, WPA Files.

30. H.R.S. Circular Letter No. 49, June 1, 1938, H.R.S. Files.

31. H.R.S. Circular Letter No. 38, January, 1938, H.R.S. Files.
32. Letter, Evans to Hoefelman, May 4, 1938, H.R.S. Files.
33. Confidential Memorandum, Evans to Regional Supervisor of the H.R.S., June 2, 1939, Joint Committee Files, Library of Congress.
34. Memorandum, Davidson to Evans, October 16, 1937, WPA Files.

# The Program of the Historical Records Survey

## THE ASSEMBLY LINE CONCEPT OF RESEARCH

In the early days of the records and research program of the WPA, two schools of thought arose with regard to the purpose and scope of the program. At Evans' invitation a meeting was held in Washington early in December, 1935, attended by A. R. Newsome, Waldo G. Leland, Robert C. Binkley, Solon J. Buck, Verne E. Chatelaine, and T. R. Schellenberg. The majority of scholars present were inclined to urge a limited program—limited not only in time and funds but in concept. Evans expressed this view nicely in April, 1938, when he said, "I think we still must recognize the fact that more rigid supervision and a less ambitious program are required when one is using relief labor than when one is purchasing labor at a high price on the open market."[1]

Two years earlier, he had written to Binkley:

I have something of a feeling that the idea that the Survey should assume the direction of a number of rather diverse types of enterprise is in danger of being overworked. I feel definitely that at the present time we have a job which we can handle creditably. I have no doubt, however, that it would be easy for us to branch out to such an extent that we would become too much of a holding corporation to function effectively in different administrative matters. I am wondering if we should not have a number of projects to handle the number of separate undertakings. . . . If there is no other way of putting these projects across, and if we are faced with an opportunity which must be seized now or never, I am willing to run in and take considerable risks in order to salvage as much as possible.[2]

This conservative attitude was again reflected in May, 1936, at a regional conference of the H.R.S. held at Chicago. In defending his concentration upon state and county records, Evans said, "My present attitude is a conservative one because I am anxious that I do not contribute to the reputation which wpa has for starting things which it cannot finish, for having eyes bigger than its stomach, and having poor administration."[3] Binkley, on the other hand, argued for a project unlimited as to type but limited geographically. Instead of attempting an inventory of all the county records in a state, he would select a particular county and inventory all records of significance, whatever their source. He seems to have thought such an attempt as a specimen project, if successful, would provoke imitation and eventually result in one or more gargantuan undertakings that would provide future scholars with ready access to all records of significance in the nation.

There were reasons, of course, in the rules and regulations regarding relief certification (the implications of which were not fully apprehended in the early days of the white-collar program) that made the kind of geographical concentration Binkley favored impossible, or at least extremely difficult. For instance, relief status was territorial, not personal, and a certified person who moved from the local subdivision in which he acquired certification did not carry his eligibility for relief to another locality. But the difference of approach between the two schools of thought involved considerations of a more fundamental character. Binkley, in discussing his point of view, wrote in December, 1938:

> It is now a matter of organizing work on a factory basis to use the minimum clerical skills that are common to the white-collar class. This does not mean that the plan for having society cash in on the special ability of those who really possess special skills is given up, but that it is no longer the key to the program. The atmosphere is a factory atmosphere.[4]

At all events, in the beginning Evans limited the aims of the H.R.S. As time went on, however, pressures from special groups with special interests, as well as the desire to gratify the wishes of sponsors, caused him to depart from his earlier resolution and to enlarge the scope of the Survey. Finally, in 1938, he could not resist the fleshpots of Egypt and, in recommending an increase of 15,000 in quota, completely reversed his earlier position. Even the increase that was granted (approximately 6,000) trebled the project personnel and resulted in the attempt to undertake a variety of projects never completed, and few of which achieved the technical excellence of the original project (the survey of county records).

The nationwide program of the survey, as it finally developed, embraced four categories of records: public records, church records, manuscripts, and imprints. In addition to these four fields of endeavor in which all states participated, there were numerous specific tasks undertaken by individual states or by a limited number of projects. The different phases of the program are discussed below, consideration being given first to those activities in which all the states engaged.

## INVENTORIES OF PUBLIC RECORDS: COUNTY ARCHIVES

As regards the work of the survey in public archives, the original manual stated as its purpose: to collect and edit the inventories of the records of state, county, municipal, and other local governments already prepared in the forty-eight states; to make inventories of the records of such governments where adequate inventories had not already been made; to prepare from the inventories mentioned a master inventory of the public records of state and local governments; and to collect and make available information on the housing, care, and accessibility of public records and the accommodations for persons who wished to consult them. Public archives—or more specifically, government archives—were defined as "papers which were once the basis of the transaction of Government business." Archives of the government of the United States were not included in the original program of the Historical Records Survey, but a separate project (the Survey of Federal Archives, WPA-sponsored Federal Project No. 4, co-sponsored by the National Archives) was initiated simultaneously with the survey to inventory federal records located outside the District of Columbia.

Information contained in the manual indicates that the original idea was to assemble unbound sets of filled-in HR forms for each county or other unit of government, copies to be deposited in the counties and states, and one copy of each form to be sent to Washington to be used in the preparation of a master inventory. In a general letter to all assistant state supervisors, March, 1936, suggestions and advice on the master inventory were solicited. This letter reflects both the development of ideas on the program and indicates the opportunity given to the states to participate in their formulation.[5]

The survey had been in operation only a few months, however, when it was decided that it would be expedient to compile and reproduce inventories for each county or other unit of government. The correspondence files for early 1936 show the development of a plan of publication; and a memorandum issued in June, 1936, by Evans advised the states of such plan. It stated that the inventories would be reproduced by mimeographing or multigraphing, and that as a general principle the inventory of public records for each county would constitute a separate publication, though permission might be granted to combine two or more counties in a single publication. Public records of state agencies were to be listed in a separate publication.

The memorandum indicated that each county inventory should have an introduction containing such information as: a brief history of the county, including the major developments of governmental organization; a brief description of the present institutions and offices of government; a summary report on the housing and care of records; a brief statement of the damage, destruction, and loss of records in the past; recommendations for improved measures toward preserving the records and making them more accessible; and a brief history of the H.R.S. project in the particular county. The main body of the inventory was to consist of a brief paragraph on each set of records, grouped according to the agency's origin. The several paragraphs devoted to the records of an agency were to be preceded by a brief statement of the constitutional or legal provisions relating to the agency or office.

Accompanying this memorandum were sample pages from an inventory for Cuyahoga County, Ohio, which was being compiled by an independent local WPA project. It was requested that each state office of the survey use the sample pages as a guide and make an inventory for a particular county as soon as possible. Following its preparation, criticisms and recommendations were to be solicited so that a final system of entry could be decided upon.[6]

More detailed instructions were issued in September, 1936, that prescribed the make-up of a published inventory as follows: title page, preface, table of contents, essays on the history of the county, governmental organization, records system, and the housing, care, and accessibility of the records, list of abbreviations, a numbered section for each office containing a statement of the legal status and functions of the office, and a summary of record requirements imposed by law with reasons for significant gaps in the records, followed by numbered entries describing the various record series. A subject or other arrangement of record entries was suggested with key-word headings to identify the different groups of record entries. Cross-references in the form of "See also" under such key-word headings were suggested in case a record or records might be classified under more than one heading. Instructions were given as to the make-up of an entry: the information to be given in the title line (entry number, record series title, inclusive dates, quantity, data on missing records, labeling of volumes, file boxes or other containers), and that in the body of the entry (description of the contents of the record series, information as to arrangement and indexing of the series, character of writing, condition of the record series if other than excellent or good, number of pages per volume and dimensions of volumes or containers, and location of the records). Finally, it was indicated that each inventory should contain an index. A suggested procedure was given to be followed in the preparation of a county inventory.[7]

The basic pattern for inventories of public archives was established by the two procedures discussed above (the memorandum of June, 1936, and *Supplement No. 4* to the manual). As editorial techniques developed in practice, however, supplements, circular letters, and other instructions so modified the original pattern that it was decided to codify all editorial instructions in a single publication. On August 10, 1940, a preliminary draft (for discussion purposes) was issued; and on May 26, 1941, the codification appeared in final form, under the title *Instructions for the Preparation of Inventories of Public Records by Historical Records Survey Projects.*[8] This volume reflects the thought of many archivists and project workers as well as the experiences of the survey over a period of more than five years, and has been used by instructors in archival courses at the American University, Columbia University, University of Illinois, and in seminars at the National Archives.

The process of producing a county or other public records inventory was not simple. Once entry had been gained to the repository, the work included: (1) original listing of the archival material in the county courthouse or other depository by the fieldworkers, almost invariably preceded by necessary sorting and arranging of records; (2) editing in the state office of the field forms submitted, forms often being returned to fieldworkers for additional information; (3) filing of the forms by county or other governmental unit and then by office, until all had been completed; (4) drafting of entries describing the records series on the basis of the edited field forms; (5) a second check of the entries against the records in the courthouse or other depository to insure accuracy and eliminate or minimize the possibility of records being overlooked; (6) historical and legal research for verifying the information submitted from the field and for writing the introductory and explanatory essays to be included in each publication; (7) collection of information for maps, charts, and floor plans and their preparation; (8) collation of essays and entries to be included in a volume, with necessary cross-references describing the record series inserted; (9) preparation of the bibliography and indexes to the volume; and (10) final editing of the complete material. The edited manuscript volume was then submitted for editorial review to the Washington office, which returned it with suggestions for revision. It was then either resubmitted or published by the state project.*

In the early days of the project the importance of legal research in the location and identification of records was not recognized. Experience soon showed, however, that when fieldworkers had itemized lists of legal record requirements and thus knew the date when a series should begin and the dates of significant changes in record requirements, their task of identifying record series was facilitated. This legal information was especially helpful when they faced such problems as: changes in record titles or in the system of labeling; evolution of a series of records into two or more specialized series; combination of two series into one; and changes in the nature of a series (for example, from original documents to recordings of the documents). Even if fieldworkers were not supplied with this information, it was necessary that the editorial staffs in the state offices know the legal impositions in order to instruct properly the fieldworkers in their collection of data.†

The preparation of inventories of county archives was the first task of the survey, and had priority over all other fields of endeavor. However, three factors retarded the tempo of the work so that inventories

---

*The informal pre-inventory work was often more tedious than the formal process. In practically every county or other unit of government where a survey of the records was made, considerable cleaning, sorting, arranging, and filing of records had to be done by the fieldworkers before they could proceed with filling in the HR forms. A newspaper article may be cited which gives some idea as to the chaotic condition of records fieldworkers frequently encountered: "A group of workers, after gaining permission from custodians, went down into the basement of the court-house in an Iowa county seat to begin work on a heap of records which were thrown helter-skelter into a room next to the boiler room. When they descended to the basement they were intercepted by the janitor. 'You're gonna muss around with that stuff in there,' he asked belligerently. 'Well, now, just a minute; that's what I use for kindlin'. I ain't gonna let you carry that stuff out. They been dumping old records in there for years. I've used it to start fires; so did the janitor before me.'"[9]

†The record-keeping practices of public officials were not always in accord with legal requirements; sometimes they did not know the requirements, and sometimes they chose to ignore them. Without such knowledge, however, it was all but impossible for the project to identify and tie together different parts of a record series.[10]

were published for only about one-fifth of the counties in the United States. The first was a complicated system of cross-references and artificial entries that, although intended to improve upon the archival practices of public officials and to aid the inquirer, greatly hindered the progress of the compilations.

In the second place, the state editorial staffs were too small in relation to the number of fieldworkers; or, in other words, the technical and supervisory personnel were not adequate to handle the quantity of material received from the project workers. The fieldwork was usually far in advance of the editing and compiling of inventories, and frequently became so out-of-date by the time the editorial staff was ready to use it that rechecking and sometimes even a complete resurvey were often necessary. Also, the editorial staff in Washington was never large enough to give prompt attention to the draft inventories submitted by the states for approval. Especially during 1937 and 1938, draft inventories accumulated in the national office to such an extent that they were returned to the states with the request that they be brought up to date. This condition proves, if proof be needed, that technical and supervisory competence was just as necessary on the H.R.S. as on other professional projects, especially if the task was to be completed.

In the third place, the tendency of the H.R.S. to enter other fields than public records caused a dispersion of effort and supervision that, if it created the immediate illusion of size, decreased the output of published inventories—the principal criterion by which the worth of the project must be judged. If the H.R.S. had limited itself to publishing inventories of the county records of all the counties in the United States, it might have today as a memorial a complete corpus.

A county inventory, as it finally evolved after a period of experimentation, included much more than the inventory itself and provided a compact historical and legal background against which the significance of the records was outlined. In the historical sketch carried in the *Inventory of the Archives of Arizona, Santa Cruz County*, for example, the following topics are discussed: geology and geography, Spanish occupation, Mexican regime, American occupation, creation of county, erection of courthouse, Indian hostilities, education, public health and welfare, transportation and communication, agriculture and irrigation, mining, population, and wealth. The historical sketch is usually supplemented by one or more maps showing the evolution of the county boundaries, and/or a map showing townships, towns, rivers, railroads, major topographical features, names of bordering counties, and other such information. The historical sketch is carefully documented, and state offices were encouraged to use the county records as source material in preparing it.

There follows an essay on the governmental organization and records system of the county, which considers the government from both a structural and a functional viewpoint. The essay is carefully documented by constitutional, statutory, and other citations, and is supplemented by a chart showing the current governmental organization in the county. In the inventory for Jefferson County, Georgia, we find the following topic headings used: legal status of the county, structural development of county government, general administration, title to property, jurisdiction of courts, law enforcement, finances, elections, education, public health, public welfare, public works, agricultural extension work, and records system.

This essay is followed by one devoted to the housing, care, and accessibility of the records. It gives information as to the location of the courthouse or other records depository, material of construction, date of erection, general dimensions, number of floors, extent to which building is fireproof, ventilation, lighting, descriptions of individual offices, vaults, attics, basements or other storage rooms, and indicates the degree of accessibility of the records. The essay is usually supported by floor plans. Data for this essay were collected primarily on WPA Form 10HR, The Building Form.*

The various offices of county government are next considered, and the essay on each office describes its creation, organization, functions, and record requirements. The statements are based primarily upon constitutional and statutory provisions, though local archives are sometimes used as supporting evidence. Defunct offices are usually given the same independent treatment as offices currently in operation. The office sections usually conform to the following arrangement: general administration, recording, administration of justice, law enforcement, finance, elections, education, health, welfare, public works, agriculture and home economics, and miscellaneous. In the inventory for Genesee County, Michigan, the sequence of office sections is: Board of Supervisors, County Clerk, Register of Deeds, Circuit Court, Circuit Court Commissioner, Friend of the Court, Probation Officer, Probate Court, Sheriff, Concealed Weapon Licensing Board, Coroner, Prosecuting Attorney, Tax Allocation Board, Treasurer, Controller, Board of Election

*A list of abbreviations and explanatory notes is included as part of the preliminaries of the volume or follows the housing and care of records essay.

Commissioners, Board of Canvassers, School Commissioner, Board of School Examiners, Superintendents of the Poor, Social Welfare Board, Soldiers Relief Commission, Health Department, Road Commission, Board of Park Trustees, Drain Commissioners, Plat Board, Agricultural Agent, Livestock Agent, Surveyor, and Dog Warden.

The essay for each office is followed by a listing of the office's records in numbered entries, grouped in general under subject headings according to the functions of that office. Most entries were compiled from data collected on WPA Form 12-13HR, Revised, Volumes and Unbound Records Form. The records series are described in entries formalized to give the following information: *in the title line*—entry number; title of record series, with the current or most recent title used as the entry title if there are varying titles; inclusive dates; quantity in terms of volumes, file boxes, file drawers, or individual documents; labeling; information as to missing and/or discontinued records; date of last entry in the series if there have been no recent entries; subtitles and variant titles; *in the body of the entry*—description of record series, including an itemization of types of information found therein; arrangement of the series; description of indexing, if any; character of writing; condition of record if other than good; dimensions; and location. Cross-references may appear in the title line or after the descriptive part of the entry, depending on whether they guide the reader to other parts of the same record series or to records that are merely closely related. If a record series has a separate index, the index is described in a separate numbered entry, with reference made to it in the record entry.

Following the last office section of an inventory is a bibliography listing all sources and other references cited in footnotes. At the end is the subject index, which guides the user to entries in which records are described.*

Usually, a single volume is devoted to the inventory for each county; but in some few cases where records were particularly voluminous, such as Los Angeles, California, more than one volume was needed. All North Carolina counties were covered in three printed volumes, and two of the Montana volumes contain inventories of the records of six counties.

The county volumes for a given state contain considerable duplica-

*Some inventories include a chronological index in which all records covering a particular decade or part thereof are described. A record entry number is listed under each decade the record covers, and underlining of the entry number in the chronological index calls attention to the initial appearance of the record. A few inventories also include rosters of county officials.

tion of essay material and also record descriptions. To eliminate such duplication and speed up production of inventories, some states during the last two or three years of operation adopted the abbreviated office essay and an abbreviated essay on governmental organization. Examples of such abbreviated-essay inventories are *Inventory of the County Archives of Tennessee, No. 1, Anderson County,* July, 1941, and *Inventory of the County Archives of Minnesota, No. 64, Redwood County,* October, 1941. States publishing these inventories committed themselves to the preparation of a comprehensive statement of the general law regulating county government—referred to in survey parlance as a "key volume"—to be published under some such title as "County Government in [*insert name of State*]." Evans, as early as September 16, 1937, in commenting on the preparation by some of the states of so-called check lists of county records required or permitted by law, stated that "it is required that every state director prepare in time a comprehensive report on 'County Government and Records in [*insert name of State*].'"[11] However, when the work of the survey was terminated, only three states—Idaho, Pennsylvania, and Wisconsin—had completed such volumes. Had all the states adopted earlier in the program the use of abbreviated essays in individual county volumes and concentrated on preparation of the "key volumes," the number of published volumes would have been considerably increased, and the bulk of the individual county volumes would have been considerably reduced.*

The final checklist of publications shows that inventories of 664 counties or parts of counties were published during the life of the survey.[12] In addition, a number of states published checklists of records required by law and other publications representing by-products of the preparation of public records inventories.†

Although inventories were published for only approximately one-fifth of the counties of the United States, data were collected by state offices on the records of practically all counties, and such unpublished data in varying degrees of publishable form are to be found in the state

---

*A few of the states attempted to step up production by limiting the information given on records series to title, quantity, inclusive dates, labeling, arrangement, indexing, and location, as in the North Carolina county volumes and in the Alabama, New Jersey, and Texas inventories.

†In addition to North Carolina, Illinois, Minnesota, and Ohio made a good showing in the publication of county inventories; these states had thirty-three, forty-four, and twenty-seven inventories, respectively, to their credit. Some of the historical sketches and essays on governmental organization in county inventories were reprinted separately for use in public schools and for other purposes.

depositories of H.R.S. materials. In June, 1942, Sargent Child stated that the best estimate that could be made from incomplete reports was that the field work had been completed in 90 per cent of the 3,066 counties in the country:

> In the tons of material which will be deposited for the duration of the war in state archives, state libraries and state universities, not only will unpublished inventories of county records be included but also tremendous quantities of rechecked transcriptions and abstracts of source material, upon which the state editors have relied in compiling the historical sketches and governmental organization essays contained in these inventories.[13]

There was some criticism of the survey for its slowness in the publication of inventories; but the publications themselves, no less than the services rendered by workers in cleaning and arranging records and in other tasks performed incidental to inventorying, received almost universal praise not only among archivists and other scholars but also among county officials. The quality of the published inventories, though uneven, is generally high; and the best of them are as good as many professional publications subsequently undertaken.*

*An exception to the precedence given to county archives inventories was made in the New England states, where the town rather than the county is the principal political subdivision of the state. No separate or special instructions were issued governing the compilation of such inventories; they followed substantially the same pattern as the county inventories.

In the field of municipal inventories, the District of Columbia, New York City, and the following states have publications: Florida (list of municipal corporations), Georgia, Indiana, Louisiana, Maryland, Michigan, New Jersey, Ohio, Texas, and Wisconsin.

The publication of inventories of the archives of special districts (such as drainage, irrigation, or school districts) by some states was anticipated but never realized. Minnesota, however, published a history of an iron-mining district (*The Cuyuna Range—A History of a Minnesota Iron Mining District*, 1940).

Since instructions relating to county inventories were also applicable to state archives inventories, no instructions relating specifically to the latter were ever issued. Because of the complexity of organization of most state governments, the preparations of such inventories required more extensive research, and accordingly there were fewer publications in this field. North Carolina published inventories for a larger number of state agencies than did any other state. Other states having publications in this field are California, Illinois, Louisiana, Michigan, Ohio, Oklahoma, and Wisconsin.

Use of public records found in courthouses and other depositories as source material for historical sketches and other essay material to be included in inventories prompted the idea of transcribing certain records in full, particularly minutes of governing bodies. Louisiana was the first state to undertake such work. In addition, transcriptions were published by the following: Florida, Michigan, Mississippi, Missouri, New Jersey, New York State, New York City, Tennessee, and Wisconsin. Fifty-six volumes in all were published.

INVENTORIES OF FEDERAL ARCHIVES

A separate project, known as the Survey of Federal Archives (WPA-sponsored Federal Project No. 4) operated from January, 1936, through June, 1937, and it must be included in any consideration of the inventory of public archives as a part of the program of the Historical Records Survey.

The act creating the National Archives empowered the archivist of the United States "to inspect personally or by deputy the records of any agency of the United States Government whatsoever and wheresoever located." Acting under this authority, and in an effort to obtain information regarding the quantity, condition, and exact location of federal records outside the District of Columbia, the National Archives, in the fall of 1935, made application to the Works Progress Administration for a project, the purpose of which was to collect the data desired. The application was approved, and late in 1935 a Presidential Letter authorized the expenditure of $1,176,000 by the project during a six-month period ending June 30, 1936. The Works Progress Administration was the official sponsor, and the National Archives the co-operating sponsor. Philip M. Hamer, at that time deputy examiner in the Division of Accessions in the National Archives, was chosen by the archivist to serve as national director of the survey.

Late in December, 1935, Hamer, with the assistance of an advisory committee composed of staff members of the National Archives and Evans, began formulating plans for the organization of the S.F.A. The first work was the preparation of Appendix C to *Supplement No. 2 to W.P.A. Bulletin No. 29*, which governed operation of the project. The purpose of the survey as set forth in this bulletin, issued January 17, 1936, was

> . . . to ascertain the exact location, the volume, and the conditions of storage of such archives (i.e., Federal archives), to identify them as regards their contents, and to furnish other information which may be of assistance in the formulation of recommendations designed to insure their safe preservation and to facilitate their use by officials and students.

The direction of the S.F.A. was placed under the authority of the national director and a staff of regional directors to be appointed on his recommendation for such regions as he should designate, and it was further provided that the S.F.A. should operate in accordance with a manual of instructions to be issued later by the national director.

Headquarters for the Washington office was established in the National Archives Building, and members of the Washington office staff, as well as the regional and assistant regional directors, were assigned to a national co-ordinating project unit. For purposes of the survey, the United States was divided into thirty-four regions, each under a regional director. Selection of the regional directors was begun in January, and completed late in March. Many were members of university faculties or on the staffs of libraries and historical societies, and could therefore devote only part of their time to the S.F.A. In such cases assistant regional directors were appointed to serve on a full-time basis. Regional headquarters were usually established in state capitals or in large cities, often in space provided by universities, libraries, or historical societies. The work of surveying was begun in the regional headquarters cities, and from there it extended to other cities and towns where federal archives were located.

In June, 1942, when the survey was terminated, 506 volumes of the inventory of federal archives had been completed and published, all in mimeograph form; eighty-one of the volumes that had been planned were still unpublished. Edited and unedited copies of most of the unpublished inventories are among the records of the Survey of Federal Archives, which have been accessioned by the National Archives. There are also unpublished inventories of records of the Post Office Department, the Civil Works Administration, the Federal Emergency Relief Administration, and the Work Projects Administration, which the Survey had not planned to publish in full.*

## THE MANUSCRIPTS PROGRAM

Manuscripts found in libraries, historical societies, and other institutions and in the possession of private individuals may possess considerable historical importance; and since many official records and semi-

*In addition to the inventories of federal archives, in states where there were sufficient numbers of customs records in various ports to warrant the undertaking and where such work would not unduly interfere with the regular inventory work, the compilation of ship registers and enrollments was undertaken. Further details concerning the history and administration of the Survey of Federal Archives, both as a separate project and as a part of the Historical Records Survey, may be found in the annual reports of the national director, published as appendixes to the *Annual Reports of the Archivist of the United States*, for the fiscal years 1936-42.

official documents frequently find their way into private manuscript collections, the importance of this category of source material is increased. Provision was made in the original survey manual for making manuscripts more accessible for research. Two forms were provided for the collection of data: WPA Form 17HR; The Manuscript Collection Form, and WPA Form 19HR, The Individual Manuscript Form. The manual stated that local project unit supervisors should list places where manuscript collections were available and issue special instructions on the care and manner of making an inventory of them.[14]

Because of the precedence given to public archives, work in this field started slowly. Evans completed the first draft of a "Memorandum on Inventory of Manuscript Collections" in June 1936. At the same time the program was considered in conferences and correspondence with scholars throughout the country. Solon J. Buck, of the National Archives, was of the opinion that a union list of manuscripts, in the sense of a card for each manuscript, was not desirable; he suggested, instead, the pattern followed by the *Guide to the Minnesota Personal Papers*.[15] At a meeting of the American Historical Association in December, 1936, the committee on historical source materials discussed with representatives of the H.R.S. problems involved in bringing the manuscript resources of the country under control.[16] In addition, the advice of J. Franklin Jameson of the Library of Congress, and of other curators and custodians of manuscripts, was sought. It was not, however, until April, 1937, when Mrs. Margaret Eliot was added to the Washington staff, that intensive work began. *Supplement No. 6* to the manual was finally completed and issued on October 22, 1937.

The data collected by the survey regarding manuscript depositories and manuscripts resulted in three types of publications: guides to depositories of manuscript collections, guides to manuscript collections, and calendars and inventories of manuscript collections. These three types of publications are considered below.*

The guides to depositories of manuscript collections were compiled from information collected on WPA Form 21HR, Manuscript Depository

---

*In the care of manuscripts, as in that of public archives, preliminary work, such as arranging manuscripts, was often necessary and, though of assistance to private repositories, naturally retarded the proper work of the Survey. Moreover, a problem peculiar to the manuscripts program arose—that of gaining access to manuscripts depositories. In April, 1938, California reported that it had been difficult to obtain the permission of custodians to assign workers to the task of examining and listing manuscripts because they had had unfortunate experiences with WPA workers. Maryland reported at the same time that the Maryland Historical Society refused any and all WPA assistance, even though only 1 per cent of the society's material was arranged and catalogued. Various ingenious devices were used to gain access to private depositories.

Form. Their purpose was to provide a list of manuscript depositories in the United States, showing for each its history, its collection policies, the nature, size, and conditions of its holdings, and other information of interest to possible users of the manuscripts. It was originally planned to publish the depository guide for the whole country as a single unit, but it was later decided to publish individual state depository guides.*

A state guide to depositories consists of a preface, a table of contents, an entry for each depository in the state, a bibliography, an index of proper names and subjects, and in some cases an index by name of collection. The data included in an entry were collected on Form 21HR in consultation with the custodian or librarian (or a representative) of the institution under consideration, and the form was required to be signed by the custodian to insure accurate information. Entries in a depository guide are arranged alphabetically by the town or city in which the depository is found and, under the name of the town or city, alphabetically by the title of the depository.

An entry is made up of several paragraphs, the prescribed number being six: first, number of the entry, name of town in which depository is located, name of the institution, if any, of which it is a part, its exact name and address, the title and name of the person in charge, and the days and hours it is open to the public; second, a brief history of the depository, fields and periods in which it collects, its policies as to the purchase, sale, exchange, and acceptance of gifts of manuscripts, and a description of the housing of the collections; third, description of the nature of the holdings of the depository; fourth, total number of manuscripts, systems of arrangement and cataloguing used, and other unpublished keys to the holdings; fifth, statement as to the availability of the manuscript holdings (indicating qualifications of applicants for use of the manuscripts, whether special permission is required, and, if so, from whom), any special or unusual rules governing their use, and the availability and prices of copying services; sixth, references to any published guides, descriptions, calendars, or other aids to the use of the manuscripts. Guides to depositories were published by nineteen states and by New York City.

Guides to manuscript collections were compiled from data collected on WPA Form 17HR. Their purpose was to provide more detailed information concerning the resources of individual manuscript depositories than was contained in the guides to depositories. A guide may cover all collections within a state, with a separate entry devoted to each col-

---

*If the number of depositories within a state was too small to justify a separate publication, two or more states were permitted to issue a joint guide. Oregon and Washington were so combined.

lection, and the entries arranged alphabetically by name of the collection under the title of the depository, or a guide may be limited to the collections of a single depository. Most of the guides—those for Iowa and Tennessee are exceptions—cover only the collections of a single depository. A collection guide includes, in addition to preliminaries, an entry for such collection arranged alphabetically and numbered serially, and an index by entry number of subjects and proper names. An entry is usually divided into three parts. The first paragraph is required to show: the entry number; title of the collection; inclusive dates, with indication as to the date span of the bulk of the collection; the quantity; the percentage arranged, and the manner of arrangement; the percentage catalogued, the manner of cataloguing, and the number of catalogue cards; the library call number or physical location of the collection if such information is needed to locate the material; its physical condition if poor enough to affect its use; a brief history of the collection, including the name of the donor and a statement as to whether it is held by gift or on loan; and the restrictions on access. The second paragraph describes the content of the collection; a long description, however, may be divided into two or more paragraphs. The third paragraph is reserved for references to any published or unpublished descriptions or calendars of the collection, to publications of any part of the collection, or to monographs or other secondary accounts based directly on the collection. Some twenty guides or inventories to manuscript collections were published.

The calendar was the third type of publication undertaken by the manuscripts program. Its purpose is to guide a researcher to the particular letters and other documents within a collection that are of specific interest and value to him. For this reason, the calendar devotes a separate entry to each document. Entries were compiled from data collected on WPA Form 19HR. A calendar is made up of a preface, which includes a brief history of the collection being calendared, a description of the arrangement and cataloguing of the collection, and information concerning any points, such as location or call number, common to all manuscripts in the collection and to which reference is omitted from the individual entries; an introduction, which includes a biographical sketch of the person whose papers are calendared and sufficient historical background of the period and subjects covered by the papers to explain their content; an entry describing each manuscript; a bibliography; and an index.

An entry in a calendar consists of three or more paragraphs. The first gives the author's name and identification if known, the place where the manuscript was written, the addressee's name and his identification if known, and the place to which sent. In the case of a diary, account book, or other such documents, some of these items, of course, would not be applicable. The second paragraph condenses the contents of the letter, diary, journal, or other document. The third paragraph describes the physical format of the document, and additional information may follow in a separate paragraph. About thirty calendars were published, some covering correspondence and papers of such colorful figures as Peter Force, Alexander Graham Bell, Gerrit Smith, General Otho Holland Williams, and Francis Bret Harte. There are also reproductions of a few diaries and journals, and Louisiana and Pennsylvania reproduced by mimeograph two manuscript collections, the Favrot papers and the papers of Colonel Henry Bouquet.

Respect for the contribution of the Negro to American life manifested itself in the H.R.S. as in the other projects in Federal One. However, the federal period had almost ended before a formal proposal for work in the field of manuscripts concerning the Negro was made.[17] Mrs. Woodward approved the plan in a memorandum of December 30, 1938, and final WPA approval was given in August, 1939. Arnett G. Lindsay was assigned to the Washington office to supervise this phase of the survey's program. The inventory was defined as a guide to manuscripts written about or by Negroes in the United States. The work was assisted by an advisory committee of Negro historians, consisting of one person in each state and a smaller representative committee in the District of Columbia, of which Carter G. Woodson was chairman.

Lindsay spent considerable time in acquainting himself with the operating procedures and methods employed in carrying out the program of the H.R.S., in observing work in manuscripts being done in depositories in the District of Columbia, in compiling a bibliographical guide to be used as a master reference work of library sources for the study of Negro life and history, and in acquiring generally the background needed to supervise the work. A tentative plan of work was submitted to Evans, but the program was abandoned when the Library of Congress project was abolished in August, 1940.

INVENTORIES OF ARCHIVES OF CHURCHES AND
OTHER RELIGIOUS INSTITUTIONS

The records of churches and religious organizations are a major source of data on American social history, and frequently the only source from which vital statistics can be obtained for the period prior to compulsory official registration. Consequently, any program for making accessible the basic source materials for research in the history of our country would be incomplete without the inclusion of church records, and it was not long before work on drafting a suitable form was begun (March, 1936). The Washington staff gave considerable supervision to preparation of the *Inventory of the Protestant Episcopal Church Records of the Diocese of Washington,* which was set up as a test and training project, and in March, 1937, three sample entries from the draft of this inventory were circulated to the states. On March 1, 1938, "Preliminary Instructions on Preparation of Inventory of Church Archives" were issued to all states. The Delaware inventory had been completed, and was to be used as a model. Final instructions, however, were apparently never completed.

The form used for the church archives inventory was WPA Form 20HR, Church Records Form. It was necessary, however, to supplement the data collected on this form by research in published works, and information obtained from present and past church officials and members. The church archives inventory series was organized on a denominational basis, with a separate volume devoted to a specific denomination or group of related denominations within a state.*

The church archives inventories usually contain a title page; table of contents; foreword by a high official of the denomination; a preface; list of abbreviations and explanatory notes; a historical introduction telling when and how the denomination came into the state or section; how the first church, parish, or synagogue was founded; how the ecclesiastical organization—diocese, presbytery, or association—developed; significant contributions to this development by individuals, especially bishops; and to what extent the denomination in the area has developed schools, institutions, men's and women's organizations, and the like. Either in this sketch or elsewhere in the volume, canonical and statutory provisions regarding the creation and custody of records are described, usually with the text or a digest of important regulations. Some of the inventories include a sketch on ecclesiastical organization, or polity, and occasionally a chapter on the housing and care of records. These

---

*In some instances, however, a separate volume was issued for an ecclesiastical division of a denomination, as for the Diocese of Fond du Lac (Protestant Episcopal Church) in Wisconsin. Permission was granted to publish such divisional inventories in order to accelerate publication. The first church archives inventory published covered the churches of a political subdivision of the state rather than those of a particular denomination, but this was an experiment. (*Inventory of the Church Archives of Oklahoma, No. 7, Bryan County,* October, 1937.)

808

introductory essays are carefully documented, wherever practicable, from sources such as convention minutes.

The main body of each inventory consists of entries with a separate entry being devoted to each church, institution, or other local unit. An entry consists of two or more paragraphs. In the heading of the entry are given the popular and legal names of the church, its ethnic and linguistic limitations, inclusive dates of the existence of the church, and address. The following paragraphs treat: the founding of the church; the name, education, and tenure of the first settled clergyman; the location and architectural style of the present and any earlier edifices; important events in the life of the parish, especially its connection with the founding and maintenance of missions; institutions; and organizations. A selected bibliography follows, if there have been publications relating to the church. In regard to records, the entry mentions the title of the series, dates covered, number of volumes or file boxes, location, and custody. When records are in the custody of a private individual and are not kept at the church, the holder's name, title, and address are given. No attempt is made to give a detailed account of the items of information shown in a record series as is done in the public archives inventories. The first paragraph of an entry occasionally lists recordings of incorporation and of property transfers as found in the public records, with reference to any acts of the state legislature bearing on the parish, and to any published court decisions specifically applying to the church.

Entries are arranged on an ecclesiastical basis, and thereunder chronologically. All the Baptist churches in a given association are listed in entries following the entry for the association itself, arranged in chronological order by date of founding (*Inventory of the Church Archives of North Carolina, Southern Baptist Convention: Raleigh Association,* July 1940). Following the entry section of an inventory are a bibliography, and chronological, geographical, and church-name indexes, and occasionally also index by name of priest or other church official. One hundred-odd church archives inventories were published by the H.R.S.

Another type of product of the church archives unit is the church directory. These directories are mostly on a statewide basis, although some states, such as California, New Jersey, and Tennessee, issued them by counties. Church directories were published by twenty states and the District of Columbia, but a few cover only part of a state.*

---

*In addition to these directories the Illinois Survey compiled, at the request of

As with the manuscripts program, difficulty was occasionally encountered in gaining permission to inventory church archives, particularly in securing the co-operation of the lower clergy. There was the matter of canonical procedure, and, in addition, there was at first some suspicion of the government's motives. In time, however, recourse to the hierarchy almost invariably resulted in the most cordial relationship. Indeed, churches of all denominations by formal resolution and otherwise endorsed and praised the work of the unit; and it was a tribute to the indefatigable energy, catholic spirit, and religious zeal of the Washington supervisor that when the central office in 1941 could no longer carry him on the payroll, a group of organizations representing many denominations donated money so that his services might be retained.*

EARLY AMERICAN IMPRINTS INVENTORY

Most pieces of early printed matter carry in the lower portion of the title page, or at the bottom of a single sheet, a note as to the place and date of printing and the name of the printer. These data are known collectively as the "imprint." In consequence, pieces of printing produced at places and dates rendering them of special interest have come to be known as "imprints." Bibliographers have for years concerned themselves with the listing of imprints; and although the efforts of Eames, Sabin, and Charles Evans may be considered monuments to scholarship, their works lack completeness, largely because of the limitations that necessarily attach to the efforts of an individual working alone. With the availability of white-collar relief workers under the WPA, an opportunity was seen to secure greater coverage.[18]

Work in the imprints field was first proposed in November, 1936, when Douglas C. McMurtrie (a typographical expert with a keen personal interest in imprints) and Luther Evans met at the Southern His-

---

the national office, a *Directory of Negro Baptist Churches in the United States,* which was published in two volumes in 1942; and the Utah Survey published an introductory volume for the church archives inventories, *History and Bibliography of Religion.* Some transcription and translation of early church records was done by Florida, Missouri, and New Jersey. Considerable work was also done in the preparation of guides to vital statistics found in church records (*vide infra,* p. 825).

*These organizations were the American Jewish Committee, the American Catholic Historical Association, the Presbyterian Historical Association, the General Council of the Congregational Christian Churches, and the Church Historical Society of the Protestant Episcopal Church.

torical Association meeting in Nashville, Tennessee. By February, 1937, Evans had agreed to make forty workers available for work in imprints, and in May the *Preliminary Statement of Plan* for the imprints inventory was issued. This was later amplified and expanded in five editions of the *American Imprints Inventory: Manual of Procedure*. As the program progressed, more workers were assigned, and local projects were initiated in a number of states.

The original plan was to make a record of imprints from early American books, pamphlets, and broadsides printed up to, and including, 1821, when Frederick Leypoldt began the listing of American publications in what is now known as the United States Catalogue. However, after a short period of operation librarians urged extension of the date limit to carry the record through 1876. This extension was approved, and for states in the Rocky Mountain region (Arizona, Idaho, Montana, Nevada, North Dakota, South Dakota, Utah, and Wyoming), where printing began relatively late, the date limit was carried through 1890.

Two products were anticipated as a result of this project: a file or union catalogue of title slips that would represent the holdings of American libraries; and published check lists drawn from the material, covering the imprints from publications of the various states and certain cities within limited periods. The several editions of the *American Imprints Inventory: Manual of Procedure* gave detailed instructions to workers in copying the desired information from the card catalogues of libraries and from the title pages of publications.

Technical direction of the work in imprints was delegated to McMurtrie, who established headquarters at Chicago in the Illinois office of the H.R.S. The office gave local authorities of the H.R.S. and all co-operating statewide imprints projects advice as to practice, received and filed the completed WPA Forms 22HR, and edited the lists of imprints co-operatively produced. Completed forms or title slips were to be mailed in weekly installments to McMurtrie, giving him and his staff an opportunity to check them currently and to make suggestions as to improvement in practice or changes in style of recording data.

Two styles of descriptions of imprints were employed, styles A and B. The latter represented descriptions as found on standard library catalogue cards and was relatively simple. The style A descriptions were more complex, and marked the ending of each line on the title page of a publication, making notes of rules, fillets, and ornaments, gave page dimensions in centimeters, and recorded the paging in detail. These were required for all American imprints dated earlier than 1801 and also for the final listing of rare imprints of a few southern and western states. This style of description, of course, necessitated working directly with the publications from which the imprints were taken, and was considerably more tedious.

The master file of title slips was built up to approximately 15,000,000 typed slips as of March, 1942, representing approximately 1,300,000 separate imprints in the period of American printing within the date limits specified. As the titles were edited, they were cleared through the Union Catalogue, which retained and filed all titles not already represented.*

Under the technical direction of McMurtrie until July 15, 1941, the second phase of the imprints program, publication, was chiefly confined to the editing and issuance of complex so-called style A check lists by the central office in Chicago. Style A lists, requiring the title page line endings, printers' devices, and bibliographical notes, necessitated almost interminable research, both in the libraries where the publications were located and in the huge file that complemented them in the central office. It became apparent in 1941 that if the million-odd titles collected were ever to be made available to the public, a more rapid method of issuing the check lists must be found. Two solutions were considered: (1) to abandon the complex Style A check lists and to issue simple Style B lists, or (2) to return the title slips to the state offices for issuance of Style A lists of titles in their own states. It was decided to choose the easier part of both alternatives, i.e., the issuance by the various state projects of their own titles in simplified Style B check lists, which they or interested scholars might refine at a later time. In more than twenty states the local staffs gave assurance that editing and publication of the Style B check lists was possible, and requested that the slips relating to imprints originating in their states be sent from the central files in Chicago. A number of check lists of imprints was published under this arrangement.

An inventory of the central files early in 1942 revealed that of the approximate 15,000,000 title slips and excerpts from newspapers, filed by states and year of publication, the following categories of materials were held: (1) active central files, comprising American imprints titles through 1876 for most states and through 1890 for a limited number of

---

*That this service was needed is proved by the fact that of titles printed in some western states, over 90 per cent were found to be new to the Catalogue. Of Chicago publications between 1851 and 1871, 85 per cent of the titles were not in the Union Catalogue.

states—7,875,000 slips, of which 77,620 related to broadsides; (2) inactive or storage files, comprising title slips of imprints of New York City, Philadelphia, Boston, the District of Columbia, and other points—6,225,000 slips; (3) materials relating to the history of the press in excerpt form—328,913 excerpts, newspaper report forms, index cards, etc.

Thirty-four check lists of imprints were published, some in revised editions, for limited periods. Using the principle of progressive bibliography, check lists were sometimes published in preliminary form, and these helped to bring other information to light. In this way the material assembled could be more quickly made available to the public, and when fieldwork and editing for a given locality were completed, the final bibliography could be published, incorporating information or titles discovered since the publication of the preliminary list. In addition to the regular check lists published, Florida and Idaho published short-title check lists of books, pamphlets, and broadsides printed in those states.*

UNION LIST OF NEWSPAPERS AND NEWSPAPER INDEXES

When research in public archives revealed a large number of issues of newspapers not included in the union list of newspapers (*American Newspapers, 1821-1936*) published in 1937, some states undertook the compilation of individual state union lists. In Louisiana the first instructions on the newspaper inventory were included in the *Louisiana Manual of the Historical Records Survey*, published in April, 1937. This manual called for the listing on WPA Forms 14HR of newspaper files found in parish courthouses and in each newspaper publishing office in the state. In May, 1940, the central office of the survey approved for duplication the Louisiana manual. During the summer and fall of 1940 an intensive recheck of all holdings and depositories of newspapers in Louisiana was made, and an entry form of presentation was developed that received the approval of the central office. Unlike the union list, which was based upon information obtained by circulating a questionnaire, that prepared by Louisiana was based upon personal examination of the newspaper files.†

---

*Some volumes were also published to serve as handbooks or reference works in the imprints program: *Location Symbols for Libraries in the United States*, September, 1939; *Location Symbols for Libraries in the United States—Additions and Corrections*, January, 1941; and *A Hand-List of American Publishers, 1876-1900*, November, 1940.

†The effort toward completeness is indicated by the fact that the Louisiana vol-

In the New England states, on the other hand, attention was directed toward the preparation of indexes to newspapers. Vermont published ten volumes of the *Index to the Burlington Free Press in the Billings Library, University of Vermont.*

Compilation and publication of newspaper union lists and indexes were locally initiated, and received little direction from the central office of the H.R.S.

## SURVEY OF PORTRAITS

The original H.R.S. manual provided a form for the listing of portraits and portrait busts in public buildings: WPA Form 16HR, Paintings and Statuary Form. At first it was not planned to issue separate inventories of portraits; but as time progressed, pressure developed in a few states to publish them. No circular of instructions was issued by the national office, however; and such work as was done was due to local initiative.

The gathering of data from which inventories or catalogues of early American portraits could be prepared was first suggested (early in the life of the H.R.S.) by Charles K. Bolton of Shirley, Massachusetts, author of *Portraits of the Founders*; and with the approval of the Washington office the collection of data on portraits other than those found in public buildings was begun in Massachusetts. Bolton generously contributed a large amount of data he had assembled over a long period; and he assisted in editing the material collected. Sylvia Schlafer, of the Massachusetts Survey staff, devoted her energies largely to the portrait survey work, and was responsible for final compilation and editing of the two volumes containing entries for 2,718 portraits, published by the Massachusetts project in 1939 (*American Portraits, 1620-1825, Found in Massachusetts*).

Connecticut and Rhode Island, with assistance from Massachusetts, published in 1939 preliminary check lists of American portraits, 1620-1825, found in those states. Other states became interested in compiling portrait inventories, and in 1940 George C. Groce, Jr., an authority on

ume adds 384 titles to the union list published in 1937, as well as numerous variations. Other southern states were encouraged by John C. L. Andreassen, regional supervisor, to inventory newspaper holdings, and several states published union lists, among them, Texas, Arkansas, and Mississippi. Pennsylvania and Utah published check lists of newspapers, and Wisconsin, a guide to newspapers in Iowa County, 1837-1940.

814

historical portraiture, was appointed to the New Jersey staff to supervise portrait work in that state and to act as national consultant for the portrait survey. He was responsible for preparation and reproduction of the *Manual of the Portrait Survey* and for devising a "portrait form" to be used by fieldworkers in the collection of data.

The *Manual of the Portrait Survey* sets forth the purpose and description of the Survey as follows:

> The purpose of this survey is to compile inventories of all American portraits which were painted before 1860. These inventories will provide (1) descriptions of each portrait including the name of the artist, with reasons for attribution (why the portrait is assigned to the artist); (2) a brief biography of the sitter; (3) the physical description of the picture, with the history of its ownership; (4) its accessibility to the public. This material will be completely indexed from four different points of view; (a) location (by city or town), (b) artists, (c) collection, (d) sitter.

In undertaking the portraits survey, the New Jersey project prepared under Groce's supervision a bibliography of early American portrait painters, 1663-1860, as an aid for project workers. This volume shows the name of the artist, kind of painter (portrait, miniature, etc., and whether he used oil, water color, or other mediums), date and place of birth and death if known, and occasionally other information. The source of information is given after each entry in code form.

This volume, published in December, 1940, listed 1,400 portrait artists, and was admittedly incomplete. It was circulated to a selected list of libraries, museums, and other institutions with the request for additional suggestions. By this co-operative method the original list was doubled. Sargent Child stated in June, 1942, that a revised edition of the volume would contain as many as 2,900 names.[19] Toward the close of the H.R.S. this list was submitted in hope of publication to the Library of Congress. The project, however, is now in abeyance.*

MICROFILMING OF PUBLIC RECORDS AND NEWSPAPERS

Early in the life of the H.R.S. it was decided to experiment with microfilming as a means of preserving old and valuable records. In

---

*States that issued publications in the portrait field were Connecticut, Maine, Massachusetts, New Hampshire, New Jersey, and Rhode Island. In addition, a worker from the central office made an inventory of the Harris Ewing Studio collection of portraits, photographs, snapshots, etc., and the Oregon project published a *Guide to the Angelus Studio Collection of Historical Photographs* in April, 1940.

1936, before non-labor funds became so limited, the Indiana staff microfilmed more than 200,000 pages of valuable county records in sixteen of the older counties at a cost of $2,000. The project was unusually providential, for the Ohio River flood early in 1937 destroyed many of the records.[20] Other microfilming was subsequently done in Indiana. Five to six hundred volumes of records in eighteen different counties were microfilmed on sixty-five rolls of film. They included minutes of the county commissioners, vital statistics, land records, and court records. Early records for the Borough of Vincennes, some dating back to 1784, were also microfilmed.*

### ANNOTATED BIBLIOGRAPHY OF AMERICAN HISTORY

Revision of Josephus M. Larned's *Bibliography of American History* had been started two years prior to the creation of the Historical Records Survey. Louis M. Hacker of Columbia University initiated this project in 1933 as a part of the New York TERA program, with the New York Public Library as the official sponsor. Work on the revision continued, though not at a steady pace, until the summer of 1935, when the project was terminated abruptly and its staff scattered.[21] As early as July, 1935, Binkley wrote to Chatelaine regarding the possibility of including work on the bibliography in the program of the proposed national project.[22] H. M. Lydenberg, director of the New York Public Library, who had supervised work on the earlier project, also wrote to Chatelaine to the same effect.[23]

In early 1936 Lydenberg interested Evans in the bibliography, and in July the project files were sent to Washington from New York. George M. McFarland of the national office staff was appointed editor-in-chief of the bibliography. In the months that followed, Lester K.

*Some of the miscellaneous records microfilmed were Estray Book, 1802-18, Clark County; Stock Brands, 1811-39, Franklin County; Manuscript of William Mitchell, 1725, and Seminary Records (in possession of the Griffith Family, Croydon), 1827-51, Harrison County; Treasurer's Book, 1812, Jefferson County; Register of Negro Slaves, 1805-7, and Poor Relief Record, 1821-32, Knox County; and Revolutionary War Pensions, Warrick County. Other than Indiana, New Jersey was the only state that attempted microfilming on a large scale. New Jersey used some 1,000 feet of film in microfilming old records, some of them dating back to 1665, 1666, 1680, 1681, 1685, and 1700. The New Jersey project also microfilmed some records, mostly in Bucks County, for the Pennsylvania project. Louisiana microfilmed birth records of the State Board of Health and of the City of New Orleans, and the New York City Project microfilmed American Loyalist Transcripts, 1783-90. So far as is known, the Kentucky project was the only one that experimented with microfilming newspapers.

Born, Donald A. Thompson, and Erik Achorn became McFarland's assistants. Survey workers from the central office staff and from the District of Columbia project, working at the Library of Congress under the supervision of Earl M. Hyde, began to check the results already obtained. These workers also forwarded to the editors new titles and transcriptions of reviews from which annotations were abstracted.

The method of work, as outlined in a memorandum of December 23, 1936, was to have workers in the Library of Congress and (in the early days) in the New York Public Library digest book reviews in selected periodicals, volume by volume, with preference given to the reviews by outstanding authorites in the field covered by the book. In general, the original language of the reviewer was retained within quotation marks. No attempt was made to balance favorable and unfavorable reviews; if competent reviewers presented contrasting views, both were given. Workers were directed to select in particular the critical, estimative portions of reviews. After reviews had been digested on cards and the cards edited, the entries were typed on letter-size paper in three copies. The original copy of each entry was then filed alphabetically by name of author, editor, or compiler; the second was placed in the classification subdivision in which it was intended to be printed; and the third copy was filed by the name and volume number of the periodical from which the review was taken.

In the preparation of the bibliography, the word "history" was interpreted in a broad sense to include not only works on politics and government but also those dealing with the social and cultural history of the country, and with its economic, scientific, religious, artistic, and literary development. Works of fiction and collections of poetry and verse were excluded. The word "American" was more restricted in extension. The bibliography, though it covers the history of the discovery, exploration, and colonization of the North American continent to the American Revolution, is limited thereafter to the regions that became a part of the United States, including its outlying possessions and dependencies. On the bibliographical side, the compilation is confined to books and pamphlets; articles in periodicals are excluded. From beginning to end the chief aim of the bibliography was to present in a massive scale and with abundant and representative detail the opinions that have been expressed in print regarding works on American history. The word "annotated" in the title is, therefore, definitive.*

---

*The titles of a considerable number of books and pamphlets for which no re-

McFarland directed the project until March, 1940, when he was succeeded by William J. Wilson. Wilson was assisted by Francis D. Horigan and a number of other workers from the Library of Congress WPA project (October, 1939, to August, 1940) and from the District of Columbia Historical Records Survey, which continued to support the undertaking until the project's suspension in July, 1941. It was intended that the entries within each classification should be arranged chronologically by year of publication beginning with the most recent book on the subject and working backward. An author index was also planned.

In June, 1941, Dan Lacy, assistant to the national director, announced that the bibliography had been completed; that final verification of entries was within perhaps six weeks of completion; that negotiations for publication were in progress; and that the volumes would be in press by autumn. He estimated that the work would appear in six large volumes containing over 80,000 reviews of some 29,000 titles.[24] The prediction was optimistic. To be sure, the bibliography, as it exists, could be brought into publishable form with but little effort. The final product, however, would lack the exactness that scholarship demands, for random checking of entries against the sources demonstrates the need for a complete and thorough check.

BIBLIOGRAPHY OF AMERICAN LITERATURE

For many years investigators in the various fields of American literature have felt the need of a new and exhaustive bibliography of American literature, both because of the inadequacy of existing bibliographies and because of the large quantity of critical material that has appeared within the past generation. The American section of the Modern Language Association had contemplated preparation of a comprehensive bibliography of American literature for a period of years; but because the several factions of this group could never agree regarding place and procedure of work, the initiation of such a project did not become a reality until the H.R.S. agreed to include it in its program.

Arthur H. Quinn, professor of English at the University of Pennsylvania, eventually interested Evans in the undertaking; and in August, 1938, a project was initiated as a unit of the Pennsylvania Historical

views could be found were collected. These unannotated entries comprise about 23 per cent of the total entries prepared, or some 6,000 items. Whether such unannotated entries should be included in the bibliography was a problem under consideration when work on the project was terminated.

818

Records Survey to prepare the bibliography. The University agreed, as co-sponsor, to supply space and equipment. The project operated for a period of a little more than three and a half years (August, 1938–April, 1942) with an average employment of forty and an aggregate employment of 250. The chief problem was that of training workers, most of whom were not initially qualified for the task. The supervisor of the project stated that it took from six to nine months to train workers to proficiency.

Edward H. O'Neill, also of the University of Pennsylvania, was appointed supervisor of the undertaking, and planned the procedure of work. He had the counsel of an advisory committee composed of members of the university faculty. For the purposes of the bibliography, O'Neill interpreted the term "literature" as broadly as possible. Historians, philosophers, nature writers, and political and economic writers, no less than those who wrote in the field of belles-lettres, were included. For each writer represented the bibliography lists individual and collected works, periodical publications, reviews, and biographical and critical studies. When the work on the bibliography was discontinued, in April, 1942, some 5,000 volumes of 250 different periodicals had been surveyed.*

INDEX OF MUSICIANS IN THE UNITED STATES

An important contribution of the H.R.S. was the compilation of the *Biobibliographical Index of Musicians in the United States of America from Colonial Times.* The index was first planned in 1936 by Keyes Porter of the central office staff. Porter was a research assistant with long experience as a librarian and a journalist, and for nearly forty years had been a student of music and musicology. His original plan embraced a work of three parts: a biobibliography, a bibliography, and a syllabus.

The list of persons included in the index was originally compiled from four standard dictionaries of American music, and to this list were added thousands of names culled from numerous volumes dealing with general and local history, histories of periods, forms (opera, symphony,

---

*When the H.R.S. was terminated, work on the bibliography was far from complete. Although none of the individual bibliographies can be assumed to be complete and the typed cards have not been checked against sources, the cards as they are should prove of assistance to inquirers.

etc.), other types of reference works and library card catalogues. Porter was assisted by workers from the District of Columbia Historical Records Survey and profited by the co-operation of the Federal Music Project, the Music Division of the Library of Congress, and the Music Division of the Pan American Union. He supervised the work until August, 1939, when the project ceased for a time because of the disintegration of the central office staff of the H.R.S. The work, however, was revived in January, 1940, under the supervision of Leonard Ellinwood and the sponsorship of the Library of Congress.

The primary purpose of the volume as finally published was to assemble under one cover the names of persons who have contributed to the history of music in the United States, and thereby to facilitiate the location of material concerning them. Over two-thirds of the sources cited in the *Index* have no individual indexes. The volume, published by the Music Division of the Pan American Union in June, 1941, has a statement by Charles Seeger, its chief, concerning the value of the publication; a preface by Harold Spivacke, chief of the music division of the Library of Congress; an introduction by Henry B. Dillard, supervisor of the District of Columbia Historical Records Survey; a bibliography giving symbols used in the index entries; and alphabetically arranged index entries (giving name, birth, and death dates if possible, and, if such dates were unobtainable, the *floruit*), field of music, and, in code form, bibliographical reference. An asterisk is used to indicate foreign birth, and nationality is given if known; and the entries also indicate any portraits, autographs, and reproductions of music in the sources cited. Following the index entries is an appendix listing special studies, biographies, and autobiographies pertaining to the persons whose names appear in the *Index*.

### ATLAS OF CONGRESSIONAL ROLL CALLS

The largest and most significant *local* undertaking of the H.R.S. was an "Atlas of Congressional Roll Calls." This work, which grew out of a casual suggestion by Louis M. Hacker, was begun in the fall of 1938. Outlines and work procedures were devised by Clifford L. Lord of the department of history at Columbia, who was consultant to the Historical Records Survey in New York City. Although headquarters for this work were first established on the Columbia campus, they were moved in November, 1939, to Hackensack, New Jersey, and in April, 1940, to Lodi, New Jersey, where Lord continued to direct the work.

Work on the Atlas involved the preparation of a series of maps portraying approximately 54,000 yea and nay roll-call votes taken in the Congress of the United States from 1789 to 1932.*

Votes were tabulated from the *Annals, Register, Globe,* and *Record* (congressional publications) and were checked for accuracy against the appropriate *House, Senate* or *Executive* journal. The *Journal* was accepted as the official record of the vote, except in cases of obvious typographical error; such errors were checked against the original vote tallies, and where the tallies had been destroyed, against the original manuscript journals in Washington. Tabulated votes, after careful checking and rechecking to assure accuracy, were used as a basis for preparation of maps. Summaries of the questions at issue, which accompany each map, identify the vote to which the map and the roll call pertain. These summaries were written from abstracts prepared largely by lawyers from the debates in the *Congressional Record,* checked and rechecked, and give the maker of the motion involved, his state and party, the date of the vote, the title and bill or resolution number of the bill involved, the *Statute* citation or indication that the bill or resolution was not passed, the effect of the motion, the result of the vote, and vote totals broken down by party; and citations to all printed versions of the roll call. The base maps, showing congressional districts, were worked out from state district acts found in the statutes of the various states; for state and territorial borders, the *Statutes at Large, Federal Cases,* and *Federal Reporter,* as well as reports of several boundary commissions, were consulted.

In final form each roll call is represented in a uniform legend on its own map. Each vote map is accompanied by a summary that identifies the particular vote, a copy of the roll call arranged by states, and citations to the text of the pertinent debates. The maps and roll calls for each Congress are supplemented by four additional maps showing state, territorial, and district boundaries, population distribution, party strength in each House, and, when available, the industrial areas of the nation.

It was planned to publish the vote maps by Congress, Session, and House, in chronological order. It was estimated that the *Atlas* as a whole would compromise some forty-two volumes of approximately eight hundred pages each. The index to the Atlas was to consist of two parts: one by subject and name arranged topically and alphabetically,

---

*Although it was originally planned to have the Atlas begin with 1789, it was decided in August, 1941, to extend the record to 1777 so as to include the votes of the Continental Congresses and the Congresses of the Confederation.

the other by bill and resolution number arranged by Congress and House.*

## SUPPLEMENT TO RICHARDSON'S "COMPILATION OF MESSAGES AND PAPERS OF THE PRESIDENTS"

Pursuant to a resolution of the Fifty-third Congress, the Honorable J. D. Richardson in 1893 began preparation of the first volume of a *Compilation of the Messages and Papers of the Presidents*. This ten-volume work was completed in its original form in 1899, and republished and brought through 1908; finally, an edition by the Bureau of National Literature, which does not appear to have been widely circulated, brought the work to 1929.

In January, 1936, Lord discussed with Evans the possibility of a project to bring the Richardson compilation up to date. He also suggested that the executive orders of the Presidents be added, and that marginal headings to Richardson's material be inserted in order to make it more accessible. The original proposal envisaged the coverage of the period from 1909 to 1936. In the next month, after some negotiation, Evans advised Lord that he would proceed at once with the preparation of instructions to the H.R.S. in New York City regarding this type of work, and suggested that Lord visit the New York City director. The project was initiated in April, 1936, as a part of the New York City H.R.S. program. At first, three workers were assigned under the supervision of Lord; and as the work progressed, the staff was gradually increased.

A manual of regulations covering the compilation was issued in mimeograph form on August 14, 1936.[26] In October, when the work was under way, Lord circulated specimens of the compilation among scholars. Solon Buck, in acknowledging receipt of the specimen sent to the Archivist of the United States, proposed carrying the publication back to 1897, where the official edition of Richardson ended. Lord replied that he could do so and still complete the manuscript by the end of the

---

*Work on the *Atlas*, more than half completed, was terminated early in 1942, and the files were moved to the Columbia University Library for storage. Volume I of the *Atlas* (*The Continental Congresses and the Congresses of the Confederation, 1777-89*) has since been published by the New York State Historical Association. Julian P. Boyd, librarian of Princeton University, in his review of the volume refers to the Atlas as "one of the most important tools ever fashioned by any nation for the understanding of its government."[25]

1937 session of Congress.[27] Authorization was granted for the extension, but the work has not yet been completed.

As early as 1936, Lord had inquired of Buck, as a member of the National Historical Publications Commission, if the commission would recommend to Congress publication of the compilation as a government document, and was apparently encouraged by the reply. More than three years later, he wrote to Buck that the undertaking was 98 per cent completed, and it represented a complete compilation of every message or communication sent by the Presidents to either house, or to the presiding officer of either house, of Congress, all proclamations and treaty proclamations, all Executive Orders of the unnumbered series with important material briefed, and a comprehensive alphabetical and topical index.[28] In June, 1940, the manuscript for the years 1907 and 1934 (a representative sampling of the compilation) was submitted to the office of the National Historical Publications Commission for examination and appraisal. The commission withheld approval and offered suggestions for revision.*

LISTS AND INDEXES OF NUMBERED AND UNNUMBERED
EXECUTIVE ORDERS

In preparing the compilation of messages and papers of the Presidents, the New York City and New Jersey H.R.S. projects collected copies of all available executive orders, both numbered and unnumbered. After the orders had been collected, Lord proposed publication; and upon approval from Washington, the New York City project proceeded with a compilation of the numbered executive orders, and the New Jersey project, with the compilation of the unnumbered executive orders.†

---

*In the commission's report it was recommended that the scope of the compilation be expanded to include the messages of the Presidents to the people as reflected in addresses delivered on public occasions, "fireside chats," statements to the press, etc.[29] The compilation remains unpublished and is on deposit in manuscript form at the Columbia University Library. The H.R.S. in New Jersey attempted a companion volume, that was to consist of a complete compilation of all messages, communications, proclamations, and executive orders issued during the second administration of President Roosevelt. The uncompleted work on this volume is also on deposit at the library.

†The only distinction between the numbered and unnumbered executive orders is that some are numbered and some are not. The numbering system was begun by the State Department in 1907 when the orders on file were arranged chronologically and given numbers, as were other orders subsequently filed with the department.

The list of *Executive Orders Numbered 1-8030, 1862-1938,* was printed in 1944, sponsored by the mayor of the City of New York and Columbia University and copyrighted by the mayor. Lord was editor, and Joseph E. Vaughan and Charles E. Baker were associate editors. This compilation was published in two volumes. In the first volume, which contains the list or abstracts of the executive orders, an introduction by the editor discusses the increasing importance of the executive order as an instrument of government, its different types, varieties in form, availability, and distinction between the numbered and unnumbered orders. Three pages of explanatory material are also included. The list of orders is arranged chronologically rather than numerically, since the latter arrangement would have meant occasional violation of logical sequence. The full text of each executive order was used as the basis of each abstract. The list gives executive order number, date, abstract of subject matter, and citation to publications or compilations containing copy of orders where orders are to be found in publications.

Volume II contains an index to the contents or subject matter of the orders listed in Volume I rather than an index to the list. Index entries are arranged alphabetically by topic and year date, with executive order numbers shown.

The *List and Index of Presidential Executive Orders, Unnumbered Series, 1789-1941* was published by the New Jersey project in mimeographed form in 1943. Lord was also editor of this volume, and the work was sponsored by the New Jersey State Planning Board and Columbia University.

The total of unnumbered executive orders is unknown, and the volume published by the New Jersey staff, as indicated in the preface, covers perhaps only a very small portion of the whole field. This preliminary list, however, can be increased as additional unnumbered orders are discovered, and perhaps in time a definitive list will be achieved. This volume also carries an introduction. The list is based upon two major sources: printed compilations of orders on special subjects, and references in other orders, numbered or unnumbered, to further orders that do not appear in the numbered series. The list is chronologically arranged, with abstract of subject matter given where

Back orders later added to the State Department collection were given in-between numbers, such as 343-A, 343-B, 343-C, 288½, etc. Many executive orders, however, never found their way into the files of the State Department, and consequently were never numbered.

possible. The index to the unnumbered orders is arranged alphabetically by topic, and each entry gives the date of the executive order.

THE HISTORICAL RECORDS SURVEY IN DEFENSE AND WAR WORK

The emphasis of the WPA upon national defense, beginning in 1940, and the eventual direction of all the energies of the agency toward the war effort were inevitable, and affected the H.R.S. no less than the rest of the program. The war work done by the survey, however, must not be interpreted as a continuation of its earlier program. Although the subject matter continued to be records, the concept was that of immediate service in the emergency and not that of historical significance.

The value of vital statistics with regard to citizenship and voting privileges, inheritance rights, parentage, legal right to marry, etc., has always been obvious, but the need for such information was increasingly emphasized during the Roosevelt era. The social legislation of the administration established new rights, such as old age assistance and retirement allowances, many of which cannot be asserted without vital statistics evidence. Later, the use of such statistics in determining the ages of men affected by draft legislation and in supplying birth certificates for persons employed in industrial war work was dramatized. In the securing, collecting, and publication of vital statistics records of churches as well as of public bodies, the work and workers of the H.R.S. performed a valuable service. Thirty-eight states in all issued guides to public vital statistics records; and twenty-one states, guides to church vital statistics. Some of the latter, however, cover only certain denominations or certain geographical areas.

The second war project initiated by the H.R.S. was a nationwide inventory of civilian organizations that might render services in home defense. The directory was to include general civic organizations, service organizations, welfare and charitable groups, auxiliary religious groups engaged in service work, chambers of commerce, national and state headquarters of labor unions and city-wide trade councils, Parent-Teacher Associations, patriotic societies, professional associations, home demonstration clubs and farm organizations, alumni groups, motorists' clubs, youth organizations, and historical societies. This work, however, came to a sudden and dramatic end in July, 1941. It seems that Mrs. Kerr, assistant WPA commissioner in charge of community service projects and also assistant to Fiorello LaGuardia, then director of the Office of Civilian Defense, had neglected to secure the latter's endorsement of the work prior to the issuance of a press release indicating such endorsement. LaGuardia's sense of procedure was outraged, and the ax fell.*

The third project undertaken by the H.R.S. as its contribution to the war crisis was concerned with the conservation of cultural resources. In developing plans for the protection of buildings and records in case of public emergency, the Public Buildings Administration's Committee on Emergency Protection of Public Buildings asked the H.R.S. to ascertain what facilities in federal buildings outside Washington would be available for storage of material evacuated from Washington. The committee subsequently expressed its gratitude to the H.R.S. for procuring this information.[30] In addition, the Committee on Conservation of Cultural Resources, created by the National Resources Planning Board in the fall of 1941, requested the assistance of the H.R.S. in protecting valuable records and cultural materials. In November, 1941, Dan Lacy resigned as assistant to the director of the H.R.S. to become secretary of the Committee on the Conservation of Cultural Resources, and other members of the central office staff of the H.R.S. co-operated with him in drafting forms to be used in the collection of data on storage space and on priority lists of records to be evacuated if the need arose.†

Although the major undertakings of the H.R.S. in its last two years were service projects of a utilitarian nature, and not concerned with history or research (except in the sense that every inquiry is a gesture of historical research), state projects were able to carry forward their publication programs; and because the volume of HR forms coming into the state offices was considerably less than in the earlier period, state editorial staffs were better able to concentrate upon publication and thus to issue more inventories, guides, and check lists than before.

Administratively, the H.R.S. was terminated in April, 1942, when the service division of the Work Projects Administration, of which the survey was a unit, redirected its program to the war effort. Permission was generally granted, however, to complete publications already in

*Although the project was discontinued on a national basis, some fifteen states, at the request of state defense councils or the governor, continued the work.

†In some states, workers completed upon short notice emergency war inventories, such as the comprehensive "Inventory of Automobile Graveyards" compiled in Michigan, to locate available scrap metal for the War Production Board. In other states, survey workers assisted in making truck and bus inventories for the War Department.

production, and some states were still issuing publications in early 1943.*

REPRODUCTION AND DISTRIBUTION OF H.R.S. PUBLICATIONS

Inventories and other publications of the survey were generally reproduced by mimeograph, multilith, or other process by the individual state projects. State projects made every effort to secure sponsor contributions to defray the costs of publication, and sponsors frequently contributed stencils, paper, ink, covers, and sometimes even multigraph or mimeograph machines. A few states—the most successful were North Carolina, Illinois, Indiana, Michigan, and Pennsylvania— were able to secure sponsorship for printing some of their publications. Contracts covering printing provided that a specified number of copies be made available to the H.R.S. for its own use. Inventories or other publications printed by private organizations could be sold by such organizations after the required number of copies had been turned over to the H.R.S. Publications were distributed to public libraries, archival establishments, universities, and other research centers throughout the country. There were one or more national depositories in every state; some depositories were interested in only certain categories (e.g., church inventories). In addition to the national depositories, there were regional depositories, which received publications undertaken in the WPA region of which they were a part.†

1. Luther H. Evans, "WPA Fashions New Tools for Research," paper delivered before the thirty-first annual meeting of the Mississippi Valley Historical Association, Indianapolis, Indiana, April 28, 1938. H.R.S. Files.

2. Letter, Evans to Binkley, April 25, 1936, Joint Committee Files, Library of Congress.

3. "Report on Luncheon Conference," Regional Conference of the H.R.S., Chicago, Illinois, May, 1936, H.R.S. Files.

*One project undertaken by the H.R.S. in this latter period, although its aim was to serve the war effort, had historical significance. Waldo Leland, in his presidential address at the annual meeting of the Society of American Archivists in November 1940, suggested that the society appoint a committee to make plans for a survey of records of World War I agencies, with the idea that an inventory of such records might be of assistance to war agencies during the present war. Sargent Child agreed to use personnel of the H.R.S. in making such a survey. A plan was prepared by the committee in co-operation with the H.R.S. The work, however, was undertaken in only a limited number of states; inventories were compiled by several states, and two (Louisiana and Minnesota) were published.

†A list of national and regional depositories is contained in Professional and Service Letter No. 63, Revised, dated December 7, 1940.

4. Robert C. Binkley, "The Why of the White Collar Program," extracts from a paper prepared for a joint meeting of the Society of American Archivists and the American Historical Association, Chicago, December, 1939, American Council of Learned Societies Files.

5. Letter, Evans to All Assistant State Supervisors, H.R.S., March 28, 1936, Joint Committee Files, Library of Congress.

6. "Editing of Public Records Inventories," Memorandum, Evans to Assistant State Supervisors, H.R.S., June 12, 1936.

7. *Supplement No. 4 to the Manual of the Historical Records Survey*, Instructions for Editing Guides to Public Records, WPA, September, 1936.

8. *Instructions for the Preparation of Inventories of Public Records by Historical Records Survey Projects*, W.P.A. Technical Series, Research and Records Circular No. 5, Vol. I, FWA, WPA, Division of Community Service Programs, Washington, D.C., 1941.

9. Des Moines *Register*, July 28, 1937.

10. Luther H. Evans and Edythe Weiner, "The Analysis of County Records," *American Archivist*, October, 1938, pp. 186-200.

11. "Legal Provisions Regarding County Agencies and Their Records," Memorandum, Evans to All State Directors, H.R.S., September 16, 1937, Philbrick and Joint Committee Files.

12. *Check List of Historical Records Survey Publications*, 1943, pp. 17-31.

13. Sargent Child, "What is Past is Prologue," a report read at the Annual Meeting of the American Library Association, June 23, 1942, p. 5.

14. *Manual of the Historical Records Survey*, p. 15.

15. Memorandum of Evans on luncheon conference with Solon J. Buck on July 28, 1936, dated July 29, 1936, Joint Committee Files, Library of Congress.

16. Philip M. Hamer, "The Discovery of Unpublished Historical Documents," An address delivered before the American Historical Association annual meeting, Chicago, December 1938, typed copy in H.R.S. files, p. 6.

17. "The Collection of Manuscripts relating to the History of the American Negro," Memorandum, Evans to Woodward, December 9, 1938, Joint Committee Files, Library of Congress.

18. Douglas C. McMurtrie, "The Record of American Imprints," Extract from the *Proceeds of the Conference of State and Local Historical Societies held at the Historical Society of Pennsylvania*, December 31, 1937, p. 1, copy in Evans' personal files.

19. Sargent B. Child, "What Is Past Is Prologue," *loc. cit.*, p. 8.

20. "Progress and Status of the Historical Records Survey," Memorandum, Evans to Hopkins, April 1, 1938, H.R.S. Files.

21. Letter, Hacker to Evans, April 20, 1936, H.R.S. Files.

22. Letter, Binkley to Chatelaine, July 30, 1935, Joint Committee Files, Library of Congress.

23. Letter, Lydenberg to Chatelaine, July 30, 1935, Joint Committee Files, Library of Congress.

24. Dan Lacy, "The Historical Records Survey and the Librarian," p. 7.

25. Julian P. Boyd, in *New York Times Book Review*, August 13, 1944, p. 10.

26. Copy attached to letter, Lord to Evans, August 14, 1936, H.R.S. Files.

27. Letter, Lord to Evans, November 11, 1936, H.R.S. Files.

28. Letter, Lord to Buck, April 27, 1940, H.R.S. Files.

29. "Report on the Technical Quality of the WPA Compilation of the Messages and Papers of the Presidents," signed by P. W. Edsall, July 26, 1940, H.R.S. Files.

30. Letter, Blakeslee to Hunter, November 29, 1941, H.R.S. Files.

# 32

## Retrospect and Prospect

An attempt to write a history of the influence since 1943 of federal and state arts programs upon public bodies, non-public institutions, and the lives and careers of private persons would require a space of time and a degree of research and composition that would equal if not excel what has been consumed in the present effort. That these arts programs, as part of the public relief programs of the depression, achieved their purpose of preserving life and at least a minimum degree of physical well-being for thousands of men and women who otherwise might have grievously suffered and that this was a work of mercy and charity, none will now deny. Moreover, few would now say that it was not right and just that those who, through no fault of their own, were unable to secure private employment and the fruits thereof, should have been given the opportunity by the public authorities to follow their several professions and to maintain that quality of human dignity and self-respect that only work—and work according to one's talents—confers. Indeed, even the hardheaded champion of laissez-faire will find it difficult not to admit that public bodies, private associations, and private individuals have benefited and continue to benefit from the experiment. As early as 1936, Audrey McMahon, writing in *Parnassus*, summarized well what the Federal Art Project was achieving:

> Three years of government patronage of the visual arts have proved several facts: that the individuality of the artist is not lost in a group effort; that the artist is deeply benefited by increased and broadened opportunity; that without this opportunity there seems to be little immediate hope for his sur-

829

vival; that the public gains educationally and materially from his efforts; that thousands of administrators of public buildings recognize the value of murals, easel paintings and other forms of art expression in their buildings and embrace the opportunity to acquire them with eagerness if sometimes without discrimination; that underprivileged children may be constructively influenced through art education; that there has been born a thirst for knowledge in the public and that of this thirst for knowledge may come a great culture.[1]

What is here said of the Art Project specifically early in its history was true many times over when it ended seven years later, and equally true, *mutatis mutandis*, of the other programs of Federal One. The fact that this present investigation has been made and this present work written and published is itself testimony to the unique place that the arts programs of the New Deal have in the history of government encouragement and subsidy of the arts in the United States. Like Ajax, Federal One stands head and shoulders above its peers; and whatever has happened since toward the same end repeats, echoes, and carries forward the earlier spirit and purpose.

## PROSPECT: THE JOHN FITZGERALD KENNEDY CENTER FOR THE PERFORMING ARTS

Between the termination of the earlier programs in 1943 and the inauguration of John F. Kennedy as President of the United States in 1961, the federal government did little directly to encourage and support the arts. To be sure, in the administration of Presidents Truman and Eisenhower proposals were made in and out of Congress and bills tossed into the hopper; but nothing of significance came of them with one exception—the John Fitgerald Kennedy Center for the Performing Arts. As early as May, 1958, Senator J. William Fulbright of Arkansas, among others, urged support of a bill to set up in Washington a National Cultural Center of the Performing Arts. The bill was passed in August of the same year, but it was not until January, 1959, that President Eisenhower appointed fifteen trustees to supervise the project; and it was not until July, 1960, that the same President named the thirteen members of the advisory committee for the proposed center. Upon assuming the presidency in January, 1961, Mr. Kennedy made it clear that he favored the plan; and in 1962 he appointed Roger L. Stevens, a New York theatrical producer, to the chairmanship of the board of trustees. On December 3, 1963, following President Kennedy's assassination, Senator Fulbright and Representative Carl Albert of Oklahoma offered a resolution, supported by President Johnson, to name the National Cultural Center in honor of the late President. In January, 1964, the bill was approved by Congress, the House adding the amendment that the Center be the "sole memorial" to President Kennedy in the District of Columbia. Congress also allotted for construction and maintenance $15.5 million in federal funds to match private contributions. The construction of the Center is now approaching completion.

## THE NATIONAL COUNCIL ON THE ARTS

This earlier move, solitary though it was, proved the harbinger of a renewed and fresh interest in the arts in the Kennedy administration, a development for which the President's wife, no less than her husband, was responsible. Shortly after taking office, the President appointed August Heckscher, director of the Twentieth Century Fund, as his special consultant on the arts. In this capacity Mr. Heckscher prepared and presented to the President a special report on the relationship between the arts and the national government.[2] In this report, after advocating a cautious policy that rejected European models both of the old regime and totalitarianism, the President's consultant emphasized the diversity and decentralization of culture and mores in the United States and advocated a program that preserved and encouraged this variety. Finally, in consonance with the traditional American preference for private enterprise, it was recommended that the role of the federal government, both in the provision of financial support and as a cultural guide, should remain purely ancillary to private subsidy and individual creativity. As part of his proposed program, Heckscher recommended a national arts foundation; and when President Kennedy found Congress reluctant to give statutory form to this suggestion, he created by executive order, on June 12, 1963, the President's Advisory Council on the Arts.

On this occasion the President suggested that the Council should investigate five specific programs and areas:

1. Examine the opportunities for young people to develop their gifts and to participate in an active cultural life.

2. Evaluate the many new forms and institutions that are developing.

3. Assess governmental policies and programs.

4. Consider public recognition of excellence.

5. Consider the implications of the national cultural scene for foreign exchange programs in the arts.

On November 22, 1963, President Johnson succeeded Mr. Kennedy as President of the United States. He appointed Roger L. Stevens to succeed August Heckscher as his consultant on the arts. Since Stevens was already chairman of the board for the proposed Center for the Performing Arts, he now assumed a double responsibility. The new President was strongly urged to carry further the cultural program of his predecessor. Accordingly, on September 3, 1964, he signed a bill that gave statutory basis to the National Council on the Arts, hitherto existing by executive order only. It was intended that the Council should function in the fields of music, drama, dance, folk art, literature, architecture, painting, sculpture, and industrial and fashion design. The Council was to consist of a full-time chairman at a salary of $21,000 per year, and twenty-five members with a per diem allowance of $75.00 and travel expenses. Its functions were defined as follows:

1. To recommend ways to maintain and increase the cultural resources of the United States

2. To prepare methods to encourage private initiative in the arts.

3. To advise and consult with other state, local, and federal agencies on methods of co-ordinating existing recources and facilities and for fostering artistic and cultural endeavors and use of the arts both nationally and internationally in the interests of this country

4. To make studies and recommendations as to how creative activity and high standards and increased opportunities in the arts may be encouraged and promoted.

Senator Jacob J. Javits and Representative John V. Lindsay, both of New York, had worked long and hard, ever since 1958, for this statutory recognition of the arts, and Lindsay commented at the time that "six years of work has come to fruition."[3]

The final step, up to now, of this movement of the federal government, formally and financially, into the realm of the arts was taken on March 11, 1965, when President Johnson submitted a bill to establish the National Foundation on the Arts and Humanities. A precedent for the proposal was sought in the National Science Foundation created by Congress in 1951. The Foundation, which is now in being, consists of three parts: a National Council on the Arts; a National Council for the Humanities; and a National Council for the Arts and Humanities, to co-ordinate the activities of the two aforesaid councils. This measure shifts the already existing National Council on the Arts from the Executive Office of the President to the new co-ordinating Council. In his proposal President Johnson was careful to warn that the government should not seek to restrict the freedom of the artist to pursue his calling in his own way.

The definitions of "arts" and "humanities" in the bill are extremely broad. The arts are to include not only such traditional fields as drama and creative writing but also photography, costume and fashion design, motion pictures, television, and radio. Under the humanities are included language, literature, history and philosophy, archeology, the history, criticism, and theory of the arts, and those aspects of the social sciences that have humanistic content and employ humanistic methods. The fundamental distinction between the two councils is that, that on the arts concerns itself with practitioners and that on the humanities with teachers. The salaries of the members of the Foundation were fixed at $28,500. The Council on the Arts and the Council for the Humanities were each to have a first-year sum of $5 million, and in addition each could be authorized to match private contributions with federal funds up to $5 million. Subsequently passed by Congress, the bill was signed by the President on September 29, 1965. Roger L. Stevens was appointed chairman of the new Foundation, and on December 13 of the same year the President and Mrs. Johnson gave a dinner and reception at the White House for its members.

The grants and awards made and projected by this new National Council on the Arts from its inception to the present are too many and too diverse to be named and described here with any attempt at completeness. They are a matter of contemporary history and bear witness to an attitude that is both generous and catholic. On December 28, 1966, Henry Geldzahler, associate curator of American art at the Metropolitan Museum of Art, reported that the Council planned the disbursement of $750,000 in grants to develop a broad program in the visual arts. These grants would include $50,000 for an art resources survey to help traveling shows visit different parts of the country; $150,000 to commission drawings for reproduction and to reproduce existing drawings for distribution through educational institutions; $100,000 to help artists to get federal housing funds; and the Council was weighing the suggestion to develop a series of 10,000 slides on art history for schools and libraries.[4] On August 29 of the same year the Council announced that it was granting $100,000 on a matching basis for commissioning prints for educational institutions and libraries; artists could get up to $2,000 for original works.[5] On August 7, 1967, Stevens announced a plan to build a $10-million artists' center on Manhattan's lower west side to provide low-income housing for 500 painters, sculptors, and other artists—this to be a joint project of the Council and a private donor, the J. M. Kaplan Fund. The average rent is to be about $110 for a three-room apartment.[6] On July 29, 1967, a $15,000 matching grant was made to the Arts Technical Research Institute to study artists materials; and on May 29, 1968, matching grants of $10,000 each were made for the purchase of works by contemporary American artists in order to bring artists' pictures where they can be seen by the people.[8] When in 1967 the Metropolitan National Opera Company, which had been attempting to bring opera to non-metropolitan centers, failed for lack of funds, the Council supported with a grant of $350,000 the American National Opera Company to undertake the same mission. The American National Opera Company had grown out of the Opera Company of Boston, founded in 1957 by Sarah Caldwell and sustained these many years by her ability and enthusiasm. Like the defunct company, the new company is to make national tours and to favor the smaller communities.[9] On June 19, 1967, the Council announced outright cash awards of $10,000 each to five writers, who were thus honored for their lifelong contribution to American literature.[10] The first instance of corporate giving to the Council was provided by the Bristol-Myers Company, which gave an unrestricted gift of $300,000. Matching this gift with an equal amount of its own funds and adding $25,000 from other private donors, the Council made an award of $625,000 to the Educational Broadcasting Corporation for educational television.[11]

That the Council is prepared to extend its program substantially both in the size of the grants and the extent of its coverage was shown when, on August 23, 1967, it recommended that Congress appropriate $130 million to support the most amibitious federal aid program for the arts ever suggested. The projects recommended included:

1. 50 permanent professional theater companies

2. The foundation of small musical groups (quartets, quintets, and twenty-piece orchestras)

3. Experimental projects in television programming

4. Aid to symphony orchestras, major dance companies, museums, composers, playwrights, novelists, poets, painters, and sculptors

Of this amount nearly $9 million would be allotted for television programming in the arts, resulting in 725 half-hour programs for non-commercial television stations; the establishment of a non-commercial radio project to explore the potentialities of radio drama by creating a repertory group of directors, writers, and actors ("Concerts, operas, poetry readings, plays and exhibitions should be available to all Americans, particularly those who live in relatively inaccessible parts of the country"); and $5 million to support such dance groups as the American Ballet Theater and the Martha Graham company.[12]

But as Roger Stevens has pointed out in an article in the *Saturday Review*, if much has been done, much remains to be done. After conceding that in 1964 there were 1,400 symphony orchestras, 5,000 community theaters, and several hundred opera and ballet companies throughout the United States, the writer goes on to comment:

In 771 American cities with 25,000 or more residents—and they comprise in the aggregate almost half of the nation's total population—only 131 had a chance to hear at least one professional symphony orchestra in a three-year period from 1961 to 1964. Only 157 had a chance to witness at least one performance by a professional theatrical company, while only 84 had a chance to listen to at least one performance by a professional opera company.

. . . One has only to recall that total U.S. federal expenditure of $5,000,000 on the WPA art project in Depression days not only produced a body of "unofficial art" now conservatively valued at around $50,000,000, but provided the inducements and training from which have come the artists who have made New York the current world capital for paintings.[13]

835

Besides the National Foundation on the Arts and Humanities, which represents by far the most direct, substantial, and continuing investment of the federal government in the arts, three other developments have occurred recently that point in the same direction: the Armed Forces Combat Art Program, the building of the Hirshhorn Museum, and the housing of the National Collection of Fine Arts in a separate building.

*The Armed Forces Combat Art Program.*—By 1967 the United States Army, Navy, Marine Corps, and Air Force had each set up an art program to record in paintings the war in Vietnam. These became known collectively as the Armed Forces Combat Art Program. More than a dozen civilians and some seventy servicemen were assigned to re-create in paintings moments of the Vietnam war. Lester Cooke, Jr., the curator of painting at the National Gallery of Art in Washington, was appointed civilian adviser to the program. The civilians are invited for stays of three or four weeks by the Office of Military History. The soldier–combat artist teams consist of five servicemen with a background in art who are sent to Vietnam every sixty days. The first showing of this art was held in the Pentagon concourse from October 30 to November 3, 1967.*[14]

*The Hirshhorn Museum.*—On October 17, 1966, a bill was approved to build a museum to house the J. H. Hirshhorn art collection, and the bill was signed by the President on November 7. Hirshhorn, a uranium magnate, presented his collection to the President the previous May. It includes 6,300 paintings, drawings, and sculptures, and is valued at up to $50 million. His gift also included $1 million for the purchase of additional art. The bill provided that the museum be called the Joseph H. Hirshhorn Museum and Sculpture Garden and be located on the mall west of the Capitol and across from the National Archives. The cost is estimated at about $16 million.[15]

---

*Most of these soldier-artists are draftees who have attended art schools or majored in art in college, and some of them find the work distasteful and frustrating. One of them is quoted as saying: "What we have to do is glorify the American G.I. What the officers here want, essentially, is a handsome American soldier stepping out of a helicopter with an American flag in one hand and a slice of apple pie in the other. They sure as hell don't want us to put down what these guys are going through."

*The National Collection of Fine Arts.*—On May 3, 1968, President Johnson dedicated the National Collection of Fine Arts in its first permanent home in the old Patents Office in Washington. The building was restored at a cost of $6 million. The National Collection of Fine Arts was created by Congress in 1946 as a branch of the Smithsonian Institution, and previously had occupied a floor of the Smithsonian's Museum of Natural History. It contains paintings, prints, and sculptures of the eighteenth, nineteenth, and twentieth centuries.[16]

PRIVATE BUSINESS AND THE ARTS: THE ROCKEFELLER PANEL
REPORT ON THE PERFORMING ARTS

It is not surprising that the increased concern of public bodies for the arts should engender a larger activity toward the same end by the private corporation. John Dewey once wrote: "As long as art is the beauty parlor of civilization, neither art nor civilization is secure."[17] The same issue was raised by the Rockefeller Panel Report on the Performing Arts, which was published in 1965. This report emphasized the arts as primarily a community concern, especially of the business world, no less than libraries, museums, hospitals, and schools. The center of support should be at the local level; financial subsidy should come first from private support within the locality; if that is inadequate, then from the local government; after that, the state government; and only last and as a last resort, the federal agencies—and then only to help the states and local subdivisions perform their task. The report recognized that in many, if not in most, cases the financial support of the federal government would be necessary.[18] In 1967, as a further instance of this corporate concern, the Business Committee of the Arts, a national advisory organization of corporation executives, was formed at the suggestion of David Rockefeller and under the chairmanship of Douglas Dillon.

Two works have been recently published on the subject of corporate giving. In the first the author, Richard Eells, touches upon support of the arts as one part of private benefaction. The second and later work is devoted entirely to the consideration of the need and propriety of corporate support of the arts. As early as 1956, in his first book, Professor Eells wrote:

> Corporation philanthropy can with good reason also lend support to the creative arts, libraries, museums, recreation, and to fraternal groups. . . .

Activities that now seem remote from managerial interests in the immediate business operation will assume more important proportions as our understanding of social, cultural, and political processes widens and deepens.[19]

Eells's later work is devoted entirely to the relationship between the contemporary corporation and the arts, and treats the subject authoritatively and exhaustively from every point of view—financial, artistic, social, philosophic, and historical. In it he writes:

A company remains indifferent to these artistic aspirations at its peril. One does not have to wait for legislation to realize that urban ugliness, water and air polluition and other disfigurements are a threat to the culture that sustains a free way of life. There is a growing feeling in the United States that business corporations should aid in meeting these problems. Stream pollution may involve violation of law. There may be no law requiring a company to beautify its buildings and grounds. Yet to ignore the incipient aesthetic norms that are becoming more and more an integral part of civic duty would be a failure of corporate social responsibility irrespective of sanctions.[20]

## THE NEW YORK BOARD OF TRADE AND "ESQUIRE"

Shortly after the publication of the Rockefeller Report, the New York Board of Trade instituted a series of annual awards to firms that made outstanding contributions to culture and the arts. The significance of this pioneering action is that it is the recognition of the business community *as such* that today's businessman is developing an aesthetic and artistic as well as a moral conscience.[21]

In January, 1967, Arnold Gingrich, the editor of *Esquire*, announced the offering of awards to business corporations for outstanding contributions to the arts. The competition had almost two hundred entries, and in the July issue of the same year twenty awards were announced. In announcing the awards Gingrich wrote:

If the American business community would earmark for cultural activities just one half of one per cent of the five per cent tax deduction allowable, this would generate $250 million annually for devotion to the arts. This roughly translates to ten times the annual amount currently allocated. In considering this proposal, think of the marvelous and delightful impact it will have in elevating the arts and bringing them to all the people on every socio-economic level. It would be one of the healthiest things that could happen in improving the quality of life in our country.[22]

Inspired by *Esquire*'s contest, *McCall's* sponsored a film version of a musical interpretation of Shakespeare's *Midsummer Night's Dream*. It was performed by the New York City Ballet, and had a premiere showing in twenty-eight cities for the benefit of the local symphony orchestras.[23]

Even private initiative for private profit was inspired to support the arts, and in the latter part of 1967 the Alabama Hotel, one of several hotels in the Bowery owned by the Lyons House group, was thoroughly renovated, the cubicles removed, and eight floor-through studios constructed for the use of artists. By December all had been rented at rates ranging from $150 to $175 per month. It was announced that a similar conversion was being planned for another Lyons House hotel.[24]

CONCLUSION

It is significant that the most recent government agency for the support of the arts is called The National Foundation on the Arts and Humanities. It is proper that the arts and the humanities should be housed under the same roof. Surely, this is a happy marriage and should bear bounteous fruit, for the purpose of each is the same. Man does not live by bread alone, nor does he live by mind alone. Man's nature, as Plato pointed out, is irascible and appetitive as well as intelligent; and one's emotions, no less than one's mind and body, must be trained and trained well. In the history of Western education until recent times, this was the task of the arts college, in which was domiciled the study of the great literatures, ancient and modern, upon which our society has rested. In the best of all possible worlds one's emotions should be in accord with right reason, and this has been the essential burden of Homer, Virgil, Dante, Shakespeare, Milton, and Goethe. By verbal definition the college of liberal arts is the college of free men, and it has been there that his emotions have been trained and brought under discipline. But the arts college is now under duress and is being gradually but effectively dispossessed by science and the computer. None would deny that science and the computer have their uses and are here to stay; but if our society is not to be impersonal and without mercy, they must be humanized by a respect for the emotional nature of the human soul. This is why the arts college must now be succored by the creative and performing arts, for they, much better and much sooner than the traditional humanistic disciplines, can reach the many. The cry of our youth today that love is better than war is not to be denied.

But here again, love alone is not enough. It, too, needs discipline, for there is something of the satyr in all of us. It is not enough to plead, as the Western young man, disillusioned by his bootless struggle for material wealth, says to that prehistoric Cretan, Zorba the Greek, "Teach me to dance!" Besides love, there must be faith and hope in the decency of the universe. There must be some mean between modern mechanical man and Dionysus sporting in the Thracian woodlands.

1. Audrey McMahon, "The Trend of the Government in Art," *Parnassus,* January, 1936, p. 6.

2. *The Arts and the National Government, Report to the President Submitted by August Heckscher, Special Consultant on the Arts,* May 28, 1963, Sen. Doc. No. 28, 88th Cong., 1st Sess.

3. *New York Times,* September 4, 1964.

4. *Ibid.,* December 20, 1966.

5. *Ibid.,* August 30, 1966.

6. *Ibid.,* August 8, 1967.

7. *Ibid.,* July 10, 1967.

8. *Ibid.,* May 30, 1968.

9. *Atlantic Monthly,* September, 1967, pp. 120-22.

10. *Publishers' Weekly,* July 17, 1967, p. 49.

11. *New York Times,* October 4, 1966.

12. *Ibid.,* August 24, 1967.

13. Roger L. Stevens, "The State of the Arts—a 1966 Balance Sheet," *Saturday Review,* March 12, 1966, pp. 24, 25. Copyright 1966 Saturday Review, Inc.

14. *New York Times,* September 15, 1967.

15. *Ibid.,* October 18, 1966, and November 8, 1966.

16. *Ibid.,* May 4, 1968.

17. John Dewey, *Art as Experience* (New York: Minton, Balch & Co., 1934), p. 344.

18. *The Performing Arts: Rockefeller Panel Report on the Future of Theatre, Dance, Music in America* (New York: McGraw-Hill, 1965), pp. 71-74, 148.

19. Richard Eells, *Corporation Giving in a Free Society* (New York: Harper & Bros., 1956), p. 132.

20. Richard Eells, *The Corporation and the Arts* (New York: Macmillan Co., 1967), p. 175.

21. *Esquire,* July, 1967, p. 6. (For a listing of the fifteen awards made by the New York Board of Trade see the *New York Times,* May 17, 1965.)

22. *Ibid.*

23. *Ibid.,* January, 1968, p. 6.

24. *New York Times,* December 29, 1967.

# Index

The following abbreviations are used throughout the Index.

ACA        Advisory Committee on Allotments
AICP       Association for Improving the Conditions of the Poor (NYC)
AFA        American Federation of Actors
AF of M    American Federation of Musicians
CCC        Civilian Conservation Corps
CWA        Civil Works Administration
CWS        Civil Works Service Program
DAR        Daughters of the American Revolution
ERA        Emergency Relief Administration (of the several states)
ERB        Emergency Relief Bureau (NYC)
ERCA       Emergency Relief and Construction Act
EWB        Emergency Work Bureau (NYC)
EWRA       Emergency Work and Relief Administration (NYC)
EWRB       Emergency Work and Relief Bureau (NYC)
EWRP       Emergency Work Relief Program of the FERA
FAP        Federal Art Project
FERA       Federal Emergency Relief Administration
FMP        Federal Music Project
FTP        Federal Theatre Project
FWA        Federal Works Administration
FWP        Federal Writers' Project
GAO        Government Accounting Office
GPO        Government Printing Office
HR Forms   Historical Records Forms
HRS        Historical Records Survey
IATSE      International Alliance of Theatrical Stage Employees
NIRA       National Industrial Recovery Act
NYA        National Youth Administration
NYC        New York City
NYS        New York State
PWA        Public Works Administration (Federal Emergency Administration
           of Public Works)

841

| PWAP | Public Works of Art Project |
|---|---|
| RCA | Radio Corporation of America |
| RFC | Reconstruction Finance Corporation |
| SERA | State Emergency Relief Administration (of the several states) |
| SFA | Survey of Federal Archives |
| TERA | Temporary Emergency Relief Administration (NYS) |
| TRAP | Treasury Relief Art Project |
| USES | United States Employment Service |
| WPA | Works Progress Administration (1935-39) *or* Work Projects Administration (1939-43) |
| YMCA | Young Men's Christian Association |
| YWCA | Young Women's Christian Association |

Colby, Merle (FWP), 673

Colcord, Joanna C., 18, 754

Colgan, Howard E. (HRS), 770

College Art Association, 345, 350, 353, 380, 405, 411, 438, 459

College of the City of New York, 353

Colorado, 290, 593, 594, 595, 596, 573n.; Colorado Springs Music Project, 77, 78; Denver, 588

Columbia Broadcasting System, 588, 624

Columbia Phonograph Company, 624

Columbia University, 377, 619, 626n.. 663, 667, 718, 759, 772, 795, 816, 820, 824; Columbia University Library 822n., 823n.; *Daily Spectator*, 667

*Comedy of Errors, A* (Shakespeare), 550, 556

"Command Performance" (FTP), 566

Commission on National Archives Survey, 755 and n., 761

Commissioner of Internal Revenue, 299n.

Committee on Art and Culture (of the Progressive Education Association), 457

Committee on Conservation of Cultural Resources, 826

Committee on Emergency Protection of Public Buildings, 826

Committee of Federal Agencies for Art Week, 479

Committee on Materials for Research of the American Council of Learned Societies and the Social Science Research Council, 755

Committee on Unemployment Relief (Philadelphia); *see* Lloyd Committee

Communists, 405, 407n., 664

Community art centers, 226-27, 380-81, 392, 395, 416-18, 423, *464-74*

Community center movement, 8

Community fund movement, 10

Community Service Programs, Division of, 315, 316, 319, 419, 788n., 826

Community services, philosophy of, 60, 100-101, 186-87, 281

Community theater, 563-65; and competition with private enterprise, 393-96

"Compilation of Bibliographies and Biographies of California Literature and Authors from Pre-Gold Rush Period to 1935" (FWP), 659

Compilation of the Messages and Papers of the Presidents (Richardson), 822

Composers' Forum Laboratory (FMP), 597, 624-25, 636

*Composite America* (FWP), 727

Comptroller-General (U.S.), 278, 280n., 286, 293, 298 and nn.

Concert Branch (FMP), 608

Conference on Education and Culture (of the Negro Arts Committee), 732

Conference on Immediate Human Needs, 731

Conference on Inter-American Relations in the Field of Music, 612

Conference on Professional, Cultural, and White-Collar Workers, 656

Congress (U.S.), 109-15, 119-21, 120-21, 200-208, 217, 227, 263, 282, 312, 427n., 513, 533-41, 674, 716

Congresses of the Confederation, 821

*Congressional Record*, 821

*Conjur Man Dies* (FTP), 558

Connecticut, 77, 78, 364, 370, 398, 431, 564, 593, 595, 709, 710, 771n., 814, 815n.; Bridgeport, 78, 94, 619; *Connecticut Guide* (under FERA), 78, 658, 693, 694, 741; Hartford, 78, 619, 658; Hartford Musicians' Protective Association, 593; Norwalk, 554n.; Westport, 348

Connelly, Marc., 549n., 654

Connolly, Cyril, 474

Connor, R. D. W. (HRS), 760

Conroy, Jack, 704, 715n.

Contemporary drama, 552-53

Continental Congresses, 582, 821n.

*Continental Congresses and the Congresses of the Confederation*, 822n.

*Continental Theatre Bulletin*, 580

Control of operations (in Federal One), 240-63

Converse College (Spartansburg, S. C.) 606

Cook, Will Marion (FMP), 613

Cooke, Lester, Jr., 836

Cooper, Charlotte G. (FAP), 374n.

Court of the Hall of Western States (San Francisco), 478

Co-ordinating Committee on Living Folklore, Folk Music, and Folk Arts of the WPA, 637

Copeland, Royal S., 657

Copland, Aaron (FMP), 625

Copyright, problem of, 273

Corbett, Harvey Wiley, 118

Corcoran Gallery (Washington, D. C.), 366

Cordell, Kathryn, 666, 674

Jazz, 355n., 584-85

Jessaye, Eva (FMP), 613

Jeu de Paume Musée (Paris), 477

Jewell, Edward Allen, 345, 352

Jews, 414-15 and n., 648, 716, 717

John Fitzgerald Kennedy Center for the Performing Arts, 830-31, 832

John Herron Art Institute (Herron Museum of Art, Indianapolis, Ind.), 373

John Reed Club, 351n., 405

Johns, Orrick (FWP), 686

Johnson, Hall (FMP), 614

Johnson, Hugh C. (WPA), 175, 406

Johnson, J. Rosemund (FMP), 613

Johnson, Lyndon B., 831, 832, 833, 836, 837

Johnson, (Mrs.) Lyndon B., 833

Johnson, Tom Lofton (FAP), 430n.

Joint Committee of the American Council of Learned Societies, 756, 760, 766

Joint Committee on Folk Arts, 637, 717-20

Joint Conference against Discrimination Practices (NYC), 412

Joint Folklore Committee of America, 580

Jones, Cecil H. (PWAP), 364n.

Jones, Edward N. (WPA), 153

Joseph H. Hirshhorn Museum and Sculpture Garden, 836

Juan Bautista de Anza (monument), 432

Jubilee Singers, 614

Judgment Day (Elmer Rice, FTP), 552

Judson Radio Program Corporation, 588

Julius Caesar (Shakespeare), 551

Julius Caesar (Handel; FMP), 589

Julliard School of Music (NYC), 589, 626

Junior League (FAP), 393

Juvenile Delinquency and Recreation Project No. 821 (Los Angeles County), 23

Kahn, Herman (HRS), 761

Kahn, Max (FAP), 437

Kansas, 523, 634, 689, 721, 722n., 736, 753n.; Kansas City, 614 and n., 634-35 and n.

Kastner, Alfred (FTP), 285

Kaufman, George, 529n.

Kellock, Katherine (FWP), 666, 668, 675, 694, 695

Kennard, Edward A. (FWP), 675

Kennedy, Jacqueline, 831

Kennedy, John F., 830, 831, 832

Kent, Rockwell, 433n.

Kentucky 523, 595, 597, 636, 721, 722n., 736, 784, 816n.; Bowling Green, 624n., Frankfort, 720; University of Kentucky (Lexington), 370-71

Kerr, Florence (WPA), 201, 210, 236, 260, 270, 305, 307, 311, 313, 316, 317, 318, 337-38, 479, 534, 536-38, 666, 688, 768, 825-26

Kerr, Margaret (FMP), 612, 643, 644

Kessler, Lillian (HRS), 787n.

Kettering, Ralph T. (FTP), 498n.

"Keys to a Contemporary Music" (FMP), 626

Kiev Municipal Orchestra, 604

Kimbal Hall (Chicago), 588

Kindler, Hans (FMP), 118

King Football (Reed Harris), 667

King Lear (Shakespeare), 550, 561

Klem, Margaret (WPA), 80, 81, 522

Knight, Henry, 350

Knott, Sarah Gertrude (FMP), 639

Knotts, Benjamin (FAP), 374n., 408, 449, 454, 456, 457, 458

Knox, (William) Franklin, 617

Koch, Frederick H. (FTP), 505, 506, 508, 564, 565n.

Kondolf, George (FTP), 528

Kubinyi, Kalman (FAP), 437

Labiche, Marin, 551

Labor relations, 404-8

Lacy, Dan (HRS), 772, 787n, 818, 826

La Farge, Henry (TRAP), 370

Lafayette, Marquis de (bust), 432

Lafayette Company (FTP), 556

La Guardia, Fiorello, 351, 589, 826

Landsmanshaften, 727

Lane, Elizabeth S. (TRAP), 370

Lang, Lester (FTP), 503, 506, 516

Laning, Clair (FWP), 73, 88, 92, 96, 98, 100, 675

Laning, Edward (FAP), 430n.

Larned, Josephus M., 816

Lasalle, Edmundo (FMP), 638

Lasker, Bruno (FWP), 652

Lavery, Emmet (FTP), 549

Lay, Joseph (FMP), 607

League of Composers, 589

League of Latin American Citizens, 639

League of New Hampshire Arts and Crafts (TRAP), 371

McFarland, Frances (FMP), 598, 599, 631, 642

McFarland, George M. (HRS), 771 n., 787n., 816, 817, 818

McGee, John (FTP), 505, 506, 511, 513, 517, 521, 574

Mackaye, Steele (FAP), 343

McKellar, Kenneth D., 200-201

MacLeish, Archibald, 425, 455

McLeish, E. E. (FTP), 517

McMahon, Audrey (FAP), 301, 305 and n., 351-54, 372, 374, 380, 386, 390, 405-7, 412, 434, 435, 437n., 458, 478, 829-30

McMurtrie, Douglas C. (HRS), 711n., 810, 811, 812

*Magazine of Art*, 436n., 455

Maier, Guy (FMP), 607, 611

Maine, 77, 78, 364, 595, 628, 629, 709, 710, 716, 815n.; Portland, 92; Rockland, 651

*Making of a Mosiac, The* (FAP), 459

*Making of a Mural, The* (FAP), 430n.

Malarial control project, 42

Man-month costs, 231-33, 328, 259, 260, 262, 290, 783, 784

*Manual for Folklore Studies* (FWP), 715

*Manual of the Portrait Survey* (HRS), 815

*Manual of the Survey of Historical Records* (HRS), 763

Manuel, Frank (FWP), 678n., 716

Manuscript editing (Biological Survey of the Department of Agriculture), 62

Manuscript of William Mitchell, 1724 (HRS), 816n.

Manuscripts program (HRS), 768, 803-7

Man-year costs; *see* Man-month costs

Maps and diagrams (FAP), 459n., 478

March, Frank (WPA), 96, 165

*March of Time* (FTP), 553

Marionettes and puppets (FTP), 494, 510, 567-68, 573, 579

*Marriage Proposal* (Chekhov), 507, 508

Marshall Field (department store, Chicago, Ill.), 453

*Martha* (Flotow), 623

Martha Graham Company, 835

Martha Washington College (Abingdon, Va.), 487

Martin, Gail (FMP), 621

Maryland, 523, 526, 593, 594, 674, 722n., 801n., 804n.; Baltimore, 409, 635n.; Baltmore Symphony Orchestra, 594n.; Maryland Historical Society, 804n.

Mason, Daniel Gregory (FMP), 619

Massachusetts, 84, 288, 364, 384, 398, 401, 414, 427, 431, 452, 460-61, 491, 513, 599, 561, 571, 594, 595, 630, 642, 671, 676, 686, 703, 710, 737, 738, 744, 771, 779, 814, 815n.; Cambridge American Folk Singers, 614n.; Lexington, 582; Lynn, 619; Massachusetts Federal Art Project Paint Testing and Research Laboratory, 460; Massachusetts Historical Society, 676; Orleans (Cape Cod), 469; Plymouth, 582; Shirley, 814; Springfield, 619; Springfield Colored Novelty Orchestra, 614; Worcester State Hospital, 642

*Max Weber* (Holger Cahill), 378

Mayer, Joseph (HRS), 755n.

Mayfarth, William C. (FMP), 606

Means test, 57, 67, 80, 95; *see also* Noncertified personnel

"Memorandum on Inventory of Manuscript Collections" (HRS), 804

Mendelssohn-Bartholdy, Jakob L. F., 623

Menominee Indian Reservation (Wisconsin), 727

Meredith, Charles (FTP), 505, 506

Mesibov, Hubert (FAP), 436, 437

"Method of Handling State Copy" (FWP), 669

*Methods Other than Profilm* (FAP), 440 and n.

Metropolitan Museum of Art (NYC), 349-50, 436n., 454-55, 458, 834

Metropolitan National Opera Company, 834

Mexican influence, 345, 354-57, 414

Michigan, 371, 462, 593, 595, 642, 644, 703, 801n., 826n., 827; Ann Arbor, 658; Grand Rapids, 614, 642; Lansing, 642; Washentaw County, 658

Microfilming of public records and newspapers (HRS), 815-16

*Midsummer Night's Dream* (Shakespeare), 839

Midtown Community Music Center (NYC), 632

Miles, Myrtle (FWP), 147, 726

Miller, J. Howard (FTP), 285, 506, 513, 576, 719

Miller, Malcolm (FTP), 576

Miller, Wallace (FWP), 675

Minnesota, 84, 387, 427, 492 and n., 523, 593, 595, 596, 627, 630, 631, 683, 736, 753n., 800n., 801n., 827n.; Minneapolis, 439, 492n., 614, 624;